Making Haste From Babylon

The Mayflower Pilgrims and Their World:
A New History

Making Haste From Babylon

The Mayflower Pilgrims and Their World: A New History

NICK BUNKER

THE BODLEY HEAD
LONDON

Published by The Bodley Head 2010
2 4 6 8 10 9 7 5 3 1

First published in Great Britain in 2010 by
The Bodley Head
Random House, 20 Vauxhall Bridge Road,
London SW1V 2SA

www.bodleyhead.co.uk
www.rbooks.co.uk

Addresses for companies within The Random House Group Limited can be found at:
www.randomhouse.co.uk/offices.htm

The Random House Group Limited Reg. No. 954009

A CIP catalogue record for this book
is available from the British Library

ISBN 9780224081382

Frontispiece: Ships, mariners and their instruments, from a sailor's guide to the English Channel and the North Sea, *The Light of Navigation* by Willem Janszoon Blaeu, published in Amsterdam in 1620 (The Old Library, St John's College, Cambridge, by permission of the Master and Fellows)

The Random House Group Limited supports The Forest Stewardship Council (FSC), the leading international forest certification organisation. All our titles that are printed on Greenpeace approved FSC certified paper carry the FSC logo. Our paper procurement policy can be found at www.rbooks.co.uk/environment

Printed and bound in Great Britain by
Clays Ltd, St Ives plc

This book is dedicated to Margaret E. Mahoney,
president of the Commonwealth Fund of New York,
1980–95

Crueltye and bloodde is in our streetes, the lande abowndeth with murthers slawghters Incestes Adulteryes, whoredom dronkennes, oppression and pride . . . even the leaste of these, is enowghe, and enowghe to make haste owte of Babylon.

—an English Puritan giving reasons
for migration to America, 1629[1]

Contents

PART FOUR
The Project

PART FIVE
America

PART SIX
The Ways of Salvation

Maps

Author's Note

A pest, a fanatic, and a hypocrite, worse than a cattle thief: that was a Puritan, said King James I of England. Despite his many talents, the king had many flaws, and we cannot trust him to describe men and women whom he loathed. We have to find a less insulting way to define them, briefly but with fairness. Without such a definition, what follows will make very little sense.

The word "Puritan" first appeared early in the reign of Queen Elizabeth, in about 1565. Puritans were people who believed that she failed to go far enough when she established a Protestant Church of England. They urged her to abolish every last trace of Roman Catholic ritual that still lingered within it. They also wished to see an end to the hierarchy of bishops that the queen had left intact.

Her Majesty had not the slightest intention of agreeing to these demands. So, if Puritans could not have the kind of official religion they wanted, they chose to look for God in private. As the law required, they went to their parish church every Sunday, but at home they prayed, discussed sermons, and studied the Bible.

Mainly, Puritans read the book of Genesis, the letters of Saint Paul, and the Psalms. In the New Testament, they also paid special attention to the Acts of the Apostles. Here they found the story of the early Church, and a portrait of Christianity in what seemed to be its most authentic form. Free from distortion by popes and cardinals, it offered a model they felt obliged to copy.

Before the English Civil War, almost every single Puritan was also a Calvinist. What did this label signify? It meant that they followed the teachings of the French reformer John Calvin, who died in 1564. A lawyer by training, Calvin began by precisely defining the nature of God. Then, with the austere logic of a judge, he explained the fearful consequences of divinity.

For Calvin, God was an absolute monarch, a king who created the universe and then sustained it at every moment by a supreme act of will. But if God was almighty, and foresaw everything that occurred, then before the beginning of time he must have decided already the fate of each human soul. This was called the doctrine of double predestination.

Like Calvin, English Puritans believed that God had divided the human race in two. Before they were born, those chosen to receive the gift of faith were set apart for eternal life. They were called the elect. The remainder of humanity were doomed to punishment forever. Try as they might, they could never obtain salvation, and so they were known as the lost.

Did these ideas make men and women fatalistic? If human beings could not change the mind of God, why bother with faith, hope, and charity at all? In fact, Calvinists reached the opposite conclusion. If Christians wanted to be sure that they belonged to the elect, it was all the more important to do good deeds and to worship correctly. To persevere in holiness gave them the best evidence that they were saved.

Among the Puritans in England, some of those who persevered the most were a small minority known as Separatists. In terms of theology, they were strict Calvinists too, but they carried Puritan beliefs as far as they would go. They argued that the Church of England was beyond redemption because of its Roman Catholic past. In their eyes, it bore the marks of Satan, not those of Jesus Christ.

Because of this, Separatists felt compelled to do more than read and pray in private. They decided to leave the established Church entirely and set up alternative congregations. Untainted by the influence of Rome, these assemblies would be pure in their membership, and in the way they worshipped. In 1593, Parliament and Queen Elizabeth made Separatism a crime.

Making Haste *from* Babylon

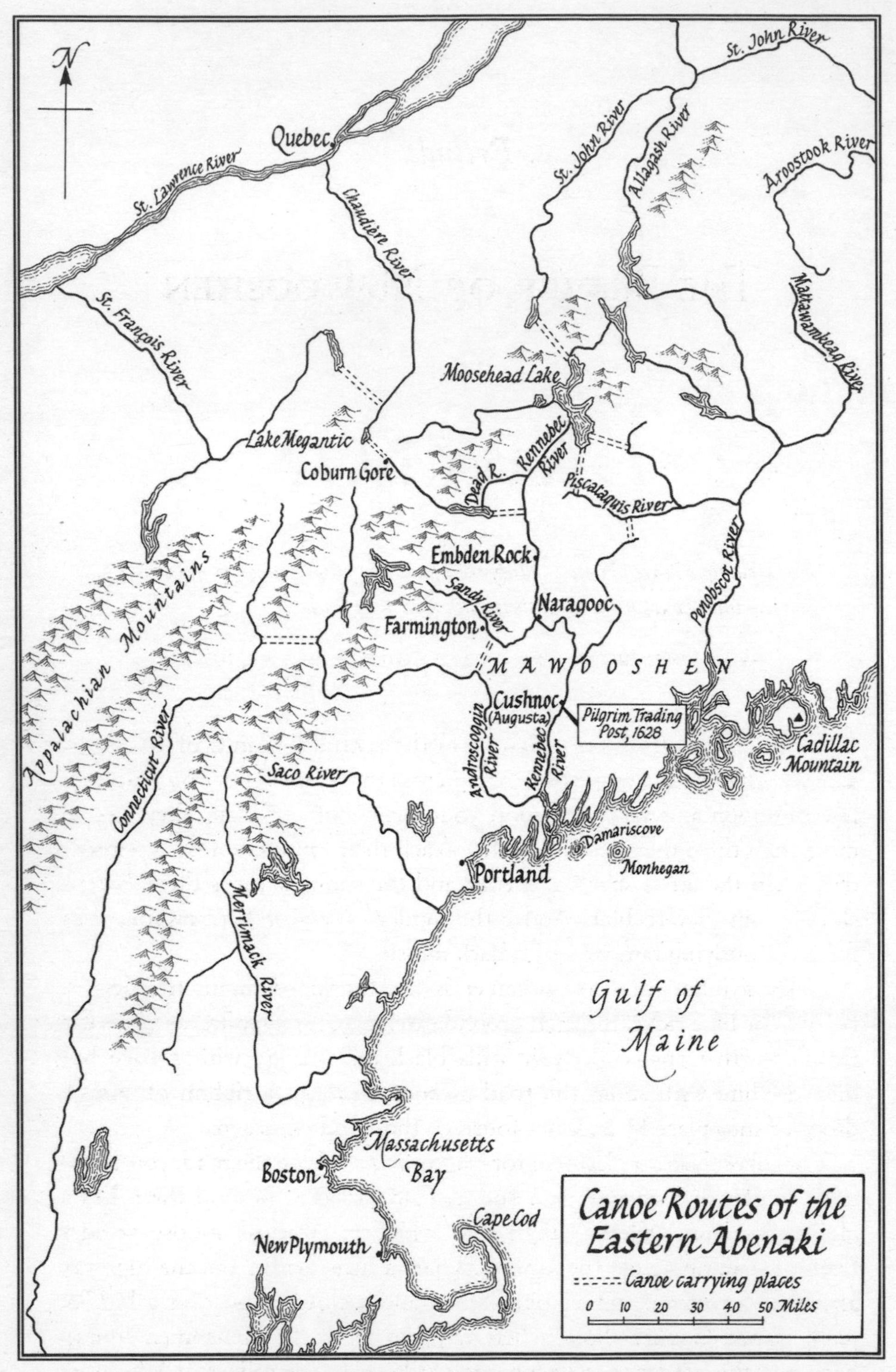

Rivers: from *Gulf of Maine Watershed Map*, Maine State Planning Office, 1991.
Canoe routes: from David S. Cook, *Above the Gravel Bar* (3rd edition, 2007).

Prelude

The Beaver of Mawooshen

The planters heare aboutes, if they will have any beaver, must go 40 or 50 myles into the country, with their packes on their backes.

—an English settler on the coast of Maine, June 1634[1]

Seventy miles from the Atlantic, in the central lowlands of Maine, if you head west along Route 2 and cross the Sandy River you will see a line of mountains far away upon your right. Built of slate, they rise to more than three thousand feet. They reach their finest color on a winter's day, when the air is sharp and cold and the sunlight turns their eastern slopes from gray to blue. Above the modern town of Farmington, they form the outlying ramparts of a dark massif.

Here the influence of the ocean ends, and the American interior begins. Behind the blue ridge, the high ground extends for sixty miles, as far as the frontier with Canada. Between hills black and shaggy with spruce but dusted white with snow, the road ascends an esker, a ribbon of gravel, dropped into place by a glacier fourteen thousand years ago.

The esker makes a platform for Highway 27. Along the road, you climb until you reach a narrow pass and a chain of lakes. Beyond them lies a gloomy wetland, called Hathan Bog, where in the dusk moose wander from the swamp across the asphalt. Then, a little farther on, the highway arrives at a plateau, and a liquor store, and a customs post, at a hidden place named Coburn Gore, where day and night the Frenchmen thump back over the border in their logging trucks. Like the valleys of West Virginia, the pass supplies an aperture, an entry into the land beyond the mountains, at the northern end of the Appalachian barrier.

At places such as this, the west begins: but where did America start for new settlers arriving from England in the 1620s or the 1630s? Maybe they saw it first from ten miles out on the ocean, with a glimpse of sandy cliffs along the eastern rim of Cape Cod, or at forty miles, if their first sighting was Cadillac Mountain, above Bar Harbor, visible to any ship bound in from Newfoundland. Or did the New World really begin later? Did its strangeness dawn upon them when they saw ice jamming a river mouth as late as April, or a belt of white wampum beads, or a field of maize, or a man in deerskin breeches, with a shaved head and a torso painted purple? The point at which the alien was glimpsed for what it was, alarming, uncanny, or sublime, might occur at any of these moments, or at none of them. Half of the early migrants simply faded and died.

There was another point when America began. The moment took place when new settlers crossed a different kind of boundary, when for the first time they could be certain that their colony was going to endure. So far as the *Mayflower* Pilgrims were concerned, this moment occurred in the territory in Maine that lay below Coburn Gore, in the year 1628. Eight years earlier, they had landed at Provincetown, Massachusetts, at the extremity of Cape Cod. Soon afterward they founded their settlement across the bay at New Plymouth. That was another beginning, but it was tenuous and frail. It took far longer for the Plymouth enterprise to make itself permanent, and to open the way for the foundation of Boston to the north, by colonists in far larger numbers.

Fraught with risk, the *Mayflower* project endured a long period of trial, experiment, and error. Deeply in debt to their backers in London, and chronically short of supplies to keep their feet shod, their muskets loaded, and their small boats afloat, they needed a commodity to send back to England to be swapped for silver coins or used to redeem their IOUs. They eventually found it, in the quantities they needed, up here in Maine. They bought it from the people who lived in the country below the watershed between what we now call Quebec and the United States. This was where the moment of maturity occurred: the place where they passed across an emotional frontier, the line that separates insecure ambition from likely success.

There was only one way in which the Pilgrims could find the money to pay their debts and finance new supplies from home. They needed the fur of *Castor canadensis*, the North American beaver. No other colonial product fetched so high a price, in Paris, in London, or in Holland. What made the skins so precious? That will be the subject of a later chapter. All we need know for the time being is that during the 1620s the price of a beaver pelt increased fourfold, to reach a peak of nearly forty shillings. That was enough to rent nine acres of English farmland for a year.

Until they had pelts, the colony at New Plymouth remained a fragile outpost, a tiny corn-growing settlement wedged between the forest and the sea. For it to become something more, the seed or nucleus for a much larger inflow of the English, they had to find beaver skins, and in Maine the valleys and the high ground supplied a vast habitat for the mammal.[2]

As many as fifty beavers may have lived in each square mile, or even more densely in places such as Hathan Bog. Alongside the esker, on every stream beavers built their dams and lodges. Today the animals have left a chain of beaver meadows, dried-up ponds, strung out along the side of Highway 27. Take the surface area of Franklin County, Maine, around and beneath the bog and the highway, and multiply it by fifty. You come to an estimate of ninety thousand of the creatures in that one county alone.

Why did the beavers of Maine become the target of exploitation, and not those of another region? The Pilgrims might have gone elsewhere, and sometimes did. Beavers will live in any setting with the trees they like to gnaw, the quaking aspen or the willow, and streams that flow down gradients a few degrees above the level. As for the date, why did it take so long for the Pilgrims to begin to penetrate the deep interior? Because it was only in 1628, and in Maine, that chance and circumstance combined to make it feasible. Access, demand for the skins, the legal right to settle, the technology of transport, the command of language, a supply of trading goods, and the presence of people able and willing to hunt: these were essential too.

As we shall see, the very early history of New England contains many hidden, forgotten corners, niches quite as remote as Coburn Gore. Most often, these spots of vagueness or omission arise because, in the British Isles, the evidence lies neglected, scattered in odd places in dozens of archive collections.

They contain a wealth of overlooked material about the origins of the *Mayflower* project and its place in the wider history of England under King James and his son the future Charles I. For the most part, British scholars have either left these very early sources untouched or failed to see their significance. They have done what the Pilgrims did not do, and left America to the Americans. This is why so much of the Pilgrim narrative remains in shadowy monochrome, like a photograph in sepia or a silent film, deprived of color, light, and sound.

Among the gaps in the story, one of the most serious concerns the trade in beaver pelts, shipped back in their thousands by way of the ports of Barnstaple, Bristol, and Plymouth in the west of England. That is why we start in Franklin County. We might begin by imagining its character, not by way of fantasy, but with the aid of available resources, scientific and archaeological, and verbal too. To help us, we might imitate the native people of the region. We might invoke the spirit of a bird to function as an airborne guide.[3]

Today more than four hundred pairs of bald eagles breed in the state of Maine. When Charles I sat on the throne, doubtless their numbers were far greater. What might she have seen, an eagle, if in the spring of 1628 she swung her head around through three-quarters of a circle and scanned the country below Coburn Gore? She saw the land of Mawooshen. That was the name given then to the region: mountain, river, valley, plain, and coast, and among them the Eastern Abenaki, who lived between the blue ridge and the ocean.

THE BALD EAGLE'S NEST

From her zenith, at four thousand feet, she sees the Sandy River bending back and forth. Fed by streams cascading down off the massif, the river swings around and doubles back but never ceases to drop toward the sea. Beyond its broad, flat valley, to the south the ground rolls out to form a plain covered by birch woods and pine, with strewn on the earth beneath them hundreds of pale gray boulders. They were abandoned, like elliptical cannonballs, by the same retreating glaciers that formed the esker.

As the ice melted and the Atlantic rose, the sea reached this far inland, laying down thick beds of silt and sand. Even now, the ocean is far closer than it seems. In the seventeenth century, long before men dammed the rivers of Maine, salmon swam all the way up from the sea to Farmington to spawn.

If our eagle of 1628 leaves her nest at the top of a tall white pine, and goes looking for game along the valley, she comes to a spot where the Sandy meets another river, deeper and wider. Before it begins its own final descent toward the sea, it flows in a sequence of long, quiet reaches between sets of falls and rapids. Each one marks a geological division, ten or fifteen miles apart, where the river suddenly alters course. For this reason, the river bears the name Kennebec. In the native language of the country the word *gwena* means "long," while the syllable *bague* refers to a placid stretch of water.[4]

Hovering above the Kennebec, the eagle probes with her eyes for a leaping fish or a squirrel breaking cover. When she finds one, she swoops down at the spot where the Sandy River meanders in from the west, near the site of the modern town of Madison. Beneath a bluff, the water forms a calm, deep pool, tinted in spring by a drifting haze of pollen from the pines. As she skims the amber surface and then swings back up into the sky with a fish in her talons, she flies over a place where the woods have been cleared, to make a wide, flat open space on a terrace thirty feet above the river.

As she climbs, the eagle pays little heed to the village of Naragooc, or the human beings stooping down to collect Maine fiddleheads, edible wild ferns gathered at this season. She ignores the circular huts along the bluff, the wooden longhouse, or the people moving to and fro between cooking fires, storage pits, and the fields of maize that loosely encircle the settlement. Instead, she rises steeply again. From her highest altitude, she can see as far as eighty miles. With the dense packing of nerve cells in her retina, she can pick out objects three or four times smaller than those detected by a human eye.

Far to the north, she sees the mountain escarpment and the dark smudge marking the site of Hathan Bog. Bare summits and icy mountain streams offer little by way of food, and so she turns toward the south. On the way to the sea, the landscape becomes a mottled rug, made up of ridges of gravel between elongated lakes. They point toward the site of the modern city of Augusta, forty miles away, with the Atlantic visible far beyond it as a distant rim of silver.

This was Mawooshen. Even the English called the country by that name. They did so in a document compiled in about 1607, most likely as a briefing paper for a failed attempt to found a colony at the mouth of the Kennebec, at Fort St. George. The word apparently referred to a confederacy of some thirteen towns and villages of the Eastern Abenaki, scattered across the zone between the Sandy River and Cadillac Mountain.[5]

Among them, the deepest inland was Naragooc, located at the junction of the Sandy and the Kennebec. Today its name survives on a modern map in the altered form of Norridgewock. When the English manuscript was written, Naragooc provided a home to as many as four or five hundred people, led by a *Zegeme,* or sachem, a chief by the name of Cocockohamas. His clan occupied a spot where the earth was unusually good. A fine olive brown tilth called Hadley loam, it formed a narrow carpet along both banks of the river, like the rich soil of exactly the same kind along the Connecticut valley, coveted by later English settlers.

At Naragooc, the Abenaki lived at the northernmost point where at the time the climate permitted the cultivation of maize. They also sat on the perimeter between the northern hardwoods, spruce, and fir and the softer oaks and pines of southern New England. Accessible by water, Naragooc was poised between corn country and the hunting spaces of the north.[6] And so in spring, when our imaginary eagle saw the village, the people who lived there would be skinning hundreds of dead beavers. Late winter was the time to catch them, with a spear driven through the melting ice, when the animals were most hungry and least cautious and their pelts were thickest.

By the middle of the seventeenth century, the trade in beaver fur had come to lie at the heart of the life of the Abenaki. At Naragooc the evidence is plain, and it takes two forms, material and linguistic. In the 1990s, when archaeologists explored the village sites beside the Kennebec, they found scores of beaver bones, from the animal's jawbone, skull, and legs. But the beaver left a still deeper mark on the language that the people spoke.[7]

It survives in the form of a lexicon compiled more than three hundred years ago by a French Catholic missionary, Father Sebastian Râle. He listed more than thirty nouns, verbs, and phrases used by the people of Naragooc to describe the animal, its skin, its behavior, and the manner in which they pursued it. They called the beaver *temakwe,* meaning "tree cutter." They gave different names to male and female adults, and they called a young beaver a *temakwesis.* They had separate words for beavers as they appeared in winter and as they were in warmer weather when their pelts had thinned. Then they were known as *nepenemeskwe,* from *nipen,* meaning "summer."

The people of Naragooc called the skin of a beaver *matarreh,* and they added extra syllables to grade the pelts into categories of size and quality. The beaver's kidneys, *rognons de castor,* had their own Abenaki word—*awisenank*—and this suggests that once skinned, the beaver was cooked and eaten: an English visitor to Maine in the 1620s compared the taste to roast lamb. Father Râle recorded phrases referring to the beaver's motion, as its tail beats the surface of a pond, as it lifts its head from the water, or as it dives back to hide. At home, the English hunted otters with packs of web-footed hounds. Râle tells us that the Abenaki did something similar: they pursued the beaver with a *chien à castor,* a "beaver dog," or in their language a *temakwekkwe.*[8]

They inhabited a place ideal for the purpose. From the highland plateau, three river systems descend to the north, south, and east: the Kennebec, the St. John, and the Chaudière, the Canadian river that drains away from the far side of Coburn Gore and down into the St. Lawrence. If the sheer quantity of mammals was the first great attraction of the region, the second lay in the ease of entry and exit along these great waterways. To the Eastern Abenaki, the chain of ponds and lakes around Hathan Bog were the high road that led from Mawooshen to Quebec and back.

After the British seized control of Canada in 1759, they sent a military engineer called John Montresor to find the path, as a means to move men and guns from Quebec to Boston and back. He found the bog and the beaver dams, but Colonel Montresor remembered how reluctant the people of Mawooshen were to disclose the secret of the forest highway.

The Abenaki, he said, were "the natural proprietors of the country... No nation having been more jealous of their country than the Abenaquis, they have made it a constant rule to leave the fewest vestiges of their route." In the early days of New England, long before Montresor, no European had trod the path at all. The first were Râle's forerunners, French Jesuits, in the 1640s, coming over the watershed southward. This was a journey a skilled Abenaki could accomplish in a week or so, if the weather were benign.

With a birch-bark canoe, eighteen feet long, fit to carry two men and one thousand pounds of cargo, the Abenaki could pole and paddle along streams as little as five inches deep. But to make canoes like these, they needed sheets of bark from birch trees at least four feet in circumference. In the seventeenth century, paper birch of such a size grew rarely in southern New England, but the trees existed in plenty in Maine. For this reason, the birch-bark canoe was chiefly a tool of the people of Mawooshen and the country that lay behind it.[9]

With their canoes, they could travel for hundreds of miles, from the headwaters of the Connecticut River in the west to Nova Scotia in the east. Up on the plateau, the belt of land around Coburn Gore could be crossed on foot. Down in the lowlands, the pattern of lakes and low ridges left behind by the ice sheets created natural canoe trails, by way of short overland carries between the waterways. By this means, the Abenaki could make detours around obstacles in the Kennebec, cross from it to another river, the Androscoggin, and reach the mountains of northern New Hampshire. In the other direction, going east from Naragooc by way of the Sebasticook, they could enter the vast basin of the Penobscot and the St. John. In turn, those rivers led them across the modern border into what is now the Canadian province of New Brunswick.

If there were boundaries to movement, they arose only from hostile opponents. In 1626, on the Hudson River, the Mohawk killed and ate seven Dutch fur traders, and two years later they ejected from the same region their foes the Mohican. So, for the people of Naragooc, the Mohawk and their fellow Iroquois fixed the limit of commerce to the west.

To the east, the St. John marked a frontier with the Micmac, known then as the Tarrentines, long the enemies of the Abenaki. They were seagoing raiders and middlemen, passing up and down the coast between the French in Canada and the people of Massachusetts to the south. Even so, between these limits there remained forty thousand square miles of uncontested country. And that was why, in the spring of 1628, our bald eagle saw the English coming up the Kennebec.

THE PILGRIMS AT CUSHNOC

If she flew south and gazed out over the ocean, she would notice white specks rising and falling on the swell. A convoy of sailing ships, thirty or forty in number, they were trawling for cod or calling at the fishing post on Damariscove Island. Behind them lay a voyage of fourteen days from Newfoundland, or eight or nine weeks if their track across the ocean had brought them without a stop from the harbors of southwestern England.

Somewhere out on the Gulf of Maine were two ships in particular. One was small, a fishing boat called the *Pleasure,* with a capacity of thirty-five tons. The other had a volume five times larger, and she was the *White Angel,* an armed merchant ship with a privateering license to take any French or Spanish vessel she met.

Both ships had come from Barnstaple, in the English county of Devon. On January 23 and 24, duly recorded by customs officers, they left their home port loaded with supplies for the Pilgrims at New Plymouth. The *White Angel* and the *Pleasure* crossed the Atlantic, handed over their freight, and began to look for a cargo to bring back. Most of all they wanted beaver skins.[10]

So did the crew of another English vessel in the region. If the eagle remained inland and wheeled over the site of the modern city of Augusta, she would pass over a smaller craft, coming upstream along the Kennebec toward the rocks that marked the end of the river's tidal reach.

The boat was bound for a small cove where a path wound up a bluff toward another flat riverside terrace. On board were guns, ammunition, and trading goods: knives, hoes, hatchets, and perhaps a few shining copper kettles. By way of rations, she would have brought casks of cider and beer and red ceramic jars, each one filled with pickled fish or olives.

The boat also carried men from New Plymouth. They were led most likely by Edward Winslow, aged thirty-two, but possibly also by William Bradford, the colony's governor, a man of thirty-eight. Probably Winslow had with him John Howland, in his late twenties, since Howland later became the manager of the Pilgrim fur business in Maine. They were English Separatists, or radical Puritans. All three had first traveled to America on board the *Mayflower,* after leaving their place of exile in the Dutch city of Leiden in the summer of 1620.

With a patent from the authorities in London, they were on their way to build a trading post to dominate the traffic in fur from the interior. Known as Cushnoc, the place can easily be found today, above the bluff, in the center of modern Augusta. In the 1980s, archaeologists discovered on the site the remains of a wooden house, a ring of timber postholes, and pieces of English red pots, dating from roughly this period. They came from Barnstaple, where shipowners gave their crews cider to drink, because it kept well on long voyages.[11]

At Cushnoc, the Pilgrims at last corrected the mistake they made when they landed inside the hook of Cape Cod. Decades earlier, an Elizabethan writer had urged new settlers to plant themselves "upon the mouthes of the greate navigable rivers," as a means of finding trading partners or a route to the Pacific.[12] This was common sense. It was what the settlers at Jamestown did when they chose a home in Virginia close to the entrance of Chesapeake Bay.

But because the *Mayflower* wandered off course, failing to reach the Hudson, her planned destination, she deposited her passengers on one of the longest stretches of shoreline on the Atlantic seaboard without a waterway reaching far inland. Eight years later, the Kennebec provided a solution. It came by way of contact with the hunting bands of the Eastern Abenaki and their network of communication. For this reason, even in later decades, when the fur trade began to slacken as competition increased and profits fell, the Pilgrims remained determined to maintain their grip on Cushnoc and its river.

They established what colonial officials in Victorian Africa would later call a protectorate. Like Uganda or Swaziland, the Kennebec valley became a region whose defense and security the British tried to control. When a French Jesuit visited Naragooc in 1650, he found that its inhabitants lived under what he called "la protection de cette colonie de Plymouth." He wished to enlist the support of the Puritan English, on behalf of the Abenaki on both sides of the mountains, in a war against the Iroquois. The Pilgrims readily agreed to help him, Catholic though he was, for the sake of the furs that came down the river.[13]

By building their post at Augusta, Winslow and Bradford began to transform forever the lands that they entered. They drew the Abenaki ever more tightly into the circuits of commerce that led back across the sea like submarine cables. The consequences were profound, and ambiguous too. Besides the bones of beavers, archaeologists found armaments at Naragooc, lumps of lead and flints used to fire a musket. The Pilgrims did not sell guns, since King Charles had strictly forbidden it, but they were not the only English traders on the coast. In the early 1630s the asking price for a beaver skin in Maine was a third of a bar of lead, or five beakers of gunpowder and two pounds of shot.[14]

Meanwhile, on the eastern side of the ocean, the results of their activities were equally far-reaching. Before Cushnoc, the French and the Dutch easily surpassed the English in the quantities of fur they acquired in North America. As many as six thousand beaver skins reached Amsterdam each year from Dutchmen on the Hudson. In Quebec, Samuel de Champlain and his French colony dealt in quantities that were still larger. Until very late in the day, the English were dabblers, barely clinging to their footholds along the coast. This first began to change in 1625, when the Pilgrims started dealing at the mouth of the Kennebec, buying pelts from the Abenaki with surplus corn. But it was the trading season of 1628 that marked the great turning point for English enterprise.

That summer, the *White Angel* and the *Pleasure* sailed home with beaver skins in quantities far larger than any their home ports had seen before. And they arrived at a decisive moment when, for other reasons, men and women suddenly began to take a far closer interest in emigration westward. That same year, because of defeat in war, events were converging in London toward a political crisis.

Puritans, mariners, and businessmen lost patience with the king's bungling of hostilities with France. They complained about squandered taxation, about dwindling civil liberties, about losses of ships and men, and about a failing economy. Most of all they feared that King Charles was conniving to bring back the Roman Catholic faith.

The following spring, in 1629, an embittered session of Parliament ended in failure from everyone's point of view. At that moment, New England ceased to be merely a zealous eccentricity. Instead, it became a Puritan demand. This was because it offered a place where alternatives might be found; but it could only do so if it paid its way.

In 1630, a much larger fleet of migrant ships sailed to Massachusetts Bay under the leadership of John Winthrop. Its organizers had closely monitored the slow progress of the settlers at New Plymouth. They began to make plans for the Winthrop colony only after they saw proof, by way of beaver skins, that New England made financial sense.

For more than five decades, the idea of a mission to America had excited energetic Protestants in England. Although little had been achieved, they had expected from the outset that religion would go hand in hand with profit. Who was the first man to think of such a project? There are several candidates, and they were French as well as English. Among them, as we shall see, perhaps the most relevant to the Pilgrims was a poet, Sir Philip Sidney.

He was a soldier as well as a writer, and he was also an eager Calvinist. In the 1580s, Sidney dreamed of a colony that would combine Christianity, economics, and patriotic adventure. His friend and biographer, Fulke Greville, spoke of Sidney's "hazardous enterprize of planting upon the main of America." Sir Philip wished to create, said Greville, "an Emporium for the confluence of all nations that love or profess any kind of virtue, or commerce." In 1586, Sidney died of a war wound, inflicted by a Spanish musketeer. He never crossed the western ocean, and so it was left to the *Mayflower* Pilgrims to build the plantation he had wished to see.

It would be godly, but lucrative too. Both Christian and commercial, it would be an instrument of empire, as well as a manifestation of faith.[15] In due course, New England became the emporium of virtue that Sidney had envisaged; but it was a complicated kind of virtue, and one that not everybody wished to share.

In this book you will find a new account of the *Mayflower* Pilgrims, their origins, and their first decade in North America. It is new in two respects. First, it draws on the multitude of neglected primary sources on the old side of the ocean. And, second, it replaces the Pilgrims within their true setting, in all its Jacobean density, in Europe as well as in Massachusetts and Maine.

This is not a simple story. Like the project imagined by Sir Philip Sidney, it has many layers, overlapping strata of piety, politics, and business. Molded by the random processes of chance, events also took the shape they did because exceptional people were involved. This, the role of character, and morale, adds yet another element of complication. Fortunately, however, we have a set of charts that can guide us through the labyrinth. The maps exist, on both sides of the Atlantic, in the tangible form of terrain.

Within the landscape lay the harsh imperatives of economic stress in an age when survival could never be taken for granted. This was true in England and in America alike. By exploring the space in which events took place, in the Old World and the New, we can begin to explain why they happened at all. We can also hope to escape from sentimentality and fiction. There is no need to indulge in mythology about the Pilgrims, when we can interrogate the land and the documents that remain. In the earth, and in the archives, we find the hard traces of motivation: assuming, of course, that we know where to look.

Perhaps Puritan New England would have happened anyway, without Cushnoc or the *Mayflower.* But, as things were, the Plymouth Colony became a permanent settlement because of the land, the animals, and the people that our eagle saw. For this reason, we start and finish on the Kennebec, among the mountains. We end and begin with the river, and the trees, with the Eastern Abenaki, the People of the Dawn, and with the *temakwe,* the slaughtered beaver of Mawooshen.

Part One

The Heavens and the Sea

ESA. 51. 22.
So spreeckt u heerscher de Heere ende u God die u wreeckt : Siet ! ick neme den tuymel-kelck , met t'samen den droesem des Kelcx mijnder grimmicheydt : ghy en sult hem niet meer drincken.

The title-page illustration from a book about the comet of 1618, published the following year by the Dutch poet Jacob Cats and called *Remarks on the Current Shooting Star.* The text beneath, from the book of Isaiah, warns of God's anger against the sinful and promises salvation to the godly. (*Boerhaave Museum, Leiden*)

Chapter One

The Year of the Blazing Star

Hung be the heavens with black, yield day to night!
Comets, importing change of times and states,
Brandish your crystal tresses in the sky.

—Shakespeare, *King Henry VI Part One* (1589–92)

An hour before dawn on November 28, 1618, a physician looked up from his house on the northern edge of London and gazed over the city between the steeples and the chimneys. Above them, in the darkness to the southeast, he saw a blazing star. It was colored a shade between green and blue, with a long white triangular tail. The comet gleamed with what he later called "a bright resplendence."

Medicine gave John Bainbridge a livelihood, but astronomy and mathematics excited him far more. An ambitious man of thirty-six, he believed in the ideas of Copernicus, and he read what Johannes Kepler wrote about the orbit of planets around the sun. In the comet he saw a chance to defend their findings. In the frost of early winter, Bainbridge tracked the apparition for four weeks, with the help of his "telescopion, or trunke-spectacle," one of the first in England. Peering through its lenses, he plotted the position of the star with a wooden cross-staff, collecting the data he needed to calculate its speed, altitude, and distance from the earth. Day by day, he watched its colors fade and the comet diminish as it soared toward the northwest. He followed it past Scorpius and the Great Bear, until it veered away into oblivion beyond the Pole Star.

Swiftly the doctor completed a book about his observations. In the manner of its time it combined algebra, verse, and abject flattery of King James. Bainbridge pointed out that the gleaming star followed a course between New Guinea and the Arctic, and this could only mean one thing. As it traveled across the sky, the doctor said, the comet promised that God would reveal to the English the shining secret of another northwest passage, the icy route that led around the top of Canada, to reach the East Indies by way of the Pacific. In the star they beheld God's gift of wealth. From the Lord, the people of Great Britain would soon receive "healthfull spices, precious Jewels, and Orientall riches," as Bainbridge put it in his most exalted prose.

Millions of others watched the comet too. From the Alps to Korea and from Iran to the Philippines we have vivid accounts of the blazing star, the brightest since the passing of Halley's comet eleven years before. A teenage student at Cambridge University looked out of a window during morning prayers, saw the comet, and thought its tail resembled a fox's brush. In China, observers called it a shining broom that swept across the heavens, while in Paris a journalist compared its round head to a burning coal, and its tail to a long sheaf of wheat. In Isfahan, the Spanish ambassador likened its green flame and its appearance each morning to the planet Venus. That year observers saw three comets, but everyone agreed that the emerald star was by far the most remarkable.[1]

From his home in Austria, Kepler first saw it break through the clouds twenty-four hours after Bainbridge, and he carefully noted its features. In Rome the Jesuits had a professor of mathematics by the name of Orazio Grassi. He spoke of the crowds that gathered on hilltops to watch the visitation from the heavens, "with no thought of sleep and no fear of the cold wind." In Florence, bedridden by gout, or arthritis, or kidney stones, his rival the great Galileo received a long line of visitors, eager to exchange their impressions of the comet for his opinion, that it might be no more than vapor exhaled from the surface of the earth.[2] Meanwhile a royal invalid, Anne of Denmark, the queen of England, lay sick with tuberculosis and dropsy. In the star the people of London saw a luminous warning of her end. Three months later, the queen was dead, and the Banqueting House of Whitehall Palace had burned to the ground.[3]

Far to the west, another group of men and women stared at the blazing star with rapt attention. Astronomy fascinated the native people of America every bit as much as it enthralled the admirers of Galileo. Describing the natives he met in Connecticut in the 1630s, the English radical Roger Williams found that "by occasion of their frequent lying in the fields or woods, they much observe the stars; and their very children can give names to many of them."[4] By the rising and the setting of the Pleiades, they constructed their calendar, fixing the best time to sow seed for corn, to plant beans, or to begin a hunting party. In their legends they gave events in the heavens a central role.

Beside Lake Huron, the Ojibwa still spoke in the 1980s of a long-tailed climbing star, which nearly ended life on earth long ago and one day will return to finish the task. In Maine, folklore collected among the Penobscot includes stories about a meteor that had warned of the outbreak of the American Civil War. We can be sure that the comet of 1618 caused just as much alarm in southern New England.[5] Nearly forty years later, in a history of the colonies, Edward Johnson of Woburn, Massachusetts, described the way the people he called Indians followed the flaming star across the night sky. Like Bainbridge, they watched it each night for four weeks until it disappeared. "They expected some strange things to follow," Johnson said.[6]

His laconic phrase conceals a world of meaning. The native people of New England split their cosmos into three realms: the sky, the earth, and a watery underworld. The boundaries between them could be crossed or penetrated by the souls of the dead, by a shaman in a trance, or by supernatural beings from above or below. Perhaps they thought of the comet as an eruption of divine power for good or ill from one cosmic zone into another. For men and women who prized the pattern of the heavens, an intervention of such a startling kind would foreshadow some great and unexpected event. Like the English expecting the death of their queen, most likely they made the comet an omen of destruction; and if they did, they were entirely correct.

According to Johnson, the comet prophesied not only the arrival of the *Mayflower*, bringing the light of salvation to the new continent, but also God's intervention to clear a space for his emissaries. "A little before the removeall of that Church of Christ from Holland to Plimoth in New England, as the ancient Indians report," Johnson wrote, "there befell a great mortality." By this, he meant a wave of epidemics, of smallpox, influenza, or hepatitis, carried on visiting ships, which began in 1616 and lasted for about three years, carving a demographic crater in the land of Mawooshen.

Before the pestilence, about ten thousand native people may have lived in the southern half of Maine. Although these numbers are conjecture, as many as 90 percent may have perished in the next two decades from sickness and in small wars. As for southern New England, before the epidemics the population may have numbered about ninety thousand. Again, maybe 90 percent of them lost their lives. Perhaps disease explains why so many beaver bones came to lie beside the Kennebec at Naragooc. The survivors among the Abenaki had to gather somewhere, and the hunting, the rich soil, and the salmon made it a fine place to do so.

Wherever it was seen, from the rivers of Maine to Manila and Beijing, the comet supplied the great sensation of the years before the *Mayflower* sailed. Connecting so many observers, from so many different cultures, with so many meanings latent in its path, the star was a social and political event, as well as a prodigy of nature. Every diplomat worth his expenses and every preacher worthy of a congregation found something to say about it. In the variety of their responses, and they were very diverse indeed, we see taking shape the complicated world from which the Pilgrims came.

On both sides of the Atlantic we have come to look upon the *Mayflower,* its voyage, and what followed as an entirely American story. We think of it simply in the light of what happened later, in the vast space between Quebec and California, making it solely a matter of American concern. This is an illusion: not a very damaging illusion, as illusions go, but an illusion nonetheless. The truth is that after the Pilgrims landed in America, on or near the boulder called Plymouth Rock, events on the western side of the Atlantic unfolded in intricate counterpoint with those taking place on the old side of the same ocean.

If we allow this dual narrative to run its course, before and after the *Mayflower,* then suddenly the picture changes. In high relief, we see the contours of a new map of the origins of Puritan America. As for the Pilgrims themselves, we discover that they were not quite the people we thought they were. "America" did not exist in 1620, and the Pilgrims were never Americans, but neither were they "English" in any simple, modern definition of the word.

Of course, they were born within the physical location known as England. The core group of Pilgrims, those who led the Plymouth Colony, came from a district as English as can be, two hundred miles north of London, at a place where three counties converge, Lincolnshire, Nottinghamshire, and the West Riding of Yorkshire. But when we peer into their beliefs and circumstances, we find that they were not narrowly English at all. Because they were Calvinists, they followed an international creed, French, German, Scottish, and Dutch as well as Anglo-Saxon, at a time when fear spilled across borders like the luster of the comet.

It was a complex fate to be a Calvinist in 1618, and faith did not bring tranquillity. The Pilgrims lived amid anxiety, phobia, and apocalyptic fantasy. They had obsessions entirely unlike our own, obsessions that the comet came to symbolize. We might prefer to think about the people of the time as men and women in our image, but if we do so, we run the risk of misunderstanding everything about them.

Of course, in their age we can find a long list of forerunners of modernity: not only the telescope, but also the invention or discovery of logarithms, newspapers, and the circulation of blood. Scientific navigation came into being, while the Dutch created a new system of global trade, linking China to Amsterdam by way of Brazil. And, as it happens, each of these innovations will find its place in the chapters ahead, because all of them played their part in the origins of New England. And yet, if we wish to see things as they were, we have to recognize that an abyss of difference divides us from the Jacobean mind.

People did not believe that they stood on the cusp of something called the modern world. In Protestant Europe they were mostly frightened, alarmed, and insecure, but for reasons bearing little likeness to our own nightmares. In the case of the Pilgrims, profound alarm gave birth to the project of migration, urging them to flee westward and to shun iniquity and defeat. As the comet appeared, Europe was approaching the great disaster called the Thirty Years' War: a war that the other side, the Roman Catholics, seemed all too likely to win.

Mother Courage and the *Mayflower*

When the comet first flew over London, the Pilgrims were trying to find the capital they needed for their plantation. Ten months earlier, they had obtained consent in principle from King James to settle within territory claimed by England in what were called "the northern parts of Virginia," meaning modern New Jersey or New York State. From their base in Holland, the Pilgrims still had to find investors willing to fund their new colony until it became self-sufficient. As they tried each avenue, speculation about the comet surrounded them. At any time, a star so brilliant would arouse intense interest, but in 1618 the conditions guaranteed that it would call forth a multitude of interpretations. The year in question opened a dangerous phase in history.

The stargazing Bainbridge had no doubt that this was so. He was one of northern Europe's rare optimists, but his optimism took a somber form.[7] Schooled by Puritans, he was another ardent follower of John Calvin, he hated the Roman Catholic Church and the pope, and he longed to see them defeated. His reaction to the comet took two forms. One was a matter of physics, as Bainbridge tried to use the comet to prove that Copernicus and Kepler were correct about the solar system, but the other concerned theology. Bainbridge made the star a prophecy of doom for most men and women, and salvation for a few.

Bainbridge listed a spate of comets in the previous century, closely coinciding with the arrival of Martin Luther, and with other significant moments in the history of the Protestant Reformation that followed. For Bainbridge, the latest comet was an emblem of Providence in action, an omen of upheaval, a sign that God was working out some vast plan of destruction or redemption for mankind. It might even be a warning of the Second Coming of the Son of Man.

No human soul could say what horrors might precede the end, but in the thirteenth chapter of his Gospel, Saint Mark supplied a clue. Before Christ returned to judge mankind, his message must first be preached in all nations, the evangelist had said. Bainbridge reminded his readers that a blazing star appeared in 1606, the year before the Jamestown colony began, and this was a promise from God that he would shine the lamp of Protestant Christianity on the heathen people of the Americas. That accomplished, the way would lie open for retribution to fall on the wicked. The comet, said Bainbridge, spoke of the imminent destruction of the Roman Church, and then all men would face the Lord.[8]

True, a few observers viewed the comet calmly, or doused forecasts such as this with cool skepticism. Grassi the scientific Jesuit disagreed with Galileo, arguing that the star was genuine and came from beyond the moon, but he also poured scorn on the Calvinists. He insisted that the star carried no theological lesson. Far away in London, James I agreed with him, dismissing the prophecies as nonsense. "Concerning the blazing star," wrote a contemporary, "His Majesty . . . swears it is nothing else but Venus with a firebrand in her arse."[9] Between royal functions, the king composed some verses, making the same point with his customary blend of learning and obscenity.[10]

Elsewhere the prevailing mood was very different, and especially in Protestant Germany. There ministers preached scores of comet sermons. Many were published, and a few have survived, their brittle pages carrying pictures of the star soaring over rivers, towns, and the sea. The words between the images conveyed a gloomy message, even darker than Bainbridge's. In the city of Magdeburg, a preacher spoke of the "grosser und erschrecklicher Comet," the great and frightful comet, and he warned that God's sword of judgment might fall at any moment.[11] At Ulm in Bavaria, a pastor told his congregation that the blazing star spoke of famine, plague, war, or earthquake, but as to which one it might be: "That lies hidden with Dear God."[12]

In the Netherlands, writers ventured specific prophecies, and they were grim too, dwelling again on the death of princes. Few believed that the gleaming object in the heavens warned of anything but bad news. Among the Dutch, the English ambassador was an industrious, clever man called Sir Dudley Carleton, who provided in his dispatches a detailed picture of the politics of his day. Even an envoy as shrewd as Carleton had little doubt that the comet conveyed a message in code from another dimension. For Carleton, it foretold the outbreak of a great European conflict. "We shall have . . . warres," he wrote home, and he was right. As the comet appeared, the opening campaigns of the Thirty Years' War began between the Danube and the Elbe. On one side were Catholic Spain and Austria; on the other, the Protestant states of Bohemia and Germany.

We need not trace in detail the sequence of events; as for their horror, the playwright Bertolt Brecht portrayed the three decades of hostilities as amply as anyone could wish in *Mother Courage and Her Children.* But in parts of central Europe, the percentage dead from violence, disease, or famine equaled the mortality rate from disease among the natives of New England. At Magdeburg, where the comet sermon had warned of a calamity, four-fifths of the population failed to survive a long siege.

Violence gathered momentum in the summer before the star appeared. In May 1618, in the episode known as the Defenestration of Prague, the Bohemians rejected Hapsburg claims to sovereignty over their country. At Prague Castle, nationalists hurled through a window the only local Catholics rash enough to defend the Austrian position. When the Bohemians raised a militia to repel an Austrian offensive, and began to threaten Vienna itself, the Austrians turned to their friends in Bavaria and Spain.

In August, Spanish troops seized the Valtelline Pass. The main road over the Alps, it gave them a safe supply line into the theater of conflict. In October, a palace revolution in Madrid brought to power a new faction eager to intervene against Bohemia. On February 3, 1619, Philip III of Spain committed his armies from the Low Countries and from Milan to the support of his allies. With that, a local squabble became a continental war between Roman Catholics and the Reformed, while Protestant England and its own Dutch Calvinist allies watched uneasily from the sidelines. A long truce between Spain and the Dutch Republic had only two years left to run, and in all likelihood the two old enemies would soon be at each other's throats again.

The fighting seemed certain to encompass all corners of the known world. Soon after the comet vanished, Carleton reported Dutch warnings that the Spanish navy was on the move. From Madrid, another English diplomat sent word that the ships were bound for North Africa to put a stop to the Arab pirates of Algiers. Perhaps the fleet was heading for the Adriatic to seize Venetian bases, or to Genoa to land troops to be sent over the Valtelline. Or perhaps the Spanish intended to attack the Jamestown settlement.

Spain relied on her annual treasure fleet, bringing silver from Peru, and this might prompt her, Carleton warned, to make a preemptive strike against colonies that might be used as a base for Atlantic privateers. "Our poore men in Virginia and the Barmudos" might be the target, said Carleton; but if his fears were justified, England could do little to fight back.[13]

In 1618 she was an impotent country, beset by dangers of many kinds. There could be no better year for the Pilgrims to seek the king's permission for their own American colony. They found allies within the highest circle of the government at home, among men who recognized the need for patriotic volunteers.

THE PRINCIPAL ADVANCER

In the autumn of 1617, from their Dutch place of refuge, the Pilgrims began to send probing messages back across the North Sea as they planned a new life in the New World. The two leading Pilgrims in Leiden were William Brewster, aged about fifty-one, and John Robinson, in his early forties. Both were strict Calvinists, from Nottinghamshire. Ten years before they had taken the radical step of setting up their own independent congregations, in separation from the established Church of England. Because that was unlawful, they fled to Holland. They took with them about one hundred fellow Separatists from the same English region, including the young William Bradford. However, neither Robinson nor Brewster was a fanatic, and neither man posed an immediate threat to the Crown. Both men could expect more than a rude rebuff from the authorities.

They were not heretics. They worshipped and chose their ministers in a free, autonomous way, but their theology aligned them with the Calvinists of France, the Huguenots, people with whom King James had friendly ties. In 1617, the leaders of the French Reformed Church were working on a plan to bring together the Protestant churches of Europe, including the Church of England, in an ecumenical union, based on a shared core of Calvinist ideas. A peacemaker by choice, James supported the scheme. It might even embrace radicals like the Pilgrims, who had the highest respect for their French counterparts. In the letters they sent to the Virginia Company, the Pilgrims played up their likeness to the Huguenots, and played down the points of divergence. This was a sensible tactic, and it yielded results.[14]

Brewster and Robinson had a friend in London called Sabine Staresmore, who acted as their agent.[15] Aged thirty-five, the illegitimate younger son of another clergyman, Staresmore belonged to a semisecret congregation based in Southwark, south of the Thames, a twilight place where people did unofficial things. The congregation recruited tradesmen, apprentices, and many women, flirted with Separatism, and tried to avoid prosecution. Staresmore himself went to prison after the authorities raided an illegal gathering. But Jacobean London was a subtle and a complicated city. Despite his views, Staresmore obtained a meeting in February 1618 with one of the most senior men in the Virginia Company, a financier in his mid-fifties called Sir John Wolstenholme.* Staresmore asked Wolstenholme to help the Pilgrims apply for the consents they needed, from the company and from the Crown, to settle in Virginia, and to do so with a measure of religious freedom. Wolstenholme swiftly agreed to help.

A description of his meeting with Staresmore survives in the great history of the Plymouth Colony written by William Bradford. Understandably, Bradford's narrative has always provided the backbone for books about the *Mayflower* Pilgrims. Later writers have often relied on it as pretty much their only source. But for all his qualities, Bradford left an incomplete account of events. We have to use the evidence from British archives to check, confirm, and amplify what he wrote; if not, incidents such as the intervention by Wolstenholme simply lose their meaning.[16]

Sir John was more than an average businessman, and the records that remain show that he had all manner of reasons to be cooperative. Although no evidence survives to suggest that he was a Puritan, Wolstenholme took his own Christianity very seriously. Near his country home at Stanmore, north of London, he built and endowed a new parish church. When he died, he left two hundred pounds for the repair of St. Paul's Cathedral, ten times the annual wages of a highly skilled craftsman. Far from distrusting the Pilgrims, Sir John recommended them for a Virginia Company grant to pay for a school for Native American children.

---

*How he pronounced his name is anyone's guess, but "Worsen-ham" seems most likely.

Besides his piety, Sir John was a practical man—his few surviving papers contain a mass of detail about the prices of pepper, silk, and indigo—and this would also make him listen sympathetically.[17] Virginia badly needed new migrants, because fever had culled the number of settlers to about four hundred. Since Wolstenholme belonged to an inner clique of investors who made a monopoly profit by selling supplies to the colonists, he had an obvious incentive to encourage the Pilgrims to head westward. He was also something of a visionary, and a patriot, worried by the fragile state of English commerce.

In business, the English lagged far behind the Dutch. Allies they might be, but the Dutch were also fierce competitors. They made better cloth than the English, they controlled the herring fisheries of the North Sea, and they fought bloody skirmishes with English whalers in the Arctic. Perhaps five times the size of England's, their merchant marine consisted of bigger but cheaper vessels, manned lightly and hired by Amsterdam traders with far more capital than their counterparts in London. And in July 1617, word reached Whitehall Palace that the Dutch had found a new South American route to the East Indies by way of a channel avoiding Cape Horn. That autumn and winter, English diplomats sent home a stream of dispatches warning that England was falling behind its opponents everywhere.

From Paris, the English ambassador reported that the French intended to create "a greate stocke and fleete for the undertakinge of remote trades, and particulerly to the West Indies." A few weeks later, he heard that the merchants of Rouen and Dieppe were planning a whaling voyage to Greenland, flouting English claims to control the area. In Holland, Carleton used his network of agents to obtain the secret Dutch log of their discoveries in Patagonia, and he sent it back to Whitehall, only to learn that the king of Denmark was also fitting out ships for a voyage to the Spice Islands. With the French and Dutch doing business there too, said Carleton, "the well will be drawne drie with so many buckets."[18]

In the opening months of 1618, the race for control of oceanic trade extended across the North Atlantic. In Paris, Champlain lobbied hard for royal support for his colony at Quebec. He asked Louis XIII for money and soldiers to help him find "un chemin raccourcy pour aller à la Chine," a quick way to China, via the Great Lakes, and to ward off his English and Dutch rivals.[19] As things turned out, the French Crown never threw its full weight behind him, but no one in London could be sure of that yet.

So, when Staresmore came to see him, Wolstenholme was busy with his own scheme to outflank Champlain and the Dutch. When a London author published the first English book on the ratios of trigonometry, vital for navigation, he dedicated it to Sir John, describing Wolstenholme as one "of the principall advancers of the Northwest discoverie," and indeed he was.[20] As a director of the East India Company, Sir John sponsored voyages to the Canadian Arctic, and when Staresmore made his approach, the quest was more urgent than ever. Wolstenholme knew about the Dutch discovery in South America, and his response was to press ahead with yet another effort to find a shortcut to the Indies.

On January 20, Sir John urged the East India Company to send a new expedition to Hudson Bay, offering to put up the bulk of the money. Meanwhile, he worked closely with a mathematician named Henry Briggs, another Cambridge man, a contemporary of John Robinson. Briggs had another theory, one that made it all the more important to secure the future of Virginia.

A Calvinist and a Puritan, Henry Briggs, like Robinson, had resigned his college fellowship during the purge of Puritans after King James first came to the throne. Briggs found a welcome in London from men of business, thanks to his own scientific expertise. He took the new tool called logarithms, first available in 1614, and showed mariners how to use them, combined with trigonometry, to calculate their course at sea. Like Bainbridge, to whom he was close, Briggs dreamed of making England the mistress of the Indies. He believed that while a route to the Pacific must exist through Canada, they could also reach the same ocean from Virginia by way of a portage across the Appalachians.[21]

Hence arose the need to plant more Englishmen in this essential region. By approaching Sir John, the Pilgrims had chosen the right man, and he did not disappoint them. Bradford mentions another revealing detail, easily missed but rich with significance. After seeing Staresmore, Wolstenholme hurried off to find a member of the king's Privy Council, the executive government of Jacobean England, to seek his support for the Pilgrim project. The statesman in question was Fulke Greville, the Chancellor of the Exchequer.

It would be hard to imagine a more willing advocate for their cause. Under Queen Elizabeth, Greville had served as treasurer of the navy, but more to the point he was Sir Philip Sidney's closest friend, the very same man who had composed Sidney's biography and recorded his enthusiasm for America. A fine poet himself, and a Calvinist of high sophistication, Greville shared Sidney's vision of godly English colonies on the same continent. By 1618 he had reached a peak of influence. He did so at a time when the political environment suddenly made the Pilgrims acceptable missionaries.

THE RIGGING OF SHIPS

For the king, 1618 had begun in typical Jacobean fashion, a mixture of high politics and farce, drenched in alcohol. In January, it was reported that James was indisposed, smitten with a sore toe, from which the pain spread to his knee. He had with him his favorite and lover, George Villiers, a young man of twenty-five, recently created Marquess of Buckingham. As he left the king's bedchamber in the dark, Buckingham fell down the stairs. He sprained his foot, vomited massively, took to his own bed for fifteen hours, and then hobbled about for several days with a stick.[22]

Buckingham gave rise to scores of anecdotes, but people wrote them down for reasons that were entirely serious. At first he was merely an exquisite courtier, but during the course of 1618 he also became a forceful statesman. His every move and mishap attracted close attention. His rise to power occurred by way of a silent coup d'état at the start of the year, a changing of the guard that secured for Buckingham the ascendancy he maintained for the next decade. It also brought to the fore in London a circle of men, including Greville, who sympathized with the Pilgrims. Their motives were partly religious, but also a matter of grand strategy. They arose from economics, and from the urgent need to strengthen the Royal Navy.

For many years, James I had spent far more than the Crown received in revenue, staving off a crisis by selling assets. But by the end of 1617 the situation was becoming desperate. From the City of London, the king had borrowed the vast sum of £100,000, enough to build twenty of the largest English warships afloat. The money bled away, mostly to pay for a royal tour of Scotland, and the City refused to lend more. The episode wrecked the credit rating of the Crown.[23] Only one option remained, a marriage between his son Prince Charles and a Spanish princess, the infanta, in return for a handsome dowry, but Spain knew that it held the upper hand. No swift agreement seemed likely. As the marriage negotiations floundered, the king at last accepted the need for financial reform.

James promoted a group of new, efficient men, allied with Buckingham, to cut expenditure and find new ways to raise money. Commissioners began to attack extravagance in the royal household, but if they were to make lasting improvements, they had to deal with the navy. Blighted by corruption, the fleet consumed far more cash than any other service, but it was ill equipped and poorly manned, barely capable of leaving harbor.

Change was required, and not only for fiscal reasons. Nearly a year before the comet, reports had already reached London of naval rearmament in Spain. Added to that was the new threat from the pirates of North Africa. They had begun to raid outward into the Atlantic, attacking English fishing vessels, taking their crews hostage, and demanding ransom. At Alicante, three English merchant ships found themselves fighting off a forty-strong Arab fleet, while more pirates were sighted only sixty miles from the coast of Cornwall.[24]

Sooner or later, England would have to mount a punitive foray against Algiers, but its ability to do so was doubtful. So, in 1618, Buckingham persuaded King James to make him lord admiral. Commissioners began to investigate the fleet, swiftly uncovering evidence of waste and embezzlement. Wolstenholme served on the naval commission, while Fulke Greville oversaw the process from his post at the Treasury. In the circumstances of the time, they had a further motive to encourage the Pilgrims, and again it was a matter of maritime concern.

Greville belonged to the anti-Spanish party at court. They were men who hoped to revive English sea power and to repeat the victories of Sir Francis Drake. His closest colleague of all was Buckingham's naval mentor, Sir John Coke, a man fascinated by warship design and logistics. Among the finest archives from the period are Coke's papers, listing the navy's requirements in intricate detail. A strong navy needed naval stores—"sea-arsenals," said Greville in his life of Sidney, and dockyards filled with "ordnance, pitch, rosin, tar, masts, deal-boards, cordage"—and Coke itemized their quantities and cost in long memoranda. Hence the importance of establishing a new colony in the northern parts of Virginia, which contained these commodities in abundance. The same year Captain John Smith, the Jamestown man, shot off one of many letters, urging the Privy Council toward New England, as a source for "all things belonging to the building and rigging of Shippes."[25]

Coke and Greville shared another colleague, a man whose name leaps from the pages of the Pilgrim narratives. Both Winslow and Bradford singled out for gratitude a politician, Sir Robert Naunton. It was Naunton, says Winslow, who convinced the king that the Pilgrims were harmless, however much they might want liberty of conscience. It would cost him nothing to let them go, since the Pilgrims would pay their own way by fishing, Naunton said. This gave the king a chance to be witty. "So God have my soul," James replied. "'Tis an honest trade; 'twas the Apostles' own calling."[26]

We have no reason to doubt that this conversation occurred. It was exactly the kind of remark that James made, and in 1618 Naunton bathed in the glow of royal approval. Another loyal adherent of Buckingham, in

January he became joint secretary of state, very nearly the highest rank within the government. Naunton saw all England's diplomatic papers, he headed its secret service, he loathed the Spaniards, he feared Dutch rivalry, and he was a close friend of Greville and Coke. We need look no further for his motives for helping Pilgrims. Without bases in America, England could not challenge Spanish control of the western ocean. And without the supplies New England might provide, the Royal Navy could not put to sea. For Naunton, most likely it was all a matter of politics and naval doctrine, with Calvinism adding the impetus of zeal.[27]

Naunton and Greville were on the same side as the Pilgrims, but of course Brewster and his colleagues were not merely tools of the English state. Even if they had been, an insolvent monarchy could not help them with hard cash. As it was, thanks partly to feuds within the Virginia Company, but also to some indiscretion on the part of William Brewster, even after royal approval it took nearly two years and two attempts for the Pilgrims to obtain the definitive patent allowing them to settle in the company's territory. For funds they had to rely on young, untried investors from London, with little capital between them. Other exiles reached America first. In August 1618, long before the *Mayflower,* another party of one hundred Separatists left for Virginia, and more Puritans followed. These ventures ended in failure, the bulk of the colonists killed by dysentery, but the principle had been established. Separatists could go to America, and the Crown would not stop them.[28]

During the years that followed the blazing star, while the Pilgrims struggled to find finance, events took an alarming course. Memories of the comet lingered, but its symbolism changed. At the time of the departure of the *Mayflower,* perhaps England's most widely read new book was *Vox Populi,* a polemic that blamed every evil of the day on the machinations of the Spanish and the pope. For its author, Thomas Scott, memories of the comet now evoked only ambiguity and doubt.

Scott recalled the excitement it caused, its sudden appearance as the war began in Germany, and the hope that the comet seemed to offer of victory over the wickedness of Rome. And yet, by the time he wrote, the outcome had been entirely different. Spain and Austria won battle after battle, until by the late summer of 1620 a Catholic army stood at the gates of Prague.

When the city fell, the refugees included an English princess, Elizabeth, the daughter of King James. Her Calvinist husband, the Elector Frederick of the Rhineland, had accepted the throne of Bohemia, and led that kingdom against the Austrians. His defeat was the most alarming blow of all. Scott remembered that the green comet carried a long tail; he reminded his readers that it was "swift in the beginning, and slow in the ending." It seemed to warn of a long, bloody, and uncertain conflict yet to come. Such was the atmosphere in which the Pilgrims set sail.[29]

In September 1620, as the Bohemian phase of the war neared its end, the *Mayflower* lay at her mooring in the finest natural harbor in England. She carried 102 men, women, and children as passengers. About half of them came from Separatist families resident in Leiden. It seems that forty-seven were adult males, with an average age of roughly thirty-eight. Her crew numbered at least seventeen, and probably more like thirty.

In Plymouth Sound, between the counties of Cornwall and Devon, the *Mayflower* prepared to leave for America under the command of her master, Christopher Jones. No record survives to show that Jones had crossed the Atlantic before; but for a while in Plymouth Sound he remained secure, among his fellow mariners in the companionship of the sea.

Chapter Two

Mr. Jones in Plymouth Sound

Plymouth is generally considered, and not without good reason, as the most capacious and secure rendez-vous in Great Britain.

—SAILING DIRECTIONS FOR SHIPS OF THE ROYAL NAVY,
FIRST HALF OF THE NINETEENTH CENTURY[1]

On Wednesday, September 6, a brisk wind blew over the sea outside the entrance to the sound. It came from the direction of an island, the Mewstone, a green pyramid of rock that leaps up from the waves like a small wet Matterhorn, situated offshore to the east. A *Mayflower* passenger called the wind "a fine small gale," and it carried the ship rapidly into the English Channel and toward the Atlantic. As Christopher Jones took her out of the haven, on her starboard side the *Mayflower* passed a headland, facing the Mewstone across four miles of water. Made of slate dotted with quartz, and topped with grass and yellow furze, Penlee Point dips and tumbles from a height of three hundred feet down into the sea.

When tankers or frigates enter or leave the approaches to Plymouth, they should keep the gray cliffs of Penlee half a mile away. At the foot of the promontory, crags spill out along the seabed to form a reef. At low tide the waves cover the Draystone, as it is known, to a depth of only one fathom. Fishermen will tell you that conger eels dwell within its crevices, waiting to bite the unwary who find them in their nets. Whether that is so or not, the reef has killed seamen in their thousands. The approaches to Plymouth contain many hazards, with ancient names—the Panther, the

Tinker, and the wicked little Shagstone, tiny, square, rising out of the water opposite Penlee—and mariners must know them all.

For two-thirds of the year, southwesterly winds sweep up from across the ocean and into the wide, deep notch in the coast that forms the sound. Mostly the winds carry a sailing vessel into Plymouth in safety, but when

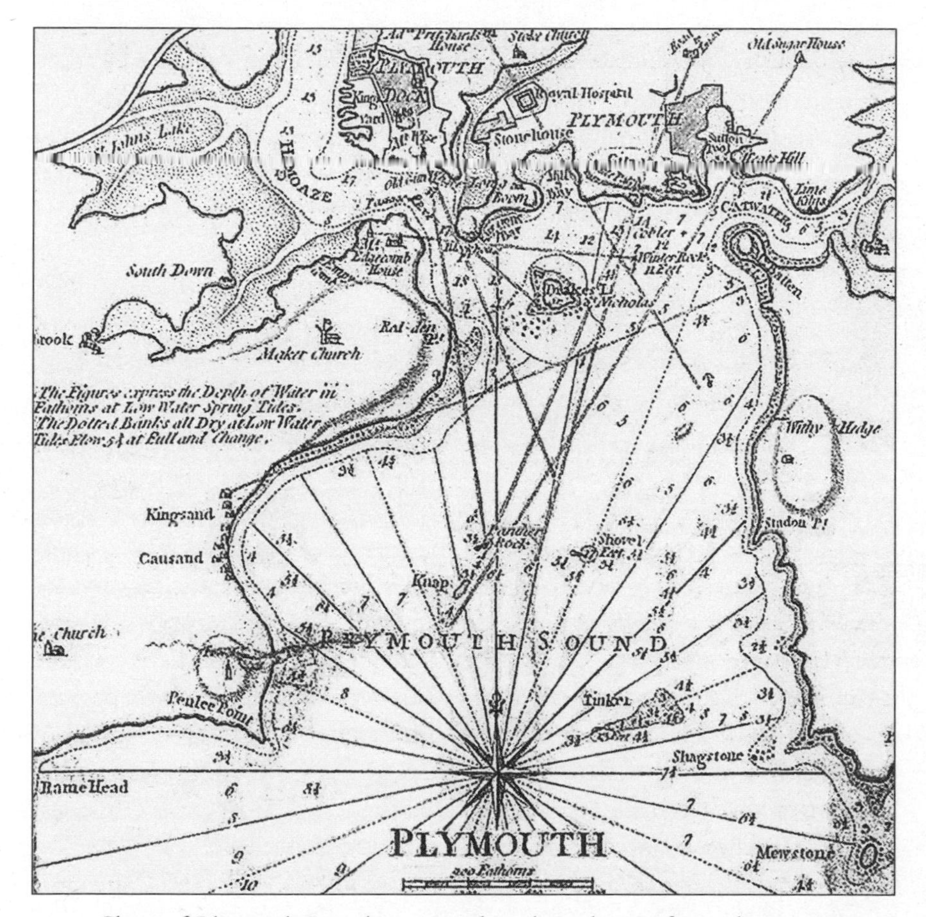

Chart of Plymouth Sound in 1782, when the only significant changes in the geography since the time of the *Mayflower* had been the building of the Royal Dockyard at Devonport, shown at the top, and the naval hospital nearby (*MR1/948, National Archives, Kew*)

they reach storm force, they will drive her straight onto the reef. Sometimes, too, the wind changes to come strongly from the east and south, while an ebbing tide pulls boats toward the west. Closer to shore another current pushes them out again as the water inside the sound piles back into the channel. When all this happens at the same time, wind one way and water another, the sea off the Draystone peaks upward to become a seething trap. A sailing ship, rudder gone or helpless in steep waves, loses her headway and slips back toward the rocks. Coastguards call the area Cannon Alley, because of the wrecks and armaments scattered offshore.

So it is along much of the rest of the coast on the way out to the west, where spurs of uneroded rock jut into the sea to form dangerous headlands. A chain of them extends as far as the Lizard Peninsula, the last English landmark before America and the most dangerous promontory of them all. In Jones's day mariners faced their greatest risks on the trip home, when they sometimes fatally mistook it for Ushant, one hundred miles to the south at the tip of France. So, the year before the *Mayflower* sailed, a Cornish squire built the first lighthouse on the Lizard.[2]

"The subtilnes of the tide imbayeth ships without prevention," said Sir John Killigrew, as he described the perils of the shore, hoping to take fees from Dutch shipowners tired of losing vessels sailing back from the East Indies. The *Mayflower* may have been one of the first ships to see his winking candles, or perhaps not. It cost ten shillings a day to keep the lighthouse shining, but Killigrew ran out of money soon after it was finished. Even so, his project made him a pioneer. Four years earlier, another lighthouse had appeared at Dungeness, at the entrance to the Strait of Dover, and these were the first of their kind since Roman lights cast their beams over the channel many centuries before. Their Jacobean revival was a sign that times were changing. So too was the voyage of the *Mayflower,* a venture forming part of a great metamorphosis of English enterprise by sea.

It was about to alter permanently, swerving toward the west, but only after a long and doubtful embarkation. Until the 1620s, more than a century after the foundation of New Spain, English skippers still remained scarce in the waters off the mainland of North America. In 1619, only six English ships made fishing voyages to the Gulf of Maine. For cod, Newfoundland still reigned supreme. The customs records list only one ship leaving the Thames that year for Jamestown, the *Bona Nova,* with a hundred settlers and a jumbled cargo of shoes, boots, hoes, and assorted ironmongery.

Only eight English ships altogether sailed to Virginia in 1619. The colony there still had little to offer by way of business, since the tobacco leaf sent home each season came to little more than fifty tons, barely enough to fill a large fishing boat. And yet by the end of the next decade, the bias of sea traffic began to change profoundly, and the passage to America at last became routine. By the middle of the 1630s, forty ships each year were leaving the port of London for Chesapeake Bay or New England. Soon each of the leading harbors in Devon had four or five master mariners who made regular crossings.[3]

The voyages traveled by English merchant ships fell into a new pattern, tilted westward. New England owed its origins to this maritime change of direction. However zealous Puritans might be, they needed sea captains willing and able to take them westward, and money to pay for the journey. Once on the other side, they had to service their debts and pay for essential items from the old country: the goods carried by the *Bona Nova,* but also glass, paper, lead, copper, Sheffield knives and hatchets, gunpowder and firearms, and most of all livestock. Alongside the beaver, and Puritans, imported cattle were the mammals that made Massachusetts what it became. Ships were needed too, more ships and bigger ships with ample hulls for carrying heifers as well as Pilgrims. Until they were available, nobody could build in New England a city on a hill.

It had to be possible to cross the North Atlantic in both directions more swiftly and more safely than in the past: in *both* directions, because to investors and indebted settlers the return journey mattered as much as the voyage out. Feasibility required experiment, and speculation. In the first thirty years of the seventeenth century, innovations such as Killigrew's lighthouse began to transform English navigation. Without this process, much of it by trial and error, Puritan America could not have come into being in the way in which it did.

Just as wind and tide converge around Penlee into a vortex of waters, but a swirl with a pattern beneath it, so a new turbine of connections began to drive events in the North Atlantic, spun in motion by new flows of trade and people across the ocean. Of all this, the *Mayflower* and Christopher Jones were physical symbols. At first sight, we seem to know little about Jones: merely the crude, random data of two weddings, nine baptisms of his children, his burial, and his lawsuits. Look a little deeper, and we find that he and his colleagues left a mass of evidence to mark their comings and goings.

In the two weeks before the *Mayflower* left for America, sixteen ships came into Plymouth, craft that the Pilgrims would have seen, bound in from Norway, Spain, Brittany, and the wine ports and salt pans of the Charente, in southwestern France. Out went another nine, heading for Dunkirk, the Basque Country, Ireland, and the Netherlands. An unknown number of small coastal boats scudded to and fro between the channel ports. These were old, familiar routes, paths deeply worn thanks to a long expansion of trade during the reign of King James. As Jones made the

Mayflower ready for departure, around him he saw the pattern of English seamanship visible in its entirety.

A Capacious Rendezvous

Somewhere moored close to the *Mayflower* was the *Patience,* skippered by Richard Barton. At the end of August, she sighted Penlee from the channel, on her way back from Alicante. Before him, as he came into Plymouth, Barton saw everything that the departing Pilgrims must also have seen: the same rocks and hills, and the same schools of dolphins, basking sharks, and canvas sails, arranged within the drowned river valleys that make the sound resemble a flooded auditorium, leading deep inland.

Like the *Mayflower,* the *Patience* was a London ship, at two hundred tons a little larger than Jones's craft. Like the *Mayflower,* she would be heavily armed against the Arab pirates to protect her cargo. It would have contained the items that Spain sent to England in the summer before wine making began: aniseed, almonds, figs, prunes, licorice, marmalade, and Spanish soap, the soft white Castile variety. Hundreds of pieces of Spanish pots and olive jars have been unearthed beneath the streets of Plymouth, with among them a broken set of blue-glazed teacups and saucers, porcelain made in China during the same era.[4]

In the nineteenth century, engineers built the great breakwater that now defends the sound. But in Jones's day the winds sped straight in from the sea without an obstacle, making it far too rough to ride at anchor in the middle. So, after the *Patience* rounded Penlee, most likely she swung to the west to enter the wide, sheltered haven of Cawsand Bay. This is a place so calm that even when a strong swell is running out at sea, the pennants of yachts berthed within it barely flutter. Long before, a Spanish raiding party had burned Cawsand village, but they left untouched the brick sheds by the beach, still standing today, where Tudor fishermen stored pilchards taken from the channel.

Cawsand made the best anchorage when the wind came from the southwest. If it changed to blow from the southeast, the *Patience* would have gone elsewhere. She would steer diagonally across the sound, making for a seamark, a stand of willow trees on a hillside. Known then and now as the Withy Hedge, the seamark still guides submarines along the deep channel that zigzags into the naval base at Devonport. At the Withy Hedge the *Patience* would turn to the north, toward the dark blue rim of Dartmoor, the granite plateau that hangs behind the sound like a curtain above a stage.

Beyond the Withy Hedge, the *Patience* would come to an island fortified with fourteen cannon. Once safely past it, four miles into the sound from the open sea, she would sail straight for a line of low gray cliffs, with above them the grass expanse of the Hoe, where Drake played his game of bowls before sailing out against the Spanish Armada. Close beneath it, at the last moment, Barton would have swung his bow sharply to starboard, under a row of more guns, pointing out over the waves from an artillery fort. Built at the corner of the Hoe, the fort had the low profile, sloping earthworks, and wide ditches recommended by the most advanced military architects.[5]

Behind the fort and the Hoe lay another haven for the *Patience.* Deep within the sound, a long placid pool curved away to the northeast, forming an anchorage, nearly one mile long. It was called the Cattewater. Either here or in Cawsand Bay, depending on the wind, Barton would have sighted the three masts of the *Mayflower,* and at her stern her square aft castle, towering thirty feet into the air. Neither ship would have entered the third available haven, Sutton Harbour, a basin flanked by piers and guarded by a defensive chain. Both vessels were too large, with about twelve feet of keel below the waterline. If either Barton or Jones had docked inside the basin at high tide, seven hours later he would have been trapped in the mud.

Carefully making his way around the *Mayflower,* Barton would have seen an aging ship. She was nearing the end of the usual working life of fifteen years. Most likely the *Mayflower* measured roughly one hundred feet long, from the beak of her prow to the hindmost tip of her superstructure. At her widest point she was roughly twenty-five feet across. Nobody can be more precise, since this was an age long before dimensions took a standard form. William Bradford says that the *Mayflower* had a volume of 180 tons, but he was not an expert.

What we can say, on the basis of surviving records, is that she could certainly fit at least 180 casks of wine into her hold, great barrels each filled with hundreds of gallons of claret.[6] Behind the gun ports in her sides and stern, if she wished to match a foreign ship of her class, the *Mayflower* also needed ten pieces of ordnance: seven cannon for use at long range, and three smaller guns charged with musket balls for close-quarter fighting. Later, at New Plymouth, Jones unloaded four of his pieces to fortify the colony. He would not have done so unless he had still more on board.

As he brought his own vessel to her berth nearby, Barton would see small boats plying back and forth from the *Mayflower* to the quayside, because Plymouth had a postmaster. Although details within Bradford's narrative suggest that the *Mayflower* spent no more than two or three days in the sound, there would still be time to write a last batch of letters up to London. The capital was only forty-eight hours away on horseback if the mail went posthaste. And since the postmaster also did business as a ship's chandler, he could supply Jones with any missing items needed for the journey. He had done just that only a few months earlier when he kitted out another English ship bound across the Atlantic that year, on an illegal voyage to Guyana in Spanish South America.

Did any of the Pilgrims go ashore? It seems that some did, but probably not many. Many weeks earlier they had already spent all their money on provisions, quarreling with one another about the cost, and about the outward customs duties they had to pay on their freight. But even from the deck they could see that the town above Sutton Harbour was new. Within a few decades, Plymouth had ceased to be just another small pilchard fishing village. Instead the town had become the sixth-busiest port in the kingdom.

Starting in about 1570, in the best havens around the coast of Devon, here and at Barnstaple and Dartmouth, suddenly the townspeople began to build new quays, wharves, harbor walls, and lanes of waterfront houses. One such, aptly called New Street, survived the Luftwaffe at Plymouth in 1941 and remains intact today. Up to a point, this new prosperity arose from the war with Spain, when Drake and his mentors the Hawkins family led the town as it became a base for warships and privateers. However, even after the king made peace with the Spanish, Plymouth continued to thrive in the Jacobean era, for reasons to be found in the voyages of ships such as the *Patience.*

We can talk about this ship, and the expanding trade of Plymouth, because of something called a port book. In 1564, to ensure that duties were paid, the Crown ordered the revenue men in each port to prepare annual reports listing every taxable cargo. The system produced immense volumes of paper, to be sent to the Exchequer in London, where they were filed and later forgotten. No historian looked at the port books until 1911, when an official inquiry revealed the lamentable conditions in which they were kept. A few scholars began to examine them, and swiftly made discoveries. This was how, at the time of World War I, historians traced in part the career of Jones and the *Mayflower* before her journey to America.

Since then, the port books have faded back into obscurity and become a neglected resource rarely touched by researchers. Often they are ragged, filthy, stained, or made illegible by heat, by damp, or by rodents. Many of the books have vanished entirely, including most of those from London. Breaks in the sequence make it hard to identify trends, and doubts exist about their accuracy, because of corruption among the customs men. All the same, and despite their flaws, the tattered books contain superb material when used with care and checked against other sources.*

The port books list the names of ships, their sizes, their masters, their destinations, the places from which they came, and the consignments shipped by each merchant. These details can be matched with other records—wills, depositions, official papers, and Puritan narratives—in such a way as to transform the familiar old story. And as it happens, a Plymouth port book has survived from 1620, ignored by historians because it fails to mention the *Mayflower.* There is nothing odd about this: the omission occurred because Jones never intended to pause in Plymouth at all.

His final port of exit was supposed to be Southampton, a hundred miles east along the channel coast. There the *Mayflower* met a smaller supply ship, the *Speedwell,* which had ferried the Pilgrims from Leiden across the North Sea. If everything had gone according to plan, the *Mayflower* and the *Speedwell* would have have left Southampton and headed straight out toward the Atlantic. Once across the other side, the *Speedwell* would have stayed on to fish and trade up and down the American coast. As it happened, soon after their departure from Southampton on August 5 the *Speedwell* sprang leaks. Both ships had to stop at Dartmouth, where the *Speedwell* underwent repairs, before they sailed out again.[7]

Three hundred miles beyond Land's End, the skipper of the *Speedwell* complained that once again she was filling with water. Back both ships went once more, and the *Speedwell* was discharged and sent home to London. This was how Jones came to be in Plymouth. The customs men did not list his ship in their annual report, because their Southampton colleagues had checked her already and collected the duties which she owed.

But even without the name of the *Mayflower,* the port book displays the forces at work in the world from which she came. The mercantile marine of England fell into three tiers or classes, depending on the size of the ship or the goods she carried. In each division England faced high risks and keen rivals. In the next four years the country underwent an economic crisis, a slump that continued to take its toll on the Pilgrims long after

*One London port book has survived in excellent condition, covering outward voyages in 1617. Lionel Cranfield, the first Earl of Middlesex and England's lord treasurer, apparently took the book home, and it became part of the Sackville Papers, at Maidstone in Kent. Every item is legible, including four references to the *Mayflower.* Overlooked by historians, it provides a complete picture of London's overseas traders, including some of those who financed the Plymouth Colony.

Pro: 3. The longitudes and latitudes of 2. places being giuen, both on the one side of the Equinoctiall, to finde their bearing and distance.

Let the Lizard in Cornewall, and an Island lying in the mouth of *Lumleys* Inlet, in *fretum Dauies* be the two places giuen, And let their course and distance be required: Admit the Latitude and Longitudes of those two places, to be as followeth:

Lumleys Inlet Latitude, No: 63. deg. 00'. Long. 309 deg.
The Lizard Latitude No: ——— 50. 10. *Long.* 17.
Their difference in Latitude ——— 12. 50' differ: lo: 68.
Which is 770'. for the difference of Latitude, and their difference of longitude is 4080'. both their differences of latitude and longitude, being multiplied by 60'. as is vsuall vpon the ordinary Chart, according to which wee will first worke.

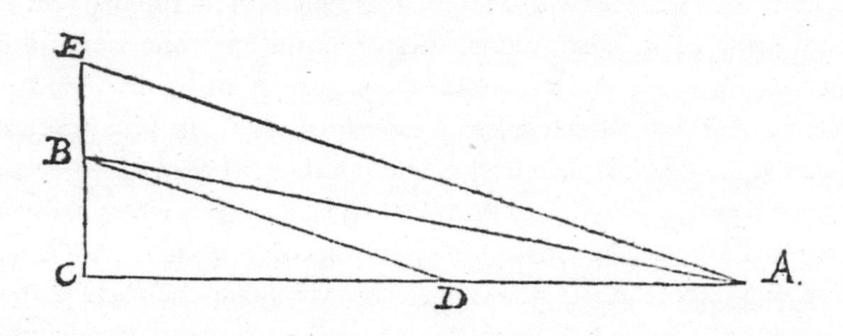

According to the ordinary Chart.

In the right angled Triangle, A B C. let B. represent *Lumleys* Inlet; and A. the Lizard point: in which Triangle according to the ordinary Chart are the 2'. lines including the right angle, B C A. giuen, together with the right angle B C A. to wit, B C. 770. minutes the difference of latitude. And C A. 4080. min. the difference of longitude; Then I say by the second Cons: of the first Axiome of the 3. booke of *Pitiscus*,

O 5 *As*

A page from the first English textbook of trigonometry, published in 1614 with a dedication to Sir John Wolstenholme, who helped the Pilgrims obtain consent to settle in America. This section explains how to calculate the distance and compass bearing between the Lizard in southwestern England and the Davis Strait in the Canadian Arctic. (*Lincoln Cathedral Library*) they reached America. As it turned out, in the end these hardships and the vagaries of war and commerce gave birth to lasting colonies. Arduous, long, and uncertain of success, the process can be followed in the careers of the men and the ships in the sound.

The *Lion* of London

Two famous mariners passed Penlee that year. History remembers Jones, but in his day the other man had far more prestige and sailed more dangerous waters. Three weeks after the *Mayflower* left for America, into Plymouth came the *Lion* of London, skippered by John Weddell. He later became the first English sea captain to take his ship to the Chinese port of Canton. In 1639, Weddell vanished at sea, most likely lost in a storm off the Cape of Good Hope, but in 1620 he stood on the quarterdeck of his first great command, within the topmost tier of English shipping.

A craft of four hundred tons, the *Lion* sailed under the flag of the East India Company. She and Weddell were bound back from Saldanha Bay in South Africa, after a year or two of trading and fighting the Portuguese in the Red Sea and the Indian Ocean. Jones would have known him, by sight and by reputation at least, since in London they lived on opposite sides of the river Thames, Weddell at Ratcliff, and Jones just across the water at Rotherhithe. Most likely the *Mayflower* crossed paths with the *Lion* on her voyage out. Before turning west to America along the fortieth parallel, Jones would have headed down toward the Azores, on a route converging with the track that Weddell must have followed home.

John Weddell belonged to England's seafaring elite, men with the skills to complete the nine-month voyage to the Malay Archipelago. On their way back, after sighting the Lizard, East India ships such as his called at Plymouth for food and water. They unloaded a little cargo, silks, spices, and perhaps some Chinese crockery, before making for the capital with the bulk of what they had. Demand for luxuries such as these led to rich profits, but it also caused side effects that, in due course, spilled over to accelerate English enterprise in the Atlantic as well.[8]

Eager to see more capacity at sea, the Crown gave a bounty to men who built new ships, five shillings per ton for each oceangoing vessel of one hundred tons or more. Records of the bounty payments show a surge of construction driven by the voyages of Weddell and his colleagues in the East India service. In 1616, English dockyards launched no fewer than seventeen oceangoing hulls, with among them two vessels of more than one thousand tons each, armed merchantmen bound for the Orient. In 1617 the boom continued, with such intensity that the king scrapped the subsidy. He saw no need to bankroll speculators with scarce public funds.

By that time, the shipwrights had already engineered a lasting increase in the size of English merchant vessels. In the final decade of the bounty, the average ship built with it nearly doubled in size, from a little over two hundred tons to four hundred. When Jones first skippered the *Mayflower*, in about 1608, she ranked as one of the largest English merchantmen at sea. By the time of her voyage to America she was slipping down the scale, smaller than all but one of the last tranche of ships that received the royal subsidy, and when John Winthrop led his fleet to Massachusetts, he traveled in a flagship twice the *Mayflower*'s size.[9] A matter of deliberate policy on the part of the Massachusetts Bay Company, the use of bigger ships was essential, as we shall see. It was only possible because of the preceding decades of experience.

As ships grew larger, expertise deepened too, with East India merchants like Wolstenholme as the chief sponsors of research. Lighthouses were only one instrument of change. Among the others were new coastal charts and tide tables, and buoys and beacons in hazardous spots, and the regular dredging of the Thames, making safer the return to England's sea approaches. In 1608, the Dutch began selling telescopes like Bainbridge's. Nine years later a London surgeon wrote the first handbook of nautical medicine. By the early 1620s, besides new manuals of advanced mathematics English seamen had the first books that tabulated the variation in the earth's magnetic field from one place to another: an essential tool for correcting errors in reading a compass.

In the same decade, the log and line first came into widespread use to measure a ship's speed and distance traveled. By way of a knotted rope paid out over the stern, they allowed the master to fix his whereabouts more precisely. In 1623 a friend of Henry Briggs first used the term "knot" to measure nautical velocity. Seven years later, the English invented the slide rule, quite literally placing logarithms in the hands of mariners. Finally, in 1631, another English mathematician published the first practical guide explaining how to follow a "great circle," the shortest distance between two positions on the globe. As an example, of course he chose the passage back across the Atlantic, from Bermuda to the Lizard.[10]

For the sake of bigger ships, as well as better pay, the finest seamen chose the East India service, but knowledge flowed westward too. Richard Norwood, the man who wrote the guide for great-circle sailors, suffered too much from seasickness to captain a ship, and so he trained as a diver. He went to Bermuda in 1613 to fish for pearls, and settled there as a surveyor and schoolmaster. New tools such as his brought the American coast within the reach of many more seamen, adding another layer of support to the new colonies when at last they began to grow.

Why did so many advances coincide? Pure research accounted for some of the discoveries, and religion played its part too: people of science saw the finding of a theorem as the pathway to the mind of God. But most of all, the momentum came from politics and commerce. For the first two-thirds of the reign of King James, traders and seamen alike had known little but prosperity, in the East India traffic and much nearer home. But England's expanding trade rested on a narrow and fragile base. Her maritime enterprise had settled into routines that left it vulnerable to competition from the Dutch and to commercial collapse in time of war. Each marine innovation came about in response to the fear of being left behind.

In the East Indies, the signs of harder times ahead were very clear. On board the *Lion,* Weddell brought home news of more trouble with the Dutch, and soon afterward it took bloody form. In October 1620, at Bantam off the coast of Java, the Dutch sank two company ships. Because of violent rivalry such as this, and because so many ships from many countries were sailing to the Spice Islands, the next decade was a disaster for the English East India traders. The market price of pepper, indigo, and silk reached a peak in London in 1622 and then sank steadily for the next seven years. Dividends paid by the company fell away. This became another reason for English eyes to swivel toward America.

For Jones, the long haul to the East Indies had never been an option, since the *Mayflower* belonged like the *Patience* to the smaller, second division of the English merchant navy. Ships of their class, based in London but using Plymouth as a port of call, stuck to a less ambitious business. And yet even for men such as Barton and Jones, the sky was growing darker. Two decades of growth were coming to an end, in a fading climate that explains why, after a comfortable career, Jones suddenly took on the unfamiliar task of carrying the Pilgrims.

The Life and Times of Christopher Jones

Christopher Jones was born in about 1570 in the port of Harwich, on the eastern coast of England. Queen Elizabeth called Harwich "a pretty town," and to her it was intensely loyal, sending three ships to join Drake against the Armada.[11] Local seamen caught lobsters, fished for cod as far away as Iceland, or carried coal from Newcastle to London. Like Plymouth, Harwich had grown wealthier still by pillaging Spanish ships, though the business it did best was to export English woolen cloth to be dyed and finished in Holland. A boy raised there would also hear stories told by explorers. When Jones was eight or so, Harwich men sailed to Baffin Island.

Pretty or not, Harwich possessed characteristics that made it ideal for the training of a seafarer. It also had a social environment that helps explain why the early colonies in America took the shape they did. Thanks to the winds and currents of the North Sea, and thanks to the silt that drifted down the coast, the entrance to Harwich contained dangerous sandbanks, with names such as the Pies, the Pole Head, and the Platters. To the north was the long pebble spit of Orford Ness, where on a single night in 1627 a storm wrecked more than thirty ships. In these testing waters Jones served his apprenticeship. His father and his stepfather were both Harwich skippers, and at eighteen Jones inherited his first part share of a ship.

He belonged to a clique of mariners and shipwrights who governed the town with harsh discipline. They sentenced five women to hang as witches in 1605, while harlots were dragged through the streets on a cart, and dice games were banned. Harwich resembled other seaports around the English coast, from Hull in the north to Barnstaple in the west, where sea captains and merchants ran local government, levying municipal taxes to pay for street cleaning, jails, and parish constables. They formed part of an international circuit of little marine republics, from the Baltic to the Pyrenees, Calvinist by inclination, from Gdansk in modern Poland to La Rochelle in southwestern France. In America, when New Plymouth and New Boston reached maturity, they formed the western extension of the same network, tossed across the ocean like the end of a coil of rope.

In his mid-thirties Jones became an oligarch himself, named as a burgess of Harwich in a new charter granted by King James. A rising man, with the help of the five-shilling bounty he built a ship of his own, the *Josian*, named after his second wife. At 240 tons, the craft was larger than average. She must have cost around a thousand pounds, a sizable sum when a ship's master hired by a merchant earned no more than fifty pounds a year, and Jones used her for trading voyages as far south as Bordeaux. Then, in 1611, he became one of a group of Harwich men who outgrew the town and moved south to the Thames. Jones made his new home at Rotherhithe, a mile downstream from the Tower of London.

By that time, he had swapped the *Josian* for a quarter share in the smaller *Mayflower*, and narrowly escaped disaster in the North Sea. In 1609, he guided her safely back from Norway through "an extraordinary great storm," with a cargo of timber, tar, and fish. As a crew member later recalled, in an effort to save the ship Jones dumped over the side a hundred planks of wood. Many weeks late they struggled back home, only to find that the man who owned the tar, wood, and rotting herring was bankrupt, unable to pay for them. When he moved to the capital, Jones found a safer, more regular trade. He also followed the tide of history.[12]

Before the 1590s, Rotherhithe and Ratcliff were country retreats, places where Londoners hunted deer and rabbits. Suddenly, as the wealth and the population of London grew, they began to fill with new houses for mariners, with alongside them abattoirs, inns, and England's first sugar refinery. In the late 1620s, a census counted nearly 120 master mariners in these two parishes alone. Excavations in the year 2000 found traces left behind by these new Jacobean citizens, immense quantities of imported pottery, Venetian glass, and some of the earliest clay tobacco pipes uncovered in England.[13] The same archaeology also unearthed some of England's first glass wine bottles, designed to be packed into crates.

Wine flowed like the Thames through the commercial veins of London. It made the fortune of the mariners of Rotherhithe. Jones's most affluent neighbor was another ship's master, named Anthony Wood, skipper of the *Rainbow,* who ranked above Jones at the very top of the parish list of taxpayers, owner of shares in three ships and a portfolio of houses on both sides of the river. Wood was another visitor to Plymouth in the autumn of 1620, sailing out of the Sound in October for Alicante, and he owed his wealth to the excellent vintages that the Spanish port supplied.[14] Alicante was the favorite drink of King James himself. A pint of it cost sixpence, close to a laborer's daily wage, and the trade was very lucrative indeed.

The largest client of Christopher Jones was one William Speight. He lived in Vintry Ward, the wine merchants' district, opposite the Globe Theatre. After buying his wine wholesale in France, shipping it home, and paying all his costs, Speight could clear six pounds of profit per ton. In May 1620, Jones and the *Mayflower* sailed back into the Thames on their last trip before carrying Pilgrims. He carried fifty tons of wine for Speight, enough to make Speight as much money as ten English clergymen earned in a year. Holding the rank of warden of the Company of Merchant Taylors, Speight owned country estates in Suffolk and tenements, shops, cellars, and warehouses in the City. At his death in 1621 he left a string of bequests to schools and the inmates of prisons, the charities supported most often by London's mercantile elite.

Men like Speight, Wood, and Jones prospered because of a surge in the intake of alcohol as the income of the landowning classes grew. At the peak of the wine trade, in 1615, London imported nearly three times as much wine as it had in a typical year twenty years previously. English customers were not only drinking more but also paying more for what they drank: during the same two decades, at La Rochelle the price of white wine doubled. Taste became more subtle too, as the English widened their horizons from claret to Sauternes, Spanish sweet wines, and brandy. The first hard liquor from Cognac arrived in London in about 1560, most likely rough stuff, like an Italian grappa, but during the reign of King James the Dutch refined it and made it an item of choice. A typical Jones voyage in 1615 saw the *Mayflower* bring back from France eighty tons of the new spirit. She carried to New England at least one keg of French or Dutch eau-de-vie.[15]

When wine ships sailed back and forth, they did more than simply fill the wallet of a William Speight. Their voyages made the Protestant maritime network deeper and tighter, binding it together with exchanges of men, women, and ideas. By the 1620s, each leading French haven along the Atlantic coast had a solid community of English and Scottish traders and brokers, with Dutchmen in still larger numbers. At the center of the web lay the city of La Rochelle, the Huguenot bastion that tied together the long loops of commerce from north to south, and from the Levant to Newfoundland.

Down from the Baltic came grain, hemp, and tar, to be sold to the French or shipped on to Spain. Back up from the Mediterranean and Gascony came currants from Greece and Turkey, iron from Galicia, and Spanish colonial goods, tobacco, or raw sugar. Along the coast to the south of La Rochelle lay immense salt marshes and the fortified port of Brouage. English ships bound back from the Grand Banks could sell their cod to fish-eating Catholics and then fill their empty holds with French salt for packing their next consignment. Or they, and the Dutch, would simply carry it back home: overcast northern nations had no salt pans to rival those of the sunnier Charente. In an age of sail, the French made the best canvas, and this too could be purchased at La Rochelle. There the English also found allies. The Huguenots had their own *armée navale,* fifteen warships ready to fight the French king.

Jones and the *Mayflower* found a place within this pattern of trade, but like the commerce with the East Indies it carried no guarantee of success. Everything, including the fortune made by William Speight, depended on finding ready takers for the only currency that London's merchants possessed. England had no gold or silver mines, and it was strictly illegal to export coin or precious metals without a license from the Privy Council.

The country's meager stocks of bullion were mostly earmarked to pay for the silk and spices returning from Asia. So when the *Mayflower* left London for France, her hold was crammed with English woolens, the nation's only substantial export. Instead of cash, Speight and his rivals used thousands of yards of raw cloth to pay for French or Spanish wine.[16]

Woolen textiles were England's strength, but also a source of vulnerability. If anything happened to deter the buyers in Europe and cloth failed to sell, the way of life of mariners such as Jones would swiftly disintegrate. A family man, Jones had to fill his ship and keep her busy. In 1620 that was rapidly becoming far more difficult than in the past.

Everything was about to go very wrong. In June, as Jones was hired to cross the Atlantic, expert observers in London could already see the warning signs of a dangerous decline in the economy. In Devon too, life was becoming more complicated, at sea and on land alike, for merchants, for fishermen, and for the soldiers in the fort at Plymouth. New problems had to be solved. As yet, very few men and women believed that North America provided the answers.

Diverse Friends There Dwelling

On September 6, as the ridge of Dartmoor vanished below the horizon, the *Mayflower* must have passed a fishing boat called the *Covenant.* In September, listed in the port book, the fishing fleet from Newfoundland came hurrying home to Plymouth, sixty-five vessels in all, traveling in convoy eight at a time. In 1620 the *Covenant* made it back first to Cawsand Bay or the Cattewater, on the very day on which the *Mayflower* left.

At thirty tons, the *Covenant* was small, from the lowest, third tier of English merchant ships. In this, she was typical of the craft that sailed to Newfoundland: the tiniest that year was a twenty-five-tonner, the *Trinitie,* a brave little vessel that took two months more to straggle back into Plymouth. Only seven of the town's Newfoundland vessels had a volume of a hundred tons or above, and none came anywhere near the *Mayflower*'s size. For this reason, cod fishing alone could never form the basis of permanent English colonies on the American mainland. The ships employed simply did not have the capacity required. Few of the Newfoundland boats could carry more livestock than a few goats or pigs.

Cod fishing yielded a good return even if the ships were small, and that was the problem. Dried and salted, the fish conveyed in the *Covenant* would fetch three hundred pounds on a Spanish quayside. And train oil, squeezed from cod, walruses, or whales, added another stream of profit.

Used to make soap for washing newly woven cloth, it sold for only twopence a pint, but it came back in batches of more than a thousand gallons per boat. Plymouth men had begun to sail to Newfoundland as long ago as the 1540s, but the cod voyages were closed circuits that did not lead elsewhere. As long as the Newfoundland trade continued to thrive, and while woolens could be bartered for wine, merchants had no need to think about mainland America. Five years before, Captain John Smith had returned to Devon from Monhegan Island, nine miles off the coast of Maine, bouncing with enthusiasm for the country he named New England. He did not find an eager reception.

Written up in a book published in 1616, his chart and his tales of Cape Cod, fish, fur, and timber failed to arouse excitement. Dashing and eloquent, John Smith did his best, touring the western ports to promote the opportunities that he had seen. Few wished to follow him, and no colonists willingly did. Later, Smith listed twenty-two voyages to New England between 1614 and 1618, from London or from Devon. They included landings on the Cape, but no one tried to found a settlement.

Three days' sail from Boston, Monhegan remained the favored destination, as a fishing or a trading post, but it could not host a colony: the rocky island measured little more than a mile long. Smith had also visited a place to the south called Accomack. He named it New Plymouth on his chart, speaking of its "excellent good harbor" and "good land," but nobody took much notice. After reading his narrative, the *Mayflower* Pilgrims aimed elsewhere, for New York Harbor, recently visited by an old shipmate of Smith's. He had sailed around Long Island and sent a report home, suggesting like Henry Briggs that the Hudson offered a route to the Pacific.

Nevertheless, although few people had grasped the point, times were changing and gradually making New England more compelling. Sometimes, cod became scarce off the Grand Banks, or disappeared entirely for a season. This happened in 1621, encouraging some adventurous traders to think again about Maine and Massachusetts. The cod voyages also became more dangerous, thanks to the pirates from North Africa.

They ambushed the fishing boats on the way home, because they were too small and lightly armed to put up a fight. In the next quarter century, the pirates took at least seven thousand English sailors captive, about half of them from Devon, and, as we shall see, in due course this helped to feed Puritan discontent with the Crown. And, once again, we find the Dutch closing in to undermine England's business. Dominating the herring grounds of the North Sea, the Dutch had mostly left Newfoundland alone. Until, that is, the year of the comet, when they began to sail to "Terra Nova," as they called it, challenging the English in their old domain.

Jones and the Pilgrims would have heard talk about matters such as these at Plymouth. Later, when the Pilgrims came to narrate their adventures, they included a typically cryptic allusion to the place. At Plymouth, they said, they were kindly entertained "by divers friends there dwelling." Who were the friends in question? The Pilgrims do not say, but two likely candidates present themselves. In their different ways, both men were looking for alternatives across the ocean. Their careers add another layer of explanation for the leap across the Atlantic that would soon occur.

The first man was the postmaster, Abraham Jennings. He was in his early forties, and he owned a quay in the center of the waterfront. As a young man, Jennings had supplied iron pots, locks, and other bits and pieces to the first Englishmen who tried to settle in New England, the failed Popham Colony of 1607, at Fort St. George in Maine. Then he apparently forgot about the New World, until the new circumstances of the 1620s aroused his interest once more.

Until then, Jennings stuck to the familiar. Dealing in cod, figs, and raisins, he bought wine from the Canaries, or shipped merchandise back from Alicante on the *Patience.* Then suddenly, in 1622, he begins to reappear in records relating to North America. A little later, Jennings bought control of Monhegan. He started to bring back beaver pelts, nine hundred in 1626, a type of cargo new to Plymouth. For some reason, he soon tired of the venture and sold the island, but his involvement was a landmark. For the first time since the Popham debacle, a substantial Devon merchant, rooted in the older European trades, had invested capital in the territory north of the Potomac. He did so in alliance with a second man, who had other reasons to look westward.[17]

To find him, the Pilgrims would have to climb up to Plymouth Fort and ask for the governor. Nobody in the realm, besides John Smith, thought more about New England than Sir Ferdinando Gorges. The fort's commander, he came from an old French family from Normandy. His fascination with America seems to have arisen entirely from patriotism, and curiosity. He seems never to have made a penny from his efforts.

At fifty-four, Gorges had been fascinated by America for more than a decade. His obsession dated back to 1605, when he met three Abenaki people, shipped back to Plymouth by an early English voyager to Mawooshen. Gorges questioned them closely about their home, and most of all about its rivers leading far inland.[18] Excited by what he heard, Gorges helped lead the creation in 1607 of the Plymouth Company, designed to operate north of the Delaware, as a twin of the London company that founded Jamestown to the south. It planted the Popham Colony, and then it backed John Smith's voyage of 1615. Beyond that, it achieved nothing, but Gorges refused to give up.

As the *Mayflower* prepared to sail, Sir Ferdinando was about to relaunch the company, with a new name and a new royal charter. The Council for New England came into being on November 3, a few days before the Pilgrims sighted Cape Cod. Packed with marquesses, earls, and a clergyman or two, in the name of His Majesty it held dominion over all the land and sea between the fortieth parallel and the forty-eighth, from the St. Lawrence to the site of Philadelphia, and as far west as the Pacific.

Because it later became extinct, abolished by King Charles, and because its papers mostly vanished, the council has never commanded much respect. Historians in America often portray the council and its creator as absurd feudal relics, intent on turning New England into an aristocratic fiefdom. Up to a point this is fair. Gorges antagonized many people, especially the fishermen of Devon, by charging fees for licenses to look for American bass and cod. But Gorges was no fool, and far from being narrow-minded, he was another visionary of a kind.

Much later, he fell out with the Puritans of Massachusetts, but to begin with he happily welcomed the Pilgrims as settlers, speaking highly of their good relations with the native people whom they met. He recruited merchants as partners, inviting Jennings to join the council. Far earlier than other men, Sir Ferdinando saw the need to build much bigger ships to service the new colonies, to be paid for, he hoped, with a loan from the East India Company.[19] If he charged fees for fishing, it was because he needed to defend the Gulf of Maine against the Spanish, the French, or the Dutch.

In 1621, Gorges made his own disappointing tour of England's west country, looking for colonists to follow the Pilgrims. He aroused as little interest as John Smith. Gorges spoke in the military language of empire, and perhaps this deterred investors. Security had to come first, he said, as he listed his American priorities: "erecting forts, placeing of Garrisons, maynteyninge shipps of warr upon the Coasts, and officers for the more safe and absolute Government of those parts." Gorges had militarized Plymouth Sound, with cannon protecting each strongpoint. Now he wished to make the North Atlantic a fortified English lake, with Virginia and New England as the armed bulwarks of a new empire.[20]

Like most of his fellow countrymen, Sir Ferdinando believed that another war with Spain was unavoidable. At Plymouth he stood in the front line. We can imagine him, pacing up and down his parapet, watching the *Mayflower* come and go, fuming at the politicians who withheld the funds he needed to man the fort and fight the pirates, and cursing the merchants who failed to share his vision of western adventure. For the time being, however, failure seemed the most likely outcome in a commercial project of any kind.

Damp and Deadness

Over the early years of the Plymouth Colony hung the shadow of depression. The voyage of the *Mayflower* took place at the moment when unease about the economy crystallized into acute alarm. Capital was scarce, and demand collapsed. Tens of thousands of weavers found themselves with no work to do. A few days before the *Mayflower* reached America, King James reluctantly called his first Parliament in six years, prodded into action by those who wanted England to join the Thirty Years' War. Raising money for rearmament should have been its principal concern. By the time the House of Commons met in early 1621, the crisis in the economy had instead become the chief topic for debate.

As unemployment rose, members of Parliament frightened one another with talk of a peasant uprising. "Looms are laid down," one wrote in his journal. "Every loom maintains forty persons . . . the farmer is not able to pay his rent, not for want of cattle or corn or money. The fairs and markets stand still."[21] Most alarming was a sudden scarcity of money. For its bullion, the Royal Mint relied entirely on private citizens bringing in plate or old coins to be recast, but the inflow of silver ceased entirely. Not a single silver coin was struck at the mint between April 1619 and March 1620, and very little in the twelve months after that. At Cambridge, departing students sold their old desks and chairs to incoming men who took their rooms. One such was the student who had described the comet in his diary. As the *Mayflower* left Plymouth, he tried to auction his furniture, but found no takers: nobody had any cash.[22]

As British governments do, King James appointed a committee to investigate. It reported that things were very bad, and offered many explanations. It said something must be done, and then the king did nothing. By the middle of 1621, western Europe had slipped into the deepest depression in six decades. As the European war made things still worse, a contemporary spoke of "that great and generall dampe and deadnesse . . . which we unhappily feele at this day."[23] In 1622, a year after returning from America, Jones died at the very bottom of the slump. He left a widow, sons and daughters, and an empty ship. Her ultimate fate is unknown, but most likely the *Mayflower* was scrapped in 1624.

Behind the slump lay many causes, but for the Pilgrims it was the consequences that mattered. In their early years in the New World, they could expect only fitful support from their backers and friends at home. In due course, seamen and merchants looked for ways to avoid another economic crisis of the same kind by widening their sphere of enterprise; and in doing so, maritime England turned its attention decisively across the Atlantic. But that did not occur until much later in the decade. In the meantime, Bradford and his comrades mostly had to fend for themselves, or try to find allies on the western side of the ocean. And if they wanted help from heaven, they had to pray to a god of thunder, the terrifying deity of Calvin.

Chapter Three

Crossing Sinai

What man, if he be to goe a long and unknowne journey, will not hire a guide to conduct him? Or to undertake a voyage by water, to the East-Indies, Guiana or the Newfoundland, but desireth the most skillful pilot to goe with him? And shall not wee seeke unto God, and desire his direction from earth to heaven? From this old Aegypt to the new Ierusalem? If we doe not, we may well wander out of our way; and split the ship of our soules upon the rocke of condemnation.

—John Barlow, Puritan town preacher of Plymouth, Devon, in a funeral sermon of 1618[1]

Nine days and nights had passed since the last full moon. The men of the morning watch rang four bells to mark six o'clock, and turned the ship's hourglass on its head in almost complete darkness. Due west, a third of the way up the vault of the sky, the *Mayflower*'s helmsman would have seen a flickering orange point. It would be Arcturus, one of the brightest fixed stars with which an expert seaman could measure latitude. Below Arcturus and to its right in the northwestern quadrant of the heavens gleamed the bulkier lamp of Venus.

Then, as dawn approached, a long, blurred horizontal shadow must have emerged from the gloom beneath the star and the planet. By seven, twenty minutes after sunrise, the shadow would have hardened into a thick gray line. From the swaying deck, Jones and his crew would have made out a ridge of land, wooded with oak and cedar.[2]

In cold but clear weather and at perhaps only ten miles, there would be no mistaking its identity. Robert Coppin, the second mate, had been there before. Eighteen years earlier another Englishman had described the headland's low sandy hills, its trees, and its shoals of cod, mackerel, and bream, and given the cape the name it has carried ever since. To seamen of Coppin's generation, Cape Cod's long sickle-shaped outline made a familiar landmark in the charts they could study before setting sail. It was, said an optimistic writer describing the voyage of 1602, a land "faire and pleasant, resembling France, temperate and well-agreeing with our constitution."[3] For ships coasting for six hundred miles from Maine to Jamestown, the anchorage behind the Cape's northern tip had offered a safe haven for at least half a decade.

Landfall came as a relief after more than nine weeks at sea, but by itself it gave Jones no cause for satisfaction, and for William Bradford and his fellow Pilgrims the sight of Cape Cod brought with it new anxieties. Because of their false starts and foul weather—for many days, the winds were "so feirce, and ye seas so high, as they could not beare a knote of saile," Bradford later remembered—they were two months behind schedule. It seems that the *Mayflower* had found her way up the long slot of deep water that today forms the main shipping lane to Boston. Slanting northwestward on a naval chart, it passes between the dangers of the Nantucket shoals inshore and those of Georges Bank far out at sea. Even so, Jones had lost his way.

They were nearly 250 miles from the destination he had hoped to find, somewhere between Rockaway Beach and Staten Island, with Manhattan beckoning behind them. And, within the belly of his ship, Jones carried a complicated human cargo, and one that might cause trouble.

Between the timbers of the *Mayflower* lay a wet, narrow space smelling of vinegar, vomit, stale meat, and overripe cheese. In daylight the lower deck resembled a long dim corridor. Partially blocked at intervals by nautical clutter, at night it was entirely dark. From deck to deck the headroom was no more than about five feet, or only four in places where the beams reached from side to side. A crouching man found his way impeded by a capstan for hoisting the *Mayflower*'s anchors, three masts, the bulkiest nearly two feet thick, and the dismantled hull of a shallop, or small boat. The rest of the crowded space was filled with human beings and their belongings.[4]

After so long at sea, the indignities of the voyage threatened to reduce them to a demoralized rabble. "A boisterous sea and stormy weather will make a man not bred on it so queasy sick," wrote a maritime author of the day, Sir William Monson, "that it bereaves him of legs, stomach and courage so much as to fight with his meate."[5] And yet everything we know about the *Mayflower*'s passage suggests that they strove to keep up appearances and to maintain decorum.

Even on the ocean, the English ranked each other in categories, carefully arranged in grades of wealth and social status. Twenty-four households traveled on the *Mayflower.* At least fifteen, with between them forty-nine members, were headed by an adult male who had lived in Leiden. The remaining nine households came from England; some apparently had Puritan leanings, of a less radical form, and it seems that some were purely economic migrants. We cannot be precise, because the passenger list does not refer to their religion, or their lack of it; it simply proceeds in order of deference. At the top were John and Katherine Carver, people of substance traveling with five servants, including John Howland, and an adopted child. At the bottom of the list sat ten single men without families, land, or skilled occupations. Sadly, because Carver failed to survive more than a few months in the New World, we know little about him, beyond the fact that he was "godly & well approved," as Bradford put it, and their first choice as the colony's governor. In the England of the period, a man of property naturally expected to serve as a local official.[6]

It seems that the discipline he enforced extended to hygiene. Next to scurvy, amoebic dysentery ranked as the worst marine affliction, the so-called bloody flux that had killed Sir Francis Drake. And yet in the *Mayflower*'s case, only one crew member and one passenger failed to complete the journey, the latter being William Butten, a boy of fifteen who died a few days before they sighted land. Perhaps, as some have argued, wine residues in the ship's planks helped prevent infection, since wine lees are mildly antiseptic. But this cannot have had more than a very marginal effect, if any at all. More likely, they held disease at bay by keeping their quarters clean, and always going up on deck to empty their bowels and bladders.

Whether or not they were hygienic, their presence created difficulties for Jones, since human beings occupied precious space. To fill out their earnings, seamen were given part of the hold for "furthing," a stock of trading goods they carried on their own account for dealing freelance at either end of the voyage. On the *Mayflower,* the colonists and their stores would have limited the room available for goods of such a kind. Since seamen resented emigrants, animosity between them might provoke a mutiny: shipboard squabbles were commonplace at the time, mainly arising from low wages or from the failure to pay them at all. In 1605 an angry English crew had refused to take a cargo of colonists to Guyana. Instead, they mutinied and marooned them on the island of St. Lucia, leaving them to starve or to be slaughtered by the Caribs.[7]

Evidence of the unpleasant atmosphere on board the *Mayflower* survives in Bradford's text. He speaks of the ship's boatswain, who was "a prowde yonge man, and would often curse, & scofe at ye passengers." This comment takes on its full meaning when we bear in mind that the boatswain was the most senior member of the crew. Responsible for sails and rigging, he conveyed the master's orders to the sailors and took charge of the loading of the ship's cargo. Under his direction, passengers came on board and stowed their possessions. During the voyage they fell beneath his control. Since he had to be able to read and write—he had to keep a "bosun's book" listing the ship's freight—his scoffing might be well-informed: from printed satires, or anti-Puritan jokes from the playhouse, he would know how best to needle a Separatist.[8]

For all these reasons, Jones would be eager to disembark his passengers swiftly. So he decided to make straight for the Hudson. Within a few hours they came to a place where the glaciers that formed Nantucket Island and the Cape left on the seabed a shifting labyrinth of sandbanks and shoals.

A man with Jones's knowledge of England's coastal hazards would not try to find his way through them without a pilot. So, when they sighted the breakers, they swiftly turned back from a point somewhere close to Pollock Rip, where the modern chart shows as little as eight feet of water. Back they went northward by night for fifty miles, passing the buff-colored ridge called the Highlands, close to the outer end of the Cape. At last the following day they rounded Race Point and entered the wide, shallow stillness of Provincetown Harbor, dotted then and now with a multitude of gulls, "the greatest store of fowl that ever we saw."[9]

Behind the calm waters of the anchorage, William Bradford saw only savagery and terror. For him, it was a wild country already chilled by the first onset of winter, "hedious & desolate," full of wild beasts and wild men. Four times on a single page of his manuscript he wrote the word "wilderness" to describe Cape Cod. In front of them lay a desert, another word from his vocabulary: no inns, no habitations, but only woods and thickets.

He likened the Pilgrims to the apostle Paul, stranded by a storm on the island of Malta, but their predicaments seemed to be very different. Paul met inhabitants who warmed him by their fire, while the Pilgrims could expect only arrows from the native people. Behind them was the ocean, vast and furious, dividing them from what Bradford calls "ye civill parts of the world." Even so, he writes, they fell on their knees and gave thanks to God.

So Bradford remembered the occasion, when he described it in the early 1630s. His first narrative of the Pilgrim arrival had told another story. It can be found in *Mourt's Relation,* the journal he co-authored with his fellow Pilgrim Edward Winslow, published in London in 1622. Intended for public consumption, to attract new investment and new settlers, it called the Outer Cape a "goodly land," and it heaped praise upon the haven. Provincetown Harbor would safely hold a thousand ships, they said. It promised rich whale fishing, cod in season, and beyond the beach freshwater and timber for cooking fires.[10]

Which version was correct? Was the Cape a goodly land or a wilderness? Neither account was objective fact of a simple kind, but in the space between the two narratives we find William Bradford himself. He lived a double or a treble life, as man of God, entrepreneur, and founder of a new commonwealth. In his account of the voyage, it was the Calvinist who held the upper hand, and because of that we can reenter his imagination and experience the arrival as he would have done.

Bradford's Voyage

Somewhere out on the ocean, amid the blast of a gale, John Howland slipped off the wet timbers of the *Mayflower.* He may have been no more than twenty-one, a "lustie younge man," says Bradford. Howland came up on deck and fell off, but before he hit the waves, he caught a rope that was trailing in the sea. It kept him afloat long enough for somebody to fish him out of the surging water with a boat hook within the short span of minutes before the cold froze his muscles and fatally weakened his grip.

Howland went on to spend five decades in America, acting as manager of the beaver trading post at Cushnoc. Lusty young John became, in Bradford's words, a "profitable member" of the community, not least when, much later, in a gunfight on the Kennebec Howland and his men killed an English fur-trading competitor. Howland lived on until 1673, surviving William Bradford by more than fifteen years. He and his wife, Elizabeth, founded a lineage with perhaps more descendants than any other *Mayflower* couple.

He ended his days on his farm close to the cove at Rocky Nook, still the quietest and prettiest place in what was once the Plymouth Colony, looking out across mudflats, wading birds, and salt marsh toward the modern town of Duxbury. When he died, Howland left his widow, ten children, and eighty-eight grandchildren, and an ample herd of cows, sheep, and goats, but he also left something else. He owned an item that, like a key, unlocks the meaning of the journey as he and Bradford understood it.

We need the key because Bradford tells the story in such an unusual way. He describes the voyage and the arrival at Cape Cod in the ninth chapter of the first book of his history of New Plymouth, but in a manner that, if we are honest, most readers will find odd, or even evasive. The more often we read it, the stranger it becomes, like a message in code in search of decipherment.[11]

Chapter 9 contains fewer than eighteen hundred words, and barely seven hundred concern the passage across the open sea. Another three hundred describe the landfall, the dangers of Pollock Rip, and the double back around Race Point. The remaining paragraphs consist of a long, eloquent contemplation of the wilderness, as Bradford first saw it. But in telling the story of the voyage, the Pilgrim left out almost every fact that most readers, then and now, would consider relevant or essential.

The name, design, and dimensions of the ship and the number of crew members: none of these appear in Bradford's history, and he says very little about Jones. We have to fill in the details from other sources, using a few clues scattered here or in *Mourt's Relation.* Chapter 9 leaves out the birth at sea of Oceanus Hopkins, son of a Pilgrim couple. It makes only the briefest mention of the death of William Butten. Bradford never talks about food, drink, armaments, pirates, the last view of land, or meetings with other craft, such as the Newfoundland ships, some of which they must have seen. He says nothing whatever about the route.

These gaps were unusual, even by the standards of his age. Travel books were popular, and navigation fascinated laypeople who had never set foot on a ship. When John Winthrop kept his journal of his voyage in 1630, he listed all the facts and figures that Bradford omits, and far more besides. Winthrop recorded sixteen calculations of the ship's latitude made, clouds permitting, with sightings of the noonday sun as the vessel, the *Arbella,* tacked westward from the Lizard along the forty-third parallel. He drew sketches of the coast of Maine and a rough map of the shore leading to the ship's destination at Salem. Winthrop even mentions the venison pies they ate when they arrived.

Bradford gives us none of this. From what must have been many incidents, during the sixty-six days between the English Channel and the Cape, he selected only very few, of which Howland's narrow escape was one. Before describing it, Bradford tells us about another lusty youth,

Howland's ungodly double, a "proud . . . & profane" seaman who jeered and cursed the seasick passengers, saying that he expected to dump half of them over the side before journey's end. It pleased God to smite the young man with disease, and he was tossed overboard himself.

William Bradford's most famous anecdote concerns a flaw in the ship. When the *Mayflower* left Plymouth, the wind was "prosperus," says Bradford, for what he calls "a season"—again, he does not say how long it was—until the ship encountered headwinds. Shaken and leaking, the ship struggled on against gales so fierce that the crew had to strike her sails and lie hull down among the steep waves, or risk losing her masts. During one of these episodes, as the *Mayflower* lay without a sheet of canvas to catch the wind, Howland came up on deck and was nearly lost. The flaw appeared amidships, when one of the beams that supported the main deck bent and began to crack.

Causing alarm and agitated discussion, the incident could not have happened at a worse moment. They were almost exactly halfway across. It would be hard to weigh the hazards of a return in winter past the Lizard against the risk of finding no means to make repairs in America. But, confident in his vessel, Jones eventually convinced passengers and crew that her timbers were sound underwater. As for the sagging beam, they heaved it back to the horizontal with an iron screw—these can still be seen today, in the few working windmills preserved in eastern England, used like a wheel jack to lift sacks of flour—and then the *Mayflower*'s carpenter wedged a post beneath it, supported by the lower deck.

And yet again Bradford leaves a hole in his narrative. The beam must have been more than twenty feet long and a foot in diameter. It would have been as heavy as six grown men. A joiner who knows English oak will tell you that such a beam will split only under extreme force from above. William Bradford never tells us how this could have happened, while the other beams remained unscathed. Perhaps the timber was rotten, which might explain why the splitting wood aroused so much anxiety. But Bradford never says that this was so, leaving rot merely as a possibility lingering in the margin. Even his account of Howland's narrow escape contains a perplexing feature. Bradford calls the rope that saved him a halyard, used to raise a topsail. Only a very shoddy boatswain would let a halyard dangle into the water, instead of making it fast to a cleat: Bradford offers no explanation.

But then why should he? William Bradford did not claim to be a seafarer. Unlike three other Pilgrims—Winslow, Miles Standish, and Isaac Allerton—he never made business trips back across the Atlantic. He did not write a sailor's yarn, dense with salty detail. For Bradford, the voyage possessed deeper meanings that mattered far more than blocks, tackle, and belaying pins. We can find the key to them in a book possessed by John Howland, listed in the inventory of his estate.

THE PILGRIMS AND THE RABBIS

The Pilgrims respected few men more than a destitute scholar called Henry Ainsworth, the author of the book in question. Like them, he was an exiled Separatist. It was said that Ainsworth lived in Amsterdam on ten pence per week, little more than a day's pay for an English field laborer. But Ainsworth was a brilliant writer, with a prose style so lucid that it can still be read with ease. Bradford called him "a man of a Thousand," modest, sociable, and friendly, "pregnant in the Scriptures as if the booke of God had been written in his hart."[12] The proof of this could be found in Ainsworth's masterpiece, *Annotations upon the Five Books of Moses,* the book that belonged to Howland, and the commentary on the Psalms that Ainsworth wrote to go with it.

The *Annotations* traveled to New England with the Pilgrims. This we know because, in 1622, William Brewster gave it to a friendly visitor from Virginia who wanted to study it on the boat home. Bradford owned another copy, and reading Ainsworth left a deep mark on him. By way of Ainsworth, William Bradford fell under the influence of Judaism, its rabbis of the Middle Ages, and their manner of interpreting the Bible and the vagaries of human life. It was because of this that Bradford wrote about the *Mayflower* as he did.

Born at the end of the 1560s, Henry Ainsworth came like Bradford and John Robinson from a family of yeoman farmers. Like Robinson, he rode up on a rising tide of erudition at Cambridge University. In 1586, a donor endowed a lectureship in Hebrew at the college where Ainsworth was a student. He belonged to a generation that took to the language with enthusiasm. Preachers trained at Cambridge liked to baffle their congregations with phrases from the Old Testament original. Even Mr. Jones, sitting in his pew at Rotherhithe, may have endured something of the kind. His parish minister enjoyed expounding the book of Job in Hebrew at enormous length.

Hebrew possessed a special appeal for Puritans. They wished to swim back up the stream of learning, and to absorb the wisdom of the Bible from as close to the source as possible, free from what they saw as Roman Catholic duplicity or errors in translation. But they did not expect the meaning of the text to be simple, and they did not simply dismiss the scholars who preceded them. Some of them did exactly the reverse. They read with sympathy the rabbis of the Roman Empire, Egypt, and medieval Spain, authors whose books were preserved by the Jews of Germany or Venice.

By 1600, England's finest scholar of Hebrew was a man called Hugh Broughton. Pedantic and abrasive, he insulted the archbishop of Canterbury, fell out with the authorities, and made his own home in Amsterdam, where his circle of contacts included Ainsworth. Eager to meet German rabbis, Broughton traveled to Frankfurt, debated Scripture in the synagogue, and made a list of twenty-two essential books by Jewish authors. Besides grammars and dictionaries, it included classical texts of Judaism such as the Midrash and the Babylonian Talmud, vast rabbinic commentaries on the Torah, the five books of Moses, and on the laws and rituals of the Jewish faith.[13] Henry Ainsworth found within them a subtle method for deepening the meaning of the Bible, and for giving resonance to daily life as well.

Inspired by the work of the rabbis, Ainsworth made new translations of the Psalms and the Torah, from Genesis to Deuteronomy. He wrapped around them a commentary, verse by verse and word by word, trying to distill every drop of meaning conveyed by their authors. He pointed out that when Jewish scholars turned the Bible into Greek, a single Hebrew term often required several Greek words in its place. This was a sign of what he called "the copiousnesse of matter" contained in the original.

For the rabbis, everything in the Bible had a connection to everything else. They compared the task of looking for the Word of God to the hard labor of dropping a bucket into a very deep well and then lifting it back by arduous effort.[14] Ainsworth developed a similar technique, calling it "the exquisite scanning of words and phrases." He drew upon many rabbis, but Ainsworth named one thinker as by far the most exquisite of all. This was the Jewish philosopher Maimonides, who lived in the twelfth century. During the Jacobean era, Maimonides came to enjoy the highest prestige among English scholars, and Ainsworth was no exception. He called Maimonides "the wisest of the Hebrew Rabbins," and in his *Annotations* he quotes him many times.[15]

Up to a point, the technique of Maimonides was familiar. Henry Ainsworth was certainly not the first Englishman to adopt it, at least in its simpler forms. For many centuries orthodox, mainstream writers had looked for depth and double meaning in the Old Testament. For a Christian, each of its stories could be read as a forecast, an anticipation or a prophecy of the ultimate truth of the Gospel. Jonah in the belly of the whale foreshadowed, for example, the descent of Christ into hell between the afternoon of Good Friday and the Sunday morning of resurrection. To this way of thinking, when the Israelites crossed the Red Sea, they enacted in advance the passage of a Christian soul to salvation. In the wilderness, God gave the Israelites manna to eat. It symbolized the bread of life, the body of Christ, or the Eucharist granted to the faithful at the Last Supper.

Ainsworth certainly thought in this way, in terms of typology, a way of reading Old Testament events as types or parallels of some later, Christian revelation. But his "exquisite scanning" went much further, into a territory far more subtle. Typology was often rigid, preprogrammed, like a spreadsheet on a laptop, mechanically making each biblical passage carry fixed meanings sanctioned by tradition. Ainsworth took from Maimonides something far more agile and nuanced. Like the authors of the Midrash, he looked not for two or three meanings but for scores of them, in a free-floating, poetic, almost playful way of reading the Scriptures. As Ainsworth said: "The Hebrew Doctors have a saying, that the Law hath seventie faces . . . and all of them truth." When Bradford read the Bible, or meditated on his life, he looked for seventy meanings too.[16]

SEVENTY MEANINGS OF THE *MAYFLOWER*

Nearly forty years after landing on Cape Cod, William Bradford began to teach himself Hebrew. "I have had a longing desire," he said, "to see with my owne eyes, something of that most ancient language, and holy tongue . . . and what names were given to things, from the Creation." To help him, he had a Hebrew grammar, bequeathed by William Brewster, and the same early American library contained a Hebrew dictionary.

Paper was scarce. For that reason, Bradford copied out his exercises on blank pages at the front of the manuscript of his history of the plantation. He covered the white space with nearly nine hundred Hebrew words, starting with eight names for God. Among his vocabulary, he carefully spelled out the Hebrew consonants of the word *midbar.* In the book of Exodus, it describes the wilderness of Sinai, crossed by the Israelites on their way to Canaan.[17]

Although Bradford came late to the Hebrew alphabet, he had known the word *midbar* for most of his adult life. *Midbar* appears in more than ninety verses in the Torah, and Ainsworth referred to it often, spelling it out in English in his *Annotations.* In Genesis, Hagar wandered in the wilderness of Beersheba, with her son Ishmael trailing behind her. In another wilderness, on the slopes of Mount Horeb, the prophet Moses found the angel of Jehovah in a burning bush. In the wilderness the Israelites turned their backs on God, and in the wilderness Christ endured temptation. From these stories, Ainsworth extracted a host of meanings, and they lay near Bradford's elbow as he wrote.

Midbar, said Ainsworth, meant a place where men go wild and go astray, a land without order, a dwelling fit only for beasts, a place where God puts his people to the test of affliction. It might also refer to "the wilderness of peoples" in the book of Ezekiel, meaning the many nations of the world, with dispersed among them the wandering Jews. The wilderness was a place of hunger and thirst, bodily starvation but also a famine of the spirit. *Midbar* symbolized the human soul lost in sin, but the word could carry opposing connotations at the same time. It referred to danger, destitution, and loss but also to salvation.

Midbar meant the wasteland across which men and women traveled to Egypt to enter servitude, but it also offered their escape toward the promised land. In the wilderness, the Israelites starved and then fed on the manna provided by God. The book of Numbers described their itinerary to Canaan, but in Hebrew its name was Bemidbar. According to Ainsworth, in the book of Bemidbar the journeys of the tribes of Israel were "the figure of our spirituall warfare; whereunto we are mustered and armed to fight the good fight of faith."

When Bradford used the word "wilderness" four times on one page, he did so with these meanings crowding in on his own imagination. When he mentions the thickets of Cape Cod, he has in mind not only the physical reality, the dense stands of pitch pine and the undergrowth of scrub oaks at Provincetown, but also the religious meaning that they might conceal. From Ainsworth's notes, he knew that the name Sinai came from the Hebrew *seneh,* or "bramble." In the vegetation of the Cape, the Pilgrim saw the brambles of Horeb and the burning bush. Ainsworth said that the brambles symbolized the Church, confined and persecuted in Pharaoh's Egypt. They meant the same perhaps to William Bradford. Tangled scrub made the Outer Cape a fearful wilderness, but also a place of epiphany. Here a Pilgrim found an echo of his reasons for leaving England, another wasteland of a metaphorical kind.

The Pilgrims believed that everything followed a plan, laid down by God before the beginning of the world, but it was a *secret* plan. That was the teaching of John Calvin. Veiled from sinful humanity, the plan was obscure, as hard to decode as a blazing star. By way of the Bible, clues might be found to the will of God, but only after prayer, study, and discussion, and with the aid of faith, itself a gift of God issued only to the elect. A Calvinist like Bradford came at experience in an exploratory manner, searching back and forth for scattered truth just as Ainsworth scanned the Bible. And when he came to tell his own story, he would do so in the same style. Even without conscious effort, if Bradford used the language he knew best, the diction of Genesis, Saint Paul, or the Psalms, he would write a resonant narrative, filled with connotation and nuance. His text would gleam with latent hints of the unseen.

A voyage was a parable, each episode an intimation of mystery. For pious men and women, the sea made visible the ways of God to man. Calvin likened the souls of the elect, chosen for salvation, to a sailor who lived through a storm, escaping death. Sinners talked about luck or good fortune, but a true Christian knew that every rescue was foreordained by God, so that a sea story might become another avenue of revelation. In the harbor towns of Devon, the preachers scattered maritime metaphors in their sermons. At Plymouth in 1620, the town preacher was a Puritan, and in his sermons he compared the human soul on earth to a seaman pursued by pirates.[18]

The sea was a fertile symbol. On the face of the waters, men found redemption and terror alike. Encircling the earth, without end or beginning, unknowably deep, a source of life and wealth, but also an instrument of punishment, the ocean evoked the majesty of God, the unfathomable power of Calvin's divinity. For his own just purposes, God made the sea the home of monsters and devils, still believed by many to be the cause of hurricanes and storms. Inconstant, uncertain, ebbing and flowing, sometimes placid, but often deadly, the ocean signified the sinful world of men, filled with unseen hazards. In the voyage of life, the soul must steer between the sands of self-love, the gulf of intemperance, and the rock of blasphemy. Sitting on the rock were mermaids, symbols of lust and earthly pleasure.

All of these similes appeared in sermons and in poetry. A ship was more than a wooden hull, topped by masts and rigging, propelled by canvas filled with moving air. She was an image of the true Church, the Church Militant, carrying as ballast the fear of God. Her sails represented faith, her masts were the cross of Christ, and the wind that blew her forward was the Holy Spirit. Her cannon were the Ten Commandments, her helm was conscience, and her compass was the Bible. A tempest symbolized the persecution of the godly, and the leaks in her planks were the wounds in the flanks of the Church caused by heresy and schism.[19]

Bradford described a real voyage, experienced firsthand, but he carried his own heavy cargo of associations. In almost every sentence, he alludes to the Bible. Was Howland an ordinary young man? Or a junior Moses, saved from the water like the prophet when Pharaoh's daughter found him floating in the Nile? Were the crew of the *Mayflower* another grumbling batch of Jacobean sailors? Or, as they debated the cracked beam, did they act out the roles of the sailors who threw Jonah into the sea?

For Bradford, trained by Ainsworth, each episode carried a plethora of meanings. In the splitting beam, he would see more than a damaged lump of wood. For him, it might represent the rot caused in the soul or in the Church, by sin or by strife. England was Egypt, the Atlantic was the Red Sea, and Cape Cod was Sinai. The stormy passage of the *Mayflower* re-enacted other voyages in the Bible: the ark of Noah, Paul's journey to Rome, and on the waters of Galilee the twelve disciples, with Christ as master of their fishing boat.

Inside the head of William Bradford, the Pilgrims mimed out these episodes of sacred history. When they reached dry land, they repeated another ancient formula. At Provincetown, the Pilgrims fell on their knees and thanked God, says Bradford. Again, behind his narrative lies a Hebrew model. It came by way of Bradford's knowledge of a Jewish ritual, the *birkat ha-gomel,* a ceremony of thanksgiving.

A First Thanksgiving

In 1618, the first prayer book for sailors appeared in print in England, written by a parish minister in the City of London. He had recently given a farewell sermon to the crew of the *Royal James,* bound for the Orient for the East India Company, and his book carried a dedication to its shareholders. Dr. John Wood gave it the subtitle *Holy Meditations for Sea-Men.* It contained prayers to be read at sea, before a battle, during a storm, or at the funeral of a crewman.

Among the prayers he included one titled "Thankes-Giving to God After Deliverance from a Tempest." The clergy often read thanksgiving prayers, and under Elizabeth it became customary to draft new ones for every blessed occasion: the end of an epidemic, the Armada's defeat, or some bloody massacre inflicted on the Irish.[20] Wood composed a seagoing version, using as raw material words and phrases from the Psalms to assemble a chorus in praise of the might and mercy of God. One psalm gave him more words than any other. This was Psalm 107, used later in the English rite for a burial at sea. It spoke of seamen engulfed by a storm who pray to God until he brings them to a peaceful harbor.

As a Separatist, wary of official worship, Bradford did not care for prefabricated liturgy read from a book. However, the Pilgrims had all grown up with thanksgiving prayers, and every Christian had a duty to say such things. If the prayers followed the Bible, no one could object. So Bradford did the same. At the end of chapter 9, after his meditation on the American landscape, he also repeats verses from Psalm 107, words that describe the journey of the Israelites across Sinai. "When they wandered in ye deserte wildernes out of ye way, and found no citie to dwell in, both hungrie & thirstie, their sowle was overwhelmed in them," writes Bradford, quoting the Psalm from the Geneva Bible, the translation used in early New England. "Let them confess before ye Lord his loving kindnes, and his wonderfull works before ye sons of men."

For the Pilgrims, these words carried a double meaning, arising from a Hebrew source. If Bradford turned to the notes Ainsworth added to Psalm 107, he would find Ainsworth quoting Maimonides. Writing about the Mishnah, the Jewish code of laws, the rabbi said that the words of the Psalm, including the verses quoted by Bradford, gave birth to the Jewish rite of thanksgiving. The Talmud listed four occasions when the *birkat hagomel* was compulsory: the healing of a sickness, the release of a prisoner, the end of a voyage, and the arrival of travelers at their destination. Ainsworth listed them too, and described the form taken by the Jewish prayer. It was a public confession of the goodness and majesty of God, of exactly the kind that the Pilgrims performed at Provincetown.[21]

A year later, most likely in October 1621, after their first harvest, the colonists held the festivities commemorated by the modern Thanksgiving. Winslow described them in two sentences. He mentions three days of feasting on game, wildfowl shot by the English, and venison killed by the native warriors who joined the celebrations. This is more or less all he says, but Winslow's brief paragraph has given birth to a weary torrent of controversy. Did they eat turkey? Did they wear pointed hats? Was the event holy or secular, a wilder version of an English harvest festival? Did they call it a thanksgiving? Or was it something the native people termed a *nickommo*, a ritual feast or dance held to avert drought or sickness, to celebrate good fortune or bring victory in war?

Most likely, it meant one thing to one person and something else to another, as communal occasions always do. But if we could ask William Bradford to define the first Thanksgiving in America, he would point to something else. He would say that it took place at the instant of arrival, at the moment on Cape Cod when the Pilgrims fell on their knees to say the Jewish prayer. And yet even this act of devotion contained an undercurrent of melancholy, of a kind often found between the lines of Bradford's text. He likened the Pilgrims on the Cape to Moses, as the prophet gazed out across the plain of Jericho. At the end of the book of Deuteronomy, from a mountaintop Moses saw the promised land. As Bradford knew well, the prophet had crossed Sinai, but he never entered Canaan. Moses died, leaving his bones in an unmarked grave on the edge of the wilderness. An identical fate awaited half the *Mayflower*'s passengers and crew.

Here we leave the Pilgrims for the time being, on the Outer Cape, approaching the first snowfall. Behind them lay a long process of formation. To find its beginnings, we have to go back two generations, and to violent death in eastern England nearly forty years before. At New Plymouth, Bradford and his comrades recalled as heroic forerunners two Englishmen who were hanged in 1583. They died on gibbets in a muddy field near the market town of Bury St. Edmunds.

Their execution came about because of the career of a man called Robert Browne. Thanks to him, Separatists like the Pilgrims came to be known as Brownists. A man who embarrassed everybody, including William Bradford, he earned the nickname "Troublechurch Browne." Time and again historians have mentioned him briefly and then pushed him quietly to one side, pretending that this infuriating, volatile character had little direct influence on the Pilgrims. It is time Browne came in from the cold, and with him the concealed history of Pilgrim origins. They lie deep within the reign of Queen Elizabeth, in England and also among the Calvinist gentry of France.

Part Two

Origins

Chapter Four

Troublechurch Browne

Nothing would bee done for a Plantation until some hundred of your Brownists of England, Amsterdam and Leyden went to New Plimouth.

—Captain John Smith, *True Travels, Adventures, and Observations* (1630)[1]

Easter week in 1580 was hot, unseasonably so. On Wednesday, April 6, at six o'clock the working day was finished, and the English were eating, drinking, or at play: or, if they were devout, they might be listening to a midweek sermon, as they were in a church opposite Newgate Prison. Later, it was claimed that boatmen felt a strange unquietness in the waters of the Thames. If so, it was the only sign that anything was wrong.

Suddenly, on the south coast, people heard a detonation like the firing of cannon at sea. For weeks, the locals had been readying defenses against the danger of a Spanish invasion. Perhaps, for an instant, they feared that this was the first salvo of a bombardment. Before the noise died away, the ground began to move under the impact of the most severe earthquake to strike England for more than a century.

It began when a fault slipped twenty miles beneath the Strait of Dover, sending shock waves south to Normandy and as far north as York. As it ended, Londoners heard ragged chimes from a hundred parish churches, as the tremor caused the bells to ring a disorderly peal. Some panicked, like lawyers dining in the Inns of Court, who ran out into the street with their knives still in their hands. Others blamed their quivering wainscots on rats or weasels. The earthquake lasted less time than it took to say the Lord's Prayer.

Only two people died. One was a shoemaker's boy, killed by a falling stone as he sat beneath the minister at Christ Church, Newgate. A serving girl beside him succumbed to her injuries later. Apart from that, damage was modest: a church tower in Kent cracked from top to bottom, flooding on the French coast, and a fallen wall at Dover Castle. But although it ranked low on the Richter scale, in the Elizabethan mind the tremor became another dreadful warning of punishment for sin.[2]

Separatism took shape during this period, the early 1580s, when its protagonist, Robert Browne, achieved notoriety. Some of those who traveled on the *Mayflower* were at school, at university, or starting apprenticeships: at least seven of her passengers were already aged between eight and eighteen. Exposed to new ideas taught by young schoolmasters, by equally youthful academics, or by preachers from the pulpit, they were also far more likely to be literate than earlier generations.

Two-thirds of yeomen and tradesmen in eastern England could read, twice as many as two decades previously, and this was the social group and region from which most of the Pilgrims came. The content of what they read made its mark as they responded to something that felt like a crisis. In the reactions to events such as the earthquake, we find a *Mayflower* mentality developing, a state of mind in which some men and women might feel compelled to seek radical alternatives to the status quo.[3]

THE WRATH OF GOD

Within twenty-four hours, a printer of sheet music rushed out a godly ballad, "moving us to repent by ye example of ye earthquake." Fifteen earthquake pamphlets appeared, with the same dire message at their heart, and the queen's bishops composed an earthquake prayer for obligatory recital.[4] Was England an especially wicked place? The shaken kingdom had many reasons to feel precarious.

England was Protestant, but its religious independence dated back only fifty years, since Henry VIII broke from Rome. When Elizabeth became queen, after the death of her Catholic sister, Mary, she restored the Protestant faith, but even so the Reformation remained incomplete and unsafe. Menaced from within by covert Roman Catholics, by vagabonds, and by the idle poor, England was threatened from outside by Philip of Spain, by the Jesuits, and by their truculent henchmen, the Irish. Or so it seemed to the Privy Council.

In February, they ordered ships back to their ports, to be ready against a Spanish assault. A few weeks before the earthquake, they told every county in England to draw up muster rolls of available armed men. When a Catholic earl began an insurrection in Ireland, word reached London that Spanish warships were gathering, heading perhaps for Bantry Bay, to join the rebel in kicking down England's back door.

Fears about the succession added another twist of alarm. Mary, Queen of Scots lived in restless captivity in the north of England, waiting if Elizabeth died to assert her own solid claim to the Crown. Unmarried, Elizabeth had no uncontested heir of the Protestant persuasion. Worse still, she was considering a marriage with a Catholic, the Duke of Anjou, brother of the king of France. Until it was abandoned in 1582, this project came and went for four years of fitful negotiation, causing all sorts of trouble. As we shall see, it helped engender new ideas about politics, ideas that flowed into Separatism and came to influence the Pilgrims.

Why did the Anjou proposal anger the Protestant gentry? Because it put at grave risk the informal constitution by which they, and England, had come to be governed. This rested on a few simple assumptions. Gentlemen would be loyal to the queen, defend the realm, pay modest taxes, and enforce the law, serving as justices of the peace, the local representatives of the Crown. In return, the JPs would run their localities as they saw fit, free from interference by cardinals, monks, and foreigners. They would also keep, of course, the Church property that they had acquired since King Henry dissolved England's monasteries.

At the apex of the system sat the queen, supreme but not omnipotent, obliged to listen to advice, ignore it though she often did. To make laws, and raise taxes, she had Parliament to help her, but more relevant were her privy councillors, and they were led by two evangelical Protestants, Lord Burghley and Sir Francis Walsingham. Burghley was the queen's lord treasurer, and Walsingham served as secretary of state.

A royal marriage with a papist threatened to break the unwritten rules of the kingdom. A French consort might bring with him toleration of Catholics, and new competitors for royal favor and the rewards of public office. That, perhaps, was why, in the months before the earthquake, the Privy Council read seething letters from Protestant squires, such as one who warned of the "serpentine subtlety" of the French and the "inevitable danger . . . of bondage, agreed upon by that holy father, the Pope."[5] In private, Walsingham said much the same, while Burghley bided his time.

Walsingham remembered that Anjou's mother had ordered the murder of the French Protestants, on the feast day of Saint Bartholomew, eight years before. Might such an atrocity occur in England too? What if Elizabeth died in childbirth, and Anjou seized power as a regent, raising the child in the Roman faith? Fears of a second massacre of Saint Bartholomew lingered all the more strongly, since refugee Huguenots had fled from France and settled in England. They made friends with Walsingham, and his Puritan allies, they told stories about persecution, and they wrote books expounding their ideas.

Such were the obsessions of the time. "God hath spoken unto us these many yeares, so many wayes, by the troubles of his Church, by the Slaughter of his Saints," wrote one author. "By monstrous births, by strange shapes . . . by foreign warres abroad, by tumults at home, and now of late by an Earthquake . . . there remaineth nothing now but the day of our Visitation. The Lord will come in his wrath, to iudge and punish us."[6] For some, however, the earthquake might also be a call for action, a commandment to complete the work of Reformation, in a land where it remained at risk. That was what being a Puritan meant.

PURITANS

For five centuries or so, since the Norman Conquest or before, England had lived a double life. Unified from the center by the Crown, and later by Parliament too, out in the provinces the kingdom divided itself into enclaves. The Church, the state, and the economy took a honeycombed, cellular form. They consisted of overlapping units, layered one over the other: the diocese, the county, the archdeaconry, the hundred, the borough, and the town with a weekly market. At the base of this system lay the most fundamental cell, the parish, with usually a single village as its nucleus.

England had nine thousand parishes, each with a church and a minister, known as a rector or a vicar. If he were lucky, the minister lived on tithes, paid by his parishioners, equal to a tenth of the gross produce of the land: grain, pulses, livestock, and everything else. If he were less fortunate, the tithes belonged to a local landowner or perhaps a college at Oxford or Cambridge, and the minister received only what they chose to give him. Money matters of this sort caused frequent quarrels, and so did another feature of the system: the fact that, in many parishes, the landowner or some other lay outsider also owned the right to nominate the minister. A parish and its tithes became property to be bought, sold, rented out, or mortgaged, by people motivated by ambition or greed as much as by religion.

In theory, beneath the queen the Church was uniform and regimented, with every parish worshipping identically. The Book of Common Prayer set out in detail the order of service. Ministers had to wear caps and white linen surplices, make the sign of the cross at baptism, and marry couples with a wedding ring. Worshippers knelt to receive Holy Communion. These old Catholic habits aroused the most frequent Puritan opposition. In practice, however, the Church was far less unified than it might seem, and rules were often bent or ignored.

In some parishes in London, in the universities, in seaports, and in market towns in the eastern counties, Protestant reform had advanced the furthest. There, where the landlord studied Saint Paul and Calvin, or hired a man who did, religion meant the preaching of the Word. In such a place worship centered on the sermon, not the Eucharist. To give sermons a sharper bite, reformers borrowed from Switzerland a new practice, called "prophesying." It referred to a meeting where clergy, and very occasionally laypeople, assembled to discuss the sermon's meaning, to fast, to study the Bible, and to pray aloud.

This was Puritanism. The word entered the dictionary as an insult, coined by a Catholic to make fun of hot Protestants who wished to do away with every last trace of Romanism. Puritans preferred to give themselves other labels: "professors of the Gospel," "professors of sincerity," or simply "the godly." They did not necessarily have special beliefs about God: Puritans were Calvinists, but so too was everyone else, at least in theory. Double predestination formed part of the Thirty-nine Articles of Religion, drawn up in 1562 with the queen's reluctant endorsement. Instead, people recognized Puritans by the way they acted, by the tone of their voices, and most of all in their demands for a new constitution for the Church. Puritans did not simply read Calvin. They wished to create a Calvinist society, with religious assemblies based on the Swiss and French Reformed churches that he inspired.

Of course not everyone wanted to be a Puritan: they were a distinct minority. Roman Catholics fought a rearguard action from sandbagged foxholes in remote locations. Even non-Catholics could blunt the edge of Reformation by choosing to cling to old ways or by ridiculing the godly. Many parishes lacked piety of any kind. In the middle of the century, recruitment of ministers had collapsed. Henry VIII had stripped the Church of assets, inflation shrank the value of clerical incomes, and religious strife made the priesthood a dangerous calling. In the 1570s, 80 percent of congregations never heard a sermon, for lack of competent men. This situation was changing, as the universities became factories for cloning clergymen, their principal function until the reign of Queen Victoria. By the early seventeenth century, preachers had been found for more than half the parishes in England; but the process was slow, many doubted the need for reform, the Church was divided, and Elizabeth could not force her subjects to cohere.

Her revenues were small, and so the queen ruled by bluff and propaganda. She did so by way of favors granted and gifts received, by manipulation, and by sometimes reluctant consent, but also by way of occasional acts of extreme violence. These were sometimes effective, but often caused more problems than they solved. Faction and feud helped to determine the course of events as bishops and courtiers rose and fell in her favor. Like a pendulum, the queen's authority in matters of religion often swung well clear of the ground. Sometimes the local bishop or archdeacon had Puritan leanings, or was simply idle or easily bullied by a local landowning elite. With patrons such as these, a professor of sincerity might hope to flout the rules of worship. But, like a pendulum, sometimes the queen's demands for due order came hurtling back.

Most famously, in 1576 she ordered a ban on prophesying, because it might be subversive. She suspended Edmund Grindal, the archbishop of Canterbury, who had dared to defend it. With Grindal in disgrace, she began to promote conservative bishops who made Puritans toe the line.

One such man was Edmund Freke, the bishop of Norwich. In the spring of 1581, he heard about a young evangelist called Robert Browne, who had begun to preach illegally in the countryside in West Suffolk. Freke had him arrested, and reported the affair to Burghley. Browne was spreading "corrupt and contentious discours," said Freke, at gatherings of "the vulgar sorte of the people . . . to the number of an hundred at a tym in privat howses & conventicles."[7] This was Separatism. In Robert Browne we see it take incendiary form, as a creed in which politics and faith reacted chemically with each other.

CAMBRIDGE MEN

Robert Browne was born in about 1550. He ended his days in prison in 1633, after the old man landed a punch on a parish constable who came to collect a local tax. In the words of an opponent, Browne was a "pestilent schismatic" who mixed with his social inferiors, inciting disobedience. It was also said, though proof was lacking, that Browne was "a common beater of his poor old wife . . . an open profaner of the Sabbath."[8] He quarreled bitterly with his own followers, and he aroused distrust, because he changed sides more than once.

Browne was a "slipperie shifter," said the hostile writer who called him a schismatic, and, worse still, he was a "wavering weathercock."[9] Much later William Bradford disowned Robert Browne, denying that he inspired the Plymouth Colony, but this was not because Bradford disagreed with what Browne had said. It was because Browne faltered, and made his peace with the authorities, and because of what Bradford called his backslidings. The Pilgrims never condemned Browne's original teachings, and in Leiden in 1618 they reprinted a radical Brownist book, written as far back as 1581 by his closest collaborator. When Captain John Smith hung the name of Brownists around the neck of the Pilgrims, he did so with fairness. Until the 1640s, as a matter of routine the English gave the epithet to any Puritan who left the Church of England entirely.

Robert Browne was not the first Separatist—there were a few in London in the 1560s—but he gave the movement its title because he was articulate, he was energetic, and at the outset he was fearless. By his own reckoning, he went to jail thirty-two times. Far from being a social outcast, he came from among the affluent gentry of the English Midlands, men whose grandsons led the fight against King Charles in the English Civil War. His sister married into a landowning family called the Pickerings, from the Nene valley in Northamptonshire, eighty miles north of London. After Browne returned to the established Church, becoming minister of a parish next to their manor at Titchmarsh, the Pickerings helped him to sue his flock for the tithes they owed him. In due course the younger Pickerings served as enthusiastic soldiers alongside Oliver Cromwell, a man who was more or less a Brownist himself.

The Brownes were gentlemen too, a little farther north in the tiny county of Rutland. They lived in style at Tolethorpe Hall, where they practiced the social graces of the time: Robert Browne played the lute with skill. His father, Sir Anthony Browne, owned nine hundred acres at Tolethorpe, sixteen houses there and in the nearby town of Stamford, more farmland by the coast, and a London residence. During the 1570s and 1580s, landowners in sheep counties such as Rutland and Northampton did extremely well as prices and rents rose steeply. Because he was a second son, Robert Browne could not expect a large inheritance—when Sir Anthony died in 1590, he left Robert only one hundred pounds—but he was comfortable. He kept three servants, and in early manhood he did not need to work. When he became a schoolmaster, it was by choice.

Apart from a rare exception like Ainsworth, Separatism was never the creed of the penniless. Besides Browne, its most famous leader was Henry Barrow, hanged at Tyburn in the 1590s, another man remembered by the Pilgrims as a martyr. The Barrows were landowners too, with a little empire spanning four counties, and Barrow's father was a stern JP with Puritan affiliations. Although he was another younger son, Henry Barrow had five hundred acres of his own, yielding rents worth five times the income of the average vicar.

Barrow and Browne certainly reached out down the social scale, especially in London, where we find shoemakers and domestic servants named among their followers. However, more often Brownists were skilled or self-employed men, including shipwrights, scriveners, and an apothecary. In the countryside, the typical Separatist came from the leading yeoman family in each village. He or she looked for leadership to an educated young gentleman-radical such as Browne, from a little higher up the social scale.[10]

Politics also surrounded Robert Browne from birth. In the fifteenth century, the Brownes had made their fortune exporting wool to Europe from Stamford. By the 1480s, they dominated its affairs, serving often as aldermen, equivalent to mayors. They left an indelible mark. Today Browne's Hospital, which they founded, still accommodates the elderly of Stamford, in limestone Gothic splendor in the middle of the town. When Stamford slipped into decline, failing to become a center for weaving cloth, the Brownes became rural landlords and lawyers. Ten times they were sheriffs of Rutland, and three times members of Parliament. Sir Anthony Browne was a JP and served as county sheriff.[11]

In the sixteenth century, a new dynasty arose at Stamford, the Cecils, who became the greatest family of Tudor England. Wisely, the Brownes made friends with the upstarts, whose lands lay immediately next to theirs, and in due course the alliance may have saved the life of Robert the Separatist. The first Cecil to arrive was David Cecil, a Welshman who fought for Henry Tudor at Bosworth and then settled near Stamford in the entourage of Henry's mother. He prospered, and also became an MP. Robert Browne's great-uncle married David Cecil's daughter: a good match, since the Cecils were amassing a great fortune. Her nephew was the most powerful of her kin, William Cecil, otherwise known as Lord Burghley.*

---

*An estate map from 1615 shows land owned by the Brownes immediately abutting the Cecil property at Wothorpe Manor, overlooking the town from the southeast. In effect, the two families encircled Stamford with their estates, as well as owning houses and inns within it.

Besides its wool, Stamford had strategic value, straddling the Great North Road. It fell within territory that Burghley took care to control. Here and elsewhere he created a web of patronage, a network of clients who gave him his eyes and ears in the provinces. He gathered about him gentry families such as the Brownes and the Pickerings: loyal men, ready to keep the muster rolls, lead the militia, and round up Catholic renegades. So, in Northamptonshire, we find Browne's close kinsman Gilbert Pickering serving as captain of horse during the Armada crisis. In 1586, the name Robert Browne appeared beside those of the Pickerings on a list of local worthies responsible for lighting beacons to warn of a Spanish attack. This may have been our man.[12]

On the face of it, to fulfill his ideals, Browne had no need to venture out of the mainstream of Elizabethan gentility. His father owned the right to appoint the minister of the parish church of Little Casterton, three hundred yards from their front gate at Tolethorpe. If they wished to make the church Puritan, the Brownes could do so, and certainly somebody stripped every vestige of Catholicism from the interior, since the plastered white walls are now as bare as can be. Indeed, by the late 1570s, the Stamford area as a whole had become a haven for the godly, where the JPs organized communal prayer and prophesying, even after the royal ban. So why did Robert Browne become a dissident? Other factors had to operate, to force him along a path of outright nonconformity.

First, by way of education, Browne became exposed to the most avant-garde species of Puritan thinking. Then, at the time of the earthquake, during the debates about Anjou, he became convinced that those ideas needed to be made still more radical, and applied immediately, without waiting for Parliament to enact reform. Finally, and like any revolutionary, he needed an inflammable situation, awaiting a spark. It existed in Suffolk, in and around Bury St. Edmunds, where, whether they meant to or not, the local Puritan squires assembled the fuel he needed.

His career began at Cambridge in about 1570, when Browne became a student at Corpus Christi College. It was small, with fewer than seventy members, and they were very young indeed. At Corpus, even the senior men, the twelve teaching fellows, had an average age of only twenty-eight. Given the need to train clergymen, and to educate the gentry, Cambridge had expanded fast, and so the number of fellows of Cambridge colleges had risen by one-third in the previous decade. Besides being youthful, they were, said an official report, "more intractable than they were wont to be."[13]

This was an understatement. In 1565, Burghley's own college, St. John's, witnessed the first of many feuds, when a young Puritan, aged twenty-seven, gave a sermon likening the unleavened bread used in the Eucharist to starch and paste. He condemned the wearing of a surplice, compulsory in the chapel. His supporters refused to wear the hated vestments, and they hissed those that did. They also spread rumors that a conservative opponent kept a girlfriend in a whorehouse.[14]

This was not an isolated case. During Browne's time at Cambridge, the most serious fracas occurred, caused by lectures given by Thomas Cartwright, professor of divinity, a man in his mid-thirties, and a Puritan. Taking as his text the Acts of the Apostles, describing Christianity as Saint Peter knew it, Cartwright called for an end to the hierarchy of the Church of England. Archbishops, bishops, archdeacons, the courts that administered Church law: popery tainted them all, and the prayer book, "an unperfecte book, culled & picked out of that popish dunghill, the Masse," in the tactful words of a Cartwright supporter.[15] He demanded a new type of church, with elected pastors, assisted by presbyters or elders, and a network of synods, linked to the Calvinist churches of Europe. Dismissed, Cartwright went into exile, in Geneva and then the Netherlands.

Controversies like these were far more than academic tiffs. Later, Browne wrote a brief autobiography, sadly lacking in precise dates or locations, but speaking clearly of the depth of feeling that flowed into these debates. He recorded his despair at what he calls "the wofull and lamentable state of the church . . . and what abuses there were in the government then used."[16] This was not empty rhetoric: Browne was entirely genuine in his commitment to seeking out the truth, whatever his critics might say.

We can be certain about this, because Browne graduated in 1572 with a bachelor's degree. To begin with, he must have intended to become a clergyman. Men rarely bothered to graduate, unless that was their career choice, and Browne could easily have obtained a living in the Church, thanks to his connections. Despite this, he refused to make the necessary compromises until the early 1590s: he even threw on the fire a preaching license that his brother had obtained for him. So the young Browne must have been sincere, and his internal crisis was very real: it was also the cause of deep anxiety, to himself and others.

Few have read his books closely, even among historians, and this is scarcely surprising. From Browne to Barrow, the early Separatists often wrote in a ranting, vitriolic style, laced with misogyny. Courageous and consistent though Henry Barrow was, in his writings the passages of eloquence and insight lie scattered amid long, wearisome tirades. They often come close to mania: he once demanded the demolition of England's parish churches, because they dated from the age of popery. Indeed, their enemies said that the Separatists were madmen. Browne, for example, worked in partnership with Robert Harrison, a Cambridge friend, who also became a schoolmaster, until, like Browne, he was dismissed. Harrison had protested when the vicar baptized his godson with the sign of the cross, but he did so with such vehemence that the authorities wrote him off as a lunatic, "trobled with a frenesey, which sicknes . . . is thought incurable."[17]

And yet bigotry and rage were only part of the story. Browne had a sharp, rigorous mind. He used charts and tables to set out his views with acute precision. Indeed it may have been this that troubled the authorities the most. Browne took the doctrines of Puritanism, and with relentless logic he pressed them as far as reason and the Bible would permit. He also immersed himself in the latest political thinking. It was expressed in the language of the Old Testament, but it was radical nonetheless. It molded his vision of Christianity, and then, most radically of all, Browne tried to put it into immediate practice.

The Covenant of Asa

In the Second Book of Chronicles, the Bible speaks of a Hebrew king called Asa. He did what was good in the sight of the Lord. When his mother worshipped an idol, Asa cut it down and burned it beside the brook of Kidron. He destroyed the altars of the heathens, he built new cities, and with the Lord's help he vanquished the Ethiopians. Then a prophet arose, called Azariah. He warned that despite Asa's good deeds, the people of Israel had forsaken God. Because they had no priests, and because they disobeyed the Law of Moses, they were in danger of defeat by their enemies. Asa listened to the prophet and gathered his people at Jerusalem. Together they sacrificed oxen, and together they made, says the text, "a covenant to seek the Lord God of their fathers with all their heart and with all their soul." In return, God gave them twenty years of peace and plenty.

In the 1570s, the most advanced Protestant thinkers seized on the books of Kings and Chronicles, finding a commentary about their own times in the stories of godly rulers of ancient Israel such as this. By far the most famous writer to do so was a Huguenot diplomat, who narrowly escaped murder in Paris on Saint Bartholomew's Day. A contemporary of Browne's, born in 1549, Philippe Duplessis-Mornay was one of the first French gentlemen to embrace the ideas of Calvin. Many decades later in New England, William Bradford spoke of Mornay with the highest respect. His fame rested mainly on a remarkable series of books he produced while in exile: books that made him an international figure. When the Pilgrim William Brewster died, he had two of Mornay's volumes on his library shelves.[18]

In London, Mornay joined the circle of ardent Protestants who surrounded Walsingham, and he became a close friend of Walsingham's son-in-law Sir Philip Sidney. Between 1575 and 1579, Mornay wrote four works, three of which were soon turned into English. In the clearest prose, Mornay redefined Christian faith as a creed based on reason, at one with the wisdom of the ancient philosophers whom he admired. For him, a church should resemble a Greek or Roman city-state, a community based on free consent, ready to defend itself by force, if need be. He likened the pope to the Gauls who captured Rome, or to the tyrants who usurped democracy in Athens in the age of Socrates.[19]

Tyranny was the subject of Mornay's finest book, and there he called on the example of King Asa. Anonymously, it appeared in Switzerland in the year before the earthquake, under a Latin title that translates as *The Defense of Liberty Against Tyrants.** Mornay pointed out that in the Bible, the Israelites chose their own kings, electing first Saul and then David. At the coronation, king and people alike entered into a dual covenant. The people and their monarch must both obey the Law of Moses and do the will of God, casting out idols and worshipping God as Moses ordained. Second—and this was far more controversial—the king was obliged to rule with justice and consent, just as Asa did, when he summoned his people to Jerusalem to ratify the covenant. If the sovereign failed to keep faith with his subjects, and with God, then the people were free to be rid of him.

If the covenants were broken, the people had to repair the breach with the Lord, even if that meant taking up arms against their king. To avoid any hint of mob rule, Mornay insisted that the people only do so under the leadership of "inferior magistrates," the godly, right-thinking men who served below the monarch. Even so, this was daring stuff, and it appealed across frontiers. It fitted the needs of Calvinists, seeking grounds

---

*The *Vindiciae Contra Tyrannos,* probably written jointly by Mornay and his friend Hubert Languet, another French Calvinist diplomat.

for resisting their lawful ruler, in France, the Netherlands, Scotland, and perhaps one day in England too.

By the time of the tremor, these ideas had begun to circulate among England's political elite. They found an audience with men such as Sidney, with Walsingham, and with the Puritans who operated close to them.* In 1579, a Puritan friend of Cartwright's published a translation of Mornay's book about Church government, and if men and women read it, they probably did so because of its politics rather than its theology. One question surpassed all others, and that was the danger posed by the possible marriage of Elizabeth with Anjou. Was a Protestant realm about to succumb to idolatry? Would priests celebrate the Mass in London? The debate about the French match reached its peak in the year before the earthquake, when the ideas of Mornay acquired fresh relevance.

In August, a Puritan called John Stubbs published a book attacking the Anjou marriage in the same stark Old Testament terms. Like Asa, he argued, the queen had a duty to uphold true religion, and to observe the dual covenant. If she did not, she would bring down on her nation the wrath of God, and if that occurred, she should be overthrown. Elizabeth took offense, and Stubbs had his right hand chopped off for sedition. In a letter to the queen, Sir Philip Sidney made the same case against the match, but he avoided mutilation by adding sycophancy, as one did. Elsewhere, however, his writings expressed the same readiness, if the worst came to the worst, to depose an erring monarch.

It was against this background that Browne and Harrison began to write. They filled their books with Old Testament kings, and they repeated the ideas of Stubbs and Mornay, echoing them by citing Asa as an ideal, godly ruler. They had little to lose, since both were marked men—Browne was in trouble for preaching at Cambridge after refusing his license—and neither could expect a flourishing career. As unemployed schoolteachers, lodging together in Norwich, England's second city, where Harrison took a job as master of an almshouse, after the queen's humiliation of Grindal they saw every sign that godliness was in retreat. Freke had arrived in 1576 and put a stop to prophesying. He suspended nine local Puritan ministers for skipping the Catholic elements within the prayer book. In the face of

*Mornay also shared Sidney's dream of founding Protestant colonies in the New World. After the massacre of Saint Bartholomew, Mornay considered leading Huguenot exiles to Canada or Peru.

all this, Browne asked a new question, and came up with an answer that eventually led to Massachusetts.

If the queen refused to reform her Church, and if the magistrates did nothing, how should *individual* Christians respond? Mornay had urged them to form their own congregations, or even leave the country, like the Huguenots fleeing from France. "Everyone Is Bound to Separate Himself from the Communion of Antichrist," ran a chapter heading in the English translation of Mornay's book about an ideal church. Browne came to the same conclusion, and, once across that mental threshold, he entered an exciting new world.[20]

Separatism had two sides, embittered and creative, and the second of these Browne began to explore. In doing so, he probably followed the promptings of another French exile, a man called Jean Morély. A Parisian lawyer, Morély had also escaped the massacre of Saint Bartholomew and found his way to London. He turned to Walsingham for help, and Walsingham found him a home in Wales with a landowning friend and kinsman of the Sidney family. Another almost forgotten man, Morély ranked alongside Mornay as one of the period's most audacious thinkers about politics and religion.*

In 1562, Morély published a book that reads like a blueprint for the Plymouth Colony. In any Christian assembly, he said, authority belonged to "le peuple tout entier"—the people as a whole—free to vote to hire and fire their ministers, without a hierarchy of bishops or a national code of religious laws.[21] Like Mornay, he compared a true church to Athenian democracy, with each congregation free to believe and to worship as it chose. Morély rested his case on the eighteenth chapter of Saint Matthew. There, the Gospel writer quoted Christ saying that a church came into existence at any moment when two or three Christians gathered together in his name. In this one verse, short and deceptively simple, Separatism discovered its founding text.

Whether or not Browne ever met Morély, or Mornay, his ideas and those of the *Mayflower* Pilgrims were identical to those of the two Frenchmen. In all likelihood, Browne came across them during the 1570s, by way of the work of another Huguenot intellectual, Peter Ramus. He was a

---

*Until quite recently, it was impossible to argue that Morély exerted any influence in England. Only in 1993 did two French scholars publish the details of his period in exile, including his ties to Walsingham.

French professor of rhetoric and logic, killed on Saint Bartholomew's Day in Paris. After leaving Cambridge, Browne retained his links with the university, where Ramus had come into fashion, and Browne clearly knew his writings well. From Ramus he learned his method of using charts and tables to express an argument visually. But Peter Ramus also stood shoulder to shoulder with Morély in heated French debates about the best way to run a Calvinist church. Ramus wrote his own treatise about religion, likening a congregation to a Greek or Roman republic, and in 1576 a batch of copies of the book arrived in England. They were shipped over by the ubiquitous Sir Philip Sidney.[22]

If we follow the Pilgrims back to their roots, we enter this ideological territory. Browne and his followers created in Norwich a church of exactly the sort that Morély advocated. Like Asa and the Israelites, they made a pact with God and with each other. As Browne later put it, "There was a day appointed, and an order taken . . . thei gave their consent, to ioine themselves to the Lord, in one covenant & fellowshippe." They wiped their assembly free from every corrupting stain of the Church of England: bishops, ministers, parishes, and tithes.

In pursuit of authentic Christianity, based on the example of the apostles, Browne and Harrison also invented their own form of worship. It seems that it was loosely based on the prophesying that the Queen had vetoed, but it lacked a rigid format, and they had no presiding clergymen. Only by way of spontaneous prayer could they prove, to themselves and to others, that their faith was genuine. How else could they be certain that they belonged to the Calvinist elect, assured of eternal salvation?

Again, Browne gives no dates, but it seems that the covenant day took place soon after the earthquake. Norwich was just emerging from three years of plague, and perhaps this added another source of urgency. So did the political climate. At that moment, Puritans hoped to win concessions from the queen, because Parliament was due to reassemble in January 1581. This too may have influenced Browne's timing. It was widely expected that members of the Commons would again call for reform of the Church, but the queen prohibited any debate on matters of religion. Soon afterward, we find an exasperated Robert Browne in Suffolk, beginning his campaign of reformation.

When Browne arrived, he found the neighborhood in ferment. The story begins with a strange incident on Christmas Eve in 1580, another episode that captures the electric atmosphere in which Separatism was born.

THE SUFFOLK PROPHET

Deep among unfenced fields of barley, eleven miles from Bury St. Edmunds, a narrow lane runs along the top of a low hill, above a village called Walsham le Willows. The farming has changed—the land is arable now, whereas then the people of Walsham reared sheep—but much else remains as it was. The pattern of roads survives, and the willow trees still grow. A footpath still follows the village's processional way, which before the Reformation linked sacred wells among the hedgerows.

Elizabethan Walsham was a lively place. It had a population of eight hundred, dwelling in cottages newly built from timber, clay, and thatch. Many still stand, their plaster walls painted as they would have been then, in earthen shades of brown and yellow.[23] Beside the lane along the hilltop lived a tenant farmer called Withers, and he had a son called William, aged eleven.

On December 24, young William Withers fell into a trance and remained unconscious for ten days, "to the great admiration of the beholders, and the greefe of his parentes." For what happened next, we must rely on a pamphlet, printed a few weeks later by the most daring Puritan publisher of the age and dedicated to one of Sir Philip Sidney's closest friends.[24]

William suddenly came round. He began to speak in a loud voice that made his bed shake. This cinematic performance he repeated once or twice a day for the next few weeks. Each time his message was the same: a warning that the earthquake foreshadowed "a farre greater Earthquake, which you shall feele a taste of shortly, unless you repent." The boy condemned pride, idleness, and infidelity, the wearing of ruffs, and the wickedness of stage plays.

Soon young William became a celebrity. Visitors hurried to his bedside, and among them were Suffolk's greatest Puritans, the county sheriff, Sir William Spring, and his brother-in-law Sir Robert Jermyn. According to the pamphlet, both were "men of greate zeale to God, lovers of religion and loyall subiectes to her Maiestie." With them came a Jermyn protégé, the town preacher from Bury, and he certified that William was a godly child.

Why did this odd episode become a brief sensation? It may have had something to do with the parliamentary session, since Suffolk's MPs were Puritan men keen to rally public opinion. Most likely, too, young William was playing his part in some local struggle for power. Far from being placid backwaters, villages like Walsham were combustible places where religious language might be used as a means to express, to incite, or perhaps to stifle conflicts of a social or an economic kind. In Elizabethan England, men and women made the Gospel serve all these purposes, and to do so they exploited the Bible's ambiguities to the full.

We may never know exactly what was going on, but the manor belonged to Sir Nicholas Bacon, older brother of the great Sir Francis. He was far from popular. Bread prices were soaring, but so too was the cost of farmland, and the Bacons, not their tenants, were the beneficiaries. During this period, they doubled their income at Walsham by using the law and an expert surveyor to force rents up as high as they would go. It might be that the Bacons and the Jermyns, who were friends, hit upon William Withers as an ally to help keep the peasantry in their place, by telling them that protest was a sin; or perhaps this is too cynical a view. Whatever the truth, in Walsham and West Suffolk there were issues to which Robert Browne could speak. Soon after the Withers affair, he turned up in the neighborhood. His intensity suited the mood of an anxious time.

Within his sermons lay an element of social protest. Among the ungodly, Browne and Harrison included moneylenders, profiteers who drove up the price of food, and those like the Bacons who were "undoers of the poore men by the lawe."[25] Browne vilified clerics who lived off the fat of the land, he spoke of a coming day of judgment, and he told his listeners that no one could make them go to church. Of course, Browne lived in a world of ambiguity. He was himself a scion of the landed gentry, and his instincts were a mixture of the anarchic and the authoritarian. His words could convey many meanings, but this may have been why he made so great an impact: because they could appeal to many different interests. To a hard-pressed tenant farmer he might sound like an apostle of equality, while to a Puritan squire he spoke of the need for law and discipline.

So it was, perhaps, with the Springs and the Jermyns, who were both godly and rich. Tudor Bury ranked as England's twelfth-wealthiest town, and they dominated local affairs, much as the Cecils and Brownes ran Stamford. Their riches they owed to the cloth trade, since the Springs were the greatest textile magnates of the early Tudor period. For their part, the Jermyns farmed sheep in four counties. Like the Barrows, the Brownes, and the Bacons they prospered from the rising value of their lands.

An active, enterprising man, Sir Robert Jermyn, when he died, left two thousand pounds to provide a dowry for even the *youngest* of his five daughters: the other Jermyn girls had all married well already. Four miles from Bury, he built Suffolk's grandest manor house. For twenty-three years he served as the county's deputy lieutenant, a trusted man, eager to repair coastal gun batteries and to maintain the queen's peace. His Calvinism took exactly the form we might imagine, and one where an American future might be traced in outline.

A Town upon a Hill

Forty years old in 1580, Sir Robert Jermyn was Suffolk's uncrowned king Asa. His only surviving portrait gives us a bearded, thin-faced man, with a hint of nervous energy. Sir Robert admired John Calvin so much that he gave a set of his works to the people of Bury, helping to found one of England's first public libraries. At Bury, he tried to build a Jerusalem as godly as Calvin's Swiss republic.

Bury was not a city on a hill, but it was at least a town on a slope, above what was left of the Abbey of St. Edmund. The monastery had been one of England's largest, built on gently rising ground above the river Lark, but now all that remained were the gatehouse, ruined walls, and an immense heap of rubble. The stone went to build new civic amenities, chief among them a covered corn market, largely paid for by the Jermyns. They had made a great deal of money by dealing in old monastic land.[26]

Jermyn and his fellow JPs based themselves at an inn, the Angel, still today Bury's principal hotel, facing the gatehouse and the ruins. From it, they governed the town as moral policemen, locking up fornicators, the idle, and the feckless. In 1571, following a national trend, and one that Burghley urged all towns to adopt, they drew up a new code of rules to stamp out sin.

They banned artisans from "loytring" and they compelled the children of the poor to become domestic servants. Unmarried women were obliged to have a spinning wheel, while vagrants were rounded up and shipped back whence they came. In the first two weeks of the new rules, the magistrates used them seventy times. They served injunctions on unmarried mothers, on a man caught by his wife watching a play in a tavern, and on "Alys Hill, wydow verraie old." Poor Alice was given a place in an almshouse, but ordered "to applye her work."[27] Meanwhile, the town issued winter clothing to the needy, ran a hospital, and gave weekly allowances to orphans. As the years went by, discipline became even tighter.[28]

The year before the earthquake, Jermyn sent Burghley a second set of rules, to show that Bury remained a well-ordered place. They laid down harsh penalties for blasphemy, swearing, witchcraft, being absent from a sermon, or making a noise in the pew. Lechers would be whipped until their blood flowed. Brawlers, scolds, and the argumentative were to be put in the stocks, but women offenders were punished most severely. They were to be carried on a stool around the marketplace before their flogging.[29] In governing such a place, the authorities might find an obvious use for William Withers. Hoax or not, poor folk who had never heard of Calvin would understand the message of the Walsham prodigy: repent, obey, or face the wrath of God, or failing that the lash.

All of this sounds like a parody, or a caricature, an appalling foretaste of the fictional Puritan New England of Nathaniel Hawthorne and *The Scarlet Letter.* An old-fashioned Marxist might say that men like Jermyn adopted religion as a ploy to keep the workers in their place. There must be some truth in that, too, but Jermyn did not have everything his own way. The events that followed came to be known as "the Bury Stirs," and the term was apt.[30] Jermyn gave his support to radical preachers, and in doing so, he encouraged protest and controversy that ultimately spun out of control. Nearly thirty years later, as we shall see, a similar pattern of events led to the flight of the Pilgrims from England to Leiden.

Religion in Bury was messy and divided. Bury had two parish churches, a few hundred yards apart, each with a conformist vicar, paid a meager stipend by the Crown. However, the citizens also employed two town preachers, whose salaries they paid themselves. Both were ardent Puritans, and one of them, called Mr. Gayton, was the man who examined William Withers. Gayton was not a Brownist, but he came close to it, and in the summer of 1581 he began his own crusade.

The larger of the two churches was called St. Mary's. With the backing of Sir Robert, Gayton climbed into the pulpit, and in Puritan style he rejected as superstitious nonsense the official regime of the Church, based on the authority of distant bishops. Again, he highlighted the democratic needs of the congregation: only the godly disciples of the parish had the right to choose the man who led them, Gayton said. Faced with this outrage, conservatives rallied to defend the vicar, and they called in the bishop's deputy, the archdeacon of Sudbury. When he protested, Jermyn told the archdeacon to mind his own business and called the clergyman a tosspot.

While this affair convulsed the town of Bury, in the countryside Browne preached illegally. Freke arrested him in April, when two of the queen's most senior judges were visiting the region. They packed Browne off to London, but the outcome was merely a reprimand. Burghley defended his young kinsman, writing to Freke to excuse his conduct: he was simply zealous, and not a troublemaker, he told the bishop. Browne promptly came back to Suffolk and started all over again. When the bishop complained once more, this time Jermyn stepped in to protect him. He warned Browne to be careful, but he did so in mild terms, apparently taking a liking to the young radical. Jermyn praised Browne as a promising fellow, a maverick, but "very fit to yield the church his profitable service."[31]

In the England of Elizabeth, nothing was simple or straightforward. On this occasion and on others Separatists found an oddly indulgent hearing in high places. Old ties of loyalty between the Cecils and the Brownes might explain this, or perhaps it arose from dislike of the bishop. Freke was a famously pompous cleric, dominated by his imperious wife, and an embezzler, or so it was said. But outweighing these personal matters lay the national interest. If the Privy Council sided with Jermyn, it was doubtless because Suffolk was a coastal county with a surviving rump of suspect papists. For Burghley, patriotism and artillery outweighed the wounded pride of clergymen.

Even so, Browne and Jermyn had gone much too far. Sooner or later, the queen was bound to intervene, and all the more so when Harrison and Browne began writing books, printed in the Netherlands and then smuggled back home. This they could do with relative ease. Norfolk and Suffolk housed émigré communities of Walloons, Calvinist weavers from Flanders who had sought asylum but retained ties with their homeland. At last, in 1582, Browne and Harrison decided to go into exile themselves. With a few dozen followers, they set off for the freer climate of the Dutch port of Middelburg, recently liberated from Spanish control. As Browne put it, in words that foreshadowed the *Mayflower,* they "all agreed, & were fullie persuaded, that the Lord did call them out of England."[32] At home, meanwhile, the controversy continued.

For two years, letters and petitions bounced back and forth between Burghley, Freke, and Jermyn, while the Puritans at Bury continued to agitate in defense of their preachers. The Bury Stirs finally came to a head in the summer of 1583. At St. Mary's, the queen became the direct target of an abusive attack that left her determined to end the Stirs once and for all. Her response took a form so cruel that six decades later in America William Bradford still remembered the events with horror.

QUEEN JEZEBEL

In St. Mary's Church, modern Bury possesses an unsurpassed museum of religious history. In the century before King Henry split from Rome, donors rebuilt and beautified the edifice. They created four chapels where masses were said for their souls. They restored the high altar, and they set up fourteen lesser altars, to Our Lady and the saints. During the Reformation, all this was torn down, the painted walls were whitewashed, and the candlesticks were sold. Even so, the Catholic past has left its evocative traces.

At the front of the church, a stone slab still protects the bones of Bury's last abbot. Sixty feet above his grave, gilded angels look down on the modern congregation from a magnificent oak roof erected in the fifteenth century. In 1583, a visitor entering the western end of the church would also have seen beneath the angels an imposing emblem of the Crown and its supremacy, between the nave and the chancel.

Supported by a lion and a dragon, the queen's arms dominated the interior. From a painting made in the eighteenth century, and preserved in the church, and from rare surviving examples elsewhere in Suffolk, we can guess the shape the arms would have taken. Painted in vivid colors on wooden boards ten feet high, they would have stood on a horizontal beam, twenty feet above the flagstones, with probably alongside them a passage from Saint Paul: "Let every soule submit hym selfe unto the auctorite of the hyer powers . . . The powers that be are ordeyred of God." A favorite text of Martin Luther's, it taught the lesson of obedience. To left and right there would have been vertical panels, displaying more biblical texts, painted in black letters.[33]

One day the worshippers arrived to find the panels daubed with a slogan from the book of Revelation: "I know thy works, and thy love, and service, and faith, and thy patience, and thy works; and that they are more at the last than at the first." What did this signify? The message took its meaning from what follows in the Bible: "Notwithstanding, I have a few things against thee, that thou sufferest the woman Jezebel, which maketh herself a prophetess, to teach and deceive my servants; to make them commit fornication, and to eat meat sacrificed unto idols."[34]

Nothing more offensive could be said about the Virgin Queen. The words implied that Elizabeth was the whore of Babylon, a tyrant, a false prophet, and a pimp, whose resistance to Puritan reform threatened her subjects with damnation. Obscene and seditious, the insult remained on the walls for three months, until Bishop Freke sent to Bury a clerical detective called Richard Bancroft. He was thirty-eight years old, a former college wrestler, and the most determined enemy the Separatists would ever have.[35]

A man of the highest importance in Pilgrim history, Bancroft later became archbishop of Canterbury. He led the efforts under King James to enforce conformity. Although he was obsessive, even paranoid in his pursuit of Puritans, Bancroft was not merely the compliant tool of despotism. He was certainly never what Puritans called a "dumbe dogge," a shallow cleric unable to preach. Bancroft amassed a library of six thousand books, he wrote and spoke well, and he worked hard. His hatred of Brownism arose from cogent argument, and not from blind prejudice or bigotry.

Bancroft believed that Separatism was spiteful hypocrisy, nonsense that would lead either to anarchy or to dictatorship. If every congregation went its own way, the schism that followed would cause an endless process of division. Christianity would fracture into countless squabbling sects. Bancroft forecast, accurately, an English civil war between denominations. He also pointed out that England was an unequal place and independent local congregations would not remain for long.

The rich would manipulate each church for their own ends, with the queen powerless to intervene on the side of fairness. Pious men like Jermyn, Bancroft said, were also landowners who oppressed the poor. And if Separatists denied the queen's supremacy, then one day they might also condone armed rebellion. He quoted from Browne and Mornay, comparing them to prove that this was so.[36]

Bancroft swiftly tracked down those responsible for the outrage at St. Mary's. Then, whatever the strength or weakness of his case, he took part in an act of vicious repression that left long memories of injustice. On June 30, Elizabeth banned the books of Browne and Harrison, making their possession a felony. A few days later, the lord chief justice began a crackdown at Bury, convicting five Puritan ministers of nonconformity, while a grand jury laid charges against forty laypeople. They fired Jermyn from his post as a JP, a disgrace that it took years, and the crisis of the Armada, for Sir Robert to live down.[37]

The worst fate awaited a shoemaker called John Coppin and a tailor named Elias Thacker, accused of distributing the forbidden books. In all likelihood, they were merely scapegoats: it seems that Coppin had been in prison in Bury since 1578, when fellow inmates heard him slander Her Majesty. They were taken outside the town to a patch of boggy ground, where the judges hanged Thacker and Coppin and burned the books. They apparently saved only one from the flames. It survives in the library of today's archbishop of Canterbury, where Bancroft's stately handwriting records its origin.[38]

Sixty-five years later, William Bradford added an extra detail to the story. According to Bradford, Coppin and Thacker bravely defied their accusers, saying this to the judges: "My Lord, your face we fear not; and for your threats we care not."[39] It seems that no other source records these words, and this suggests that they came from an oral tradition, carried on board the *Mayflower.* And between the Plymouth Colony and Bury St. Edmunds there may exist a still more direct connection.

On May 9, 1568, a couple called John and Margaret Carver took an infant to be baptized at Rougham, a nearby village. The child's name was John, and the Carvers were Jermyn family retainers. When Sir Robert's father died, he left forty shillings to "Margerie Carver," alongside a bequest to the man who kept his rabbits. It is possible, though not certain, that the John Carver born at Rougham was the same John Carver who sailed on the *Mayflower* and became the first governor of New Plymouth. At his own death in 1614, Sir Robert Jermyn remembered in his will "my servant John Carver."[40] To serve in the household of a man as rich as Sir Robert carried no stigma: the people who ran his estates would command respect in local society. The Pilgrim John Carver's origins may always remain a mystery, but if the boy born at Rougham was our man, then at the time of the hangings he was an impressionable fifteen.

Robert Browne eventually came back to the British Isles. As Bancroft predicted, he split with his supporters, and then he upset the Scots; in Edinburgh even the Presbyterians found him impossible, and locked him up. Protected by Burghley, and then by the Pickerings, Browne withdrew to the English Midlands and became a reluctant conformist. For forty years he served as vicar of Thorpe Achurch, in the meadows by the Nene, occasionally lapsing back into dissent, until his last violent clash with the law.

Meanwhile, his books made a deep impression, read by Barrow and others.[41] Browne left a network of converts and followers in London, in Norwich, and along the eastern coast, in the region where many of the *Mayflower* passengers originated. Bancroft, for his part, acquired a resolute loathing of everything for which Browne stood. In 1593, he assisted in the process that led to Barrow's execution, and then a decade later he set in motion the sequence of events that led to the exile of the Pilgrims.[42]

In the Bury Stirs, we find a pattern that came to be repeated. In terms of theology, a Brownist did not really differ from a Puritan. Both groups of people wished to create a godly community where piety kept sin and disorder at bay. For this reason, and because of a shared hatred of Spain and the pope, a patriotic squire such as Jermyn might shelter or encourage a nonconformist such as Browne. From time to time, however, events acquired a momentum of their own, as religious dissent took an exceptional form that caused alarm at the highest level of church and state.

At that point, in a pocket or cell of the kingdom, a crisis might occur, when politics and local strife combined to cause an explosion, a sudden collision with authority. In such a situation, the local Puritan leaders, men like Sir Robert, would find themselves unable to prevent a drastic purge from above. In such a crisis, a committed group of zealous men and women might choose the path of outright Separatism, followed by emigration. This was very rare indeed, but it happened in the case of the Pilgrims as well as Robert Browne. The decisive events occurred in the valleys of two rivers in the north of England.

Chapter Five

Men and Women of the Clay

England, from Trent and Severn hitherto,
By south and east is to my part assign'd;
All westward, Wales beyond the Severn shore,
And all the fertile land within that bound,
To Owen Glendower; and, dear coz, to you
The remnant northward, lying off from Trent.

—Shakespeare, *King Henry IV Part 1* (1597)

There is a place on the outer end of Cape Cod, close to a trailer park twenty miles from Provincetown, where a narrow stream winds slowly down toward the marshes beside Wellfleet Harbor. Before it passes through a culvert under a country road, it measures no more than a yard across. Nothing remains nearby to suggest that the site has any historical significance.

In December, the month when skies are at their clearest on the coast, the brook soaks its way forward in an icy brown mess of fallen leaves. And yet for William Bradford, who stepped across it on December 7, 1620, the stream came as a blessing, a merciful relief from the sandy dryness of the Cape. He carefully noted the event in *Mourt's Relation.* "We saw two becks of fresh water . . . the first running waters that we saw in the country," Bradford wrote.[1]

His account of these opening weeks in America contains details so exact that today one can follow on foot the path he took. Living in an age before pesticides and tractors, William Bradford had to know land with an

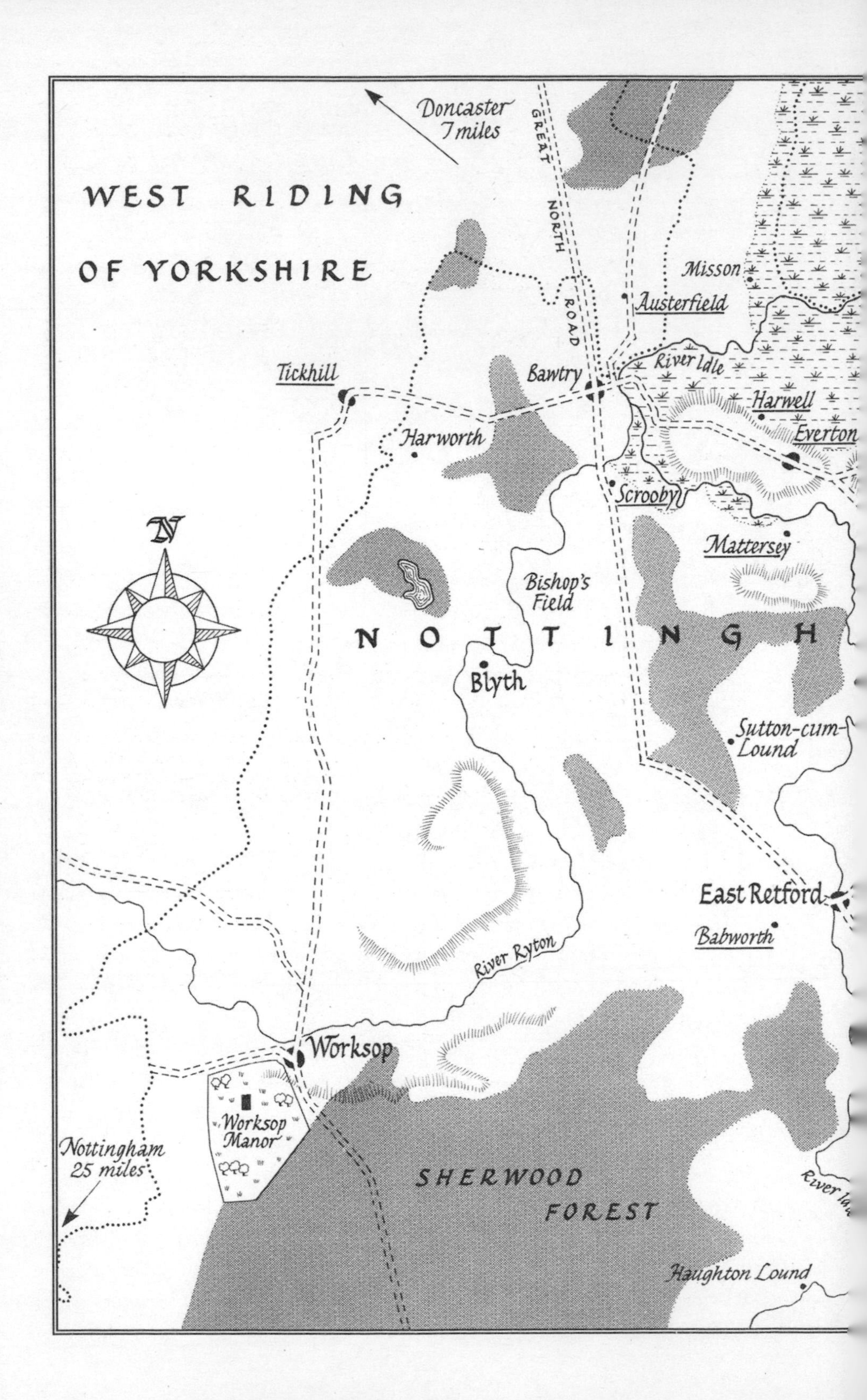

Doncaster
7 miles
WEST RIDING
OF YORKSHIRE
GREAT NORTH ROAD
Misson
Austerfield
Tickhill
Bawtry
River Idle
Harwell
Harworth
Everton
Scrooby
Mattersey
Bishop's Field
N O T T I N G H
Blyth
Sutton-cum-Lound
East Retford
Babworth
River Ryton
Worksop
Worksop Manor
Nottingham
25 miles
SHERWOOD
FOREST
Haughton Lound

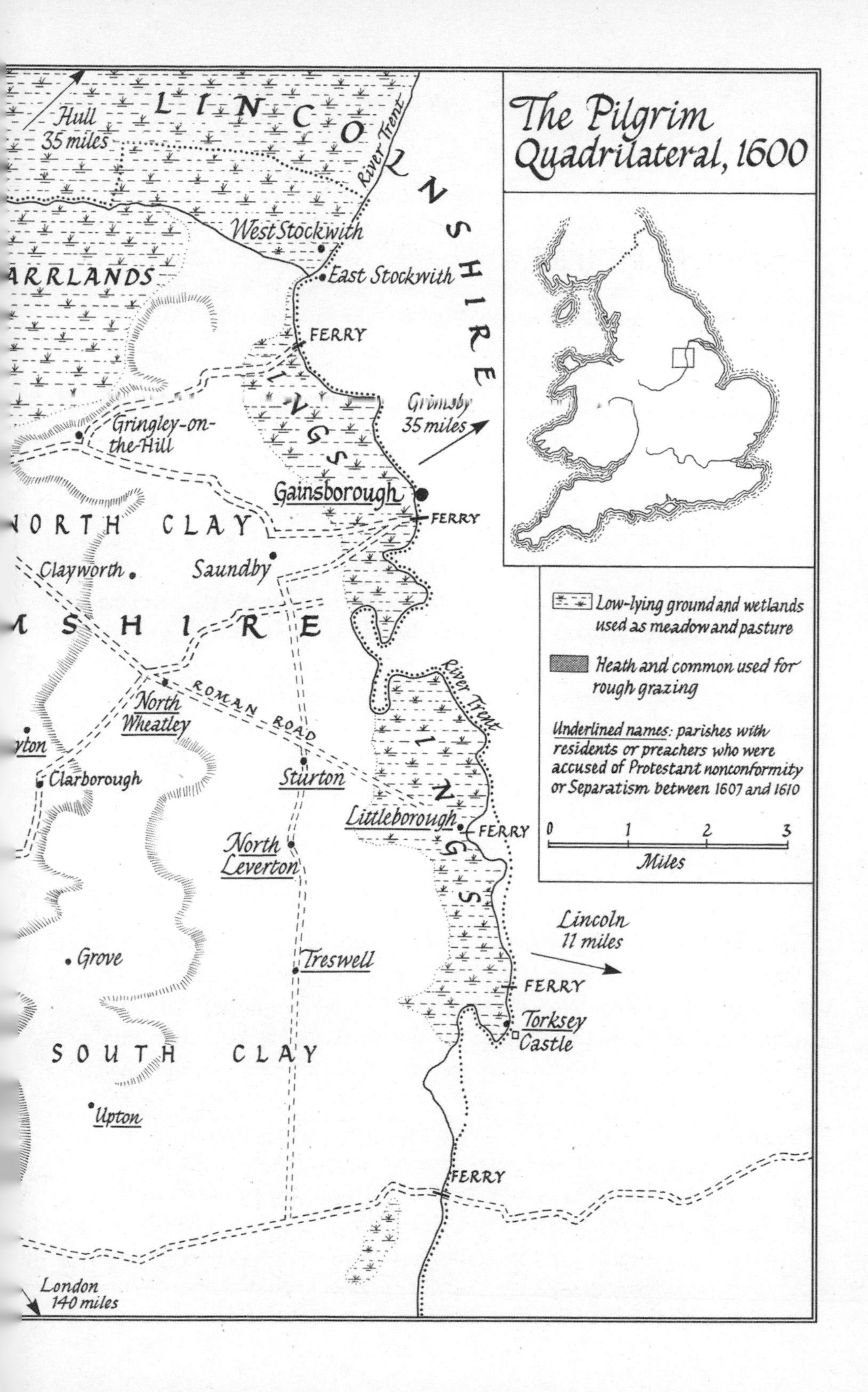

The Pilgrim Quadrilateral, 1600
Hull 35 miles
LINCOLNSHIRE
River Trent
West Stockwith
East Stockwith
ARRLANDS
FERRY
LINGS
Gringley-on-the-Hill
Grimsby 35 miles
Gainsborough
FERRY
NORTH CLAY
Clayworth
Saundby
MSHIRE
ROMAN ROAD
North Wheatley
Clarborough
Sturton
Littleborough
FERRY
North Leverton
Grove
Treswell
Lincoln 11 miles
FERRY
Torksey
Castle
SOUTH CLAY
Upton
FERRY
London 140 miles
Low-lying ground and wetlands used as meadow and pasture
Heath and common used for rough grazing
Underlined names: parishes with residents or preachers who were accused of Protestant nonconformity or Separatism between 1607 and 1610
0 1 2 3
Miles

intimacy that few of us share today. This is why he carefully examined each slope of the new country, soil that he might have to cultivate one day by hand, with an iron mattock or with a plow drawn by oxen. He catalogs the trees and the russet surface of the Cape, its ponds, and even the texture of the ground. Describing the Provincetown Hook, Bradford speaks of the "excellent black earth" a spade deep, and this is true. Drive a blade into the cordgrass on the edge of the salt marsh, and up comes wet, dark peat.

When he talks about the stream, Bradford displays his origins by using a dialect word. To call it a "beck" marks him out as a man from what he called "the North Parts" of England. This word for a stream rarely appears on a map of the country south of the Trent, the river that divided the two halves of the kingdom. Born and raised nearly two hundred miles from the capital, William Bradford and his *Mayflower* colleague William Brewster came from a region of wetland, heath, and wide open fields of red clay, just inside the North Parts.

Of course, people could migrate to Massachusetts without being born in that part of the country. The great majority of those who colonized New England originated elsewhere, chiefly in East Anglia, much nearer to London, but numbers mattered less than leadership. It was leadership that made a new venture a success or a deadly fiasco, and the men who led the Plymouth Colony came from a precise, distinctive zone, with special tensions, limits, and possibilities that shaped their upbringing and their attitudes. They came from a place where the land carries many meanings, inscribed by glaciers, by floodwaters, by politics, and by religion.

THE SCROOBY MISTAKE

This is the eastern edge of England's mining country, green and black, a mixed terrain of wildlife and machinery, spoil heaps, woods, and pasture. Mostly, the coal mines have closed, the tips made over for cubicled housing in brick and tile, but the country still has its rabbits, its foxes, its retired miners with emphysema, and its peaks and falls, made from a coupling of industry and nature. Historians will tell you that the *Mayflower* Pilgrims came from Scrooby, in the northern corner of Nottinghamshire. This is not false, but by itself it says nothing about the country or its character. Least of all do the books mention coal, the embarrassing resource that has left the region looking as it does today.

Come to Scrooby by car, twenty minutes from the old railway town of Doncaster, and you will see little that the Pilgrims might recognize, and a very great deal that they would not. Three thousand yards to the west, a tall blue and gray tower overlooks the village from the summit of a ridge. Visible fifteen miles away, it overwhelms the limestone steeple of Scrooby's medieval church. Built only twenty years ago, the tower holds the winding gear for the shafts of Harworth Colliery, Britain's deepest coal mine. Used only occasionally now, because of lurking methane gas and buckled rock, the shafts descend three thousand feet. At the bottom, the seams dip away under the earth, shelving downward to the east and beneath the North Sea, bearing hundreds of millions of tons of virgin coal.

At Scrooby, Nottinghamshire, the medieval church of St. Wilfred, viewed from the northwest. At the left, the lane leads toward Scrooby Manor, while on the right is the cottage known as the Old Vicarage, partly dating from around 1600. Behind the low stone wall beside the lane is the old village pound, used to keep stray animals. (*Photography: Nick Bunker*)

Eight miles away in the same direction, plumes of steam rise over another ridge. They come from power stations in the valley of the river Trent, located there for the sake of access to coal and water. Not far to the north, an airport sits on a low plateau, above Austerfield in Yorkshire, the place where William Bradford was born. Before it became an airport, its hangars kept the Vulcan jets that carried the hydrogen bomb for Britain. Enter the village of Scrooby, and again you will find the relics of the Pilgrims half-hidden and overshadowed by the vestiges of a much later age.

The church remains, gray, small, and squat, built mostly in the fifteenth century, with the eroding heads of angels perched around its windows. Nearby is a cottage with a timber frame, dating from about 1600, which Brewster may have helped to build for the parish minister. Part of Brewster's home still stands, at Scrooby Manor, out-of-bounds to the casual tourist, though a tumbled heap of broken masonry remains visible behind the garden wall of a house nearby. Beyond the wire, a soggy depression marks the site of a medieval moat, with fishponds to right and left, but the blatant, dominating feature of the place is the railway. The main line from Edinburgh to London slices noisily down the western edge of Austerfield. Then it passes within two hundred yards of the manor at Scrooby, cutting it off from open country to the east.

The railway runs where it does because it follows the path of the Great North Road, the old highway to Scotland. William Brewster lived here because he was the postmaster at Scrooby, stabling the horses that carried the king's mail from London to the Scottish capital. Scrooby stands at a gateway between north and south, where the English Midlands meet the Vale of York. The railway, the coal mines, and the airport with its runways facing Germany and Russia are modern signs of the strategic value of the place.

Long before the era of the Pilgrims, people had already molded the landscape for centuries, including the Romans who laid a road across the wetlands. Scrooby, and the land around it, were sought after for reasons that differed from one period to another: game for hunting, or proximity to the sea, or the deep geology of coal. Whichever resource mattered most, at any given time, the district was never minor or irrelevant.

Little of this history has left its mark in books about the Pilgrims. This is because it clashes with an orthodox version of the Scrooby story, a version dating back to 1849. In that year, a Presbyterian minister called Joseph Hunter published the first account of their roots. He depicted the Pilgrims as simple folk from an obscure place with little or no past to speak of, and certainly no scars left by industry or warfare. Hunter identified Scrooby as the home of William Brewster and the site of the Separatist assembly that formed the nucleus of the *Mayflower* community. In doing so, he fashioned a naive and mistaken image of the people in question.

"They were but inconsiderable persons at home," Hunter wrote. "There is scarcely anything to be told of their early history, besides the very small facts . . . which make the history of men who are of but small account in the midst of a larger and advanced population." Oddly patronizing, Hunter set the tone for the writers who followed him.[2]

Hunter was an excellent archivist, but he lived at a time when historians took little interest in people who ranked below the upper reaches of the landed gentry. As a result, he made errors and oversights. Because Scrooby was a small village a long way from London—in 1603 it had little more than two hundred residents, or forty households—he portrayed the Pilgrims as a tiny, humble band, arising in some spontaneous way from rural tranquillity. Hunter made them sound isolated, or eccentric. He gave the impression that nothing more could be found out about them.

None of this was fair, but Hunter's work had an enduring effect. Another English writer, William Bartlett, picked up his material and made it popular, in a book of 1853 called *The Pilgrim Fathers.* An illustrated best-seller on both sides of the Atlantic, it added the visual elements of pointed hats, wide linen collars, and the landing on Plymouth Rock. Bartlett gave wide currency to the same mistakes about Scrooby, and both men distorted or misunderstood William Bradford's account of events.

Bradford never refers to Scrooby by name. He did not pin the Separatists to the village with Hunter's degree of precision. Bradford says that they came from "sundrie townes & vilages, some in Notinghamshire, some of Lincollinshire, and some of Yorkshire," implying that the movement was wide and diffuse, as indeed it was. Joseph Hunter chose to focus on a single detail, of a kind he could easily verify from the archives that he knew best. Bradford says that the Separatists met at Brewster's home. The house in question was a manor owned by the Church of England. He did not identify it, but Joseph Hunter lived nearby, and he recognized that Bradford was referring to Scrooby Manor. It was a valuable property belonging to the archbishop of York, and Hunter rapidly found proof that it was the spot Bradford had in mind.

Hunter traced William Brewster's father as a taxpayer at Scrooby during the reign of Elizabeth. By 1849, Hunter had become the deputy keeper of the Public Record Office in London, and there he also found the accounts of the Crown's postmasters. These revealed the payments of the younger William Brewster's salary. They ended in the autumn of 1607, immediately before he went into exile in the Netherlands. It also emerged, from the archbishop's archives, that Brewster's father was the archbishop's bailiff. The Bradfords were easy to find, because the parish register of Austerfield survives. It lists the baptism of William.

At that point the story seemed almost complete. A century ago, the loose ends were apparently tied up by two more clergymen, one an American and one a Briton. The American was a Congregational minister called Henry Martyn Dexter. A Yale man, he searched the archives again, and in York he examined the records of the prosecution of the Pilgrims. His book—*The England and Holland of the Pilgrims,* published in 1905—remains the best starting point for anybody studying their background.

The British scholar was a Unitarian called Walter Burgess. In two books that appeared as long ago as 1911 and 1920, he unearthed new evidence about Robinson, and about another local Separatist called John Smyth. Burgess widened the field of inquiry, but not by much, since he took little interest in politics or in social history. After Burgess, British scholars added very little, for understandable reasons: no matter how much the Pilgrims may matter to Americans, by leaving England they made their exit from the historical stage of their homeland. And, since Hunter had a high reputation, and Dexter had written a very fat book, it was hard to imagine that they had overlooked anything significant. The exception, five decades ago, was a fourth clergyman, an Anglican called Canon Ronald Marchant, who wished to understand how the Church ran its affairs in the area.

Marchant examined a rich but at that time a rarely visited archive, the papers left by the archdeacons of Nottingham. They presided over the Church courts that tried people accused of offenses such as adultery, blasphemy, or low-level witchcraft. The papers contain a host of anecdotes, about fornicating vicars, foulmouthed scolds, and men charged with playing football or spreading dung on a Sunday. Here we find scattered references to Puritans, shedding more light on the Pilgrims. Marchant reproduced them, but his research was limited, few have read his book, and he left the Scrooby myth intact.[3]

Although Scrooby played its part, it was not the center of the movement. Nor were the Pilgrims a tiny, isolated congregation dwelling in a narrow little district about which nothing more can be said. Actually, the community of dissent extended across a much wider area. Its fulcrum lay in nearby towns that were far larger at the time. And when it came to leadership, the local Separatists looked to four men, rather than two. Brewster and Robinson worked with two partners and colleagues, John Smyth and Thomas Helwys. A clergyman, Smyth was a talented writer with a daring religious imagination. Helwys came from a local yeoman family that had risen to create within three generations a chain of estates across three counties and prospered in business in London.

It was Thomas Helwys who led the flight of the Pilgrims to Holland in 1608. Because he did not reach America, because he fell out with Smyth, and because many records have been overlooked, history has almost forgotten him. Almost, but not entirely: in America, Baptist scholars rightly remember Helwys, and John Smyth, as pioneers of their form of worship. Often Americans think of the *Mayflower* as a northern event, something that took place above the Mason-Dixon Line and mattered mainly to people who later formed the blue side in the Civil War. In fact, southern and Chicago Baptists can trace their origins to the same tract of land by the Trent. This makes the region still more intriguing.

Why did these things happen here, so far from London and in what looks like a backwater? Open and defiant separation from the Church of England was very rare indeed, and emigration was even less likely. Mostly, nonconformists found ways to stay within the Church by means of compromise or subterfuge. So why did Separatism take root around Scrooby, at a precise point in history, early in the reign of James I, at the moment when Shakespeare was writing *Coriolanus*?

Of course, the Scrooby region was never really obscure at all, but these were very unusual events, and we have a great deal of explaining to do. The best place to start is with our feet placed firmly on the ground. For want of a better term, we might call the region the Pilgrim Quadrilateral.* It covers some ninety square miles. In 1603, it had a population of about fourteen thousand, divided among some thirty parishes.[4] Its highest hill rises to three hundred feet, but most of the land is far lower than that, often only a few feet above sea level.

The Quadrilateral has immense skies, thanks to the low horizon, and soft light, because of the reflection of the sun from lush grass and shallow water. It is a land of two rivers, the Trent and the Idle. In those days it was rich territory for cattlemen and hunters, coveted by rival noblemen and squires who vied for supremacy. Far from being a placid enclave, it bore a closer likeness to a troubled county in Faulkner's Mississippi.

Behind and beneath it all lay the necessities of the soil. As a great historian once put it, in early modern England agriculture was a vast mountain range, and in front of it other forms of activity were merely minor peaks. But rural productivity remained meager by the standards of a later age. Yielding far too little, each year the average acre gave rise to fewer than

---

*Most of the area in question fell within an administrative unit called the Hundred of Bassetlaw, part of Nottinghamshire. However, the Pilgrim movement spilled over the county lines, into Lincolnshire and the West Riding of Yorkshire. It also included people from other districts in Nottinghamshire a long way from Scrooby. To call the people involved the Bassetlaw Pilgrims would be incorrect: Pilgrim Quadrilateral makes more sense, which is why the phrase has been coined for use in this book.

fourteen bushels of wheat, a fifth of the amount that farmers can grow on the best land in eastern England today. Fourteen bushels were only a bushel or two more than the yields medieval farmers had achieved, before the Black Death three hundred years earlier.

By bringing more land into use, during the second half of the seventeenth century the English gradually made famine a thing of the past. But in Brewster's day it remained a lingering threat as the kingdom's population rose, from three million in 1560 to five million eight decades later. Poor harvests made the mid-1590s miserable years. Then another grain shortage sent prices soaring, at the very moment when the Pilgrims were on the verge of going into exile. This was not the reason they left, but it had implications that they could not evade: nobody could, in an England still so overwhelmingly agrarian.

We can probably never entirely disentangle the mixed motives of the early settlers in New England. Their ambitions for betterment were religious, economic, and political at one and the same time. Separatists like the Pilgrims were men and women who wanted to improve themselves: that was the essence of what Robert Browne had said. It was their duty to create a more perfect form of society, disciplined and fraternal, like the early Christian world he saw in the New Testament. But what did this mean in practice, in the world as it actually was in a region such as the Quadrilateral? Religious ideals could never be pursued without thinking about material well-being as well.

How could a human being be godly if he or she lived in a place that was so obviously not? In a sense, the problem was brutally simple, as it always is for emigrants: the risks of remaining at home began to outweigh the dangers of going somewhere else. The England in which they lived was starting to polarize between landowners and large tenant farmers, on the one hand, and a landless laboring class, on the other. As the gap widened, so the penalty for failure became more and more alarming.

An enterprising yeoman might, by hard work and shrewd speculation, gradually assemble enough land to rank as a gentleman. Equally well, his family might sink down the scale, because of excessive debts, because a breadwinner died young, or because they simply had too many children. Because the land was still so unproductive, and because farm rents and the price of food rose far more rapidly than wages, the downward spiral might relegate them to degrading poverty. It has been estimated that between 1500 and 1620, the income of an English laborer fell by more than half in real terms. This created spiritual hazards, as well as the risk of destitution.[5]

How could such a society fail to cause strife, conflict, and sin? And how could people be godly if they were poor, illiterate, and bullied by godless superiors? The social evils caused by poverty were all too obvious in the Quadrilateral, as we shall see. So too were the startling flaws of the men set above the population, in positions of authority.

If we begin with things as they were, and not with the Scrooby myth, it will be easier to see why someone might wish to leave such a territory. The *Mayflower* story is the record of the extraordinary manner in which a group of people broke out of confining limits. Those boundaries were very specific, rooted in the landscape from which they came. The only way to grasp the meaning of the country is to walk across it patiently, from east to west, with an eye educated by what the archives contain.

The River and the Clay

The river Trent defines the eastern edge of the Quadrilateral. Shakespeare called the Trent a "smug and silver" stream, and so it may sometimes appear, but it has a fluid drama of its own. From south to north, falling slowly in wide curves, from a Tudor ruin called Torksey Castle to the town of Gainsborough, the river drops only ten inches in each of the eight miles between the two. At this point, where it divides the counties of Nottingham and Lincoln, the current is slack, but the river is unstable.

For millennia, its course has shifted back and forth over a plain two miles wide, creating bends a mile across and then chopping through them at the neck to form isolated lakes that dry out into boggy hollows. Although the Trent has thirty miles to go before it reaches its estuary, it is tidal as far as Torksey, with a foaming bore that charges up the river after a high tide in the North Sea. All this has made the river a very ambiguous resource. Being tidal, the Trent is rich with fish and fowl. In Brewster's time, salmon swam in its waters alongside sixty breeding pairs of swans. But because it is tidal, and because the estuary into which it flows drains one-fifth of the surface area of England, the Trent has often flooded with disastrous effect.

Elderly farmers recall how after the last great inundation, caused by melting snows after the harsh winter of 1947, the land became an elongated lake stretching fifteen miles north to the steel town of Scunthorpe. Even so, hazardous though the river can be, the same floods made the valley wealthy and sought after. They laid down deep beds of fertile alluvium, forming earth that clots after rain into heavy dark brown double cubes.[6]

Before modern farming, the land was too dense and too wet to be plowed for corn. So in Brewster's day the Trent valley was cow country.

Here by the river they fattened livestock before the drive to Doncaster, the largest cattle market in the north, or the long journey on the hoof down to London.[7] As early as 1560, a drover took sixty head from the Quadrilateral to the capital. Nine-tenths of the land by the river was given over to grass, either for grazing or as hay meadows, on land known then and now by a local dialect word, the "Ings." Today a rim of dikes protects the Ings, but a painting from 1835 shows how they would have looked in the reign of Elizabeth. Trodden into mud at its edge, the Trent was a magnet for horses, red cows, fishermen, and guns, a coveted locale for watering cattle and for field sports.

Thanks to the grass, the villages by the Trent were large and thriving.[8] As towns grew, and their citizens ate more meat, the price of hay doubled in England in the twenty years before the Pilgrims went into exile. "Of all other grounds, none are as profitable as medow," wrote the author of a surveyor's manual, a book that Brewster took with him to Massachusetts. Rents along the riverbank were the highest in the region, but greed for meadow and pasture had its darker side. The archives show frequent disputes, sometimes fought in the courts and sometimes with fists and pitchforks. Villagers squabbled about their rights to graze cattle on the Ings, and members of the landed gentry argued about the terms of leases and bad debts.

As we shall see, conflicts of this type, about land and status, played their part in the birth of the Pilgrim movement. Behind all this lay that same economic fact. A gap was widening between those who had land, either as owners or as large, secure tenant farmers, and those who were landless or lacked firm tenure. In the Quadrilateral, farm rents increased by perhaps a third in the ten years after 1594. This raised the stakes in all the conflicts of the region. Competition for land made the rich still wealthier, and made failure more devastating, giving each controversy about ideas an urgency it might otherwise have lacked.[9]

If the Pilgrim movement had a center, it was not at Scrooby but here by the Trent. The largest incident of religious disobedience at the time occurred about ten miles from Scrooby, at Treswell, a Trent valley village. Here, in 1610, some twenty-seven residents refused to attend sermons given by a new vicar. They were fined a shilling each. The Treswell twenty-seven most likely drew their inspiration from preachers farther down the Trent, in two larger settlements on either side of the river, at Sturton and Gainsborough, at the northeastern corner of the Quadrilateral.

The larger of the two was Gainsborough, where the early Baptist John Smyth organized his Separatist congregation. The area's leading market town, with about seventeen hundred inhabitants, Gainsborough serves as a test tube where we can see Pilgrim origins come into crystalline form.

Gainsborough stood on the right bank of the river, just across the county boundary in Lincolnshire. It owed its stature to its location. Although it lies inland, Gainsborough was a seaport too, at a time that saw a boom in coastal traffic. Gainsborough could handle vessels as large as eighty tons, dealing in coal, lead, and grain, and life in the town was dynamic. Because the parish register contains an unusually rich amount of detail, it can be seen in high relief. Starting at the moment when Separatism was at its height, in 1607, the parish clerk helpfully recorded the occupations of all three hundred men who died, married, or fathered newborn children during the next three years. Nearly a fifth of the men worked in trades reliant on cows: tanners, glovers, shoemakers, and no fewer than thirteen butchers. Twenty-three of the men listed were boatmen, fishermen, or shipwrights, and there were eleven tailors and six blacksmiths.

Later, an opponent mocked John Smyth because he was "made minister by Tradesmen, and called himself the Pastour of the Church at Gainsborough," and in this there was more than a grain of truth. Gainsborough was a commercial town of self-employed craftsmen and shopkeepers, based on the cattle trade but open to the outside world, by sea, by river, and up and down the Great North Road.[10]

For this it paid a high price. In each of six epidemic years between 1587 and 1610, the grave diggers of Gainsborough consigned seventy people to the ground, compared with about twenty-five in a normal year. As a result, the average death rate was far worse than the norm for England at the time. Low-lying market towns in wetlands close to highways or to rivers suffered severely from infectious disease, imported from outside and fed by poor sanitation, or transmitted by mosquitoes: a form of malaria was common. William Brewster's mother came from Doncaster, situated on the Great North Road and next to a marsh, and in 1583 a pestilence killed a quarter of its inhabitants. In Gainsborough, the other side of the coin was an even higher birthrate, far outstripping deaths. The town's population grew by about fifteen surviving infants each year. Even this was a cause for concern, because so many of the births were illegitimate.

From the number of entries marked "base" in the register, it seems that the people of Gainsborough copulated out of wedlock with twice the gusto of the average English town, leaving double the usual number of bastards. In August 1607, the local archdeacon summoned the churchwardens to report offenders. Of the thirty-one people named, the seven accused of some form of religious dissent were outnumbered by the eight accused of premarital sex or adultery, the four drunkards, and the eleven men charged with plowing or hay making on Sunday. Most wicked of all was Janet Rogers, arraigned "for suspition of keeping a bawdie-house & herself being ye queane." Behind this lay a national scandal. Rates of illegitimacy soared in England under Queen Elizabeth, to reach a peak in about 1600 before dropping away after about 1615. As a place of transit, Gainsborough offered more temptations than most.[11]

It was an ungodly community in which, paradoxically, a new religious movement was all the more likely to gain ground. Moral danger, the random but ever-present threat of sudden death, the entry of new ideas by way of contacts with the outside world, the hope of advancement, and the fear of squalor: these were all features of a town like Gainsborough. A man or woman was as likely to embrace an evangelical vocation here as he or she might have been in an urban ghetto in the twentieth century. The reasons might be the same: the yearning to carve out a space for respectability, and to gather allies against sin and the devil.

The same was true of Sturton, across the river in Nottinghamshire. It was a smaller place, but even so it was the largest village in the Quadrilateral, with about 650 residents. John Robinson was born here, John Smyth taught at the village school in 1602, and Sturton gave birth to the *Mayflower* passenger Katherine Carver, who married the first governor of New Plymouth. As we shall see, it was a troubled, violent parish, where the vicar brawled in the main street and armed men ran off each other's livestock, but by the standards of the time it was prosperous. Again this helps explain why it became another center for religious enthusiasm. Prosperity was insecure, and those who achieved it could not assume that it would continue indefinitely.*

Visit Sturton today, and the signs of past affluence are unmistakable, in the shape of its medieval church. Unusually grand, it has a tower so tall that it can be seen from the castle battlements far away at Lincoln. In 1593, the village had fifteen men wealthy enough to pay the subsidy, the principal tax levied by the Crown and Parliament. Among them were John Robinson's father, also called John, and his father-in-law, Alexander White. Robinson married Alexander's daughter Bridget White, taking her with him into exile in Leiden, and Bridget's sister Katherine became in due

---

*At some time in the eighteenth or early nineteenth century, the village came to be known as Sturton le Steeple, the name it bears today.

course the *Mayflower*'s Mrs. Carver. Sturton had more taxpayers than any other village in the Quadrilateral. It was and remains a large parish, of more than four thousand acres, with an excellent situation.[12]

To the east, a wide bend of the river created an expanse of grassland more than a mile across, known as the Upper Ings and the Out Ings. Drained by a lattice of ditches, the Ings were divided into long rectangles of meadow and pasture, with their short side along the water, and here the cattle fed. This was valuable land, but the secret of Sturton's success lay in a combination of assets, and soil of many different kinds. To the west, the ground begins to rise gently, up a long shallow gradient, toward the top of an escarpment that runs north and south, parallel with the Trent. High, dry, and easily worked for grain, with copses of oak on its summit, the escarpment has been known as the North Clay since the early Middle Ages. Its color and its characteristics added a second defining feature of the Pilgrim country, and another source of wealth.

After harvest, the empty fields of the North Clay resemble vast rashers of raw bacon hung out to smoke on the hillside. Beneath the earth is a soft sedimentary rock, and it frays at the surface into a red soil, which crumbles easily and does not impede the plow. The land drains freely into streams that fall down to the Trent and give the villages fresh water. So distinctive is the land that medieval writers simply called its inhabitants "Men of the Clay." Likewise, the soil, its pigment, and the crops upon it determined the name of the nearest market town to the west, Retford, and the names of villages nearby: North and South Wheatley, Clayworth, and Clarborough.[13]

Sturton lay astride the clay ridge and the river meadows, encompassing cornfields, orchards, woods, and grass, with ample manure from its livestock. If a farmer could assemble a mixed portfolio, combining each type of land, he could do very well: and so it was with the Whites. When Katherine Carver's father died, in about 1595, he owned nearly 160 acres of land in and around the village. He owned two houses, six cottages, two gardens, and two orchards, and he rented more land across the river. On the slopes of the escarpment, Alexander White had arable land, while out on the Ings he owned pastures and meadows. The hay alone would have brought in roughly twenty-two pounds a year, about three times the earnings of a field laborer. If he sold all his land on the open market, it would fetch close to six hundred pounds, enough to place him within the top 1 or 2 percent of England's population.

And yet even the Whites were insecure. Holdings as large as theirs could provide a good standard of living, but they could not guarantee its maintenance from father to children. At his death, Alexander White made over the bulk of his estate to his widow and eldest son, Charles, but there remained three younger sons and four unmarried daughters. To the daughters, including the future Bridget Robinson and Katherine Carver, he gave sixty-seven pounds each, and at least two of them found solid husbands. But the younger sons each received a meager yearly income of two pounds, intended to be paid from the profits of the White properties. The problem was typical. As the birthrate ran ahead of a family's means to support its offspring, the younger sons and the unmarried daughters had to seek alternative routes to security and status.

One of the younger sons, Roger White, became a Separatist and went to Leiden, exchanging letters with William Bradford in America. Meanwhile, those Whites who stayed at home became industrial pioneers in coal mining. Forty miles away across the county they rented another estate, at Beauvale Priory near Nottingham. By the 1590s, this was already an active coalfield, and so the Whites went into the trade. Leases survive, showing that Katherine Carver's nephew Charles White Jr. rented the rights to sink mines at Beauvale, using horse-driven engines to pump water from the shafts.

This was the social stratum from which the leaders of the Plymouth Colony came. They were the nouveaux riches of rural England. If they had luck and aptitude, they might prosper in villages where rising profits flowed from the land, but there were limits to advancement. The cruel statistics of fecundity and early death stacked the odds against them. At the same time, these conditions planted seeds of incentive to work and better themselves, by way of coal or by way of exile. If William Bradford had stayed in England, it is hard to believe that he would have floundered in passive idleness. Like his teacher John Robinson, he might well have married a White, and ended his days as another coal-mining entrepreneur.[14]

The Idle Wetlands

At its northern extremity, the North Clay ends in a conical hill, called Gringley Beacon. From its top, a shepherd gazing down would see to the west another floodplain. Through it flowed the Idle, the second river of the Quadrilateral. From the steep side of the escarpment, the clay fields overlook the Idle valley, a low-lying basin that extends like a concave green dinner plate as far as Scrooby, three miles away. This was William Brewster's immediate neighborhood. Like the land by the Trent, it was pasture and meadow, but damper still. And again this had its implications for the Pilgrims in the coastal wetlands of New England.

In winter, heavy rain often floods the valley. Almost overnight, the river can turn from a stream fifteen yards across to a chain of ponds ten times that width, with wild swans feeding among the drowned crops. In Brewster's day, before modern drainage, this happened all the more often. The paths across the valley were merely narrow filaments of gravel lined by scrubby trees, where men and women gathered willow wands for basket weaving. Many traces survive in the archives of the constant struggle to maintain the fields and tracks, and to keep them dry. In 1648, after winning the Civil War, Parliament sent commissioners to survey Scrooby Manor, confiscated because it was Church property. The manor house had mostly been demolished. What was left was "built of Bricke & Timber & much ruinated," and nearby they found "parcells of meadow . . . wasted by the overflowing of waters."

In William Brewster's day, the leading resident of Scrooby was a man called Richard Torre. He acted as business manager for the area's richest magnate, Gilbert, seventh Earl of Shrewsbury, arranging shipments of lead from the earl's mines to Europe. When Torre died in 1602, he left twenty shillings to his neighbors, "towardes the mendinge of the hye waye into the Inges," enough to pay six laborers for a week's work on the path that led out of Scrooby to the east. Two years before that another man, from Mattersey, the next village, fell afoul of the archdeacon's court for cleaning out a ditch on the Sabbath. In 1606, a woman from Clayworth was charged with failing to attend her parish church. Her excuse, accepted by the judge, was that in winter the way was "so dangerous that without dainger to her health she cannot resort."[15]

Even now, the green wetness of the plain has sounds, shades, and textures that, at times and fleetingly, invite us back into the world Brewster inhabited. Come on foot to Scrooby from the east, or wander to the south, and you will see on the horizon a chain of seven medieval church towers. They encircle the lowest part of the valley. Each tower pokes up like the small gray horn of a cow, and they mark dry spots on the rim of the wetland where islands of the same gravel supplied sites for building.

One of these church towers is at Scrooby, and another is at Austerfield. Between them the river Idle bends in a wide U, curving around to the northeast toward its junction with the Trent, through what are known as "Carrs," another dialect word. Created by the last glaciation, twenty thousand years ago, the Carrlands mark the northern frontier of the Quadrilateral, but this is a damp, blurred frontier without a rigid frame. The eye is always drawn away into the far distance, over alternating bands of dark and light green as far as a man or woman can see.

At their farthest extremity, the glaciers ended about fifteen miles south of the city of York. They left only a ridge of moraine to make a low barrier across the country from west to east. In front of the glacier, meltwaters collected in a huge lake. When it emptied, and formed the estuary of the river Humber, the lake bed filled with peat from rotting vegetation, forming wetlands known as the Humberhead Levels. Rivers flowing out of the glacier, off the hills, and across the lake bed created a braided pattern of peat and sand, leaving the low humps and levees where the churches and causeways can now be found.

How did the wet, flat geography and the vast skies affect the minds of those who lived there? It is impossible to say for sure, especially now that drains and pumps have tamed the Levels, but some elements of their mental life can be reliably imagined. Because to the east the Levels melted into an estuary, the sea and what lay beyond it were far closer than they appear on a modern map. Between Scrooby and Austerfield, there were wharves on the Idle at Bawtry, another river port where packhorse routes converged, carrying wool and minerals for shipment down the rivers to the ocean. Because of the direction in which the valleys bend and the waters flow, those who lived nearby looked eastward toward the North Sea, and the region's chief seaport, at Hull. The Idle basin was a place with a wide perspective, facing outward. It was not an enclosed, landlocked zone of introversion.

For centuries, in fact, the Levels had a reputation for nonconformity, as a place where hunting and gathering vied in importance with stationary farming as a way of life. Austerfield lay on the edge of Hatfield Chase, a royal hunting forest, often submerged, where in the reign of King James red deer in their hundreds swam in flight from men pursuing them in flat-bottomed boats. Where islands rose above the water, the people herded cattle or foraged in the wetlands for shellfish and eels. On account of their independence, and their occasional lawlessness, they came to be known as borderers, stilt walkers, or free dwellers. By 1830, engineers had already drained most of the Chase and the Carrs, but at the time of the American Civil War a newspaper in Doncaster carried a series of articles that recorded the details of this older way of life. The writer interviewed men and women whose memories stretched back into an environment that the Pilgrims would have recognized.

Their England was not yet a domesticated place, but a landscape with wild features, and these he recorded. Otters four feet long lived on the Idle, close to Scrooby, where men hunted them with spears. They stalked the otters along the riverbed, using a long pole to vault across deep streams. Stag hunting continued on the Carrlands until as late as 1762. Beds of rushes sheltered pike and twenty species of wild duck, and the Carrlands supplied a rich habitat for tens of thousands of wildfowl taking refuge from stormy weather out on the North Sea. Trout swam in a brook that flowed past Brewster's back gate. In the summer, he would hear the high-pitched whistle of the osprey, a migrant from Africa, swooping down with black-and-white wings six feet wide to take fish from the waterways. The last osprey in the valley was shot near Austerfield in 1856. Even within living memory, after World War II, the clumps of sedge at Scrooby between the trout stream and the railway were thick with the nests of snipe.

Historians often write about the early English settlers of America in a cerebral way, or with a sentimentality that the Pilgrims would have found very odd. In fact, they came from the old, feral England, as it was before the railways, and as it still exists in vestiges today. The *Mayflower* carried two dogs to America, not as pets, but as hunting dogs: a spaniel for retrieving game birds and a mastiff for running down deer. When Bradford spoke of "the innumerable store of fowl, and excellent good" that the Pilgrims found at New Plymouth, he knew what he meant. Scrooby had a village poacher, prosecuted three times in 1605 and 1607 for shooting hares and geese and killing swans without a license.[16]

When the Pilgrims explored Cape Cod and the forest behind New Plymouth, they were excited young men, wandering freely in a game-filled land that echoed on a vastly larger scale the semi-wilderness they knew in the land of their birth. In America, herons rise blue and serene from the marshes at Wellfleet, and they have their transatlantic cousins in the herons that alight on the Idle.

Southern New England was also formed by glaciers, and their aftermath created a similar pattern of wetlands, low hills of sand, and wide shallow estuaries, ideal for migrating birds like the wetlands between Scrooby and the sea. When settlers crossed the Atlantic, they followed paths taken long before by vagrant sandpipers. Sometimes the birds fly back and forth from America and feed in England, probing for mussels on the mudflats along the Humber.[17]

The Forest and the Open Fields

Not all the land was wet. Three miles west of Austerfield, there grew until 1820 an ancient oak called "the jutting tree," and by tradition it marked the northern end of the royal hunting forest of Sherwood. The legal boundary of the forest lay farther south, but the tree made perfect sense as a marker. Sherwood was a forest, used for hunting, because the rock beneath it is acidic sandstone, fit only for woodlands of oak and birch. The rock began close to the jutting tree, extending past Scrooby and south in a long strip as far as the city of Nottingham, where the castle sits on its most conspicuous yellow outcrop. Because the sandstone was hard and dry, the Great North Road ran along its eastern margin, above the marshes, but it also created heaths and wastelands close to Austerfield. They formed a no-man's-land between north and south, long viewed with official distrust.

If the legends of Robin Hood have any basis, it derives from outlaws in this part of medieval England. Today the name Raker's Field on the map marks a spot, behind Harworth Colliery, that was licensed by Richard the Lionheart as a tournament ground. Bands of men from Yorkshire met their rivals from the south in legalized fights that had to be banned when they became deadly brawls. In Bradford's day, highwaymen plied their trade on the Great North Road, pillaging travelers until King James ordered a purge of innkeepers who harbored them. For six weeks in 1605, judges sat at Doncaster and Sheffield to put on trial and hang the felons whom they found.[18]

So, long before he reached New England, the young Pilgrim had already lived on a frontier of a sort, in a village where life was arduous and rewards were small. Austerfield bore little resemblance to the fat cattle country along the Trent. Again, the village has left behind it a footprint of early documents, while the terrain preserves memories of its own that open a window into the world he knew.

Near the church where William Bradford was baptized, a narrow track called Low Common Lane veers away from the road. Follow the lane until it dwindles into a path, and three things catch the eye. The first is the hedge that lies along its eastern side. It contains a host of species—hawthorn, holly, wild blackberries, and more—and then a stand of oak and beech. Hedgerows like this take centuries to establish, and so in Low Common Lane we encounter remnants of the Jacobean landscape. The second signature of the land is bracken, spilling across the path's western side. The third is a dead rabbit, slung over a fence by its throat.

A rabbit killed with a shotgun can sum up a page of a history book. With about 130 residents, divided among some twenty-five households, Austerfield was one of the tiniest townships in the Quadrilateral. It had so few people, so much bracken, and so many rabbits because so much of its soil was sand. Ten minutes' walk from the church, in an arc around the village, quarrymen have dug huge pits, and they reveal that the topsoil is thin. Exposed beneath it lies sand the color of burnished copper, pockmarked by rabbit holes. Not all the land was quite as difficult as this—to the east and south, the soil is darker, near the Idle—but most of the parish offered little to the farmer.

The northern half of Austerfield consisted of thickets and rough pasture known as High Common. Here the villagers cut hay and gathered firewood, while their pigs rooted for acorns. To the south, between High Common and the church, lay the Ridding Field, the site of the sand pits, where William Bradford's uncle Robert rented seven acres. Again, "ridding" was a dialect word meaning a clearing hacked from a forest, and again the soil was sparse. It was unsuitable for wheat. So they grew rye and peas to make the best of the sandy conditions, but next to the Great North Road the ground was fit only for trees. A strip of woodland lay along the highway.

On a modern map it still bears the name the King's Wood, because Austerfield was a royal manor, and the Bradfords were tenants of the sovereign. The Crown occasionally surveyed its estates, and sometimes the results survive, as they do at Austerfield. Because of this, and because before they died the Bradfords made detailed wills, the family's changing fortunes can be plotted over time. They did well during the sixteenth century, but Austerfield did not offer much by way of opportunity. Under King James, the Bradfords faced the likelihood that life would become harder still. Against this background, the young William left and went into religious exile.

William Bradford had a great-great-grandfather called Peter. During the reign of Henry VIII, he lived in the wet lowlands to the north of Doncaster. There he grew barley and raised sheep. A good Catholic, at his death he bequeathed his soul to "god Almightie and to owre ladie saint Marie and all tholie company of heaven." His family multiplied and fanned out across the countryside. They accumulated horses and more sheep and a broken line of land to the south of Doncaster, as outright owners or as holders of a lease. In doing so, they were typical of large tenant farmers in the first half of the reign of Queen Elizabeth. Because leases were long, with rents set many years before, a tenant selling his produce for rising prices could prosper and acquire freehold property himself. At his death in 1578 the Pilgrim's great-uncle Robert Bradford gave his daughter forty pounds and an income of six pounds per annum, after leaving the bulk of his assets to his widow.

At some time before 1560, the Pilgrim's grandfather, also called William, moved to Austerfield, where he joined a small, intermarried elite of yeoman farmers, ranking above the landless field hands. Grandfather William had two sons, another William and another Robert. In 1584, William married Alice Hanson, also of Austerfield. Their first child was William Bradford the *Mayflower* passenger, baptized on March 19, 1590. When the boy was less than a year old, his father died, and two years later his mother, Alice Bradford, wedded an Austerfield man called Robert Briggs.

In 1599, Austerfield had only four villagers affluent enough to pay the taxes voted by Parliament, and three of these were William Bradford's grandfather, uncle, and stepfather: John Hanson, Robert Bradford, and Robert Briggs. When more deaths struck the family, the boy was passed from one man to another. Alice died in 1597, and so young William entered the care of John Hanson, Austerfield's wealthiest tenant. When in turn Hanson died in 1602, the twelve-year-old Pilgrim went to live with his uncle Robert.[19]

What effect did the chain of bereavements have on the boy? We have no idea what emotional damage might have occurred, if any, but we do know that he stood to inherit his father's property, such as it was, making him independent at twenty-one. We can also locate the Bradfords precisely in the social scale of their time.

Like most of the Crown's land, Austerfield had been neglected, its rents packaged up and sold off on derisory terms on a long lease to a remote absentee. In 1608, in a vain effort to restore the solvency of James I, the lord treasurer commissioned a new survey of royal manors, to see what income they would yield if they were managed commercially. Along with the will of William's uncle Robert—he died in 1609—the document tells us what kind of people the Bradfords were. Their upward mobility had apparently ceased.

On the royal manor, Robert Bradford owned a house and a little under eleven acres of plow land and meadow, and he rented another twenty-three acres. A holding of this size made him no more than a minor yeoman: independent, making perhaps fifteen pounds a year, twice as much as a laborer, but without a safety cushion against disaster in the event of a string of poor harvests or a bout of cattle plague. At his death, Robert Bradford had two maidservants—to one he left a cow called Daisy, and to the other a horse—and he owned a team of oxen. Besides that, and his tenancies, he had very little.

At Austerfield, he enjoyed the status of a village elder, but only because this was such a small place, and because he was lucky enough to find a careless landlord in the shape of the Crown. The survey showed that Bradford paid less than nine shillings in rent, while he should have been paying forty. His kinfolk, the Hansons, had the same good fortune. For their seventeen acres they paid less than six shillings, about a seventh of the rent the surveyor thought was a fair amount. This situation clearly held risks of its own, if the Crown tried to push the rents up as high as they would go when the tenancies fell due for renewal.

Small yeoman farmers like the Bradfords had little status, and far less security than the Whites of Sturton. Uncle Robert left behind him an eighteen-year-old son and three teenage daughters, cousins of the future Pilgrim. An estate of his size would not support a dowry. All three Bradford daughters died unmarried, and in the conditions of the time they would have had to work as domestic servants. Robert Bradford's will said that his children should receive "tuition" from neighbors, but "tutor" could mean a guardian or an employer, rather than implying any element of education.

Perhaps all this explains why, when the young William Bradford became an ardent Puritan, he found his family less than sympathetic. Nearly a century later, the Massachusetts historian Cotton Mather wrote a short biography of the Pilgrim, and despite its brevity it contains details that carry us back into the harsh realities of rural life. Mather says that Bradford encountered the "wrath of his uncles . . . [and] the scoff of his neighbours." According to Mather, after an illness at about the age of twelve William Bradford began to read the Scriptures, and then he came under the influence of a local Puritan clergyman, Richard Clifton. It is easy to see why this upset his family. As an only child, with what Mather calls a "comfortable inheritance," the young William should have been helping his kin, perhaps by marrying a cousin. This was all the more necessary if the rents they paid were about to shoot up.[20]

That was the way things were in the Jacobean countryside, just as they would have been in County Clare in 1870, or Calabria in 1900, or as they are on the plains of northern India today. And yet in another sense Austerfield was very distinctively English, in a way that shaped the attitudes of the people who lived there. It was what historians call an "open field" village, like Scrooby and Sturton. For perhaps five centuries or more, men and women had farmed in the same way, according to the medieval field system of the English Midlands. This too had its implications for William Bradford.

In an open-field village, the farmers divided the land for grain into many hundreds or even thousands of strips. Each strip occupied about an acre. They were arrayed asymmetrically across the land so that the furrows followed the natural slope. That way, rainwater drained by itself across the contours, emptying into ditches at the field edge. In each village the strips were grouped into three or four great open fields, sometimes a mile wide, with no fences or hedges within them, spaces entirely different from the uniform rectangles that long ago replaced them.

At Scrooby, the open fields covered the dry and rising ground to the west of the Great North Road, with woad for blue dye grown nearer to the village. Austerfield had three open fields—the Ridding Field, the West Field, and the Low Field—arranged in a ring around the parish church. Robert Bradford rented six or seven acres in each one, so that his strip holdings lay as much as a mile apart. They were scattered among those of his neighbors, as the system decreed, so that each man had a share of good or bad ground.

Open field farming was not some kind of communism. All the villagers were tenants of a landlord. At Austerfield and Scrooby the farmers were commercial, buying and selling cattle, hiring extra grazing land for cash when they needed it, and sometimes subletting cottages to one another. Pragmatically, the open field system survived not as a form of socialism but because it saved time on fencing and ditching, the bane of an English farmer's life, in a rain-soaked country that relied on livestock for fertilizer and protein.[21]

Certainly, they managed the land in a communal way, but again this was simply pragmatic. Out of experience, they planned the farming year jointly, with everyone plowing, planting, weeding, and harvesting at the same time. They moved their cattle only when necessary, at fixed dates. By doing so, the village made the most of its labor, keeping fences to a minimum, ensuring that everybody had a stake in the yearly outcome. All the tenants had rights to scavenge and to feed their beasts on the meager soil that formed the commons of Austerfield, but this too was subject to rules. No one could keep more than an allotted number of sheep or swine. To enforce the regulations, they had a manorial court. With a jury of tenants, it levied fines on those who tried to dodge the system by putting a few more animals on the common or by cutting more than a fair quantity of wood.[22]

How this system affected the way people thought and felt we cannot know for sure, but the mental world of William Bradford had characteristics that we can realistically guess. The first was the pervasive anxiety of a system under threat. During his teenage years, a few landlords and large tenant farmers were just starting to enclose the open fields in villages within twenty miles of Austerfield. They cast greedy eyes on such spaces as

High Common, with a view to a new, more risky kind of system, where enterprising men did as they pleased with their land. Fair or unfair, this was likely to bring unsettling change.

Austerfield was small but not isolated, since London already exerted a magnetic force, as men from the region went there and back to do business. Aside from the Crown, the largest landowners were the Frobishers, including the Arctic explorer Martin Frobisher. With his plunder from raiding the Spanish in the West Indies, he bought the manor next to Austerfield, and in Bradford's boyhood the Frobishers owned half the houses in the village.[23] Even so, places such as this were inherently conservative, because of disciplines of an economic kind. The open field system imposed rules, and it required team spirit. As it came under threat, relationships were bound to become more fraught.

Families would almost inevitably persecute those of their members who showed signs of being different. If a landowning youth like William Bradford displayed too much independence, bucking the constraints of kinfolk and community, and especially if he spoke the language of piety, the conflict was likely to be all the more unpleasant. At Austerfield the surviving records suggest that people lived on rye bread, pea soup, weak beer, and in wintertime a little pork and bacon. Being told by a Puritan that they were ungodly was doubtless more than they could tolerate.

William Bradford grew to manhood in circumstances such as these, but economics and rural envy were not the only forces that formed his mind. From Austerfield he would have learned other things too. Life among the open fields gave rise to a precise awareness of nature, the habit that the Pilgrim took with him to Cape Cod.

Men and women of his period knew the trees, flowers, animals, and wild birds of the countryside in intricate detail. They had a huge, largely forgotten vocabulary of words for each and every species. Prescientific, it survives best of all in Shakespeare, in the scenes portraying the madness of King Lear and in the names of the wildflowers gathered for a garland by the drowned Ophelia: "crow-flowers, nettles, daisies and long purples." This was not imaginary: because plows drawn by oxen required a large turning circle, and because the wetter parts of the soil were left untilled, the open fields were fringed and hemmed by ribbons of color, thickest where the livestock left their droppings. And beneath the corn, the clay required its own ample lexicon.

Within the open fields each patch of soil possessed a label according to its dampness, its dryness, its use, or the landmarks that gave it an identity. A little of this lingers on in early surveyors' plans of Sturton, from the eighteenth century, and in the list of Alexander White's real estate. Within the Low Field and the West Field at Sturton were "House Furlong," "Robinet Furlong," "Four Sandhills Furlong," and "Nether Bolgate." In open fields with no fences between the strips, men and women needed such a plethora of terms to define the spaces they occupied. The sought-after grazing land was parceled out precisely too, in small lots, each with its own designation.[24] All of this went with Bradford to America, and again it helps explain the care with which he described the New World.

There was also something Shakespearean about the narratives that unfolded in the Pilgrim Quadrilateral. The years that saw the local birth

The parish church at Sturton le Steeple, Nottinghamshire, seen from Freeman's Lane to the northwest. According to local tradition, the Robinsons lived close by, near the left-hand edge of the picture. In the foreground is land known in 1600 as Wybern Dale, where Alexander White, father of the *Mayflower* passenger Katherine Carver, owned a *close,* a fenced area probably used for livestock. The picture has been edited to remove electric power lines. (*Photography: Nick Bunker*)

of Separatism were a period of abrasive conflict. This was especially true of Sturton, the home of John Robinson and Katherine Carver. People fought for grazing land, for the tithe revenues of the Church, or for the rights to levy tolls on river traffic or goods sold on market day. They competed for precedence, quarreling over symbols of rank within a local hierarchy. In the stories the village left behind, again we can begin to see why people might wish to emigrate, and how little Christianity in the neighborhood resembled a Puritan ideal.

The Breaking of the Pews

Two muddy roads met in Sturton by the parish church. One was the old Roman highway from Lincoln, which crossed the Trent by way of a ferry before heading over the North Clay to Bawtry. The second road ran north to south, parallel with the river. On May 16, 1594, the vicar of Sturton, John Quippe, was leaving the church when he saw by the crossroads a gentleman called George Lassells. Aged thirty-three, Lassells was lord of the manor of Sturton. Lassells carried a pistol, while Quippe had only his walking stick.

There are two versions of what happened next. The first, and the more likely, says that George Lassells flew into a rage. He felled the vicar and rained blows down on him. Struggling to escape, Quippe, a man in his mid-fifties, asked what might have provoked the attack. Lassells told Quippe that he was "a vyle priest" and accused him of reporting the Lassells household to the authorities for failing to come to church. The story Lassells told was different—he accused the vicar of assaulting him—but a fracas there clearly was, and it was neither the first nor the last. George Lassells was the eldest of at least eight brothers. They fought their neighbors, and they fought each other, leaving behind them a long chronicle of violence.[25]

A word must be said about the sources. The details of the brawl come from the records of the Court of Star Chamber, where Lassells sued Quippe. On at least thirteen occasions George Lassells, his father, or his siblings were parties to litigation in that court, which heard case after case filled with stories of mayhem. Historians must be skeptical about some of these anecdotes of bloodshed, because lawsuits in the Star Chamber were apparently used as a form of intimidation. Complaints filed with the court were not given under oath, and so false accusations were often made as a way to smear an enemy. However, at Sturton we have other sources, and they corroborate the picture of a troubled village. George Lassells was a bully, and a predatory lecher. Such were the local rulers of the Pilgrim country.[26]

A stream of incidents in 1605 convey a picture of life as they lived it. On January 12, a laborer from Sturton called Henry Arnold appeared before the local JPs, charged with a felony. He confessed, so they sentenced him to be whipped by the parish constable "till his body be bloody." The constable failed to carry out the punishment, and so in April the justices put the constable in the stocks, and they ordered a flogging for two Sturton men accused of theft. Meanwhile, an unholy scene had occurred in Sturton Churchyard involving George Lassells—or rather, Sir George, as we must call him, because King James had given him a knighthood.

One Sunday in Lent, after evening prayer, the villagers found Sir George arguing with a manservant called Biggs. "Young man, I will teach you to behave," said Lassells. "I am too olde to be taught by you," Biggs replied. "I never offered 40 shillings and a gowns cloth to one of my maids to occupie her as you did." Among those present was John Robinson, the preacher's father. Three lawsuits for libel followed, and produced a stream of testimony on oath, from Robinson and others. It appears that Sir George had approached a serving girl one morning, as she made the beds. In exchange for sex, he offered her money, a bodice made of taffeta, and enough material to make a pair of sleeves to go with it. The story was all the more credible because Sir George had a history of mistreating his employees. In 1604, the JPs at Retford had summoned Sir George to appear before them for failing to pay his servants their wages. Lassells was a JP himself, which makes it virtually certain that these allegations were true.[27]

At Sturton, even the parish church became a site of combat. The state of the building was a disgrace. It was a common problem in the period, when the Reformation had made men and women more reluctant to mend leaking roofs and broken windows. In November 1597, the people of Sturton gathered to discuss repairs, and they decided to erect new pews. A churchwarden, called Dickens, installed a private pew and sat in it every Sunday until Christmas. As the vicar celebrated the Nativity, his prayers were interrupted by uproar in the aisles. One Isabell Sturton clambered into the pew, claiming that "tyme out of mynde" her ancestors had occupied the spot. Dickens told her to move and threatened to punch her in the face if she did it again. She and her menfolk waited, and then did what they had to do. One night in February, someone crept into the church and smashed the pew to pieces.[28]

Behind all this lay a story of dispossession, a chain of injustice that destroyed whatever harmony this village may once have enjoyed. In the time of Henry VIII, the lord of the manor at Sturton was Thomas, Baron Darcy. A valiant soldier, Darcy held firm Catholic beliefs. He opposed Henry's divorce from Catherine of Aragon and he objected to the dissolution of the monasteries. When the king's greed caused an insurrection in the north in 1536, Darcy sided with the rebels, but he also tried to bring about reconciliation with the king. He was courageous, but he was naive.

Darcy failed to allow for the ambitions of the Lassells family. Minor landowners near Worksop, at the opposite corner of the Quadrilateral, they hitched their cart to the horse of Protestant reform. George Lassells, grandfather of Sir George, acted as an informer, alleging that Darcy had conspired with the rebels. Darcy was beheaded, and his estates were taken by the Crown. As a reward, the Crown gave George Lassells the whole of Darcy's land in the North Clay.[29]

Men who had behaved in such a way were bound to be unpopular, but for other reasons too the village became unstable. The parish contained more than one manor, and the Lassells family had made enemies. Their rivals were a dynasty called Thornhagh, who lived as lords of the manor at Fenton, half a mile from Sturton crossroads.*

By 1600 the Thornhaghs had amassed an ample estate in the neighborhood, and they bought more land whenever they could. Wealthier than the Lassells clan, the Thornhaghs also outranked them in status and in education. They sent their sons to Cambridge, and their mortal remains still lie in the place of honor at the eastern end of Sturton Church. The two families waged a long war for domination of their little world. Over the space of thirty years, Lassells and Thornhagh sued each other time and again, exchanging accusations of fraud, barn burning, and abduction of each other's cattle. By the early seventeenth century, the feud had come to center on the church tithes, but the conflict was entirely irreligious.

As always, the villagers had to pay by way of tithes a tenth of the produce of the land. At Sturton, the Church gave the Thornhaghs a lease of the revenue in return for a yearly rent. This angered the Lassells family beyond endurance. During the harvest of 1600, George Lassells told his men to gather the peas and beans that grew amid the corn, and he refused to give the compulsory tenth to his rivals. Then, one autumn day, two men from the Thornhagh household rode down to the Trent to hunt with a hawk.

By the river they met George Lassells, leading a gang armed with swords and pikes. In the fight that followed, Lassells and his men killed the hawk, and then to add another insult, they stole a spaniel belonging to the Thornhaghs. The Thornhaghs went to court, filing with the Star Chamber a diatribe that filled a parchment thirty inches square. In the Church

---

*Thornhagh was pronounced either "Thorney" or "Thorn-hay."

courts, they began another lawsuit, demanding their fair share of Sturton's green vegetables.[30]

These tales of vendetta in the countryside might be trivial if they were isolated affairs, but in fact they were typical of the landscape from which the Pilgrims came. Worst of all was the rivalry between the Earl of Shrewsbury and his enemies, a family called Stanhope. It reached its climax in 1593 in a pitched battle by the Trent. Among those who fought for the earl were Richard Torre of Scrooby and the Lassells family: no mêlée was complete without them. In the reign of Elizabeth, the county of Nottingham acquired a reputation as one of the most turbulent in the realm. Under King James its infamy continued.[31]

In those days, a happy and peaceful shire needed a dominant aristocrat to mediate between the squabbling gentry and to plead the county's case before the king. If the poor were lucky, the nobleman in question would organize food supplies in hungry years and hear their complaints against exploitation. He would also try to make sure that the JPs who undertook most local government did their job as they should, rather than making it a pretext to serve their own greed and ambition. Nottinghamshire had no such man to lead it. Instead, the local aristocracy were divided, each rival magnate seeking his own self-interest and each hoping to emerge as the king's favored grandee in the region.

In due course, the Pilgrims fell victim to the toxic conditions created by this local battle for power. By far the most dangerous of the rival magnates was Gilbert Talbot, the seventh Earl of Shrewsbury. As we shall see, the earl stood to gain the most from a purge against religious dissent, and he hated Puritans with venom. But before we come to that, and to the events that forced the Pilgrims out of England, we have to look more closely at their early lives. In America the leading layman among the exiles was William Bradford's mentor, William Brewster. To him we must now turn, and to his misbehaving father, William Brewster the bailiff of Scrooby.

Chapter Six

THE MAKING OF A PILGRIM

Late in the afternoon, we rode through Brewster . . . Who has not heard of Brewster? Who knows who he was?

—HENRY DAVID THOREAU, VISITING THE CAPE COD TOWN OF BREWSTER IN 1849[1]

To the west of Scrooby, the largest of its open fields stretched away over a ridge toward the town of Blyth. It was called the Bishop's Field. Somewhere hereabouts a scandalous incident took place one day in the 1580s. Somebody saw a young woman take off her shoes and tights and place them in a bush. Barefoot and bare-legged, she crossed the field toward a balk, a strip of soil left unplowed between the corn to allow people and cattle to pass to and fro. Among the wildflowers she found an older man waiting. He was William Brewster, gentleman of Scrooby, the father of the Pilgrim, and the young woman was "Mr. Willm Brewster's whore."

Or so she was said to be. In about 1587, old William Brewster sued a local woman for libel, for repeating the gossip about his alleged fornication between the furrows. Among the undated court papers are four witness statements from women in Blyth who heard the tale. The girl was a maidservant who worked for a lady in Blyth called Jane Marshall. It seems that Mrs. Marshall spread the story around the neighborhood, saying that if her maid was pregnant, then Brewster must be the father.[2]

At the time, his son was about twenty-one. The future Pilgrim was living in London and serving on the staff of a member of the Privy Council,

William Davison, the queen's new secretary of state. If he heard about his father's disgrace—if that is what it was—we will never know his reaction. The episode certainly never appeared in later histories of the Plymouth Colony. Whether the story was true or not, the incident casts a harsh light on the environment in which the Pilgrims came to maturity.

We cannot write a conventional biography of William Brewster. He left no private letters. No physical likeness survives, and we know very little about his inner life. But we can sift through the elements that went to make him what he was, including the circumstances of his father. In fact, such an undertaking is essential, because Brewster was indispensable, as a member of the core group of Separatists who supplied leadership in America. Without an understanding of the man, and the forces that created him, the reasons why the colony succeeded will remain elusive.*

His protégé William Bradford had no doubt that this was so. When Brewster died in New Plymouth in 1644, at the age of about seventy-seven, Bradford composed a eulogy that awarded him much of the credit for the settlement's survival. Brewster, he says, was a man "seasoned with the seeds of Grace and vertue." Tough and resilient, in mind and body, brave but also canny and resourceful, he was an inspiring teacher, modest and sociable, and discreet as well as devout. He also had an education: he possessed, said Bradford, "knowlidge of the lattine tongue and some Insight in the Greeke." Once again, there is no reason to doubt the truth of what Bradford writes. The colony could not have maintained its morale, essential for survival, if it had lacked leadership of high caliber.[3]

How did William Brewster become the man he was? Or, to put it another way, what was he trying to achieve, first as a Separatist and then as an American, and why did he want to achieve it? The answer may run something like this: when the Pilgrims settled in the New World, they were looking for more than Christian liberty, however they might define it. They carried with them a blended ideology, an amalgam between religious beliefs and secular concepts of virtue, gentility, and heroism. These ideas were borrowed from ancient Greece and Rome and then refashioned to suit the needs of the Elizabethan era.

Brewster, as we shall see, became exposed in his teens and twenties to new thinking about what it meant to be civilized and courageous. Welded

---

*The best attempt at a biography was made by another English clergyman, Harold Kirk-Smith, in his useful book *William Brewster: "The Father of New England"* (Boston, Lincolnshire: 1992).

together with Calvinism, it gave him a powerful creed, a Puritan compound of Saint Paul and the stoic austerity of Roman heroes. Life in Nottinghamshire was unheroic, and unholy. For a man of William Brewster's social rank it also contained barriers to advancement. Puritanism offered, perhaps, an alternative, the opportunity and the means to escape from what he thought of as moral squalor. It might also provide a new way to define "gentility" and "virtue," words that resonated widely in the discourse of the period. To see what Brewster was trying to escape from, we return briefly to his father's lechery.

Gentlemen and Lechers

This peccadillo in the long grass was not an isolated case. If old Brewster seduced a serving girl, he was only one of many gentlemen who did so. At Sturton, George Lassells had at least attempted the same thing, and others certainly accomplished it. In 1592, the archdeacon prosecuted Thomas Sturton, a member of the family that claimed the troublesome pew. He admitted fathering a child with a servant, "Dorothy Style, fornicatrix," taking her into his bed night after night while Mrs. Sturton was away caring for a sick neighbor.[4] In the Quadrilateral, the sexual exploitation of young women was casual and commonplace. The authorities recognized it as something that required firm action.

At the end of the century, in the face of conditions close to famine, the queen and Parliament enacted the first of a series of poor laws. They obliged each parish to look after paupers and to collect a parish tax for the purpose. As a result, in the Trent valley in the late 1590s we begin to find churchwardens taking a few pence a week from each taxpayer to be doled out to the needy. As the cost of welfare rose, it became all the more essential to find the fathers of illegitimate children. So the JPs started to name the culprits. A sordid company of local gentlefolk began to file through the courtroom. In the summer of 1607, just before the Pilgrims made their first attempt to leave the country, churchgoers at Blyth could enjoy the spectacle of a gentleman called Valentine Revell sitting in the stocks. The justices sentenced Revell to a stocking for fathering a bastard, and ordered him to pay the mother twenty pounds.[5]

When the pioneer Baptist John Smyth wrote about his reasons for becoming a Separatist, social evils such as this featured high among them. According to Smyth, the parishes along the valley of the Trent were filled with "infinite sorts of sinners . . . adulterers, Theeves, Murtherers, Witches, Conjurers, Usurers, Atheists, Swaggerers, Drunkards, Blasphemers."[6] He exaggerated a little (outright homicide seems to have been rare), but in a village such as Sturton he clearly had ample evidence of sin.

When John Smyth drew up his list of sinners of different kinds to support his condemnation of the Church of England, he did so as a way to support his argument that by permitting the wicked to worship alongside the godly, the Church betrayed the sanctity of the congregation. Actually, the authorities in the Quadrilateral tried hard to punish moral offenders, and with renewed vigor after the accession of King James. But the archives that they left behind serve only to show that Smyth was describing things he saw with his own eyes.

In the last three months of 1607, as the Separatists reached the peak of their activity in the area, the archdeacon's court at Retford prosecuted forty-one people. Among them more than half were charged with fornication. When the Retford JPs met for their quarterly session on October 9, with Sir John Thornhagh in the chair, they dealt with another twenty-three offenses, with drink-related matters to the fore. Included among the defendants were seven people accused of brewing without a license. Five were charged with assault or fighting. As for conjurers and witches, a laborer's wife came up before the justices, prosecuted for using charms.

Low-level sorcery often appears in the local records, with references to fortune-telling or the use of magic to cure sick cattle. Occasionally, women found themselves accused of malevolent witchcraft. Austerfield had a village witch, reported to the archdeacon in 1589 by William Bradford's uncle; she was a widow who tried to inflict dysentery on her victims by burning pieces of their excrement. But while this sort of case was very rare, harmless white magic was an everyday occurrence. John Smyth took special offense at people who tried to put a stop to rabies by writing the Lord's Prayer on a piece of cheese, and feeding it to mad dogs.[7]

So if old Brewster was a sinner, there were many like him, and Smyth drew his portrait from life. If immorality in Gainsborough helps explain why pious tradesmen turned to Smyth to lead them in worship and prayer, the same was doubtless true on the west bank of the Trent as well. However, many other people besides Puritans objected to sexual misconduct, drunkenness, and witchery without reaching his conclusions about the need for a new form of Christian community. Sin aroused just as much anger among the Anglican bishops. This was especially true of Browne's old enemy Richard Bancroft, who embarked on determined campaigns against malefactors in London. So there must have been more to the motivation of Separatists such as Brewster and Smyth than simple moral outrage at the sin they saw around them, essential though such outrage was.

If we turn old William Brewster's libel case on its side, so to speak, and think about what it meant to sue for defamation, then it will become easier to understand why Puritanism appealed to men and women in such places as the Quadrilateral. When Brewster the bailiff filed suit, he joined a long procession of people who used litigation as a way to defend their good names.

The Church courts dealt with cases of sexual defamation, and after 1560 the number of new lawsuits began to soar in the archdiocese of York. People called each other whoremongers or adulterers or accused each other of carrying venereal disease, and those whom they insulted fought back with a writ alleging slander. By the 1590s, plaintiffs in the region were filing at least two hundred lawsuits of this kind each year.[8]

Slandered men and women asked the court for help because they set enormous store by honor, status, and reputation. Families rose and fell, with their fortunes determined by access to land, by patronage, or by luck. They were exposed to random crises of a moral, an economic, or a pestilential kind. For this reason, it became all the more urgent to achieve rank, to cling to it, and to defeat those who tried to take it away.

Litigation became a way of defending status, but if that was too expensive, or the prospects were uncertain, ritualized violence offered another avenue of redress. Dueling was a craze as feverish as the resort to law, forcing James I to pass the first anti-dueling statute in 1609.[9] Perhaps we might view Puritanism in the same light, as a strategy for protecting reputation. If a family chose to be godly, they gave themselves a discipline that reinforced respectability. Piety and a moral code might keep a household untainted by sin and dishonor; and Christian evangelism created its own form of prestige, an alternative hierarchy of esteem.

Issues such as these possessed a special urgency for people like the Brewsters. They inhabited the grayest of gray areas within the social hierarchy, the foggy mezzanine between the lower reaches of the gentry and the upper ranks of the yeomanry. One form of status mattered more than any other, and that was the right to call oneself a gentleman.

Everybody wanted to be a gentleman, or a gentleman's wife or daughter. Local leadership belonged only to those who ranked among the gentry, or within the even more exclusive social tier made up of aristocrats: earls, marquesses, and dukes. In Elizabeth's reign, there were only about sixty peers of the realm. Aristocrats and the gentry combined amounted at the most to less than one in twenty of the population. While the tiny size of the elite made membership all the more intrinsic to self-worth, it also caused all the more argument about the eligibility of those who aspired to it.

Although the gentry remained a tiny minority, it was a minority in motion. Some families climbed the social staircase, while others slid backward into the unwashed multitude. In Yorkshire, during the reign of Elizabeth one hundred new families claimed to have entered the gentry, but many of those who called themselves gentlemen had doubtful grounds to do so. A case in point to the south at Sturton was Charles White, brother of the *Mayflower*'s Katherine Carver. In 1614, heralds from the College of Arms carried out one of their occasional investigations of the Nottinghamshire elite. In the marketplace at Retford, they publicly reprimanded Charles White for falsely claiming to be a gentleman.[10]

If everybody had agreed on an economic test, based on the number of acres owned, then White might have escaped humiliation, but such a test did not exist. People disagreed profoundly about the definition of gentility. Was it a matter of blood, of education, or of wealth? If it was the third, how much land *did* a gentleman need? Should entry to the elite be a reward for meritorious service of some kind? Once a man was a gentleman, was his status guaranteed forever? Or could he forfeit his rank, thanks to debt or disgrace? Was there such a thing as a Christian gentleman? If so, how did he behave, and what did he believe? Did a lady simply take on her father's or husband's rank, whatever it might be? Or could she aspire to gentility of her own, a composite of beauty, charm, accomplishments, and cash?

At Scrooby, these questions had no easy answer. In the eulogy that Bradford wrote for Brewster, we find a typically intriguing sentence describing the dead Pilgrim's life in the Quadrilateral. Brewster, he said, "lived in the Country in Good esteeme among his frinds and the Good Gentlmen of those parts especially the Godly and Religious." What exactly did Bradford have in mind, when he used this string of loaded words: "esteem," "good," "gentle," and "religious"? Who were the "good gentlemen" of whom he spoke, but whom he does not name? What did it mean to be a "gentleman" in a place where gentlemen went about fighting, whoring, smashing pews, stealing spaniels, and rustling cattle?

As for the Brewsters, people might very well question their right to be regarded as genteel at all. They never served as JPs. Their only real estate was apparently some property in Doncaster, belonging to the Pilgrim's mother, but they had to go to court to prove their title even to that. Fifteen miles from Scrooby lived a lawyer called Sir John Ferne, legal counsel for the borough of Doncaster, and in 1586 he published a book, *The Blazon of Gentrie,* which summed up the most snobbish of attitudes toward families such as the Brewsters. According to Ferne, the gentry consisted of no fewer than twenty-three grades, ranked according to their lineage, occupation, and record of military service. Highest among them were those of perfect blood ancestry, with five generations of forebears each entitled to bear a coat of arms. At the very bottom, Ferne placed a suspect order of gentry, "gentlemen of paper and wax," men who scarcely deserved the title at all. This was the place where we would find the Brewsters, clinging to the ladder's lowliest rung.[11]

By way of occupation, old William Brewster had two jobs. Neither automatically qualified him for the status of a gentleman, and his grip on at least one of them was frail. As bailiff of the archbishop's manor at Scrooby, he collected the rents and ran the manorial court, where his principal task would be to arbitrate in disputes between tenant farmers. This sort of thing carried little prestige, and William Brewster quarreled with his employer. In 1588, the archbishop of York died, his widow began to sort out his affairs, and she raised queries about Brewster's expenses. He reacted by filing suit against her, and she responded by accusing him of "evill words" and false accounting. If he lost his post as bailiff, he still had another position—before his son, he served as the Crown's postmaster—but this was not especially well paying. Nor did the post confer social rank on the man who held it. His daily stipend added up to little more than thirty pounds a year, about the same as a country vicar. If he supplemented his earnings by hiring out horses and guides, or by keeping an inn at the manor, then his genteel status would become even more questionable.*

For the young Brewster, the future Pilgrim, another set of opportunities existed, but they came by way of his mother's relatives, not those of his father. In about 1564, William Brewster the bailiff married a widow called Mary Simkinson. In about 1566 she gave birth to young William. Before her first marriage, Mary Simkinson was called Mary Smythe, and she belonged to a successful family in the port of Hull. Her brother John Smythe, the Pilgrim's uncle, was a merchant, trading wine and other cargoes between Poland, Norway, La Rochelle, and Spain, and he served three terms as mayor. Another of the boy's uncles was Francis Smythe, a clergyman, minister of a wide parish on an island in the marshes between Scrooby and the Humber. He was also a Cambridge University graduate, from the argumentative college of St. John's, and his sons studied there too.[12]

---

*Historians have often said that as well as becoming postmaster, William Brewster the Pilgrim succeeded his father as bailiff at Scrooby Manor. Actually, no documentary evidence for this has been found. In view of his father's quarrel with the archbishop's widow it seems unlikely.

Through his mother, therefore, Brewster came from a civic echelon of literate local ministers and businessmen. From them, and from his schooling, he might acquire a richer and more adequate idea of what it meant to be a gentleman. As we shall see, it was probably with their help that the young man obtained his place at court with William Davison. In the town of Hull, we find a trail that eventually led all the way to the coast of New England. The route went by way of education and politics.

For Goodness and Religion

We know nothing about William Brewster's childhood. The Pilgrim enters the archives for the first time on December 3, 1580. On that day, he became an undergraduate at Cambridge himself, at the college of Peterhouse. He did not take a degree, and he remained at the university for little more than a year. However, we know what ideas he encountered. At his death his library in America still contained books that were in vogue at Cambridge when he was a student.[13]

Among them were new books about courtesy, gentility, and civilized behavior, and especially a work written by an Italian humanist, Stefano Guazzo. Within its pages, Brewster would encounter an alternative definition of rank, depending on neither wealth nor heredity. First published in Italy in 1575, the book soon reached England, where it came out in translation in 1581 as *The Civile Conversation.* Its language and its message bear a striking similarity to the eulogy composed after Brewster's death by William Bradford.

Guazzo was a lawyer, working for the Dukes of Mantua. His book celebrates gentlemen who acquire gentility by way of diligent public service to their city or to their nation. Far from slotting individuals into fixed places in a hierarchy, Guazzo says that the best men are those "who from verie lowe place with the ladder of their owne vertue climbe to most respected highness. As manie Popes, Emperours and Kings have done being the sonnes of verie meane men." His ideal gentleman has the qualities that Bradford saw in Brewster—piety, learning, discretion, humility, and generosity—but also the specific kind of bravery that he displayed in New England.

Guazzo said that the finest gentlemen were those who shunned wealth and fame, and instead did battle with "povertie, ignominie, pain and death." In a passage echoed by Bradford, he taught a lesson that spoke directly to the plight of Separatists. "Those poore Gentlemen are to be pittied," says Guazzo, "who by some mischance & evill hap, not by their owne fault, are become poor and low." Relevant to the Pilgrims, exiles who left home to follow a life of hard labor in foreign lands, this sentiment appears in the Brewster eulogy as well. According to Bradford, his mentor was "tender-harted and Compassionate of such as were in Missery but especially of such as had bin of Good estate and Ranke and were fallen into wante and povertie either for Goodnes and Religions sake or by . . . Injury and oppression."[14]

These ideas could acquire an incisive edge if they were hammered together with evangelism, and with political philosophy, to form an ideology of valor and resistance, derived from ancient history. For any educated Elizabethan, the icons of courage were the Roman heroes whose stories they read in Latin at the grammar school. We find men of such a kind alluded to in William Bradford's history of the colony, where he cites the inspiring example of noble Romans like Cato and Seneca, who died in defense of the Roman republic or in defiance of a tyrant. And in Brewster's youth, there was another new book—again, he owned a copy of it in New England—that plainly advocated a more open society where rank and gentility were won by merit and hard work.

It was called *De Republica Anglorum* (Concerning the Republic of the English). A manual for politicians, it analyzed the workings of government in England from top to bottom. First published in 1583, it went through another eight editions in the next forty years. The book was written by Sir Thomas Smith, a lawyer and diplomat, and its most striking feature was its title, suggesting that England itself was a republic, albeit a republic presided over by a queen. Remarkably, too, Smith analyzed society in simple, economic terms. If England prospered, said Smith, it was because its social hierarchy was flexible and open. In England, men could climb up from one rank to another and alter their status, simply by making money.

Smith said bluntly that if somebody had an income of £1,000 a year, then he was a nobleman. To qualify as a knight, all he needed was £120. Gentlemen simply had to pass a very basic test. In order to live, did they have to do manual labor? If not, because they survived on the rental income from their land, or because they had a learned profession, or even a business in the City of London, then they ranked as members of the gentry. Gentlemen, said Smith, "be made good cheape in England."

He even found an honored place for yeoman farmers in the social order. In Smith's eyes, the yeomen had earned respect as the foot soldiers of medieval armies, and they continued to play a vital role in government, as jurors and constables and by choosing members of Parliament. For Smith, Parliament lay at the heart of the English republic, and among the yeomen he praises that stout class of patriots, the "forty-shilling freeholders," farmers with enough land to allow them to vote in a county election. The leading Separatists in the Trent valley came from exactly this social grade. The village of Sturton had eight forty-shilling men. Among them was John Robinson, father of the Pilgrim pastor.[15]

So, in the books he read, and in the ideas that circulated around him, the young William Brewster encountered competing visions of what it meant to be virtuous and to be genteel. And, in the conditions of the Scrooby region, the endless squabbles, and the shabby conduct of the local gentry, he could see how far reality fell short of any moral principles at all. We can understand why he might turn to the radical, evangelical solution offered by Puritans. He might come to see Puritanism as a means to shape an alternative, richer ideal of what it meant to be a Christian gentleman. It would be based on effort, enterprise, public service, or honest commercial success, a hybrid of the values of Sir Thomas Smith and Guazzo.

However noble a set of ideas may be, they will not survive without an environment in which they can take effect. The events in the real world that shaped the young man took place in the realm of war and sectarian conflict. Two rebellions occurred, with consequences that cut across the social landscape of his youth. Their effects must have reinforced the motives that made the young Brewster a Puritan.

The first was the Northern Rising, a futile attempt by Catholic noblemen to depose Elizabeth and place Mary, Queen of Scots upon her throne. It was a debacle, and it led to a Protestant backlash, a backlash that created a local Puritan movement. The second rebellion was the revolt against Spain by the Netherlands. Here the critical year was 1572, when the Calvinist privateers known as the Sea Beggars began a guerrilla war on Spanish shipping. Eager to help them, the Protestant seaport of Hull readily entered the fray. In the year in question, the town's mayor was John Smythe, the uncle of William Brewster.

Republics of the Godly

In December 1569, eight thousand troops approached Scrooby from the south and from the west. They came under the command of Edward Clinton, Earl of Lincoln. From each stop along the route, including Scrooby, Clinton sent dispatches back to Whitehall Palace, because he was advancing up-country against six thousand Catholic rebels.

In November, the rebels tore up the Protestant service books in the cathedral at Durham. They did the same in nearly eighty churches across the North Parts. They restored the Mass, and received the pope's forgiveness for their past obedience to the heretic Elizabeth. In the end, the Northern Rising failed chaotically, after the Privy Council moved the Queen of Scots out of reach. However, the episode left a deep mark, and not only on the families of seven hundred people hanged as traitors.

The rising had shown that the North Parts remained unconquered by Protestant reform. A new archbishop arrived at York, in the person of Edmund Grindal, a firm Calvinist who had taken refuge in Germany during the reign of Mary Tudor. Writing to Burghley, Grindal expressed his horror at the popery he found among the northerners, with their rosary beads and archaic funeral rites. They had three evil qualities: they were ignorant, they were stupid, and they were stubborn. They displayed, said Grindal, "great stiffness to retain their wonted errors."[16]

Grindal began a campaign to convert the north, with new clergy, new schools, and discipline imposed on the disobedient. To help him, from 1572, he had the new lord president of the Council of the North, which acted as the right arm of the Privy Council in the region. The new president was the so-called Puritan earl, otherwise known as Henry Hastings, third Earl of Huntingdon. Another keen Calvinist, he sheltered Puritan writers, and he encouraged prophesying, those sessions of Bible reading, dialogue, and prayer so dear to the evangelical Protestants of the age.

For more than twenty years, Huntingdon waged a relentless war against what remained of the Roman Catholic faith. By the time he died in 1595, as many as thirty priests and eight laypeople had been sentenced to death by hanging at York. No record remains of any Protestant nonconformists meeting the same fate, although technically the laws applied to them too, if they published open attacks on the Church of England or on the queen's supremacy.

For most of the reign of Elizabeth, therefore, men and women in this region could function as Puritans with little fear of interference. This was especially so around Scrooby, within the area policed by the archdeacon of Nottingham. It was very rare indeed for a Puritan to be prosecuted for the offenses of which they were usually accused. The archdeacon took little interest in rooting out nonconformity, unless Catholics were involved. In 1587, he carried out an inspection of the area, covering some fifty parishes. Nearly half replied with simply two words, "Omnia bene": "All is well." He probed no further, although some of these parishes had Puritan ministers known to have flouted the rules of worship.[17]

Things began to change a little in the 1590s, when rules against nonconformity became more strict. But even then, the penalties meted out were mild. In 1593, a new archbishop ordered an inquiry into the conduct of the parish clergy, and in the Quadrilateral his officials found three ministers with Puritan tendencies. Among them was William Bradford's friend Richard Clifton, rector at Babworth, seven miles from Scrooby. A decade later Clifton became one of the core group of Separatists, revered by Bradford. When he arrived in Holland, says Bradford, Clifton was "a grave and fatherly old man . . . haveing a Great white beard and pitty it was that such a reverend old man should be forced to leave his country."[18] In the 1590s, he escaped with nothing more than a mild rebuke.

Clifton failed to wear the surplice, and during baptism he left out the sign of the cross. He admitted both offenses, but the judge simply dismissed him with a warning. His case was trivial compared with the opposite threat of popery. Nor did the authorities make anything more than a token effort to coerce or to chastise laypeople. Between 1596 and 1603, the court prosecuted in only sixteen cases where men and women had gone missing from their parish church. The bulk of these cases had nothing to do with belief. They concerned men caught in the alehouse or playing cards during evening prayer, or opening a shop or working in the fields on the Sabbath. Even if a person was convicted, the penalty for nonattendance was small: a fine of one shilling, and this was often waived.

William Brewster the Pilgrim benefited from the same lenient policy. Early in 1598, after three years of failed harvests, the archdeacon relayed to the churchwardens a questionnaire, circulated to every parish in England. Far from being some tyrannical tool of oppression, it was chiefly intended to ensure that parishes were doing their best to help the poor. In April, the Scrooby churchwardens turned up among wardens from more than twenty villages, on the day when responses were due to be given. They reported Brewster and several others for the offense of "sermon gadding," the Puritan habit of forsaking the parish church to hear a better preacher elsewhere. They also accused Brewster of "publicly repeating" sermons, a practice frowned upon by conservative clergymen. The archdeacon's court summoned Brewster to explain, then sent him away with a verbal warning. No further action was taken.[19]

This was typical. By far the dominant theme in the region was the official campaign against the Catholic faith. The Brewsters and their kin the Smythes of Hull were immersed in this process too, as active participants in the same campaign against the old religion. Just before Grindal left York, he gave old William Brewster the post of bailiff at Scrooby; it is most unlikely that he would have done so unless Brewster was seen as a safe pair of hands, with sound opinions. And later, when Brewster became postmaster, he must have received the full endorsement of the Puritan earl, for reasons of national security.

Apart from the military importance of the Great North Road, and the need to safeguard the royal mail, Scrooby needed a reliable man for another reason. Long after the Northern Rising, the Privy Council continued to worry about Catholic dissidents, men and women perhaps merely biding their time before another insurgency. Bawtry, between Austerfield and Scrooby, was regarded as "a dandgerous place," so dangerous that in 1578 it became the subject of a special report to Burghley from an intelligence officer.

Bawtry contained, said the writer, two families of suspect Catholics, "a trybe of wicked people . . . Traitors, rebells, feugetyves, conspirators." They were the Mortons and the Thurlands, and the officer listed their names and misdeeds. Their young men made covert trips to Rome, and traveled back and forth across the north of England: alarming behavior, since the Queen of Scots was only twenty miles from Bawtry, in captivity at Sheffield. Both families were neighbors of the Brewsters and the Bradfords: William Bradford's uncle Robert rented land from the Mortons. In the local records, their names appear frequently as Catholic recusants, cited for failing to attend their parish church. Hence the need to have a trustworthy man to watch the mail at Scrooby.[20]

In such an atmosphere, the local Puritans could hope to do far more than simply live a quiet and pious life. In alliance with the authorities, they might even take the reins of power themselves. This was the case at Hull, where Brewster's kinfolk did exactly that. In the town, the Smythes and their neighbors built a marine republic of their own, with the approval of Grindal and the Earl of Huntingdon. Godly, disciplined, and patriotic, it became another forerunner of the Plymouth Colony.

Merchants ran the town. Of the twelve aldermen, more than half were overseas traders, dealing with Russia in the north, and the Canaries in the west, and they sent whaling voyages to the Arctic. As mayor of Hull, Brewster's uncle was a powerful figure, since Hull was the kingdom's fourth-busiest port. Events at Hull mirrored those occurring at Bury, and in other godly republics where magistrates strove to create what Smythe and his colleagues called a well-ordered commonwealth. Burghley used a less pompous phrase, calling places like Hull "good towns," but the message was identical. A good town punished drunkards, set the poor to work, and kept its streets clean. It employed a godly preacher who gave sermons three times a week, with the residents obliged to attend.

During Smythe's first term, he put in place regulations allowing him to punish the lazy, the tipsy, or the lecherous. Soon, like Bury, Hull had more than fifty rules designed to keep its people within the confines of the straight and narrow. To assist them, Hull appointed a red-blooded Puritan as parish minister. He refused to wear the surplice, and he tried to end the Catholic practice of bell ringing. When some of his flock rang the bells on All Saints' Night, the vicar and the mayor turned up to stop them. A scuffle followed, and the minister threw a punch at a passing sailor. If this was a little undignified, the jail provided another weapon against the enemy. In 1577 the prison at Hull held twenty-two Roman Catholics.[21]

If asked to justify their severity, Smythe and his colleagues would point across the sea to the Netherlands, where the revolt against Spain was at its height. During Smythe's second term, Hull welcomed two warships operated by the Sea Beggars, allowing them to resupply. Every night the townsmen slung a chain across its harbor mouth in case of a Spanish attack. They could not allow renegade Catholics to form a fifth column: or so they would argue.

For the career of William Brewster, the politics of Hull may have been decisive in a very direct and personal way. In 1584, during Smythe's last term as mayor, Hull chose as its high steward the most fiery Protestant member of the Privy Council. This was Walsingham, the queen's secretary of state, a man who eagerly supported English intervention to help the Netherlands. The post of high steward made him Hull's friend and patron at court. In return, Hull paid Walsingham a fee and accepted his influence over the town's affairs. Within less than a year, the young Brewster joined the staff of William Davison, who was Walsingham's closest subordinate. We can guess, though no documentary proof exists, that Walsingham did the mayor of Hull a favor, by finding a job for his nephew, in return for his appointment as high steward. The relationship between Davison and Brewster had profound consequences for the future.

Davison came from a modest background, and he owed his advancement to merit. He carried out difficult diplomatic missions, and he married well: his wife was a cousin of the Earl of Leicester, the queen's favorite, and Leicester in turn was close to Walsingham. Both men, and Davison, had Puritan leanings. A man in his fifties, Davison counted among his personal friends Sir Robert Jermyn, the Puritan squire, and also John Stubbs, the man who lost his hand for insulting the queen.

Brewster became very close to William Davison, and late in the summer of 1585 he traveled to the Dutch Republic in his retinue. Bradford's eulogy says that Davison treated the young man "rather as a son than a servant . . . and . . . Imployed him in matters of Greatest trust and Secrecye."

During the five months he spent with Davison in the Netherlands, the future *Mayflower* passenger encountered men and situations of a kind that could not have been more suitable for the training of a colonist. Among them he met not only the Earl of Leicester but also the gentleman whom many regarded as England's paragon of virtue, the poet and soldier Sir Philip Sidney. Sidney was Leicester's nephew, and he married Walsingham's daughter. Leicester, Walsingham, and Sidney formed a close network of kinship and political sympathy, with Davison affiliated too.

On the afternoon of September 3, 1585, William Davison disembarked at the port of Flushing, in the Dutch province of Zeeland. In the coming weeks, Brewster was at his side at every moment. Brewster took part in a Puritan crusade, a crusade that Davison did his best to advance, and a crusade that served as another forebear of the *Mayflower* project.[22]

Valiant in the Lord's Cause

Three times in the last five hundred years, British commanders have led their troops across the Dutch island of Walcheren. It has two sizable towns: Flushing, at its southwestern corner, and Middelburg, a little way inland. A glance at a map will soon tell you why this elongated patch of mud and sand has so often invited attack, and why the fighting has often been bloody. Extending for nearly forty miles, Walcheren and the smaller islands to its east form the northern bank of the estuary of the river Scheldt. They control the long approach to the port of Antwerp.

In the sixteenth century, Antwerp had the busiest docks in western Europe, forming an entrepôt between the Baltic and the Mediterranean. Thanks to its Calvinist zealots, Antwerp also served as the chief point of origin of the Dutch revolt. This made the Spanish all the more determined to recapture the city. After a long siege, the Spanish army under the Duke of Parma forced Antwerp to surrender in August 1585. The news reached London a few days before Davison left for his mission across the North Sea.

By the time he set foot in Flushing, elements of the Spanish army had advanced to within thirty-five miles of the town. Short of supplies, Parma was weaker than he appeared, but it was widely expected that he would soon press home his advantage. Either he would thrust north on land to isolate Walcheren, or he would make an amphibious assault across the Scheldt. In October, Davison sent home reports that Parma was assembling flat-bottomed boats to serve as landing craft, and bundles of timber to serve as bridges across canals.

Parma could count on the low morale of the people of Zeeland, exhausted by a long war, and on help from Catholics who remained behind the Dutch front line. The English sent over a military engineer to inspect the fortifications, and his dispatches were gloomy: he found "the common people without obedience, the soldier in miserie and disorder for want of pay, the Governors weary, & tired for lack of good assistance." He described flawed and feeble defenses, while the Dutch commanders were divided.[23]

All of this tested Davison's diplomatic skills to the utmost. The previous year, after long debate, the queen finally agreed that England must help the Dutch rebels, to prevent Spain from occupying the entire eastern side of the North Sea. She authorized an oceanic naval war, with Drake unleashed against the Spanish in the Caribbean. At the same time, an English expeditionary force of seven thousand men prepared to go to the relief of the Dutch Republic, with Leicester in command.

Grand strategy is one thing, and politics quite another. The Dutch did not trust the queen, suspecting that she was secretly making peace with Spain. Elizabeth did not trust the Dutch, believing that they intended to do the same. Wisely, too, the queen feared that the cost of war might bleed her dry, if the campaign descended into a quagmire of trench warfare. So Elizabeth agreed to help the Dutch only if they handed over two so-called cautionary towns, fortified places controlling the mouths of the nation's great rivers. One of these was Flushing, with nearby the artillery fort of Rammekens, guarding the Scheldt. The other was Brill, thirty miles to the north, with its cannon sweeping the mouth of the Lower Rhine. With Brewster in attendance, first Davison had to ensure that the Dutch ratified the treaty, signed in August, which contained these terms. Then he had to take possession of Brill and Flushing and garrison them with English troops.

On arriving at Flushing, Davison hurried north to The Hague. He obtained the necessary Dutch agreement, and then he made his way to Brill. It was desperately short of armaments, with only seven cannon and two barrels of gunpowder. The English soldiers who arrived to man the walls were raw and poorly trained. Worse still, as Davison received the keys of the town, he found himself squabbling with his own general in the field.

English troops had been coming ashore for more than a month. As they marched inland, they came under the command of the queen's finest soldier, Black Jack Norris, who bore that name because of his dark hair, his vicious temper, and his savagery in Ireland. Brave but arrogant, Norris wished to lead the army out against the Spanish, to secure the Rhine crossing at Arnhem. Davison disagreed: he preferred caution. He wished to concentrate the available soldiers at defensive strong points. He also wanted to displace Black Jack, in favor of his kinsmen Leicester and Sidney, when they arrived later that autumn.

Three private letters survive from Sidney to Davison, dated 1586. In Sidney's handwriting, and signed "your loving cosin," they were letters that the young Brewster must have seen. Between the lines lay a common ideology of militant Calvinism, in which both Davison and Sidney believed.[24]

A man quite as fiery as Black Jack, Sidney had two ambitions. Either he would sail with Drake against the Spanish, and plant his godly colony in America, or he would lead a Protestant alliance in Europe against the same papist enemy. The queen vetoed the first alternative, and he never sailed from Plymouth. Instead, with the avid support of Walsingham and Davison, he joined Leicester's expedition, as military governor of Flushing. In doing so, Sir Philip carried across the North Sea the hopes of English Puritans, eager to put into practice the doctrine of sacred resistance to a tyrant by aiding the Calvinist Dutch against Philip of Spain.

At least two hundred English gentlemen followed Leicester to the Netherlands, bringing with them county detachments of infantry and cavalry. Among them was Sir Robert Jermyn, keen to redeem himself from his disgrace at Bury. He saw the expedition as a religious duty. As he wrote in a letter to Davison in August, listing the troops who were on their way from Suffolk: "all which and the rest which shallbe employd in that service, I praye God to blesse with his reward that thei may be valiant in the Lords cause, & fight his battailes with corage." His Puritan friends, the preachers, had rallied to his side, preaching farewell sermons, in which they told the soldiers "how to use this calling & profession of a soldier in true Dutye to God & to their soveraigne."[25]

Davison and Sidney shared these sentiments entirely. Both men were friends of Mornay, the French ideologue of rebellion. A briefing paper survives, apparently from Davison's files, that uses Old Testament rhetoric like Mornay's to describe the coming campaign. Again they drew inspiration from a Hebrew king, but this time Hezekiah, who destroyed the altars of the pagans and renewed the covenant with God. So too the Earl of Leicester would root out from the Netherlands the last vestiges of popery. Once on Dutch soil, both Leicester and Sidney hastened to put in place Protestant reforms of a kind far more radical than those permitted at home. To serve the garrison at Flushing, Sidney opted for a church along Huguenot lines, governed jointly by ministers and by lay elders. For the

Dutch Republic as a whole, Leicester called a national synod, with the aim of making Calvinism compulsory and discipline rigid.[26]

As so often, circumstances hindered the work of godliness. Sidney did not reach Flushing until November 18, when bad weather blocked the harbor. He had to wade ashore at Rammekens and then walk three miles to the town. He found Davison at his wit's end with worry. After occupying Brill, Davison had entered Flushing in October, with the help of five ragged companies of infantry. Riddled with disease and short of food, the troops were forced to sleep in churches because, filled with refugees, the town had no billets. Departing Dutch soldiers had left their barracks in a filthy state. On Davison's first night in Flushing, when the gates were locked, the keys were given to William Brewster to keep beneath his pillow: a detail recalled by Bradford in America sixty years later. The people of Flushing were restive and possibly hostile, and the English garrison was three hundred men short of adequacy.

Davison had very little cash. So he ran up huge debts with local merchants, writing out IOUs that he hoped Burghley would honor. Meanwhile, the military engineer had sent back to England his pessimistic report: walls too long, ramparts easy to climb, cannon defective. That autumn, Black Jack captured by storm two Spanish forts near Arnhem, but at the cost of heavy losses. As winter approached, he withdrew toward Flushing to spend the winter seething with anger at his demotion. Another long delay followed, until Leicester finally arrived with the bulk of the expeditionary force, on December 11. By that time, Sidney had sunk into depression, demoralized by the lack of men, money, and supplies.

William Brewster was an eyewitness of all these events. He also saw at the closest of quarters the first of a sequence of disasters that led to the failure of the expedition, and left the Dutch even more dangerously exposed to a Spanish offensive. The catastrophe occurred when Leicester ignored the queen's instructions and agreed to become governor-general of the Netherlands. It led to furious arguments. First Leicester quarreled with Elizabeth, and then he fell out with the Dutch, because of the high-handed manner in which he behaved.

At Flushing, Leicester slept in Davison's house, where they began talks with the Dutch about the role that Leicester would play. Brewster was part of the English delegation as Leicester embarked on a triumphal procession across the Netherlands. Feted with banquets, pageants, and odes composed in his honor, Leicester arrived on January 3, 1586, at the city of Leiden.[27] Again Brewster stood at the center of things, lodging with Davison in the home of Paulus Buys, the leading government official in the province of Holland. An ardent supporter of the Anglo-Dutch alliance, Buys wanted Leicester to take on the leadership of the Dutch Republic, and Sidney agreed enthusiastically. Fascinated by ancient history, Sidney argued that his uncle should become a dictator, like the men who saved Rome from the likes of Hannibal.[28]

On January 15, with Davison standing by, Leicester accepted the Dutch offer of the governorship. When the outraged Elizabeth ordered Leicester to resign, the earl promptly placed the blame on Davison. Recalled by the queen, he left Flushing for England a few weeks later. He was a sick man and in temporary disgrace, but Sidney and his Dutch friends kept him abreast of events with a stream of correspondence. Davison took home a gold chain, a gift from the Dutch, and he entrusted it to William Brewster, who wore it as they rode to Whitehall. In the autumn, as the pendulum swung again, Davison returned to royal favor, and the queen promoted him to sit alongside Walsingham as her second secretary of state. Brewster remained in his service.

Meanwhile, Leicester had achieved very little in the Netherlands. An English officer betrayed the frontier fortress of Deventer to the Spanish, while Leicester angered the Dutch by banning their merchants from trading with the enemy. He also waged a futile campaign against Parma in the river country north of Arnhem, and during it he lost Sir Philip Sidney. One September morning, as a screen of English cavalry led by Black Jack and Sir Philip patrolled the country around the town of Zutphen, the mist parted. It lifted to reveal a much larger force of Spanish musketeers and pikemen. In the skirmish that followed, a musket ball smashed Sidney's left thigh, and twenty-five days later he died in agony from gangrene. The earliest report reached Davison in England in the first week of November 1586. It fell to him to console Sir Francis Walsingham.[29]

By this time, events were overtaking Davison himself. His tenure as secretary lasted only four months. It coincided with the trial and execution of Mary, Queen of Scots. For this Queen Elizabeth made him the scapegoat. The chain of events was complex, and Davison's role in the death of Mary remains open to varying interpretations. But we can be sure of one thing: Davison went on trial in March 1587, charged with issuing the death warrant without the authority of Elizabeth. Convicted, Davison spent eighteen months in the Tower of London, before the queen allowed him to retire to private life. Throughout this period, William Brewster stuck with him, "doeing him many offices of service in the time of his troubles," as

Bradford put it. In return, when old William Brewster died, Davison helped ensure that the younger William succeeded his father as postmaster at Scrooby. He took up the position in 1590.[30]

Debts, disease, and short rations, clashing egos, complicated politics, and impossible logistics: these were the realities of the Leicester expedition. As we shall see, they bore a close resemblance to the early history of New England. Even the science of military engineering had its relevance to the Plymouth Colony, with its fort and its artillery facing the forests of the interior. What better training could William Brewster have received for the challenges he would experience in America?

During his years with William Davison, Brewster also encountered the militant ideals of the international Calvinists of the 1580s in their most highly developed form. He entered the world of Mornay, Walsingham, and Jermyn, men for whom theology and patriotism were simply two sides of the same anti-Spanish coin. Far from being an abstraction, something purely theoretical, their ideology found its embodiment in the life and death of Sir Philip Sidney. On a Dutch battlefield, Sidney had displayed a belligerent kind of Christian fortitude: one that William Bradford would later celebrate in his account of Brewster's own adventures.

So what became of the young Puritan? In the 1580s, Brewster could expect an excellent career, as a trusted servant of a great official. Barely two decades later, the same man was a refugee, in exile in Leiden, the city where he had been a member of Leicester's entourage. Men such as Davison never had to be Separatists. Why did it become the fate of William Brewster? Why did he find Brownism unavoidable?

This question has an orthodox answer. After the death of Elizabeth, along came the coercive King James, the monarch who harried the Puritans out of the land. Or so the story goes. He certainly wanted them gone, and his arrival set in train the events that led to the settlement of New England. But this did not happen in some simple, mechanical way, and the explanation is far from straightforward. King James was a very complicated man. We begin at the end of his reign, when the corpse of the Anglo-Scottish king lay on an autopsy slab.

Part Three

Separation

Chapter Seven

The Entrails of the King

No kingdom lackes her owne diseases.

—James I, *Basilikon Doron* (1603)[1]

His skull was so hard and so strong that the surgeon had to struggle to break it open with a chisel and a saw. He found a swollen brain packed tightly inside the thin film of cells that enveloped its surface. The white matter filled the membrane, spilling out onto the table under the surgeon's hands. He prized out the dead man's heart, and the onlookers saw that it was unusually large. They found that his lungs and gallbladder were black. One kidney was sound, but the other had dwindled to such a tiny size that the surgeon had to rummage for it in the dead man's bowels. When at last he located it, he picked out two small kidney stones.

Although the departed had passed away three months short of his fifty-ninth birthday, he was already senile in body. Gravely weakened by arthritis, he suffered from kidney disease, and possibly he had endured a series of small strokes. It seems that a larger stroke killed him, after eight days of fever. Only his liver remained entirely normal. This the royal doctors expected, since the case notes record the feel of the organ—"naturally good, big, bloody and strong"—when tested by hand during the king's lifetime. Despite his many years of heavy drinking, the postmortem revealed no sign of fatty liver or cirrhosis. The tissue was as fresh and healthy as a young man's.

They removed his vital organs and his viscera, for separate burial in a casket. Then they embalmed the cadaver and placed it inside a sheath of lead. They encased the lead box in an oak coffin, filled with spices, its surface wrapped in purple velvet studded with gilded nails and hinges. On Monday, April 4, 1625, eight days after the death of the king at his country home in Hertfordshire, the cortege set off for Whitehall Palace. Drawn by six black horses, the hearse traveled through pouring rain some sixteen miles southward, past London to the river Thames. At last, that evening, the coffin arrived in the royal apartments, where the monarch would lie in state.[2]

The dead sovereign was the first King James. Whenever the *Mayflower* drama is replayed, he always appears somewhere on the stage, as the villain or sometimes the comic accessory, and rightly so. If James had never lived, men and women would still have migrated to America, but their precise motives and the pattern of events might have taken a very different shape. For that reason, we have to delve into the king's character, to find what lay behind his antipathies, including his hatred of the Puritans. In doing so, we reenact the intense curiosity felt by the people of his age.

Throughout his lifetime, since his mother, Mary, Queen of Scots, last saw him when he was ten months old, the body of the king was the object of the piercing gaze of strangers, for what it might reveal about the destiny of the state. Because monarchy obliged the king to display himself to his subjects, James always dined in semipublic, in front of those admitted to the royal apartments. His love of hunting on horseback meant that he was often seen in the open air too.

Privacy of a kind existed in the bedchamber, which James said should not "be throng & common," but instead a place where the king could meditate and speak discreetly. And yet even here he would not be alone. "Kings' actions (even in the secretest places) are as the actions of those that are set upon the stages, or on the tops of houses," James told Parliament in 1610, and this was literally true.[3] In the bedchamber, Stuart kings had about them a half-dozen gentlemen-in-waiting.

So, over the course of his reign, first as king of Scotland and then after 1603 as king of England too, many thousands of people saw James. Often they wrote down their observations. For this reason, and because so many portraits survive—at least fifteen oil paintings, besides medals, busts, and the like—we can re-create a remarkably reliable picture of his appearance and his mannerisms. He also bequeathed to posterity an archive of evidence about his long feud with Puritans and Brownists. Because King James wrote copiously in four languages, much of it comes from his own pen.

James published two books containing attacks on the likes of Robert Browne. In the second, titled *A Meditation upon the Lord's Prayer,* and dated

1619, James gave a pithy account of their origins. He wrote with a lucidity that modern historians would do well to emulate. "Our Puritans are the founders and fathers of the Brownists: the latter onely boldly putting into practise what the former doe teach," he pretty accurately said, and he threw in for good measure an insult or two aimed at what he called "these innumerable sects of new Heresies, that now swarme in Amsterdam."

Much earlier, in his manual of kingship called the *Basilikon Doron,* James piled up an even larger heap of abuse of Brownists and Puritans alike. Rash, brainsick, and heady, vain, proud, and pharisaical, ungrateful, fanatical, seditious, and conceited, they were "very pestes in the Churche & common-weale," said the king. And, in case readers failed to take the point, his editor inserted an extra little caption, calling Puritans "an evill sorte."[4]

Why did James hate nonconformity so much, and why did he feel compelled to venture into print? Queen Elizabeth, that mistress of delegation, never stooped to verbal combat with Separatists: for her, a couple of public hangings every ten years did the trick quite well enough. What made James behave so differently, with less physical violence, but with so much more emotion?

He acted as he did because he wished to defend the hygiene of the realm. Aptly enough for a king who spent his later years in almost constant physical pain, James tended to speak about his kingdoms in the language of the body and medicine, in terms of anatomy, well-being, and morbidity. In doing so, he did more than merely repeat medieval clichés that compared the realm and its people, the body politic, to a frame of human flesh and blood.

Men and women at the time used figurative language so freely and with such verve that it was impossible to say where metaphors finished and reality began. They did not think in terms of rigid lines of demarcation between soul, mind, and body, or between matters that were personal and those that were political. Nor did they slice up their experience into segregated zones, as we do. They did not insist on sharp boundaries between fields of knowledge, each one with its academic police ready to handcuff those who dare to cross their borders. In the eyes of Jacobeans, God had created everything, and so everything was connected to everything else. For them, an educated man or woman was a person who tried to see things as a whole.

So it was with King James. He never used one metaphor where five would do. "What God hath conjoined, let no Man separate," he said in 1604, as he urged his first Parliament to unify England and Scotland by force of law. "I am the Husband, and all the whole Isle is my lawful wife: I am the head, and it is my body: I am the shepherd, and it is my flock, I hope therefore, no man will be so unreasonable, as to think . . . that I, being the Head, should have a divided and monstrous body." In the eyes of King James, a Christian king performed the role of a bridegroom, a father, and a pastor; he was God's lieutenant on earth, he was the origin of justice, and he was the source of wealth and well-being..

From the heart of the kingdom, the sovereign pumped the blood of mercy through the arteries of the state. That being so, he also served as the doctor of the nation. James called the monarch "the proper Phisician" of his kingdom, with a duty to cure it from sickness, and this he meant entirely literally. He used the phrase not in some work of learned theory but in his most famous and practical text, *A Counter-blaste to Tobacco* of 1604, his fierce attack on the practice of smoking.

A king and a philosopher, a monarch but also a human being, James experienced dominion as an alternating condition of power and fragility. "I am a Man of Flesh and Blood, and have my Passions and Affections as other men," he said in 1607, and this was an understatement.[5] Often succumbing like a Shakespearean hero to waves of emotion emitted from an obscure source, James felt the troubles of his realm in his skeleton, his nerves, and his intestines. His views about health and medicine formed a seamless whole with his wider doctrine of government, and with the ideas that caused him to loathe religious nonconformists.

King James thought of Puritans as a disease, which at its worst took the form of the Brownists. But before we venture into the depths of his mind, there is a story of surfaces to be told swiftly. It concerns events that took place between the Puritan crusade to the Netherlands, and the execution of Henry Barrow in 1593, and then, a decade later, the purge of nonconformists overseen by King James.

THE ROAD TO HAMPTON COURT

Barrow the Separatist went to his death in a season of defeat for the Puritan cause. Another change in political fortunes had occurred, with the decline of the party at court who sympathized with Puritanism. Leicester and Walsingham died, in 1588 and in 1590; Davison languished in disgrace. The Puritan clergy lost their most powerful defenders. They also faced a determined foe in the form of John Whitgift, archbishop of Canterbury, with at his side the implacable Richard Bancroft.

Soon after the defeat of the Armada in 1588, an underground Puritan printing press began running off anonymous pamphlets. They were filled with abuse against the bishops of the Church of England, penned by someone who called himself Martin Marprelate. Amusing for the first few pages, until the polemic begins to pall, *The Marprelate Tracts* denounced the bishops as swinish rabble, sauceboxes, petty popes, and lying dogs, men guilty of corruption and embezzlement. The author called for a much deeper reformation, of the kind that Puritans in Parliament had long been looking for. He also gave Whitgift and Bancroft the opportunity they needed to embark on an all-out attack on Puritans within the Church.

Neither man was a bloodless bureaucrat. Both were evangelical Christians. A man renowned for his charity, Whitgift had been a defiant Protestant during the reign of Mary Tudor. He became a convinced Calvinist, making his name with lectures intended to prove that the pope was the Antichrist. And far from being a careerist, Bancroft had a reputation for being blunt and combative. Often passed over for promotion, he did not become a bishop until the late age of fifty-three. However, both men had come to believe that Christianity depended on an efficient, disciplined, well-financed hierarchy, with the bishops as commanding officers. Their attitudes hardened and became authoritarian. The Marprelate affair made them all the more convinced that they were right.

As the leading mainstream Puritan, Thomas Cartwright tried to distance himself from Marprelate, but to no avail. Bancroft's hunt for the author soon turned up embarrassing evidence against Cartwright and his friends, men known as "forward preachers." Bancroft was able to show that they were building in secret a parallel church of their own, a presbyterian club of clergymen and supporters among the landed gentry. When the time was right, they would step out of the shadows and remake the Church of England as a presbyterian assembly. It would be run by preachers and lay elders, with not a trace of old Catholic ritual, not a bishop in sight, and very little role for the queen. This, said Bancroft, was sedition of a revolutionary kind.[6]

In 1590, the Church authorities jailed Cartwright and eight other forward preachers and stripped them of their posts as parish clergy. Their lawyers mounted an excellent defense, tying the prosecution in legal knots, and in due course they were released, after three unpleasant years in prison but without the trials reaching a conclusion.

Even so, the affair dealt a body blow to the Puritan movement. And when Parliament met in 1593, Archbishop Whitgift got what he wanted, a new statute aimed directly at the most radical Puritans and Brownists. For the first time, the law entirely banned private religious gatherings—

"unlawful assemblies, conventicles or meetings under pretence of any exercise of religion"—and imposed penalties of banishment or prison.

Despite this, the forward preachers left trailing behind them a mass of loose ends. Many years later, they resurfaced and made fresh connections. Puritan books were still read, and Puritans survived in the universities and elsewhere, despite a hostile climate. They often met bafflement, irritation, or anger among their neighbors, people who liked a little Catholic ritual and preferred a lenient religion that did not demand endless devotion. The strongholds of the Puritans were quite few and far between. But although they had a narrow base, they put down deep roots. In places, we find a critical mass of Puritan ministers and supportive local gentlemen, yeoman farmers, and town tradesmen. They were the kinds of people who later supported the New England project, or even made the trip themselves.[7]

Elizabeth died, and King James came south in 1603 to claim the throne. That summer, the survivors among the forward preachers began a campaign to persuade the king to take the Church down a Puritan path. Their manifesto was called "the Millenary Petition." It listed more than thirty changes that they wished to see. Some came from the old Puritan agenda, such as calls for an end to the sign of the cross in baptism or to bowing at the name of Jesus. Others were economic, intended to increase the incomes of the parish clergy by ending practices such as the leasing out of tithes, the kind of thing that had caused so much trouble at Sturton. The petition also contained one particular demand that neither James I nor the archbishop could possibly accept.

The petitioners wanted to ease the burden of "subscription," the rules which required that clergymen swore that the Book of Common Prayer was entirely the Word of God. If this change were made, it would remove the most powerful weapon in the armory of discipline. Bancroft had become the bishop of London, he was Whitgift's most likely successor, and he had his own project of an entirely contrary kind. He wanted a much tougher set of rules to impose moral and religious discipline, and he intended to enforce it with subscription.

However, the king did not simply reject the petition out of hand. A man who usually relished the exchange of ideas, he convened a debate, which took place at Hampton Court Palace in January 1604. At this event, James exploded with the infamous outburst in which he issued threats against the Puritans who attended, pledging that he would "harry them out of the land." This was an incident so notorious in Pilgrim history that in 1921, during American celebrations of the *Mayflower*'s tercentenary, an actor dressed up as King James repeated the same words, accompanied by bagpipes, to an audience including President Harding. Time and again, writers about the Pilgrims have quoted or misquoted James, uncritically and without asking what he meant, and without examining the quality of the source.[8]

The sentence appears in a semiofficial account of the event, approved by Bancroft, and written by a clergyman called William Barlow. He and Bancroft intended to mock and belittle the Puritans, making them out to be pedants, with the conference portrayed as a total defeat for the Puritan cause. Barlow reports James's exact words as follows: "If this bee all, quoth he, that they have to say, I shall make them conforme themselves, or I will harrie them out of the land, or else do worse."[9] The most revealing clause is the first—"if this bee all"—because Barlow wished to suggest that the Puritans were trivial, and their complaints petty.

Barlow says that James became exasperated by the leading Puritan spokesman, a wordy academic who wished to make minor amendments to the Thirty-nine Articles of Religion. This, says Barlow, seemed "very idle and frivolous" to the king and his bored privy councillors. They relieved the tedium by laughing over an old joke to the effect that "a Puritane is a Protestant frayed out of his wits." The king's threat to harry them out of the land was apparently something similar. It seems to have been a heavy-handed effort in sarcasm from an irritated monarch who had endured two full days of circuitous pomposity. If so, it was entirely in character for James.

As it happens, the conference was not an annihilating defeat for Puritanism. Most famously, it led to James's authorized translation of the Bible. It also gave rise to a list of small reforms, such as a pledge to make the ecclesiastical courts fairer and not to excommunicate people for trivial offenses. Measures like these helped to cool the heat of controversy, and so, after the purge of Puritans ended, in about 1608, England enjoyed a decade of relative calm in matters of religion.

However, in the immediate aftermath of Hampton Court, these elements of compromise paled by comparison with Bancroft's energetic attack on dissenters. Whitgift died soon after the conference, leaving Bancroft to carry on the campaign against all those who disturbed peace and good order. First, he pressed ahead with inspections of every aspect of cathedral and parish life, covering drunkenness and fornication, as well as signs of religious laxity. At the same time, in 1604, the king issued two proclamations against nonconformity. He insisted that everybody follow the Book of Common Prayer to the letter.

This allowed Bancroft to use the tool of subscription. He gave clergymen a deadline of November 30 to sign up to full acceptance of the prayer book, or face dismissal. Meanwhile, Bancroft had prepared another weapon: a new, steel-plated set of canons, laws, and regulations for the Church, intended to seal off every loophole through which a Puritan might creep. For example, they imposed new duties on parish churchwardens to report offenses such as private conventicles or unlicensed preachers. This made it far harder for villagers to turn a blind eye to each other's nonconformity.

These new rules were not simply a matter of sterile coercion. Since Bancroft was an evangelical himself, he wished to repair the shaky morals of the parish clergy and to see sermons preached every Sunday and in every parish. If he could carry out these reforms, he would make pious men and women far less likely to look for Puritan alternatives. So, for example, his canons included strict rules barring clergymen from taverns and from gambling, together with a requirement for every church to have a pulpit. And splendid new pulpits did indeed appear. Within a few miles of Scrooby, for example, churches in the villages of Tickhill and North Wheatley possess sturdy Jacobean examples. Erected in 1608, they remain in excellent condition today.

However, Bancroft's canons contained a flaw. Because Puritan sympathizers might oppose them, the king never submitted the canons to Parliament for approval. They became law only by way of his personal decree. For this reason, uncertainties lingered about their legality, and opened the way for protests by the same lawyers who defended Cartwright. Even within the Church, men had their reservations.

In the north, in the archdiocese of York, doubts expressed by high-ranking opponents meant that not until March 1606 did the canons come into force. This delay allowed Brewster and his allies to carry on their activities far longer than they could have done in the south. They were able to build a far wider movement than would otherwise have been possible.[10]

By the time Bancroft became archbishop of Canterbury, in December 1604, the deadline had passed for clergymen to subscribe. Within the next five years, mostly during the first twelve months, he achieved the dismissal from their parishes of about eighty ministers who resolutely refused. In a sense, this was a trivial number, less than 1 percent of the parish clergy at the time; but, again, the numbers matter less than the commitment of the small minority involved. The victims of the purge included four Puritans living near Scrooby, associates of William Brewster. Among them was the white-bearded Richard Clifton. What's more, Bancroft swept up within his net the universities of Oxford and Cambridge, seeking to rid them of nonconformity as well. In due course, two Cambridge men, John Robinson and John Smyth, led the Separatists of the Quadrilateral out of the Church of England.

Before that, we have to return to King James, and look more deeply for the secret of his animosity toward the Puritans. His beliefs about religion and the Church carried an intense emotional charge. To appreciate why this was so, we begin with the suffering man, and not with his disemboweled carcass under a surgeon's knife.

Our Master Lear

Ill health obsessed the king and his leading subjects. In the opening months of 1605, at the height of the great purge of Puritans, and as Shakespeare began to plan the writing of *King Lear,* we find one eminent man after another beset by bodily afflictions. In January, the bishop of Winchester complained about his sciatica and his flatulence, while Lord Cobham had the gout. The insomniac Lord Zouche tossed and turned with measles and a heavy cold, while Sir Bevis Bulmer caught a burning fever. William Brewster's boss was Sir John Stanhope, head of the Royal Mail, and in March he suffered from colic and cramps. The Earl of Dorset consulted his doctors about some unspecified illness. They gave him "physic and fomentations" intended to open his pores and make him sweat.[11]

During these months disease was rife, though as so often its exact type cannot be established. Although London was free from plague, an epidemic struck the western port of Bristol, and in the Pilgrim country the town of Worksop suffered ten months of contagion. Only six miles from Scrooby, in Worksop that year fifty-three people died, forty-nine from something tersely called "infec" in the parish register, compared with sixteen deaths in a normal year. As was the custom, the JPs placed a levy on the other parishes nearby to raise money for the town. We can be sure that the Pilgrims were well aware of the calamity.[12]

Men and women lived with death leaning over their shoulders, but the king's health always gave most cause for alarm: very much so, in 1605. Of course, he had two sons, Prince Henry and Prince Charles. But they were only eleven and four years old, while his daughter Elizabeth was not yet nine. If a minor succeeded to the throne, the king's death would plunge the realm back into the uncertainties that dogged the closing years of the old queen's reign. Later that same year, the Gunpowder Plot came close to ending his life, by blowing him up as he opened a new session of Parliament. But even without that notorious conspiracy by Roman Catholics his survival was never certain. With his passion for the chase, James always ran the risk of a fatal accident—while on his way south, two years before, he broke his leg in a fall—and in 1605 he suffered from a series of heavy colds. His courtiers nervously watched his habit of heavy drinking in the open, while he was perspiring after many hours in the saddle.

At this point King James was only thirty-nine. As the years went by, allusions to his worsening health came to feature ever more often in the eyewitness accounts that survive. If we exclude mocking comments made by opponents, we come up with a comprehensive portrait of James in middle age. He was a man of medium height, broad shouldered, but with a slender body and spindly legs. He had a sparse light brown beard the same color as his hair. He was apt to walk about in circles, something first noticed when he was in his teens. Later in life he did so while leaning for support on a good-looking young man. James was inclined to cough and splutter because of mucus and catarrh, and to gobble his food because he lacked teeth. Prone to stomach upsets, he broke wind frequently, from both orifices. He also suffered woefully from diarrhea, blamed by his doctor on excessive drinking.

Like the king's physical health, his turbulent feelings were also on display. They were documented in 1623 in notes made by his principal physician, the French doctor Theodore Turquet de Mayerne. He recorded the king's chronic stomach upsets and the pain he suffered when he threw up his food, pain so severe that apparently it covered his face with red spots. Mayerne also commented on his attacks of anxiety and depression, after a death in the family or a political setback.

In 1610, the king endured a disappointing session of Parliament, when the Commons blocked plans for reform of the royal finances. After dissolving the assembly, James collapsed in early 1611, vomiting twice a day and suffering more than a week of diarrhea, with unusually watery, bilious feces. Most alarming of all were symptoms of mental distress: chest pains, palpitations, and "moestitia," meaning "grief" or "sadness." He suffered even worse agonies after the death of the queen in 1619. A multitude of ailments struck him simultaneously. As always, he suffered from runny bowels, and severe melancholy, but also from inflamed kidneys, an acute bout of arthritis, a rash of small white ulcers on the back of his throat, and, ominously, an intermittent pulse.

After editing James's letters, a modern scholar described him as "one of the most complicated neurotics ever to sit on either the English or the Scottish throne."[13] By middle age he would have presented an insoluble riddle for a psychoanalyst. By then, James had endured painful illness in his childhood—he could not walk until he was six—and a host of attempted coups, bereavements, and conspiracies. His mother Mary was beheaded. His father was murdered, strangled while his house was destroyed by an explosion, and of course James I came close to dying in a similar way in 1605. His opposite numbers in France, Henry III and Henry IV, both fell to the assassin's dagger. And as it happens, the second of these murders occurred in 1610, not long before James's collapse the following year.

Was he a coward? That was his reputation. Referring to the autopsy, a diarist mentioned the inflated size of James's heart to explain why the king was "soe extraordinarie fearefull." Famously, James wore a quilted doublet to hinder an attacker's knife. People took these traits as signs of a yellow streak, but that was unfair. Hunting on horseback is not a pastime for the timid. Few men had better reasons than James I for succumbing to occasional attacks of panic. But who could say precisely which of his fears were neurotic phobias and which had some objective basis? Nobody could define the boundary where rationality ended and chronic anxiety or depression began.

Almost inevitably, a man so insecure might waste his energy in a futile quest for emotional support—and this James did, time and again. He might turn to alcohol or ceaseless physical activity, such as hunting. This was habitual for James. He might look for comfort from younger men, as favorites or lovers: he leaned on them in more ways than one. Or perhaps he might take refuge in fantasy and cast himself in the role of a philosopher king, dreaming of an imaginary empire of perfection where everyone obeyed his wise instructions. This James did too, as we shall see.

For James I, Separatists and people like them came to symbolize the poison of disorder and discontent that threatened to contaminate his ideal monarchy. In this there lay an element of paranoia, and if we reach that conclusion, we have the authority of Shakespeare. From *Lear* and *Othello* to *The Winter's Tale,* he provided a commentary on the character of powerful but frightened men, and the devastating effect of their anxieties. His audience cannot have failed to see that Shakespeare was exploring in heightened form the daily plight of their sovereign.

In an age when monarchy was personal, the inner life of the king had implications of the most far-reaching kind. And when King James wrote about Puritans and Brownists, we find him using language that mingles theology, political calculation, and obsessional neurosis. We see it most clearly when he uses the terminology of medicine.

PATHOLOGY AND THE PILGRIMS

In his case notes, Mayerne said that King James laughed at doctors. Even so, this unhealthy man took care to choose as his physicians the medical luminaries of the era. King James favored not only Mayerne himself, a star who treated Cardinal Richelieu for gonorrhea, but also William Harvey, the man who first described the circulation of the blood. Most frequently of all, James selected men who had new things to say about the nature of disease, linking it to poor hygiene, to contamination, or to defective chemistry inside the body.

The king's interest in public health was entirely genuine. When the City of London chose a lord mayor, the new incumbent came before the king to be praised or chastised; and in the early 1620s, the mayors found themselves being berated by His Majesty for the City's failure to clean up the open sewer known as the Thames. As king of Scotland, the young James employed as his court physician a man who blamed the plague on polluted drinking water. And in 1618, James sponsored Britain's first official compendium of drugs and elixirs, a project that embodied his concern for the well-being of his subjects. Like Bancroft's canons, it was intended to promote uniformity and to serve as the guarantor of health and good order.

Mayerne, Harvey, and the London College of Physicians prepared the book, which came to be known as the *London Pharmacopoeia.* Appropriately, it included a formula for distilling Scotch whiskey, but it was a serious work that went through many editions, often revised and updated. "Desirous in all things, to provide for the common good of our subjects," the king decreed that he would do away with "all falshood, differences, varieties and incertainties in the making or composing of Medicines." For that reason, he gave the book the force of law, with a proclamation that made it a crime to concoct potions that deviated from a list of standard recipes.[14]

When he spoke in this way about the common good, King James drew on new theories, ideas that were absurd and even bizarre, but capable of developing along a scientific path. Chemical medicine, as they were known, originated with the Swiss metallurgist known as Paracelsus. He died in 1541, but by the end of the century his system of thought had deeply influenced the medical establishment in England. During the reign of James I, it came close to being accepted as official orthodoxy. Most of the king's favored doctors were Paracelsians. Among them was Mayerne, trained in Paris by a French Paracelsian by the name of Joseph Du Chesne. In 1605, Du Chesne's principal book appeared in London in translation.

Of course it was nonsense, an esoteric farrago of garbled theology, alchemy, and magic, but it contained the seeds of progress. It also had affinities with the king's own attitudes and emotional commitments.

Du Chesne said that sickness arose from chemical dysfunction, a toxic chain of cause and effect open to investigation in the laboratory. Following Paracelsus, he believed that the material world arose as the product of three essences—salt, sulfur, and mercury—mixed and compounded by heat and by alchemy. Du Chesne explained that salt was dry and solid, mercury was moist and fluid, and between the two was sulfur, sweet and clammy. Combined together, in food, wine, and sperm, they created a human being.

The liver absorbed food and drink, and from the salt within them it synthesized a hot white juice. This became blood and flowed up through the veins to the heart, as if the body were a system of tubes, glass vessels, and retorts, heated by a flame. The heart cooled and purified the blood, added sulfur, and then transmitted it to the brain. Like a distiller making cognac, the brain slowly heated and refined the blood and added mercury. With the process complete, the liquid became rich arterial blood, ready to flow outward to refresh each limb.

Odd though they were, Du Chesne's theories possessed a degree of logic. Since the body was a chemical machine, of course it gave rise to waste products, just as men found ashes or sediment when they smelted copper or brewed beer. Among the dregs of human biology, said Du Chesne, were saliva, urine, and sweat. Left within the system to decay, these congealed to form what Du Chesne called "superfluous humours," noxious excrements liable to violate the balance of body and mind: in the kidney, they produced the stones that inflicted so much pain on King James. Trapped in the liver, the humors would accumulate and rise up to infect the brain, causing "long madness, burning frenzies, setled melanchollies . . . and many such like." As for the second cause of disease, that was obvious: poison, or lethal waste matter implanted from outside.[15]

What did all this have to do with politics? Not much, we might think, but Du Chesne and Mayerne would have disagreed. So would King James. Both Mayerne and Du Chesne were intensely political, and served as physicians to Henry of Navarre, the Huguenot leader and later the king of France. French royal doctors saw commentary on public affairs as part of their profession, and they applied the doctrines of medicine to the exercise of power. Observation first, to identify the symptoms; next, the application of theory to decide the cause; and then the choice of therapy: that was how a doctor went about his job. The king should follow the same procedure to eradicate the maladies that afflicted his people.[16]

For Du Chesne, the body functioned best when its internal functions bubbled freely away, without interference, following their natural course. So too in the language of King James the realm prospered when the balm of his wisdom flowed outward like pure spring water, circulating from one end of his kingdom to the other, without interruption by the disobedient. When James condemned tobacco smoking, he did so using ideas of the same kind. Tobacco, said the king, contaminated the natural fluids of the human body, and smokers harmed not only themselves but the nation. "Sucked up by the nose, and imprisoned in . . . braines," smoke left an oily deposit in the lungs, which poisoned the mind and made men lethargic. By purchasing the weed from foreigners, they undermined the economy of the realm. By inflicting a smelly torment upon their wives, they endangered the holy institution of the family.

For King James, Puritanism resembled the addiction to nicotine. Like the superfluous humors described by Joseph Du Chesne, the Puritans were sediments, dregs, or dross, by-products of an alembic malfunction in the organs of the body politic. Willful Puritans upset the king because they followed their private, individual inclination, rather than accepting the established wisdom of the community, sanctioned by statesmen and embodied in the Church. Puritans behaved, in other words, like tobacco smokers, devoted to their own obsession regardless of the cost that fell upon themselves and others.

This idea, that Puritans were diseased, came to have wide currency. It was expressed in pungent form in one of the most popular books of the period. *The Anatomy of Melancholy* appeared in 1621, and its author, Robert Burton, devoted a chapter to the victims of spiritual malaise. According to Burton, the Brownists were "a company of blockheads," men and women who "will take upon themselves to define how many shall be saved, and who damned in a parish." Incited by the devil, their outlandish ideas were symptoms of mental illness, the fever of religious melancholy. To bring it about, Satan used the infirmities of the body: Burton claimed that brain sickness arose from a distempered liver.[17]

Sick and deluded, a Puritan became an agent of infection, giving rise to quarrels and division: or so it seemed to King James as well. Left free to do their worst, they would deface the body politic and shatter the hard-won unity of the realm. Although Tudor kings and queens had valued peace and uniformity, for James they became an obsession that he experienced with an almost physical intensity. Here was a monarch who had come to understand the perils of discord during his period north of the border, when Scotland stumbled from one plot and one civil war to another until the young James engineered a degree of stability.

In the opening years of his reign in England, James tried to complete a great scheme of unification to make his authority seamless in every corner of the British Isles. Because Puritans endangered the fulfillment of such a project, he wanted them gone, and they were not the only ones. As Jacobean exiles, the Pilgrims had many equivalents: as we shall see, refugees took their leave of Donegal and Edinburgh as well as Scrooby.

A Perfect Union of Persons

When King James crossed over the frontier on his way south after the death of Elizabeth, he entered political territory of a kind that was almost entirely new. Three hundred years before, Edward I had briefly created an English empire by conquering Wales and Scotland, but it failed to survive for more than a decade. In 1603, James believed that God had given him a duty to re-create a unified Britain, beneath one monarch, and not merely in name alone. Unification had to be thorough, and deep, so that the king could promote common standards of civility, sobriety, and God-fearing obedience, rolled out into each enclave of his domain. This was what James had in mind when he told Parliament that he wished to see England and Scotland become "a perfect Union of Lawes and persons."[18]

Unification seemed to be a practical necessity. Border thieves and raiders passed back and forth between England and Scotland, evading extradition. Until the two countries were united, it would be impossible to put a stop to their activities. In Ireland, meanwhile, 1603 marked the end of the Nine Years' War between the English and the Earl of Tyrone, the leader of Catholic resistance, but in English eyes the country remained unpacified and alien. It seemed likely to rebel again as soon as the moment presented itself. At home on the mainland, the king's peace varied in quality from one place to another, depending on the energy and talent of the JPs in each county.

James acted with vigor to put a stop to social evils and to make the rule of law uniform across his kingdoms. In the north, he convened a new border commission, and it began to track down and string up the outlaws of the region. In England the king issued a host of proclamations, thirty-two in the first nine months of his reign, and more than eighty in the first five years. Among them were measures for dealing firmly with such enemies to good order as highwaymen, pirates, drunkards, unlicensed alehouse keepers, and speculators who endangered London by building ramshackle, fire-prone dwellings. As Bancroft pursued the Puritans, the king ordered the JPs to redouble their efforts against all forms of offenders, and often they did so with alacrity. In the Quadrilateral, in April 1604, the JPs at Retford prosecuted thirty individuals for brewing without a license, including five from Scrooby.

Of course the Gunpowder Plot against King James made the process of coercion more urgent. On both sides of the Irish Sea, dissident Catholics seemed to pose the greatest danger to the Crown. And so the king's lord deputy in Dublin began a policy of intense persecution of the old religion. Legalized theft of territory, executions of priests, the beating to death of Roman Catholics on the doorsteps of their churches: all of these took place. And in Ireland, the quest for uniformity led to a famous incident in Donegal that oddly resembled the case of the fleeing Pilgrims.

Forgotten by everyone else, but never by the Irish, it came to be known as the Flight of the Earls. It involved the two great Gaelic magnates of the north: the old rebel Hugh O'Neill, the Earl of Tyrone; and Rory O'Donnell, the Earl of Tyrconnell. Goaded by the authorities, and possibly hoping to find military support from Spain, in 1607 the earls boarded a ship at Lough Swilly and set off for exile in Rome. They left Ulster to the mercy of English colonists. This was only one of many episodes of exodus, enforced or voluntary, or somewhere in between.

In Scotland, James had already used the tactic of ejection many times against rebellious nobles or Calvinist troublemakers in the Church. The years after 1603 witnessed a new array of banishments or occasions when people fled because the Crown left them no alternative. In 1609, for example, the king and the Scottish parliament banned lawless "Egyptians" and ordered the Gypsies to quit the kingdom or be hanged. They dealt in much the same way with the Graemes, an extended Anglo-Scottish clan of border raiders. More than seventy Graemes suffered deportation to the Netherlands, where they were supposed to serve with English regiments. They deserted and came home, and so the Crown arrested fifty families of Graemes: men, pregnant women, and children. They marched them to a distant harbor and shipped them out to Roscommon in the west of Ireland.

The same year, in Edinburgh, the authorities jailed six ministers for illegally convening the General Assembly of the Church of Scotland. They packed the six men off to France and to Holland, where one of them lived close to the Pilgrims in Leiden as minister of the city's Scottish congregation. Many English Roman Catholics were compelled to leave as well.[19]

Like the painful stones within his kidney, men and women such as these irritated King James, and so they had to go: earls, Catholics, Gypsies, Graemes, and Presbyterians alike. Again, this was a consequence of his doctrine of sovereignty, and it found a parallel in the medical theories that fascinated the king.

Because Du Chesne, Mayerne, and the chemical doctors pictured disease as the product of superfluities, waste matter retained within the body, or poison coming from outside, they favored medicines designed to expel them from the patient. Enemas and laxatives figured high on their list of recommended drugs. When the king's son Henry fell ill in 1612, Mayerne diagnosed his fever as the result of eating too many melons, grapes, and oysters. He gave the boy a purge made of senna and rhubarb, then opened his veins and bled him. Prince Henry died soon afterward, but Mayerne's prestige survived. So did the concept of purgation.[20]

For James, the language of ill health supplied a rationale for banishment and exile. If the king was the doctor of his realm then, said James, he too should search out the "peccant humours" responsible for disorder and do his best to cast them away. If the kingdom succumbed to contagion, then the remedy was for the monarch "to purge it of all those diseases, by Medicines meet for the same." The consequence was rejection for all those who clouded his vision of perfect uniformity. Among them were the Scrooby Pilgrims and many others: a battalion of Cordelias forced out by their King Lear.

For William Brewster and his friends, events came to a head in the Quadrilateral in 1607. A new archbishop of York arrived, a man devoted to the service of King James. He encountered the evangelists Smyth and Robinson and the Puritan network to which Brewster belonged, and again the consequence was exile. Into the story came another Separatist. This was Thomas Helwys, the forgotten leader of the Pilgrim flight from England.

Chapter Eight

Disobedience and Contempt

> *. . . after the example of the Apostles, beeing shut out of Churches by the magistrate, we have gathered together the faithful into houses, and we have builded the true Jerusalem . . . it is lawfull in favour of the Trueth to make assemblies against the laws: no lesse then for good Citizens to assemble themselves against a tyrant usurping the commonwealth*
>
> —Philippe Duplessis-Mornay, *A Treatise of the Church* (1579), a book owned by William Brewster in New Plymouth

Travel up the Idle valley from Scrooby, and eventually, if you cling to the river, you will find by the water's edge the mossy rubble of an ancient chapel. Its ruins lie in what was once a deer park, spanning both banks, with an Elizabethan mansion at its center. The house vanished long ago, and a little way downstream an abandoned coal mine has left its heap of detritus at a place called Haughton Lound, where the Idle bends between boggy fields dotted with cinders and clumps of reed. Long before the colliery, it belonged to a family named Ellwes, or Helwys, as they also called themselves.

Their estate was small. When William Ellwes died in 1557, in his will he described himself as a farmer, staking no claim to be a gentleman. All the same, the Lound was good for farming, and Ellwes built a portfolio of tenancies, from Scrooby southward, mostly rented from the archbishop of York. William had four sons, and three of them rose with such speed that for once the word "meteoric" is fair.

People mocked the family as upstarts, but they attracted scorn only because they did exceptionally well. The eldest son, John, attached himself as a bailiff or a steward to the family who owned the chapel and the mansion. By trading in the soaring land market, he made himself a gentleman, with a manor house near Sturton. The youngest boy found his way to the capital and made a fortune, ending his days in 1616 as Alderman Jeffrey Ellwes, sheriff of London. The second son, Edmund, married an heiress and became a local official for the Exchequer. He acquired not only a coat of arms, but also Calvinism of a fervent kind.

Edmund probably wrote an intense anti-Catholic tract, published soon after the defeat of the Armada. It forecast the end of the world, with Queen Elizabeth leading the forces of the godly. And when Edmund Helwys died in 1590, he left behind a remarkable will, animated by the same religious zeal. Most wills began with a brief preamble, expressing faith in God and hope of resurrection. In his case, it covered nearly a page of manuscript, filled with quotations from Saint Paul and Saint Augustine. As Calvinists did, Edmund called himself a wretched sinner, and the world "a dirty stie, a grave of thorns . . . nothinge but feare, shame, tears, labour, sicknesse . . . and death." On page two, he gave instructions for preserving his social status after his passing. He owned a pew at the front of the parish church. He wished to be buried beside it, with his arms engraved in brass on the slab.[1]

Edmund left his estate to his son Thomas, and Thomas Helwys became a Separatist. Born in about 1570, he died in London in about 1614, almost certainly in prison, accused of sedition. William Bradford never mentions him, but Bradford left out a great deal, and especially the names of those, such as Helwys, who later developed more extreme forms of Brownism in exile. Despite this, Robinson acknowledged Thomas Helwys as the man who led the flight of the Pilgrims to Holland in 1608. According to Robinson, Helwys "above all other guides, or others, furthered this passage into strange countries; and if any brought oars, he brought sails."[2] This was literally true, since he hired the boat and planned the escape.

We do not know how and why Helwys became a Puritan, but in 1593 he entered Gray's Inn in London, where young men went to train as lawyers. Not everybody at Gray's Inn was a Puritan, but many were. Most famous was Nicholas Fuller, one of the "benchers" who ran the inn's affairs. In the 1590s, Fuller led the legal campaign to free Cartwright and the forward preachers from imprisonment. In Parliament, he fought against the new statute, passed in the year when Helwys entered the inn, which made Separatism a crime. Later still, we shall find Nick Fuller playing his part in the events that led to the flight of the Pilgrims. For the moment, the relevant point is that ties existed between lawyers and Puritans of the most radical kind.

Instead of practicing as a lawyer, however, Thomas Helwys came home, to live forty miles from Scrooby at Broxtowe Hall, close to the town of Nottingham. Despite his father's rank, they did not own their lands, but rented them on a long lease, and so Helwys was less wealthy than his uncles. He ran a small herd of only four hundred sheep. As for his private life, tongues wagged: it was said that Thomas had not lawfully married Joan Ashmore, the woman with whom he lived. Before their irregular wedding, Joan was his housekeeper, and in 1598 they were accused of fornication. This was an offense that might lead to a humiliating penance in the parish church. But no action was taken, and Helwys remained a protected member of the gentry. Six years later, a laborer took a dislike to Thomas Helwys and assaulted him. The JPs gave the man twelve months in jail.[3]

Helwys belonged to a web of Puritan-leaning landowners and lawyers spun across three counties. They must have been the people Bradford had in mind when he spoke of the "Godly and Religious" gentlemen who viewed Brewster with such respect. Their center of gravity lay around Sturton and Gainsborough, and by the early seventeenth century the most prominent was Thomas's cousin Sir Gervase Helwys, son of John, a JP and a man with ambition. He lived at Saundby, between the two places, though his chain of property extended to the Humber estuary. As Puritans did, he acquired the right to appoint the ministers at Saundby and at Babworth, where Brewster's friend Richard Clifton was the incumbent clergyman. When Clifton was dismissed, Sir Gervase replaced him with another Puritan with a history of infringing the rules that regulated worship.

At Gainsborough, his counterpart was another ambitious man, Richard Williamson, son of a local draper. Born in about 1560, he also entered Gray's Inn, where he rose fast, to rank alongside Fuller among its most senior lawyers. He picked up Puritan sentiments, and he married his daughter into a famous family of Puritan clergy. Under King James, he became Sir Richard Williamson, living between the capital, his hometown, and York, where he joined the Council of the North. He belonged to the same network as Sir Gervase. Williamson protected local Puritan ministers, and he wielded authority as a JP for Nottinghamshire.[4]

It would be possible to add more names and to follow this network indefinitely, to and fro and down to London, but it would be tedious and unnecessary. All that matters is that by 1605, when the purge of Puritans began, Brewster and Helwys had a circle of kinsmen and friends entrenched in positions of power and influence, men who, like them, had only recently joined the ranks of the gentry. They were not, however, quite powerful enough.

Above them ranked the two greatest aristocrats of the region, men divided by religion and by old antagonisms: Gilbert Talbot, seventh Earl of Shrewsbury, and Edmund, Lord Sheffield. Both had motives for wanting to end the period of toleration that Puritans had long enjoyed.

Two Rivals

Half a day's walk from Scrooby stood another Elizabethan mansion long since destroyed. Worksop Manor was very tall, and it was very new, completed only in 1586. Ninety feet above the ground a great chamber looked out across the landscape, with a view so fine that Burghley's son Robert Cecil called it the fairest gallery in England. Richard Torre of Scrooby supervised the workmen who built it, because it belonged to his master.[5] He was George Talbot, sixth Earl of Shrewsbury, unhappily married to his countess Elizabeth, known to posterity as Bess of Hardwick.

The sixth earl died in 1590, survived by the countess, who lived on until 1608. His son Gilbert inherited not only the title but also his father's difficulties with the queen. Under the Tudors, by way of loyal service against rebels and the Scots, the Talbots became the greatest family in the north, but in the 1580s they dwindled in authority and prestige. Queen Elizabeth gave George Talbot the task of taking care of Mary, Queen of Scots, but the two became a little too friendly. Elizabeth grew suspicious. When Gilbert became the seventh earl, he found himself exiled from court and denied the highest offices in the region.

In the eyes of Elizabeth, he suffered from two flaws: Roman Catholic sympathies and a vile temper. Gilbert Talbot married an ardent Catholic, who imported holy relics, and he quarreled with medieval ferocity. In 1598, during a duel with swords in Worksop Park, a local gentleman skewered the bowels of a Talbot family friend, and so the seventh earl assembled a hundred armed men to pursue him. The incident came close to causing a neighborhood civil war when the duelist gathered his own allies in the county. They were led by Talbot's great rival Edmund, Lord Sheffield, the most powerful magnate in the region to the east, between Lincoln and York. He raised his own band of sixty men, and more bloodshed was only narrowly averted.[6]

Despite this, and much more acrimony, when James became king Gilbert Talbot began to regain royal favor. Both James and his queen stayed at Worksop, on their way south from Scotland, and the king knew that the Talbots had treated his mother well. Talbot was close to Robert Cecil, the king's most trusted statesman. And so, very soon, James began to give Gilbert Talbot the offices he wanted and the power that went with them, making him a privy councillor.

Around Austerfield and Scrooby, the seventh earl was an awkward and intruding presence. He levied river tolls on the Idle, and in the Bawtry and Austerfield survey of 1608, high above the name of Robert Bradford, we find that of Gilbert Talbot. The seventh Earl of Shrewsbury owned Bawtry Hall, five cottages and twenty acres of land nearby, and he commanded a following among the gentry. He counted among his supporters not only the violent Lassells family but also the Mortons, the local Catholic renegades. More remarkable still was the hold that his stepmother, Bess, exerted over the economics of religion in the area. An inventory of her assets, made at Hardwick in 1609, shows that she claimed ownership of the rectories and the tithes of five parishes nearby, including Scrooby and the next-door parish of Everton. She had also purchased the right to nominate the minister in each one. Most likely, she bought all these properties from the Crown in the 1590s, as the queen scavenged for money to pay for the war in Ireland.[7]

These were real estate transactions. It seems unlikely that Gilbert Talbot and Bess of Hardwick hatched a great scheme to dominate belief and worship in the Pilgrim Quadrilateral. Even so, for a local Puritan the revival of the Talbots could only cause unease. Gilbert's dislike of their kind made itself very clear in 1604, in an exchange of unpleasantness with Lady Isabel Bowes, an heiress and perhaps the most eminent Puritan gentlewoman in the north. They wrote to each other about the Hampton Court conference, but their letters swiftly descended into personal abuse. Talbot insulted Lady Isabel in crude terms and warned her not to meddle with sedition. Besides his loathing for Puritans, Gilbert Talbot also had a rival in Lord Sheffield; and soon he found an opportunity for combining the two animosities. It arose from a mixture of religion and local jealousy.[8]

Aged thirty-eight in the year when James became king, Sheffield was the son of a great beauty, Lady Douglas Sheffield, adulterous mistress of the Earl of Leicester. He became the most powerful man in the north of England during the critical period when Separatism began to take root in the region. Even so, he spent much of his adult life struggling with debt. Much of it was incurred to support the ladies of his family: his embarrassing mother—he had to mortgage four manors to pay her an annuity—and his six daughters, who needed dowries. His troubles deepened after he built his own country house, at Normanby, towering above the Trent near

Scunthorpe. From here, he claimed as his sphere of influence all the country between York and Lincoln, and especially the cattle land to the north and east of Austerfield. But his financial position grew steadily worse. When James became king, Sheffield pestered him with requests for posts that might give him an income, until at last the king made Sheffield president of the Council of the North in September 1603. Unfortunately, the Sheffields had their own awkward religious profile. This too had its consequences.[9]

Lord Sheffield had married another ardent Catholic, with Catholic rites, and so he came under suspicion himself. As a means to clear his name, he renewed the campaign against those of his wife's religion: as many as nine hundred were indicted at York in 1604. However, Sheffield had strayed too far in his eagerness to prove himself a good Protestant. As Bancroft removed the Puritan clergy in the south, it emerged that Sheffield had once employed just such a man as a tutor to his children. The preacher in question, called Bywater, later reappeared as a Separatist in Amsterdam, but before doing so, he gravely offended King James. In January or February 1605, Bywater sent the king an insulting book, advocating Puritan reform.

In prison in the Tower of London, Bywater mentioned his link to Lord Sheffield. Hurriedly, Sheffield sought to clear his name. He wrote to Cecil to protest that, yes, he had employed Bywater, but the man was dismissed when he denounced his master for wasting his time with falconry.[10] Meanwhile, as his rival Gilbert Talbot stood ready to supplant him, if Lord Sheffield fell from favor, suddenly the Puritans and their sympathizers in the north began to attract unwelcome attention from King James. The problem arose from an undiplomatic letter written by the archbishop of York.

His name was Matthew Hutton, and by this time he was an old man, close to death. Even so, at the end of 1604 Archbishop Hutton wrote to Cecil seeking leniency for Puritans, on the grounds that they were patriotic allies against the influence of Rome. Unwisely, in passing he criticized the king's deer hunting, for damaging poor men's crops. Worst of all, the letter must have circulated widely, because several copies survive, including one among the papers of Gilbert Talbot. It would appear that the Earl of Shrewsbury spread stories to the effect that Hutton and Lord Sheffield were conniving with Puritan ministers.

King James reacted as we might expect. That winter, as he roamed the countryside in search of animals to kill, he received one annoying petition after another from squires defending the Puritan clergy. Losing patience, with them and with his officials at York, on February 19 he issued a reprimand to Hutton and Sheffield, telling them to enforce the law against Catholic and Puritan alike: with "diligence and constancie," he said, "against the disobedient both of the one sorte and of the other." In their different ways, Sheffield and Hutton were both weak men, and especially Sheffield because of his debts and the threat posed by Gilbert Talbot. Inevitably, they felt obliged to placate the king. In doing so, they ended the years of official complacency concerning Brewster and his network.[11]

At York, when the archbishop dealt with a nonconforming clergyman, he used his Chancery Court. It generally met on a Friday, no more than once a month. Suddenly, in March 1605, the meetings became much more frequent, with eight in less than six weeks, beginning soon after the king's reprimand arrived. Swiftly, the court called before it five Puritan ministers from Nottinghamshire to answer charges of nonconformity. Four of them refused to sign up to Bancroft's test of loyalty: Richard Clifton of Babworth, Henry Gray of Bawtry, Robert Southworth of Headon, and Richard Bernard of Worksop. Each village lay within twelve miles of Scrooby. In April, the archbishop dismissed all four from their parishes, and the first three men on the list were excommunicated.[12]

At a stroke, national and local politics came together and swept away the local platoon of Puritan ministers supported by Brewster and his friends. No action was taken yet against laypeople, because Bancroft's canons had not come into force. Indeed, if matters had ended there, the emigration to Holland and America might not have occurred, since nobody in the area had yet taken the radical step of leaving the Church of England entirely to become a Separatist. For that to happen, the locality needed its own compelling equivalent of Robert Browne.

Leadership of such a kind soon arrived in the shape of the preaching radicals Robinson and Smyth. Both had excelled at Cambridge, and in their late twenties they had every prospect of a lifetime of advancement in the Church. Then both men, and especially Smyth, became outcasts and pariahs, with wrecked careers. So, at the end of 1606, or thereabouts, they decided to take the path of illegality. Early the following year they led the act of separation. They took with them Brewster, Helwys, and the most radical Puritans in the Quadrilateral.

MR. ROBINSON AND MR. SMYTH

It would be hard to exaggerate their importance. Although he never crossed the Atlantic, John Robinson remained from afar the mentor of the

Plymouth Colony. And if any single person can claim to have launched the Baptist faith in the English-speaking world, then John Smyth was the man.[13] Born in about 1575, John Robinson definitely came from Sturton, and some evidence suggests that Smyth was born there too, though his name is too common to permit an exact fix of his ancestry. Smyth was the older man, by about six years, judging by the dates at which they entered the university. Smyth became a member of Christ's College in 1586, and Robinson arrived at Corpus Christi in 1592.

Both men belonged to the lowest tier of Cambridge students. They were sizars, or promising boys with little family money, permitted to enter the university if they could pay their way by doing chores for richer young men. From the college records, it seems likely that Robinson owed his place at Corpus to another dynasty of aristocrats, the Manners family, Earls of Rutland. They had feudal rights over Sturton and treated the village as part of their sphere of influence. In 1590, Corpus began to attract the sons of noblemen, including Roger Manners, fifth Earl of Rutland, who joined the college in that year. In all probability somebody at Sturton recommended the young Robinson to serve as a sizar for the earl.

A college like Corpus might offer a clever sizar a swift route to success. If he displayed outstanding aptitude for Greek and Latin, he had every chance of obtaining a fellowship and then moving gracefully onward into a career in public service. At Corpus, this was all the more likely because of the prestige of its new master, John Jegon. A staunch Calvinist, marked out for greatness by Burghley, Jegon was the son of a weaver, but he rose to become the bishop of Norwich. His brother Thomas Jegon acted as Robinson's tutor, the young man worked hard, and the Jegons rewarded him for it.

Within four years, Robinson achieved the rank of scholar, and in 1598 Corpus made him one of its eleven fellows. In rotation he served his turn as college lecturer in Greek and then as dean. Five minutes' walk away at Christ's, John Smyth had done just as well, becoming a fellow in the autumn of 1593 and remaining on the faculty for the next seven years.[14]

By itself, a fellowship did not count for much, since Christ's and Corpus were far from rich, and each college suffered periods of financial difficulty. Fellows had their rooms, and food and drink, but their pay was small, and if they wished to marry, they had to resign. But while at the college, they had the leisure and the opportunity to make friends and allies, and to look for a job to become available elsewhere. Best of all, they might find a post as minister of a large and wealthy parish, or as a "lecturer," a clergyman hired by a town or city government to preach sermons to its citizens.

So it was with Smyth and Robinson. In 1600, Smyth left Cambridge to become city lecturer at Lincoln, with an annual salary of forty pounds, eight times his pay as a fellow at Cambridge, plus the rent for his house and the right to graze his cows on the communal heath. He married soon afterward, and children followed. As for Robinson, after his year as dean he held no further offices at his college, but instead, as he neared the age of thirty, he began to ask for long leaves of absence. He took three months off in the autumn of 1603, he resigned his fellowship in February 1604, and then a few days later he married Bridget White of Sturton. He found a post at Norwich as deputy to the minister of St. Andrew's Church, a man called Thomas Newhouse. This was a distinguished parish, and it should have made a splendid base, in a city famous for clean streets and godliness.

It might seem that both Smyth and Robinson had found their niche. In fact nothing could be further from the truth. At Lincoln, John Smyth fell afoul of city politics. For many years, the city had been divided into factions: a small group of wealthy tradesmen, Puritan by inclination, squabbling with townspeople with no desire to belong to a godly republic. Drink apparently played its part. The leaders of the popular party included men who ran malt houses and spent their days in the tavern. It seems that behind the politics lay disputes about how many alehouses to allow in the city, how much beer could be brewed, and how much the city should spend on welfare payments for the unemployed.

Never a man to mince his words, Smyth gave sermons that aligned him with the Puritans. He spoke against "profanity, oppression of the pore, drunkenes, poprye, or any other sinne," but it seems that he personally insulted one of the leaders of the opposition. His friends tried to make Smyth lecturer for life, but they lost control of the city council, voted out of office by a large majority. In 1602, the new mayor fired John Smyth and reported him to the bishop of Lincoln as a nonconforming Puritan.* Although he petitioned the king, and appealed to Lord Sheffield, the episode blighted his career forever.[15]

In 1603, the archbishop of Canterbury took away Smyth's license to preach, and he lost his livelihood. By this time, he had buried one son and baptized at Lincoln an infant daughter. He called her Mara, the word that in the Hebrew Bible stands for "bitterness." His health was poor. Again and again, Smyth had reported sick for weeks at a time while at Christ's

*John Beck, the mayor who dismissed Smyth, was barred from office in 1609 for "inordinate and excessive drinkinge . . . the lothsome & odyous sinne . . . which tends to the overthrow of the cyttie."

College. It seems that he suffered from some chronic disease, perhaps the tuberculosis that, according to Bradford, ended his life when Smyth was little more than forty.

Meanwhile, John Robinson fared little better. On the face of it, his position at Norwich should have been ideal, a first step toward evangelical fame in a place where the clergy and the city fathers were sympathetic. Thomas Newhouse had been a colleague of John Smyth's at Christ's College, and like him he preached enthusiastically, giving every Thursday a lecture steeped in Calvinism. By way of predestination, God had chosen the elect, and damned the rest, the reprobate, to hell, and this was justice, said Thomas Newhouse. John Robinson never wavered from the same creed, and so he should have fitted in at St. Andrew's with little trouble.

This was all the more true since by now his old master John Jegon had come to Norwich as the bishop. And yet somehow Robinson offended his superiors. His period in Norwich remains mysterious, with few entirely reliable sources, but it seems that he fell victim to Bancroft's purge. Early in 1605, Jegon began investigating his clergymen for traces of nonconformity. Soon afterward, Robinson paid a visit to Sturton, and gave a sermon at Retford. Somebody reported him to the authorities for doing so without a license; presumably, Jegon had already withdrawn it. By this time, both Robinson and Smyth had more or less reached the end of their careers as ministers within the established Church. Even so, Separatism remained a daring and dangerous step to take.[16]

Men and women did not become Separatists in a blinding moment of insight and conversion. All too often, historians have written about the *Mayflower* as though leaving the established Church were a move people often made in Jacobean England, simply because the Church was irksome, or unsatisfying, or because it lacked evangelical excitement. In fact, separation was exceedingly rare, and especially for career clergymen such as Smyth and Robinson. They abandoned the Church of England only after a long period of anxious meditation, and after trying every other option.

As far back as 1597, three of Smyth's colleagues at Christ's complained about him to the university for opposing the wearing of the surplice and the use of the sign of the cross in baptism.[17] So, by that time, he was already a mainstream Puritan; but it took him another decade to make the leap into Separatism. Before he did so, he underwent an intense nine-month period of thought and discussion, beginning in the summer of 1606. By then, he had tried alternative careers, as a schoolmaster and a physician, until the authorities vetoed those as well. Robinson's history is less clear, but he studied alongside the leading Puritans at Cambridge for nearly ten years. No record has been found of any nonconformity on his part during this period.

People became Separatists because they believed that it was essential for salvation; but salvation itself was a mystery. Nothing about it was simple. First, each Christian had to determine, by way of prayer and introspection, which group he or she belonged to, the elect or the damned. As Newhouse put it at St. Andrew's: "Hearing this voyce dailie sounding in the Church, that there is a number of men in the counsell of God rejected, wee are to examine oure estates, and to make question: whether it be we or not?" Only those who had authentic faith could be sure that they were among the elect, and not the excluded multitude. But faith was not a tranquil state of mind: it was a dynamic process, unfolding over time, by way of a long adventure toward maturity. Smyth and Robinson became Separatists because, gradually, they lost confidence in the conventional English parish as a place where they could follow such a path.

Most likely by way of the work of an older fellow of Christ's, William Perkins, it seems that both Smyth and Robinson came under the influence of a German Calvinist, Zacharias Ursinus. Another forgotten man, he was in his day the leading theologian at the great university at Heidelberg. Ursinus spoke of salvation as the product of a sequence of different kinds of faith. Each stage had an emotional tone of its own, assembled from alternations of hope and fear, shame and guilt, despair and longing. The effects of faith included both joy and deep anxiety. For Ursinus, and for Robinson and Smyth, true faith included uncertainty: one of its distinguishing marks, said Ursinus, was "the strife and conflict within us of . . . faith & doubtfulness." The others included belief in the Holy Trinity and predestination, of course, but a human being must first display a sincere desire for salvation.

Struggle and doubt were signs that the yearning for faith was unfeigned, while another might be found in perseverance in good deeds. Since a true Christian possessed "an earnest purpose of obeying God according to all his commandments," as Ursinus put it, he or she had also to display charity and to practice self-denial.

It seems that Robinson had a special talent for taking subtle ideas such as these and expressing them forcefully, in plain language. William Hubbard, the first official historian of New England, referred to Robinson's "polished wit, ingenious disposition and courteous behaviour." So, when he came to write an essay on faith, Robinson summed up what Ursinus had said about his relationship with doubt. "We are not here to imagine an idea of Faith, free in this infirmitie of our flesh from doubting," he wrote. "The tree may stand, and grow also, though shaken, and bended with the wind: so may Faith."[18] His essay appeared in a book that came to be one of the most widely owned at New Plymouth.

In themselves, none of these ideas were unorthodox, but John Smyth added an extra element that most definitely was. His first altercation with his bishop arose when he questioned the value of repeating the Lord's Prayer, a central, compulsory part of the Anglican service book. Smyth worried about its misuse not only in the church but also in the countryside, where conjurers chanted it over sick cattle, as well as feeding it to rabid dogs. His qualms deepened into profound unease about *any* prayer read from an official liturgy.

For Smyth, prayer should be "conceived," by which he meant deeply felt, rewritten, and re-created anew by each believer to express a faith deeply personal. Again, this followed logically if faith was seen as a dynamic oscillation within each human soul, but it was a dangerous thing to say. Many years before, Richard Bancroft had condemned "conceived prayer" as an unruly kind of worship that would lead to chaos. John Smyth openly advocated the practice, in a book published in 1605.[19]

Eventually, both Smyth and Robinson clambered over a last mental barrier. They began to read the work of Browne, Barrow, and Ainsworth. Like them, Robinson and Smyth came to focus sharply on the eighteenth chapter of Saint Matthew, and its message that a true church existed whenever two or three people gathered in the name of Christ. Like Browne, they came to believe that *only* when people assembled in such a way, and freely made a covenant with each other and with God, did they follow the path of Christianity. Once they reached that point, they became committed radicals. Bishops, Church laws and canons such as Bancroft's, compulsory tithes, the parish system, ecclesiastical lands and property, the entire economic basis of the Church of England: all of them had to go, in pursuit of authentic worship and faith, the only assurance of election.

Neither man underwent this process of thought in academic seclusion. They were responding to what they saw around them. Self-evidently, or so it seemed to them, the parish church could not be a congregation of the elect if it allowed the ungodly, people perhaps like the Lassells family, to worship and to take the Eucharist alongside true Christians. And, especially in the case of John Smyth, both men were reacting to the unfairness with which they were treated.

By the spring of 1604, Smyth had settled firmly at Gainsborough, where he practiced medicine, and fathered two more daughters. He found friends among the local Puritans, gentry and tradesmen alike. In the absence of the usual vicar, who was sick, they persuaded Smyth to preach. Early in 1606, somebody told the bishop that Smyth had done so without a license. Local gentlemen rallied to his defense, including Williamson and Sir Gervase Helwys, who signed letters praising him. Regardless, the authorities called Smyth before an ecclesiastical court. He was convicted of being "contumacious." In November they barred him from working as a physician without a license from the bishop.[20]

So John Smyth began his climactic period of reflection. He traveled ninety miles south to Coventry to consult a group of moderate Puritan clergy to hear their arguments for remaining in the Church. At about this time, possibly on the way home, he fell seriously ill and took shelter with Thomas Helwys at Broxtowe. There, in February 1607, he preached illegally in a parish church nearby; then Smyth vanished from the local archives, as he and Robinson turned their backs on authority.

In America, Bradford described the events that followed with tantalizing brevity. The act of separation occurred, he says, because of what he calls "the tiranny of the Bishopps against godly preachers and people in silenceing the one and persecuting the other." This was an entirely accurate description of the treatment of John Smyth. If we had more documentation about Robinson, we could probably say the same about him. "The Lord's free people," Bradford wrote, "joyned themselves (by a Covenant of the Lord)." They formed two distinct churches of their own, entirely Separatist.

One led by Smyth met at Gainsborough, while the other was convened at Scrooby Manor by Clifton, Robinson, and Brewster. Two letters survive, one by Thomas Helwys, that give some idea of their style of worship. It was an all-day exercise, beginning at eight in the morning and ending at five or six in the evening, in two sessions divided by a two-hour break at noon. They sang psalms, but most of all they worshipped by "prophesying," reading a biblical text, with each participant standing up to discuss it: a radicalized version of the Swiss practice invented many decades earlier and advocated by Browne.[21]

These were not tiny groups of farmers, plowmen, and their wives assembling in cottages in remote hamlets. Since Scrooby Manor was a station of the Royal Mail on the highway, it would have been hard to hide the gatherings, while Gainsborough had one of the busiest grain markets in the region. News of what was going on soon reached a wide public. As early as January 1608, an anti-Puritan published a book in London that alluded to the affair, and he mentioned the involvement of the local gentry.

"Hear you not of Teachers and people in the farthest parts of Lincolnshire and Nottinghamshire etc. who are flatly separated?" the author wrote. He mentioned "a Gentlewoman of place, who is said to be absolutely gone from the Church," and it is conceivable he was referring to Lady Isabel Bowes. She had ties with radical Puritanism and certainly knew John Smyth. When examined as a whole, the evidence suggests that this was a conspicuous movement, gathering momentum. A series of strong personalities converged and then collided, across a swath of land where tensions had reached the breaking point.

The Drews of Everton

Along the Trent valley, between March and August 1607, episodes of public disobedience, anger, and agitation began to come to the attention of the authorities. On the Lincolnshire side of the river, at Torksey, a Puritan clergyman gave an angry sermon. He called his flock "sinfull Sodomites," because they objected to another Puritan who had preached in the same pulpit before him. Not far away at Retford, a woman was cited before the archdeacon's court for standing up one Sunday and haranguing the minister in front of the congregation. At Gainsborough, a tradesman found himself in trouble for failing to doff his hat in church.

When each one is looked at in isolation, after four hundred years, episodes like these seem tiny, trivial, or even comic. But within them lay a pattern.[22] For the first time, the rigor of Bancroft had begun to bite hard on laypeople in the region, as well as on what remained of the Puritan clergy. The result was protest and dissent. It was this—the involvement of the laity, and the organization they established—that made the events which followed remarkable, with no obvious parallel at the time.

Nobody knows the precise date when the act of separation occurred, the moment when Brewster and the rest felt that they must quit the Church of England for good. However, it probably took place in March. At that time, the critical dates were those when men and women were obliged to receive the Eucharist, a ceremony that served as a test of obedience. It only took place five times a year, and between Christmas and Easter week in 1607 a long interval elapsed of more than three months without any Eucharist required.[23] No record survives of trouble at Christmas, but several incidents of refusal occurred at Easter. The festival fell on April 5.

Two days later, in accordance with Bancroft's new rules, the churchwardens of Everton tersely reported that four men and one woman had failed to take Holy Communion. At least one of the offenders was a member of Brewster's dissident group at Scrooby. This incident displays far more clearly than any other the social origins, and perhaps the motives, of the men and women who formed the nucleus of these early Pilgrim congregations.

Two miles from Scrooby, Everton sat on the top of the North Clay, above the Idle wetlands. A smaller version of Sturton, it was another open field village with a rich mixture of grazing land, meadows, and cornfields, with woods on the higher ground. It was a place where rents were high too, but where the farmers could enjoy a standard of living much better than at Bradford's Austerfield, forty minutes' walk across the valley. Among them were a prosperous yeoman family called the Drews. They were men and women who grew wheat and rye, reared sheep, and held radical views.

The Drews lived a few hundred yards from the church, in a hamlet called Harwell. It occupies the crest of a sandy ridge between the cornfields and the meadows. At the family's head was Richard Drew, a man of modest education who could not sign his name. Even so, he was pious and affluent enough when he died in 1616 to leave three pounds, fifteen weeks' wages for a laborer, toward the schooling of poor children of the parish.

Feather beds, kitchen scales, mattresses, rugs, carpets, and red curtains figured among the possessions of the up-and-coming Drews. They were some of the first people in the region to have in their houses a room called a parlor. Among Richard's sons in 1607 were three young men in their twenties who all became defiant Puritans. Robert and John were two of the five Evertonians who did not receive the Eucharist at Easter, and Roger was named in July for refusing to go to church at all. John Drew, aged twenty-three, seems to have been the most outspoken. Later the authorities locked him up in the cells at York Castle for being a Brownist. Banished by the Privy Council in 1609, he headed for the Netherlands to join Brewster and his comrades. And although his father, Richard, does not seem to have been an active rebel, he did what he could to shield his sons. He incurred a fine of two shillings.[24]

Why should such a family opt for refusal and resistance when the vast majority of their equivalents in England did not? Most likely, the personal influence of Brewster had a great deal to do with it. The Drews must have known him for many years, because the archbishop of York was lord of the manor at Everton, and Brewster's father would have collected the rents. They must also have known Richard Clifton, because his brother John was another Evertonian yeoman. According to Cotton Mather, after his illness at the age of twelve, Bradford began to listen to Clifton "not far from his abode." In all likelihood, he simply forded the Idle and walked up the wooded slope to the same village.

Why was Everton a haven for dissent? Another explanation was political, though the politics were very local. If the lord of the manor was an absentee, like the archbishop, then in practice the yeoman farmers could run their own affairs. This they did at Everton, where little authority existed but their own. All but one of the large tenants and landowners at Everton came from families known to be Puritan sympathizers. The Drews and their friends dominated the parish church, serving as churchwardens, while John Drew kept the parish funds. In 1609, long after the Pilgrims went into exile, the vicar of Everton was still complaining about the nonconformists, including John Clifton.

They were self-employed men, large tenant farmers, or tradesmen who had become used to independence, in matters of belief as well as in the running of their open fields. Something similar occurred in Gainsborough too, although there the politics were urban. In August 1607, a Gainsborough man called John Noble was reported to the authorities for failing to take Holy Communion for twelve months. He also refused to remove his hat during Sunday service, a gesture often made by Puritans.

John Noble was a man of substance, one of Gainsborough's largest taxpayers. He was a draper with a shop in the middle of the town and business contacts in London. One of the founders of the town's grammar school, he served as parish constable. Again, he valued independence from outsiders. In alliance with Sir Richard Williamson, and with another local attorney called Edward Aston, from 1605 onward John Noble fought a long and angry legal battle with the lord of the manor, one Sir William Hickman, a newcomer from London who charged exorbitant levies on market traders and tried to ban Noble from doing any business at all. It was Hickman who reported John Noble for nonconformity.[25]

All three men—Aston, Noble, and Williamson—belonged to the local Puritan network. Aston later stood bail for Joan Helwys, the Separatist, when she was arrested. We can fairly assume that John Noble was one of the tradesmen who worshipped with John Smyth. It seems that Gainsborough had not merely a few nonconformists but an active Puritan party, men tied together by business and common self-interest as well as religious friendship. Not all of these men became Brownists. But they had every reason to sympathize with separatism, if the movement had a godly, disciplined tone and served as a weapon against social evils.*

The Old Hall at Gainsborough, Lincolnshire, viewed from the north, showing the bay window of the great hall, built in about 1465. (*Photography: Nick Bunker*)

Most of the local gentry apparently agreed. In their role as JPs, they turned a blind eye to Brownism. Under ecclesiastical law as it stood, the judges who sat in the archdeacon's court could impose only limited penalties, small fines or excommunication, and they had no power of imprisonment. However, if an offender persisted, the archdeacon could send him or her to the JPs to be dealt with more severely. Alternatively, the JPs could prosecute themselves, using the criminal law against Catholic recusants or

*Without documentary evidence, historians have often said that Smyth and the Separatists worshipped at Gainsborough Old Hall. A magnificent fifteenth-century brick manor house, it still stands close to the parish church. It belonged to Sir William Hickman, which means that the story is unlikely to be true if it refers to events in 1607, in view of Hickman's attitude to John Noble. However, Smyth commanded widespread respect in the town, and so he would certainly have been a guest there in earlier years. In any event, the Old Hall retains its exceptional importance as one of the finest late-medieval buildings in England.

Separatists. In Nottinghamshire, their sessions were fully minuted, and the minutes survive in their entirety. They show no trace of any action against Brewster or his friends.

Not, that is, until October 1607, when at last they began to call a few Separatists before them. By that time events had moved on. At a much higher level the authorities had become aware of the civil disobedience in the Quadrilateral. The lenient old archbishop of York had breathed his last. When a new man came to take his place, he tackled the problem with urgency.

Dangerous Schism

In early July, the new archbishop left London for the north. When the decisive encounter came, in November, it involved a direct confrontation with a defiant Brownist. However, this was not a simple clash between dictatorship on the one hand and ardent faith on the other. It was a confrontation between two sets of equally evangelical Christians. It arose from a wider conflict about the basis of the authority of the Church, and about constitutional law.

Aged about sixty-three, the new archbishop, Toby Matthew, came from another family of tradesmen. In his teens he made his name as a scholar of precocious brilliance: men called it "half a miracle," so swiftly did he take his master's degree. As the young dean of an Oxford college, he made himself popular with his generosity, and for what one observer called his "cheerfull sharpnes of witt," involving a taste for outrageous puns.

As he worked his way up through the hierarchy, mainly in the far north at Durham, Toby Matthew lost neither stamina nor enthusiasm. Although he often fell ill, with rheumatism, toothache, and catarrh, he keenly pursued his vocation as a preacher. In the space of forty years he delivered nearly two thousand sermons, preaching regularly even in his seventies, when he might have left the task to juniors.[26]

And yet the diligent Toby Matthew was never his own man, and the Gospel reached the ears of his congregation filtered through a sieve of politics. As bishop of Durham, Matthew had met King James the moment he came south across the border in 1603, he traveled with him to London, and he preached frequently at court. Most recently, he had risen from his sickbed in April 1607 to give a sermon to the young Prince Henry. His spell in the south the previous winter was the result of politics too, as he lent his support in Parliament to the king's final, doomed attempt to legislate for the complete union of England and Scotland. So we can fairly assume that Toby Matthew saw himself as the king's instrument, seeking loyally to impose the Crown's authority.

As he traveled up the Great North Road, he passed through country troubled by unrest of another kind, causing alarm at Whitehall Palace at the very time when reports of Brownism were also beginning to arrive. In towns and villages less than a day's ride west of the highway, the spring and summer of 1607 witnessed the most serious popular revolt of the reign of James I. It was known as the Midland Rising. It flared up in May, before being swiftly crushed in June, with Gilbert Talbot playing a leading part in its suppression. A spate of hangings followed. Behind the rebellion lay material realities at their cruelest and most basic, at a point when the fall in the real incomes of the laboring poor had very nearly reached its lowest point.

In 1607, with the price of grain rising sharply, landlords in parts of the Midlands were making matters worse, by raising rents and by enclosing open fields and turning them over to grazing land. Crowds of people numbering in thousands gathered to break down hedges and to fill in ditches. Economic protest though it was, suspicions were aroused that one or another group of religious dissenters, Catholic or Puritan, had fomented the unrest. In the autumn, as the price of bread soared again after another poor harvest, to reach its highest level since the 1590s, the Privy Council continued to worry. No evidence links the Pilgrims to protests against enclosure, but the Midland Rising created a climate of unease that may help to explain why the archbishop acted as he did.

For his part, Toby Matthew had a reputation as a man "industrious against Papists." At York he found a weapon against them in the form of the Court of High Commission, a tribunal with wide powers against religious offenders. Thanks to new legislation, action could be taken far more effectively than in the past. Applying solely to Roman Catholics, the statute became law in 1606 as part of the Crown's response to the Gunpowder Plot. It obliged them to take a new oath of allegiance, requiring them to disown the authority of the pope. Armed with this, Matthew stepped up the campaign against the old religion to new heights.

While only a handful of arrest warrants were issued against the Separatists, the lists of those relating to Catholics fill scores of pages in the archives of the High Commission. As many as sixty such cases, covering two hundred individuals, appear in the records relating to a single session of the court in June 1607 alone.[27] More than a century ago, when a visiting American scholar examined the same minute book at York, he published only the few entries relating to the pursuit of the Pilgrims. He suppressed the evidence of much harsher treatment of those of a different persuasion.

Henry Martyn Dexter, the writer in question, passed over in silence the material that deals with the anti-Catholic purge. His motives for doing so were all too obvious. When Dexter's book appeared in Boston in the early 1900s, its pages were strewn with barbed asides against the pope and the Catholic religion.[28] Among the details he omitted were, for example, the relative numbers of prisoners in the cells. Only four Brownists were imprisoned, but they shared the jail at York with fourteen "recusants in the castle," Catholics detained for "superstitious errors & disobedience," and for refusing to take the oath of allegiance.[29]

Henry Martyn Dexter was a New England Protestant, at a time when in Boston and New Haven prejudice against Italians and Irish Catholic immigrants was commonplace. It serves no purpose today to chastise him for that. However, by detaching events from their context, Dexter misrepresented and misunderstood the material he studied, and because the archives at York have received little attention, his errors have never been corrected. By failing to reexamine the original records, later historians have left intact a vague, naive account of the affair.

The fact was that the Brownists did not go to jail simply for being radical in their religious views, or for creating a Separatist community at Scrooby. They did so because they attacked the legal authority of the Church, and in terms based on a defense of civil liberties that applied across a far wider domain than religion alone. When the final crisis came, it concerned politics and law, rather than faith or theological dissent.

Toby Matthew presided over his first session of the High Commission on August 13. He went straight to work against Catholics, and then he headed north to the town of Ripon, one of their strongholds, where four days later he dealt with them again. A recess followed in September. In October he reconvened the court, and on the sixth of the month he handled fifty-six cases of Catholic nonconformity, covering some 170 individuals: in the margin, the word "fled" appears next to three names.

At first, the archbishop used mild measures against the Separatists. Rather than bullying his opponents, he tried to convert them. During the recess, he traveled south to Nottinghamshire. He gave four sermons, preaching at Bawtry against the Brownists on September 10. Then back he came to York, where he fell ill with his old ailment of catarrh. Then, in November, a Brownist came up before the High Commission, in the shape of a gentleman called Gervase Nevyle, the first to be imprisoned.

He was "a very daungerous schismaticall Separist Brownist & irreligious subiect," said the court, but that was not why they sent him to jail. They locked him up because he refused to testify on oath. In this respect, the Nevyle case was evidently unusual, and sensitive. The clerk neatly wrote out a verbatim report, much longer than the brief notes that he normally made. Specifically, he referred to the fact that Nevyle offended the archbishop by refusing to be sworn, by making "contemptuous speches," and by declining to answer questions. The clerk gave the substance of what Nevyle had said: he insulted the archbishop by "protesting . . . againste his authoritie (and as he tearmed it) his antichristian hierarchie."[30]

Why did his case require careful handling? First, Nevyle was well connected. His contacts included the lawyers of Gray's Inn. More than one Gervase Nevyle appears in the records, but our Separatist was almost certainly a young man of twenty-one, Gervase Nevyle of Grove. This was a village on the North Clay, where the Nevyles were lords of the manor: it appears that they also owned land at Everton. At Grove, they allowed a radical Puritan to serve as minister, one of the men dismissed by Archbishop Hutton in 1605. Even more to the point, the young Gervase was the nephew of the Gainsborough lawyer Sir Richard Williamson, who served on the very same court, the High Commission, that was about to hear his case.[31]

Second, it seems that Gervase Nevyle was remarkably well-informed about the law. By using the words he did, he made an uncomfortable connection between his case and a great legal controversy that was raging in London, fascinating advocates and irritating King James. Far from being a despotism, Jacobean England was intensely legalistic, and political debate often found its principal arena in the courts. When Nick Fuller represented Puritans in the 1590s, he defended them by arguing that the legal apparatus of the Church was unconstitutional. In 1607 the issue was revived when he defended a merchant from Norfolk who, like Nevyle, refused to give sworn testimony when charged with Separatism. In Parliament, and in a book printed unlawfully, most likely in Amsterdam, Fuller called for the outright abolition of the High Commission.

In language very similar to Nevyle's, Fuller said that the court was unjust, arbitrary, and unlawful. The High Commission contravened Magna Carta because it did not allow trial by jury. It had no right to imprison defendants, he claimed, since Parliament had never voted freely to give it powers to do so. Worst of all, the court compelled the accused to give testimony on oath before they knew the charges against them: it forced them to incriminate themselves, flouting an ancient privilege of English defendants. According to Fuller, the High Commission had no right to try offenders of any kind, whether they were Catholics or Brownists, adulterers or bigamists, or publishers of unlicensed books.

Fuller's campaign reached its climax in the summer and autumn of 1607, at the very moment when the authorities at York began to take action against Brewster and his comrades. In June, the House of Commons came close to voting to do away with the High Commission, and of course Toby Matthew knew this situation intimately: he was sitting in the House of Lords. In July, the authorities arrested Nick Fuller, and then in October the High Commission in London sent him to prison. His friends obtained a writ of habeas corpus, and the case went to the leading forum in the realm, the Court of King's Bench. They decided against Fuller on November 24, but the controversy continued, when the following month his illegal book turned up in England. The authorities rearrested him in January 1608, and this time they charged Nick Fuller with sedition.[32]

King James took all this very seriously, because the High Commission operated with his direct authority. Attack the commission, and you attacked the royal prerogative. This explains why at York the commissioners treated Gervase Nevyle with such great care. By speaking as he did, the young man put them on notice that he intended to protest, like Fuller, against their right to exist, and to do so in constitutional terms. On Christmas Day, the commissioners met and gave special instructions concerning the minutes of proceedings against the "disobedient or contemptuous." In future, they would be kept in a chest with three locks in the archbishop's registry. Evidently, they expected a legal challenge. If it came, they needed to be sure that they could defend themselves, with a written record of the offending words uttered either by Nevyle or by any Roman Catholics who tried the same tactic.[33]

Freedom to worship as they wished was, without doubt, the goal that the Separatists were seeking, but civil liberties of different kinds depended on each other. If Fuller won his campaign, then the High Commission would lose all its jurisdiction over moral offenses, or tithes, or prohibited books, as well as its powers to coerce those who would not go to church. If he was victorious, then Parliament would gain in power and prestige, while the Crown would see its prerogative diminished.

William Bradford did not spell this out at length, but he recognized that the Separatists were doing more than simply trying to evade prosecution. When he condemned Bancroft's canons and the Church courts for being anti-Christian, he also said that they were "unlawfull." By employing that specific word, Bradford makes the same connection between Separatism, due process, the authority of Parliament, and the right to a jury trial.

Undetered, the High Commission continued to close in. In December, they went after Brewster and a second man at Scrooby, Richard Jackson. They issued warrants for their arrest, on charges of Brownism, but both men had vanished: Brewster had resigned his office as postmaster. In their absence the commission fined them twenty pounds, a substantial sum.[34] It was the same penalty they imposed on Roman Catholics who failed to turn up to answer charges. By doing so, the High Commission made it plain that they intended to use the full rigor of the law against the Separatists, exactly as they did when dealing with their Catholic counterparts.

This was very new: the records from Nottinghamshire show nothing like it in the previous thirty years. It also created another alarming prospect: the risk of death by hanging. As we shall see, the authorities never came close to employing the death penalty, but it is quite likely that by the end of 1607 some of the Separatists *believed* that they were in danger of the noose.

One thing can be said with certainty: the Pilgrims ran no risk of death by fire, since the penalty of burning at the stake applied only in cases of heresy. Nobody ever accused the Pilgrims of that. Nor could the High Commission hang a man or woman for Separatism. It was against the law to attend "unlawful assemblies, conventicles or meetings" for religious purposes, but this was not treason. It was not even a capital crime. The penalty was imprisonment until the defendant confessed, took an oath not to repeat the offense, and then returned to worship in the parish church. After three months in jail, those who refused could be handed over for punishment either to the JPs or to the king's judges at the county assizes, where a jury trial might be required. Even if found guilty, the offenders faced not death but banishment. They only became felons, liable to face the death penalty, if they returned without permission.[35]

However, the Separatists ran the risk of conviction for a different offense. Nevyle used words that might give rise to a charge of sedition because, like Fuller, he questioned the lawfulness of the court. Saying what he said in court was not a crime, but it might be if the Separatists were found to be spreading the same talk in their area, or if they put it into print. So, when the Crown charged Fuller with sedition, the Pilgrims had to think very carefully. Even sedition was not automatically a felony: Nick Fuller was released and died a wealthy man. But from their reading, especially of Ainsworth, who carefully listed the sentences imposed on earlier Separatists, Robinson and Smyth knew that the Crown had used the law against sedition to send Henry Barrow to the gibbet.

Even if this were not so, Archbishop Matthew remained an intractable foe. He kept Nevyle in prison, still refusing to testify. Unable to find Brewster, the High Commission arrested Joanna Helwys and John Drew of Everton. They appeared in court on March 22, 1608, they refused "to take an oath to answeare according to lawe," and they were also detained in York Castle. Meanwhile, Robinson preached illegally at churches near Sturton, in November 1607 and again in March 1608. Then his name too disappears from the records that remain.

By now, the Separatists had already made their first, abortive effort to leave the country, in the autumn of 1607. This in itself, the act of emigration, was probably illegal, though the precise Jacobean letter of the law is hard to reconstruct. Since at least the 1540s, the Privy Council had required people to obtain a license before traveling overseas, but the register of licenses has mostly failed to survive: the relevant entries in the archives relate chiefly to Roman Catholics suspected of heading for Flanders to enroll in the Spanish army. We do not know how, if at all, the rules were applied to seamen or merchants. But whatever the law may have said, Bradford makes it plain that the Separatists expected harbors to be closed against them.

They hired a ship to meet them in a secluded haven, somewhere close to the town of Boston in Lincolnshire. Only after a long delay did the ship arrive, by night, but the skipper had betrayed them. Customs officers boarded the vessel, stripped and searched the Separatists, both men and women, seized their books, money, and belongings, and took them to the town under arrest. The local justices asked London what to do: after a month in custody, most were set free, under orders from the Privy Council. According to Bradford, seven remained in prison, to be tried at the assizes, but they were also released.

Little trace of this episode remains among the archives: merely a single scrap of manuscript, undated and overlooked, but preserved in the county record office at Lincoln. It lists fifteen Separatists, accused of "certaine unlawfull assemblyes" at Boston, "maliciously and with seditious intent," language drawn from the Elizabethan statutes against religious nonconformity. Among the fifteen were Richard Clifton and Thomas Helwys, and somebody called "W.Br.g": William Brewster, gentleman, perhaps. Alongside them was another interesting name, that of Leonard Beetson, from Boston, a draper, who shortly afterward joined the town council.[36]

Beetson was neither famous nor important, but other material survives about him that helps place all this in its context. Much later, Beetson became a close friend of John Cotton, the Puritan vicar of Boston who, in the 1630s, sailed to the new town of the same name in America.*

*When Beetson made his will in 1625, dying shortly afterward, he left twenty shillings to "our revrent Pastor John Cotton Vicar of Boston."

Sixty miles of countryside lie between Boston and Scrooby, and so this scrap of paper and the mention of Leonard Beetson suggest that by 1607 Brewster and Helwys had already built a far-flung movement. Their extended network linked them directly to the local municipal rulers of a distant town that many years later became one of the principal sources of English settlers in Massachusetts, a decade after the voyage of the *Mayflower.* It seems that the original organization of Separatists was far larger than scholars have recognized. The ties between the Separatists and the later migrants to New Boston may have been much closer than those described in standard histories of these events.

No further attempt at escape was possible during the winter. Conditions were atrocious: "most miserable . . . frost and snow for many weeks . . . such weather as no man could travel through," as Toby Matthew put it in his diary. Then, in the spring of 1608, Thomas Helwys led a party of Separatists who tried again. This time we can describe the episode exactly as it happened, and again with new sources beyond William Bradford.

Chapter Nine

Stallingborough Flats

Betweene Grimsbe and Hull . . . was a large comone a good way distante from any town.

—William Bradford, describing the site of the flight of the Pilgrims by sea from England in 1608

It was May 12, a cold Thursday, about four in the afternoon. The flood tide had peaked, the brown foam of the river had turned to a rapid ebb, and the wind had begun to blow from the higher ground upstream. The moment had come for ships bound down the estuary to slip their moorings, and to look for the deep channel toward the open sea.

The *Francis,* a sailing barge built to carry coal, swung at her anchor in the shallows in Stallingborough Haven, on the south bank of the Humber. Here a stream flowed slowly down between salt marshes, where sheep grazed three or four to the acre. At the point where it entered the river, the stream carved a deep trench, winding out through the mud of the haven until it merged with the breakers. On the mud, churned into rust-colored puddles like dung beside a cattle trough, an onlooker would have seen black-and-white wading birds picking out cockles with their long beaks.

This was the widest point on the estuary, nearly six miles across in the year 1608, far wider than today, but the width was deceptive. At the flood, each tide carried in from the North Sea many hundreds of tons of silt, to be washed out again with the ebb. But the frequent storms stemmed the outflow, and the red and brown clay particles dropped down to form a cordon of shifting mudflats. Stallingborough Haven lay at the thin, northernmost tip of the largest of the flats, a long wedge of mud that fanned out southward along the shore as far as Grimsby, five miles away.

Covered with shallow water at high tide, when seen from a distance at low tide the flats seemed to form a solid, dry beach, but again the appearance was misleading. Anybody trying to cross them would find that a man's boot sinks deeply into the upper layers of the wet silt. A soft ooze, it has a color and a thickness that resemble dirty pink heavy cream.

The mudflats shelved downward with only the gentlest of gradients. Even two thousand yards from the shore, in places the water was barely three feet deep. For this reason, the mayor and burgesses of Hull, the chief port of the Humber, had placed a buoy or a beacon on Burcom Shoal, a mile or so out into the estuary from Stallingborough. It warned mariners to follow the seaward channel to its north. But in the dark, in the frequent fogs, or caught between tides and winds beating against each other in opposite directions, even a local skipper with a flat-bottomed craft could find himself stranded by sandbanks that constantly moved and might baffle the most experienced pilot.[1]

So it had been with the *Francis.* She came from Hull, farther up the river, her master was Henry Spencer, and the customs records describe her as a vessel of fifty tons, capable of long coasting voyages from Tyneside to the Thames. And yet the falling tide had trapped her on Wednesday on the flats at Stallingborough. Seeking refuge from a heavy swell, she had entered the haven and found herself grounded, unable to move until Thursday noon.

In the ordinary way of things, the delay might have caused little harm. The usual business of vessels the size of the *Francis* was to pick up coal, either from Newcastle or from the quaysides by the river Trent, and then to ferry it to Hull or all the way down to London to feed the kitchen fires of the capital. There as well as in Yorkshire the winter had been harsh, the coldest perhaps for more than forty years, freezing the river at London Bridge. Whatever the date of Spencer's arrival, demand would be keen, as householders filled their cellars for the following year.[2]

On this occasion, however, the ship's cargo consisted not of coal but of human beings and their belongings. Spencer docked at Gainsborough on Monday, and then the following morning, May 10, he received aboard ten women, three children, and two men, one old and one young. As she passed down the Trent, and then into the Humber, the *Francis* must have made more stops at the creeks and river ports along the way, because by the time she reached Stallingborough on Wednesday, she was filled with between eighty and a hundred passengers. Their bed linen, chests, and trunks came with them, amid the coal dust, and they were seasick. Shallow though it was, the Humber had a foul reputation for choppy voyages.

Because of the people, another sailing vessel waited in the estuary not far from the shore, somewhere close to the spot where today a light vessel has replaced the old Tudor beacon. She intended to take the passengers of the *Francis* across the sea, to her own home port. She was foreign, this other craft, a Dutchman bound back to Amsterdam, and most likely smaller than the barge she had come to meet. She was a hoy, the name given to a tiny Dutch ship with a single mast, rigged fore and aft, the sort of bustling little thing we see today crowding the foreground of oil paintings by Frans Hals.

As the tide ebbed, she hoisted her anchor and her sails, but before she did so, a rowboat put out to meet her. The two oarsmen and the boat belonged to the *Francis,* and they carried as many as sixteen men who had been waiting on the shore, pacing up and down above the mud. They had come on foot over the chain of low hills, the Wolds, which run parallel to the coastline a few miles inland. At about four o'clock they clambered out of the rowboat and into the Dutch hoy. As they did so, they looked back and saw a troop of armed men, on horseback and on foot, hurrying down toward the haven. The members of the troop carried guns and bills, an infantry weapon of the day, a curved blade mounted on a long wooden shaft.

The armed men were most likely the local militia, under the orders of the Grimsby justices. To reach Stallingborough, they had to cross a wetland that stretched back behind the shore for as much as two miles, as far as the parish church at Stallingborough village, and then curved down along the coast in Grimsby's direction. A bridle path or two led across the marsh, between the grazing livestock, but the land was so flat that anybody walking along the path would be visible from a long distance.

When he saw the militia, the master of the hoy swore loudly. He hoisted his anchor and set his sails. Off he went toward the North Sea, taking with him his sixteen Englishmen. They left behind on the *Francis* their belongings, their comrades, their wives, and their weeping children. The Dutchman and his passengers reached his home port safely, but only after a difficult passage, buffeted by gales, which took them far out to the northeast, close to the coast of modern Norway or Sweden. Meanwhile, the eighty people left at Stallingborough divided into two groups. While the able-bodied men among them scattered and fled, the women and children and their leaders remained behind to face the magistrates.

THE CASE OF THOMAS ELVISH

On Friday, May 13, the justices questioned the master and crew of the *Francis,* probably at the town hall of Grimsby. They also brought before them Thomas Helwys, the man who led the attempted escape. Diligent servants of the Crown, the two JPs sent down to Whitehall Palace a copy of the depositions taken from Helwys, and his servant, and from Spencer and one of his crewmen. The event they record was nothing other than the flight of the Pilgrims from the coast of England, the episode of suffering and escape that William Bradford later chronicled with such emotion in his history of the Plymouth Colony.

As so often, Bradford passes over in silence his own role in the incident. However, so intensely does he describe the voyage of the hoy to Amsterdam that it seems likely he was on board and witnessed the events. It has always been thought that his narrative provided the only version of this affair, the distant precursor of the landing at Plymouth Rock, but this is not so. In fact, the depositions have lain forgotten and forlorn among the English State Papers for four centuries. They expand on Bradford's story, adding far more detail and confirming the accuracy of what he writes. They also place the episode firmly back within its historical setting.[3]

Until now, readers have examined the depositions perhaps only twice: when they were cataloged in the reign of Queen Victoria, and then when they were microfilmed, a few decades ago, along with the rest of the Privy Council's working memoranda. It may seem remarkable that the depositions have gone unnoticed, but the reason is very simple. The relevant catalog entry gives not the slightest indication of the importance of what lies behind it.

The catalog appeared as long ago as the 1850s, in the form of the Calendar of State Papers for the early years of the reign of James I. It was compiled by a busy archivist called Mary Green.[4] At the time, the Pilgrims had only recently attracted interest from historians in England, and Mrs. Green may have known nothing about them. She produced more than forty volumes of calendars, and the speed with which she worked meant that she could not dwell for long on each of many thousands of documents. By this time Joseph Hunter, the Englishman who knew most about the Pilgrims, was sick and elderly and rarely seen among the archives: he died in 1861. Even if Mrs. Green had heard of Helwys (and that is unlikely), the allusion to him was easy to miss. Jacobean writers wrote the name with an anarchic variety of spellings—Ellwis, Helliwis, Elwaies, and so on—and at Grimsby the justices found a version of their own. They described him as "Thomas Elvish of Basford in the county of Nottingham gen." In the index of the catalog only the name Elvish appears.

Whatever the reason, the papers have never been closely studied. And yet, from these documents, and from the scientific geography of the Humber then and now, it is possible to reconstruct what happened as it really

From the Jacobean state papers, the original depositions taken in May 1608 from Thomas Helwys (spelled "Elvish" here) and his servant, after their arrests at Stallingborough Haven. The official stamp dates from the reign of Queen Victoria, when the papers were numbered and cataloged. (*SP 14/32, fol. 82, National Archives, Kew*)

was, with no call for mythology. This material, and Bradford's narrative, are the main sources for this chapter's description of the flight from Stallingborough. On the Humber, the haven and the stream can be found today behind the steel piers of the oil tanker terminal at Immingham, visible when the fog clears, with behind it on the drained marshes a long row of factories making latex gloves and vinyl paint.

Of the two Grimsby JPs, the more active was a landowner by the name of Thomas Hatcliffe, who signed off the report to the Privy Council. His family labored beneath a curse, or so it was said, because they had taken stone from a demolished church to build their manor house in the village that bore their name. And indeed, the Hatcliffes soon died out, and their home has vanished, leaving nothing but a weedy mound. Their graves lie lost beneath illegible inscriptions in the tiny vestry of Hatcliffe Church, in a wooded valley a few miles inland. But in his day, people had to pay attention to Thomas Hatcliffe, because he was member of Parliament for Grimsby, and the leading local gentleman in a remote neighborhood where vigilance was essential, to protect the interests of the realm.[5]

Because of the silting up of the estuary, by the seventeenth century the havens and creeks along the coast of Lincolnshire had long since ceased to be commercial ports. Even Grimsby was semi-dormant, its harbor choked with mud. Its revival to become the world's busiest fishing town did not occur until two centuries later, when engineers built new docks. But precisely because they were so quiet, the inlets along the coast made places of secret entry and exit for smugglers or for Roman Catholic plotters. A long way from roads and houses, Stallingborough Haven made a perfect spot for shipping in and out illicit cargoes.

In the spring of 1608, it fell to Hatcliffe and his colleagues to keep an especially close eye on places such as these. Stallingborough lay beneath the jurisdiction of the customs men at Hull, but the chief officer there was under investigation for corruption. What's more, the poor harvest of 1607 and the cold winter that followed gave rise to fears for the next year's crop. For this reason, the Crown banned exports of grain and told local justices to arrest ships breaching the order. Then, in April, the Privy Council instructed magistrates to stop travelers leaving or entering by sea and to make them swear the oath of allegiance to the king before allowing them to go on their way.[6]

This seems to have been a measure prompted by the flight of the Irish earls from Donegal, and by fears of another war with Spain. Hatcliffe's inner thoughts will never be known, but perhaps we can understand why, when he heard about a group of people loitering on the seashore, he sent the militia to intercept them. Perhaps he thought they were papists on their way to join O'Neill and O'Donnell in subversive exile on the continent of Europe.

The true story took a little time to emerge. Under examination, Thomas Helwys flatly refused to answer, for fear of incriminating himself. Much the same was true of his servant, Edward Armfield, who later turned up as a Separatist in Amsterdam. Despite prolonged questioning, he revealed only two details, minor in themselves, but such as to help us reconstruct what took place. Armfield said that he spent Tuesday night at Caistor, a market town on the Wolds. This means that he and the men who came overland had walked thirty-five miles across country in more or less a straight line from Gainsborough. Thomas and Joan Helwys seem to have done the same. They arrived at Stallingborough on Wednesday, to spend a cold night with Armfield in a shepherd's hut.

The justices found Spencer and his crewman much more helpful. They revealed that Thomas Helwys had hired the *Francis* at Gainsborough on Monday, May 9, to take down the river a cargo including goods belonging to his cousin Sir Gervase. This in itself was a startling detail, which must have raised eyebrows in the courtroom, because that year Sir Gervase Helwys was serving as county sheriff for Lincolnshire. We do not know what he thought about his name being dragged into the affair like this; but his involvement may help explain why later, when the dust settled, the authorities quietly allowed Thomas Helwys to slip away to the Netherlands.

Sir Gervase was not a Separatist, but he must have been fully aware of what the Brownists were up to. In 1609, the year after the escape from Stallingborough, he made Thomas a potential beneficiary of his will, implying no disapproval of what he had done. Nor did any of this do lasting harm to Sir Gervase, who in due course became lieutenant governor of the Tower of London. He ended his life on the gallows, hanged for his role as accessory to murder in the infamous Overbury affair, a sensational case of poisoning in the Tower, but that is another story. Poor Sir Gervase, by all accounts not the cleverest of men, seems to have played merely the role of a dupe.

Perhaps that was also the way it was in the spring of 1608. According to Henry Spencer, early on Tuesday, May 10, the *Francis* took on board the first contingent of Brownists, the fifteen men, women, and children who embarked at Gainsborough. He was reluctant to say more, but the rest of the details were filled in by his crewman Robert Barnby, who had helped take the rowboat out to the hoy. He confirmed that the refugees had filled the *Francis,* that they had numbered between eighty and a hundred, and that the skipper of the hoy said that he came from Amsterdam.

The depositions say nothing about what happened next, but the mere fact that they survive at all means that the documents must have reached

London. Once again, the Privy Council had to ponder the fate of the Separatists. Once again, they reacted with moderation, just as they did when the Pilgrims were caught trying to sail from Boston. They did not unleash an all-out attack on nonconformists in the north. The explanation lies in the fine detail of the politics of the age.

The arrest of women and children created an awkward dilemma for the king's ministers, a point that William Bradford makes very plain. From the moment they were taken prisoner, they became a grave embarrassment, these "poore women in . . . distress," as Bradford describes them: "weeping & crying on every side, some for their husbands, that were carried away in ye ship . . . others not knowing what should become of them, & their little ones; others againe melted in teares, seeing their poore little ones hanging about them, crying for fear, and quaking with could." They posed a legal problem too, because they had committed no obvious crime, since they were women whose duty it was to follow their husbands: or so a lawyer like Nick Fuller might argue.

Was it an offense for them to try to quit the realm without the obligatory license? The legal position was muddled and uncertain. Nobody had codified England's many laws, which were full of contradictions, and of course they had also laid down since 1593 that banishment was the penalty for Brownists. Hence in theory the people arrested at Stallingborough should be exiled anyway, making it nonsense to prosecute them for seeking to leave the country.

What if the justices simply released the womenfolk and the children? That would create a new problem of another kind. With their husbands gone, the women would have no means of support. They had already sold their homes to finance the escape. Destitute, they would become a burden on the local taxpayers wherever they settled, and so nobody would wish to take them. Due in part to the new poor laws, English villages were becoming increasingly hostile to outsiders, to vagrants and beggars who might demand the welfare payments that the law required. Bradford says that the women and children were shunted from one JP to another, and from one place to the next.

This was understandable. Less so is the fact that even the ringleaders escaped stern punishment. No record survives of any pursuit or criminal prosecution of John Robinson or of John Smyth, and after his interrogation it seems that Thomas Helwys was merely released on bail. All three men surfaced in Amsterdam during the summer. Brewster and Robinson must have been in hiding in England before that, since William Bradford clearly says that they were among the last to reach the Netherlands. Smyth, however, may have been one of the men who sailed from Stallingborough, because he appears to have been in Holland as early as June, within weeks of the incident.*

In fact, the authorities took most interest in Joan Helwys, perhaps because she had already been in prison before jumping bail to join the flight from Stallingborough. Even so, she was allowed home, and then she vanished again, leaving the High Commission at York with the task of recovering her bail money from the men who stood as sureties. She, too, later turned up in Amsterdam at her husband's side. Back home, the seventh Earl of Shrewsbury kept watch on suspected troublemakers: the Talbot Papers show that he intercepted mail sent back by Helwys from Holland.

With Joan Helwys gone, only three of the Brownists—Nevyle, Drew, and Thomas Jessop—remained in the cells at York Castle, awaiting trial. It would seem, from one source, that they appeared before the judges at the assizes in York in July, but again they avoided harsh treatment. Less than a year later, on May 25, 1609, the Privy Council simply ordered Lord Sheffield to release the three men and banish them from the kingdom, as "sectaries . . . in matters of religion," the punishment they should have received at the outset. It was a course of action entirely in line with the policy of exclusion that King James had followed many times, in all three of his kingdoms.[7]

Nevyle and his comrades left for Holland, and with their departure the first act of the Pilgrim drama came to a quiet close. Periodically in the next decade or so, laymen and laywomen were hauled up before the ecclesiastical courts in the Quadrilateral, accused of nonconformity. Perhaps a Brownist underground eked out a shadowy existence in the area. As late as 1618, ten years after the crisis, there were reports of private conventicles at Clarborough, on the North Clay between Scrooby and Sturton, and a man from one of the Trent valley villages was arraigned "for beinge a separist."[8] We can also find subterranean affiliations between the Separatists of 1608 and later Puritan activists in the region. Even so, with the departure of Brewster, Helwys, Smyth, and Robinson the movement lost its local leadership. Not until the 1640s and the English Civil War did Nottinghamshire provide another challenge to authority of so blatant a kind.

---

*It is conceivable that the ecclesiastical High Commission in London prosecuted both Robinson and Smyth, because some of their activities took place in the Diocese of Lincoln, south of the Trent. Sadly, the London commission's records were almost entirely destroyed during the early 1640s.

For us, however, one question remains unanswered. Why in 1608, in the face of such a defiant gesture, such a drastic act of civil disobedience, did the Privy Council do so little and act so leniently, especially in the case of Thomas Helwys? To find the answer, we have to look at events through the eyes of the most powerful man in England after the king. This was the lord treasurer, Robert Cecil, Earl of Salisbury, the minister whose job it was to respond to the reports from Grimsby. In the troubled spring of that year, Cecil had on his hands an Irish rebellion and a minor fiscal crisis, and Puritan agitators were a sideshow. Furthermore, Robert Cecil and the Crown could afford to be merciful. They had already won their war on dissent. Or so they thought.

The Humber estuary at Stallingborough Haven, Lincolnshire, seen in May 2008 in fog at the same time of day and in the same tidal conditions as those when the Pilgrims embarked for Holland. The Immingham docks are located immediately to the north. (*Photography: Nick Bunker*)

ROBERT CECIL AND THE PILGRIMS

In 1608, Cecil found himself dealing with an almost perfect duplicate of the situation that confronted his father, Lord Burghley, some twenty-five years before, in the case of his kinsman Robert Browne. As it happens, a document has survived that casts a bright light on Cecil and his leadership, at precisely this moment. It paints a clear picture of the manner in which decisions were made at the very heart of Jacobean politics. The document is a detailed daily journal of Cecil's activities between May and July, and it exists for the following reason.

After James came to the throne, Robert Cecil gradually tightened his grip on the levers of power. The period of his greatest influence began barely a week before the events at Stallingborough, on May 4, when he added the post of lord treasurer to his existing roles as Secretary of State and privy councillor. His appointment came as an immense relief to the second-in-command of the royal finances, the heroically named Sir Julius Caesar. Wearied by the king's lavish spending, Sir Julius spent long nights of insomnia worrying about a royal bankruptcy, but in Robert Cecil he saw a man who would bring reform. At forty-four, and despite his weak appearance—he was small and humpbacked—Cecil was in his prime. He acted with determination. Within a matter of weeks, he put in place a battery of new taxes—on trade in luxury goods, spices, and exotic fruits—he hastened the collection of debts due to the Crown, and he ordered the survey of royal manors, such as Austerfield.

Awed by Cecil's intellect and hard work, Caesar kept a diary of his first eleven weeks in office. It covers the period during which the dispatch about the Pilgrims would have arrived from Hatcliffe. We can be sure that it came to Cecil, because the supervision of port and customs fell within his role as finance minister. He certainly knew all about the corrupt officer at Hull. Cecil's papers include a long letter dated April 30, which accuses the man of allowing the shipment through the port of contraband goods. Since Cecil himself had issued the orders banning the export of grain, he took a close interest in any news that arrived from coastal regions.[9]

By far the most pressing issue of the month was that bloody perennial, the Irish question. In early May, news reached London of a rebellion in Ulster, led by the young Gaelic nobleman Sir Cahir O'Doherty, aged twenty-one and the lord of Inishowen, the peninsula forming the easternmost portion of Donegal. After the Flight of the Earls, colonial officials continued to taunt and provoke the Gaelic gentry, including O'Doherty, until they pushed him too far.

At two on the morning of April 18, O'Doherty led ninety rebels in a surprise attack on the tiny English settlement at Londonderry. Swarming up from the Bogside, his followers took the fort, burned the town, and killed the governor. After Derry, the young warrior gathered a force of five hundred men, and with them he ranged across the northwest of Ireland, probing toward the English territory within the hinterland of Dublin. Sir Cahir had the makings of a hero, but in July he fell to a musket ball. His defeated followers fled, and the English displayed the rebel leader's head on a spike. Even so, the affair caused alarm in London. It might foreshadow a much larger insurgency, led perhaps by the exiled Earl of Tyrone, returning with a Spanish army at his side.[10]

If Hatcliffe promptly sent his report down to the capital, it would have arrived on or about Wednesday, May 18. The king was about to leave for Windsor Castle, and so that evening the lord treasurer welcomed the royal family to his own mansion by the Thames. Because James's love of hunting kept him away from London for long periods, during his visits to the capital Cecil tried to spend as much time with the king as possible. On this occasion, James would want to know what Cecil was doing about O'Doherty, while Cecil would be looking for royal approval for his new taxes.

Assuming, too, that the depositions had arrived, Cecil would have been able to tell the king about the news from Lincolnshire. The next full council meeting took place on Sunday, May 22. This must have provided the first opportunity for its members to discuss the Pilgrims. And, indeed, the diary of Sir Julius Caesar records that immediately afterward, on Monday, Cecil sent a number of dispatches to the north. Caesar says that they dealt with finance—Cecil wished to stop illegal felling of trees in the royal woodlands—but they might also have included his instructions, whatever they were, about the prisoners at Grimsby.

Of one thing we can be sure. During these crowded weeks, Robert Cecil impressed observers with his decisive manner. On June 2, he presided over a session of the Exchequer, the law court that dealt with cases having to do with taxation, and Cecil performed with what Sir Julius calls "admirable dexterity, quick apprehension and sound judgment." It seems that he displayed the same qualities on June 5, when he led an all-day session of the Privy Council, in the presence of the king. The meeting ended with orders to send four thousand pistols and muskets to Ireland, to reinforce the English garrisons.[11]

A man of Cecil's caliber, one who acted in such a way, would not have failed the test that the Pilgrims imposed on him. Their choice of a departure point showed that they hoped to escape detection, but Thomas Helwys did not behave like a weakling. His behavior had been an affront to authority. If Cecil quietly let Helwys and his accomplices go, despite their temerity, he must have had a motive. He would have thought carefully before deciding to let the matter drop, and to allow the Separatists to travel to Holland as they wished.

Happily for them, in matters of religion the lord treasurer was a flexible man. Indeed, Robert Cecil was so pragmatic that even the historians who have studied him most closely have found it very hard to say what he believed. Observers said as much in his lifetime, too. Only six months before Stallingborough, the king accused Cecil of being a Puritan himself, in one of those half-joking letters that James was inclined to fire off at his officials as a way to keep them guessing about his private thoughts. Others took the opposite view, that Cecil was a secret Roman Catholic, a man prepared to do anything to preserve the fragile peace with Spain. He was certainly a close friend of the man in the north who took the toughest line against the Puritans, the overbearing Gilbert, Earl of Shrewsbury. Even so, the baffling Robert Cecil made no effort to hand the earl the heads of Puritans on a dish.[12]

Most likely, he let the Pilgrims go because nothing was to be gained by making them stay, and because he did not want to give them a platform for oratory. Like his father, Cecil held the post of chancellor of Cambridge University. That being so, he might well have known the two intellectuals John Robinson and John Smyth, at least by reputation, and the bishops could have supplied any more information he needed. Highly intelligent and articulate men, the two preachers might stir up an embarrassing fuss if they were placed before a tribunal.

At this very moment, as we saw, the most brilliant lawyers of the day were hoping for a fight about the jurisdiction of the archbishops of Canterbury and York, for which the case of the fleeing Pilgrims would provide an excellent opportunity. For Robert Cecil it may have seemed far better, in the circumstances, to let them wander off into impotent exile in Amsterdam. Being the ardent Protestants they were, they would pose no threat to national security. They did not wish to see a toppling of King James, in favor perhaps of a papist invader.

Evidence from the playhouse adds weight to this interpretation. Two years later, at the Globe Theatre, a London audience saw the first performance of *The Alchemist,* the comic masterpiece of Ben Jonson. It mocked the Separatists of Amsterdam and Leiden. Most of all it made fun of a pastor by the name of Tribulation, a character who quotes from the same German theologians who inspired Robinson and Smyth. No one would have chuckled if they and their like were not already familiar targets for satire. That, perhaps, was what Cecil expected: that the Pilgrims had most to fear from the old anti-Puritan weapon of ridicule.

Part Four

The Project

Chapter Ten

The Tomb of the Apostle

So long as we be on earth we are strangers and exiles.

—Bishop Lancelot Andrewes, 1611

Two weeks out from Stallingborough, the Dutch hoy that carried the Pilgrims approached a narrow channel, the Spaniards' Gat, which led around the very northern tip of Holland. The channel passed between the white sand dunes of the mainland and a humpbacked island called the Texel, topped by the steeple of a church. Ships coming in from England had to pick their way carefully here among shifting mud banks, as hard to predict as those of the Humber. Once through the gat, the hoy would turn sharply to starboard and begin her final approach along the coast of the Zuider Zee, toward the river mouth that led to Amsterdam.

As the hoy crossed the North Sea, far to the south another group of exiles from King James had already reached their destination. These were the fugitive Irish earls, and they had arrived in Rome. They sat at the right hand of the pope, below the spacious dome of Michelangelo.

On May 19, 1608, the Earl of Tyrone and the Earl of Tyrconnell came to the Vatican to behold the making of a saint. St. Peter's was not yet the basilica we see today, with its long nave thrusting out like the handle of a sacred implement, from the base of the dome to the piazza, ringed against heat by its white oval colonnade. When the earls first saw the Vatican, the western bays and chapels of the nave had not yet been erected, and men were still building the facade. The church remained as the Florentine sculptor intended it to be.

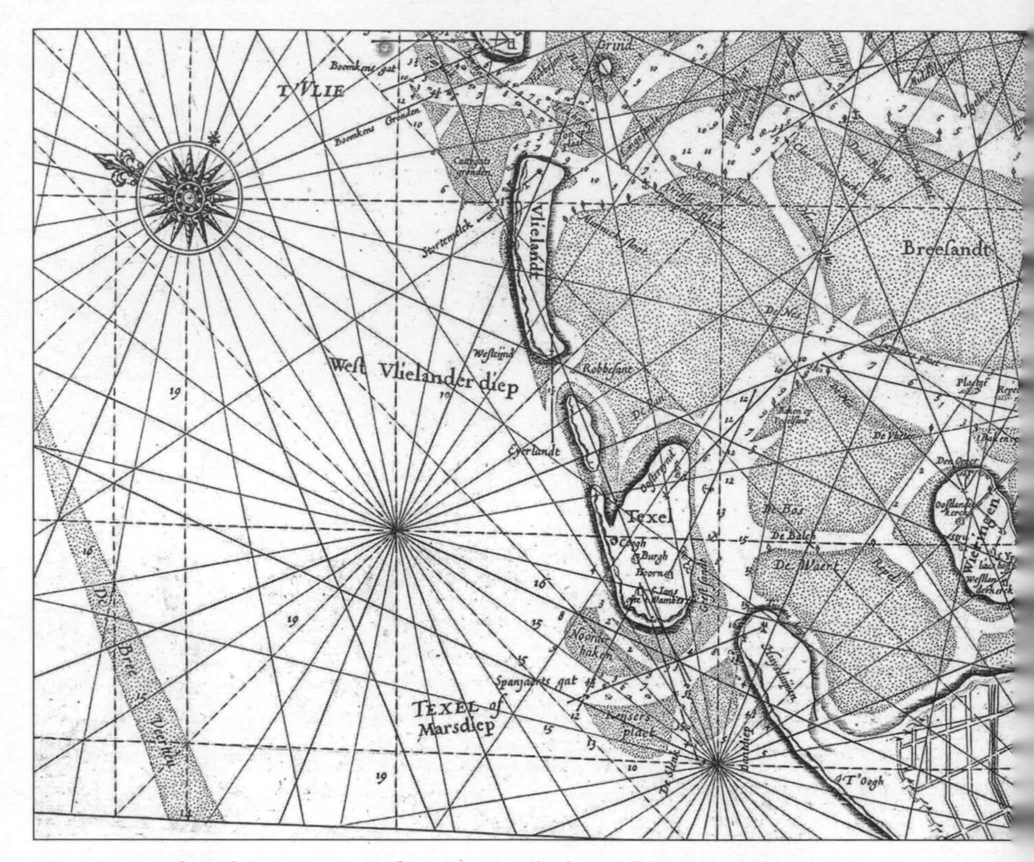

From *The Light of Navigation* of 1620, a Dutch chart of the approach to Amsterdam from the North Sea, showing the island called the Texel and the channel known as the Spaniards' Gat, through which the Pilgrims would have passed in 1608 (*The Old Library, St. John's College, Cambridge,* by permission of the Master and Fellows)

The earls climbed up the steps to a wide platform. They entered a building laid out like a simple Greek cross, symmetrical and balanced, without the vast dimensions it later acquired. As they paused below the steps, or as they knelt in the sunshine that lit the space within, they saw the dome shoot up above them into the blue sky in its grandest and most assertive form. It sprang up to the heavens directly from the earth, with nothing but the scaffolding outside to deflect the gaze of the devout.

Pope Paul, the fifth pontiff to bear that name, had told his nephew to invite the Irishman to the ritual which took place that day above the sepulchre of St. Peter. The nephew, Scipione Borghese, was of course a cardinal. There were thirty-seven in Rome: Tyrone and Tyrconnell visited each in turn in their first weeks by the Tiber. On this occasion, Cardinal Borghese

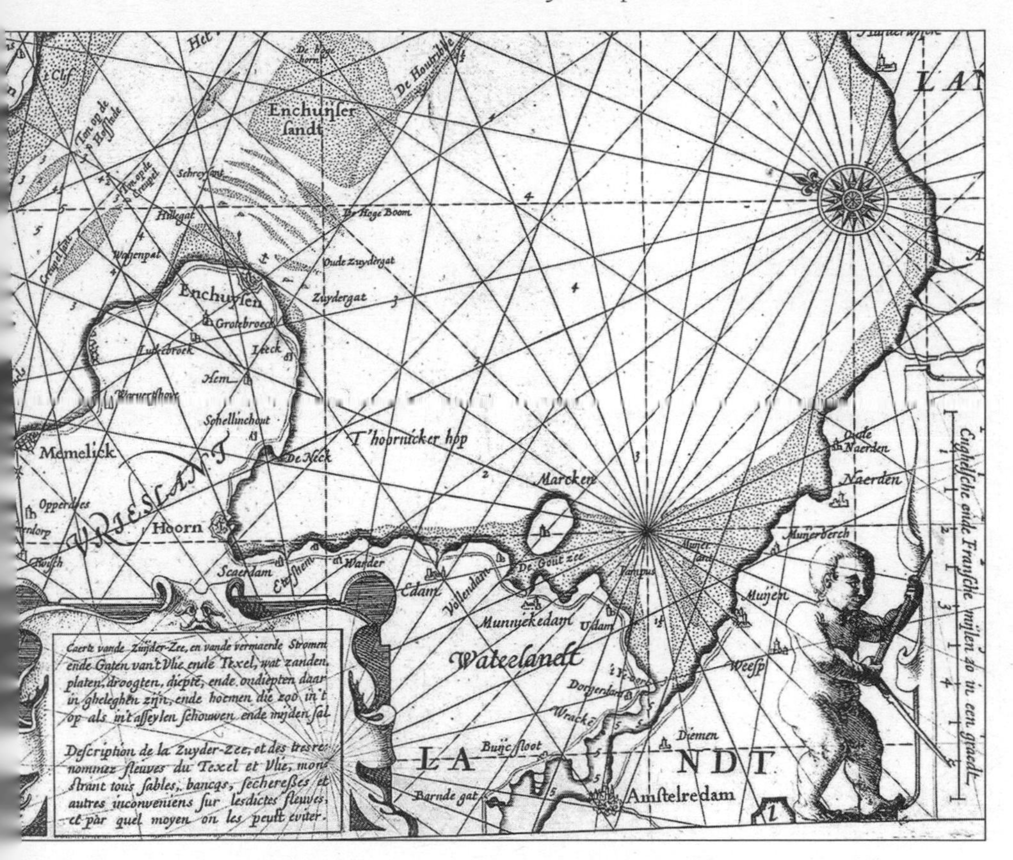

sent a gentleman to collect the earls and their countesses from the palazzo where they were lodged. He delivered them to their stalls, close to the Spanish ambassador. There they listened to the Mass, intoned by the pope and sung by the choir, "the most melodious in Christendom," in the words of one of the Irish party.

It was not the first time the earls had entered the presence of Pope Paul. He was a tall man, at fifty-five running slightly to fat. His beard was sharply pointed, and his hair closely cropped beneath his cap or his tiara. Soon after their arrival, the Irish party had trooped past his throne, ninety strong, some doubtless still with their long hair and woven mantles, each one kneeling in succession to kiss the papal foot. But the canonization of Santa Francesca Romana was by far the grandest occasion of their first few months in Italy.[1]

The young Countess Catherine of Tyrone came with the pope's niece, and she sat among the great ladies of the city. Enchanted by the event, perhaps she forgot for a little while her husband's many adulteries and his frequent intoxication. There she heard the Angelus bell, and also the bell that faintly rang to mark the mysterious instant when the bread and wine became the flesh and blood of Jesus Christ. She witnessed too the veneration of the new Saint Frances, a Roman matron of the fifteenth century revered for her works of charity, for her visions, and for the life of poverty she led in a convent cell.

And when the Irish left, and when the lurching image of the saint passed out of the basilica, the earls took with them gifts from the pope's own hands. He gave them a silver basket, a pair of white doves, a golden bottle of wine, and a gilded loaf of bread. Outside, the Swiss Guards blew their trumpets and they beat their drums. Above the river, the guns of the Castel Sant'Angelo fired a simultaneous salute. Irishman that he was, the eyewitness who described the event remarked with admiration on the superb Italian horses—"beautiful, mettlesome and wild"—that drew their carriages through the streets.

Every detail of the ceremony would have scandalized the Pilgrims: the bells, the nepotism, the marble theater of hierarchy, and most of all perhaps the Angelus, the triple Hail Mary. For them, it was the worst type of idolatry, the faithless automation of a formulaic prayer. As for the reception of the earls, nothing could have differed more from the first weeks spent in the Dutch Republic by the exiles from the Trent.

John Smyth set up his headquarters in Holland in the back room of a bakery, a place where they made ships' biscuits, not gilded bread. There he lived until his death four years later. No civic welcoming party came to meet him on the quayside, and the new immigrants attracted little interest. English Separatists had been arriving individually or in small groups for a decade or more, and by now several hundred already lived in Amsterdam.

In their participants, these two episodes of exile could not have been more unlike. The Irish were warriors, cattle breeders from the farthest Atlantic cliff edge of Europe, while the Pilgrims were minor gentry, yeoman farmers, tradesmen, and servants from market towns and lowland villages. For their livelihood, the earls could count on a modest but adequate annuity, paid by the Pope but financed by Philip III, the Spanish king. For the arriving Pilgrims, on the other hand, the second priority after accommodation was to find work. This had to mean manual labor in a country where, although the real wages of artisans were twice as high as in England, the jobs involved were tedious, repetitive tasks, mainly in textiles. As William Bradford put it later, "It was not longe before they saw the grimme, and grislie face of povertie coming upon them like an armed man."[2]

And yet the two stories had odd similarities. Both groups of emigrants had a chronicler who recorded the terrors and the hardships of the voyage by sea. The Pilgrims of course had Bradford, who told of "the fearful storm" between Stallingborough and Amsterdam, when for days on end the sun and stars were invisible, until they went down on their knees and prayed for salvation. Six months before, as they left Lough Swilly, the earls had their own narrator, a bard, the family historian of the Maguires, writing in the Irish language.

Harassed by contrary winds all the way down the west coast of Ireland, past Connemara and Kerry and across the channel, the earls and their companions had also resorted to devotion, but of a very different, Catholic kind. Somewhere between England and France, beset by a storm of their own, they fastened to a rope a golden cross filled with holy relics, and they trailed it along in the swell behind the ship. They too reached harbor safely, in thirteen days, almost exactly the same duration as the Pilgrim voyage.[3]

Behind both migrations lay unifying themes, and the parallels between the two were far from being merely coincidental. In both cases, the Jacobean regime's drive for uniformity squeezed out of the realm those who would not fit in, just as in Scotland it pushed into exile dissident Calvinists and Gypsies. Freedom of worship was a goal the Pilgrims shared with the Irish earls. In words that mirror those of the Brownists, Tyrone told Philip III that "with regard to matters of conscience," the English forced his people to abandon their beliefs, to take part in heretical ceremonies, and to swear allegiance to James as the head of the Church. Those who refused were imprisoned, or worse.

In writing to the Spanish king, the Irish earl addressed a man who had his own experience of pogroms.[4] His forebears dealt wickedly with their Jews, expelling them from Spain in the year when Columbus reached the West Indies. And in 1609, within eighteen months of the letter from the earl, the king of Spain issued another decree, casting out of his territory the Moriscos, Arabs who remained in Andalusia, after the reconquest of the province by his ancestors. In the course of the next six years, Philip III sent as many as 300,000 Moriscos into exile. They died of hunger or disease, or they were murdered when they reached North Africa.[5]

And so the Pilgrim flight from Stallingborough was only one of a multitude of dispersals, like the sailing of the *Mayflower,* and later the Great Migration of Puritans to Boston. If we could draw a demographic map to chart the patterns of diffusion, we would see the voyages of Brownists, across the North Sea and then the Atlantic, as a pair of small directional arrows among many other movements of displaced humanity.

Landless workers walked over the frontier from overcrowded France into less thickly peopled Spain, to fill villages left vacant by migrants to Madrid. The Spanish capital more than doubled in size in the first half of the seventeenth century. So did London, brimming with new entrants from the shires. Black slaves in Lisbon, Christians in Algiers, Armenians everywhere from Venice to Bengal, French and Dutch Protestant weavers in Norfolk, Welshmen in London, and Scots in Antrim or Roscommon: we would find them all on such a map. Like tidemarks on the sand, traces were left by flows of human beings, often channeled and diverted by the decrees of monarchs, but mostly lying beyond their ultimate control.[6]

Exile did not mean escape, and emigration did not put an end to politics and hardship. In Italy, the Earl of Tyrconnell died very soon. In the summer, he went down to the sea at Ostia, to avoid the July torpor of the city, and there in the insect-ridden marshes he caught a fever. Tyrone lingered on, drinking hard, trying to gather money and men for an armed return to his native land, until his own death in 1616.[7] As for the Pilgrims, they continued to agitate, as best they could, in the country where they settled.

Their shrewd old enemy Bancroft knew that this would be the case. In 1606, he had already written to the English ambassador in the Dutch Republic, urging him to stop Puritan exiles printing seditious books for secret dispatch back to England. In the case of the Pilgrims, Bancroft was right to suspect the worst. He also predicted that when Separatists were free to do as they pleased, their communities would splinter into a multitude of sects. He was correct in this as well.[8]

Less than a year after reaching Holland, John Smyth swerved away along a new and even more radical path. He insisted that even the rite of baptism of children was tainted by popery, because the infant did not give free consent. Only adults could do so, and therefore Smyth insisted on rebaptizing himself and his followers. This alarmed most of those who looked to him for guidance. Soon he split from Thomas Helwys, and the English Separatists in Amsterdam broke into fragments as Bancroft had foreseen. In the spring of 1609, to escape the quarrels and controversy, John Robinson and William Brewster led their own community to the industrial center of Leiden. There, eight years later, politics caught up with them again, in a divided city.

Chapter Eleven

WHY THE PILGRIMS SAILED

In Leiden . . . all these disorders, both in church and state, had their beginning.

—SIR DUDLEY CARLETON, JANUARY 1618[1]

In 1617, England's envoy at The Hague was a man of forty-three, a collector of tapestries and a linguist, an acute observer of people and affairs. One day in January, Sir Dudley Carleton left his embassy in the city and joined a crowd on horseback and on foot. Gawkers, artists, and men of science, they were hurrying down to the seashore to poke with their sticks a prodigy of nature.

On the western side of The Hague, beyond the last loop of a tram, today the beach at Scheveningen has an air of superannuated opulence, pacified by a pier and titillated by a casino. It was different then, when only a shoal of fishermen's cottages lay scattered along its inside edge. That winter, almost every day the wind blew from the southwest, bringing mild, wet weather to the south of England, but gales to the coast of Holland. The tides and the storms fettered Dutch ships to their harbors. They also caused the stranding of whales, at least four of them, here and along some forty miles of coastline, from Rotterdam northward.

One of the whales had come aground at Skeveling, as the English called the place, unable to cope with its name in Dutch. Skeveling was nearest to The Hague, and so it was the Skeveling whale that Carleton went to see. Most likely it was a sperm whale. The artists painted the creature, while

Sir Dudley recorded its dimensions: sixty feet long, and thirty feet around its middle.

Of course he mentioned the whales in the dispatches he sent to Whitehall Palace. As always, Carleton noted the meaning that people gave to natural events. Men and women remembered the beaching of whales at historic moments, when the Dutch began their rebellion against Spain, and then again when the two sides signed a truce. What did the whales signify? "They are thought to prognostique both famine and plague," Carleton wrote. An abundance of rats duly appeared by the Rhine, around Cologne, and then a pestilence that moved fatally northwestward down the river: it was probably either bubonic plague or smallpox. At Leiden, the number of burials leaped up, to reach its highest level in a decade. Then human beings added calamities of their own: riots and disorders, which carried the Dutch Republic to the brink of civil war.[2]

Sir Dudley had landed at The Hague twelve months previously, after five years as English ambassador in Venice. In Italy, by making peace between Spain and the Duke of Savoy, Carleton laid the foundations for a brilliant career. As ambassador to the Dutch Republic, he occupied a post of the highest prestige. The Anglo-Dutch alliance was the cornerstone of English foreign policy: he was entrusted with its safety. To his dismay, on arrival he found a country riven by dissension. His brief was to keep the Dutch united, with their frontier defenses intact against Spain. It was not a hopeless task, but Sir Dudley could achieve his mission only by taking sides in a violent struggle for power between Dutch factions.

Sixteen-seventeen was also the year when the Pilgrims first decided to leave Holland and to take their chances far away in North America. Perhaps they too saw the whale, since the sands of Scheveningen are less than fifteen miles from Leiden. Whether they did so or not, the Pilgrims found themselves pitched back and forth by the same winds of Dutch internal strife. This was certainly not what they expected when they first came here, a year after the flight from Stallingborough. All the same, by settling in Leiden they had entered an environment that might in time destroy them, a habitat as hostile as a beach to a stranded whale.

A CITY OF EXILES

William Bradford called Leiden a "fair, & bewtifull citie, and of a Sweete situation," and for some of its residents it was. It had a vast pinnacled town hall erected only fifteen years before the Pilgrims arrived. For its great university it possessed a lofty auditorium, with behind it a scientific garden for herbs. Leiden also had intelligent civic leaders. In 1611, on the northern flank of the city, they laid out a new town with streets and canals arranged in a grid pattern, where they built twelve hundred new homes for weavers and their families. In foresight, this far exceeded anything undertaken in England at the time. However, Bradford wrote in terms that were too glowing. A few pages later he makes this plain himself, as he describes the Pilgrim motives for leaving the city to go to America, but as so often his narrative leaves many things unspoken.

No town in Europe had industry more dynamic than Leiden's. The demand for new housing arose because the city grew at alarming speed. The university was founded in 1575, soon after Leiden survived a siege by the Spaniards. At that time it had a population of ten thousand. By 1622, the number of inhabitants had soared to forty-five thousand, thanks to floods of immigrants coming to work in its textile industry. If we wanted a later city to compare with Leiden, what might the closest likeness be? Chicago in 1890, perhaps, a new metropolis with the same extremes of inequality, the same volatile politics, and a religious divide. To complete the parallel, we would have to assume that a Spanish army occupied Milwaukee, waiting to attack.[3]

The rulers of Leiden understood perfectly well the economic forces that made their city what it was. Their favorite artist was Isaac Claesz van Swanenburg, and in the middle of the 1590s they commissioned him to portray the source of the city's wealth in a magnificent oil painting.

Hanging today in the town's museum, the picture shows the walls and windmills of Leiden at sunset, with above them St. Peter's Church, situated in the quarter where Robinson and Brewster lived. In the left foreground we see an old lady clad in dowdy woolens, colored black, brown, and maroon. Van Swanenburg paints her shrinking backward, as if she were fading into the gloom. Front and middle stands a tall young woman, wearing a white tunic emblazoned with red crossed keys, the Leiden colors and coat of arms. She offers a welcome to a slim young girl who enters from the right. The young girl wears a bright green blouse and a billowing pink skirt. As graphically as anyone could wish, the scene explains the secret of Leiden's success.

Fresh and attractive, the girl represents the so-called new draperies, light woolen fabrics, easily cut in a variety of designs. Woven in Leiden in rolls, nearly thirty yards long, white in their raw form but dyed with brilliant colors, these fabrics were known as *says.* They weighed much less than other woolens, and their popularity reached a peak in the early seventeenth century. Middle-class people, enriched by trade or rising rents, began to want new outfits with fashions that changed from year to year. They also began to wear undergarments. *Says* were ideal for both. Beginning in the late 1570s, the city of Leiden seized control of the trade, making itself the foremost producer in Europe. This happened after the siege, when a free, fortified Leiden opened its gates to refugees, driven there by war and persecution.

Painted in the 1590s, Van Swanenburg's depiction of the new draperies arriving in Leiden. Above the old lady's head we see the Pieterskerk, close to the homes of William Brewster and John Robinson, with the town hall to the right. (*S 423, Stedelijk Museum De Lakenhal, Leiden*)

The decisive episode occurred after the sack of the textile town of Hondschoote, near Dunkirk, where more *says* were made than anywhere else. In the 1560s, the weavers of Hondschoote became ardent Calvinists, pillaging churches and killing priests, and when the time came they joined the revolt against Spain. In support of the rebels a French army arrived in 1582 but the troops soon fell out with the townspeople. They sacked and burned Hondschoote, destroying nine hundred workshops, and the *say* weavers fled: some to England and to Germany, but most of all to Leiden. The city welcomed them warmly, and it gave them religious freedom: not absolute religious liberty, because that never existed in the Dutch Republic, but at least the right not to join a state church. Holland did not have one. With the weavers from Hondschoote came the fabric symbolized by Van Swanenburg's maiden.[4]

As a result, Leiden grew rich. As the years went by and demand for its cloth continued to grow, the city continued to attract new immigrants. They came not only from Hondschoote but also from Bruges, Ghent, and Ypres, and then from Antwerp after it fell to Parma in 1585. In due course, Leiden readily allowed the Pilgrims to settle in the city.

Robinson's group numbered about one hundred, of whom about twenty-five came from the Idle and Trent valleys. They reached Leiden in May 1609, after the city politely ignored a protest from the English ambassador, Sir Ralph Winwood, Carleton's predecessor. Both men, it should be said in passing, were reluctant oppressors of English religious exiles, interfering with them only when pestered to do so by an outraged king or archbishop. Carleton spoke with respect about the most eminent English Puritan exile, William Ames, whose sermons he attended. Not quite a Separatist, though not far from it, Ames was on friendly terms with Robinson. Despite being a nonconformist, for eight years he acted as chaplain to the commander of the English regiments in the Netherlands.

For its part, the city of Leiden had an obvious, unsentimental motive for offering asylum to the Pilgrims, because temporarily the city had lost momentum. Between 1602 and 1604 a long epidemic killed five thousand of its inhabitants. The output of *says* fell sharply, and took several years to recover. Robinson and his colleagues arrived at a time when Leiden was starting to grow again, but remained short of labor. Most of the Pilgrims found work as artisans, and some clearly worked very hard indeed.

A case in point was William Bradford. He hired himself out to a French silk weaver, until he reached the age of twenty-one. Then he sold his land in England and used the money to start up on his own. His business went badly at first, absorbing all his capital, but by 1612 he could at least afford to buy his own small house. This was success of a kind, since only two-fifths of families in Leiden were homeowners. Bradford wove fustian, a mixture of linen and wool, and he must have done so energetically. When he sold his house in 1619, it fetched 1,250 guilders: not a large sum, but equivalent to four years' wages for a laborer. In 1623, Leiden levied a property tax on householders, and if he had remained in Holland, William Bradford would have been eligible to pay it. Only a dozen fustian weavers were affluent enough to enjoy this doubtful privilege.

By settling in Leiden, Bradford and the Pilgrims entered another vortex, driven by international flows of goods and people: a fabric of migration in which religion was the warp, money was the weft, and politics served as the shuttle of the loom. For the majority of emigrants, the textile industry offered by far the most viable avenue of escape from whatever they were fleeing. Weaving was only one facet of an industry built on a multitude of roles, with slots for men, women, and children, whatever their aptitude, dexterity, or physical strength. So we find the English in Leiden working as processors of wool as well as weavers, and there were many other opportunities, in shearing, spinning, dyeing, and "fulling," or beating and kneading cloth in tubs or pits with fuller's earth.

Workers of each kind needed helpers and suppliers, makers of soap or shears or the lads who brought beer to quench the thirst of men combing wool, an exhausting business. Van Swanenburg painted all of this as well: in the Leiden museum, immediately opposite his allegory of the old and the new draperies, visitors will find his crowded cycle of paintings of the many stages of cloth manufacture, from the import of raw wool by sea to the sale of the final product by haggling merchants. He completed the last one in 1607, two years before the Pilgrims arrived.

Van Swanenburg portrayed a thriving, confident city, but it had a dark side that he did not expose. The vortex might all too easily become a whirlpool where the migrants were the most at risk of drowning. In a trade depression, or during a war, demand would wilt, slashing the income of textile workers, who were paid by the piece. This happened during the European slump in the 1620s. The output of *says* in Leiden reached a new peak in 1617, bobbed up and down for six years, and then collapsed. Never again did it equal the heights attained in the year of the whale. The fustian trade did better, taking up some of the slack, but only after its own troubles between 1620 and 1622. Meanwhile, the price of bread in Leiden soared, more than doubling in the next decade, thanks to the resumption of war with Spain.

Furthermore, by coming to Leiden, a refugee found himself at the bottom of the social hierarchy. In Leiden wealth and influence belonged to very few. More than half the city's property was owned by a narrow class of no more than 250 people, led by the brewers and overseas merchants. Among them were a tiny group of the super-rich, fourteen magnates who each possessed, on average, assets worth 160 times the value of Bradford's house. In England, the typical Separatist was somebody rising like the Drews of Everton, but in Holland the ladder was blocked from above.[5] No Englishman could penetrate the clique of oligarchs who ran the towns, and neither could most of the Dutch.

Inequality led to bitter antagonism. This began to take a violent shape as economic conditions worsened. After the Dutch signed their truce with Spain in 1609, weavers and brewers in Spanish-held Flanders and Brabant were suddenly free to begin to fight for market share against the Dutch towns of the north. Competition forced weavers to make cheaper cloth, so that even during the boom years profits may have fallen despite rising sales. As wages dropped, unrest grew among the workers at their looms and in the breweries. It led to a first explosion twenty miles from Leiden at Delft.

To pay for repairs of their harbor, the port from which the Pilgrims later sailed, the authorities at Delft imposed a tax on flour in 1616. At the same time they refused to place a duty on imported wine, drunk by the rich. Workingwomen marched on the tax collector's office, with their children at their side, beneath a flag made from a long blue skirt. They attacked the town hall, ripping up records and smashing windows, while the burgomaster hid in a back room. Order was only restored when troops arrived from The Hague, and even then the ringleaders escaped over the walls of Delft by night.[6]

William Bradford lived in Holland during a period that saw an angry deepening of social division. As for the beauties of Leiden, they could certainly be found, but nearby lay insanitary squalor. Disease was yet another peril facing exiles who worked in the textile trade. People died far more often in the towns than in the country, and so a path of emigration to urban Europe might well be a road to nowhere. If the Pilgrims were to survive, they needed to break away from the sixteenth-century pattern of escape undertaken by way of industrial toil in a back street. The risks they faced if they did not were all too obvious in the stinking suburb where William Bradford and John Carver made their homes.

Life by the Back Canal

Modern Leiden has a long, wide, and crowded thoroughfare called the Haarlemmerstraat. A few minutes by bicycle north from the town hall, on the way to the railway station, the street curves from west to east through the heart of a low-lying area once known as Marendorp. Long before the Pilgrims arrived, Marendorp had ceased to be a village. By 1609, it was an industrial neighborhood, identified by the city fathers as a place to put the smelliest textile trades, those that turned canals into sewers of effluent. Fulling was one of the most horrid, and today in Marendorp you will still find a street called Vollersgracht: in English, the Fullers' Canal.

Narrow little lanes lead northward out of Haarlemmerstraat, and among them is Paradise Alley. Walk up it, and after forty paces you come to another long street, running parallel with the Haarlemmerstraat, but much quieter. It used to be called Achtergracht, or Back Canal. Even now it is obvious, from the curved surface of the pavement, that a watercourse runs beneath it, about six paces wide. This was where William Bradford lived.

The Achtergracht was what the Dutch called a *stincknest.* Even in the seventeenth century, the authorities wanted to brick it over because it was so noxious, thanks to human sewage as well as waste from industry: William Bradford's privy emptied by way of a pipe leading down into the canal. Pollution was worst by far in hollows such as Marendorp, where the canals could not drain freely. The same was true near the home of William Brewster, in an alley known as Stincksteeg, much closer to the center of Leiden, where most of the Pilgrims lived. Only sixty paces from Brewster's doorstep was a stagnant canal, another Vollersgracht, which had to be covered over in stages after 1595, because it smelled so dreadfully.[7]

Of course there was more to Marendorp than open sewers. It made sense for Bradford to move to the district, along with seven other Pilgrim families, because on the Haarlemmerstraat was the hall where finished fustians were inspected and displayed for sale. And close by, the city authorities had built something else that was very new, and very Dutch: purpose-made dwellings for the working class, two minutes from Bradford's house. They occupied a site where, in the Catholic Middle Ages, monks and nuns had lived in three cloisters in Marendorp. After the Reformation, the city confiscated their property and turned the space over to become a cattle market, a leper hospital, and then a housing project.

Between 1581 and 1606 nearly six hundred new homes for weavers appeared in Marendorp. Mostly they were very small indeed. Closest to Bradford was a complex called the Mierennest, or the Anthill, where a convent had once stood. In 1596, the authorities jammed more than sixty new dwellings into the plot that the monks and the lepers had occupied. Built of brick, with a steep roof, the weavers' cottages measured twenty-two feet by eleven, with two rooms at street level, with space for a weaving loom in the front, and a bedstead and fireplace for cooking at the rear. A ladder led up to an attic bedroom. They were cheap, letting each week for the same as it cost to feed one person with the staple diet of rye bread for seven days.

New as they were, these weavers' houses captured the ambiguities of Leiden. In a sense they were the product of enlightenment, planned and built to last. At the same time, they embodied division, holding the artisans at a distance, segregated from the wealthy, who lived on the higher and healthier ground around the Breestraat, beside a free-flowing river. Worst of all, the Back Canal harbored infection.[8] Centuries later, in 1832, the city suffered an outbreak of cholera, spread by bacteria in water contaminated with feces. A map of the incidence of death shows that the overcrowded weavers' lanes in Marendorp were among the worst affected. Paradise Alley and the streets around it became in time the city's most infamous slums, to be shamed as such by Dutch journalists in the 1930s. Nobody would have called them that in 1617, but even so Leiden had the makings of a death trap.

Understandably, historians have always lingered over the deaths at New Plymouth in the winter after the *Mayflower* reached America. But most of the English Pilgrims at Leiden stayed put and never crossed the Atlantic. They numbered about three hundred. In 1624, they faced a catastrophe of their own, the worst epidemic since the siege by the Spanish. In the space of two years, the plague killed eight thousand people, nearly one in five of the inhabitants. Among those who died was John Robinson, in the late winter of 1625: he was in his early fifties. A decade later, it happened all over again, when fourteen thousand people died in the Leiden epidemic of 1635.

William Bradford gave four reasons to explain why he and his comrades left the city. At the top of his list was what he called "the hardnes of ye place": poor conditions, endless work, and a harsh diet. Rye bread was eaten at Austerfield too, but there at least they could cook their own bacon, and their cows gave them milk and cheese. He also mentions a gradual weakening of morale, as in Leiden the Pilgrims aged prematurely, because of the hardships of manual labor. He lived before the language of industrial disease, but this may have played its part. Exposed to flax dust, workers with linen suffer from byssinosis, a lung disorder that causes a chronic cough.

Third among Bradford's grounds for departure came the burdens inflicted on children. In Leiden, they had to work from an early age. In Nottinghamshire, even the smallest boys and girls hand knitted woolen stockings, but there was a world of difference between cottage life among the open fields and the toil of fetching and carrying in cramped Leiden. Worst of all, Bradford mentions the fact that the young might take to crime, or choose to ship out on Dutch vessels bound for the East Indies. In the seventeenth century, half of those who did so never returned.

Finally, William Bradford speaks about the hopes the Pilgrims had of conveying the Gospel to the New World. We will return to this in due course, when we explore the motivation of the investors in London who financed the voyage of the *Mayflower.* Edward Winslow, meanwhile, added a list of arguments of his own for quitting Leiden: the fear of losing an

English identity, the lack of education for the young—Leiden did not have an English grammar school, like the one Winslow attended—and lastly the irreligion of the place. As he and Sir Dudley both pointed out, in Holland greed and competition transformed the Sabbath into a working day.

By the year of the whale, the Dutch Republic had ceased to offer a safe haven. The riot at Delft was merely a mild forerunner of what lay in wait. Less than eighteen months later, the city of Leiden became a battlefield. Years of rising tension, social and religious, led to a bloody crisis that added a last incentive for removal to America. Ironically enough, in Leiden the violence began on the city's annual day of thanksgiving. Within a few weeks, the Pilgrims were deep in their talks with the Virginia Company in London as they sought permission to settle across the Atlantic.

THE ARMINIAN BARRICADE

In Leiden, October 3 marks the anniversary of the lifting of the siege in 1574. It remains a public holiday, celebrated with herring and vegetable stew, the first meal the survivors ate after the Spanish retreated. Public holidays had a way of turning sour. So, expecting trouble, on the day in question in 1617 the burgomasters of Leiden installed squads of armed guards in the Breestraat, at either end of the town hall.

Kitted out in the city livery of red and white, these guards were known as *waardgelders.* They were a new force, about three hundred strong, raised by the authorities only four weeks earlier, because the burgomasters did not trust the city's militia. On the afternoon of the holiday, a crowd gathered to jeer at the *waardgelders.* They mocked them for failing to wear the orange sash, the great symbol of Dutch patriotism in the revolt against Spain, led as it was by William the Silent, Prince of Orange.

When one of the *waardgelders* yawned in the face of an aggravating boy, the crowd took offense. Shouting "Long live Orange," they pelted the guards with stones, and so the *waardgelders* began to fire shots over their heads. They struck and killed somebody watching from an upper story. Soon a riot was under way, causing two more fatalities that night. Seeing that they had lost control, the burgomasters called in the old militia to quell the disorders, only to find that after doing so, the militia refused to stand down. Two days later, the burgomasters began to build a redoubt in the Breestraat. Occupying the town hall, they sealed off the space outside with barricades, manned by the hated *waardgelders* and protected by two cannon pointing down the street.[9]

All of this happened only two hundred yards from Brewster's front door in Stincksteeg. During 1617, similar riots flared up in one Dutch town after another, beginning in February, when in Amsterdam a mob ransacked the home of a rich merchant. Incidents of arson followed, and the authorities discovered caches of homemade bombs, bags of gunpowder fitted with matches. Looking on in horror from The Hague, Carleton sent anxious dispatches back to London, often in cipher—Dutch intelligence opened his mail—warning that the country was disintegrating.

Behind all this lay religion: sectarian controversy intertwined with social unrest. For the English Separatists, the situation created new hazards of three kinds. One was obvious: the risk of falling victim to random violence in the street. The second was a matter of national security. If, as seemed likely, the Spanish intended to go to war again when their truce with the Dutch expired in 1621, then a divided republic might swiftly be overrun, ending religious freedom for people such as they. And, last but equally dangerous, the Pilgrims might find themselves forced to take sides and end up among the losers in a civil war whose outcome could not be foreseen.

Theology supplied the origin of the conflict. In the 1590s, some liberal Dutch pastors began to file away the sharp edges of Calvinist doctrine, raising doubts about the idea of double predestination and flouting the official doctrine of the Dutch Reformed Church. This they could do, because that church had never been made compulsory. It could never compel everyone to accept its rigid Calvinist confession of faith. Many of the republic's leaders never joined it at all. Those who did not included the central character in the drama of 1617, the Dutch statesman Johan van Oldenbarnevelt, the republic's prime minister in all but name. Seventy years of age and a veteran of the revolt against Spain, he distrusted the clergy and resented their ambition to dominate the state.

Oldenbarnevelt could not accept the idea that God created some human souls purely for the sake of damning them to hell. Nor did he wish to be dictated to by the Dutch Reformed Church, however patriotic it might be. And so, from about 1607, he sided with the liberals, or Arminians, led by the Amsterdam preacher Jacobus Arminius. Known also as the Remonstrants, the Arminians argued that God might choose to save everyone, and that human beings could freely assist God in doing so. More to the point, the Arminians were happy to accept that the state, led by Oldenbarnevelt, reigned supreme.

In all of this, Oldenbarnevelt played with fire. Theology stirred up emotions, and he had made many enemies: he was a brilliant lawyer, but by birth he came from a landowning family in the rural east of the republic, and he was an elitist. Nobody hated him more than the popular hero of the Dutch, the son of William the Silent, Prince Maurice of Nassau, fifty years of age in 1617. A brilliant general, and a determined foe of Spain, Prince Maurice was also amoral, an undiscriminating lecher, and a man happy to use religious strife as a weapon in a contest for power.

As Carleton put it, the disorders arose from "a schism in the church, countenanced and maintained by faction in the state." Prince Maurice threw his weight behind the Counter-Remonstrants. They were the popular

England's ambassador at The Hague, and later secretary of state, Sir Dudley Carleton (1574–1632), from a portrait painted in about 1620 by the Dutchman van Mierevelt (*Print in author's collection*)

Calvinist party, anti-Arminian, a loose and unruly alliance of the Dutch Reformed Church, the urban working class, and merchants eager for another war with Spain, not least because they wished to take control of the trade with the Indies, East and West.[10]

Each of the violent clashes of 1617 involved a sectarian fight between these two religious factions. The Amsterdam riot, for example, erupted because the rioters heard that an Arminian pastor was preaching in the house they attacked. At The Hague, thousands of Counter-Remonstrants occupied the city's largest church, opposite Oldenbarnevelt's mansion, and held it by force. Much the same was true at Leiden. There, and at other cities, the ruling oligarchy and the burgomasters were Arminians, and they mobilized their *waardgelders* to defend themselves against a popular rebellion. The barricades around the town hall at Leiden came to be called "the Arminian fence," and the city became a sort of Dutch Belfast, divided by physical barriers as well as those of creed and class.

How should the English exiles respond? Their sympathies lay entirely with the Counter-Remonstrants, because the Pilgrims were orthodox Calvinists, sharing the same stark dogma of double predestination. Their friend Ames acted as tutor to the sons of an Amsterdam merchant called Reynier Pauw, leader of the anti-Arminians in that city and a close ally of Prince Maurice's. At Leiden, William Bradford loathed the Arminians, blaming them entirely for the unrest. John Robinson took an even more direct role in events, actively supporting the Counter-Remonstrants in fierce debates at the university. His friends included the most orthodox Calvinist professors, ardent supporters of Prince Maurice.[11]

On the other hand, the English were merely foreigners, powerless and with little money. If they backed the wrong horse, they might find themselves in serious trouble. It should not be surprising, therefore, that the Pilgrims began an urgent debate about the idea of leaving for America, or that they found it very hard to reach a consensus. Which course of action was the more dangerous? To sail to the New World, where the traumas in Virginia gave little cause for confidence? Or to remain at Leiden, where anything might happen and where the economic climate was already difficult, and might soon become disastrous? The puzzle was all the harder to solve because the Dutch crisis offered a positive opportunity.

Suddenly the Pilgrims found themselves in full agreement with King James about a religious question. From the very outset, both Carleton and the king supported the Counter-Remonstrants, and not merely because they felt that the Arminians were troublemakers, hairsplitters who endangered peace and prosperity. They also disliked Oldenbarnevelt. He often irritated the English by being too close to France or negotiating hard in disputes about trade. It was also rumored that Oldenbarnevelt took bribes from the Spanish. For England, the much younger Prince Maurice seemed far more attractive in every way.

By the autumn of 1617, Maurice had made it clear that he would use force if necessary to defend the Counter-Remonstrants. With the army behind him, the prince was bound to win, an outcome that would suit the English very well. A military dictatorship led by the prince would unite the Dutch Republic and ensure that it stood firm against Spain. In all of this there lay a certain irony, which people noticed at the time: that, among the Dutch, King James was aligned with exactly the kind of Calvinist zealots whom he most disliked at home. For the Pilgrims, the situation had obvious benefits, all the same, by making them more acceptable to the English authorities. The king counted as his allies in Holland the very same Calvinist clerics who lived close to John Robinson and considered him their friend.

So, that autumn, the Pilgrims sent John Carver back to London, along with another exile, Robert Cushman, who made an arduous living in Leiden combing wool. Cushman and Carver began the talks with the Virginia Company. They took with them the Seven Articles, a declaration of belief that explained how conventional the Pilgrims were in their theology. As so often, Bradford does not give the date, but the mission appears to have taken place immediately after the riots in the Breestraat. On November 12, the company's treasurer, Sir Edwin Sandys, wrote a friendly letter back to Robinson and Brewster, praising the Seven Articles and promising to help.

Things did not go badly for the Pilgrims in the ensuing months. With the help of Sir John Wolstenholme, Fulke Greville, and Sir Robert Naunton they received royal consent to go to America. They had little hope of obtaining support by way of capital from the Virginia Company, but in Leiden they found themselves on the winning side. During 1618, Prince Maurice gradually isolated Oldenbarnevelt and the province of Holland, where the Arminians were strongest, while he mobilized his own base of supporters.

In the summer and autumn, he disarmed the *waardgelders,* and in September the Arminian barricade came down. The following month Prince Maurice ousted the burgomasters of Leiden and installed a new town council. Huge crowds turned out to carry him into the city, "with much applause of the people," Carleton told Naunton: "The boys marched about the town with a flag and a drum . . . felling Arminians by the score."[12] Prince Maurice toppled Oldenbarnevelt, having him arrested on a charge of treason. After a show trial, Oldenbarnevelt was beheaded in May 1619.

By this time, however, the Pilgrims themselves had stumbled off course. As we shall see, they had a good chance of finding merchants in Amsterdam ready to finance the voyage, but in London their period of royal approval turned out to be brief. King James did not prohibit them from sailing to America, but he did find a new reason to be very angry with William Brewster.

In 1616, Brewster hit upon a promising scheme, combining evangelism and the profit motive. At first, he had suffered worse than most in Leiden,

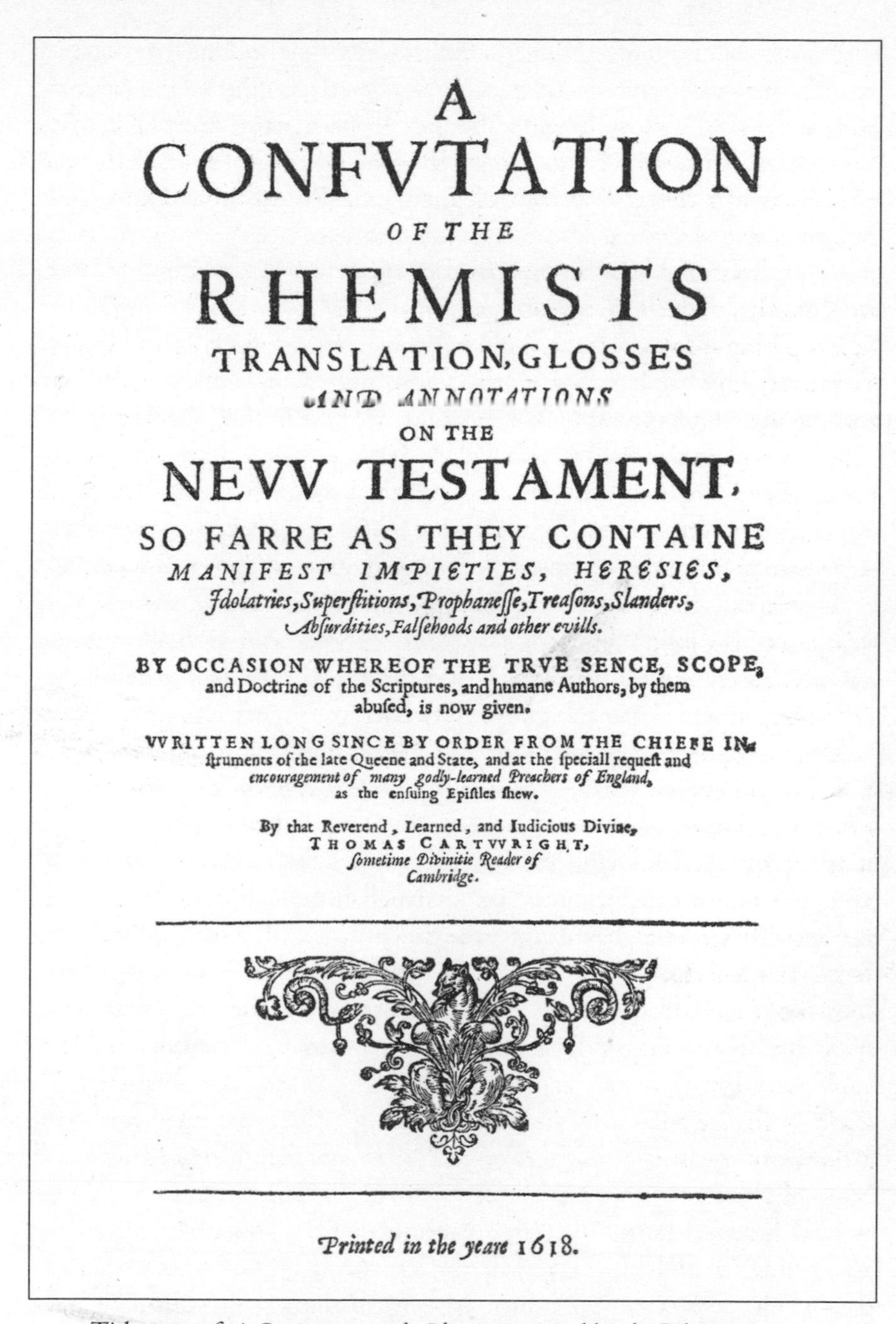

A
CONFVTATION
OF THE
RHEMISTS
TRANSLATION, GLOSSES
AND ANNOTATIONS
ON THE
NEVV TESTAMENT.
SO FARRE AS THEY CONTAINE
MANIFEST IMPIETIES, HERESIES, Idolatries, Superstitions, Prophanesse, Treasons, Slanders, Absurdities, Falsehoods and other evills.

BY OCCASION WHEREOF THE TRVE SENCE, SCOPE, and Doctrine of the Scriptures, and humane Authors, by them abused, is now given.

VVRITTEN LONG SINCE BY ORDER FROM THE CHIEFE INstruments of the late Queene and State, and at the speciall request and *encouragement of many godly-learned Preachers of England,* as the ensuing Epistles shew.

By that Reverend, Learned, and Iudicious Divine,
THOMAS CARTVVRIGHT,
sometime Divinitie Reader of Cambridge.

Printed in the yeare 1618.

Title page of *A Confutation of the Rhemists,* printed by the Pilgrims at Leiden. This copy belonged to the poet Edward Benlowes (1602–76). A Royalist during the English Civil War, Benlowes was not a Puritan, but he was fiercely anti-Catholic, and this seems to have been the book's appeal. (*The Old Library, St. John's College, Cambridge,* by permission of the Master and Fellows) because of the strain of keeping his large family—he and his wife brought with them five children—and because as a gentleman he had never done manual work. Gradually, he built a reputation as a tutor, teaching English to wealthy Danes and Germans studying at the university. Then, with backing from another Separatist, a minor landowner from Kent called Thomas Brewer, he went into the book trade. In early 1617, the Pilgrims began publishing titles at Leiden, mostly expensive, finely bound volumes for sale to academic Puritans at home.

The Pilgrim Press issued about nineteen books. By far their biggest seller was a thick, handsome folio by the great Thomas Cartwright, bearing the ponderous title *A Confutation of the Rhemists.* Written in the 1580s, and commissioned originally by Puritan sympathizers, including Walsingham, it was an anti-Catholic commentary on the New Testament. Although nothing in it was subversive, it fell afoul of a system of censorship introduced in 1586, when the Star Chamber decreed that printers must obtain a license from the archbishop of Canterbury for any title they sold. John Whitgift banned Cartwright's book, fearing that it might enhance his reputation. It languished unpublished until 1618, when Brewster revived it and began shipping copies back to England.[13]

Although it was unlicensed, the *Confutation* must have sold openly and well, because nearly sixty copies still exist, fifteen of them in college libraries at Oxford. It would have been impossible to smuggle a book as hefty as this in such quantities. It seems that Brewster had found a profitable niche: books a little too hot for English publishers to handle, but not scandalous enough to bring the full weight of authority crashing down. The following year, however, the Pilgrims went too far. On his list, Brewster included books by a Scottish author, works bound to infuriate a king who had suddenly become especially sensitive to criticism.

THE PERTH ASSEMBLY

For many years, the king had complained about scurrilous pamphlets printed abroad, mostly by exiled Catholics. There was, for example, a rebellious crew of Irish Franciscan monks who ran off seditious books in Gaelic from a printing press in their Belgian monastery, causing a mild furor in 1614.[14] Then, the following year, a pocket-size title went on sale at the Frankfurt Book Fair, written in excellent Latin, accessible to every educated European. It was a comic sensation.

Titled the *Corona Regia* (Kingly Crown), it was a satire aimed directly at King James. In October, an English informer in Brussels overheard two

Jesuits chuckling about its contents. A few copies reached England and enraged the king. For the next two years he made his diplomats devote much of their time to tracking down the anonymous author. Besides making fun of the king's pretentiousness, not least his posing as a peacemaker, the *Corona* mocked his heavy drinking, his habit of smacking his lips, and his vomiting after meals. Worst of all, the author broke a taboo by openly calling James a homosexual, with a preference for juveniles.[15]

Scores of dispatches remain to show how great a fuss this caused. King James became even angrier when the theological civil war among the Dutch gave rise to pamphlets that reminded him about the defects of his own state church. At this point, James was pursuing his cherished plan to unite the Protestant churches of Europe. He took very unkindly to any suggestion that he had failed to bring religious peace to the British Isles. His fury became still greater if any writer touched on religious affairs in Scotland, his old domain.

In the spring of 1617, James rode north to Edinburgh on his extravagant royal tour. In advance, he had sent up a list of changes he wished to see in the Church of Scotland, to make it more closely resemble English practice. Again, he wanted uniformity between his kingdoms, but he horrified the Scots by suggesting that they kneel to receive Holy Communion and by proposing to give more power to bishops. Leading the opposition was a prolific and popular minister called David Calderwood. Events soon followed a familiar pattern.

James summoned Calderwood before a Church court. Calderwood did not attend, and so the king had him dismissed, banished from Scotland, and branded a rebel.[16] In hiding in Scotland, then in a safe house in Holland, Calderwood wrote book after book attacking the king's plans for the Scottish Church. He found a willing helper in William Brewster and the Pilgrim Press.

By this time, the young Winslow, aged only twenty-two, had arrived in Leiden, after about five years as an apprentice printer in London. It seems that he came to work with the Pilgrims as a compositor in 1618, setting the type for their publications. Soon afterward, at about the end of that year, the Pilgrims began to print Calderwood's books. This time they were definitely contraband, smuggled back across the North Sea. The operation must have been successful, because today the library at Edinburgh University owns four copies of the most controversial, the *Perth Assembly*, and Glasgow has another three.

The Pilgrims had picked a fine time to upset the king, since his agents were still trying to find the men responsible for the *Corona Regia*. Meanwhile, Prince Maurice had seized power in The Hague, and with the support of King James he convened a synod at Dordrecht, with a view to settling the dispute with the Arminians once and for all. The synod began to assemble shortly after the comet lit up the night sky at the end of 1618, and the blazing star only made the delegates more quarrelsome. Despite the fall of Oldenbarnevelt, civil disorders continued, lasting far into the following year: in the worst incident, the army shot dead four Arminians in the town of Hoorn.

Against this background of unrest, James feared that the synod might fail or reach the wrong result. If it did so, then pamphleteers on all sides might be to blame for inciting controversy. Before the synod, therefore, he urged the Dutch to clamp down on public debate about religion, by Dutchmen and exiles alike. This was all the more necessary, since Europe was sliding into war and James needed a peaceful, united Dutch Republic as his ally. In December, Carleton persuaded the Dutch authorities to issue a decree banning English exiles from printing books and sending them home.

Brewster and the Pilgrims took no notice and printed Calderwood's books regardless. Illegal copies began to turn up in Scotland. Until now, Sir Dudley Carleton had left the Pilgrims unmolested, even though he must have known of their activities: one of his best agents was an expatriate English Puritan. The same was true of Carleton's superior at Whitehall, Sir Robert Naunton. He was a friend of the Pilgrims, not an enemy. Neither man displayed any eagerness to persecute the exiled Separatists. But at last, under orders from the king, in February 1619 they had to take action. And yet even then Carleton dragged his feet, risking the anger of his sovereign.

On February 26, Naunton wrote to Carleton to tell him that the king was furious about another libelous book in Latin, apparently written by a Scottish nonconformist and printed in Holland. Carleton went to Prince Maurice to complain. He soon discovered that Calderwood was the likely author, but he did not hurry to track down the publisher. Not until July did Carleton report that the guilty party was "one William Brewster, a Brownist, who hath been for some years an inhabitant and printer at Leyden." Brewster, he said, either had printed *Perth Assembly,* which was freely available in Leiden, or would know who had. Poring over the books in question, and comparing their typeface with that of the *Confutation,* the ambassador decided that all three books came from the Pilgrim Press.

But Brewster was nowhere to be found. According to Carleton, a few weeks earlier the Pilgrim had left for London. This was false: in fact, Brewster seems to have spent the whole of the spring and early summer of 1619 in England, where the Pilgrims were trying to close their deal with the Virginia Company. This they did on June 9, when the company granted them a first patent for a plantation. Then Brewster slipped back to Holland, where he lay low. He surfaced briefly at Leiden at the end of August, when at last he was spotted by Carleton's informants.

Even with the help of the Dutch, and after a reprimand from the king, Sir Dudley failed to detain the Pilgrim. After the authorities bungled an attempt to arrest him, Brewster went into hiding at Leiderdorp, a rural suburb only two miles from the Achtergracht. He reemerged in America, after traveling on the *Mayflower,* and the Pilgrims avoided mentioning his name in their early reports about life in New England. His backer Thomas Brewer was easier to find. In mid-September, his books, papers, and printing type were seized, marking the end of the publishing house.

Even so, Brewer escaped harsh treatment. Because he was a member of Leiden University, he could be locked up only in the university's own prison. Carleton had to negotiate hard before the university would allow Brewer to be taken to England for questioning. Sir Dudley had to give assurances that the English Crown would treat him well, meet his expenses, and release him after three months. Not until November 12 did the university finally deliver Brewer to an English officer, Sir William Zouche, for the journey to London. Even then, John Robinson came with him as far as Rotterdam. Far from putting Brewer in handcuffs, Zouche bought him drinks as they waited for the weather to clear.[17]

Like their friend Ames, the Pilgrims had made powerful allies among the Dutch. Given the politics of the day, Carleton had no wish to offend them for the sake of an affair that had blown over. With Robinson lending his support, the synod at Dordrecht had also ended well, settling the religious dispute in favor of the Calvinists and Prince Maurice. With that accomplished, and Oldenbarnevelt dead, Sir Dudley hoped to strengthen the Anglo-Dutch accord by striking deals with the prince to end the disputes about fishing rights and the East Indies that endangered the relationship.

For their part, the Dutch reminded him that King James was penniless, while they were rich: the Dutch paid the wages of English soldiers in their country. If James wished to play in the politics of Europe, the only card he had was his friendship with the Dutch, and they knew this perfectly well. So did King James. He fulfilled his pledges to Brewer, who was released unharmed. As for the Pilgrims, in the months ahead they came even closer to their Dutch friends. Until April 1620, less than six months before the

Mayflower left Plymouth Sound, they were still hoping to sail to America under the Dutch flag. If they had done so, their future might have taken a very different form.

Fair Offers from the Dutch

When Bradford came to write his history, he touched briefly on an alternative proposal. He says that "some Dutchmen made them faire offers aboute goeinge with them."[18] In fact, as Winslow later explained, two sets of Dutchmen came up with two alternatives. The first was for the Pilgrims to leave Leiden, but to remain in the Dutch Republic, and to move south to Zeeland and the town of Middelburg.

This would have made some sense. In Zeeland the political and religious leaders were refugees themselves, exiles who had fled north from the Spanish many years before. Pro-English and pro-Puritan, they had already offered to help by intervening with Prince Maurice on behalf of Thomas Brewer. When the Pilgrims communicated with England, they did so by way of Middelburg, which had an English business community. The man who carried their mail was John Turner, concierge of the English merchants' house. His name turns up in the customs records, ferrying over from London cargoes of pewter and English beer.[19]

Neither Bradford nor Winslow explains why the Pilgrims rejected the Zeeland offer. The reasons were most likely very simple: prospects would be no better there than at Leiden, and if the Dutch and the Spanish went to war again, Middelburg was even closer to the front line. A second proposal carried more weight. It came from the New Netherland Company, which saw in the English exiles potential settlers for the islands that it knew existed at the mouth of the Hudson. Once again, however, the Pilgrims found themselves caught up in the vagaries of politics.

Ten years before, Henry Hudson had first sailed up the river that bears his name and told merchants in Amsterdam about it. Since then, Dutch seamen and merchants had made voyage after voyage, with varying success, trading for furs up the Hudson as far as Albany and often clashing with the native people. More creatively, the Amsterdam skipper Adriaen Block made accurate maps of the coastline, from Manhattan as far as Marblehead Bay to the north of Boston.

So, in 1614, a consortium of Amsterdam merchants with interests in fur and whaling formed the New Netherland Company with a patent from the authorities in The Hague. It gave them exclusive rights for three years to explore and to trade in the zone between the fortieth and the forty-fifth parallels, from the Delaware north to Nova Scotia.[20] By 1620, their time had run out, before they could establish a permanent base. The Pilgrims offered one last chance. In February, the company told Prince Maurice that they had found at Leiden an English preacher—John Robinson—willing to take four hundred families to the Hudson River. There, they said, he would plant "a new commonwealth" under Dutch protection and convert the natives to Christianity. To make the idea more appealing, they mentioned the abundance of timber, ripe to build oceangoing hulls. From Prince Maurice, they needed two Dutch warships to protect the Pilgrims from rivals, including King James, who claimed the same territory for England.

Expressed in such a way, the project had not the slightest chance of approval. With war against Spain approaching, the prince needed no more quarrels with England. In any event, plans were already being made for a much larger venture, a West Indies Company, led by such men as Ames's friend Reynier Pauw, to challenge the Spanish in Brazil and elsewhere. On April 11, after consulting the prince for less than twenty-four hours, the Dutch authorities vetoed the Robinson scheme.

Even so, their talks about the project gave the Pilgrims a glimpse of a new opportunity. For the first time, they crossed paths with the mammal that came to be their salvation: not a beached whale, but the North American beaver.[21]

Chapter Twelve

The Beaver, the Cossack, and Prince Charles

The bever . . . is as bigge as a dogge, long, gentle, of blacke and shining haire, with a very long taile, and feete like a goose.

—Pierre de La Primaudaye, *The French Academie* (1618), a book owned by Miles Standish in New Plymouth[1]

In 1591, a yeoman called John Hall went to the gallows for theft, committed on a highway leading out of London. His punishment was routine, but his felony was not. In Middlesex, where Hall was indicted, each year seventy criminals met their end by hanging, but in his case the stolen property contained something new and still very unusual.

The items he took were clothes fit for a man of style: a pair of sea green satin breeches, a velvet jerkin, and a black silk and mohair cloak lined with taffeta. They belonged to a clergyman, one Everard Digby, fellow of a Cambridge college and author of England's first coaching manual for swimmers. The stolen goods were valued at fourteen pounds at a time when the average minister earned little more than twice that in a year. Among them was the finest fashion accessory of a gentleman: a beaver hat worth twenty shillings, or one pound.[2]

Hall was perhaps the first man in England hanged for stealing a hat made of felt from the fur of a beaver. First reported in Paris in 1577, beaver hats reached London a little later, in the early 1580s, perhaps on the heads of the Duke of Anjou and his entourage when he came to seek the hand of Queen Elizabeth. From the very first they fascinated those who saw them.

In 1583, the chronicler of exploration Richard Hakluyt inspected in Paris a haul of furs brought back from Canada. He described "divers beastes skynnes, as bevers, otters, marternes, lucernes, seales," and coming as he did from a nation of shopkeepers, Hakluyt swiftly appreciated the trading opportunity that the French had found in North America. As for the hats, the earliest literary reference in England dates from the very same year. Amid ranting disapproval, the writer recognized the commercial draw of this new luxury.

In *The Anatomie of Abuses,* Philip Stubbes condemned the wicked vanities of maypoles, the theater, and the ruff. Among the marks of sin, he included extravagant hats, and especially the new variety made from beaver felt. "And as the fashions bee rare and straunge, so are the things wherof their Hattes be made," he wrote. "Some of a certaine kind of fine haire, far fetched and deare bought . . . Bever hattes of 20, 30 or 40 shillinges price fetched from beyond the seas."[3] Stubbes spoke like another true Englishman, censorious but eager to appraise this new commodity in cash.

Whether or not the beaver hat was an emblem of vanity, it rescued the Plymouth Colony from extinction. By the 1620s, the beaver hat had ceased to be a foppish, eccentric novelty, and instead it became an almost universal object of codified desire. As Coco Chanel once said, a hat is more than just something you wear in the street. Its shape, its color, its style, and its erotic charge, the material from which it is made, its price, its maker, and the conventions that govern the display of a hat have a host of meanings in the life of their time. The beaver hat was far more than an item of headgear. When worn in London, it served as a gilded fetish, bearing little resemblance to the austere black cone familiar from Puritan imagery.

At the peak of their activity, in the 1630s, the *Mayflower* Pilgrims sent more than two thousand beaver pelts home to England, where their sole use was to make a hat. Without the fur trade, the colony would have failed, and the name of the ship would have faded into oblivion. This is something historians have long acknowledged, but only in passing and with little comment. More than fifty years ago, in the classic account of merchants in the new colonies, the Harvard historian Bernard Bailyn referred to the central role the beaver played in the opening phase of Puritan settlement. Nobody has followed Professor Bailyn's lead, and the early days of the New England fur trade remain a neglected subject, alluded to and then forgotten.

In the 1990s, a brilliant French-Canadian scholar, Bernard Allaire, used the superb archives of Paris and provincial France to examine the French end of the business. The English records are more fragmentary, but they complete the picture. We start with a set of manuscripts preserved in the library of the archbishop of Canterbury, at Lambeth Palace in London.[4]

Bacon's Beaver Hats

Among the most curious archives at Lambeth are the Bacon Papers. They include bills for beaver hats of the highest quality, supplied between 1594 and 1597 to Anthony Bacon, elder brother of Sir Francis Bacon, the philosopher and politician. The novelist Daphne du Maurier, the author of *Rebecca,* wrote a biography of Anthony Bacon, an exotic figure, a spy as well as a member of Parliament, and a man touched by scandal. He was a homosexual at a time when death might be the penalty. Indeed the bills include items for trimming and lining two old beaver hats belonging to a young manservant who was apparently Bacon's lover.

The hats came from two haberdashers, a father and son called Richard and Samuel Arnold: or rather, *le Chapelier Mr. Arnould,* as the latter liked to be known.[5] Anthony Bacon never paid his bills on time, and so the Arnolds kept sending new invoices for silk, velvet, and taffeta nightcaps, as well as for beaver hats and their repair. Because they did so, the Bacon Papers document the early beaver hat almost as completely as we might wish.

Anthony Bacon bought fourteen hats from the Arnolds, five made from beaver felt and nine made from wool, but the beaver hats were by far the more expensive. They cost five times as much as the inferior woolen model. Even the cheapest of Bacon's beaver hats carried a price tag of thirty-five shillings. It was big, black, and lined with taffeta. Above the brim, it had a hatband made of "Sypres," meaning a transparent, gauzy crepe silk, imported from the Middle East via the island of that name. A forty-two-shilling hat came with a finer surface, and an even more extravagant interior: "a blacke smoth bever lyned with velvet with a duble Sypres." The most expensive cost forty-six shillings, and sat grandly on the wearer, because it was black, smooth, and "lynd with tafyta and quylted in the head and a three pleat Sypres band therto."

When beaver hats wore out, or fashions changed, they could be repaired, re-dyed, and lined with new material. The cost varied from as little as one shilling ("for mendinge an old bever") to as much as sixteen, for a hat dyed and lined with taffeta and velvet. Because it could be reconditioned, and its shape or trimmings modified, the beaver hat became a flexible marker of status. Among the invoices, the cheaper alterations applied to the hats worn by Bacon's young friend, while the more expensive were Bacon's own. In an age obsessed with rank and degree, the beaver hat's adaptability gave it a special appeal. Soon hatmakers found a host of ways to give each hat a character of its own, with gold and silver wire and silk in many different shades. A dull old hat with obsolete trimmings would tarnish its owner's status, while a new beaver hat would elevate it. The same prestige applied to the men who sold the hats, and the Arnolds were far more than mere artisans.

Beaver hat makers were prosperous people, and the Arnolds lived for four decades in the wealthiest wards of the City, west of St. Paul's Cathedral, where they ranked among the highest taxpayers, near neighbors of Shakespeare. The Arnolds stood at the very top of the hierarchy of the Company of Haberdashers, the body to which by tradition hatmakers belonged. With as many as 1,500 members, in a city with a population of no more than 200,000, the Haberdashers came second only to the Merchant Taylors as the largest and most powerful of London's livery companies. In the 1590s, Richard Arnold served twice as warden of the company, and he belonged to the committee that ran its affairs.

They were aristocrats of commerce, the Arnolds, and they embodied links between exploration, luxury, and the Protestant faith. When the king granted a patent to the Newfoundland Company, among its thirty founding members were four haberdashers and eight merchant taylors. At his death in 1618, the *chapelier* Samuel Arnold left five pounds to "my loving ffrend Mr. Samuell Purchas, Minnister of the parish at St. Martens at Ludgate." A cleric of many talents, Purchas made his name as a zealous anti-Catholic pamphleteer, but also as the editor of *Purchas His Pilgrimes,* a sprawling compendium of seamen's and travelers' tales from all parts of the world. First published in 1617, it was read by the Pilgrims. It contained a sea captain's description of the neighborhood of New Plymouth, written only a year before the *Mayflower*'s voyage.[6]

Later historians have often portrayed Puritan merchants as troubled souls, afflicted by an inner conflict between religion and the stress of commerce. This does not seem to have worried men such as the Arnolds. As senior haberdashers, they supported Puritan clergymen, such as John Downam, a divine who acted as the company's spiritual adviser and wrote books that William Brewster collected: in America, Brewster owned seven copies of Downam's sermons and manuals of prayer. At the same time, they sold beaver hats with no sign of unease. Godly the haberdashers might be, but they saw nothing wrong in making a profit from the lure of the exclusive.

Versatile, sensuous, durable, but chic, visibly expensive but open to subtle reinvention, the beaver hat became a Jacobean version of the tweed suits designed by Miss Chanel. Worn by women as well as men—a portrait of Anne of Denmark, King James's queen, shows her wearing a splendid plumed example—it retained the status of a fashion classic for nearly two centuries. It did so because new aspirations found an outlet by way of the special qualities of the fur. Half the history of England in this period can be found written on the surface of felt hats.

THE WOOL OF THE BEAVER

I said that beaver hats were first heard of in Paris in the 1570s, but this is not strictly true. People wore them in the Middle Ages—King Henry III had "a beaver hat of the greatest beauty" in 1261—but they suffered a long eclipse after about 1450, when hunters all but wiped out the animal in Europe and western Russia. When they arrived in London in the reign of Elizabeth, beaver hats swiftly revived a passion for sleek and gleaming felt, and that was the core of their appeal: the gloss and texture of a material long affiliated with monarchy and wealth.

For many centuries, felt signified power and prestige, like the tall felt hat that the Greek writer Xenophon saw on the head of the king of Persia. When the three wise men visited Jesus, they might have kept warm with something of the kind, because another Greek speaks of the felt turbans worn by Persian priests, or magi. These associations between felt, monarchy, and spiritual power had their origin in the very nature of the stuff. The best felt required not only the finest wool but also a long, exhausting process of preparation. The hairs had to be sorted and sifted, kneaded and molded into a mat, and then bound together by rolling to form a dense, smooth surface. Owing to the effort and expense involved, felt making stood far above weaving in the hierarchy of textile manufacture.[7]

Because of the life the animal leads, beaver fur has a special aptitude for the purpose. "Water is his natural element, and he cannot trust himself far from it with personal safety," wrote the American naturalist Lewis H. Morgan, in a superb account of the beavers he met in the 1860s, when he was a director of a railroad company. Beavers spend nearly five hours each day swimming and foraging for food, and in Canada they sometimes remain beneath the icebound surface of their ponds for nearly half the year. So the beaver must keep warm and waterproof. Their tails must be big, to serve as a rudder or to thrash the pond water as a distress signal, but this requires a large surface area, prone to heat loss. Hence within the beaver's tail are thick layers of fat and networks of blood vessels that circulate warm blood and retain heat at the animal's core. The fur plays an essential part too, by way of insulation and protection.[8]

It comes in two forms. Shielding the beaver from injuries are the outer guard hairs, two inches or more in length. Too coarse to be used for felt, the guard hairs were discarded by hatmakers. Beneath them lies the inner fur, or beaver wool, like the soft down on the breast of a duck. This was the secret of the beaver hat. An average square inch of the wool contains nearly three thousand hairs, making beaver fur much finer and denser than a rabbit's. When the poet Ben Jonson wished to describe a woman's beauty, he likened it to newly fallen snow, swan's down, or "the wool of the beaver," and this was wonderfully apt. The fineness of the beaver wool gave its felt a smooth, silken quality that invited a stroking hand.[9]

Within its anus, the beaver has a gland that produces a creamy, viscous substance, a grease that lubricates the fur, making it waterproof. This too makes the end product ideal for wearing on the head. It also lacks the scaly layer of protein, which covers rabbit hairs like a sheath. Felt made with rabbit fur was coarse, and hatters preferred not to use it, until in the eighteenth century they discovered that a solution of mercury and nitric acid would remove the scales. Before that, beaver fur reigned supreme. It gave by far the best felt, resilient but pliable, fit to make a wide variety of shapes, to form the curves, crowns, and brims of hats of many different kinds. Its only rival was Peruvian vicuña, prized by the Incas and their Spanish conquerors.[10]

Beaver hat making had a language of its own to express the sequence of thirty expert steps needed to produce the finished item. Because the hatters of France were the masters of the trade, the principal source for our knowledge of the craft is an article in the *Encyclopédie* published by the French philosopher Diderot in 1753. Although some innovations may have intervened, between the time of Bradford and the age of Louis XV the process seems to have remained broadly the same. Indeed only with the help of Diderot's description can we understand what William Bradford says about the skins that he shipped home.[11]

Diderot's article makes a distinction between *castor gras* and *castor sec.* The *castor gras* appears under the name of "coat beaver" in Bradford's history. It refers to a beaver pelt that has been scraped, greased, and worn inside out like a coat by a Native American hunter, such as those who lived by the Kennebec. Rubbed and abraded and smeared with sweat, the guard hairs fall away. The hunter's perspiration gives the beaver wool beneath something that Diderot called "a particular quality . . . best for hat making."

The *castor sec,* or "parchment beaver," is a pelt that has remained unworn and been left to dry in the sun. Coat beaver was the more valuable commodity, fetching, according to Bradford, some twenty shillings per pound, compared with about fifteen for an unworn pelt. When mixed with *castor sec* in a ratio of one to four, the coat beaver gave the fur the body and firmness needed for strong, glossy felt.

To remove what remained of the guard hairs, and leave just the beaver wool—the *poil fin*—required first the use of a knife three feet long, wielded by a man. Then a woman took a shorter knife and carefully finished the job. Pinning the outstretched pelt to an easel, she separated the *poil fin* from the beaver's skin. She cut as near to the root as possible, taking the utmost care not to pick up tiny fragments of skin—*chiquettes*—which might cause imperfections on the surface of the felt. She divided the wool into three grades, depending on the part of the pelt from which it came.

On the beaver's abdomen grew pale fur known as *fin blanc,* best for gray hats. On the animal's back was the dark *beau noir* most suitable to make a jet-black model. Between them, on the flanks of the beaver, hatters found the finest, longest wool, known as *l'Anglois.* It was so long that it could be mixed half and half with silk and knit into clinging, sheer, luxurious stockings to suit the finest legs. Or, if kept by the hatter, *l'Anglois* made the grandest beaver hats, called *chapeaux à plumet.* They had a slightly raised pile like brushed velvet. And at this point in the process, any necessary blending could be done, by adding vicuña or fine wool from Spanish merino sheep, to make the raw material for a species of felt hats known as *demi-castors.* These appeared on the market early in the seventeenth century as a cheaper substitute for the best beaver variety.

When the various grades of fur had been sorted, there followed the most delicate maneuver of all. They used an instrument called an *arçon,* shaped like the bow of a violin, to sift the cut beaver wool into a mass of clean, fine hair free from dirt or tangles. The craftsman vibrated the string of the bow through the *poil fin* above a panel made of willow to form dense pudding-shaped piles of hair called *capades,* each an inch thick. A raw beaver skin of about 1.7 pounds yielded half a pound of usable *poil fin.* At least one pound was needed to make the four *capades* required for a single hat.

Next, the hatter inserted the *capades* into a conical canvas mold, called a *feutrière,* or "felter," resembling a lamp shade. Then, against the sides of the felter, with his thumbs and fingers he kneaded the wool until it formed a firm sheet of an even consistency. He soaked each sheet in a mixture of wine lees and water. He rolled it flat on his workbench, carefully checked it for points of weakness, and repeated the process. Next he used a wooden mold to shape the felt into a hat. He began with the crown, formed over a pointed or curved wooden block. Then he bent and stretched the sides and brim. At last the hat was recognizable. It was sanded, brushed, trimmed with scissors, dyed and sealed with glue and gum, left to stand in a steam bath, and then dried again in a stove. Passing next to the milliner, the beaver hat was ready to be adorned with the linings, hatbands, and plumes described in the Bacon Papers.

Buckingham, the Beaver, and Prince Charles

If men and women wanted beaver hats, they did so only because they wanted many other luxury goods as well. In Anthony Bacon's bills, the beaver hat dressed itself in silk, in a counterpoint of elegance of complementary kinds, the shades and textures of the fabric and the felt enhancing each other's expensive appeal. Like London's thirst for wine that kept Christopher Jones in business, the English gentry's greed for silk served as a sort of stock market index. It connoted affluence, and imports of silk soared during the reigns of Elizabeth and her successor. By 1600 London was said to have three hundred silk weavers, ten times more than in the 1550s, and by 1627 an expert on English trade saw this as one of the kingdom's most essential industries. "I will here remember a notable increase in our manufacture of winding and twisting only of forraign raw silk . . . in the City and suburbs of London," wrote Thomas Mun, a director of the East India Company, its principal importer. "At this present time it doth set upon work above fourteen thousand souls."[12]

Only a minority could afford silk, of course. Nevertheless, the landowning classes were becoming wealthier, and so were London's small but dynamic class of large overseas traders, not to mention lawyers enriched by a boom in litigation. Prosperity of this kind became available to allow the purchase of luxuries, among which the beaver hat was one of the most prominent. The most visible sign of the new enthusiasm for consumption was the first designer shopping mall, in the shape of London's New Exchange. It was opened in 1609 by the king himself. Located in the Strand, appropriately close to the site of the modern Savoy hotel, the New Exchange offered everything the Jacobean consumer could desire: two arcaded floors of retail outlets, with milliners and haberdashers on the upper story. In 1622, the Council for New England decided it needed new office space, and so it chose the New Exchange: where else?

Luxury goods were far more than frivolities. Before the invention of steam power, at a time when agriculture dwarfed every other activity, if the state wished to make the economy grow more rapidly, it had very few means at its disposal. The productivity of farmers grew painfully slowly as they fought a yearly battle against the weather, weeds, and pests. When handicrafts like beaver hats were perfected, they at least helped to circulate wealth, and they created some well-paid jobs for those who made them.

Unlike those who worked on the land, skilled men and women in the luxury trades did not waste the winter months in idleness. They also helped improve the balance of payments, a subject that worried statesmen endlessly. If a brisk retail trade promoted manufacturing, and generated exports that earned bullion from abroad, then so much the better. But of course this required the input first of raw materials, carried home by sea. The goal was to create a trading nation that shipped back from its colonies goods such as raw silk and raw sugar, fish oil, walrus oil, fur, and potash, and sent them out again as finished products: taffeta, marmalade, satin, soap, hats, and gunpowder.

Hence luxury goods were a tool of policy, and the yearning for them led to North America. Hating tobacco as he did, King James hoped that silk would replace it as the staple product of Virginia. Worms wriggled their way to the New World in their thousands, sailing alongside human emigrants, to take part in silk-farming trials beside the Chesapeake. As for the beaver hat, nobody did more than the king's son Prince Charles to stimulate demand, and so, perhaps ironically, the royal family played its part too in securing the future of Puritan New England. During the years when the Pilgrims first planned the *Mayflower* project, and then began to execute it, the beaver hat reached its apotheosis of glamour. It did so in the apparel of the prince.

Wasteful expense was a hallmark of the reign of King James. Royal fecklessness reached its most extreme point in 1617, thanks to the royal visit to Scotland, and the Crown's deficit came to nearly £140,000 for the year. This was a huge sum. The numbers become still more scandalous when we remember that England was at peace, and when we see how much Prince Charles spent on clothes, wall hangings, and accessories for his household. In the space of fifteen months, he lavished no less than eleven thousand pounds on his wardrobe: for one thousand pounds less, the East India Company could build two ships fit to sail to Java, each one six times larger than the *Mayflower*.

Five volumes of the wardrobe accounts of Prince Charles survive, in manuscript form in the National Archives in London. Beautifully written, immensely detailed, but never published, they depict in all their splendor the garments that the prince wore. We read of his tennis suit, delivered in

1618, made from nine and a half yards of green and light blue satin, striped with silver. Lined with taffeta, the suit was stitched with seventy-two silver buttons and trimmed with seven yards of ribbon and a yard of lace. In all, it cost eighteen pounds and nine shillings to kit out the prince for a game, excluding the racket.

Alongside the tennis suit, we find four pairs of yellow silk tights, for which he paid a total of six pounds. His robes for attending Parliament had to be perfumed, and this cost ten pounds and eight shillings. Of course, he needed to redecorate at St. James's Palace, and for this tapestries were an ornamental necessity. To make his twenty-one new wall hangings required 2,384 skilled man-days, and for this the bill came to £159. Close by, in the same accounts, we find listed the beaver hats bought by Prince Charles, and the prices paid: sixty-four beaver hats in 1618, fifty-seven in 1619, forty-six in 1623, and forty-three in 1624. They cost about fifty shillings each, before allowing for the hatbands and the plumes, which added perhaps another thirty-five. At the time, eighty-five shillings was the same price as the most expensive horse sold at a country fair, or eleven weeks' wages for each of the men who wove the hangings.

These beaver hats bore little resemblance to the tall, pointed specimens seen in imaginary Victorian paintings of the Pilgrims. French sources, and portraits of Charles I, suggest that by the mid-1620s the up-to-the-minute beaver hat was a model called a *mousquetaire.* It had a low, rounded crown and a very wide brim, sometimes sweeping up or down in an elegant curve, and it was adorned with a gold or silver hatband and ostrich feathers. The hats changed their color from year to year, matching the shades of the prince's suits of clothes. From this we can see how the court of King James and his son acted as the arbiters of taste, setting fashions that diffused through the remainder of genteel society.

The beaver hats purchased in 1617 were mostly black, with one white beaver model lined with taffeta. To go with them, the prince's staff ordered brightly colored hatbands, in crimson and gold, rose pink, nutmeg, and silver. Red seems to have been the color of the season, because the prince also purchased a suit of crimson satin. To adorn a favorite hat, he bought a rich plume for his personal use, for seven pounds. In 1618, the colors changed to green. The grandest hat that year was "a grassegreene Beaver lyned with taffeta," doubtless for the prince himself, and it cost seventy shillings. Green remained in vogue in 1619. The accounts include bills for four white beaver hats for pages, each with a green and gold hatband. That same year the prince's pack of beagles wore green collars and strained at green leashes as they trotted to the hunting field.

Four years later, the beaver hat reached its moment of ultimate splendor. It did so in circumstances that show how it became an international style, transmitted between the royal courts of baroque Europe. In 1623, Prince Charles and the Duke of Buckingham paid an ill-fated visit to the king of Spain, so that the prince could woo the king's sister, the infanta. Their wardrobe expenses alone came to more than £9,344, because they had to clothe eight footmen, three grooms, and twenty-six gentlemen-in-waiting.[13]

To grace some outdoor gathering in Madrid, they ordered a great tent, a pavilion made of silk and velvet. Beneath it the prince sat in a velvet-upholstered chair embroidered with gold and silver. The tent was tawny in color, and so too were the costumes of his retinue. From a London haberdasher, Prince Charles bought twenty-six silk-lined black beaver hats for his gentlemen-in-waiting. They had twenty-six hatbands embroidered with silver and twenty-six "faire plumes of tawny and white." To match their plumed hats, they wore suits and cloaks of tawny velvet trimmed with silver lace, silk stockings, and twenty-six pairs of tawny garters.

By the 1620s, the beaver hat had become an item as essential to the dignity of rank as a crown and scepter were to medieval monarchs. For that same reason, it became an emblem of status for members of the peerage and the landed gentry too, and so we can roughly quantify the demand for pelts. By this time, after the death of Anne of Denmark, there were in effect three royal households—the king's, the prince's, and Buckingham's—and let us assume that each one needed fifty hats each year. Perhaps the hundred-odd peers of the realm bought half as many, say twenty-five each. Say, too, that the twenty thousand or so families of the landed gentry each ordered just one.

We come to a minimum requirement of nearly twenty-three thousand beaver hats each year. These figures are guesses, but they serve their purpose, conveying the order of magnitude of the trade. At the very least, the English needed each year about the same number of beaver skins, even if they blended the felt with Spanish wool or vicuña. Where was the fur to be found? There were only two possibilities, and one lay at the far end of an especially perilous sea voyage.

Convoys to Russia

On October 20, 1621, boatmen on the Thames saw moored in the river five ships that had recently returned from the distant north. They came from the White Sea port of Archangel, six weeks away from London, and their journey there and back took them around the North Cape of Norway. The voyage to Arctic Russia was shorter by five hundred miles than the passage to America, but extreme cold, fog, the currents around the North Cape, and the danger of pack ice rendered it far more dangerous. It was undertaken for the sake of access to products that only Russia could supply.

On board, the five vessels carried the skins of hundreds of seals, ermines, and squirrels and that of a single wolverine. Most precious of all, on board a ship called the *Encrease,* were two thousand sable skins, imported by a man named Ralph Freeman. They made sable muffs, prized accessories since Queen Elizabeth ordered one of the first from Paris. For London's hatters, Freeman brought home nearly four thousand beaver wombs, the segment of fur from the animal's abdomen.[14]

Freeman was the uncrowned king of the fur trade. More than half the pelts that came into the Thames that autumn were his. He served his turn as lord mayor, he belonged to the board of the East India Company, and he invested in Virginia and Newfoundland. At his death Freeman left legacies equivalent to about eleven thousand acres of farmland. His supremacy in fur came about because, in 1620, he led a consortium that bought the exclusive rights to send ships back and forth from London to Archangel, rights that belonged to the Muscovy Company. With this deal, Freeman acquired complete control of English trade with Russia, and he kept it for the next decade, giving his rivals a new incentive to look westward across the Atlantic.[15]

From the moment that beaver hats became fashionable again, in the last quarter of the sixteenth century, a choice existed with regard to the source of pelts, and the principal countries concerned took different routes. The French went west. They obtained their skins from North America with a chain of supply that led from the St. Lawrence to the Louvre, by way of a royal hatmaker, based in the Rue de la Lingerie in the heart of Paris. In London, the haberdashers chose to take their skins from the east, from Archangel, but by the early 1620s this was becoming a less and less attractive option. A new source was necessary, even before Freeman made it essential to find an alternative.

Archangel was never an ideal trading partner. Ice closed the White Sea for eight months of the year, and so ships bound out from London would sail in convoy, between April and June, aiming to reach the port in time for its summer trade fair. They had to hurry back, or risk being trapped when the sea froze, and it was all too easy to stray out into the North Atlantic, or founder along the hazardous eastern coast of the British Isles. By 1620, the Archangel fair had become one of the busiest in Europe, with forty-odd ships arriving each year, both English and Dutch, but they did business there only because Russia had lost its more obvious outlets to the west. In 1581, the Swedes captured the Russian port of Narva, on the Baltic about 150 miles west of St. Petersburg, and it was because of this that Ivan the Terrible first established a haven on the White Sea.[16]

For the English, the Archangel connection rapidly became a strategic necessity, even though their relationship with the Romanovs was far from untroubled. For their masts, pitch, rosin, and rope, England's navy depended almost entirely on the link. So did the East India Company, for the ships it launched from its slipways into the Thames. In an average year in the reign of James I, the Royal Navy bought four hundred tons of cordage, and the best was made from Russian hemp. Grown by peasants in the hinterland of Smolensk, it was spun into yarn in fishing villages in winter and then carried fifteen hundred miles by sledge to Archangel to be sold. A single warship needed fourteen barrels of tar and two tons of rosin each year to seal and grease its timbers. This too had to come from Russian forests, and as England's merchant fleet expanded, its needs multiplied also.

This was why both Elizabeth and James I tried to maintain friendly relations with the tsars. The connection was simply too important to lose, not only for the sake of the Royal Navy, but also for the access that Archangel gave to the overland silk and spice route to Persia, by way of the Caspian Sea.[17] Sadly, the Kremlin did not make a safe, reliable ally, because of Russia's internal instability, and because of its frequent wars with the Swedes and the Poles. In 1617, the Swedes forced the Russians to hand over the entire coastline from Latvia to Finland. The following year, the Poles attacked Moscow and carved a vast slice out of the western territories of the tsar. In order to fight the Poles, in 1618 the beleaguered tsar asked James I for a loan of £100,000. Since James was even more insolvent than usual, he asked the City of London's merchants to raise the money. This they did, but it was a heavy burden and repayment was by no means guaranteed.

The Russians drove hard bargains, and especially in the fur business. It evolved side by side with the commerce in naval stores, and with the small but luxurious trade in caviar from the Volga basin, but the tsars kept it strictly under their control. This was so from the moment in the early 1580s when Russian fur trappers began to look for pelts in Siberia. By that date, trappers and hunters had hunted to extinction fur-bearing animals on the western side of the Urals. So, looking mainly for sable, they crossed

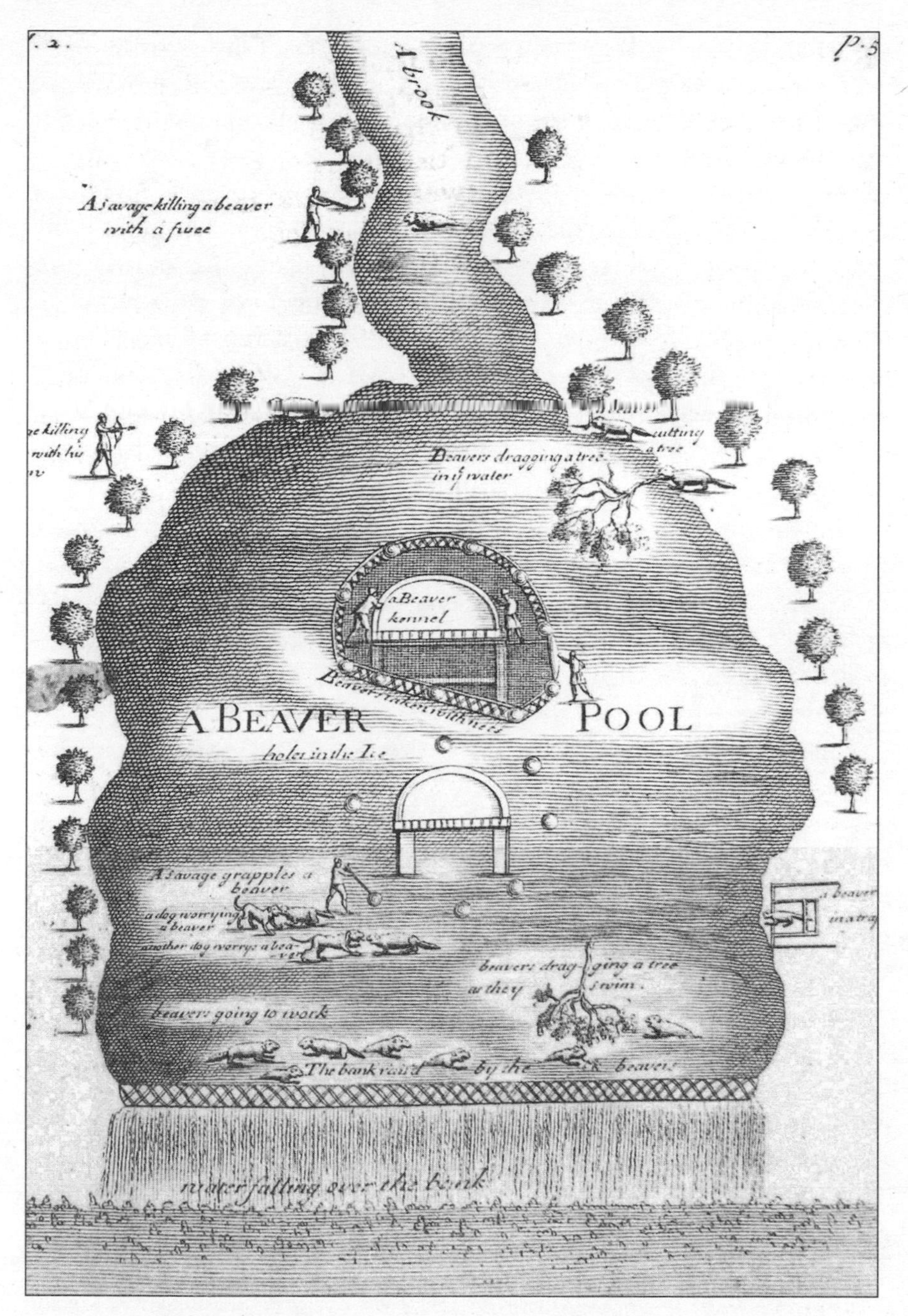

From *New Voyages to North America* (1703), by Baron de Lahontan, perhaps the most realistic early European representation of beaver hunting, showing beavers being speared through holes in the ice, shot, trapped, and pursued by dogs. A French soldier, Lahontan went to Canada in 1683 and traveled as far west as Minnesota. (*London Library*)

the mountains, led first by the Stroganov family, merchants from Moscow, who created a private commercial empire in the east. Unleashed by the Stroganovs, in 1581 the Cossack general Ermak conquered the Tartar stronghold of Sibir.

Three hundred miles beyond the Urals, Sibir was the gathering point for vast quantities of fur. Ermak sent back to Moscow a rich tribute of sable, black fox skins, and two thousand beaver pelts, and the tsar responded by making the conquest of Siberia a goal of Russian policy. Cossacks, traders, and trappers built a network of forts and blockhouses to draw these immense spaces within the pale of Muscovite dominion.[18] Once that was achieved, the tsar made money in three ways. He imposed a fur levy on the native people, he took a tithe from private traders, and he

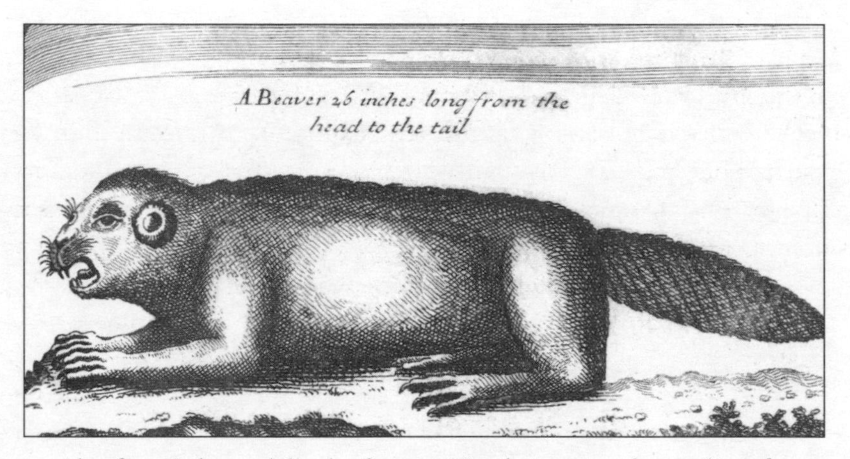

Also from Lahontan's book of 1703, a North American beaver (*Special Collections, the Albert Sloman Library, University of Essex, England*)

purchased skins for the imperial account or for resale at a big markup to foreign merchants. To prevent foreigners from trying to sneak into Siberia by the back door, in 1619 the tsar banned voyages to the east of Archangel, along the northern coast.

By 1620, the Cossacks had reached the rivers that feed Lake Baikal, close to the longitude of Beijing, and the speed of their advance must have caused problems of its own. As they went, they ravaged the wildlife they found. It was said that by the mid-1620s they had wiped out the beaver as far east as the Yenisey and Tunguska valleys, and a glance at the map shows that this region lies two thousand miles from Moscow. Given that beavers are easily trapped and killed, this was entirely possible.

Their dams make obvious targets, and they have the effect of changing the current of water downstream, alerting a trapper to their presence. Another fatal weakness of the beaver was its preference for certain trees and shrubs. Why does the beaver choose to munch the quaking aspen and the willow? Because their wood is digestible and packed with nourishment, and the willow contains salicylic acid. The active ingredient of aspirin, it is eaten by beavers to give their bodies a natural medicine. All a trapper had to do was to break a hole in the ice near the beaver lodge and poke a willow or an aspen branch into the water. Lured to the edge of the pond, the hungry beaver made an easy target for the spear.

If this holocaust of mammals had reached the Yenisey by the 1620s, then as furs became more distant, the price must have risen: the data lie hidden, perhaps, in the Russian imperial archives. Even if it did not, English haberdashers had another motive to consider America as an alternative. At Archangel, the Russians would accept nothing but hard currency. So the ships that sailed from London had to take bags of Spanish coins: the *Sea Venture,* for example, left for Russia in 1617 with nearly four thousand pounds in pieces of eight.[19] Carrying bullion required a warrant from the Privy Council, because of the national shortage of precious metals, and because the East India Company had first call on silver: their suppliers of spices and silk in the Indies insisted on it. When English stocks of bullion collapsed in 1620, the situation must have become almost impossible.

By the time the *Mayflower* sailed, the English merchants who traded with Russia had mostly been forced out of business. Again the Dutch played their unhelpful part. The Muscovy Company did not deal exclusively in furs or naval stores: starting in about 1610, it also sent whaling expeditions to Spitsbergen, between Norway and Greenland, for the sake of whale and walrus oil. But soon the Dutch arrived, and the two countries found themselves fighting an undeclared war in the Arctic. Claiming priority in the same waters, Dutch whalers attacked the Muscovy Company's ships, wrecking its trade, and set fire to its post at Archangel.

Typically, King James added to the confusion by granting a new whaling charter to a Scottish consortium, led by a favored courtier, to compete with the Muscovy Company. The wars between the Russians, Swedes, and Poles also took their toll on the company, damaging Russia's trade. What remained went mostly to Amsterdam. By 1618, three-quarters of the ships that made the summer run to Archangel came from the Netherlands. In the spring of that year, unable to fund their share of the loan to the tsar, the Muscovy merchants had to seek a rescue by way of a merger with the East India Company. The latter agreed, reluctantly, because it needed to protect its supplies of Archangel rope.

As things turned out, the merger failed to serve its purpose. By the end of 1619, the Muscovy Company had collapsed, suffering from heavy losses, and the East India men decided to exit the business. They sold the whaling stations to the investor group led by Ralph Freeman, and with them the right to trade back and forth to Archangel. Recorded in the board minutes of the East India Company, the deal was done in February 1620. With this transaction, Freeman cornered what was left of England's commerce with Russia, in fur, rope, and caviar. He controlled it throughout the 1620s, sending out six or seven ships each season.[20]

On June 22, as Jones made the *Mayflower* ready for sail, the Virginia Company put out a promotional pamphlet. It contained the following sentence: "The rich Furres, Caviary and Cordage, which we draw from Russia with so great difficulty, are to be had in Virginia, and the parts adioyning, with ease and plenty."[21] The words speak for themselves. Because of beaver hats and rope, because of Freeman, because of the tsars, and because of the shortage of bullion, the easier voyage to America became a compelling, attractive proposition, for merchants and mariners alike.

Chapter Thirteen

IN THE ARTILLERY GARDEN

O master, if you did but hear the pedlar at the door . . . He hath ribbons of all the colours i' th' rainbow; points more than all the lawyers in Bohemia can learnedly handle, though they come to him by th' gross; inkles, caddisses, cambrics, lawns: why, he sings 'em over as they were gods or goddesses; you would think a smock were a she-angel.

—SHAKESPEARE, *THE WINTER'S TALE* (1611)

We have Prince Maurice to thank for the Plymouth Colony. If the Pilgrims had sailed as Dutchmen, they might have created a settlement in Brooklyn, or camped out upriver trading furs, but this would not have been New England. Eccentrics already, in the eyes of their countrymen, the Brownists of Leiden would have become traitors too. These were years when Dutch and English seamen were fighting each other not only for whaling but also for the spice trade in the Moluccas. The general in The Hague saved them from becoming soldiers in a trade war, but in doing so he left them with only one option. It turned out to contain perils of its own.

He drove the Pilgrims into the unreliable arms of a trader from the City of London. This was Thomas Weston, aged thirty-five, and he led a company of investors, numbering about seventy. The figure comes from Captain John Smith, who says that they were a mixed party of gentlemen, merchants, and tradesmen. They financed the Pilgrims with what the contract called an "adventure." French in origin, the term referred not to the voyage but to the risk taken by the investors, who ventured their capital to support the colony. At La Rochelle, Frenchmen who invested in Canada looked for a return on their capital of about 30 percent. Weston must have hoped for something similar. A decade later investors in New England still wished to make profits on that scale, because risks were high and they needed a reward to match.[1]

Until 1628, the colony at New Plymouth ran up heavy losses, and by the time it broke even, most of the investors had long since died, withdrawn, or sold out. By 1626, the seventy had already dwindled down to six, who stuck with the project until it began to prosper. Two of them bought country property at Clapham, on the south side of the Thames, and made themselves landed gentlemen with the help of the profits they eventually made. To begin with, however, Thomas Weston was one of the first of many Britons who promised far more in America than they could deliver.*

From the outset, the colony was a commercial project, as well as a mission inspired by religious ideals. Weston wished to make money, as the contract put it, from "trade, traffic, trucking, working, fishing" on the American coast. Far from being a commune, the *Mayflower* was a common stock: the very words employed in the contract. All the land in the Plymouth Colony, its houses, its tools, and its trading profits (if they appeared) were to belong to a joint-stock company owned by the shareholders as a whole.

When the final value of the assets was determined, after seven years, the investors and the colonists would divide them up: that was the plan. All of the participants, those who stayed in England and those who had come to America, would receive a dividend in proportion to the number of shares they owned. Those who had no capital, but simply came on the boat, were deemed to have a single share. If any investor injected more cash, he or she would receive extra shares accordingly. It was not the same thing as a modern corporation, but a likeness existed, and not least in the dubious character of the man who acted as chairman of the board.

By birth, Weston ranked as a gentleman, but his wealth was scanty. His behavior was even worse. Somebody he crossed said that Weston was "soe subtile & unconscionable soe that he might accomplish his owne ends he cared not what bonds he or anie for him entered into for he would keepe

---

*From the limited data that survive, it is impossible to say exactly how much money the investors and the Pilgrims sank into the Plymouth Colony before it broke even. In 1624, Captain John Smith gave a figure of seven thousand pounds, which is probably not too wide of the mark. This was equivalent to the market price of more than fifteen hundred acres of English farmland.

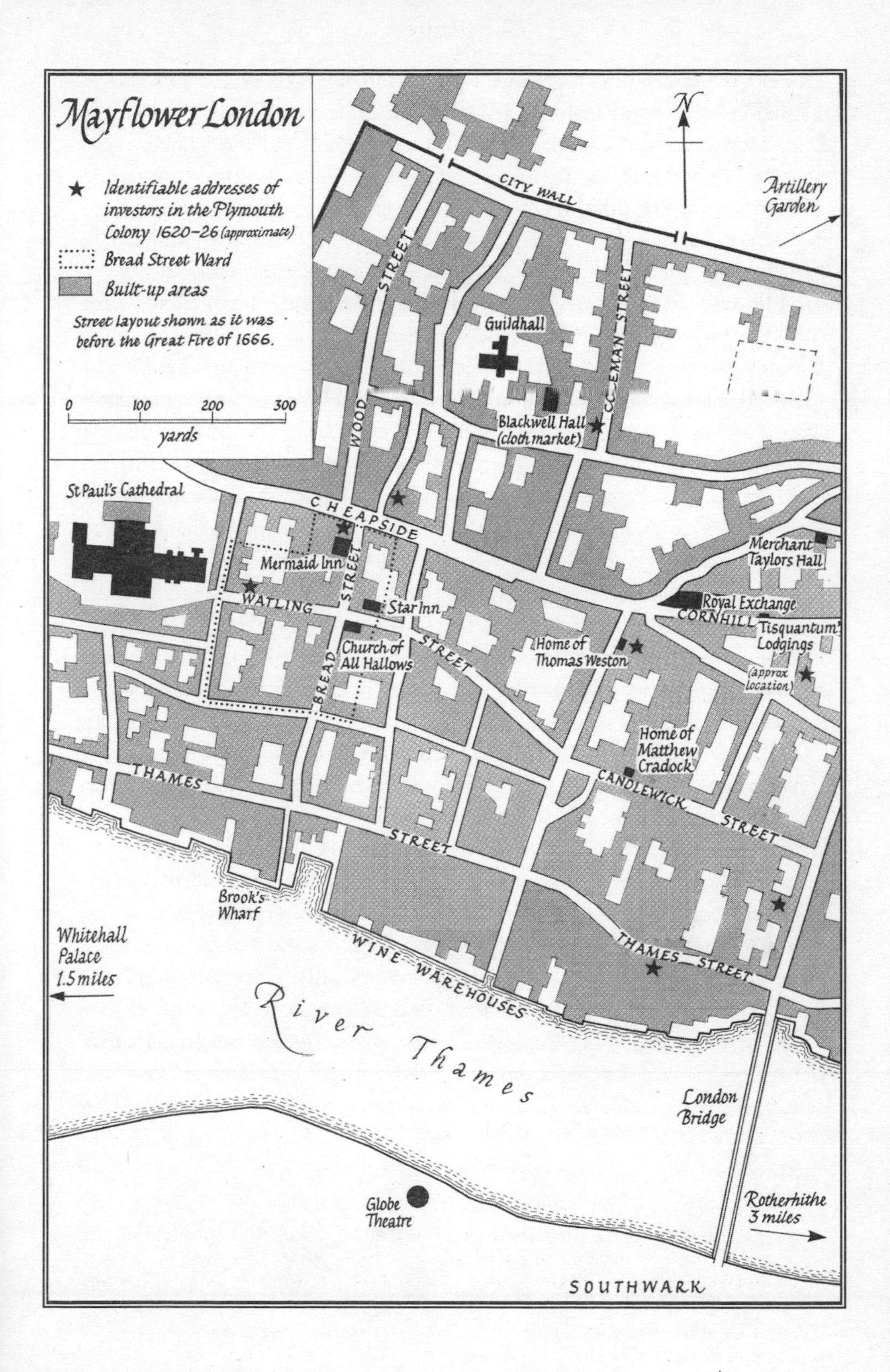
Mayflower London
Identifiable addresses of investors in the Plymouth Colony 1620–26 (approximate)
Bread Street Ward
Built-up areas
Street layout shown as it was before the Great Fire of 1666.
0
100
200
300
yards
N
CITY WALL
Artillery Garden
WOOD STREET
COLEMAN STREET
Guildhall
Blackwell Hall (cloth market)
St Paul's Cathedral
CHEAPSIDE
Mermaid Inn
WATLING STREET
BREAD STREET
Star Inn
Church of All Hallows
Merchant Taylors Hall
Royal Exchange
CORNHILL
Tisquantum's Lodgings (approx location)
Home of Thomas Weston
Home of Matthew Cradock
CANDLEWICK STREET
THAMES STREET
Brook's Wharf
WINE WAREHOUSES
Whitehall Palace 1.5 miles
River Thames
London Bridge
Globe Theatre
Rotherhithe 3 miles
SOUTHWARK

none."[2] Bradford rather more gently labels Weston a man "embittered in spirit," but either way history's verdict has been hostile. Because he first sabotaged and then abandoned the Pilgrims after they reached the New World, Weston ranks next to King James as the villain of the piece.

Even if he was, Thomas Weston had some extenuating circumstances. Only in the 1970s did a British genealogist find Weston's date and place of birth, in 1584 at Rugeley in Staffordshire.* Without that information, his background and his career could not be reconstructed. For this reason, pretty much everything written about the early days of the Plymouth Colony is incomplete, and much of it is misleading or inaccurate. Weston definitely failed in commerce in the early 1620s, he was certainly a smuggler, and he may have been a felon, a gunrunner. Nobody would freely choose him as a business partner. But if we put Weston and his colleagues back in their correct setting, they lead us to the heart of Jacobean England as it was.[3]

What sort of place was it? To find an artistic mirror, again we might turn to Shakespeare, and *The Winter's Tale.* The play has many meanings of a subtle kind, but it also contains documentary elements, assembled from the mundane realities of the day. Among its characters we find the peddler Autolycus, described in the lines quoted at the head of this chapter. In Autolycus, Shakespeare gives us the beginnings of a consumer culture, by way of a growing market for cheap household items—pins, needles, thimbles, ribbons, and the like—carried up and down the land on the backs of men such as him. The investors who financed the *Mayflower* included merchants who fed the likes of Autolycus with the wares they carried.

They also bought and sold woolen cloth. That too we find in *The Winter's Tale,* where the drama unfolds amid the bleating of sheep. Jacobean England had ten million of the animals, numbering twice as many as its human population. "Divide our native commodities into ten parts," said the greatest lawyer of the age, Sir Edward Coke, in Parliament in 1621, "and nine arise from the sheep's back." Coke did not exaggerate by much. Three-quarters of English exports did indeed consist of woven cloth, and Thomas Weston depended on it, as did most of the men who financed the voyage of the *Mayflower.* When their world seemed to be collapsing, they turned to America. Since some of them, but not Weston, were Puritans with their own evangelical ties, their commercial motives went hand in hand with piety of a very distinctive Jacobean kind, both militant and patriotic.

---

*Peter Wilson Coldham, in an article in the *National Genealogical Society Quarterly.*

Dick Whittington and the *Mayflower*

Let us imagine that one summer evening Shakespeare left his home in Stratford and walked down to the Avon. Fourteen stone arches carried a highway across the river, and on the bridge he would see a chain of horses, steaming with sweat. Traveling twenty miles each day, the horses came from the Shropshire market town of Shrewsbury, near the Welsh border. On their backs they carried bundles of fabric known as Welsh cotton, though in fact it was made of coarse wool, with a fluffed surface.

Hill farmers raised the sheep whose fleeces made the stuff. In their shacks in winter they spun and wove the wool before selling it to the drapers of Shrewsbury who finished it and dressed it and packed it. Early every Wednesday morning, from August to October, off went the horses on the eight-day trek to the capital. On Thursdays and Fridays, merchants in London bought Welsh cottons at Blackwell Hall, the City's bourse for cloth, and they shipped a third of it to France: mainly to Rouen.

It was shoddy material, often attracting complaints, but the customers were poor. Rouen served Normandy and the Île-de-France, and like the rural workers in England the forgotten peasants of this region were losing ground as each year went by, their grim standard of living growing ever more intolerable. Welsh cotton sold well to the laboring masses because it was cheap and it was warm. Since France had four times as many inhabitants as England, and Welsh cotton also sold through Amsterdam, the trade was substantial. Hundreds of thousands of yards of cloth left English harbors each year. This was how Thomas Weston made his living, as an exporter of the same rough textiles, sourced from Shrewsbury.[4]

Only forty miles separated the town from Weston's birthplace at Rugeley, and the two places had close ties. One of Weston's brothers served his time as an apprentice in Shrewsbury, qualifying there as Simon Weston, draper, in 1617. Perhaps the saddest of all the stories from the terrible early months in America had its origins in this same connection. On board the *Mayflower* traveled four infants, Ellen, Jasper, Richard, and Mary More, the unwanted offspring of a failed marriage in a Shropshire village, sixteen miles from the town where Simon Weston lived.

Among the boys and girls, the oldest was eight and the youngest was four. Their great-grandfather was another draper in Shrewsbury. In the summer of 1620, their parents were divorced, on grounds of adultery, and the children were declared bastards. A family retainer took them to London and handed them over to Philemon Powell, Weston's servant and factotum. Weston received a hundred pounds to cover their passage and to finance the purchase of shares in the colony. The first child to die was Jasper More, in Provincetown Harbor, and only one of the children survived the first American winter.[5]

Thomas Weston also dealt with a Shrewsbury cloth merchant named John Vaughan. Thanks to Weston, in 1622 Vaughan incurred heavy losses. Litigation followed, and the affair and its consequences left behind a mass of legal documents, filled with evidence of the loosest of commercial morals. They show that Weston ran a precarious business, dealing in Welsh cottons bought on credit and then shipped to Europe, along with assorted haberdashery. Sometimes he handled exotic cargoes, whale fins, or tropical wood used to make dyes, but he had a handicap, and one that was common. He had far too little capital. This was his undoing, and very nearly that of the Plymouth Colony. Thomas Weston started off as yet another younger son from a marginal family with few connections.[6]

By the time of King James, the Westons had lived at Rugeley for at least two hundred years, as the lords of Hagley Manor. Behind a motel, at the drab edge of modern Rugeley, a little park encloses a pond, with an island in the middle: all that remains of the Weston residence, and its medieval moat. But from the surviving features of the landscape, and because a stream still feeds the pond, we can imagine the life the Westons led on the edge of the dense woodlands of Cannock Chase. Beside the brook, and above the house, stood the manor's water mill, while the town's livestock market lay a few yards away, across a street still called Sheep Fair today. Thomas grew up surrounded by cattle, sheep, and horses.[7]

But mention Rugeley to a Jacobean, and if a word came to mind, it would not be "sheep" but "papist." Staffordshire was, and has remained, an area with more than the average English complement of Catholicism, partly thanks to local noblemen who clung to the old religion. It would be ironic, to say the least, if we found that the man who backed the *Mayflower*'s voyage was raised in that same faith. So he probably was. While his private beliefs may forever remain unknown, the following facts can be established.

In 1648, officials seized the estates belonging to his eldest brother, Sir Richard Weston, after naming him as a Catholic. Thomas Weston's mother came from a part of Lancashire that also held out as a Roman Catholic enclave, while his aunt married into the Wolseleys, who were Catholic gentry. The two families remained close, doing land deals together. Rugeley had a hard core of awkward Romanists, and in 1616 the authorities prosecuted six Catholics in the town for refusing to go to church, and another twenty at Cannock. None of this proves that Thomas Weston remained a

Roman Catholic, since he also had early Puritan ties: as a youth, he worked for a leading Puritan iron merchant in the capital. But, at the very least, he came from a suspicious background.[8]

Nor were the Westons particularly wealthy. Their land ran to little more than two hundred acres, and they did not serve as JPs, one of the defining marks of a solid gentleman. Their hopes centered on Richard, who went to Oxford. Excelling in the law, he became a judge with a knighthood under Charles I, grew the estate, and built a new manor house. For the younger sons a less exalted future lay in store: there were six children, and that was too many.

In England in the seventeenth century, the average member of the landed gentry fathered two male children from each of his two marriages, but the professions were much smaller than they later became, and no standing army existed to absorb surplus youths. Each year, genteel occupations such as the law, the Church, the government, and the navy recruited between them no more than five hundred new entrants. In time, demographic facts such as these encouraged men and women toward America, but for the Westons there was only one available option.

Before Thomas Weston's father, Ralph, died in 1605, he decided that Thomas and three of his brothers should become apprentices. This was the only way to maintain their status as gentlemen. To avoid working with their hands, they had to build a career in commerce, as an apprentice draper, haberdasher, or the like.[9] The Westons sent Thomas to London to train under another Shrewsbury man, Rowland Heylin, a godly donor to good causes and a leading figure in the Company of Ironmongers.

Jacobean London swarmed with apprentices, thirty thousand or so, and at the time of Ralph's death they found their dramatic incarnation in Dick Whittington. It seems that the year 1605 was also the date of the earliest performance of *The Legend of Whittington*, telling the folk story of the provincial youth who walks to London with his loyal black cat. Dick becomes an apprentice, overcomes hardship, survives ill-treatment, and makes a fortune with the cat's clever help in the West African trade. He marries the boss's daughter and ends up as lord mayor three times over. Soon Dick was a household name, with a ballad version of the story set to music. Clearly the play spoke directly to the predicament of many young men, including Thomas Weston.

It was becoming much harder to find a place as an apprentice, and still more difficult to make a success of what came later. Competition between gentry families bid up the "premium," a fee paid up front to the master to whom the boy was apprenticed. It might come to as much as one hundred pounds, the price of twenty acres of land. Once accepted, an apprentice often lived a menial life, little better than an unpaid kitchen porter, with no guarantee of ultimate entry to his chosen trade. Less than half of London's apprentices finished their training. This was the case with the Pilgrim Edward Winslow. Another boy from a minor gentry family in the West Midlands—the Winslows lived only forty miles from Rugeley—he was apprenticed at eighteen to a London printer. He quit after only five years of the customary seven and took off for Leiden, where the Pilgrims had work for a young man with his skills.

Besides death, the most common reason for dropping out was brutally obvious: a lack of capital with which to start a business of one's own. In his will, Ralph Weston stipulated that when his sons completed their apprenticeships, they should each receive one hundred pounds "for a stocke to set up with." Far too small a sum, this would barely fund a shopkeeper in London. A Shrewsbury draper needed four times as much, and an overseas trader to Whittington's Africa might require two thousand pounds. As for ironmongery, the business involved far more than selling odds and ends of hardware: Heylin and his like ran iron foundries, supplying shipyards and construction sites, but this was far beyond the capacity of Thomas Weston.[10]

He finished his apprenticeship at the age of twenty-five, but it seems that he never bought or sold an iron rod for his own account: if he did, no evidence has been found for it. Instead, Weston took advantage of the so-called custom of London, which allowed a freeman of one company to do business in the trade of any other: this is why, for example, we find merchant taylors dealing in wine, and salters importing goatskins while skinners exported woolens. By 1612, Weston was doing the same, selling textiles to the French and the Dutch. For capital he had to rely on the flimsiest resources.

London had nothing that remotely resembled even a Victorian bank, let alone a modern example. So men like Weston paid their way with private bills of exchange—postdated checks, or IOUs—which circulated like an unofficial currency, bought, sold, and swapped between merchants often hundreds of miles apart. If chains of packhorses linked Welsh hill farms to London, they had their counterpart in these loops of credit that wound back and forth from one city and town to another. Weston paid for Welsh cottons with a bill dated many months in the future. He hoped to redeem it when he sold the cloth in France or the Netherlands, either by shipping home goods that an English merchant wanted or by obtaining a bill from a Dutchman or a French trader, an IOU that Weston in turn could sell in London.

This sounds complicated, and it was. If the economy grew, and everybody's sales expanded, the multiplication of credit could carry on indefinitely. But if the economy faltered, even for a moment, and ready buyers failed to appear for English cloth or French wine or Dutch copper kettles, then credit would begin to vanish like sand down the throat of an hourglass. Since men gave personal guarantees for each other's bills, the system might disintegrate if a few large merchants failed to meet their obligations. At that point, the hourglass would empty entirely; and, as we shall see, exactly this occurred in the early 1620s.[11]

Thomas Weston managed to survive in this fashion for seven years or so. The few surviving customs books from London refer to him often. Between the spring of 1616 and the autumn of 1617, we find him sending twelve cargoes from the Thames to Rouen, Amsterdam, and Hamburg. Half of his consignments were cottons like those from Shrewsbury, but he also dealt in hundreds of sheepskins, and he shipped out six gross of garters and fourteen dozen pairs of plain leather gloves, on a vessel aptly named the *Sheep.* Occasionally, Weston dealt in quite high grades of cloth, but mostly he traded at the bottom end of the market. This was not the way to make one's fortune.[12]

By far the largest profits flowed from luxury imports, spices, silks, and wine, sold at high margins to the wealthy. Again, this required capital and connections, and in practice a small elite controlled the richest trades, men such as Sir John Wolstenholme. In theory a small merchant might accumulate capital from trading profits, earned by hard years of graft. But in practice an array of monopolies, cartels, and legalized forms of racketeering occupied the commanding heights of the economy.

For Weston, the most relevant monopoly was the one operated by the Fellowship of Merchant Adventurers of England. Eager to encourage weaving at home, Tudor monarchs had given the fellowship an exclusive right to send undyed, unfinished white woolens to the Netherlands: a very big business indeed, which reached its peak in 1614, when their sales to the Dutch exceeded the entire tax revenues of King James.

Joining the fellowship was difficult and expensive, and far beyond the means of Thomas Weston. This left him with only two options. Either he stuck to selling Welsh cottons, where profits were mediocre, or he could engage in "interloping." By virtue of a statute from the fifteenth century, any merchant could legally sell woolens to the Low Countries, provided he paid a fee to the fellowship and complied with their regulations. It was not a crime to interlope, and the interlopers, including Weston, traded openly and paid their taxes.

However, if circumstances changed and times became harder, the fellowship might try to enforce their monopoly more strictly. If they did so, they would push men like Weston to the wall: and that was what occurred, propelling him across the North Atlantic. It happened in the following way.

As soon as Robert Cecil became lord treasurer, he began to devise schemes for strengthening the royal finances, but the Crown and Parliament could not agree on measures to close the budget deficits that the king habitually ran up. Cecil died, taking with him to the grave the ashes of fiscal rectitude. In 1614, James made a last attempt at reform, by way of the so-called Addled Parliament, but he and its members soon fell out with each other, and so he dissolved the assembly. Forward stepped Alderman William Cokayne with a plan to strengthen the economy, to outwit the Dutch, and to replenish the Exchequer, all at the same time. It came to be known as the Cokayne Project.

Cokayne persuaded the king and the Privy Council to terminate the monopoly enjoyed by the Fellowship of Merchant Adventurers. In its place, Cokayne would create a new monopoly, to finish and dye white woolens before exporting them across the North Sea. This would create English jobs for English workers, while King James would receive a royalty for each roll of the stuff, yielding a sum uncannily close to his wardrobe bills and those of his son combined. Everybody would be happy, including the interlopers and members of the old fellowship, since they would all be invited to join, pledging their capital to the new venture. In June the Addled Parliament ended, a few weeks later the Cokayne Project began, and soon it proved to be disastrous.[13]

Hearing of the scheme, the Dutch bought all the raw cloth they could find and banned imports of Cokayne's new product. The members of the old fellowship went on strike, refusing to buy woolens from England's weavers. Cokayne's investors failed to supply new capital, and unsold cloth piled up in workshops and warehouses. Soon acute observers suspected that the project was a fraud, simply aimed at elbowing aside the fellowship and transferring their business to Cokayne, with no finishing and dyeing done at all, no investment, and no new employment. In 1616, as Shakespeare fell ill and died, in the weaving districts business faltered, and came to a stop.

Thousands of workers lay idle, and the king concluded that Cokayne had cheated him. His project was, James told the Privy Council, "playne

Cosonage." The word "cosonage" meant "theft," and James told them to put a stop to it. For another year, the crisis continued as the Crown negotiated a solution. At the opening of 1618, the old merchant adventurers struck a new deal with the king, agreeing to pay him fifty thousand pounds in return for their old monopoly. At the same time, as part of the deal they insisted that the Crown halt trading by the interlopers, including Thomas Weston.

At first, the interlopers stood their ground, even when sent to jail. In The Hague, Sir Dudley Carleton heard stories of the affair, about defiant interlopers who "claime and challenge free trafficke by the lawes of the realme and theyre birth-right, and divers of them are committed to the Marshalsee for refusing to enter into bond to desist." Weston's name appears on a list of six offenders reported to the authorities in June. No record seems to survive of official sanctions against him, but it looks as if his business collapsed. The fragmentary customs records that survive show no trace of exports by Weston in 1619.

As we have seen, William Bradford often forgot to give chronology, and so we do not know exactly when Weston first made contact with the Pilgrims. But we do know that a link between them existed, by way of a haberdasher named Edward Pickering, who kept shops in London and Amsterdam, and acted as Weston's agent in Holland. A Separatist himself, and involved with Weston since about 1612, Pickering became a strong supporter of the Pilgrims, leaving money in his will to help them. The introduction must have been his. Weston needed a new source of income to replace what he had lost when interloping ended, and Pickering had friends in Leiden who needed help. Between them, it seems, they recruited the rest of the *Mayflower* consortium.[14]

Peddlers and Pilgrims

We have the names of forty-six investors in the Plymouth Colony, chiefly from a list of forty-one men and one woman compiled in 1626 and contained in a letter transcribed by William Bradford. From information elsewhere, we can establish the origins or occupations of eighteen. Tentatively, we can identify the backgrounds of another five whose names, like John White, are too common to prevent uncertainty.

A handful, perhaps no more than three or four, were religious radicals like the Separatists. Most of the rest were either mainstream Puritans or men with no pious enthusiasm either way. When it came to North America, it seems that none possessed prior experience of any kind. In 1620, the

Virginia Company made a list of its own shareholders, and no overlap exists with the names of those who backed the Pilgrims. Captain John Smith implied that they were small traders and minor members of the gentry, and this seems to be correct, but not entirely. In the City of London, two of the young men who financed the *Mayflower,* John Pocock and John Beauchamp, both in their late twenties, were rising stars. Like the mariners in Plymouth Sound, they left a mass of evidence in their wake. By way of their careers, the *Mayflower* finds her place in the wider history of England at the time.[15]

Both men stand out from their colleagues because, in 1626, they were among the very few investors still prepared to commit more capital to the Pilgrims after years of losses. We start with John Beauchamp, aged about twenty-eight in the year of the voyage. His name appears nearly thirty times in Bradford's *History,* and he worked closely with Weston. Though he never went to America, the Pilgrims granted him land at Scituate, between Plymouth and Boston. His brother-in-law helped to found the Cape Cod town of Sandwich.

We know almost nothing about his character besides a comment by a fellow investor that Beauchamp "seemed somewhat harsh." His will contains evidence of stern paternal piety: he urged his children not to marry without their mother's approval, "as they expect a blessing from God the ffather of us all without whose blessing nothing can prosper." He was also a Puritan, and in the 1650s the Cromwellians made Beauchamp a justice of the peace. But while his inner life remains obscure, his business career is quite another matter.

Beauchamp came from the same world as Autolycus. His family were the most prosperous yeoman farmers in a village called Cosgrove, fifty miles from London in Northamptonshire, a county where the low undulating hills supported sheep in immense numbers. When John Beauchamp's uncle Christopher died in 1622, he left a ewe and a lamb each to a daughter and two granddaughters, and ten shillings to the poor of "Cowesgrave," as he called his township.

A solid man and a churchwarden, Christopher Beauchamp left nearly three hundred pounds, not bad for a yeoman, and the Beauchamps ranked among those wealthy enough to pay taxes and vote. Although they were rural, they were far from isolated. Just as the Great North Road ran along the edge of Austerfield, the ancient highway of Watling Street passed close to the boundary of Cosgrove. Along it walked peddlers heading north toward Chester and Liverpool, while packhorses plodded past them on their way south to London.

John Beauchamp was a third and youngest son, and when his father died in 1614, he received a legacy worth only eighty pounds, even less than Weston's. By that time he was already apprenticed as a salter, but with what must have seemed like only modest prospects of success. His eldest brother inherited the family's land, but died young in 1625. A second brother, a London haberdasher, died the same year, probably from plague, and left only feeble legacies of a few shillings.[16] John, however, did exceptionally well. Like Weston, he traded as an interloper, exporting cloth, but Beauchamp made his fortune in another way, as an entrepreneurial pioneer. Within less than a decade, Beauchamp rose to become by far the largest London importer of the sorts of goods carried by traveling salesmen such as Autolycus.

With his roots in the countryside, Beauchamp began by sending rural commodities to Amsterdam: fleeces, horsehair, and black rabbit skins. Using the same Dutch ships that carried woolens for Weston, he exported stockings, of the kind farming families knit by the fireside as a way to earn a little extra money. Then back from Holland he brought merchandise to feed the peddlers of the kingdom as they built their networks of consumption, selling lightweight articles to housewives and provincial shopkeepers. In 1621, we find Beauchamp importing from Holland an assortment of tennis balls, pins, needles for securing bundles on a horse's back, and six thousand thimbles. By 1626, as he tried to keep the Plymouth Colony afloat, his business had grown from these modest beginnings to reach an unrivaled scale.

Ship after ship sailed into the Thames carrying items for John Beauchamp. Among them were hundreds of the "inkles" and "caddisses" found among the wares sold by Autolycus: an inkle was linen tape used by seamstresses, and a caddis was woolen tape for stocking garters. We find, for example, the *Cornelius* of Amsterdam unloading for Beauchamp a cargo of caddis ribbons, inkles, hairy goatskins, plates, sewing needles, nearly seventeen thousand thimbles, and more than 200,000 iron tacks. Alongside Beauchamp another *Mayflower* investor, James Sherley, plied the same trade, dealing in similar items. They apparently worked together, and their business volumes far outstripped those of other London importers of the same merchandise. Sherley and Beauchamp were the pair who bought a country place in Clapham with their profits from the fur trade.

If men like this supported the *Mayflower,* then a riddle can be solved. Among the twenty-one households that traveled on board the ship, five had no documented ties of any kind with the Leiden congregation, and several came from country locations a long way from London. How did they hear about the venture? If the backers were men such as Beauchamp and Sherley, whose peddling contacts roamed the country, then the mystery vanishes.

Take, for example, William Mullins, a shoemaker from Dorking in Surrey. Twenty-six miles from London, Dorking had a grain market, and a firm chalk road that led toward the capital. Mullins was a small businessman who carried with him to New England a stock of boots and shoes, together with his wife, son, and daughter. For buckles and laces, he would have turned to wholesalers like Beauchamp. This is how talk of the *Mayflower* project must have circulated, carried by tradesmen and peddlers on foot between the open fields along the highway.[17]

We can also see why the trade in beaver skins might appeal to Beauchamp. Haberdashery, goatskins, and hardware might sell well, but the margins were narrow, and anybody could enter the trade. Silk, spices, and luxury goods lay within the protected domain of the monopolies, mainly the East India Company. Tobacco was out of the question, its import controlled by another monopoly, and the economics made it a waste of time. In 1620, Spanish leaf was far cheaper than Virginia's: tobacco sold retail in London for less than it cost to grow the plant in Jamestown, while the Crown came close to banning tobacco altogether.[18]

By contrast, the fur trade offered excellent prospects. Demand was strong. No bullion was necessary if the skins came from Native Americans, rather than difficult Russians. All they needed was a patent for settlement, from the Virginia Company or from Sir Ferdinando Gorges, both of whom were eager to help, since they needed settlers to colonize New England or to replace those who had died at Jamestown. The import duty was low, at sixpence per beaver skin, and the king smiled on the trade. Best of all was the wide gap between the cost of the skins at five shillings each and the market price of the hat, which fetched at least eight times as much. Within the tactile chain of manufacture lay a wide margin of profit. A North American venture offered an opportunity for Beauchamp to raise his commercial game, at the expense of the beaver king, Ralph Freeman.

Thoughts like these must have passed through the minds of the investors, but so too did evangelism. London also contained the young John Milton, raised the son of a scrivener in Bread Street, at the mercantile heart of the city. Around the corner from the future author of *Paradise Lost* lived another young merchant, John Pocock. A Puritan like the Miltons, and an investor in the Plymouth Colony, Pocock definitely did not see the *Mayflower* simply as a chance to make money.

Bradford did not care for Pocock, or so it seems, since his name surfaces rarely in the Pilgrim narratives. If so, the feeling was mutual. Pocock wished to remain inside the Church of England and reform it from within. During the first six years of the Plymouth Colony he and his friends viewed Bradford and the Leiden Brownists as unreliable extremists. Nevertheless, Pocock showed courage of his own, and Bradford was wrong not to acknowledge it.

A political activist, later arrested as a tax rebel against the Crown, John Pocock supplied the link between the Pilgrims and the much larger migration led by John Winthrop in 1630. He invested in both, he financed the Atlantic trade in beaver fur, and he embodied the Puritan culture of London, the environment that went to shape the poet Milton. It was most probably Pocock who recruited Captain Miles Standish, a veteran of service with the Dutch, to act as the colony's military commander in America. In his leisure hours, John Pocock served as a part-time soldier himself.

The Puritan Militiaman of Bread Street

If you wished to enter the City of London from the north, you came by way of Bishopsgate. Close to it you would find a patch of open ground called the Artillery Garden. Here, beginning in 1611, the young businessmen of the City drilled each week with their weapons, as members of the Honourable Artillery Company, a volunteer fraternity with a fine reputation for discipline and skill with arms. If war broke out, and the Spaniards invaded, they would supply the cadre of officers commanding the trained bands, raised from London and the surrounding counties. It was a privilege to be enrolled in the artillery company. John Pocock was a member, and apparently John Milton entered the regiment, too, in 1635.

Pocock joined the artillerymen in 1619 and served alongside a young haberdasher called Owen Rowe, who was Edward Pickering's apprentice and thirty years later signed the death warrant of Charles I. Their names appear together on the scroll that records the membership. Drawn up in 1635, it lists as soldiers in the company no fewer than nine investors in the Plymouth Colony, together with the printer who employed Edward Winslow, and another printer who published *Mourt's Relation*. When the English Civil War began, the same company and the same kinds of men led the London militia for Parliament against the king.

Sponsored by the Lord Mayor, the Honourable Artillery Company had a paid commander in Captain John Bingham, a soldier who had served for many years in the Netherlands under Prince Maurice. It seems sensible to assume that Miles Standish came to the *Mayflower* project by way of a recommendation from Bingham to Pocock. Like the artillerymen, Standish saw no conflict between soldiering and godliness. In fact, the artillery company commissioned sermons on the connection between the two, such as one they heard in 1617. "We are all Souldiers, as wee are Christians," said the preacher. "You beare both Spirituall Armes against the enemies of your Salvation, and Materiall Armes against the enemies of your Countrey."[19] Standish could not have asked for a better summary of his own philosophy, and we may assume that Pocock endorsed it too.

He lived within the core of the City, in an environment that combined commerce, learning, and religion, where all the elements that went to create the Plymouth Colony could be found in close proximity. Pocock spent his adult life in the shadow of St. Paul's Cathedral, at the London end of Watling Street, in Bread Street Ward. If Puritan London had a nucleus, you would find it here, at the crossroads where Watling Street and Bread Street met.

When news arrived from America, it came here first, because four doors away from the intersection was the Star Inn, used by carriers from the western ports of Barnstaple and Plymouth. If they were godly, visitors might pause for a Calvinist sermon at the church of All Hallows, Bread Street, where Milton was baptized in 1608. And if they had sons to educate, they need only turn the corner and walk to the end of Watling Street. There they would see St. Paul's School, a charitable institution that charged no fees. At the school Milton read Homer and Virgil during the day, while in the evening he studied music with his father, an amateur composer who published settings of biblical texts for the voice and viol.[20]

Here a visitor would also find the center of the cloth trade. Watling Street housed "wealthy Drapers, retailors of woollen cloathes both broad and narrow," said a contemporary. Among them at the King's Arms lived a merchant taylor called John Harrison. Childless, John Harrison employed the young John Pocock. The boy came from a village called Chieveley in Berkshire, west of the capital, an area where under the Tudors local drapers had begun to grow rich from the mass production of textiles in workshops in the towns of Newbury and Reading. Among them, it seems, were the Pococks, who bought their own small estate in 1566. Comfortably off, the family found John his niche with Harrison, whose firm he joined in 1607 as an apprentice.[21]

From the King's Arms, Harrison ran a network of "chapmen," small retail dealers in provincial market towns, from Exeter in the south to Preston in Lancashire in the north. They distributed drapery made by Harrison's cloth workers, and the business flourished. Pocock served his time as an apprentice alongside another boy called Ralph Longworth, and after Pocock finished his training in 1615, they went into business together, with a loan of two thousand pounds from Harrison as capital. When Harrison died in 1619, and Longworth in 1620, John Pocock took over the operation as a whole.

He also shared Harrison's evangelical religion. "Puritan" is a word that must be used carefully to speak about Londoners in the 1620s, because times had changed, definitions had become less clear-cut, and men and women did not always tell the truth about their beliefs. Puritan or not, Harrison belonged to a group of merchants who clustered around evangelical Calvinists in city parishes. One such man was the spiritual leader of Bread Street Ward, Richard Stock, the rector of All Hallows who baptized the poet.

Richard Stock belonged to a network of ministers who inherited the name "forward preachers" from the old Elizabethan Presbyterians of the 1590s. A few of these survivors of the old Puritan movement were still alive, and they found shelter and support with men such as Stock. He had made his name as a verbose anti-Catholic, but he was also a diligent pastor and no respecter of persons—it was said that he would denounce sin "even to the faces of the greatest, both in publike and private"—and he built a loyal following.[22]

Among the merchants who listened to Stock was another draper, Nathaniel Wade, who lived around the corner at the sign of the Bear in Friday Street. At his death Wade left thirty pounds to his "loving friend" Richard Stock, and the bulk of his fortune, including the Bear, to his widow. In 1623, Mary Wade married John Pocock, the rising young merchant from only two hundred yards away. This must have cemented Pocock's standing as one of the neighborhood's most substantial citizens. An evangelical ally of Richard Stock's, he worked with him on a project that closely resembled the Plymouth Colony, in motivation at least. It was aimed not at America but at Lancashire, in northwestern England, where Harrison's family had originated.

When Harrison died, he made John Pocock an executor of his will, while Stock supervised Pocock's work. With no children to provide for, Harrison bequeathed his fortune to charity. In 1620, therefore, Pocock carried out Harrison's scheme to build a new Merchant Taylors' School near Liverpool, with no fees for the boys beyond an initial shilling, supported by an endowment of rents from houses in Bread Street Ward.

Godly Puritans still saw the north as a backward wasteland of popery and ignorance, and Harrison's school was one of many founded with the aim of putting this right. They compared this with the work of taking the Gospel to the New World. As a politician put it, "There were some places in England which were scarce in Christendom, where God was little better-known than among the Indians."[23] As the *Mayflower* crossed the Atlantic, and Pocock signed off the bills for the school, the Merchant Taylors commissioned verses in honor of Harrison, resonating with the sense of mission that we find in Bradford as well. Harrison's bequest, the Latin says, was inspired by "love of Country, love of Virtue, love of Learning, and the love of Religion."

This sort of thing was hardly subversive. Nobody could object to an educational charity. However, the motives that lay behind the *Mayflower* or the school might one day spill over into politics, if circumstances changed. If men like Pocock came to believe that the Crown and the Church of England were outright enemies of the work of godliness, rather than simply idle or inadequate, then a more radical maneuver might be needed. Stock, for example, helped to lead a group of London merchants and clergymen, the so-called Feoffees for Impropriations, who bought rectories around the country, and used the tithe revenues to pay the salaries of Puritan preachers, as a means to create an evangelical church within a church. One day this sort of thing might lead to a clash with the authorities, if the archbishop of Canterbury tried to forbid it.*

For the time being, events had not reached a moment of decision requiring outright civil disobedience, or exile, for mainstream Puritans such as John Pocock. For him, and for young Whittingtons like Beauchamp, the *Mayflower*'s voyage was an experiment, a shrewd gamble by means of the fur trade to thrust themselves into the front rank of commerce. At the same time, the new colony would fulfill evangelical goals by bringing the Sermon on the Mount to a land that had not heard it. Even so, New England was not yet a desperate necessity, since ways and means such as education could still be found to do the Lord's work in abundance at home.

Within less than a decade of the *Mayflower*'s voyage, a crisis occurred in which New England suddenly became just such a necessary option. At that point, Pocock and his neighbors in Bread Street Ward would have to

---

*The Pococks became very close indeed to Richard Stock. When Stock made his will in April 1625, he left Mrs. Pocock thirteen shillings and four pence to buy a Bible, while John Pocock witnessed his signature. Since Stock was a central figure in the evangelical culture of his day, these details suggest that the *Mayflower* project was far more tightly linked to the mainstream of Puritan activity in London than historians have hitherto recognized.

take their stand as political rebels. In 1620, however, that moment still lay very far in the future. Instead, informed men and women were mostly looking not west but east, across the North Sea toward a continent sliding into war and economic calamity.

The *Kipper* and the *Wipper*

In January, King James issued the usual secret instructions to an English diplomat on his way to Madrid. "Informe yourselfe of all such Preparations as there be made, which wil be of three sorts: Mony, Men and Shipping," wrote the king, in case another Spanish Armada was in preparation. Then he turned elsewhere, to a more urgent source of anxiety: the ambassador, he said, needed to monitor "the present affaires of Germany: wherof the Eye of the Christian world is like cheifely to be fixed."[24]

And so it was. As the Thirty Years' War began to escalate, the effects of the conflict in Germany rapidly spilled across frontiers. In the fourth week of July, as the Pilgrims left Delftshaven on the *Speedwell,* heading for Southampton to meet the *Mayflower,* the Spanish and Bavarian armies began to march toward Protestant Bohemia. Long before they reached Prague, the economic damage done by the hostilities had already begun to take its toll in England, despite the nation's neutrality.

The war caused a chaos of hyperinflation, which came to be known in German as the *Kipper und Wipperzeit,* the "time of the Kipper and the Wipper." *Kipper* meant "tilting" and *Wipper* meant "wagging," and the words referred to deception, practiced by goldsmiths who played tricks with their scales, swapping sound coins for lightweight or counterfeit duds. Hundreds of mints debased their coinage as a way for local rulers to raise funds to pay for armies and weapons. At its worst, the process became a panic of competitive devaluation, as mints fought each other to attract bullion and then to coin it into as much currency as possible. As money lost its value, prices soared, increasing six- or sevenfold. Wages lagged far behind, and in southern Germany the real incomes of manual workers fell by two-thirds.[25]

When their truce with the Netherlands ended, in 1621, the Spanish Crown imposed an embargo on Dutch shipping; and since the Dutch were the principal carriers between the Baltic and the Mediterranean, this caused the depression to deepen still further. England had begun to feel its effects far earlier than that, in the spring of 1620, as a result of the inflationary crisis in Germany and Poland. London merchants who traded to Gdansk found that English cloth simply would not sell. The rising value of the pound killed their exports, and they were soon petitioning the Crown for help. This was why, six months before the *Mayflower* set sail, the Shrewsbury drapers were already in difficulties, as cloth piled up unsold at Blackwell Hall.[26]

The price of wool began to drop sharply. So did the price of grain, because of a series of excellent harvests. As the *Mayflower* gathered her supplies, a bushel of wheat fell to its cheapest price in fourteen years. Even this had its darker side, as tenant farmers found their incomes collapsing while their costs did not. As farm incomes fell, farm rents, which had been rising steeply in England for fifty years or so, at last began to stabilize, but not quickly enough to bring relief.

Against this background, between June and August, the Pilgrims made their final preparations and closed their deal with Thomas Weston. It is easy to see why the negotiations took place in a fraught, bad-tempered atmosphere. Along with the families recruited in England with no Leiden connections, Pocock and his colleagues insisted on sending with the colonists a Puritan merchant from Essex, Christopher Martin. A man with a record of minor clashes with the local church authorities, Martin apparently joined the expedition in order to reduce the influence of the Separatists. He also acted as supply officer, purchasing provisions but quarreling with John Carver about their cost and where to buy them.

Meanwhile, Weston was determined to strike the hardest bargain he could. He insisted that in the New World the colonists should work seven days a week for the joint-stock company, with even their houses treated as company assets for division after seven years. As for the Pilgrims, in the conditions of 1620 it was impossible for them to borrow in order to complete their purchase of supplies. In June, they had about £350 less than they needed, a very substantial shortfall, severely reducing their resources for the first winter in America: in the summer of that year, one pound sterling bought either forty pounds of butter, or sixty candles, or a dozen geese, or more than one hundred gallons of beer.[27]

When Bradford came to write about their final weeks in England, he said nothing about the economic collapse that was occurring around them. As we shall see, it nearly caused the destruction of the colony, because it wrecked the finances of Thomas Weston, which had always been fragile. But another Separatist who traveled to New Plymouth gave his own, less famous account of the motives that might lead an immigrant to America. He laid heavy stress on the hardships of the period.

The author was Robert Cushman. He did not sail on the *Mayflower*: instead, worried about the lack of supplies and the lateness of the season,

Cushman was one of a group who turned back with the *Speedwell* when her skipper refused to proceed. He eventually went to New England in 1621, and preached a sermon at New Plymouth. Published in London the following year, his text was an appeal for new settlers to follow the Pilgrims. Cushman kept a grocer's shop in England before combing wool in Leiden, and his sermon went straight to the economic point.

In England, he said, "the rent-taker lives on sweet morsels, but the rent-payer eats with a dry crust and often with watery eyes." Unemployment rose and vagrant beggars multiplied in a fractious, divided country beset by "envy, contempt and reproach," and by the malaise of litigation. He blamed all this on poverty and overcrowding. "The straitness of the place is such, as each man is fain to pluck his means, as it were, out of his neighbour's throat," he said. "There is such pressing and oppressing in town and country, about farms, trades, traffick etc; so as a man can hardly any where set up a trade, but he shall pull down two of his neighbours."

This was language much harsher than Bradford's. The two men fell out before the *Mayflower* left England, when Cushman mishandled negotiations with Weston, accepting his terms too readily. And yet in Cushman's language perhaps we find a rare, authentic echo of the speech of Jacobean men and women in streets, in taverns, and in market squares during these years of destitution.

For Cushman, a refuge from sin and strife lay in what he called "a spacious land, the way to which is through the sea." There we must follow the *Mayflower,* as she rounded the Provincetown Hook and entered the wide, calm haven behind the sand hills, where Christopher Jones let his anchor slip at last on the morning of November 11, 1620.

Part Five

America

Chapter Fourteen

Comfort and Refreshing

Though this had been a day & night of much trouble and danger unto them; yet God gave them a morninge of comfort & refreshing (as usually he doth to his children) . . . on munday they sounded the harbor, and founde it fit for shipping; and marched into the land.

—William Bradford, describing the first arrival at New Plymouth[1]

Almost the first thing they saw was a school of whales. Every day they played around the *Mayflower* as she lay at anchor at Provincetown, like the little fleets of dolphins she must have passed ten weeks before along the coast of Devon. There were so many that Jones compared Cape Cod Bay to the whaling grounds of the Arctic. "If we had instruments and means to take them, we might have made a very rich return," the Pilgrims later wrote, but for the time being, the whales were spared. Harpoons and nets were among the items they had failed to bring. When they tried to shoot one of the creatures from the deck, the gun exploded into pieces in its owner's hand.

A century later, in the 1740s, a local shipowner, Benjamin Bangs, kept a remarkable journal of his own, an account of the bay as the Pilgrims would have known it. Bangs described the great schools of blackfish, the Cape Cod name for pilot whales. At the time of year when the *Mayflower* arrived, Bangs often saw them fill the waters between Provincetown and the shore five miles away at Truro, each one as much as twenty feet long. When the wind changed to come from the northwest, it left them stranded in

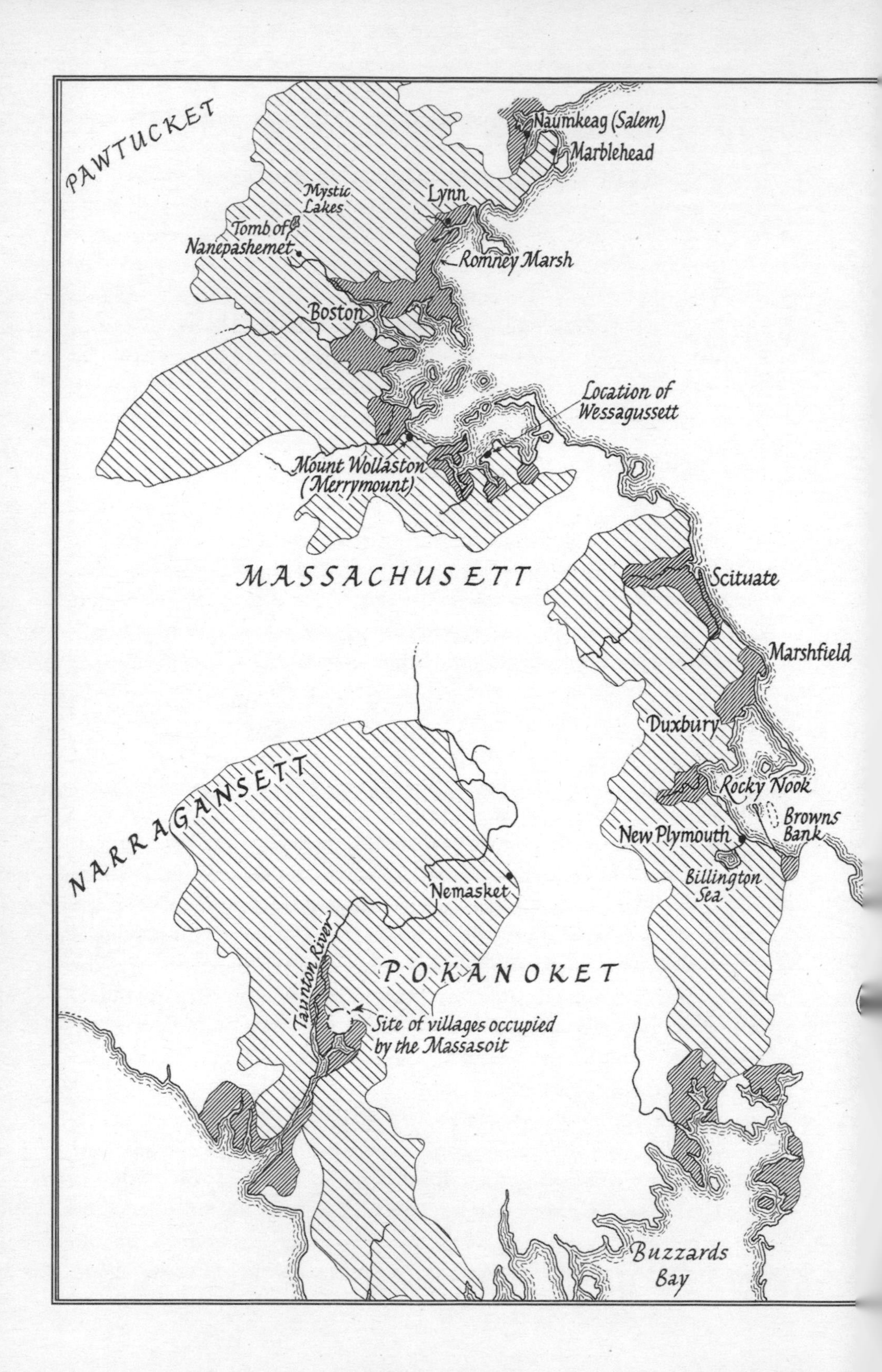
PAWTUCKET
Naumkeag (Salem)
Marblehead
Mystic Lakes
Lynn
Tomb of Nanepashemet
Romney Marsh
Boston
Location of Wessagussett
Mount Wollaston (Merrymount)
MASSACHUSETT
Scituate
Marshfield
Duxbury
Rocky Nook
Browns Bank
New Plymouth
Billington Sea
NARRAGANSETT
Nemasket
Taunton River
POKANOKET
Site of villages occupied by the Massasoit
Buzzards Bay

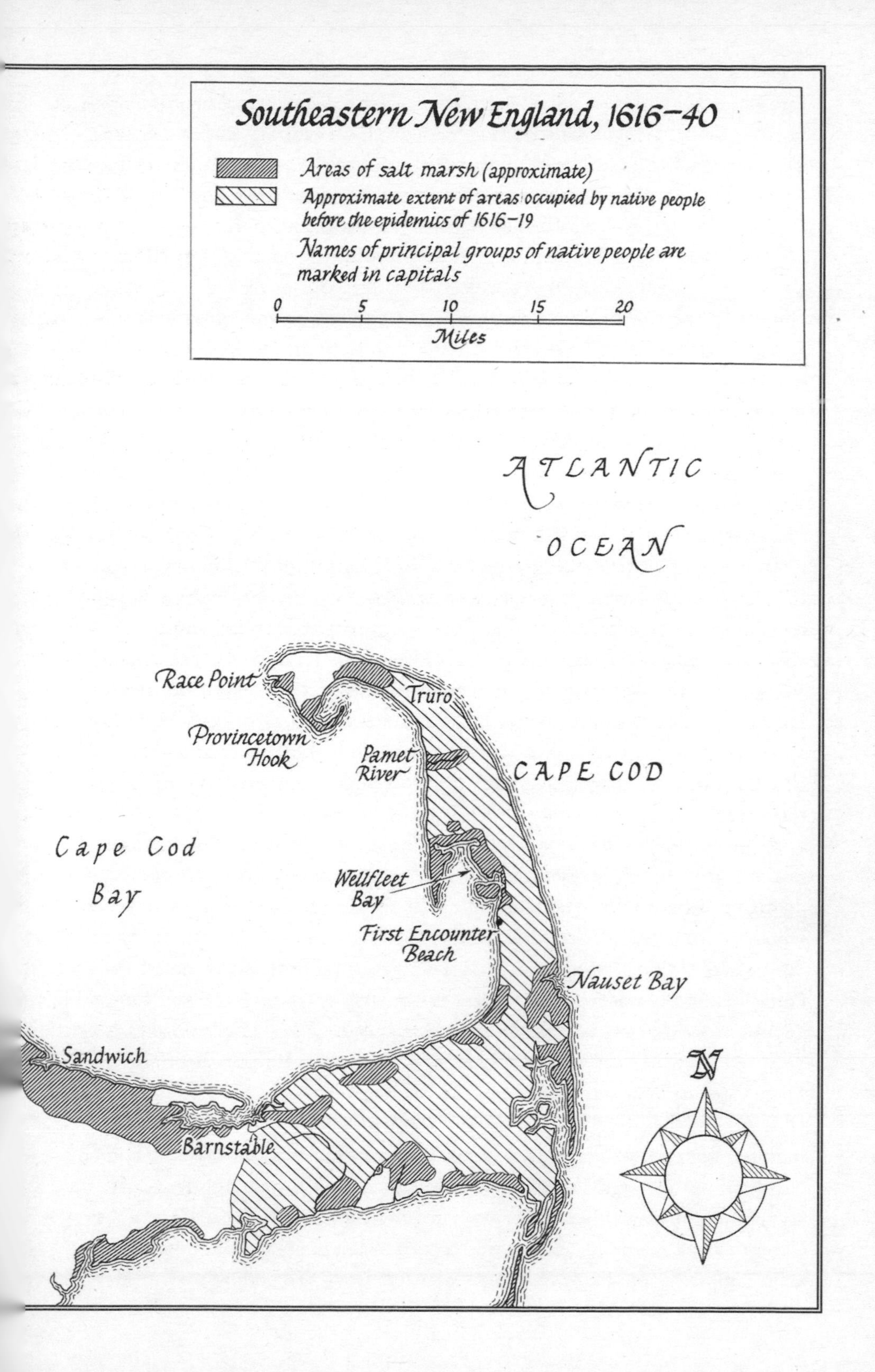
Southeastern New England, 1616–40
Areas of salt marsh (approximate)
Approximate extent of areas occupied by native people before the epidemics of 1616–19
Names of principal groups of native people are marked in capitals
0
5
10
15
20
Miles
ATLANTIC
OCEAN
Race Point
Truro
Provincetown Hook
Pamet River
CAPE COD
Cape Cod Bay
Wellfleet Bay
First Encounter Beach
Nauset Bay
Sandwich
Barnstable
N

immense numbers along the beach. On a single day in late October 1747, the people of Truro killed six hundred of the creatures. As far south as Wellfleet, incidents of slaughter on an even vaster scale continued until as late as 1912, when in the age of petroleum the pilot whale at last began to lose its value as a source of oil for lighting or for lubrication.[2]

The blackfish might stand as a symbol of the strange new world that the Pilgrims entered. It was an altered and vastly magnified version of what they knew in the old. Pilot whales belong to the same marine family as the dolphins of the English Channel, but here in America these creatures existed in numbers unimagined, just as the falls and the sweep of the Kennebec River in Maine far surpass the valley of the Trent. Reading the works of Captain John Smith had prepared the Pilgrims up to a point, but previous English seafarers like Smith had mostly come to this part of the Atlantic coast much earlier in the year. They had never described the blackfish, and never traveled far inland.

In the pilot whales, the Pilgrims saw what Smith told them they would find: an abundant store of value in nature, holding out the promise or the temptation of riches. For the first time, they also realized how unprepared they were, how few tools they had, and how long it would be before anything better than survival could be achieved. A long process of education lay in wait. It was going to be a matter of trial and error, mistakes and successes, improvising and adapting. They took old skills and English models and either made them fit the New World or discarded them if they did not.

Captain Smith made one dangerous omission. He had neither endured nor put into words a northeastern American winter, and while the Pilgrims must have known something about the climate, they had little with which to compare it. Although the Thames sometimes froze, it was a rare event, like the great frost at Christmas in 1607, chronicled in detail precisely because it was unusual. It was not a customary feature, like the ice that blocks rivers in New England between January and March. Cold of a very un-English severity was the second thing the Pilgrims noticed on Cape Cod, straight after the whales.

It began when they had to wade ashore at Provincetown—the earliest detailed chart shows that water deep enough to float a ship began only half a mile from the beach, and even a small boat had to stop a long way out—and then it became steadily more acute. By the first week of December, more than six inches of snow covered the land. In a small boat men found that damp clothing froze on their backs like iron, and coughs and catarrh evolved into fatal illness.

In his account of their first winter in America, Bradford only mentions scurvy by name as a cause of death among the colonists. However, he also refers to the filthy condition of the sick. At sea, for whatever reason, they had escaped the mariner's scourge of amoebic dysentery, but Bradford's comments suggest that the disease struck them with its full force after their arrival in New England. If scurvy was the principal agent of mortality, then the dreadful fact is that it could have been avoided. By 1620, ships' surgeons in the East India service were already well aware that lemon or lime juice prevented the disease, although it took another century or more before the Royal Navy began to carry fruit rations on every long voyage. Dysentery was quite another matter: apart from trying to keep themselves clean, and drinking water to ease the dehydration caused by diarrhea, the Pilgrims could do nothing about it.

By the time the spring returned, forty-four of the passengers had died, and nearly half the crew. The first four to succumb, including Dorothy Bradford, William's wife, had died before the Pilgrims first saw New Plymouth. The fate of Dorothy Bradford—she fell into the sea and drowned—remains mysterious, but the other three were those we might expect to perish soonest. They were either old or very young. The first was Edward Thomson, a servant, probably in his teens, who died on December 4, but the next was seven-year-old Jasper More, and then James Chilton, on December 8: in his mid-sixties, Chilton was perhaps the oldest man on the *Mayflower.*[3]

And yet, as disease began to take its toll, the Pilgrims also made their journeys of discovery. The fourth expedition finally took them to Plymouth Bay, on December 10, and led to their choice of a place to settle. There are two ways to tell the story of what occurred. We can simply follow the familiar sequence of episodes, narrated many times by many writers, as they explored the Cape on foot, and then with the shallop, and fought their first fight against the native people at First Encounter Beach near Wellfleet. Or, alternatively, the opening weeks can be seen as a series of meetings with objects or creatures like the blackfish, phenomena that, like the number of pilot whales, defied an English imagination.

Ranging and Searching

First, the outline of events. To sustain a colony, the Pilgrims needed timber, game, fresh running water, a flat expanse of earth for corn, shoals of fish, and a harbor—and, if they could find them, a wide river leading inland, and native people willing to sell skins. Some of these elements existed on the Cape, but the full combination most certainly did not. South along the shore, the mouth of the Pamet River was visible from Provincetown, but after a few miles it led to a dead end. It was tidal and salty, and around it the ground was dry. That was the damning flaw of the place: rain simply vanishes into the sandy soil. Provincetown has little water of its own, and although Truro has aquifers, they lie deep beneath the surface.

Added to that, the terrain was exhausting. An outwash of gravel and sand from melting glaciers created the Outer Cape, and to the south it formed a wide, dense belt of low hills in their dozens with no obvious route through them. It was unattractive as a place to settle. Even in 1790, Provincetown had fewer than five hundred inhabitants. The entirety of Cape Cod all the way to Sandwich had little more than seventeen thousand, so that much of the land lay empty.[4]

The first expedition was simply a landing, fifteen or sixteen armed men going ashore on November 11 to reconnoiter the hook, where they found the black earth that so impressed them. The second was more ambitious, and began on November 15. Again it involved only sixteen men, but over three days they saw their first native people in the distance, found signs of graves and cultivation, and reached the Pamet. Most famously, they discovered a buried cache of corn and a ship's copper kettle. They filled the kettle with corn and carried it back to the *Mayflower* slung on a pole between two men to serve as seed the following season. They intended to pay for it, and indeed they did so eventually, but not before the incident caused their clash with the natives.

The shallop remained unfit for use until November 27, but then a third expedition was possible, more than thirty strong. The boat followed the men as they marched along the shore. Again they found corn, and more graves, but also their first native encampment, two houses made from bent saplings covered with mats. They were uninhabited, but filled with bowls, trays, dishes, pots, and an English basket. When they returned to the ship on November 30, they began to debate what they had seen: the time for urgent discussion had arrived, because as the weather grew worse, further missions by sea would become impossible. Supplies were running low, disease began to appear, and the *Mayflower* could not be relied on to linger on the coast. If they were to leave Provincetown and find a new place to settle, they would have to do so very swiftly.

They decided to make a last journey of discovery, by sea around the inside of the Cape. Most of all, they wanted to reach an estuary, which the second mate of the *Mayflower* believed he had seen on an earlier voyage.

Led by Standish and Carver, but also including Bradford, Howland, and Winslow, the party set out on December 6. They did not find the estuary—none of any size existed nearby—and they lost their mast and were nearly wrecked in a gale at the entrance to Plymouth Bay. But they did find the site of New Plymouth, where at last they landed on December 11. The *Mayflower* followed on December 16, the Pilgrims began to come ashore, on or near Plymouth Rock, and so the colony began.

New Plymouth did not have an estuary, but it was the best place they could find. Dense woodland lay behind it, and the site had flowing water—as always, Bradford singles out for comment "the runing brooks"—and it had an adequate harbor, ringed by sandbanks but accessible with practice. Inland they found cornfields left by the native people, most of whom had died in the epidemics. It was also defensible, thanks to Burial Hill.

Several hundred yards inland, the hill rose above the cornfields and might serve as a redoubt. This must have seemed all the more necessary, because during this last expedition the Pilgrims had come under attack, at First Encounter Beach. As they broke camp at dawn on the sands, a party of thirty or forty native people attacked them with a hail of arrows. Led by Standish, the party had to fight them off with their muskets.

Such was the bare schedule of the journeys that the Pilgrims made, but their engagement with the Cape took another form as well. There was a narrative, a plot that unfolded as the Pilgrims looked for a suitable site to settle, but they also encountered a succession of new and bewildering images and objects. Of these, by far the most disturbing was a Native American grave that they found on November 30 somewhere in the flatland along the Pamet valley. Winslow, assuming he was the author of this section of *Mourt's Relation,* described it with a precision highly unusual at the time. This was a sign of how odd he felt it to be.

Seeing traces of a recent burial, they began to dig. They found first a mat, then a bow, and then another mat. Beneath it was a board more than two feet long, painted and carved, with incisions or slots at one end that made it resemble a crown. Between the mat they found layers of household goods: bowls, dishes, and trays. Underneath them was another mat, which covered two bundles. The larger one contained a sheet of canvas, a cassock of a kind worn by sailors, and a pair of breeches. Inside them were the skull and almost entirely decomposed body of a man.

To their astonishment, the skull had strands of yellow hair. Around the body there were European goods: a knife, a pack needle for securing baggage, and pieces of iron. Dark red powder, with a strong smell, covered the remains. They found the same powder in the second, smaller bundle, encasing the bones and the head of a small child. Strings and bracelets of white beads enveloped its limbs, and beside the remains was another small bow. The Pilgrims took some of the finest articles and filled in the grave.

Archaeology did not yet exist in England, even in rudimentary form. Nearly forty years passed before a doctor from Norwich, Sir Thomas Browne, published in 1658 the first account of prehistoric and Roman remains plowed up by English farmers. Not until the 1680s did a museum curator in Oxford begin to write reports about stone tools found in the earth. And yet Winslow took notes of painstaking accuracy, giving details that can be exactly verified from later excavations. The twin burial at Pamet closely resembles a similar interment found at Marblehead, near Salem, in 1874. The excavators discovered the same powder and beads, a similar mixture of native and European goods, and the same manner of placing a child beside an adult.[5]

Perhaps the dead at Marblehead and at Pamet were victims of the epidemics that had swept the coast: the Pilgrims saw many graves, suggesting that some appalling catastrophe had befallen the inhabitants. And yet Winslow displays not so much horror as fascination, as well he might. No contrast could have been greater with the burial practices of his homeland.

By 1620, the churchyard of an English parish remained the resting place of the vast majority—the wealthy had taken over the chancel, inside the church and at the front—but it had become an unholy space, used for keeping geese or pigs or grazing cows. At Sturton in Nottinghamshire, women beat their laundry on a slab in the churchyard, beside a well. Few grave markers of any kind existed: only very rarely does one find a gravestone set up before 1660. If the churchyard dated back to the time of the Norman Conquest, by now it might contain thousands of skeletons, with no record of their resting place. Every plot had many occupants.

After the English Civil War, attitudes began to change, but in the grave digger's scene in *Hamlet,* Shakespeare portrayed Jacobean cemeteries as they were, muddy and unkempt, with their scattered bones and skulls and shallow, reused graves. Inside the church, another regime existed for the wealthy, and in the four decades before the *Mayflower* there was a rush to build carved monuments, with the painted effigies that still survive on so many tombs. Even so, it was the effigy that mattered, and the inscription. The physical remains of the deceased were an irrelevance.[6]

For Calvinists, this was entirely logical. For them, death was final and absolute, an instantaneous divide, the point at which the soul passed entirely beyond the reach of human beings, either to damnation or to eternal life. It might make sense to erect a carved monument as a commemoration of rank, or to flatter the living members of the family, but caring for the corpse served no purpose. In the graves he found on Cape Cod, Edward Winslow encountered people for whom exactly the opposite was true, for whom the dead might be ever present. For them the ornamentation of the cadaver was a duty. They left precious trading goods with the remains as a mark of respect for the departed.

Within the next three years, Winslow's readiness to pay close attention to the customs and the language of the native people whom he met came to be an essential asset of the Plymouth Colony. It was critical for their survival. Equally fundamental was another early event: the signing of the Mayflower Compact, that document sometimes exalted as the origin of American democracy, and more often these days dismissed as an irrelevance.

The Mayflower Compact

If the first creatures they saw were the pilot whales, the first thing they did was to sign the compact, before the first men landed, before the women went ashore to wash clothes, and before the carpenter began to reassemble the shallop. Like the blackfish, the compact was a mingling of the familiar and the very new. The Pilgrims took English models, and then radically transformed them to fit new conditions.

Forty-one adult males put their names to it, because Carver and his colleagues wished to put a stop to argument and grumbling in the ranks, dissent that might give rise to mutiny. The problem arose because the *Mayflower* had strayed north beyond the domain of the Virginia Company, entering territory where the patent for the colony had no legal force. Because of this, says Bradford, some of the "strangers" on the ship—meaning men who had not come from Leiden, but joined the party in England—pointed out that they could not be compelled to obey orders.

So, to maintain unity and discipline, they drafted and signed the compact. When *Mourt's Relation* appeared in London, it included the text, but the authors added a preamble that puts the situation very clearly: "it was thought good there should be an association and agreement, that we should combine together in one body, and to submit to such government and governors as we should by common consent agree to make and choose."[7] As we shall see in a moment, the words the writers chose were loaded with significance.

The compact was what an English lawyer would call an enabling document. It was not a constitution as such. They drew up a combination or a covenant, creating "a civill bodie politick," and they gave it the powers to make "just & equall lawes, ordinances, Acts, constitutions & offices" for the general good of the colony. But they did not say exactly what those rules would be. For this reason, and because it was clearly improvised, it has become commonplace for historians to play down the importance of the document, as though it did not have a fundamental role to play.

It is also fashionable to claim that writers and politicians in the north invented a Pilgrim myth in the nineteenth century. It is said that this Yankee myth gave the *Mayflower* and New Plymouth far more significance than they deserved, compared with Jamestown, or with the Great Migration of the 1630s. Some argue that the Mayflower Compact was no more than a short-term, temporary measure, drawn up in a hurry, containing nothing new and nothing original. That being so, the argument runs, it could not possibly be the foundation stone of American democracy, but was simply one source among many.

We can debate the legacy of the compact as it was seen by later generations, or we can ask how a Jacobean Englishman or Englishwoman might have regarded it. Did *they* think it was merely a temporary fix? Or was it much more? Would the Mayflower Compact have struck *them* as something new and different? If it did, and if it contained some radical elements, going beyond the usual English way of running a town or village, then the case for the compact is proven. If it was new, it was new. If it possessed originality, then it deserves to be given back its status as the earliest manifesto for a distinctive, American form of democratic government.

What did the document mean to William Bradford? It was certainly improvised, but in his eyes there was nothing mythical or temporary about it. For him, the compact always remained fundamental, a permanent, necessary source of authority as long as the colony lasted. If it had simply been a short-term fix, the compact would have ceased to matter in 1630, when the Plymouth Colony obtained a definitive new patent from the Earl of Warwick, as president of the Council for New England. Instead, Bradford and Winslow made it plain that the compact remained very much alive.

In 1636, they codified the rules of the Plymouth Colony in a new Book of Laws. On page one, they called the Mayflower Compact "a solemne & binding combinacon," and they treated the compact and the Warwick Patent as the double-barreled source of the colony's right to exist and to run its own affairs. If one or the other could claim seniority, then it was the compact, not the patent. This was because the compact depended on the vote of the governed, while Warwick issued his patent under authority delegated from King Charles.

In the same Book of Laws, they added an extra paragraph that explains how they interpreted the documents. They say that they came to America as "freeborne subjects of the state of England." Helpfully they explained the meaning of the words. Freedom meant that nobody could force on the colony any "imposicon law or ordnance"—and, incidentally, an imposition meant a tax—except "by consent according to the free liberties of the state & Kingdome of Engl. & no otherwise." In other words, obedience to the law required freely given consent, just as it did in the paper they signed at Provincetown.

In a crisis, if the Pilgrims could not agree to a law passed in England, and if they had to choose between obedience and liberty, then the king would have to yield. In the Book of Laws, they wrote out the form of words used when every new freeman of the colony swore allegiance to it. All the men pledged "to advance the growth & good of the severall plantations," but they also swore to be "truly loyall to our Sovereign Lord King Charles." Some time later, doubtless during the English Civil War, they neatly crossed out the mention of the king. Although the Mayflower Compact began with a promise of loyalty to the monarch, in extremity he could be deleted from the constitution, while the consent of the governed could not. The people outranked the Crown.

All of this happened a very long time after the landing at Cape Cod. It might be thought that the question of resistance to the Crown never arose at the moment when the compact was signed. Actually, it *did* arise, or almost certainly so, in the mind of William Brewster. Because of his education and his career, Brewster stands out as the man most likely to have drafted the document. He owned works by an author notorious for justifying rebellion in circumstances where the sovereign failed to honor his side of his bargain with his subjects.

In 1622, the archbishop of Canterbury ordered the public burning of books written by a German Calvinist called David Pareus, professor of theology at Heidelberg. They were, said the archbishop, "seditious, scandalous and contrary to the scriptures," but four volumes by Pareus sat on Brewster's library shelves at New Plymouth.[8] Among them was the most seditious of them all, the professor's commentary on Saint Paul's letter to the Romans. No book within the Bible carried more weight with the Pilgrims than this one, and David Pareus gave it a startling new interpretation.

In a famous passage, Saint Paul told Christians to obey their rulers, the powers that be, because they were divinely ordained. Boldly, Pareus reread this to mean that the same Christians had a *duty* to overthrow a tyrant, and especially an irreligious one, because such a man was clearly an enemy of God. "Obedience hath certaine limits," Pareus wrote. "When tyrants go about to force their subjects to manifest idolatry, or to some wickednesse, against the expresse word of God; in this case the scripture commands us, that in no wayes we obey such tyrannical Edicts, but that every man, according to the condition of his calling, make resistance."[9] Of course, Brewster did not insert anything of such an outspoken kind in the Mayflower Compact. All the same, if this was the world of ideas within which he lived, then we would expect to find them leaving radical traces within the words he did employ. And so we do, though mingled and blended with other language that was more common.

At Provincetown, they had to find a substitute for the patent granted by the Virginia Company. So whoever drafted the compact modeled it partly on the words these patents usually contained. Examples survive, from 1619 and 1622, when the company gave planters the power "to frame and make orders ordinances and constitucions." Although the original patent granted to the Pilgrims has been lost, it would have included a similar clause. Whoever drafted the compact simply carried over the same language. This was because the need for it arose only from an accident of seafaring, and not from defects in the original document.[10]

Any educated Jacobean would have noticed something else as well. When the Pilgrims used the term "a civill bodie politick," and awarded themselves the power to make laws and ordinances, they used phrases from the royal charters that gave English boroughs their rights and powers. Early in the reign of King James, many towns renewed their charters, tightening up the wording to prevent legal challenge by people who, for example, disliked paying local tolls or taxes. They included towns that Brewster and Christopher Jones knew intimately: Doncaster, Harwich, and Retford. All three obtained new charters between 1604 and 1607. If New Plymouth was a sort of colonial borough packaged up and shipped across the Atlantic, then again it made sense to use the same sort of language.

So was the compact trite and commonplace, a ready-made replica of the arrangements by which any town in England already ran its affairs? No, most definitely not. A mass of legalese, designed to thwart any hostile litigation, an English borough charter often ran to four thousand words, twenty times longer than the compact. It was intended to be exclusive. Most of the new charters placed the right to rule in the hands of a few citizens, like the oligarchy to which Jones belonged at Harwich. That was not the case at Provincetown. Brief, clear, more a statement of principles than a charter, the compact carried the signatures of the vast majority of the men on board, and it treated them all equally. Menservants did not sign, and because dates of birth are missing for many passengers, we cannot be certain exactly how many adult males made the crossing. But at the very least the forty-one signatures accounted for 90 percent of the men on the *Mayflower.*

During the reign of Elizabeth, experiments in democracy took place in small English towns and villages, but in this respect, the number of those who signed, the Mayflower Compact went far beyond them. A case in point was Blyth in Nottinghamshire, three miles from Scrooby. Like the Plymouth Colony, Blyth had a common house, a common store of arms, and an annual election. Every April the townspeople gathered to choose a mayor, and they recorded the outcome in a town book that still survives. In 1587, the lord of the manor of Blyth died without an adult male heir, and the people of Blyth seized their chance to assert themselves.

They rewrote the language used for an election to make it clear that the townspeople could freely elect whomsoever they wished, without following a recommendation from the local landowner. Again, the words they used closely resembled those of the compact. At Blyth, the citizens decided that in future the mayor would be "chossen by the consent of all the inhabitants . . . he will endeavoure himself to doe the best that he cane for the common wealthe of the towne." They widened the franchise, from eleven voters in the 1570s to as many as ninety-two in the 1590s. Even so, the electorate represented less than one-third of the adult males at Blyth, so that "all the inhabitants" meant something far less than it did at New Plymouth.[11]

Although it drew on experiments like the one at Blyth, the compact went much further, simply by allowing every freeman full participation. As for its guiding principles, they flowed from another, deeper source in the political ideas that Brewster came cross either at Cambridge or during his time with William Davison. Brewster, as we saw, owned a copy of the manual of government written by Sir Thomas Smith. In the 1560s and 1570s writers such as Smith and Sir Philip Sidney began to speak of England as though the realm were really a republic, like the ancient city of Rome. Of course they had a queen, but she ruled by way of consent, expressed through Parliament and the Privy Council—or so they suggested. According to Smith, in a sentence evoked at Provincetown in the language of the compact: "A common wealth is called a society or common doing of a multitude of free men collected together and united by common accord and covenauntes among themselves, for the conservation of themselves aswell in peace as in warre."[12]

When the Pilgrims picked the term "association" to describe the document they signed, again they chose a word with a loaded meaning embedded in the politics of the Elizabethans. Only in the 1580s did people start to use the word in this sense, to mean a paper signed by a number of people with a common purpose. This usage of the word became current in the name of the so-called Bond of Association drawn up by the Privy Council in 1584. Drafted by Burghley and Walsingham, it circulated up and down the country, attracting the signatures of thousands of local dignitaries and members of the gentry. They swore to resist by force of arms anybody who made an attempt on the life of Queen Elizabeth, or tried to claim the throne.

Two decades ago, the British historian Patrick Collinson showed that the Bond of Association was itself a republican document. It was drawn up in such a way that, if worse came to worst, and Elizabeth died without an heir, the signatories of the bond would elect a new Protestant sovereign. Brewster entered public service, working for one of Walsingham's closest aides, during the period when the bond was very much a talking point.

Were all these echoes of earlier documents merely unconscious or coincidental? Perhaps they were: but given what we know about Brewster, it seems unlikely. Assuming that he drafted it, he assembled the Mayflower Compact from a mosaic of the best precedents he could find. He made it simple and clear, but he also filled it with resonance. He did not insist on a religious creed, or require sectarian faith from those who signed it. In 1620, a Roman Catholic could have put his name to it without offending the pope, since all the compact demanded was a brief, ecumenical nod in the direction of King James. It contained not a single phrase with a specifically Puritan meaning or source.*

The Pilgrims drew up the agreement in a new location, at the moment of creation of a new colony. They did so in terms that, two decades later, could be used as a rationale for outright resistance to the Crown. This, the right of disobedience, existed within the language of the Mayflower Compact from the very start. Most radically of all, they produced a document that nearly every man signed, including those who in England were only laborers. This was all very new indeed, as new and different as a school of pilot whales.

---

*The Mayflower Compact uses the word "covenant" to refer to the agreement between the colonists. Although the word could have religious connotations, equally often it simply meant a legally binding contract.

The Meeting with Samoset

As the winter went on, hardship and deaths continued. After the *Mayflower* arrived at New Plymouth, five weeks passed before the first Sunday when the Separatists could gather for a Sabbath assembly on land. Until that point, the colonists remained mainly on the ship, where so many of them had died, six in December and another eight in January. In the meantime, they had laid out a settlement with two streets and plots of land around them. On Christmas Day, they began to build a common house to hold stores and provide temporary shelter. They also started to make an emplacement for cannon on the hill.

Thanks to atrocious weather and the toll taken by sickness, each of these tasks took far longer than it should: the common house remained unfinished until January 20. At times as few as six or seven men and women remained on their feet. As the number of deaths neared its peak, they began to see signs of more activity among the native people of the interior. Up to that point, they had caught glimpses of fires in the distance, but now, on February 16, a man out shooting wildfowl saw a band of twelve warriors. He took cover, then hurried back to the colony to sound the alarm. In the next few days the Pilgrims made ready to receive an attack. It was at this point that Jones and his seamen unloaded four pieces of artillery from the ship and dragged them up Burial Hill.

The onslaught never came, but death from disease continued. They were still dying in March, thirteen that month, even as the weather began to brighten. Edward Winslow's wife, Elizabeth, died on March 24, the last day of the old year 1620, as the English reckoned their calendar at the time. On March 3 they heard birdsong, and on March 7 they planted their first vegetables. On the same day Governor Carver led their first fishing and hunting expedition to Billington Sea and the other ponds close by. Within weeks he too would be dead, apparently from a heart attack while working in the fields in April. Less than two months later, his widow, Katherine Carver, of Sturton, died too.

Bradford never said much about John Carver. Only one seventeenth-century historian gives us even the briefest character sketch, and that was William Hubbard, author of an official history of New England, begun in 1682. However, Hubbard clearly had sources that have since been lost, and so his comments about Carver carry weight. Hubbard writes about his piety, his humility, and his public spirit, but also he refers to the man's "public purse." Carver, he wrote, "disbursed the greatest part of that considerable estate God had given him for the carrying on of the interest of the company."[13] Carver also lived long enough to accomplish the principal duty of any colonial governor: diplomatic affairs, the making of pacts and treaties. Shortly before he died, he reached an accord with Massasoit, the foremost sachem of the native people of southeastern New England. It came about by way of the intervention of two intermediaries.

On Friday, March 16, "a fair warm day," as they completed their fortifications, at last the settlers saw a man break cover close to their huts. He was tall, with long black hair swept back from a shaved forehead, beardless, and almost naked, except for a leather loincloth. He carried a bow and two arrows, one tipped with a warhead and the other not: that was symbolism. This was a man the English mariners on the coast of Maine called "Somerset." It was no doubt a garbled, joking sailor's version of whatever his name was in his own language.

Three years later, far away near Boothbay Harbor in Maine, an English naval officer met Somerset, or Samoset, as Winslow knew him. The officer, Captain Christopher Levett, remembered Samoset as a sachem himself. He was a leader among his people, eager to talk and trade beaver pelts, and to make an alliance with Levett against their enemies, the raiding Micmac from farther up the coast. Captain Levett recommended him as a man "very faithfull to the English." Samoset, Levett said, had "saved the lives of many of our Nation, some from starving, others from killing."

Samoset also spoke English, learned from the seamen at Monhegan. Already, English and French were becoming the trading dialects of the coast, as the economies of western Europe began to annex the region. Algonquian is a family of different languages, and as Levett pointed out, two native people from settlements separated by as little as seventy miles could understand each other no better than the English could the Welsh. Today, the Native American linguists who keep alive the ancient tongues of Rhode Island or Massachusetts do not claim to know the languages of Maine or Quebec. As Levett remarked, "They were glad to use broken English to expresse their mind each to other."[14]

So it was with Samoset. He strode up to the Plymouth colonists, and he began to pour out a description of the coast, its people, its chiefs, and their military resources. By now, he clearly knew that these details fascinated the English, just as they enthralled Ferdinando Gorges at old Plymouth fifteen years before. Samoset asked for beer, and so the Pilgrims gave him brandy: doubtless they and the sailors had long since finished off the *Mayflower*'s ale. That afternoon Samoset began to explain the politics of the hinterland, and the reasons why the native people had seemed so likely to attack.

He told the Pilgrims that bitter recollections remained, arising from the activities of Thomas Hunt, an earlier visitor. Hunt was a ship's master who came with Captain John Smith on his voyage to New England in 1614. By the time the Pilgrims came ashore, Hunt himself was dead. He was lost at sea or succumbed to disease in 1619, after a trading voyage or two to Russia: his will survives, and so does a record of the bullion Hunt carried to Archangel. In his lifetime he almost destroyed New England before it began.

Thomas Hunt was a religious man who made bequests to pay for Good Friday sermons by "a godlie preacher" in his hometown.* However, in Cape Cod Bay, at the site of New Plymouth and farther east and around toward Hyannis, under cover of commerce in 1614 Thomas Hunt tricked onto his ship some twenty-seven people. Twenty came from Patuxet, the native name for Plymouth, and seven from among the Nauset, who lived along the Cape. Hunt took them captive and carried them back across the Atlantic, to be sold as slaves in Málaga: as Captain John Smith put it, Hunt "sold those silly Salvages for Rials of Eight."

Stories of the incident spread around the region, and worse was to follow. Another English skipper massacred a trading party of native people with a barrage of shot from his "murderers," small shipboard guns carried for use at point-blank range. Because of episodes such as this, in 1620 another ship's captain sent out by Gorges, Thomas Dermer, very nearly met his end at the hands of the inhabitants of Martha's Vineyard. Not long before the arrival of the *Mayflower*, he lost all his crew and had to flee south to Jamestown.

It was not surprising, then, that the Plymouth colonists encountered hatred and distrust. However, among the captives taken by Hunt was another native, a man about to join Samoset in helping them bargain with Massasoit. This was Tisquantum, the Native American who became famous as Squanto, the friend of the Pilgrims.[15] At Málaga, Spanish monks saved him and his fellow prisoners from slavery, and Tisquantum found his way to London. There he learned English, and met a different kind of merchant, before he shipped back to America with Dermer. Thanks to what he saw by the Thames, he stood ready to mediate between the Pilgrims and the native people inland.

In the meantime, in the same city of London, Thomas Weston faced a gathering crisis of a different kind. As the depression deepened, men like him found their affairs disintegrating. They turned to dangerous expedients, including some that took them outside the law.

---

*Aldeburgh, in Suffolk.

Chapter Fifteen

The Mystic and the Thames

You may guesse in what case we are (for all our fair shewes) when neither Lord Maior, Alderman, farmers no nor whole companies, as the East Indian . . . are able to hold out and pay their debts.

—John Chamberlain to Sir Dudley Carleton,
November 10, 1621[1]

Very early one morning, in the darkness between one and two, a barge filled with heavy sacks approached a wharf beside the river Thames. The sacks weighed ten tons, and if any had split or burst, they would have spilled a fine white powder onto the mud or the timbers of the jetty. A group of men waited for the barge at a spot on the north bank almost opposite the Globe Theatre. Their leader was Philemon Powell, aged about twenty-five.

There was, it seems, some delay, an altercation by the water's edge. At last a deal was struck, and Powell and his accomplices loaded the sacks into carts or wheelbarrows. They trundled them along the lane that sloped up and away from the river toward the sheds and houses of Bread Street Ward, where that night they made their delivery.

On the wharf with Powell was Andrew Weston, younger brother of Thomas. Both men were under surveillance. An informer patrolled the wharf, Brook's Wharf, between Stew Lane and Queenhithe, a few hundred yards upstream from London Bridge. He spotted Powell and the sacks, which contained alum, more scientifically known as aluminum sulfate. It was a chemical essential for the textile trade, because it helped to fix dyes into woolen cloth.

Smuggling alum was a racket, one of many in Jacobean England, a contraband activity that could yield a profit of nine pounds per ton, before paying off those whom you had to pay off. This, it seems, was one of the ways in which Thomas Weston tried to recoup the losses he made from the voyage of the *Mayflower.* The legal records describing the incident give it no precise date, but others that survive show that Weston was dealing heavily in alum in the spring of 1621. He had every reason to turn to desperate alternatives, because the expedition to New England had been a commercial fiasco.

As the settlers emerged from their first winter, in London their backers soon learned that the venture had fallen at its first hurdle. The *Mayflower* made a swift return passage, leaving America on April 5 and docking back in England on May 6, but she came back empty, with neither fish nor fur. That was the worst possible outcome for Weston and his associates. One mishap they could cope with, but only one: the error in navigation, which had caused Jones to disembark his passengers a long way from the intended destination by the Hudson.

The investor group quickly dealt with that. They obtained a new patent for the colony from the Council for New England. The council happily granted the permission required for the Pilgrims to occupy a spot north of the fortieth parallel: the document, the so-called Peirce Patent, hangs today in Pilgrim Hall at Plymouth, Massachusetts. This, however, was just a legal matter, necessary but not sufficient. It did not pay their bills, and as the economy shrank, the investors found their resources diminishing too. Instead of writing off the Pilgrims instantly, they began to assemble finance for a second voyage, to reinforce the colony. Even so, it took another two months to prepare the second ship, the *Fortune,* and she was small.

She had a volume of only fifty-five tons. Although she carried thirty-five new settlers, she was almost entirely devoid of supplies and trading goods. The *Fortune* did not reach New England until November. When she did so, at first she hovered oddly around Cape Cod, causing alarm: reports from the native people suggested that she was a hostile French vessel. William Bradford armed his men, loaded the cannon on Burial Hill, and prepared to blow the Frenchman out of the water.

At last the *Fortune* entered Plymouth Bay, and she was passed as friendly. Her passengers swiftly panicked after seeing the conditions at the colony and after listening to the customary words of encouragement from the *Fortune*'s crew, seamen as jaundiced as those on board the *Mayflower.* They very nearly reembarked and left, until the *Fortune*'s master talked them out of it, promising in an emergency to carry them on down the coast to Virginia. Even so, as Bradford recorded, "ther was not so much as Bisket, cake, or any other victials, neither had they any beding, but some sory things . . . nor over many cloaths." But at least they added labor. Almost all the passengers were grown men but young, and they had their uses: one of them was Philip De La Noye, the distant ancestor of Franklin Roosevelt.

In London, the depression worsened. Since England had no banks, there were no banks to fail, but there were many loans to foreclose and many speculators on the brink of ruin. Within the *Mayflower* investor group, the stronger men such as Pocock and Beauchamp clung on, and staked their hopes on the *Fortune,* but they had built sound businesses with deep roots in provincial supply and demand. Thomas Weston had not. He spiraled down toward insolvency. Worse still, he offended the authorities, by way of "wilful contempt and abuse offered to the State," as they put it when later they issued a warrant for his arrest.[2]

Was Thomas Weston a rogue? Perhaps, but if he was, he had good company. That year, many men saw their businesses go under, and it should not be surprising that commercial ethics went the same way as their money. In the same month that the *Fortune* reached New Plymouth, the Lord Mayor of London fled his creditors, emptying his house and vanishing one dark night. As for the alum scam, it was commonplace: in 1620, the Crown prosecuted more than a hundred merchants, up and down the length of the kingdom, for illegally shipping in four thousand tons of the stuff. The fraud, if that is what it was, arose because of the way in which the Crown had riddled the economy with perverse regulations and monopolies, creating incentives for cheating.[3]

There were alum mines in Yorkshire, and they were considered to be strategic assets for the kingdom. Sadly, the owners failed to make a profit. So King James took the mines into state control and then farmed them out to a private monopoly, which paid him a rent. To ensure that they could afford to do so, James banned imports of European alum—the Pope, as it happened, owned the best available—and he insisted that English customers pay a fixed price per ton: twenty-six pounds. Meanwhile, the English monopoly exported its alum to continental Europe and dumped it on the market for eleven pounds less.

So, of course, men such as Weston picked it up abroad, mainly in Rouen, and shipped it back. They passed it off as Yorkshire alum bought legally in England, and sold it for twenty-four pounds per ton to customers in the cloth trade. This could easily be done because English alum was white, while the pope's was red.

Of course a racket as lucrative as this could not be expected to last. Unhappily for Weston, in April 1621 the king gave a new patent to a man called Guest, making him an official searcher for alum. Guest would receive a reward for each ton of contraband he found. A copy of the patent survives, in the immaculate archives of the Lord Treasurer of the time, Lionel Cranfield, along with a set of documents that relate to Weston. The informer at Brook's Wharf contacted Guest, it appears, and Guest filed a lawsuit against Weston in June in the Court of the Exchequer, the forum that handled matters relating to royal revenues. Guest demanded unpaid customs duties on the smuggled alum, and tried to impound the consignment. Predictably, Weston had bought it on credit: if he lost the case he faced ruin.

For merchants such as he, reliant on IOUs, the only working capital available was reputation. Once that was gone, they were virtually doomed. Of course, the Exchequer jury found against him, and so Thomas Weston's affairs began to unravel. For one thing, the two men who bought the alum from Powell were throwing all the blame in his direction, insisting that Weston alone was liable for the heavy penalty imposed by the court. It came to no less than £345, a huge multiple of the profit that Weston had hoped to make. The sum was far beyond his reach.

Weston survived for a little while, since he had a few weak cards left to play, and a last flimsy line of credit, but the inevitable could not be delayed for long. As we shall see, Weston reached his lowest ebb in the early months of 1622. At the same time the Plymouth Colony very nearly collapsed, and for reasons that were closely related. In the meantime, before the *Fortune* arrived, Bradford and his comrades had begun to lay some foundations for the future. Even so, nearly seven years of uncertainty lay ahead, until at last the turning point came in 1628.[4]

Samoset and Tisquantum

When the Pilgrims met Samoset in March 1621, they gained access to the networks of trade between the native people, the French, and the English that circled back and forth along the shores of the Gulf of Maine. This was not a new phenomenon. At least as early as the 1590s, sachems from among the Micmac to the east and north had begun to act as middlemen, translators, and procurers of beaver pelts. However, there was something very unusual about Tisquantum. It swiftly emerged after Samoset introduced him to the Pilgrims on March 22. It transformed a fraught and dangerous situation.

In the six days since he first came striding out of the forest, Samoset had been entirely friendly, but on this part of the coast his value was limited. He was not a local man. With him, on March 18, he had brought five warriors: tall long-haired men like him, but dressed differently, with deerskins wrapped around their shoulders and long leggings that Winslow likened to the trousers worn by the Gaelic Irish. They offered the Pilgrims a few skins, but these exchanges remained hesitant on the English side, with Carver and his men still nervous about the danger of an attack. At one point, two or three warriors appeared a few hundred yards away on the top of Watson's Hill, making threatening gestures, until Standish took out a patrol and warned them off with his muskets. A better intermediary was needed.

Tisquantum arrived with Samoset, bringing a few skins to trade and some fresh dried red herring—Winslow carefully noted details such as these—and he too spoke English. In his case, however, he had learned it in a remarkable location, while staying at the London home of John Slany, a merchant who ranked far above the likes of Weston in the commercial hierarchy.

Slany lived on Cornhill, at the very center of the City, barely five minutes' walk from Bread Street. Since 1610, he had been treasurer of the Newfoundland Company, a small colony, even smaller than New Plymouth. It was so small that even in 1617 the annual supply ship from England carried among its stores only twenty-four gallons of beer.

Slany owed his stature not to this disappointing venture but to his position among the Merchant Taylors, the largest of the London livery companies. We do not know the exact dates of Tisquantum's period in London, but it seems to have been in 1617. In that year Slany, aged about fifty, served as one of the company's three wardens, while in 1619 the Merchant Taylors chose him as their master, a post carrying so much prestige that the Dutch ambassador attended his election.

A man of substance, John Slany had close ties to the largest clients of Christopher Jones: in 1619, Jones's associate William Speight joined the ruling committee of the same company, and John Slany's brother Humphrey imported wine on the *Mayflower* less than nine months before she sailed to America. The records show that Slany knew John Pocock well, since Pocock was a rising man among the Merchant Taylors. We can also be sure of something else: that if the social life of the City of London bore any resemblance to the same thing today, then Tisquantum would have swiftly become a celebrity, in the street, in taverns, or paraded at formal dinners.[5]

Was it simply a coincidence that Tisquantum turned up again at New Plymouth in the spring of 1621, just as the Pilgrims emerged from their first winter? Perhaps: but it seems equally likely that ships which arrived off Maine or Virginia in March knew about the *Mayflower,* that news about her traveled up and down the coast, and that Tisquantum came looking for the Pilgrims when he heard the word "London." At this point, Jones and his command were still anchored in Plymouth Bay. As soon as Jones and Carver heard the name "Slany" from Tisquantum, they would have known that they had found someone they could trust.

Tisquantum spoke the language of the Wampanoag, the people led by Massasoit. He could describe in detail the city from which Jones had sailed, with its merchants, its ships, its king, its wine, and its weapons of war. He could also explain that while most Englishmen might be vicious hypocrites like Thomas Hunt, an occasional exception could be found. At the Newfoundland Company, Slany gave specific instructions that native people should be treated with respect.

However Tisquantum came to be there at exactly the right moment, he made the essential introduction to Massasoit. That same afternoon of March 22, with sixty of his warriors the sachem himself appeared above the settlement, most likely again on Watson's Hill. Actors in a pioneering drama, playing parts in a scene to be repeated many times in the ensuing history of the British Empire, from the Ganges and Lucknow to the African veld, the Pilgrims made peace on behalf of the Crown of England.

They had no Maxim guns or Enfield rifles, but they did have Standish, his muskets, and the ordnance unloaded from the *Mayflower.* They also had a small stock of trading goods, knives, bracelets, a copper chain for Massasoit, and alcohol too: Winslow mentions the brandy they gave the sachem to drink. And, of course, they had Tisquantum as translator.

In the name of King James, Edward Winslow crossed the Town Brook toward Massasoit and then opened the negotiations, offering trade, a peace treaty, and an alliance against his enemies. This Massasoit required, because of the dangers he faced from his enemies to the west, the Narragansett of Rhode Island. Hostages were exchanged as sureties, with Winslow remaining on the perilous side of the water. Then Massasoit forded the stream, under an armed escort led by Standish, and walked up the short but steep slope toward the English houses.

His conference with John Carver took place in a half-finished dwelling in the colony, where the Pilgrims had placed a green rug and some cushions. Again, it was a scene awaiting reenactment many times in a later period. To the beat of a drum, Governor Carver kissed the hand of Massasoit. As the sachem returned the compliment, they sat down on the cushions and the rug, and Massasoit ate and drank the food and liquor he was offered.

According to *Mourt's Relation,* the deal they struck contained six heads of agreement: essentially, a pact of nonaggression, and an alliance against enemies who might attack either the Pilgrims or Massasoit and the Wampanoag. We have to say "according to," because no record exists from the side of Massasoit to show how he understood the terms of the arrangement. As *Mourt's Relation* also emphasizes, at this early stage the language barrier remained high. Tisquantum lacked a perfect command of English. Although in London some men had studied the languages of the Algonquians, the vocabulary they knew came from Virginia, where the idioms and diction were entirely different.

For the short term, the agreement reached on March 22 evidently marked a turning point, since the military threat from Massasoit fell away. That is as much as we can honestly say. The peace held: but how and why did it do so? Even Bradford, describing it more than two decades later, offered no explanation. The reality, perhaps, was that the English at New Plymouth had accepted a territorial boundary, whether they understood it or not.

They were about to learn far more about the geography of the land they entered. They would soon see the limits it placed on them, but also the opportunities it offered.

The Mission to Massasoit

Even today, in a car or on a bicycle and with a map, you may lose your way very quickly in the labyrinth of bogs, woods, and hillocks that stretch away west and south behind the town of Plymouth. Like the interior of Cape Cod, it was a very un-English landscape, but with an extra difficulty: here the ocean was invisible, and without it the land offered no directions.

Follow the Town Brook on foot, as the Pilgrims would have done, and after a mile and a half you will come to a spot near a grove of majestic pines where suddenly the vegetation thins and a horizon appears. This is the place where the brook flows out of Billington Sea, the wide still pond where John Carver went to hunt.

Then on the far side of the water, the terrain becomes entirely incomprehensible. Today, bulldozers have opened clearings many hundreds of yards wide to make artificial bogs for growing cranberries, separated from the road by the narrow slits of drainage ditches. A skirt of suburban housing encircles the rim of Billington Sea. Even so, it is easy to understand why the Pilgrims did not try to cross this landscape until the midsummer of 1621, and with a native guide.

In hollows in the forest lie pond after pond—Darby Pond, Ricketts Pond, Trockle Pond, and many others with no name on the map—and since one pond, ridge, and thicket looked very much like another, the risk of losing their way again was simply too great. Even the native guides sometimes strayed off course, in the dark or when the weather was poor.

If there was a clue to the topography, perhaps it lay in the fact that a watershed existed on a belt of high ground rising to two hundred feet, about three miles west of Billington Sea. A man could find his way out of the maze simply by following brooks downstream: except that the streams lose themselves in swamps.

If you chose the wrong one, you would end up far off course, in the river valleys leading over into Rhode Island. Nor was the water safe to drink. Winslow noted that the native people took it only from the headwaters near a spring, because the gradients were shallow and animal droppings could easily poison a sluggish stream.

Fifteen miles of country such as this separated the colony from Nemasket, now known as Middleborough, the first stop on the trail that led inland. Winslow called it "a town under Massasaoit," but the name Nemasket seems in fact to refer to a tract of land, not a settlement. It was defined not by ownership or title but by its physical character and resources. It means a fishing place, and indeed Nemasket was a low-lying spot, surrounded by meadows and swamps, in the basin of the Taunton River, which flows into Narragansett Bay. The Pilgrims first saw it on the afternoon of July 3, on their way to a second meeting with Massasoit, at his summer base forty miles from Plymouth, between the sites of modern Providence and Newport.

By now, Bradford was worried about the corn harvest. So he would have been at Austerfield, since midsummer was the time in England when grain and bread prices peaked, as the last season's corn was exhausted. Tisquantum had shown the settlers how to plant and fertilize maize the Native American way, in small mounds mingled with nitrogen-fixing beans and squash, manured with fish. However, the harvest was still a month or so away, and Bradford feared that he would be unable to pay debts to the native people who came to trade at New Plymouth. So he decided to send Winslow on a mission to Massasoit to explain the situation politely, and to ask him to limit the number of visitors to those who brought skins. He also wanted help in finding the Cape Cod people from whom the Pilgrims had taken corn in November, so that they could also repay that debt.

The visit was successful, a matter of gift giving, tobacco smoking, singing, games, and a demonstration of skill with firearms by Winslow's men. Massasoit willingly agreed to do as they asked, and Winslow went home, arriving back at New Plymouth on July 7. The wider significance of the episode lies in the superb description of the country given by Winslow, and published the following year as part of *Mourt's Relation.*

In England, narratives of travel had become popular, and Winslow had served his apprenticeship with a printer called John Beale, who specialized in the genre. Beale counted among his authors Thomas Coryate, who walked all the way from Constantinople to the court of the Great Mogul at Agra and then sent his journals home on an East India Company ship. Perhaps Beale's most prestigious title appeared in 1617, when Winslow was still with him. The work of another travel writer, it was a magnificent edition of the journeys of Fynes Moryson. It was from this book that Winslow learned that the Irish wore trousers.* Moryson served as a soldier in Ireland under Queen Elizabeth, rising to become secretary to the English commanding officer against the Earl of Tyrone. His account of Ireland remains a leading source for Irish history, not least because it describes the Gaelic way of fighting a guerrilla war in bogs and forests.

Hence, when Winslow came to tell his story, he knew the value of precise observation of military affairs, an alien culture, and a foreign landscape. Ireland's pattern of settlements, its land tenure, its language, and its mobile cattle farming differed radically from England's. At Nemasket, and then later around the Mystic River north of Boston, Edward Winslow encountered another highly distinctive way of life, as odd to English eyes as that of the Irish. Like Moryson, he took copious notes recording its characteristics.[6]

Guided by Tisquantum, Winslow reached Nemasket after a six-hour trek. The first thing he noticed was the agriculture. Maize was growing in

---

*Describing the native people he met, Winslow says that they wore "long hosen up to their groins, close made . . . altogether like the Irish trousers." Moryson wrote this about the Irish: "Among them the Gentlemen or Lords of Countries weare close breeches and stockings . . . their said breeches are so close, as they expose to full view, not only the noble, but also the shamefull parts."

abundance—from eighty yards, one of his party shot a crow that was damaging the crop—but besides corn bread the native people gave him shad roe and acorns. At sunset he saw men catching bass at a fish weir on the Taunton River. The following day they reached the tideway, and Winslow carefully recorded this too. It was essential to know how easily a ship or a shallop could ascend the river, since French skippers were known to use Narragansett Bay and might either attack Massasoit or compete for his friendship.

Farther downstream, they came upon more food, men and women carrying baskets of crabs and shellfish, and at the next settlement the people gave them oysters. Winslow soon recognized that despite the variety of things to eat, at this season calories and protein were in relatively short supply. At Massasoit's settlement, some forty people, including the English, had to dine on two large fish caught by the sachem himself.

However, Winslow could see equally well that they could tolerate a period of shortage before the harvest, provided all the resources of the land were mobilized. The men and women whom he met were living active, energetic lives with few signs of hardship. And in due course, when the harvest came, the Pilgrims discovered that the outcome was much better than they could have expected.

They found that an acre of maize produced far more nutrition than an acre of wheat or rye in the environs of a place like Austerfield. In the spring, they planted only twenty acres of maize, and another six of English barley and peas, the latter with seeds imported on the *Mayflower.* In England, even before allowing for rents and tithes, a plot of land this size sown with wheat would barely feed twenty people, at most, and the farmer required additional meadow and pasture to feed his livestock. In America, using the methods learned from Tisquantum, the Pilgrims achieved maize yields that were high enough to satisfy nearly three times that number of settlers. Tithes, rents, and landlords were blissfully absent.

"Our corn did prove well," said Winslow, describing their first harvest with British understatement. They had every reason to celebrate in the autumn, with the festivities commemorated by today's Thanksgiving. Soon the abundance of New England became a common theme in accounts of the new colonies. So much so that thirty years later, in 1651, an English writer called for farmers at home to copy the techniques used across the Atlantic, because of the high yields extracted from "Indian Corne" by using fish fertilizer on spring-sown crops.

He gave a long list of American produce—pumpkins, squashes, watermelons, and whortleberries—that he wanted to see grown in old England.

Cranberries he liked best of all, a fruit "as big and red as a cherry . . . very good against the scurvy and very pleasant in tarts." However, all of this had to be learned from experience, and abundance had to be re-created anew each year: the native people they met could only live as they did because of centuries of effort and self-education.[7]

Even in southern New England the quality of the soil varied immensely from place to place, and some spots were far less fertile than others. The wide belt of land behind Billington Sea was a case in point, a place where the sandy earth drains far too rapidly, creating a thin reddish brown topsoil, far too dry and too acidic for farming. Because of distance and the topography, it was impractical to fetch fish to fertilize the ground, or cartloads of crushed oyster shells to neutralize its chemistry, techniques available on the coastal strip. Inland this could not be done, and so the forest remained wilderness, a wide buffer zone between the Pilgrims and Massasoit.

During the months that followed Winslow's mission to Massasoit, the Pilgrims began to learn that the land they had entered consisted of a mosaic of environments. They often varied profoundly from each other, but they also differed in their combination of contrasts and similarities with landscapes at home in the old country. At Nemasket and around the Taunton River, they entered a region that would have made a far better place to settle, thanks to its waterways and the diversity of food sources available in the estuaries feeding down into Narragansett Bay. This was country an Englishman could recognize.

It had affinities with the wetlands Bradford knew from eastern England, where in 1620 there still existed a way of life not unlike the customs of Massasoit and his people. Eels, cockles, and Whitstable oysters, as any Londoner could tell you, were for centuries a staple of the eastern English diet as well. All the same, and attractive though it was, the estuarine zone west of New Plymouth was off-limits, the domain of Massasoit. It was also insecure, because of the proximity of the hostile people beyond him.

As they continued to explore, the Pilgrims ventured as far as Nauset, near the elbow of Cape Cod. That too was territory they could not use, but for different reasons. In July, the teenage John Billington, from an English family of fen dwellers, made the mistake of trying to explore alone the enveloping tract south of New Plymouth. The boy wandered off and lost his way. He survived for five days on berries, until he met some native people. They bundled him off to the east, along Cape Cod, and deposited him with Aspinet, the sachem of the country around the modern towns of Orleans and Eastham.[8]

By way of Massasoit, word reached the Pilgrims of his whereabouts, and so a party set out from New Plymouth by boat to find him. Pausing along the way at Cummaquid, the place now known as Barnstable, they heard more stories of the crimes of Thomas Hunt when they met a weeping old woman whose three sons had been among his captives. It was a time for inadequate apologies from the English—"we gave her some trifles, which somewhat appeased her," as *Mourt's Relation* puts it—and a moment for recognizing that diplomacy had its limits.

When they reached Aspinet, they encountered suspicions that could not be allayed entirely. These were the people from whom they had taken corn the previous November, and with whom they had clashed at Wellfleet. As they beached their boat on the shore, the Pilgrim delegation found themselves surrounded by warriors, including a man who had owned some of the stolen corn. They promised to pay him back after the harvest, but their attempts to trade for fur yielded very little.

As night fell, down to the water came Aspinet, escorting the young John Billington. With him came a band numbering one hundred, half of them armed with bows and arrows and half of them not. The armed men cautiously kept their distance, while the unarmed contingent accompanied Aspinet to the boat, where they handed over the boy, his neck adorned with beads. In return the Pilgrims gave English knives to Aspinet and to one of his people who had looked after the youth. There the matter ended, among promises of peace but little warmth. Off the Pilgrims sailed to Plymouth, stopping again at Cummaquid to refill their water bottles and cement their relations with the local sachem.

The Nauset affair had another implication. Evidently, the Pilgrims could not expect to enjoy here the amicable alliance they had built with Massasoit. Over and above that, Aspinet had also barred them from the excellent habitat that existed beyond the beach. To the east, behind Eastham and Orleans and on the Atlantic side of Cape Cod, lies Nauset Harbor, a place of great natural beauty that the Frenchman Samuel de Champlain had surveyed many years before.

It was a locale so appealing that many years later, in 1644, the Plymouth Colony very nearly decided to move there, deserting entirely the Town Brook and Burial Hill. Defensible and sheltered by a barrier beach, the harbor at Nauset possessed resources like Narragansett Bay, if on a smaller scale: freshwater from ponds and streams inland, bay scallops, plenty of clams and mussels, and soil richer than elsewhere on the Cape. This too, however, lay off-limits to the Pilgrims in 1621, securely held as it was by Aspinet.

At Nauset they also learned that their ally Massasoit had difficulties of his own. Just as in Ireland chieftains like Tyrone were not absolute rulers, but men first among equals, so Massasoit was in reality the leading man among a confederation of sachems. They owed him loyalty but not obedience. He did not rule his territory from a capital. Instead, he and his people moved as and when they needed to, with seasonal settlements made up of houses that could be dismantled and shifted as rapidly as they were built.

From Aspinet, and then at New Plymouth, the Pilgrims heard two extra pieces of news, alarming but informative, adding more detail to the picture they were assembling of the land they had entered. First, they learned that the Narragansett had invaded Massasoit's territory and toppled him—or so it seemed, since Massasoit had disappeared. Second, they heard that another sachem of the Wampanoag, a man called Corbitant, had staged a coup d'état at Nemasket. He seized Tisquantum and two other men friendly to the Pilgrims, Hobbamock and Tokamahamon, holding a knife to Hobbamock's chest. Somehow, Hobbamock escaped and fled the fifteen miles to New Plymouth, where he brought word that Tisquantum was most likely dead.

On August 14, amid pouring rain, Standish marched out of the colony with a rescue party of between ten and fourteen armed men. His orders were simple: capture Corbitant, and cut off his head if it turned out that he had killed Tisquantum. About three miles from Nemasket they halted and rested until nightfall, planning to surprise Corbitant by surrounding his house at midnight. Hobbamock was guiding them, but in the dark and in the rain he lost the path. When they picked it up again, they were so tired, wet, and dispirited that Standish fell his men out to eat the thin rations in their packs. Rested and refreshed, they pressed on, reached the house, and encircled it.

Standish forced an entry, only to find the house full of men, women, and frightened children. In the confusion, three of them slipped away and received sword or bullet wounds from the men outside. On the inside, two of the English panicked and let off their firearms, terrifying the occupants, who screamed for mercy while the women among them clung to Hobbamock.

As the smoke cleared, and Standish searched the house, Hobbamock explained that all they wanted was Tisquantum and Tokamahamon. It soon became clear that neither was dead. Corbitant had done no more than threaten them. Hobbamock climbed onto the roof and called out for both men, who soon appeared. Meanwhile, Corbitant's men had fled, and he was nowhere to be found.

It also emerged that reports of Massasoit's defeat had been exaggerated. His whereabouts were still unclear, but he was alive and remained the grand sachem of the Wampanoag. Chaotic though the incident was, the affair at Nemasket served its purpose by making it plain that Tisquantum and others under Pilgrim protection were untouchable, by force of English arms. On September 13, Corbitant was one of nine sachems, from as far away as Martha's Vineyard, who apparently signed a treaty at New Plymouth making peace with the Pilgrims and swearing allegiance to King James. We have to say "apparently" because, again, we cannot know what this treaty signified to men such as Corbitant, or how they would have defined loyalty to a distant English king. Neither Bradford nor Winslow mentions this treaty specifically, and the only record comes from a book published nearly fifty years later, in 1669, by Bradford's stepson. No text in Corbitant's language exists.

And yet something important had clearly occurred, the passing of another landmark, whatever it meant to those involved on the native side. Immediately afterward, the Pilgrims felt confident enough to send an expedition northward. They intended to make peace and to trade for beaver fur with the native people of "the place by the great hills," the meaning of the word "Massachusetts," the people among the marshes and estuaries surrounding the modern city of Boston, and along the valley of the Mystic River. This was an episode filled with meaning, for what it revealed by way of tragedy and anticipation.

The Grave of Nanepashemet

On October 21, 1862, on a farm in what is now the Boston suburb of West Medford, some workmen were removing topsoil when, less than three feet down, they uncovered human bones. They found the remains of four adults and a child, buried on gently sloping land not far from the body of water now known as Lower Mystic Lake. At that time, the Middlesex Canal ran for twenty miles between the Mystic River and the Merrimack, linking Boston to the mill town of Lowell. The canal passed close to the spot where the graves were found.

One of the skeletons far surpassed the others in the quantity and richness of the goods buried alongside it. The bones were those of a man of about sixty, crouched on his side in the familiar, fetal position, his head facing westward. Among the items beside him were an iron arrowhead, a stone knife, and a soapstone pipe nearly six inches long, with a mouthpiece made of finely rolled and beaten copper. Nearby lay a matted bunch of deer's hair, all that survived from a tobacco pouch. It contained a substance that still smoked when they applied a lit match.

The farm belonged to a family called Brooks, Massachusetts politicians and heroes of the Revolutionary War. Among them was the Reverend Charles Brooks, a minister and local historian. He swiftly recognized the importance of such a discovery in this spot. Around Medford, farmers often plowed up stone drills and arrowheads, and Brooks knew that just before the arrival of the Pilgrims the valley of the Mystic was densely inhabited by native people. They were the Pawtucket, led by a great sachem called Nanepashemet.

His name meant "Moon Spirit." At his death in 1619 or thereabouts, Nanepashemet commanded allegiance across a great swath of land that stretched as far west as the Connecticut valley at Deerfield. His influence extended from the Charles River in the south as far as the Piscataqua River and New Hampshire in the north. Before the epidemics, tens of thousands of people had made their home here, owing loyalty to the Moon Sachem.

Brooks sent the skeleton with the pipe to Harvard, where the university had recently set up its Museum of Comparative Zoology. In December 1862, he spoke about the find at a meeting of the Massachusetts Historical Society, speculating that the bones from what he called the "Indian Necropolis" belonged to Nanepashemet himself.[9] This may have been wishful thinking, but there could be no doubt that the land around the Mystic ponds had once been a Native American stronghold. Twenty years later, workmen digging another hole for the Brooks family at West Medford came upon eighteen more skeletons, with weapons and tobacco pipes, dating, it seems, from the earliest period of contact with Europeans.

Nothing remains, barring a street called Winslow Avenue, to record the first visit made by the English to the tomb of Nanepashemet, on September 21, 1621, but the early settlers understood the importance of the place. Nearly a decade later, when the Massachusetts Bay Company began to allocate slices of land to its investors, they gave the north bank of the Mystic to one of their richest supporters at home, Matthew Cradock. The choice of this spot for Cradock's plantation showed just how attractive the land was felt to be. Its qualities were equally clear to the Pilgrims from the moment they first saw it. In order to reach it, however, they had to first leave the sphere of influence of Massasoit and enter what might be hostile territory.

Bradford picked ten men, with Tisquantum and two other native people as interpreters, and on September 18 he sent them north by boat to find a woman. They were looking for the widow of Nanepashemet, known to the English as the Squa Sachem. Because she outlived her first husband by more than three decades, she may have been no more than thirty at the time, and like Massasoit she had her enemies.

Her late husband, Nanepashemet, had not died from natural causes. It seems that the Micmac from the east and north had probed this far along the coast and killed him during a raid. Because the Pilgrims left only a brief account of their visit to the Mystic valley—even combined, the two accounts left by Bradford and Winslow run to fewer than thirteen hundred words—it is hard to say how much they knew about this before they set off. But it looks as though they saw an opportunity to replicate the alliance they had made with Massasoit, offering the Squa Sachem a measure of protection, backed by English guns and ammunition.[10]

On the morning of September 19, the Pilgrim expedition landed somewhere on the shore south of Boston. They aimed to make contact with Obbatinewat, the most northerly of the sachems who looked to Massasoit as leader. This they did only to find that while he was friendly, he too lived in fear of the Micmac, and he had his differences with the widow of Nanepashemet. Nevertheless, he agreed to help, and on the twentieth they crossed the bay between the islands that dotted Boston Harbor. They sent out scouts to reconnoiter the country on the other side. On the twenty-first, they went ashore, on one or the other bank of the Mystic River—it could have been either, because, as its name implies, Medford was a crossing place—and then they marched inland.

Today, thanks to cars and to a dam named after Amelia Earhart, the river valley has been tamed or violated, depending on your point of view. Floods no longer spill over the marshes and meadows as once they did, and the Atlantic tide no longer gives the Mystic Lakes a saline tang, as it would have done in 1621: the water is clear and fresh to the taste. However, enough of the topography remains intact, even beneath the avenues of Medford, to explain the area's immediate appeal to any Jacobean Englishman with an eye for land.

Edward Winslow mentions two hills. Nanepashemet had lived on one of them, in a house raised on a wooden scaffold built on planks and poles. On the other, where apparently he lost his life, there was another dwelling, abandoned after his death. Nearby the Pilgrims found his tomb. It lay in a glen or a valley, inside a fort protected by a high palisade, by a ditch four feet deep crossed by a single footbridge. Inside was the house where the Moon Sachem lay buried.

It may never be possible to know the locations exactly, since it seems that only rudimentary maps survive from the colonial period. But in 1865 the Pilgrim historian Henry Martyn Dexter identified the site of the first hill as Rock Hill, beside the Mystic. There, ten minutes' walk east of the commuter rail station at West Medford, it can still be found, and it made an obvious bastion. A steep granite outcrop, softened by lichen and partially obscured by modern houses, birch trees, and Norway maples, Rock Hill climbs in steps and ledges to a height of more than a hundred feet above the flat bottom of the river valley.[11]

At its base runs the Mystic Valley Parkway, wide and noisy but not quite as poisoned by gasoline as it might seem at first. Undeterred by the automobile, in late October a squawking colony of migrating waterfowl live between the road and the river, Canada geese, feeding in their dozens. A thin covering of grass extends across the valley bottom, but a single scoop of soil shows that the earth is a dark alluvium which made this an ideal place to grow corn. Winslow mentioned the crops of maize, and later English visitors described the splendid fishing hereabouts, and the game that filled the woodlands.

On arrival, the Pilgrim party looked for the Squa Sachem, but instead they met the frightened survivors of the people of Nanepashemet. They were mostly women, with their harvest only just complete, the corn in heaps. The Englishmen did their best to calm them down, and a rapport of some kind was established. According to Winslow's narrative, the women boiled cod for the colonists, but it took time to persuade them to summon down their menfolk to open a trading relationship. When at last one man came, he too shook and trembled in fear. He was prepared to sell skins, but he would not say where the Squa Sachem had gone.

According to Winslow, Tisquantum suggested stealing the skins, because the man and the women were hostiles. It seems that the Pilgrims did not follow his advice. Even so, the women sold the coats from off their backs, coat beaver perhaps, the best kind of pelt for a hat, and then they covered their nakedness with branches. As Winslow put it, "They are more modest than some of our English women are." Still the Squa Sachem remained elusive, and that was the end of the expedition. That night, with rations running low, the Pilgrims set sail back to New Plymouth.

Ruefully, they took with them the realization that this, the hinterland of Boston, offered the environment that should have been theirs from the outset, much more suitable for livestock, corn, and hunting than the terrain surrounding the Plymouth Colony. They had also seen the route of what later became the Middlesex Canal: a natural highway along woodland paths toward streams and rivers leading to far better beaver country than the sandy wastes of southern Massachusetts. In the words of William

Bradford, "They returned in saftie, and brought home a good quantity of beaver, and made reporte of ye place, wishing they had been ther seated."[12] Nevertheless, they had done the best they could, and they had found the commodity that the investors in England wanted most.

The Fate of the *Fortune*

After the commercial failure of the *Mayflower*'s voyage, Bradford and the Pilgrims knew that it was imperative to get a cargo of fur and timber back to London as soon as possible. They swiftly turned the *Fortune* around and sent her home with pelts acquired along the Mystic River and from Massasoit. After giving his sermon, Robert Cushman sailed back with her on December 13, 1621, taking two hogsheads of beaver skins, otter skins, clapboard, and sassafras, worth about four hundred pounds. Then, five weeks later, disaster struck her too, when on January 19 she met a French warship off the coast of the Vendée, to the north of La Rochelle.

Cushman and the *Fortune* were unlucky, but the circumstances were typical of the period. Navigation remained imperfect, and naval affairs were always liable to disrupt or divert the path of western enterprise. The French skipper caught them not far from the fortified Île d'Yeu, but this lies more than 350 sea miles from Land's End and the Lizard Peninsula. It seems that the *Fortune* had made a familiar error. She mistook the long snout of Brittany for the southwestern end of England, and then she strayed off down the French Atlantic coast at the worst possible time.

Under the law of the sea, even though England and France were at peace a French captain could legally seize the *Fortune* if she was a pirate, or in reprisal for plunder taken by English ships, or if she was aiding France's enemies. Only two months previously, as part of their defiance of Louis XIII, the Huguenots of La Rochelle had sent out their *armée navale* to fight the royal fleet, and given it a thrashing. The king's ships fled back into harbor, while the Huguenots prowled up and down the coast. The fortress on the Île d'Yeu remained in the hands of the Crown, but any English vessel coming close was liable to search and seizure in case she was ferrying supplies to the rebels. The French warship stopped and boarded the *Fortune* and carried her back to the island.

It soon emerged that she was neither a pirate nor carrying contraband. All the same, the French governor seized her guns, cargo, and rigging. He locked her master in a dungeon and kept Cushman and her crew under guard on board the vessel. He also confiscated the manuscript of *Mourt's Relation*. After thirteen days, he let them go, with the book but minus the beaver skins. They made it back into the Thames on February 17, 1622. They found commerce in London paralyzed by the depression and the *Mayflower* investors in deep trouble, and none more deeply so than Thomas Weston.[13]

By this time he was already nearly ruined, and the loss of the *Fortune*'s beaver fur dealt the final blow. When the alum racket blew up in his face the previous summer, Weston wrote one IOU after another as he tried to carry on trading, but he had very nearly reached his limit. For many years, he had expected the Pilgrims' friend Edward Pickering to guarantee his debts, but by the time the *Mayflower* reached America, their ties were already weakening. Each man came to distrust the other. In March 1621, Pickering came over to London to try to settle their differences, and an agreement was patched together; but as his problems mounted, Weston continued to issue bills of exchange, which he expected Pickering to honor. By early 1622, the relationship had collapsed entirely, after a heated argument in London. Weston killed it for good by having Pickering arrested for debt, and at about the same time he broke with the rest of the *Mayflower* investors. He sold his share in the venture for whatever they would give him. By this time, the Shrewsbury draper John Vaughan was chasing Weston for payment for a consignment of Welsh cotton, and he owed still more money to the men who had bought his smuggled alum and to the Crown. The authorities were determined to recover Weston's unpaid fines and customs duties.

Few men attempted anything as daring or as dangerous as his next maneuver. As the *Fortune* docked in London, Weston made one bold last gamble. The records of what happened remain in Cranfield's papers, as crisp and legible now as they were four hundred years ago.

Weston had fitted out another ship, the *Charity*, to sail from Portsmouth with a cargo of settlers and artillery, accompanied by a smaller fishing vessel called the *Swan*. Perhaps with his elder brother's help—Richard Weston was by now a successful London lawyer—he obtained an export license from the Privy Council to send the cannon to New England. Issued on February 17, 1622, the day on which the *Fortune* reached the Thames, the license covered thirty pieces of ordnance. They included big guns each weighing nearly two tons. Allegedly intended for the use of the Plymouth Colony, the consignment came from the royal arsenal at the Tower of London, but it never reached America. It appears that Thomas Weston planned to run the guns elsewhere and then sell them to the highest bidder. There would be many takers in the North Atlantic, Arab pirates, Huguenots, Dutchmen, or Spaniards, all of them in need of extra armaments.

News of the imminent departure of the *Charity* came to the attention of the man who ran the alum monopoly. They reminded the Lord Treasurer about Weston's debts to them and to the king. Weston had vanished from his London home, and from what Mrs. Weston told them on the doorstep, it seemed that he was preparing to flee to New England. Lionel Cranfield swiftly alerted the authorities in Portsmouth, and they found Philemon Powell, posing as the purser of the ship. With him were eighty colonists, bound for New Plymouth and Massachusetts Bay.

Under arrest, Powell refused to talk. Because this was a very serious matter, Cranfield sent an Exchequer judge down to Portsmouth to interrogate the suspect. Unimpressed, Powell kept his mouth shut, claiming that by law no servant could be made to give evidence against his master. On March 21, the exasperated judge reported back to Whitehall. Three days later Lord Cranfield ordered Powell's detention in the Fleet Prison in London.

Thomas Weston, meanwhile, had managed to evade arrest, hiding behind the silence of his accomplice. He had the gall to petition Lord Cranfield for Powell's release, arguing that he was losing five pounds for each day that the *Charity* lingered in Portsmouth Harbor. Then Weston disappeared entirely, only to surface briefly in New Plymouth the following year, after crossing the Atlantic disguised as a blacksmith. Most likely, he traveled on a Devon fishing vessel, and then he quietly slipped off one or another ship at one of the fishing posts along the coast of Maine.

Meanwhile, in the spring of 1622, the rest of the *Mayflower* investor group were wondering what to do next. Some were close friends of Pickering, who wanted to file suit against Weston: that autumn Pickering did so, issuing a futile subpoena. His case had little prospect of success, seeking money that Weston did not have, and tortuous litigation in London could not save New Plymouth. Whatever the long-term outlook, the colony urgently needed supplies that year. The investors did the best they could.

Led by James Sherley and John Pocock, at first they struggled. They could barely assemble enough money to pay for twenty tons of stores and send thirty passengers across the ocean. So in the spring Robert Cushman approached John Peirce, the London merchant who had obtained the new patent of 1621 from the Council for New England. Peirce agreed to help finance another voyage, and somehow he and the *Mayflower* investors raised four hundred pounds. This was still a modest sum, but at least it was enough to buy thirty tons of supplies and trading goods and a ship called the *Paragon*.

Even so, she did not leave London until October 1, and the voyage ended almost as soon as it had begun. The ship had barely reached the English Channel when she sprang a leak in a gale. Two weeks later she was back in the Thames. Her second attempt fared little better, and nearly ended in catastrophe. In January 1623, the *Paragon* set off again, with 109 passengers, many of them women and children. By the middle of February, she was only halfway across the Atlantic when she came close to sinking in another storm. At the storm's height, to save the ship, the master cut away the mainmast. With three men at the helm, the *Paragon* struggled back to Portsmouth, but minus her superstructure, shorn away by the sea.[14]

Hearing of her return, Pocock and Sherley promptly told Peirce to repair the vessel and send her out again within fourteen days. When he did not, they went to court and sued him. Their attempt to rescue the colony ended in yet another exchange of recriminations. Four years later Peirce was still demanding compensation in the courts. An extra reason for the animosity lay in the fact that Peirce had apparently tried to double-cross both his fellow investors and the Pilgrims.

Six months before the *Paragon* sailed out on her first voyage, Peirce had gone to the Council for New England and asked them to amend the patent in such a way as to make himself and his business partners the landlords of the Plymouth Colony. It seems unlikely that this was outright swindling; probably Peirce simply wanted a sort of insurance policy, an element of collateral for the money he put up to finance the ship and her stores. When the Pilgrims, Sherley, and Pocock complained, the authorities upheld the original patent. Even so, the dispute rumbled on until John Peirce died.[15]

The *Paragon* affair had been a shambles, but during the course of 1622 the Pilgrims had achieved something else, less tangible but with far-reaching effects of its own. Quite apart from founding a new colony, they had also helped to invent journalism in its modern form.

TWO GREYHOUNDS AND THE *WEEKELY NEWES*

When the *Fortune* reached London stripped of her cargo, she still had on board the manuscript of *Mourt's Relation.* It rapidly found a publisher. Fresh, exciting, and narrated in the clearest English, it told with a mass of visual color and the odd joke or two the story of the colony's first year. The book began in England, on the way out of Plymouth Sound, and it ended in America after the first Thanksgiving and the mission to the Mystic. It went on sale in London, at a shop in Cornhill only yards from the home of John Slany, at the very time when a new vogue for topicality created a ready market for this sort of thing. The city's bookstores were just beginning to sell periodical news sheets, or *corantos,* as they were known. The publisher the Pilgrims found was a man schooled in this new segment of the trade.

London had fewer than twenty printers, but the city had ten times as many booksellers. Under King James their business grew almost as fast as sales of wine and silk. In 1620, more than 400 new books hit the streets to satisfy a rapidly expanding reading public. And in their search for new titles, printers like Winslow's former employer John Beale tried pretty much everything.

Beale published not only travel writers, such as Fynes Moryson, but also self-help books (*Directions for a Maide to Choose Her Mate,* of 1619), as well as sermons, sheet music, ballads, histories, how-to books on arithmetic and handwriting, and cautionary tales of city life. Another Beale title was something called *The Roaring Gallantes, Contayning a Short Narracion of the Lifes and Deaths of William Nicholls and John Welsh, Broker:* sadly, no copy seems to survive. However, perhaps the boldest of London's book entrepreneurs were two men called Bourne and Butter. They became the founders of the English newspaper.[16]

Edward Winslow certainly knew Nicholas Bourne, because at his bookshop Bourne stocked the titles that Beale had printed. Everyone in the business knew Nathaniel Butter, because he was the most audacious and flamboyant bookseller of his time. Butter began to publish sensational news as far back as 1605, when he issued a gruesome account of a murder in Yorkshire, with a sequel describing the execution of the culprit. In 1608, after publishing the first edition of *King Lear,* he followed it up with *Newes from Lough-Foyle in Ireland.* It chronicled the equally bloody career of O'Doherty, the rebel from Donegal.

Books such as these were one-offs, not periodicals, but then in 1618 the first *corantos* went on sale in Amsterdam to meet the demand for regular news about the war breaking out in Germany. As the *Mayflower* lay at anchor off Provincetown, the first English translations of these *corantos* appeared in London. The following autumn, the first true English newspaper was born, when on September 24, 1621, someone called "NB" published the first issue of a weekly. It was called the *Corante* and subtitled *Weekely Newes,* but it apparently survived for only seven editions. Most likely, "NB" was either Bourne or Butter, sheltering behind initials in case of official disapproval.

Then, in May 1622, as the Pilgrim manuscript sat in a printing shop awaiting the typesetter, a second wave of periodicals began to appear. Soon afterward, Butter and Bourne joined forces to dominate the new market. On October 15, they began to publish a weekly newspaper called *The Relation.* It ran without a break until the summer of 1624, when the first editor died during an epidemic. Filled with news of foreign wars, natural disasters, and the doings of kings and queens, it firmly established a taste for topical sensation, available to anyone who could afford twopence to buy a copy. Butter and Bourne had their own connections with the Pilgrims; and in London they did more than anyone else to create the environment in which the Plymouth manuscript found readers.

Of course, the two men lived in close proximity to the *Mayflower* investors: that came about simply because London was so densely concentrated. Nathaniel Butter lived in Bread Street Ward, where he attended the same church as John Pocock. The newspaper office was Butter's shop, at the sign of the Pied Bull on Watling Street, a few yards from Pocock's front door. It was Bourne, however, who supplied a direct link with the Pilgrims, an affiliation they could not do without.

For nine years, Nicholas Bourne had an apprentice called John Bellamy, a young man with radical views. Many years later, when he was Colonel John Bellamy, part of the Puritan leadership in London during the civil war, it was revealed that in his youth Bellamy belonged to the group of semi-Separatists who met across the river in Southwark. These were the very same people who acted on behalf of the Pilgrims in the year of the comet, in their early negotiations with the Virginia Company.

John Bellamy clearly knew Edward Winslow, and like his employer he knew a commercial opportunity when he saw one. Early in 1620, Bellamy finished his time as an apprentice, but he went on working with Bourne until, at some time in 1622, he set up his own shop a few yards away, at the sign of the Two Greyhounds in Cornhill. There he began to publish and sell books. Among the very first was the Pilgrim narrative. Close behind it came Bellamy editions of the works of William Bradford's beloved author, the Hebrew scholar Henry Ainsworth, volumes bound and printed with such skill that they remain a pleasure to examine today, on paper with barely a mark of age.[17]

At the end of June, as the second wave of newspapers started to go on sale, John Bellamy obtained his official license to print the story of the Plymouth Colony's adventures. It bore a title intended to appeal to exactly the same appetite for vivid news of current affairs.

Although historians call it *Mourt's Relation,* when it first appeared on bookstalls, it carried a much longer title. Cascading down the page in such a way as to attract even the most jaded browser, it ran for eight paragraphs, filled with the names of Indian chiefs. Of course it began as though it were a *coranto:* the book, said the title page, was *A Relation or Iournall of the Beginning and Proceedings of the English Plantation Setled at Plimoth.* Two years later, they came up with a simpler title for Winslow's second book of Pilgrim adventures, but it was directed at the same audience. John Bellamy published that book too, and it was called *Good Newes from New-England.*

For the next twenty-five years, Bellamy went on issuing books relating to North America. He did so far more consistently than any other London publisher and printer. No method exists for quantifying the impact they had, but we can be sure of one thing. Colonies did not survive by themselves. They needed supplies, reinforcements, and new flows of stores and capital, and so they needed publicity too. Without the Pilgrim books published by John Bellamy, this would have been lacking. Since Bellamy learned his trade from Bourne and Butter, we can say with confidence that Puritan America relied on journalism from the very start: almost as much as it depended on the beaver, on Tisquantum, and on Massasoit.

Chapter Sixteen

DIABOLICAL AFFECTION

Three things are the overthrow and bane, as I may term it, of Plantations . . . 1. The vain expectation of present profit . . . 2. Ambition in their governors and commanders, seeking only to make themselves great . . . 3. The carelessness of those that send over supplies of men unto them, not caring how they be qualified: so that ofttimes they are rather the image of men endued with bestial, yea diabolical affections, than the image of God, endued with reason, understanding and holiness.

—EDWARD WINSLOW, 1624[1]

The Pilgrim fort on Burial Hill looked east across the sea and west toward the forest. As late as 1830, an official map showed that even then the light and shade of the woodlands behind New Plymouth reached to within a thousand yards of the water's edge. In the time of William Bradford the cleared margin between the beach and the trees was far narrower still. One August day in 1623, a sentry posted on the parapet of the fort would have seen emerging from among the oaks and pines a procession of men and one woman. All of them were naked from the waist up.

They numbered as many as 120, and they were painted, some black and some yellow, but mostly a purple-red, the color of mulberries. Their dark uncut hair was greased with oil. On their shoulders or behind them they carried or dragged as gifts the carcasses of slain deer and a turkey. At their head, most likely, was Massasoit, with his long knife slung across his muscular chest on a cord. The black skin of a wolf would have encircled his shoulders, while behind his neck there hung a pouch of tobacco.[2]

As he descended the wooded slope toward the Pilgrim town, and followed a path that led along the north side of Burial Hill, Massasoit would have looked up and seen on a pike above the fort a severed human head, a few months old. In the summer sky close to it a scrap of linen flapped or dangled in place of a flag. The linen too was colored red, but red of a different shade, the dull red of dried blood.

What Massasoit made of the severed head we cannot say, but the intention of the Pilgrims was clear. On August 14, Massasoit, his warriors, his fellow sachems, and one of his five wives joined in celebrating the second wedding of William Bradford. The governor made sure that the head and the blood-soaked rag were starkly visible above the fort, as reminders to Massasoit that the Pilgrims were men of terror as well as men of God. For this period, the most detailed source is Edward Winslow's *Good Newes from New-England,* and its opening paragraph praises the work of divine providence for "possessing the hearts of the salvages with astonishment and fear of us." But anxiety and alarm were not one-sided, and the English felt them too.

Writing for public consumption, Winslow manfully defended the colony's achievements, and especially those that concerned security. Profits remained elusive, but the Pilgrims were "safely seated, housed and fortified, by which means a great step is made unto gain," he wrote. As we shall see, much of *Good Newes* is military history, an account of the exploits of Miles Standish as he quelled an attempted assault on the Pilgrims by the people of the Massachusetts. It was the head of a Massachusetts warrior that Standish and Bradford stuck up on a pole, and his blood that dyed the linen. But interwoven with this chronicle of violence were other themes that preoccupied Winslow and William Bradford alike. In the second period of the colony's history, the fear of conspiracy or civil strife became for them an overriding concern.

During the first eighteen months in America, the secret of survival was morale. In the next phase, this remained the case, but the relevance of morale expanded to encompass more than physical endurance. It widened to include the need to prevent the colony from falling victim not to external forces, but to its own internal discontents, or worst of all to a combination of the two. This was the motive for the brutal gesture of erecting a decapitated head on a spike. It was something far from customary in the England of the time, where felons were hanged but decapitation was reserved for the most dangerous of offenders, English traitors or Irish rebels. It was a gesture of deterrence, aimed perhaps at some of the colonists as well as at Massasoit.

Two troubled episodes dominated the long second act of the drama at New Plymouth. The first, and most notorious, was the fight at Wessagussett, at the southern end of Boston Harbor, when the failure of a colony founded by Thomas Weston led to bloody conflict with the native people and to the stern reprisals meted out by Captain Standish. The second episode concerned the mutinous activities of two newcomers. These were a settler called John Oldham and a clergyman, John Lyford, sent out to New England by the London investors to minister to the spiritual needs of the colony.

Most accounts of the Pilgrims canter swiftly through the Lyford business. They treat it as a tedious, slightly baffling diversion, scarcely worthy of the space and the intense emotion that William Bradford committed to it. But while later historians have found the Lyford affair unworthy of close attention, for Bradford it represented a spiritual danger more potent than any attack with arrows and spears. For Bradford and Winslow, the common motif linking Lyford and Wessagussett lay in what Winslow called "diabolical affections," the inner agencies of degradation that threatened to subvert the work of godliness.

In the person of John Lyford, we also encounter another man who, like John Pocock, embodied connections between the Pilgrim narrative and the wider history of Britain at the time. Lyford came to New Plymouth after nearly a decade in Ulster, where he was engaged in a colonial project of another kind. The early years of New England coincided with imperial beginnings elsewhere, in India and Ireland. As we shall see, the links between these three locations were close, direct, and very personal.

Disorderly Wessagussett

Phase two of the Plymouth Colony began in the winter of 1621–22, a few months after the departure of the *Fortune,* and in ominous fashion. The Narragansett people of Rhode Island made apparent threats of war, sending over a sheaf of arrows wrapped in the skin of a rattlesnake: Bradford sent it straight back, stuffed with bullets. Doubts also arose about Tisquantum when he fabricated a story that Massasoit was planning his own attack, apparently as a means to restore his own status as a necessary mediator. This enraged Massasoit. Under the terms of his pact with the Pilgrims, he had every right to demand that Tisquantum be handed over to him for punishment.

This Bradford refused to do, but the incident served as a reminder of how frail such alliances might be and how insecure the colony remained.

As yet, Bradford had no idea of the fate that had befallen the *Fortune,* but he knew how little the colony possessed by way of resources. In order to survive, and to live at peace with Massasoit and the other people of the region, the colony needed supplies and trading goods from home and new settlers who were able-bodied and self-sufficient. In fact, during that year and in 1623 the colony suffered a drain on what small reserves it had, and one that very nearly brought it to its knees. For this, they could thank Thomas Weston.

By now Weston was a ruined man and a fugitive. Even so, and with financial help from Beauchamp, he managed to send across the Atlantic another small craft, the *Sparrow.* She made landfall in Maine, joining the rest of the modest English fishing fleet in those waters. Somehow, too, Weston saved Philemon Powell from prison and secured the release of the *Charity* from arrest at Portsmouth, along with now only fifty or sixty passengers.

With the *Swan,* the *Charity* duly set sail and reached New Plymouth in midsummer, but when she arrived, the thirty guns were missing. Their fate remains a mystery, but Weston's foes were quick to allege that the worst possible crime had been committed. Weston's brother Andrew sold the cannon "for extraordynary and excessive gaine to the Turkish pyrates or other enemyes or strangers," the Pilgrim investor James Sherley claimed in legal papers. The guns were certainly sold to someone, but no proof exists that the buyers were pirates. Gunrunning to corsairs was an offense that would have sent the Weston brothers to the gallows, but no serious attempt was made by the Crown to pursue them. The authorities knew that the cannon had not reached New England; but they cared far more about the money the Westons owed in unpaid fines and taxes.[3]

Before he went to ground, leaving his wife to cope with years of litigation, Weston wrote a final letter to Bradford, dated April 10, 1622. Carried on the *Charity* or the *Swan,* and arriving nearly three months later in New England, it consists of excuses, diatribes against his enemies, and empty pledges of help. Weston also candidly admitted that the latest reinforcements he had sent to America were not England's finest. "Now I will not deney that ther are many of our men rude fellows, as these people terme them," he wrote. "Yet I presume they wil be governed, by shuch as is set over them; and I hope not only to be able to reclaime them from yt profanenes that may scandalies the vioage, but by degrees to draw them to god."

Whether Weston meant this seriously we will never know. Wary as ever, Bradford did not believe it. For him Weston's letter marked his final loss of confidence in his former backer. When Weston turned up at New Plymouth, in disguise, he cadged some beaver skins and supplies before heading to Virginia. Perhaps Weston had done his best, but he created for the Pilgrims more problems than he solved. On the *Charity* and the *Swan,* he sent over raw new settlers with inadequate supplies, and in doing so, he put the colony in grave danger. The native inhabitants of southern New England could not afford to allow into their land parasites who upset the economy they had created.

If the Pilgrims added something to the life of the region, by way of trading goods, or by assisting the native people against enemies inland or up the coast, then they might serve a purpose. If, on the other hand, the English became a leech on the area's resources, consuming other people's corn and game and offering little in return, then they had no legitimate reason to be there and should be expelled. This is a truth that Edward Winslow recognized. Perhaps this was because he had read widely in the new travel books, such as Moryson's, which pointed out that those who went to strange lands must pay their way and learn the customs of the country.

Weston's new settlers failed this test at a time when the Plymouth Colony could least afford to make mistakes. Within a few months of the arrival of the newcomers, the Pilgrims reaped their second harvest of corn from the little fields laid out around New Plymouth, but it was meager. Crop raising in England and America alike required intense labor, by way of weeding and the application of manure, and in the New World without carts and livestock everything had to be carried and done by hand. But during the growing season of 1622, again the Pilgrims found their attention diverted from cultivation to defense.

An English ship fishing on the coast brought news from the south of a native uprising, which came close to destroying the settlement at Jamestown. Bradford promptly ordered the construction of a blockhouse on the top of Burial Hill, with emplacements for six cannon. The effort required took precious time away from agriculture. Since they were mostly too poorly nourished for manual work, the effect was all the worse, leaving food reserves depleted. Bradford also blames Weston's new settlers for stealing corncobs as they hung on their stalks in the fields, but the facts of the case are disputed.

There is an alternative version of what took place more sympathetic to Weston's men, and written by a different type of migrant. The author was an English lawyer and adventurer, Thomas Morton. He arrived in New England at some point in the middle of the 1620s and made himself the leader of a small fur-trading settlement at Mount Wollaston, between

New Plymouth and Boston. In due course he quarreled violently with the Pilgrims.

As far back as Nathaniel Hawthorne and beyond, historians have argued about Morton, his reliability, and the true explanation for the mutual hatred between him and William Bradford. Since Morton was a man who enjoyed drink, dancing, and making fun of Puritans, and since he may have been another Roman Catholic, it is hardly surprising that his account of events fails to match the story as told by a Separatist. Nonetheless, Morton must be treated with respect. Published in London in 1637, but apparently written much earlier, his book *New English Canaan* contains details that can only have been learned by somebody who knew the landscape intimately, and had listened carefully to the native people around the shores of Boston Harbor. He differs fundamentally from Bradford.[4]

Morton agreed that Weston's men were wasters—"many of them lazy persons," he writes—but he accuses the Pilgrims of pushing them out of New Plymouth, because they might topple the Separatists from their position of control. According to Morton, Weston always intended that the beaver fur trade should be the basis of the colony, and the men he sent were entirely suitable for that purpose. The Pilgrims, Morton says, wanted to keep the fur trade for themselves, and they resented the need to share sparse supplies with the newcomers.

Whatever the reason, that autumn the Weston men left and founded a village of their own, at a place called Wessagussett. The name means "at the edge of the rocks," and so it is: a few hundred yards from the settlement site, close to the shore lie a cluster of rocks exposed at low water.[5] Today Wessagussett goes by the name of North Weymouth, beside an Atlantic inlet called the Fore River, ten miles south of downtown Boston. Like many another colonial location, the banks of the Fore River have long since become industrial, lined with oil tanks, a power plant, and what was once a naval shipyard. Nonetheless, the geography survives, never entirely subdued, and the seascape retains its beauty, with the familiar New England counterpoint of overcast eggshell skies and speckled sandy woods.

As so often, at first the site seems unremarkable, just a small wooded dell behind some houses. To find Wessagussett, simply head east from the town of Quincy, across the steel girders of the Fore River Bridge. After half a mile, turn left at the next Dunkin' Donuts. Climb over the crest of a low ridge, which runs from west to east parallel with the shore, about fifty feet above the beach, and look down across the river, toward the ocean. Between the ridge and the high-water mark was a flat strip of land about two hundred yards wide, and on it they established the Weston colony. Today white suburban houses cover the slopes and obscure the view inland, while a low concrete seawall defends the houses from the tide. But the ridge screens out the noise from the highway, and so with the help of old maps and a little imagination it is possible to appreciate the qualities of the place.

It was defensible, because North Weymouth is a peninsula between the curves of the Fore and Back rivers. Marshes and swamps left only a narrow neck of dry land along which it could be approached on foot. Wessagussett had excellent access by sea, because the Fore River made a good natural harbor. Sheltered from storms by islands and by the promontory of Hull to the east, the river has a gray sandy bottom, ideal for anchors. At low tide a wide expanse of mud and sand offered shellfish for the taking, and Wessagussett was renowned for oysters and mussels. The islands were rich with berries, and lobsters filled the bays and coves. Besides the availability of food, the site had a fourth attraction, freshwater. The dried-up bed of a stream can be found straying down through the dell to the sea.

In many ways Wessagussett outshone New Plymouth as a place to live. It was also far closer to the Charles, Mystic, and Merrimack rivers, which led inland toward opportunities for trade. But unlike New Plymouth, Wessagussett was not an empty space. Its qualities rendered it ideal as a village site for the people of the Massachusetts, and some of them already lived nearby. Most visible among them were Wituwamat and Pecksuot: tough and courageous men, determined to protect their domain, but occasionally brutal too. They made short, cruel work of the ship's company of two French vessels that had ventured into the adjoining waters.

When the first ship ran aground, the warriors made servants of her crew. They forced the Frenchmen to eat food fit only for dogs, until they wept and died. When the second ship arrived, hoping to trade, the warriors pretended to bring a bundle of beaver skins, and then with hidden knives they murdered her crew as well. The master of the ship put up a fight, hiding in the hold, and so they burned him out, butchered him too, and incinerated his vessel.

Settling in this dangerous location, Weston's men swiftly built houses and a palisade, but they had arrived too late in the year to plant corn. So, that November, the Pilgrims and the new arrivals used the *Swan* to make a joint expedition in search of corn and beans, paying for them with knives, scissors, and beads. They intended to sail around the elbow of Cape Cod, south through the shoals, and then westward toward Buzzards Bay, but the weather was bad, and the shoals as baffling and treacherous as before.

Then, as they traded near the modern town of Chatham, the Pilgrims lost Tisquantum.

In the words of William Bradford, he "fell sick of an Indyean feaver, bleeding much at ye nose (which ye Indeans take for a simptome of death) and within a few days dyed there." It has been argued that Tisquantum was poisoned, but this is no more than conjecture. His was only one of many bleak deaths in 1622, in what seems to have been another epidemic. According to another source, the native people suffered another "great plague," Standish went down with a fever but survived, and Weston's brother-in-law, one of the new settlers, died suddenly at New Plymouth. Massasoit himself fell gravely ill soon afterward, with a similar nose-bleeding symptom.

Whether or not Tisquantum died of natural causes, his death removed the man who knew the English best, thanks to his period in London, a city where he had probably spent more time than any of the surviving Pilgrims, bar Winslow and Brewster. Indeed, if we wish to speculate, it is not impossible that as a business venture the voyage of the *Mayflower* was partly Tisquantum's idea. At the house of John Slany and at Merchant Taylors' Hall, Tisquantum would have been very conspicuous. It is inconceivable that he would have escaped the attention of the investors who backed the voyage.

It also appears from the Newfoundland Company's papers that Slany was a sympathetic host who would have listened carefully to what Tisquantum had to say. But this is a guess, and no more. We do know that in losing Tisquantum, the Pilgrims lost their finest translator and their best intermediary. When he passed away, they abandoned the trading expedition to the south.

Instead, less ambitiously, the *Swan* sailed back to the north, to trade in Boston Harbor, and then along the inside of Cape Cod Bay between the modern towns of Barnstable and Eastham. So they spent the autumn and the winter. Standish and Bradford made more forays in search of corn, by boat or overland, as far west as the northern shore of Buzzards Bay. And as they did so, it became increasingly clear that they and Weston's men had antagonized the native people of the region. The most alarming incident occurred in March 1623. It involved Miles Standish.

Recovered from his sickness, in a small boat Captain Standish rounded the headland that forms the southern end of Plymouth Bay, on his way to the native settlement of Manomet. His task was to collect corn that Bradford had purchased. Standish found the corn, but not the cordial welcome he expected. He walked up from the beach to the house of the local sachem, taking with him two or three of his men but prudently leaving the rest with his boat. He had been at the house only a little while when in came two warriors from Wessagussett.

One of them was Wituwamat, the killer of Frenchmen. He took the English dagger he carried around his neck, a dagger confiscated from Weston's men, and he gave it to the sachem. Then he spoke at length, in riddling language that Standish could not comprehend but that the sachem greeted with enthusiasm. As Winslow tells the story, Miles Standish knew that an insult was intended, and most likely something far worse. Among the guests that night was a warrior from the Pamet River, a man who in the past had treated him as a friend. On this occasion, he boasted that he had a great kettle "of some six or seven gallons." He said that he would happily give it to the Englishman, as though the colonists were poor inferiors.

Refusing their invitation for his men to come up to the house, Standish hurried back to his boat, paying women from the village to carry the corn down to the water. The man from the Pamet insisted on coming with him, to sleep with the English. Fearing an assassin's knife, Standish remained awake, pacing up and down throughout a freezing night, in the orbit of his campfire. The following morning Standish sailed straight back to New Plymouth with the corn. It seemed that a crisis was approaching. In the eyes of William Bradford, the blame lay fairly and squarely with Weston's men at Wessagussett.

That winter, they began stealing food from the native people who lived nearby, digging up their storage pits at night. How many thefts there were is a matter for controversy. Bradford and Winslow suggest that there were several. Thomas Morton mentions only one, when a settler found a native barn in the woods and took a capful of corn. But even a single case of theft would be enough to gravely damage the reputation of the Pilgrims. Far from showing them to be rich and powerful, endowed with special skills, it would suggest that the English were small, shabby men, forced to barter or to steal. Worst of all, stealing was the opposite of giving; and for the native people of the coast, the surest sign of honor was generosity.

A decade or so later, somewhere in this region, the English radical Roger Williams witnessed a *nickommo,* a ritual feast or dance. At its heart lay the making of gifts, and it was the act of giving and not of receiving that brought good fortune. As Williams wrote, the hosts of the *nickommo* would "give a great quantity of money, and all sorts of their goods, according to and sometimes beyond their estate . . . and the person that receives this gift, upon the receiving it, goes out, and hollows thrice for the health and prosperity of the party that gave it, the master or mistress of the feast."[6] We can begin to see what the warrior from the Pamet was saying when he boasted about the great kettle that he said he would give to the English soldier. He was taunting Standish about the poverty of the colonists, and about their lack of means to make ritual donations.

He mentioned a kettle because kettles made of brass or pure copper had long been some of the most-sought-after European goods. A document in the British National Archives serves to make the point. The ship's master who warned the Pilgrims about the native uprising in Virginia was John Huddleston, a man employed in taking emigrants to Jamestown and bringing back tobacco to the Thames. Sailing to America in 1619, he carried a hefty consignment of copper, weighing "four hundredweight and four score pounds," in the form of bars and "rundletts," meaning large kettles, mainly used at home for distilling brandy.[7]

In native America, copper was more than just another mineral, and a kettle was more than a kettle. Some five thousand years ago, native peoples began smelting copper and using it to make knives, fishhooks, and ornaments, in locations close to Lake Superior, where copper ore lay not far beneath the soil. Copper resists corrosion, it can be worked easily, and it shines with a luster that does not fade. Most precious of all was its color, recalling the red of blood, making it a symbol of life, healing, and fertility. Copper kettles were versatile, with many uses, for cooking, as urns for the bones or ashes of the dead, or as a raw material. Melted down or cut into strips, kettles could be refashioned entirely, as they were by the Kennebec, in villages such as Naragooc.[8]

New England and the St. Lawrence lay far away from the copper of the Great Lakes, and so here copper had an extra scarcity value. Once again, the French were far ahead of the English in recognizing its potential. From the archives of provincial France, the Quebec historian Laurier Turgeon found that as early as the 1580s, French and Basque ships' masters were bringing across the Atlantic copper kettles in their hundreds. Trading goods needed to be rich and plentiful, and so too did the gifts the Europeans were expected to make. But, as Bradford and Winslow frankly admitted, their stock was scanty, and poor in quality, compared with the ample French supplies of kettles, hatchets, and clothing. As we shall see, it was only when the Atlantic ports of France were closed by war that the English were free to take the lead in North America.

For the time being, in the spring of 1623, the survival of the Plymouth Colony remained anything but guaranteed. The previous autumn, into the bay had come a ship called the *Discovery*. Her master sold the Pilgrims what stock he had, but many years later Bradford still ruefully recalled the high prices he charged for knives and beads, and the very low price he gave them for beaver pelts. Worse still, Weston's men at Wessagussett squandered their own supplies. They used them to trade with the native people, paying too much and bidding up the price of corn.

In perhaps his finest piece of narrative, William Bradford remorselessly depicted the squalid failure of their settlement. They sold their clothes for food, they sold their bedding, and at their worst, they abandoned their huts and scattered like nomads among the woods and along the shore, to live on clams and groundnuts. Weakened by hunger, one man was unable to free himself from the mud of the beach where he was foraging for shellfish. He was found dead, from exposure or drowned by the tide. Their leader took native women as concubines, or so it was said. Losing all fear of the English, and all respect, Wituwamat's people took what little food the colonists had found and stripped them of what blankets they had left.

Bradford wrote in what he calls a "plain style," but this did not mean that he lacked artistry. A technical, literary term, "plain style" referred to a mode of writing based on Latin models, and especially Seneca, a favorite author in the Plymouth Colony. Developed by authors such as Sir Francis Bacon, the plain style influenced the composition of essays such as those of John Robinson. It was a type of prose intended to convey some moral or religious lesson as forcefully as possible, using the familiar, material language of everyday life. So, in the long passage that describes the collapse of Wessagussett, Bradford writes with unusual power and intensity, filling three manuscript pages with long, loose sentences, the longest stretching to nearly two hundred words.

Written in Jacobean plain style, the sentences tumble and unwind through a maze of semicolons and subordinate clauses, their wandering syntax imitating the dissolution of the company of men at Wessagussett. Bradford gives these straggling paragraphs shape and coherence by framing his account with phrases from Scripture. As always, we have to read him with the Bible at our side. Without it, we risk missing entirely the point Bradford wishes to make.

"It may be thought strange that these people should fall to these extremities," he writes in his opening sentence, and the word "fall" takes us straight to the book of Genesis. We remain in that territory when Bradford describes with contempt the behavior he found most humiliating: the readiness of Weston's men to enslave themselves. "Others (so base were they) became servants to ye Indeans, and would cutt them woode, & fetch them water," he writes, adapting verses from the book of Joshua that describe the bondage of the Canaanites. Nearly one thousand words later, Bradford rounds off the narrative with a proverb, the moral of the story, and one that again uses the same motif: "A man's way is not in his own power, God can make ye weake to stand; let him that standeth take heed lest he fall."

These sentences condense two verses from the letters of Saint Paul to the Romans and the Corinthians, while concealed inside them lies another hidden allusion to the wilderness between Egypt and the promised land. Bradford quotes almost verbatim from the tenth chapter of 1 Corinthians, where Paul referred to the sinful Israelites who ignored the law of Moses and turned to idolatry and fornication, suffering death as a result. When Bradford likened the journey of the Pilgrims to the crossing of the Red Sea, his message conveyed praise and celebration, overlaid with awe. The affair at Wessagussett was its wicked opposite.

An unholy, inverted image of the Pilgrim passage to America, the fate of the Weston colony served only to prove that its victims were outcasts, sinners damned to exclusion from the ranks of the elect. Since Bradford was a Calvinist, he believed that their fate was predestined, an episode of retribution that made manifest God's unswerving justice.

Does all this make William Bradford unreliable as a historian? Not really, since Bradford never pretended to be anything but a follower of Calvin, and we have other accounts of the same events, by Edward Winslow and by one of the Wessagussett men, Phineas Pratt. If anything, these narratives and Morton's make the Wessagussett story still more distressing. Morton dwelled at length on a notorious incident when Weston's men hanged one of their own number for stealing corn from the native people, in the hope of placating them. Bradford only mentions this in passing, but this was characteristic. For Morton, and even more so for Winslow, detail mattered for its own sake, or for the sake of the reader: for William Bradford, details took their significance from the spiritual lesson they taught.[9]

The Healing of Massasoit

In the spring and summer of 1623, the Pilgrims drew back from the edge of catastrophe by restoring their prestige in the eyes of the native people. The means they used were a combination of humanity, violence, and faith. While the humanity was Edward Winslow's, the violence belonged to Miles Standish. The gesture of faith was a gamble, but it succeeded.

While Standish was at Manomet, the Pilgrims heard perhaps the worst news they could imagine. Word arrived that Massasoit was ill and close to death. Winslow recognized this as a moment of definition, when the colonists had to take the initiative, either to help their friend or to salvage something from the disaster that his death would mean. With Hobbamock at his side, he swiftly traveled on foot the forty miles to Massasoit's village. There he found that sickness had struck not only the sachem, but also his people.

Edward Winslow was not a physician, and this was just as well. An English doctor would have opened Massasoit's veins and bled him, a painful, upsetting, and useless process that could only have hastened his end. Instead, Winslow tried to feed Massasoit. For two days the sachem had neither eaten nor slept, and he had temporarily lost his sight. A practical man, Winslow happened to have with him what he calls "a confection of many comfortable conserves." These, one guesses, were pickled fish, pilchards possibly, used by the English as seamen's rations. With the point of his knife, Edward Winslow pried open the clenched teeth of Massasoit and shoved the pickles into his mouth.

Winslow would have liked to give him liquor too, brandy most likely, the universal remedy of Jacobeans. Sadly, he had dropped the bottle on the way. Instead, he dissolved some pickles in water and gave the sachem that instead. It worked. Within thirty minutes, the stricken sachem revived, and his sight returned. Massasoit gave orders for his men to fetch more supplies, chickens and another liquor bottle from New Plymouth. In the meantime, Winslow improvised again. Massasoit wanted game stew, but Winslow felt that his patient was not yet ready for it.

A man of brilliant intuition, Winslow concocted an odd bouillon of corn flour, strawberry leaves, and sassafras and fed a pint of it to the grateful sachem. Soon Massasoit was happily sitting on his latrine, where he deposited three small turds. Winslow counted them carefully, telling his English readers about them in the book he published the following year. Relieved from his burden, the sachem went to sleep.

The following day, Winslow tended the others in the village who were sick, and then in the evening he shot a duck. He plucked it and sliced off its breast to make a broth to give to Massasoit. Unhappily, the duck in question was fatty, as ducks so often are. Winslow knew that duck fat could be nauseating, but Massasoit ate the broth just the same and threw it back up immediately. Then the sachem had another nosebleed, for four hours. Once again Winslow waited, knowing that the death of Massasoit might mean his end as well. Happily, the bleeding ceased, and the sachem slept again. When he awoke, Winslow washed and bathed him. Soon Massasoit was sitting upright and beginning to regain his strength.

Winslow's courage was all the more significant because so many people witnessed it. Reports that Massasoit was gravely ill had traveled a hundred miles and brought a host of visitors to watch his last moments. Instead, they saw him recover, and they heard his fulsome thanks. Reaffirming his alliance with New Plymouth, at a critical moment, the incident restored the reputation of the Pilgrims as men with some form of spiritual power, access to resources of some special, valuable kind.

Winslow says that the native people used the word *maskiet* to refer to the medicine he had given to Massasoit. Besides meaning medicine, the word *m'ask-ehtu* also meant grass, or a green thing, or something raw or uncooked. It connected the ideas of health, life, youth, and benevolent fertility. Winslow had something finer than a copper kettle: he had the power to channel the forces of nature into healing, and he had done so freely and generously, as one should.*

On his way back to New Plymouth, he paused at the home of the sachem Corbitant, once an enemy of the Pilgrims who now welcomed him warmly. There for the first time Winslow talked about religious belief with the people of the region, a conversation he reported straight back to London. With not a trace of bigotry and no sign of a sneer, Winslow records that he discussed with them the Ten Commandments. They approved of all except the seventh, the prohibition of adultery, which they considered unrealistic. They agreed that the English God was the same as their own supreme power, the benign divinity they called Kiehtan, the Creator God from the warm southwest, bringer of corn, beans, and new life.

And yet the power of the English might have a darker side, and so too might their God. If the English could cure, they could also destroy.

The Killing of Wituwamat

Winslow's mission had been accomplished, but he returned to New Plymouth with another alarming message. Massasoit had revealed the secret of the insults endured by Miles Standish at Manomet. Angered by thefts of corn, and possibly too by the desecration of graves, the people of the

---

*For the definition of *m'ask-ehtu* and other native words, the principal source is an unsung American classic, J. Hammond Trumbull's *Natick Dictionary*, published by the Smithsonian Institution in 1903.

coast had decided to push the English back into the sea. The alliance apparently included all the native people who lived along the coastline from Provincetown, around the arc of Cape Cod, and as far as the Mystic River. It seems that Wituwamat and Pecksuot had persuaded their own sachem to give the order for an attack on the colony at Wessagussett. It would be followed immediately afterward by the annihilation of New Plymouth.

Confirmation of the story told by Massasoit soon arrived, carried by Phineas Pratt. As cold, hunger, and sickness began to kill the men at Wessagussett one by one, their quarrels with the native people became ever more bitter. Pigs were killed, knives were drawn, and the native people taunted the English. From the woods, now white with snow, they watched and waited for the right time to strike. Overconfidently, Pecksuot made the error of threatening the English too blatantly, assuming that none of them would have the courage to try to flee to warn the community of Plymouth. On March 23, 1623, Pratt did so, making his escape from Wessagussett, through the swamps between the Fore and the Back rivers, with his pack on his back.

As the crow flies, the distance from here to New Plymouth is about twenty-five miles, through the modern towns of Marshfield and Duxbury, but nobody could hope to cross it on foot in a straight line. The terrain consisted of alternating bands of woodland, relentlessly identical, with few landmarks. With the howling of wolves in his ears, Pratt had no compass, and clouds covered the sun. For navigation he had to rely on a brief sighting of the Great Bear. Cutting through the forest were three rivers. Their waters are shallow and slow moving, but salt marshes make the estuaries formidable obstacles to a man on foot, impassable at high tide. Not until three the following afternoon did Pratt reach his destination.

He arrived to find the Pilgrims already preparing an expedition for the relief of Wessagussett. The day before, as Pratt struggled through the swamps, the colonists at New Plymouth had convened their annual meeting. The leading item on the agenda was the threat of an attack. Should they try to forestall it with a preemptive strike? After long debate, they decided to leave the decision to the three leaders, Bradford, Isaac Allerton, and Standish. They chose to take the offensive. Standish and eight men would sail to Wessagussett to rescue the settlers. They would kill Wituwamat, cut off his head, and bring it back to serve as a warning to any other enemies of the Plymouth Colony. It was a very small force, but Standish planned to use deception. He would pretend that he was on a trading mission.

Standish and his force found Weston's small ship, the *Swan*, empty and at anchor in the Fore River. They fired a musket. From the woods and the beach there appeared some of the survivors of the colony, men who had left the palisade and were living in native wigwams. Unarmed and apathetic—"like men senseless of their own misery," Winslow says—at first they denied that they needed help. Questioning them, Standish found that the best men among them were still at the plantation, and so he went to find them. He gave them rations of corn and offered them sanctuary at New Plymouth, but he also ordered them to remain inside their palisade and say nothing to the native people.

The weather was vile, with rainstorms. In the wet, an attack with muskets could not be made. And as they waited, one of Wituwamat's men came boldly up to Standish, carrying beaver skins to trade. He could soon tell that Standish had not come to do business, and he reported back as much to his comrades.

Once again, Wituwamat and Pecksuot made threats with their blades, boasting about their murders of Frenchmen and English alike. They came up to the palisade and sharpened their knives in the open. They waved them so close to the faces of Standish and his men that they could see every detail of the weapons. Edward Winslow records that the knife of Pecksuot was ground down at its tip like the point of a needle. That of Wituwamat had on the end of its handle the likeness of a woman's face. At home he had another, decorated with the visage of a man. With these knives he had killed the master of the French ship that beached near Wessagussett.

The confrontation ended in bloodshed the following day. According to Thomas Morton, Miles Standish persuaded the two warriors to eat, serving them pork. Edward Winslow's version of events makes no mention of a meal, but somehow Standish managed to entice Wituwamat and Pecksuot into a room in one of the houses built by Weston's men. There was another warrior with them as well as Wituwamat's younger brother, aged eighteen. Standish had three of his men with him, and Hobbamock too, and although much smaller than his opponents he also had surprise on his side. No sooner was the door fastened than Miles Standish ripped the stiletto from around Pecksuot's neck. As Standish grappled with him, finally stabbing him to death, the other three Plymouth colonists fell on Wituwamat and the unnamed warrior. They killed them too, after a wild struggle for possession of the knives. Then the Englishmen took Wituwamat's brother and strung him up to die by hanging. They found and killed another native, and some of Weston's men killed two more.

About half a mile east along the shore from Wessagussett, a hill rises between the swamps and the river to a height of about 150 feet. Today it has a long view across the bay toward downtown Boston. There, most likely, they fought the last round of the battle. Seeing a column of warriors advancing to take the hill, Standish and his men raced them to the top. Standish got there first, and the warriors retreated, took cover, and let fly with their bows and arrows. Until this point Hobbamock had taken no part in the fighting. Now, as he came under fire himself, he pulled off his coat and gave chase. Standish and his men squeezed off two musket rounds against a warrior who showed himself from behind a tree, aiming an arrow at the captain. The warrior fled back into the swamp. The fight was over, save for a last exchange of insults.

The battle of Wessagussett, if we can call it that, took the lives of seven men of the Massachusetts people. Two Englishmen fell, not in combat, but because they were Wessagussett men who had been living in a native village. They were killed by their hosts after news arrived of Wituwamat's death. All that remained was for Miles Standish to sever the warrior's head from his body and sail back with it to New Plymouth, where they mounted it on its spike. Delighted by the outcome, Bradford took one final step. He sent a blunt warning to Obtakiest, the sachem of the area around Wessagussett, telling him not to damage the houses or the palisade that Weston's men had erected. Any further plots against the English would be dealt with in the same determined fashion.

THE SECOND THANKSGIVING

Only a few weeks before, with the healing of Massasoit, the Pilgrims had revived their wilting status as men of spiritual power. Now, with their fierce suppression of the conspiracy, they also regained their reputation for strength and bravery. They reminded the people of the coast about stories told by Tisquantum, about the plague and pestilence that the English could summon up at will. In the weeks after the fighting, the terror caused the native people to scatter for safety into swamps and remote wasteland. As they did so, a new epidemic swept across the southeastern corner of New England. The victims included three of the sachems of the region, men who had been linked to the conspiracy. According to Winslow, one of them before he died drew the following conclusion: "the God of the English was offended with them, and would destroy them in his anger."

Winslow noted the loss of life from sickness and was inclined to agree with the sachem. Nor was this the last of the disasters that befell the region in that year. From time to time, southern New England suffers long droughts, coupled with hot weather. In the summer of 1623 it endured a dry spell of exceptional severity. Not a drop of rain fell on New Plymouth for seven or eight weeks, between the middle of May and the middle of July. For men used to English arable farming, such conditions were unknown, coming as they did from a country where the most common problems are late frosts, a cold spring, and heavy rain before and during the harvest. In Massachusetts the drought was very unusual: even in 1965, the driest year in the twentieth century, nearly three inches of rain fell at New Plymouth during the same summer months.[10]

With their keen eyes for terrain and vegetation, Winslow and Bradford vividly recorded the effects. "Ye corne bigane to wither away . . . at length it begane to languish sore, and some of ye drier grounds were partched like withered hay," Bradford wrote. Winslow remembered how the cornstalks lost their color and how the dry heat stunted the growth of the beans planted in their midst, scorching them like fire. And yet, once again, something close to a catastrophe became an event seen in hindsight as a blessed opportunity. It gave the colonists the chance to demonstrate once again the power of John Calvin's God. They did so by means of a festival of prayer. It took the same form as the public worship with which, four decades earlier, pious Englishmen and Englishwomen had responded to another natural disaster, the great earthquake during the reign of Elizabeth.

Winslow and Bradford carefully described what happened at New Plymouth. More bad news had just arrived from someone who had spotted the signs of a shipwreck farther up the coast. The Pilgrims feared that this was the supply ship from England, sent by the London investors, the *Paragon,* which they knew had already failed twice to cross the Atlantic. If the *Paragon* had foundered, and if the crops failed too, then the colony was doomed. Was this the wrath of God, a deadly rebuke for misdeeds or for disobedience of some unknown kind? In search of an answer, they began with the kind of arduous self-examination that Puritan thinkers recommended, aimed at exposing the marks of sin within each lonely conscience. Then, as a group, they set aside a working day, a Wednesday, for what Bradford calls "a solemne day of Humilliation."

Humility decreed eight hours of fasting, prayer, and meditation, a procedure referred to by Winslow as an "exercise," a term dating back to the early years of Puritanism in England to refer to a day of sermons and abstinence. Fasts of this kind were cherished by Puritans, not only for their own sake, but also as a means to bind together the people of a godly republic. At New Plymouth the results were immediate and effective. In the morning, when the exercise began, the sky was cloudless and the heat extreme. By late afternoon, clouds had begun to converge from the sea and from inland. That evening, rain began to fall—"soft, sweet and moderate showers," says Winslow—and for fourteen days it continued, interspersed with intervals of warm sunshine. The withered crops recovered, and so did the colony's morale. They reaped an excellent harvest of corn. "Such," says Winslow, "was the bounty and the goodness of our God."

Hobbamock saw what happened and spread the word. Coming so soon after the healing of Massasoit, and then the slaughter at Wessagussett, the day of fasting and its fertile outcome completed the restoration of the prestige of the English. Or so it seemed to Bradford and to Winslow, who describes the reaction of Hobbamock and his compatriots: "He and all of them admired the goodness of our God towards us." Soon afterward, Miles Standish made another voyage up the coast and came back with supplies bought from fishermen. With him he carried the good news that the *Paragon* had not been lost, but had made it back to England, battered but still afloat. The Pilgrims set aside a second day of solemnity, as a public thanksgiving. By the time they reaped their harvest, still more reinforcements had arrived.

They were welcome, but they still fell far short of adequacy. In late July and in August, two ships reached New Plymouth, the *Anne* and the *Little James,* sent over by the investor group, which had found a new leader in Beauchamp's friend and partner, James Sherley. Between them, they brought another sixty-odd passengers, another mixed band of men, women, and children. Godly and ungodly, weak and strong, again they were undersupplied. Again they arrived too late in the year to go to useful work.

The *Anne* was a ship of 140 tons, and the Pilgrims sent her straight back across the ocean, laden with timber and with the few beaver skins they had managed to obtain. The *Little James* remained. She had the task of cruising back and forth along the American coast, fishing and fur trading in the service of the colony. Aboard her was an enthusiastic Englishman from a family of landed gentry with their seat in the county of Essex, to the northeast of London. He was very young. His letters home reveal the disappointments that befell him, and the colony, as another year of misadventure began.

THE WRECK OF THE *LITTLE JAMES*

A pinnace of forty-four tons, brand-new and fresh from the shipwrights, the *Little James* carried six small cannon, each with a bore of about two inches, firing a ball a few pounds in weight.[11] Her men had six muskets. After a stormy three-month voyage, she moored in the bay just in time for the young man in question to attend the governor's wedding. A friend of John Pocock's, his name was Captain Emmanuel Altham. He made an excellent impression on William Bradford, with his good manners and his polite gentility.

The pinnace had another man, a master mariner, to sail the ship, but Altham was keen to learn. On the journey over, he studied a manual of navigation, and he urged his family to send him the very latest English books of discovery. Thanks to the moving and eloquent letters that Altham wrote to a brother, we possess our account of the wedding, the arrival of Massasoit, and the early appearance of New Plymouth.

Fascinated by what he found, and most of all by the native people, by their weapons, by their singing and dancing, and by their nakedness, Emmanuel Altham spoke with admiration of Massasoit. He called the man "a great emperor among his people." Massasoit was, said Altham, "as proper a man as was ever seen in this country, and very courageous." They feasted together on fruits and venison, in pies and roasted in steaks. As any English adventurer would, Altham asked the sachem for a boy to send back to England. Wisely, Massasoit said no.

For his relatives in England, Altham carefully described the colony. He saw twenty houses, of which four or five were "very fair and pleasant," the newly built fort with its six cannon, the palisade built from stakes eight feet long, the foraging hens, swine, goats, cornfields and plentiful timber, and lobsters fished from the bay. He praised William Bradford and what he called "the company of honest men" whom he found gathered around him. He mentions the bloodstained flag and the head of Wituwamat, impaled on its spike, and he included in his first letter a summary account of the killings at Wessagussett. Altham warned too of the fear of native attacks from the sea. He spoke of the illicit trade in firearms along the coast. The Englishmen at Monhegan had sold guns, shot, and powder to the Abenaki or the Micmac, and so too had the French. Altham saw just how dangerous this was, and it seems to have sowed the first doubts in his mind.

He came with high ideals, and religious sentiment fills his letters. "I was called by God to this place," Emmanuel writes from New England, in May 1624. His values were inscribed within his very name. Two of his brothers had been Cambridge students, at the Puritan bastion of Emmanuel College, and the head of the college was a family friend. From his family, the young man inherited not only exalted notions of virtue but also ambitions for worldly success. The Althams originated as London merchants and lawyers, headed by one James Altham, sheriff of London in 1557. In the early years of the reign of Elizabeth, James Altham bought the ample country estate at Latton in Essex where the family lived for many centuries. By inclination they were moderate Puritans, and by the time Emmanuel left for America they ranked among the county's ruling elite. His eldest brother, Sir Edward, the man to whom he wrote his letters, sat year after year as a JP. Among their kinfolk by marriage they counted Oliver Cromwell.[12]

Failure was not an option for young Altham, but the fear of it fills his letters. He made his investment in the Plymouth Colony with the proceeds of his inheritance. Born in 1600, on reaching the age of twenty-one, the young Emmanuel received two bequests from his parents. They amounted to four hundred pounds from his father, and from his mother another one hundred pounds and an assortment of household silver, bed linen, blankets, pillows, two feather beds, and two coverlets, "one of them fitt for to lay on his own bedd." The failure of the colony to produce a swift return meant that when new capital was needed, Emmanuel Altham had to turn to friends and family retainers for more. He tapped for cash not only the local parish minister, a Puritan, but also the family's senior tenant farmers. Hence the need for his regular letters. They were intended to be passed on to the men from whom he raised the money.[13]

Courteous, clever, and endlessly enthusiastic, young Altham wrote home in terms that were gleefully bullish. As well as describing Massasoit, he spoke of the vast shoals of fish, cod, turbot, and sturgeon he had seen offshore. Timber, he thought, could be sent back to England and "raise great profit," and still more money could be made by setting up a saltworks on the coast and selling the salt to fishermen. Most of all, he hoped to find rich supplies of fur—from beavers, otters, foxes, and raccoons—by trading to the south and west, as far as the Hudson River. Sadly, Emmanuel Altham was prone to exaggerate. His appraisal of the prospects was absurdly optimistic.

He claimed, for instance, that as many as four hundred ships were already fishing each year off the coast of Maine. This is a figure recent historians have repeated, but in fact it was a wild overestimate, by a factor of at least ten. No more than forty English vessels, at the very most, sailed each year to the waters off New England, since Newfoundland remained the chief destination for them and for the French. Nor was there any point in shipping a cheap, low-margin bulk cargo like timber some three thousand miles, unless it consisted of tall trees as masts for ships. A vessel as small as the *Little James* could not carry those. The economics of the crossing meant that fur, not cod, made the difference between profit and loss. And, as it turned out, her voyages in search of skins were a fiasco.

Emmanuel's second letter was dated March 1624. During the winter, things had not gone well. The *Little James* sailed around Cape Cod, as far as modern Rhode Island, but Altham too lacked the kettles, hatchets, and woolens that the native people wanted in exchange for pelts. He could not compete with the Dutch, who could pay them a much better price. He had also begun to detect signs of weakness in the Plymouth Colony. Half its inhabitants were women and children, and many of the men were idle, or so he said. The vast bulk of the work fell on the shoulders of a few led by Bradford. And, thanks to some drunken sailors, they had suffered yet another disaster, and one of a uniquely English kind.

By the early 1620s, the English had already begun to celebrate with bonfires on November 5 the event referred to earlier as the Gunpowder Plot. This was the day in 1605 when the Roman Catholic Guy Fawkes was arrested with explosives in the cellars of Parliament, attempting to blow up England's elite, including the king. The saving of the monarch swiftly became the pretext for an annual ritual of Protestant fervor, with a few drinks thrown in. It appears that on November 5, 1623, some visiting seamen marked the anniversary with a bonfire party. They were "roystering," says Bradford. They had chosen to do so in a thatched wooden hut, located next to the colony's storehouse. He does not say whether or not, as was the custom, they burned stuffed effigies of Guy Fawkes and the Pope. The flames caused a chimney fire, the thatch was set ablaze, and three or four houses were burned to the ground, with everything inside. The storehouse survived, thanks to swift work with wet rags. Even so, New Plymouth lost one-sixth of its housing stock.

Altham himself had a narrow escape, and one that served as an omen of worse still to come. It took place at sea, just outside Plymouth Harbor, thanks to Brown's Bank, a shifting sandbar where the chart shows a depth of only four feet. In Bradford's day seamen already knew of its hazards, and they gave it its name, to commemorate some otherwise forgotten Jacobean. Its perils may be seen at their worst during one of those windstorms, the tail of a hurricane, that beat up along the coast from the Caribbean in the autumn. From the top of Burial Hill, in a fifty-knot wind and through the driving rain, the sands of Brown's Bank show up as two parallel lines of surf, about two miles away, surrounded by water the color of a lead coffin lid.

As the *Little James* arrived back from Rhode Island, the weather was calm. Her master chose to drop anchor at the entrance to the harbor. Then the wind began to rise and became a gale, and the anchors lost their grip. Driven by the storm toward Brown's Bank, the *Little James* seemed lost. Frantically, the hands chopped through the mainmast, at the level of the deck, and cut away the rigging. The pinnace was saved. Stripped of her mast and tackle, she anchored again, and the anchors held until the wind changed and she could enter harbor. There she spent the rest of the winter, in freezing weather. The crew existed on short rations, apart from some roast wildfowl, with no alcohol and only cold water to drink. This, too, was dangerous, in another way. Altham described the grim consequences.

When the crew of the *Little James* signed up for the voyage, they agreed to a spell of six years with the Plymouth Colony, but as shareholders rather than wage earners. In other words, they expected to make their money by receiving a slice of the vessel's profits from fishing and trading. In the meantime, the investors paid for their food, drink, and clothing. Because the *Little James* was armed, the seamen also believed that they had a chance of taking prize ships, French or Spanish, as far south as the West Indies. However, under the law of the sea, this was only permitted with letters of marque issued by the Crown, and the *Little James* had no warrant of the kind. On the way over, young Altham refused to pillage a French ship sailing home to La Rochelle, and so by the time they reached America, the crew was restless. On board were a gunner named Stephens and a carpenter named Fell, two men who knew that they were indispensable. At New Plymouth, they led the crew out on strike to demand an interim payment of cash. To calm them down, a deal was cut, but only after Bradford promised to pay them himself. During the long, hard winter, discipline collapsed entirely.

In the spring of 1624, Altham took the *Little James* eastward to Maine, but with a sullen, hungry, and rebellious crew. In the anchorage at Pemaquid, they mutinied, threatening to kill Altham and the master and to blow up the ship.[14] They forced Altham to sail back by small boat to New Plymouth to find more supplies. With some bread and peas, Altham and Edward Winslow hurried back to Pemaquid. They were within a day's sail of the *Little James* when word reached them that a second storm had struck the vessel, in the harbor at Damariscove, where English seamen ran a small fishing station. On April 10, during another gale, in the dark the *Little James* had slipped her anchor cables once again. The wind and waves drove her onto the rocks. As she toppled over, the sea smashed two great holes in her timbers. The master and two men were drowned, and Stephens and Fell mutinied again, refusing to help salvage the vessel.

Even now, not all was lost. Ships' masters who called at Damariscove inspected the *Little James* and decided that she was fit for salvage. They sent a message to William Bradford, offering to do the job if the Plymouth Colony would meet the bill, in beaver skins. Bradford sent the pelts and work began. All sailing ships carried carpenters and coopers, and they made great barrels, sealing them tightly. At low tide they made the casks fast to the *Little James,* until the rising waters lifted her off the rocks. All hands set to, and they hauled her off to a sheltered spot where the craftsmen patched her up. Within six weeks of the shipwreck, she was afloat once more, almost as good as new.

This was a minor triumph of enterprise and pluck, but the incident finished off any hope of a happy ending for Captain Altham. In the wreck, the *Little James* lost her four small boats, vital for doing business on the coast, her salt, her codfish, and all her few supplies and trading goods. Altham lost his precious books and most of his belongings. There was nothing for it but to sell the craft, to one or another of the Englishmen he met on the coast, in return for enough supplies to get them all back across the sea with a small cargo of fish. When they reached London, Fell and Stephens left the vessel "in the river of Thames in very disordered and evil manner." They promptly sued James Sherley and the Plymouth Colony for forty pounds, by way of the wages Bradford had promised.[15]

Young Altham lingered on in America for another year, trading in a modest way for skins. With his last letter, he sent home a native tobacco pipe, and he asked his brother to mention his name to a former governor of Virginia, a man with Essex connections who was planning to found a new plantation. Emmanuel thought he might be useful, with his hard-won knowledge of the land and its people. Even so, a sense of melancholy pervades his final paragraphs. Saddest of all was his loss of faith in his fellow man. "It is my resolution to adventure this ways again," he wrote. "But never to have any other but myself to be the chief manager of it, for a honest man had better deal with savages than seamen, whose god is all manner of wickedness."

Soon afterward, Emmanuel came home to Latton, after losing his inheritance and the money he raised from the local tenantry. Like a character from a novel by Joseph Conrad, he wandered toward the rising sun. In 1630, he found a place with the East India Company as military commander and agent at a fever-ridden place called Armagon, on the coast of India, at a salary of fifty pounds a year. It was the first piece of land the British acquired in the subcontinent, but again Captain Altham encountered little more than disenchantment and defeat.

When he arrived, he found India in the grip of famine, because the monsoon had failed three times. At Armagon, he was supposed to trade cloves from the east for Indian calico, but disease and hunger had laid the country waste. The local rajas were unsympathetic, and the fortifications and the English settlement amounted to little more than a heap of mud. He rebuilt the defenses, making an eastern replica of New Plymouth, with a round fort armed with twelve cannon pointing out over a lagoon, just like the Pilgrim guns that faced Cape Cod. There by the tropical sea his bones must lie today, in some forgotten graveyard. Emmanuel Altham died at Armagon in January 1636. Four years later the company dismantled his parapet, removed the artillery, and abandoned the post. They moved forty miles south and built a new base at Fort St. George, or Madras, as the British came to know it in later centuries.

Before he set sail for Asia, Captain Altham made a short will—"my returne beinge doubtfull"—taking care to mention a debt of forty shillings, which he owed to a settler in New England. He left everything else to his family. In the autumn of 1637, news reached London of his death, but another two years passed before the East India Company agreed to give the Althams the money due for his pay. It seems that he rebuilt the fort without obtaining permission, and the company objected to the cost.[16]

EDWARD WINSLOW'S ATLANTIC

The loss of the *Little James* came as a terrible blow for the Pilgrims. Their harvest prospered, but not the trade on which they relied. Once again, the diabolical emotions of a few, the ship's company, had fatally impeded the activity of godliness. And yet, looked at from another perspective, the crowded events of the past twelve months had at least served to clarify the colony's requirements. They now knew what would work and what would not. Between the autumn of 1623 and the wreck of Altham's ship, Edward Winslow had been back and forth across the ocean. In London he was able to explain, with the help of his writing, the model that the colony needed to follow.

Before he left America, the Pilgrims had already taken steps to inject new energy into their farming methods. In 1623, they abandoned an early, communal system for growing food. Instead they opted for individual enterprise, with each household allocated its own private slot of land. We will need to look at this again later, in a little more detail, because for any

English community in the seventeenth century nothing mattered more than the health and prosperity of agriculture, on whichever side of the Atlantic they happened to be. Even religion depended on it, as any bishop or parishioner could tell you. Without tithes and episcopal land the Church could not be financed. And even after the Pilgrims abolished tithes in Leiden and at New Plymouth, they still had to live, pay their bills, and feed and house their pastors.

Winslow conveyed a simple message: from home, they needed cattle, bulls, oxen, and cows to add to the swine and the chickens that Altham saw rooting about beneath Burial Hill. American corn, bass, bluefish, lobsters, and the like could sustain a large settlement, but nutrition was only half the story: morale required a more diverse diet. No sane Englishman would travel three thousand miles to live in a subsistence economy fed with corn and clam chowder. And, if they wished to achieve a further leap forward in their production of food, so as to release a surplus for trading, then they required livestock as beasts of burden and as sources of richer manure.

Besides livestock, they also needed trading goods, in much larger quantities and of a much better quality. Without them, they had little hope of unlocking the country's resources of beaver skins, and fur was indispensable. It had become ever more clear that beaver pelts were the only currency that could pay for the animals imported from England, and service the Pilgrim debts. By way of the fur trade, Winslow wrote, "I dare presume . . . that the English, Dutch and French return yearly many thousand pounds profit."

In fact Winslow was guilty of exaggeration of Altham's kind. Certainly the French and the Dutch were prospering in the beaver trade, but even now the English had still barely made a start. Because so many of the customs records from these years have vanished, it is impossible to say precisely how many American skins were reaching British ports. The documents that do survive suggest that they were very few. Most arrived on French vessels, while Russia still supplied the bulk of the raw material for English beaver hats.

We find, for example, that between March and September 1622 fewer than ninety beaver skins arrived at old Plymouth, in Devon. These came from Canada on board a French ship, the *Magdalene* of La Rochelle. In the same period in 1624, only two consignments entered the same port, and the pelts were only about seventy in number. If anyone had been likely to make a go of the fur trade, it would have been Abraham Jennings, the Plymouth man who had bought the post on Monhegan Island. And yet the customs books show not a single beaver pelt coming back from Monhegan in the first three years of the Jennings period on the island. We know from other sources that *some* beaver skins were brought home to Devon. They must have arrived during periods for which the customs records have vanished. But if the trade had been substantial, it would have left some trace somewhere. None exists in the remaining documents.[17]

As for the Pilgrims, they had managed to send skins home to England only in small quantities. For this the loss of the *Fortune* was only partly to blame. During the long months before Wessagussett, the voyages and overland journeys made by Standish and Bradford were wasted time. So was the abortive mission of the *Little James.* Winslow's task in London was to put a brave face on all this, and to rally new support, but he did not hide the underlying truth. He made it perfectly clear that only a very determined effort and a much larger commitment of capital could give New Plymouth the impetus it needed.

Winslow's mission was a step forward in itself, since the thinking that lay behind it gave the colonists at last a clear set of objectives for the future. And yet, as it turned out, another crisis was just about to befall them.

The Lyford Affair

In January 1624, as at last the English economy revived, the London investors fitted out the *Charity* for another voyage. Besides trading goods, ammunition, and brandy, she carried the first of the livestock that the colony needed. Winslow brought back three heifers and a bull: the challenge of conveying a reluctant, rampant animal between the decks across the ocean can scarcely be imagined. Besides the cattle, Winslow ferried back to America a new and troublesome type of human import. Sherley and his colleagues sent over a clergyman in his forties, the Reverend John Lyford, to act as a minister at New Plymouth. With him came his wife, Sarah, and their own litter of young children. Lyford's arrival soon led to a quarrel of such intensity that it very nearly caused the disintegration of the colony's group of supporters at home.[18]

James Sherley tactfully described Lyford as "a preacher . . . an honest plaine man, though none of ye most eminente." From the outset his status was doubtful. As Sherley knew well, neither Bradford nor Brewster could possibly accept as a pastor a man who had not been selected by a vote among the Pilgrim congregation. That was a fundamental tenet of Separatist belief. At best, Lyford could function only as a sort of guest preacher by invitation. At worst, an angry feud was likely if he dared to administer the sacraments of baptism or the Eucharist.

According to William Hubbard, writing in the 1680s, Lyford did exactly that, baptizing the infant son of William Hilton, an innkeeper who came over on the *Fortune.* Though not a Leiden Pilgrim, Hilton was not some ungodly rascal—he praised his fellow settlers for their piety—and in seeking his son's baptism, he was simply doing what almost all English parents did. They viewed with terror the prospect of a child dying unbaptized and going straight to hell. To an advanced Calvinist, this was foolishness. To them, sacraments had no effect in themselves, but were simply marks or "seals" of God's covenant with man, and no sprinkling ritual could bind the Lord's power to save or damn a child as his justice decreed. On his side, William Hilton had centuries of prudent village custom.

For Bradford, in any event, far more was at stake than a difference of opinion about the liturgy. Although he does not mention the Hilton baptism, his account of the Lyford affair runs to eighteen vitriolic pages of his manuscript. This is far more space than he gives either to the voyage of the *Mayflower* or to the events of the first winter in the New World. Many years later, when he meditated on the episode as he wrote his narrative, Bradford remained a very angry man. The furious language he used against John Oldham and John Lyford far exceeds in severity anything he found to say about Thomas Weston.

They were evil, profane, and perverse, says Bradford, but Lyford was more than merely a hypocrite and traitor: he ranked as something infinitely worse, a human manifestation of the Antichrist himself. William Bradford rarely uses the word "malign," but he employs it twice to condemn the behavior of John Lyford and his accomplice. Protestant writers made the word a term of condemnation reserved for the Roman Catholic Church—"the Church Malignant"—by which they meant a perverse and willful sect in rebellion against God.[19]

Whatever else John Lyford may have been, he was definitely not a Roman Catholic. That will become very clear, but for the moment we have to start with William Bradford's account of events. According to him, trouble began almost the moment the man stepped off the boat, in the spring of 1624. Bradford shows Lyford hawking his humility from one end of New Plymouth to the other, begging to be allowed to join the Pilgrim church, greasing his path with a long confession of his sinful past. According to Bradford, he admitted that he had been "intangled with many corruptions . . . and blessed God for this opportunitie, of freedom and libertie, to enjoy ye ordinances of God in puritie among his people." From the first, Bradford had misgivings—false confessions of faith were not unknown among Separatists and Puritans—and soon his doubts were vindicated.

Bradford noticed that Lyford was often in the company of Oldham, an independent settler who had shipped himself over in 1623. Oldham had already angered the Pilgrims by sending back to England letters filled with allegations about the failings of the colony, religious and otherwise. Indeed, Oldham may have been responsible for Lyford's arrival: certainly someone had complained that the sacraments were absent at New Plymouth. Then, when the *Charity* was about to set sail for home, Lyford was spotted scribbling letters to be sent back to London.

Fearing the worst, William Bradford set a trap and allowed Lyford's letters to sail with the ship. The *Charity*'s master was an ally. A few miles offshore he paused while Bradford followed in a small boat, boarded the vessel, and opened Lyford's mail. "Full of slanders, and false accusations," the letters showed that in league with a faction among the investors at home Lyford and Oldham planned to launch what amounted to a coup d'état, religious and political. Lyford intended to destroy the colony's religious independence and bring it back within the hated authority of Anglican bishops and the official Church of England. His suspicions confirmed, Bradford returned to the shore.

He bided his time until Lyford and Oldham overplayed their hand. First there was a brief fracas, when Oldham refused guard duty and pulled a knife on the governor. He was clapped in the colony's jail, but released. Inevitably, perhaps, the climax came on a Sabbath day, when John Lyford and his co-conspirators refused to join the Pilgrim congregation. Instead, they set up their own church, with Lyford as the minister.

This was another familiar situation, which the Separatists had encountered many times in England and the Netherlands. But here in America it was much more dangerous, because the foundations of New Plymouth were still so flimsy, and internal strife might invite attack. Lyford left Bradford with no choice. In June or July, Bradford convened the colony and put Oldham and Lyford on trial, with Lyford's letters as the evidence. In those letters, Lyford threatened to reopen an old deep wound of division by alleging that Bradford and the Leiden men were militant Brownists, unable to live patiently with those not of their persuasion. Bradford and his friends were sectarian schismatics, or so Lyford claimed, narrow-minded men who kept the colony's provisions to themselves and refused to allow any form of worship but their own.

The trial could have only one outcome. Oldham and Lyford were condemned to expulsion: immediately in the case of Oldham, and with a six months' postponement for Lyford, for his wife and children's sake. Lyford staged a second repentance, and then with equal predictability he began to stir up trouble again, writing another agitating letter to London. Finally, in 1625, the Plymouth Colony banished him. The Lyfords briefly made their home in the north, with a new band of colonists at Naumkeag, later known as Salem. From there they moved to Virginia, where Lyford died in about 1628.

Every detail of the narrative given in the last six paragraphs comes from Bradford, but Thomas Morton tells a different story. He says that Lyford was a moderate Puritan himself, a diligent preacher, and a hardworking man, "honest and laudable." Morton of course had his own ax to grind, but other evidence suggests that although Lyford was flawed, he was not the simple villain depicted by Bradford. His condemnation by the colony led to a turbulent series of meetings among the investors in London. Lines were drawn in the sand, with John Lyford finding powerful supporters.

Read carefully, Bradford's narrative makes it plain that the majority backed Lyford, who had as his advocate a well-known lawyer, John White. White was a man of substance, a staunch Puritan and also a politician. Elected to Parliament in 1640, for the radical London seat of Southwark, White made his name as an outspoken foe of the bishops and the king. Of course, lawyers will represent even those with whom they disagree, but if White defended Lyford, then it seems all the less likely that Lyford was what Bradford made him out to be, the tool of authority at home. In reality, John Lyford was a Puritan himself. He came to America from the north of Ireland, where he took part in a colonial adventure to which Puritans gave their full support.

Ten years before the voyage of the *Mayflower,* the Crown launched the plantation of Ulster on land taken from the Catholic Irish, led by the O'Neills of Tyrone. Beginning in 1610, nearly four million acres of land were divided up and allocated anew. Some of it went to the native Gaels, but much larger quantities were awarded to English and Scottish settlers and to old soldiers who had taken part in the long wars under Elizabeth. John Lyford served in Ulster as minister of a parish made up of fertile land in the county of Armagh, territory confiscated by the Crown. Known as Loughgall, the parish acquired a savage history of its own, and one that continued far into the twentieth century.

NEW ENGLAND, NEW IRELAND

Early one evening in the spring of 1987, at the very top of the long, sloping main street of Loughgall, a mechanical digger rammed a bundle of high explosive through the steel fence of a police station. The blast destroyed the compound, but it was followed by a long volley of automatic fire from assault rifles. When it came to an end, British soldiers had inflicted on their enemy the largest single defeat sustained by the Irish Republican Army during the recent Troubles. They shot dead eight men: seven members of the IRA's East Tyrone Brigade, and one bystander.

Not so long ago, in bars in Irish districts of north London, you might have heard a nationalist ballad that commemorated the Loughgall Ambush, as the incident came to be known. It occurred close to the end of a long chain of bloodshed and reprisal, which began with the wars and confiscations of Elizabeth and King James.

In 1795, Loughgall became the birthplace of the Orange Order, following the so-called Battle of the Diamond, a series of clashes between Catholics and Presbyterians. Much earlier still, in 1641, Catholic rebels committed their own atrocities against the occupying power in the same village. These conflicts had their origin during the era when Lyford served as rector of Loughgall. At that time, County Armagh became a contested space, as a result of the forced entry of new settlers divided from the native people by language and by religion.

These are sensitive matters. It is best to tread carefully among them. A likeness seems to exist between the Gaelic Irish and the native inhabitants of America. Both peoples suffered dispossession at arrogant British hands. About that, no room for doubt exists; but when we move from generalization to detail, the picture swiftly acquires far more by way of light and shade. No wise writer ventures into Irish history with simple interpretations. The same is true of America's dealings with its native inhabitants.

For many years, historians on both sides of the Atlantic have drawn parallels and made comparisons between these new English colonies in Ireland and the foundation of Virginia at the same time. It has been argued, convincingly, that the new Irish plantations served as a template for the development first of Jamestown and then of the colonies in Massachusetts.

Some of the same men were involved as backers of both projects, and many affiliations existed. John Winthrop, the founder of Boston, had an uncle, another John Winthrop, who settled on the Munster Plantation in the far south of Ireland in 1595. Some evidence also survives to suggest that Edward Winslow's father was an early citizen of Londonderry. More relevant still is the case of John Slany, the merchant who lodged Tisquantum. In 1613, Slany served on the ruling executive of the Merchant Taylors' Company when they agreed to invest one thousand pounds in the same Ulster plantation. The following year he belonged to the "Committee for the Irishe Business," overseeing the company's lands at Coleraine.[20]

It might be tempting, therefore, to combine the course of colonial history in Ireland and in America, and to make them a single narrative of imperialism. It would also be rash, since many of the episodes in question remain subjects for dispute, with the bare facts still open to controversy and disagreement. And, whatever occurred in Ulster in 1610, or in America in 1620 or 1630, an immense and crowded space of history intervened between those events and the modern era. There were many forces at work of a kind undreamed of by King James, and many causes of later conflict in Ireland that have nothing to do with Puritans and Jacobeans.

Nevertheless, in the case of John Lyford we uncover a forgotten or unknown connection. By doing so, we add an essential extra dimension to the Pilgrim narrative. In selecting John Lyford to go to New Plymouth, the investors in London deliberately chose a clergyman directly involved at the very sharpest end of the annexation of Ulster, after the flight of the Irish earls to Rome.

Once again it seems to have been John Pocock who recruited Lyford, just as it was Pocock who probably hired Miles Standish. Bradford gives no clue to Lyford's ancestry, but the name is uncommon. This narrows down the field. A large family of Lyfords lived as landowners in the county of Berkshire, a few miles from the Pococks at Chieveley. When John Pocock's father died, a man called Arthur Lyford was among those who signed off the document listing his real estate, and the Berkshire Lyfords were also Merchant Taylors in London, before buying their rural property.

Three other Lyfords from the same family became Jacobean clergy, and the villages where they lived are less than thirty miles from Oxford. There at the university a John Lyford graduated with two degrees in 1597 and 1602, from Magdalen College. Although Cambridge was the more Puritan of the two places, Oxford had many Puritans too, and Magdalen was their stronghold. The Lyford who studied at Magdalen was almost certainly the same man who sailed to America.[21]

We do not know what he did straight after Oxford, but in 1613 John Lyford went to Ulster to become a minister in the Church of Ireland. The church in question was Protestant, and of course administered by bishops. Governed by King James, it commanded the respect of only a tiny minority, since very few of the Irish had any intention of joining it. Even so, the

Crown believed that a Protestant reformation might be achieved in Ireland too. For this reason, the king allowed the Church of Ireland to become a haven for Puritans, men whose zeal might prove useful in converting the reluctant natives.

So, if a clergyman felt uneasy wearing a white surplice or making the sign of the cross, then off to Ireland he would go. For Puritans, the greatest attraction lay in a loophole in ecclesiastical law. Protestant clergymen in Ireland did not have to sign on the dotted line and pledge their support to the Book of Common Prayer, or to the articles of faith of the Church of England. And, in the second and third decades of the seventeenth century, close ties existed between the Puritan preachers of London and their comrades in northern Ireland. Many letters passed back and forth between them. We can be sure that John Lyford was a Puritan, and not some kind of Episcopalian enforcer.

He found his niche in Ulster thanks to a new archbishop of Armagh. The new man, Christopher Hampton, came to Ireland with a brief to hasten the work of reform. His task was to appoint new preachers, and to give the Protestant settlers the parish clergy they needed. As archbishop, he took possession of St. Patrick's Cathedral, founded in Armagh by Ireland's saint many centuries before, on the rock above the city. Hampton revived the ancient title of prebendary, a rank he gave to three men, among them John Lyford. Each prebendary had a special chair, with his title inscribed above it, in the choir of the cathedral. Although it has often been rebuilt—the Irish set fire to the cathedral more than once—their prebendal seats remain in the edifice today.[22]

Each man received an income from an Irish parish. John Lyford became prebendary of Loughgall, a post with some prestige. It entitled him to take the income from the tithes and clerical land in the village, seven miles from Armagh, and he had the title of rector. This was an excellent living, worth as much as sixty pounds a year. Lyford owned what the Ulster archives call a "sufficient parsonage house," with attached to it an apple orchard.[23]

Apples grow in their millions in this part of Ulster, and Loughgall became one of the most-sought-after tracts of country in the new plantation. Even in the twenty-first century, the stone walls of the planter estates still neatly divide the farmland roundabout. This remains perhaps the best surviving example, on either side of the Atlantic, of a colonial landscape as it was three hundred years ago. Loughgall remains a charming place, often voted Northern Ireland's best-kept village, with Georgian houses and a little Victorian school built by its principal landowning family, the Copes. They too were Puritans, and famous for it. Sir Anthony Cope, the man who bought Loughgall, became an outspoken Puritan member of Parliament during the reign of Elizabeth. She sent him to the Tower of London in 1587 after he introduced a bill calling for a Presbyterian reformation.

His family made their home in Ireland on stolen property, because Loughgall lay within a tract of country known as the barony of Oneilland. As its name suggests, it belonged to the Tyrone O'Neills, as it had for many centuries. After the flight of the Earl of Tyrone from Lough Swilly, King James seized Oneilland, and it fell within the new Ulster Plantation. The Copes took the largest slice. For the next three centuries they remained at Loughgall, as local stalwarts of the Protestant ascendancy. Such beginnings are hardly likely to give rise to a peaceful history.

Opposite the gates of the Cope estate, the tall west gable end of Lyford's church still stands, overlooking a muddy green valley. Few visitors from outside Ulster find their way to Loughgall, but those who do will see that the ruined church was intended to withstand attack. Supported by massive buttresses, even now it bears the marks of combat. During the rising in 1641, the Catholic Irish burned it to the ground. They took Loughgall and led the Copes away to confinement. They killed one of Lyford's successors as prebendary, stripping him naked and hurling him into the river Bann at Portadown. A few years later, an army of Scottish Calvinists recaptured Loughgall, and this time they burned the whole village.[24]

Loughgall existed on a frontier, next to the most defiant region of Gaelic Ireland. Two or three times larger than those of an English parish, the official limits of Loughgall sprawled as far as the Blackwater River, a natural line of defense. Within Lyford's clerical jurisdiction lay the royal fortress of Charlemont, an outpost not unlike the Plymouth Colony. Commenced in 1602 to control the river crossing, its earthworks still overlook the Blackwater today, while near Loughgall the Copes left the limestone ruins of a bawn, or fortified house. From the brow of a hill, it commanded a windswept view as far as the Mourne Mountains.

We can start to see why John Pocock and his associates selected Lyford as the first pastor of New Plymouth. He was used to operating in hostile territory. With his background in Ulster as a chaplain and a missionary, he came with the right experience and with Puritan credentials. But this simply made his dereliction all the worse. During the angry meetings in London, it emerged that John Lyford had misbehaved at Loughgall. A young woman came to him for advice about choosing a husband. As scandalous clergymen so often do, the minister invited her for private counseling. According to William Bradford, Lyford "satisfied his lust" on the young woman, and what was worse, he did so in an unnatural way: according to Bradford, Lyford "endeavoured to hinder conception."

Soon more evidence came to light. Mrs. Lyford revealed that when they married, her husband already had an illegitimate child. He made their marriage a misery by interfering with one maidservant after another. Sordid too, in Bradford's eyes, was the manner in which Lyford masqueraded as a Puritan. In Ulster, he says, Lyford "wound himself into the esteem of sundry godly, and zealous professors . . . who having been burdened with the ceremonies in England, found there some more liberty to their consciences." When they discovered his guilty secret, they ostracized Lyford, and he was forced to leave Ireland. That was how he became available to go to New Plymouth.

How reliable is Bradford's story? If this had occurred on the English mainland, public records might have preserved some independent evidence. In Ireland, the vast bulk of them were lost in the civil war in 1922, during the siege of the Four Courts in Dublin. Only fragmentary papers remain, revealing that the Copes at Loughgall underwent colonial misadventures of their own, running up huge debts in their first two decades. They confirm that a new parish minister replaced Lyford at Loughgall in about 1621. They also contain a small but telling detail which suggests that Bradford was entirely correct about his character.

In 1639, a decade after the death of John Lyford, his son remained under the care of guardians. On the boy's behalf they gave a power of attorney to a pair of leading citizens of Dublin. It fell to them to claim rents due to the family from real estate in the north. Oddly enough, the property included land at Levalleglish, a subdivision of Loughgall, in the valley below the ruined church and the police post.

Later records show Levalleglish as land owned by the Church of Ireland for the support of each parish minister during his period of service. When Lyford died, the land should have been given back to the authorities, but there were ways and means for clergymen to enrich their families at the expense of the Church. It seems that Lyford adopted the corrupt practice of granting ecclesiastical land to his children at a low rent and on a long lease that stretched far beyond his own lifetime. This was commonplace in Ireland—Archbishop Hampton did it at Armagh, to benefit his brothers—but it was very damaging. It siphoned off income intended to support a dynamic Protestant ministry. By 1623 the abuse was causing so much trouble that the Crown wrote to Hampton banning it. The letter still survives in the library of his cathedral.[25]

With this the story becomes complete. If Lyford embezzled from the

Church, he committed the sin for which God struck dead the guilty in the Acts of the Apostles. A squalid lecher and a charlatan, he threatened to infect the Plymouth Colony with the evils that Bradford and Brewster had seen at home, in the neighborhood of Scrooby. Like a bacillus, John Lyford carried with him the degraded English ways that they had tried to leave behind. Like Weston's men at Wessagussett, he might cause the colony to revert to iniquity—or so Bradford must have believed. That was what he meant by malignancy, and that was why his anger rose to such a pitch.

Although Bradford was victorious, the Lyford affair took its toll on the Pilgrims. Because of the rift it caused with Pocock and his group, the episode deferred once again the point at which the colony reached maturity, with happy, cooperative investors at home. Miles Standish made an abortive trip to London in 1625 in an attempt to raise new capital, but he found a city stricken by plague and money hard to find: he was obliged to borrow at an interest rate of 50 percent. As controversy about Lyford dragged on, the Plymouth Colony still seemed no closer to making a profit or to paying down its borrowings in London.

To rid themselves of their debts, which had reached as much as thirteen hundred pounds, they would need to ship home three thousand beaver skins. This was a vast amount, apparently far beyond their reach. During the trading season in 1625, the investors sent over the *Little James* and another ship to fish for cod. The *Little James* carried home about five hundred beaver pelts, but the cargo never reached its destination. In the English Channel, almost within sight of Plymouth, she was captured by pirates, and the skins were sold for four pence each in the bazaars of Algiers or Tunis: another disaster, in a year that also brought from Leiden the news of the death of John Robinson.

Five years on from Plymouth Rock, the colony could feed itself, and life was tolerably quiet and orderly, but its future remained far from certain. Depending on England for stores and supplies, the settlers could not survive indefinitely on borrowed money. True, they had acquired a high reputation among powerful men at home. In 1623, the colony received another visitor, a man called John Pory. A pioneering journalist who worked as a civil servant in Virginia, he earned extra money by circulating private newsletters to members of the aristocracy. Pory told them about the Mayflower Pilgrims, giving enthusiastic accounts of their achievements, with a special emphasis on their piety and hard work. Twenty years later, when he came to write his history, William Bradford remembered him with deep gratitude. Pory, he said, "did this poore plantation much credite, amongst those of no mean ranck."[26]

This sort of praise was valuable. It was also justified, but more was required than reputation. By the end of 1625, the Pilgrims needed a turn in their luck. This was about to occur. That same year, Edward Winslow led a first Pilgrim trading mission into the Kennebec River, selling surplus corn grown around Burial Hill. He returned from Maine with beaver fur weighing seven hundred pounds, equivalent to the pelts of about four hundred animals. By opening this new avenue of trade, Winslow assured the future of the colony, but for reasons that, as yet, nobody in New England could possibly foresee. They arose from events three thousand miles away, in Paris, in London, and along the coast of France.

Chapter Seventeen

If Rochelle Be Lost

My most deare and loveinge Husband . . . I am sory for the hard condishtion of Rochell. the lord helpe them and fite for them and then none shall prevayle against them . . . the lorde who is a myty god and will destroye all his enimyes.

—Margaret Winthrop, writing to her husband, John, founder of Boston, Massachusetts, February 1628[1]

On the right bank of the river Gironde stood the citadel of Blaye, facing the vineyards of the Médoc. With its artillery, the fort controlled the approach to the port of Bordeaux. Since before anyone could remember, custom had decreed that foreign ships must unload their cannon at Blaye before sailing upstream to the city. Only on their way back downriver to the sea could they collect their guns and hoist them back on board. In 1626 the governor of the citadel was the Duc de Luxembourg, and he found the regulations highly convenient. In the autumn, the duke told his men to detain the entire English wine fleet in the estuary. Because they were disarmed, the ships fell into his hands without a shot being fired.

In Paris, waving aside the protests of an English diplomat, the king's chief minister, Cardinal Richelieu, pretended that the duke had acted without authority. The French also pointed out that he had some justification for what he did. Not long before, English warships had boarded three French vessels returning home from Spain and carried them off to Falmouth. Even so, no one could seriously claim that the duke's response was proportionate. He imprisoned in the Gironde 135 English ships, and another 45 from Scotland, with four thousand mariners aboard them. Like La Rochelle, Bordeaux had a resident community of English businessmen, and they stared ruin in the face. They had already loaded the ships with the new season's wine and paid for their cargoes with borrowed money. On November 30, they wrote in despair to their ambassador in the capital, warning of "the utter overthrow of a great number of worthy marchants."

During the following winter and spring, England and France approached and then crossed the threshold of war. The "great Arrest att Blaye," as the incident came to be known, was simply the most blatant of a series of provocations that each country offered to the other. The sequence of insults and counter-insults had begun nearly eighteen months previously, soon after the marriage of Charles I to Henrietta Maria, sister of the French king. Behind the posturing and the bluster lay serious causes for division between the two countries. And, because of what it led to, a chain reaction of resented taxes, commercial ruin, military disaster, and civil disobedience, colored by religious animosity, the war with France had remarkable side effects in North America.[2]

Events on the old side of the Atlantic supplied the final impetus that secured the future of the Plymouth Colony, and paved the way for the much larger colony of Massachusetts Bay. This process happened in two ways. As a consequence of the French war, politics and religious tension at home gave migration to America a new urgency for a zealous group of activists. And, at the same time, the war led to a surge of Atlantic activity by merchants and mariners. They found a new incentive to cross the ocean when the war caused a sudden and steep rise in the market price of beaver fur in Europe. Carefully recorded by William Bradford, it made mercantile eyes turn westward at a time when the Pilgrims urgently needed the new resources they had to offer.

None of this would have happened as it did without the Anglo-French conflict, or the role within it played by the city of La Rochelle. So we start by asking how it was that the war came about at all, inflicting on England its strategic nightmare: simultaneous hostilities with Spain and France, the strongest powers on the continent of Europe.

From the outset, the marriage between Charles and a French princess caused embarrassment. Understandably, she insisted on bringing with her to Westminster an entourage of Catholic clergy to attend to her devotions and lead her retainers in worship, as the marriage treaty had provided. In July 1626, to placate outraged English opinion, Charles expelled her courtiers and her priests. This deeply offended her brother, King

Louis XIII. He also knew that the Duke of Buckingham was secretly encouraging conspiracies against him inside France. In all this, far more lay at stake than merely injured pride.

England had gone to war with Spain in 1625, but the campaigns led to one debacle after another. Worst among them was a disastrous expedition against the port of Cádiz. By way of his marriage to Henrietta Maria, Charles hoped to rescue the situation by signing a military pact with the French. Instead, Louis signed a secret treaty with the Spanish. This was a prelude, it seemed, to some grand alliance of great Catholic nations against their much smaller Protestant opponents. And, by the end of 1626, Richelieu had also initiated a great rebuilding of the French navy. This project seemed to have three motives. Each of them endangered the interests of Great Britain.

Dispatches from the English embassy in Paris suggested that the French intended to make themselves "maisters of the Narrowe seas," from Flanders to the coast of Spain. Second, it seemed that Louis XIII and Richelieu wished to revive the imperial ambitions of Henry IV and annex for France a lucrative share of the oceanic trades to the Indies. With this aim in view, the cardinal set up a colonial company, headquartered at the naval base of Morbihan, in Brittany, and in the spring of 1627 he reorganized the fur trade to French Canada around it. He put the whole of New France in the hands of this new monopoly, the Cent-Associés, with capital supplied by investors, including the beaver hat makers of Paris. But the most obvious cause for war was a third factor, something that provided perhaps the most important motive for the naval rearmament the cardinal had begun.[3]

French historians disagree with their British counterparts when it comes to apportioning blame for what happened next. Nearly eighty years ago, the keeper of the archives at La Rochelle wrote the classic account of the war and the siege. He argued that Buckingham provoked an unnecessary conflict.[4] Richelieu, he said, never intended to extinguish by force the city's independence, or to impose Catholicism. He simply wanted to make the Huguenots disarm their warships and agree to stop plotting against his master, King Louis. The cardinal began preparing for a siege only when Buckingham appeared on the French coast with an English fleet and army. Britons tend to take a different view. They argue that Richelieu always intended to suppress the liberties of La Rochelle. He could not attain his other goals while the Huguenots remained a potential cause of civil war.

For the history of New England, the British view has most relevance. This is not because it is more accurate, but because it was what the English believed at the time. It certainly looked as though the cardinal had a master plan for subjugation of the place. In the same month as the arrest at Blaye, word reached Whitehall that Richelieu had sent fifteen hundred soldiers to reinforce the forts that the French Crown had built to encircle the city. It seemed only a matter of time before he began an assault on it; and if La Rochelle were to fall, then the implications for England might be severe.

Of course, defiant La Rochelle would never succumb without a long fight. Protected by the sea to the west, and by marshes to the north and south, the Stalingrad of the Huguenots had deep earthwork ramparts of the most modern kind. Six bastions outside the walls allowed the defenders to halt an attacking army with enfilading fire. Supply ships could come and go through its narrow, fortified harbor mouth. Beneath the streets lay a catacomb of tunnels and cellars, reached by a staircase in the thickness of the battlemented walls of the Hôtel de Ville.

Only one tactic was feasible. That was to starve the city into surrender. So, before a siege, the cardinal and his commanders needed to make careful preparations for a blockade. First, they would have to occupy the Île de Ré, an island that controlled the entrance to the harbor. They sent twelve companies to hold their strongpoint on the island, the fortress of St. Martin, in February 1627. The arrest at Blaye seemed to fall into the same pattern. A warning shot, aimed at barring the English from internal French affairs, it put out of action ships that Buckingham might have mobilized in support of La Rochelle.

Even so, the English had three reasons for wishing to intervene, and Protestant solidarity was only one. A second was simple, and political. Like rooks on a chessboard, the Calvinists of La Rochelle pinned down the French armed forces, endangering their flank and rear. A conquered La Rochelle could no longer keep the French Crown in check. And, third, and despite occasional squabbles between the merchants of La Rochelle and those of England, the French port remained an irreplaceable economic partner.

Before their voyage to America, Christopher Jones and the *Mayflower* relied on it for business, on the wine it exported and the English cloth it received. In the harbor of La Rochelle, mariners like Jones found the bolt that riveted together the long chains of commerce between the Baltic, the Mediterranean, and the far side of the Atlantic. If Cardinal Richelieu subdued it, there would be nothing to stop the French from excluding English ships entirely from their ports. With his new men-of-war to back him up, Louis XIII might insist that all cargo coming in and out of French ports travel in French hulls, manned by French sailors, claiming back his nation's seaborne traffic. In the words of an English member of Parliament, alarmed by the prospect, "If Rochelle be lost . . . what a blow shall we receive."[5]

God, Taxes, and America

On the eve of the Puritan exodus to America, nothing held the attention of the politically aware more firmly than the fate of La Rochelle. Chronicled in the weekly news sheets, the reports from France arrived in a country already embittered by defeats sustained in the hostilities with Spain. Worst of all were the burdens suffered by coastal towns. These burdens, and the other stresses caused by war, helped to push their citizens toward dissent, but also toward the new opportunities that might be available in the west.

In January 1627, for example, the townspeople of Barnstaple sent their leading citizen to protest to the Privy Council about their plight. They listed seven grievances. Chief among them were the heavy costs of billeting and feeding soldiers coming home from Cádiz. The men and their officers spent eight months in the town and left behind them a heap of unpaid debts, which Barnstaple carefully totaled down to the last shilling. The town suffered too from a breakdown in trade caused by the war, from the "imbargoes in Spaine and in France, the troubles of late at Rochelle, and the many great losses . . . by Turkish piratts." Similar complaints arose from other coastal towns, not to mention the unpaid seamen of the Royal Navy. In February, they marched to London. They demonstrated outside Whitehall Palace and threatened to pillage Buckingham's house if he did not pay their wages.[6]

Behind all this lay a familiar but unsolved cluster of difficulties, a tangled mess of problems that fused arguments about religion with disputes about finance and political doctrine. Fiscally, the English state remained weak. Nobody had found a reliable way either to pay for a navy or to manage it with consistent competence. Indeed, the maritime shambles gave Barnstaple its incentive to complain: the town was trying to give reasons why it could not afford to pay ship money, the tax levied on seaports to finance the king's fleet.

For the Crown that winter, the most pressing problem arose from the dismal end of the last parliamentary session. It was terminated by an angry monarch in June 1626. Charles halted the session because the House of Commons was calling for Buckingham to be impeached, blaming him for the losses at Cádiz. But he did so before Parliament voted him any new taxes to finance the war, either the existing hostilities with Spain or the new conflict likely with the French. This had fateful consequences, as we shall see, because the king had to find another way to raise money. And above and beyond the question of money, as always there loomed the question of God.

In the same week in which he dissolved Parliament, Charles issued a proclamation banning public debate on fundamental issues of theology. Perhaps this was intended as an evenhanded measure, to silence troublemakers of all kinds; but Calvinists read it as an attack specifically on them. For the next eighteen months, until he recalled his legislature, King Charles presided over his subjects in an atmosphere made acrid by distrust, sectarian and political. Puritans began to interpret his every move, and Buckingham's, as steps along a road toward a despotic monarchy along Spanish lines: a despotism that would free him from any parliamentary veto. Worse still, they might be planning to return England to some form of union with the hated Church of Rome.

In the months after the arrest at Blaye, these controversies came to center on a single issue. During each year of the war, it cost about £300,000 to keep the navy afloat, with caulked seams, primed and loaded guns, and tolerably able seamen. But in 1626, it seemed only a matter of time before the fleet would be called on to mount its most ambitious operation since the reign of Elizabeth, in the shape of the relief of La Rochelle. Where was the money to be found? Without Parliament to assist them, Charles and Buckingham had to find another source of income. They turned to the so-called forced loan, levied by royal decree and without the need for a parliamentary fuss.

This was an old medieval and Tudor device, a loan demanded from the same taxpayers who usually paid the levies voted by the House of Commons. The loan was forced inasmuch as those who refused to lend would be sent to prison. It was simply a tax by another name, and it formed a tight bottleneck for Puritan anxieties. From October onward the loan met with stiff resistance. In the front rank we find men deeply engaged in the affairs of the Plymouth Colony.

It seems that they opposed the loan for two reasons, but neither sprang from pacifism. They were perfectly happy to fight the Spanish, and no Puritan wished to see Calvinist La Rochelle hoist the flag of surrender. But, leaving that aside, they wished to see the war run with efficiency; and they wanted to fight it with taxes voted by Parliament. Behind this lay a matter of principle about the limits of the monarchy's power to rule without Parliament's consent, but also a question of tactics. Puritans had few sticks with which to beat the king, and Parliament was their most effective.

In the last forty years, historians in England have shown how profoundly difficult it is to make generalizations about the politics of this period, and about the motives men and women possessed for doing what they did, including settlement in America. Labels like "Puritan" became ever harder to define, and the records contain many gaps. People often shifted their allegiances and acted for reasons of self-interest, and personal or local loyalty, rather than with granite integrity. However, the forced loan posed one very distinct threat to any Calvinist, and especially to those men and women who feared that the Church of England was sliding backward, toward reconciliation with the Vatican.

Parliament supplied a stage, where men acted and where they made their histrionic speeches in advocacy of their faith. If the king could raise money without it, he could do away with Parliament entirely. That would leave the Protestant religion bereft of its sharpest English weapon. Men and women were bound to find this all the more alarming if they belonged to the Puritan minority who felt that the English Church had never been Protestant enough in the first place. In such terms we can find a simplified account of the issues at stake. And simplified or not, no room for doubt exists about the connection between loud opposition to the forced loan and equally vocal support of the Puritan deployment to Massachusetts.

Among the opponents, the most illustrious, and the richest, was the Earl of Warwick, a man of Puritan sympathies, and also a keen financier of privateering voyages against Spain. By this time, he had assumed control of the Council for New England, as its president. From that position he did his best to accelerate trade and colonization. He smoothed the path of the Pilgrims, among others, by awarding them a revised, expanded legal patent protecting their rights of settlement. And earlier, in the late autumn of 1626, Warwick acted as ringleader of a group of noblemen who very nearly forced the Privy Council to abandon the forced loan entirely.

By far the most energetic of the group was a young Puritan aristocrat who, as a result, spent two years in the Tower of London. He later became an ardent supporter of the new colony in Massachusetts Bay, which drew many of its early migrants from among his tenants and his friends. He also had a curious connection with the *Mayflower,* a link with the Pilgrims that left its mark in one of the most tantalizing sentences William Bradford ever wrote.

The nobleman in question was the Earl of Lincoln, Theophilus Clinton. His sister Arbella sailed with John Winthrop in 1630 and gave her name to his flagship. The earl seems to have known the Pilgrims since as far back as the spring of 1619, when they were trying to finalize their legal patent from the Virginia Company. According to Bradford, the first patent for the Pilgrim colony was issued in the name of somebody whom he calls "Mr. John Wincob (a religious gentleman then belonging to the Countess of Lincoln, who intended to goe with them)." The countess was the young earl's mother, but the records of the company helpfully add an extra detail. They show that Weyncopp (as they spelled his name) carried with him a recommendation from the earl himself.[7]

At that time, Theophilus was very young indeed. Nineteen years old, he had inherited his title only a few months beforehand. It is hard to know what to make of his involvement with the Pilgrims at such an early stage in their history. The Clinton family papers have disappeared entirely, it seems. All we have is the hint from Bradford that the Leiden community had friends and supporters among the aristocracy, as well as among the anti-Spanish party at court. But whatever his motives before the *Mayflower* sailed, by 1627 the young earl had become a very combative Puritan indeed.

As the new year began, Warwick and his friends quieted down, at least in public. Not so the young Earl of Lincoln. His territory lay in the southern half of Lincolnshire, not far from old Boston. Here the earl incited resistance to the loan by circulating a pamphlet that attacked the measure in outspoken, radical terms. Addressed "to all English freeholders," and most likely written by the earl himself, the text accused the Crown of seeking to engineer "the overthrow of Parliament and the freedom that we now injoy." According to the author, "If it goes forward we make ourselves and our posterityes subject to perpetuall slavery."[8]

These were fighting words. They found eager listeners in the county. In March, commissioners acting for the Crown named dozens of people who refused to pay up. They included the mayor and nine citizens of Boston, and the same John Wincob who had applied for the Pilgrim patent in 1619. Alongside him among the protesters was William Coddington, who later traveled to America and founded Newport, Rhode Island. They also included the earl's estate manager, Thomas Dudley, the second resident governor of Massachusetts Bay. He was accused of sheltering two of his colleagues among the earl's staff, men wanted by the Crown for distributing the pamphlet.[9]

Despite the efforts of the Earl of Lincoln, resistance to the loan never became a genuinely national movement. When they added up the cash received, the officials in the Exchequer found that they had received four-fifths of the sum they were seeking: a good result for King Charles. Like the Puritan movement, opposition to the loan tended to be narrowly based, in specific locations. But in these places the roots of protest went very deep. This was nowhere more true than in parts of the City of London, where taxpayers had recently faced an irksome demand for money for twenty warships. The most dissident ward was Bread Street.

In July 1627, more than six months after collection of the forced loan began, the authorities reported that only thirty-two men in Bread Street Ward had agreed to pay up, including John Milton, the poet's father. More than one hundred refused. This made Bread Street Ward by far the most unwilling part of the city for which records have survived. And if the area's protest against the loan had a leader, it must have been the *Mayflower* investor John Pocock. Three days after the report was written, the Privy Council issued a warrant for his detention in the Fleet Prison.[10]

They ordered him into internal exile in the north of England, along with twelve other men from the city. Pocock apparently said no to that as well. His name figures on another list, dated September 30. It gives the names of thirty-five opponents of the loan who failed to report to their appointed places of house arrest. Pocock rubs shoulders on the schedule with the most eminent parliamentary critics of Buckingham, and his conduct of the war, men who later became his allies and associates in investment in New England.

The appearance of John Pocock in company such as this tells us how much had changed in the two years since Charles I ascended the throne. All the evidence suggests that Pocock was not only a shrewd trader but also, at less than forty, a man on the verge of entering the elite of the City of London. He had every prospect of reaching the same rank as John Slany, and becoming master of the Company of Merchant Taylors. His personal wealth had recently risen again, when his father died, leaving him the bulk of the Pocock family land in Berkshire. In his dealings with William Bradford and the Pilgrims, hitherto Pocock had behaved as such a man would, holding extremism at arm's length.

And yet now, during the controversy over the forced loan, Pocock displayed open contempt for authority. What had happened? John Pocock had not altered his religious stance. Far from becoming a Separatist, he remained a member of his parish church in Watling Street, serving as a churchwarden.[11] The blame for his new radicalism lay fairly and squarely with King Charles and Buckingham. Whether they were autocrats or simply inept, they set in motion a chain of events that pulled men such as Pocock across an invisible boundary. They entered a new political space where respect for the monarchy was very tenuous.

For the time being, the disobedience offered by men such as Pocock was passive, a matter of saying no. He was released from custody after several months of what seems to have been mild confinement at home. Even so, this new political environment was a place where men like him could begin to imagine more active resistance. This would be necessary if the Crown became an outright enemy not only of the rule of law, whatever that might mean, but also of the Protestant faith. Put simply, the forced loan compelled the Pococks and the Clintons to think more deeply than before about the proper limits of royal authority, about the value and the role of Parliament, and about alternative places to go if their homeland became intolerable. Against such a background, divisions between mainstream Puritans and the Separatists would tend to dwindle in significance. They were overshadowed by issues that reached more surpassing heights.

So far, events had not yet reached a point of acute emergency. But if that were so, perhaps it was only because the fate of the Huguenots still hung in the balance. If Buckingham achieved victory at sea, or defeated the French on land, then his critics might forget the outrage caused by the forced loan. In the summer of 1627, as Pocock pondered what to do about his impending arrest, all eyes were turned toward the coast of France. In the final week of June, an expeditionary force set sail from Portsmouth, bound for La Rochelle, with Buckingham in command. On board one hundred ships, the fleet carried seventy companies of infantry and a small force of cavalry. Buckingham commanded the *Triumph,* his brother-in-law sailed on the *Victory,* and close beside them was the *Hope.*

Nothing but humiliation lay in store. Far to the west, on the other hand, William Bradford and his comrades were about to achieve a series of victories, in a campaign of a very different kind. During the next twelve months, as the war killed ever more men in Europe, the Pilgrims set up their beaver post at Cushnoc. They wove a new network of connections that led back across the water, giving them a firm grip at last on the commerce they needed. By the summer of 1627, they were ready to seize the opportunities the war was about to create.

WAMPUM, BRASS KETTLES, AND MONMOUTH CAPS

On August 20, 1627, a ship in the Thames called the *Marmaduke,* master John Gibbs, loaded a cargo of supplies to be sent westward to the Plymouth Colony. In the customs book of the port of London, we find itemized the contents of her cargo. The details give us a profile of the Pilgrims as they were, exactly so and without mythology or sentiment, and without the need for another narrator to add layers of distorting commentary.

For adults, the *Marmaduke* carried four dozen coarse shirts, three dozen woolen waistcoats, twenty-four pairs of men's woolen stockings, and three dozen short coats. For children, she brought to New England two dozen plain hats. The men received two dozen Monmouth caps, a flat, round knit item of a kind often worn by sailors. Because Winslow and his colleagues had always enjoyed their duck and turkey shooting, the goods on board the *Marmaduke* included four hundredweight of lead birding shot. Some residents at New Plymouth must by this time have built houses with glazed windows, or they were planning to do so, because also among the freight were "glass leades," to the value of twelve pounds.[12] On board were eight dozen pairs of new shoes, but no women's garments appear on the list of goods. This seems odd, but there may be an obvious explanation, as we shall see.

Back in the old country, men such as Brewster, the son of a rent collector, were used to keeping a written tally of who received what, to prevent village quarrels about fairness and status. In 1627, they divided their stock of cattle and shared them out carefully between twelve household units. Each one had exactly thirteen members drawn from two or three families who lived and worked together.

When they did so, they listed the members of each household, making 156 names. The details contained in the list match those in the manifest of cargo on the *Marmaduke*, down to the number of pairs of shoes carried for adults. From the two lists, of cargo and people, it seems that the colony possessed a balance of gender, age, and marital status ideal for a plantation on the verge of a breakthrough to prosperity, in an agrarian age where success required physical toil.

In these early days, New Plymouth resembled a town on the edge of a new oil field, serving drilling platforms out at sea, but still waiting to find out whether the company geologists were right about the reserves. The place was very masculine, by economic bias and by way of demographics. It seems that about fifty-seven of the residents were adult males, aged sixteen or more. There were only thirty adult women. Only two female adults in the colony lacked husbands, but as many as half the men, twenty-eight, were unmarried.

This accounts for the contents of the cargo on the *Marmaduke.* When they fitted out the ship, the investors only bothered to send over men's shirts, waistcoats, and stockings for the unmarried laborers, those with no wives to sew, mend, and make garments. Everyone else, we may assume, wore homemade clothing. As for their ages, we cannot be entirely precise; but the average man seems to have been only about thirty, meaning that they were in their physical prime. Among the thirteen male leaders of the colony, listed first in each household, men like Bradford, Standish, Brewster, and John Howland, the average age was only about ten years older than that.

Hardship had winnowed out the weaker settlers. Exhausted older men died in the harsh first winter, or because of the arduous labor of the early years. Then the migrant ships, the *Fortune* in 1621 and the *Anne* in 1623, carried younger ones without families, perhaps escaping from unemployment in England or in Holland. Among the nearly seventy children in the colony, at the time of the cattle division nearly thirty were aged between eight and fifteen. They were old enough to do chores and simple farmyard tasks and to wear the "plaine hatts" from the *Marmaduke.* So, by 1627, the colony possessed an ample able-bodied labor force, with few unproductive mouths to feed. It had the means to grow more corn than it needed and the resources to defend itself with arms.

Their corn surplus gave them currency of a kind for buying fur, and they had recently found another. It took the form of wampum, tubular beads of white and purple. They were fashioned by the native people of the coast from shellfish, either northern whelks or hard-shell clams.[13] They could be found in multitudes along the coast of southern New England, and for at least nine hundred years forms of wampum had been trafficked into the interior, reaching sites as far away as Michigan. After Europeans arrived, the volume of the trade grew rapidly. Objects made from wampum became bulkier and more opulent. Wide, long multicolored wampum belts appeared, made from as many as two hundred beads or more. A native counterpart of the beaver hat, they were sought after as marks of status and for the hint they gave of beauty and of spiritual power.

It seems that the Dutch began systematically to exploit this new resource with the help of extortion. In 1622 a Dutch trader abducted a native chieftain and demanded a ransom of a huge quantity of wampum. During the next four years, the Dutch invented a lucrative pattern of exchange, swapping cloth from Holland for wampum on the shores of Narragansett Bay. Carried up the Hudson River, it made a ready form of payment for furs. Once sold to the Iroquois, the beads spread the taste for wampum belts into a deep hinterland, adding more momentum to the trade.

At about the same time that the *Marmaduke* reached New Plymouth, the Pilgrims established a small trading post near the modern town of

Bourne, Massachusetts, at the westernmost end of Cape Cod. It gave them swifter access to the Dutch along the coast. They bought wampum from Isaack de Rasières, the chief agent in America for the New Netherland Company. As de Rasières explained, he willingly sold them the beads as a way to deter the Pilgrims from entering Rhode Island and building their own supply chain. For both sides the deal made sense. With the wampum, their corn, and trading goods from England, Bradford could look forward to an excellent season for business on the Kennebec. Suddenly the moment of opportunity had arrived.

In 1627, the price of beaver skins began to soar on the eastern side of the Atlantic. Sadly, the records from England track only the volume of fur imported. We have only scattered indications of the rising price of beaver hats: by the early to mid-1630s, in London they cost about five pounds each, double the amount paid by the Prince of Wales some fifteen years previously.[14] In France, however, the archives of the notaries of seaports contain far more detail, to show how the maritime war drove up the value of each pelt.* In 1621, a pound of beaver fur fetched only about five English shillings. Although the price crept up, it was still less than eight shillings in 1625. In 1627 it more than doubled, to nearly eighteen. It went on rising to reach a peak of more than twenty shillings in 1628, a price that held firm for another two years.[15]

The Pilgrims fully understood the benefits they stood to receive. As William Hubbard put it, writing in the 1680s, "having lived with the Dutch in Holland, they were naturally addicted to commerce and traffic."[16] In his own narrative, Bradford identified 1625 as the point of deepest frustration for the colony, but also the moment at which the corner was soon to be turned. And toward the end of 1626, Bradford and his closest colleagues took steps that gave them the financial stability they needed, if they were to reap the reward of the upturn in the market for pelts.

To put it bluntly, the Plymouth Colony was bankrupt. But if it could keep its boats afloat, and find new working capital to pay for copper and wampum, it could generate cash from beaver skins to pay at least a portion of its debts. So the Pilgrims sent the *Mayflower* passenger Isaac Allerton back to England with the authority to reconstruct their balance sheet. In London in November, he signed a new deal with the forty-one investors who remained. It was the kind of arrangement a modern insolvency lawyer would recognize.

---

*The average pelt weighed about 1.7 pounds.

First, they wrote off all the equity capital sunk into the project since 1620. Then they jointly agreed that the debt owed by the Pilgrims came to eighteen hundred pounds, a sum that must have been far less than the amount they had actually borrowed. They set a repayment schedule with nine equal installments, with the last one due in 1636. The money would be paid every September to five men led by Pocock and Beauchamp, acting as agents for the remainder of the consortium in London. In return, the investors at home abandoned all their claims on the colony's assets in America: in other words, their land, livestock, and equipment.[17]

It was possible, of course, that the Pilgrims might fail to meet the schedule for repayment. So in July 1627, at about the same time as the cattle division, the settlers gave the responsibility for finding the money to a small group, known as "undertakers." Led by Bradford, Standish, and Allerton, the undertakers agreed to pay the sums required in London. They made themselves personally liable in the event of a default. In exchange, the rest of the settlers gave the undertakers the profits of the trade in beaver fur for six years. They would also receive an annual rent assessed in corn or tobacco. After 1633, the rent would cease, and the fur trade would revert to the colonists as a whole. From England, meanwhile, the necessary working capital arrived, by way of additional loans from Beauchamp, Sherley, Pocock, and a few others. They demanded high rates of interest, but nevertheless they lent money.[18]

Under the terms of Allerton's deal with the investors, the first installment of two hundred pounds fell due only in September 1628. Until then, the Pilgrims had a breathing space of two years. It turned out to be enough. By the time Allerton climbed up the steps of the Royal Exchange in London to meet the deadline, the battle for La Rochelle was nearly over. Its consequences in North America were only just beginning.

Part Six

The Ways of Salvation

Chapter Eighteen

The Prophecy of Micaiah

God is about a great worke, yea to make a great change in the world.

—John Preston, sermon on Isaiah 64, 1627[1]

On the last Sunday in October 1627, in the Chapel Royal at Whitehall, the congregation saw a gaunt, brown-haired, bearded man climb into the pulpit to preach before King Charles. Exhausted by fasting and long hours of study, the preacher had turned forty only a few days before. He was already frail and sick, with less than nine months to live. His doctor recommended tobacco, but it brought him no relief. A complicated fellow, the preacher suffered periods of listless melancholy, while at other times his eyes shone with enthusiasm.

Fragile though he was, that day he gave perhaps the most provocative sermon ever delivered within the precincts of the palace. An eyewitness said that he spoke "like one that was familiar with God Almighty." As the war with France approached a moment of catastrophe, he denounced an impious kingdom and its erring ruler, calling on them to repent or to face the wrath of heaven. In doing so, he gave the Puritans of his generation a compelling language in which to describe their mission to North America.

The preacher went by the name of John Preston, but in London that autumn onlookers called him "Micaiah," after an Old Testament prophet. The Micaiah of the Bible "seldome prophesied good," and he foretold the grisly fate of the tyrant Ahab, whose blood was licked up by the dogs in the street. John Preston accepted the comparison, and like the sermons preached by ancient holy men to Hebrew kings, his own address caused a sensation. It became all the more notorious when he was banned from preaching a sequel. Soon afterward, a political crisis began. As events unwound over the next two years, they telegraphed their consequences across the Atlantic, adding the last elements needed to complete the preconditions for colonies that would endure.[2]

With their expeditions up the Kennebec, the Pilgrims opened the western arc of a new circuit of trade, making it feasible at last to achieve the settlement of New England by well-equipped settlers in their thousands. But before the process could reach its fruition, with the Great Migration of the 1630s, a new and more intense climate of feeling needed to exist, widely diffused among supporters of the project.

New England would not expand and prosper if it remained the eccentric errand of Separatism, headquartered in Holland and commanding only a few adherents. Exile needed to become an enthusiastic, emotional vocation, widely felt by dynamic members of the aristocracy, by men of business, and by a core of energetic and enterprising gentlemen and yeoman farmers. This was where John Preston left his mark, and this was why his timing was so relevant. By preaching as he did, and by way of his network of contacts, he did more than any other single minister to convince men and women that the Lord was calling them across the sea.

One preacher from the period remains famous, John Donne at St. Paul's Cathedral, but in his own day Preston vied with Donne for admiration as an evangelist. When Miles Standish died in Massachusetts, the sermons of John Preston accompanied *The Iliad* and Julius Caesar on his bookshelves.[3] Since he was also an educator, holding the post of master of Emmanuel College, Cambridge, where the Althams studied, Preston spread his influence widely as his pupils entered public life. Because of his talent, and his following, he could not be ignored, and so for many years he enjoyed a degree of royal favor. He was a useful man on those occasions when the Crown wished to open a dialogue with Puritans or their political allies.

John Preston greatly amused King James by using the logic of Aristotle to prove that the king's hounds were capable of thinking like philosophers when they tracked deer by their smell. Thanks to his wit and intellect, Preston became a chaplain to Prince Charles, a post that made him eligible to preach from time to time in front of the royal family.

Gradually, however, in the middle of the 1620s, Preston fell from grace, as the king and the Duke of Buckingham ceased to bother to placate those of a Puritan disposition, while new clerics from the opposing party rose in their estimation. Preston apparently pondered the idea of exile himself, to some Calvinist place of refuge in Europe. In the end he decided to remain, and so, in the autumn of 1627, he came to take his stand at Whitehall.

To appreciate the occasion, we must begin with the venue. An amalgam of old and new, the Chapel Royal served as an emblem of the new regime that Buckingham and King Charles wished to create amid the clutter of the past. Like the monarchy and the Church of England, the chapel had a Tudor core, but a Stuart facade. By the late 1620s the new surfaces had come to matter most. They symbolized a disquieting process of change that Charles set in train, as the young monarch tried to refashion church and state to embody his ideals of deference, decorum, and good order.

Close to the private apartments of the king, the chapel lay among a labyrinth of brick buildings erected a century earlier in the reign of Henry VIII. Coming upstream along the Thames from the City of London, visitors landed at a jetty where boatmen unloaded supplies for the nearby privy kitchen. They climbed up a narrow passageway that led to the pantry and the great hall, until forty feet from the riverbank they came to the chapel, also built of brick. It was entered by way of a winding corridor that kept the king warm and dry as he came to worship. None of this had altered since the time of Elizabeth.

But while the exterior remained unchanged, the space within had not. It let fall upon the visitor something very new, and very different, a vision of color, a miniature foretaste of the ceiling of the Banqueting House, a few hundred yards to the north, where the Flemish master Rubens began to decorate the ceiling two years later.[4] Inside the Chapel Royal, the walls were speckled with leaf green paint, suggesting foliage. The organ case was blue. So was the ceiling, and from it hung gold pendants. Today no relic of this remains at Whitehall, where the last traces of the building vanished under concrete many years ago, but a private equivalent survives at Rycote Chapel in Oxfordshire. It gives us some idea of the appearance of the Chapel Royal.

At Rycote, we find an elaborate oak pew, apparently built to honor a visit by King Charles in 1625. Above it stands a great wooden canopy, also colored a deep azure, studded with gilded stars made by applying playing cards. Doubtless at Whitehall the decoration far exceeded this in splendor. In the Chapel Royal, in the 1620s, the king's painter cleaned and restored the furnishings and the pictures. He refreshed in gold and brown the figures decorating the walls. He added shadows, and subtle effects of light and shade. An image of Joseph looked down on the congregation, with nearby the king's coat of arms, carefully retouched.

What did all this mean? Had King James and his son begun to flirt with the Catholic faith, with its images, its candles, and its bells? No, they had not: neither Charles nor his father had the slightest intention of abandoning his supremacy over the Church of England. Nor did their bishops. If the Chapel Royal symbolized anything, it was not a return to popery but an increase in the authority of the monarch.

By restoring the chapel, the early Stuart kings created an orderly space where visual grandeur signified the miracle of salvation, under the governing hand of God, bishop, and king. This was the way King Charles wished England to be. He wished to rule a peaceful kingdom where men and women knelt in their proper places, receiving in return the benefits of royal justice.

Mirage this might have been, but it was not the worst mirage we can imagine. Charles had an absurdly hierarchical vision of the world, but again it makes no sense to take sides in the controversies of four hundred years ago. Without those conflicts, the Puritan settlement of New England would not have occurred, but their quarrels are not ours. The tragedy lay in the collision of the deeply felt faith of Charles I and, on the other hand, the equally earnest convictions of those who opposed him, men such as Bradford. To them, the values symbolized by the Chapel Royal were at best mere affectation. At worst, they were a form of sacrilege, tainted by Catholicism, as wicked as those the Earl of Tyrone saw in Rome.

So, when John Preston rose to speak that Sunday morning, he did so in a setting rich with symbolism. There he was, the wheezing Puritan, wearing no doubt a black gown beneath the white surplice required in the chapel, preaching among the grand insignia of royal religion. The theater of the moment cast him as an Old Testament prophet, like Azariah, telling unwelcome truths to King Asa about the need for sacrifice, repentance, and the renewal of vows.

One issue overshadowed all others: the fate of Buckingham's expedition to France. Since July, his army had clung by their fingertips to trenches and encampments on the fortified Île de Ré, astride the approaches to La Rochelle. The duke had made little progress in subduing the French garrisons on the island, and still less in securing a beachhead on the mainland. The names of his ships, *Hope, Victory,* and *Triumph,* had turned out to be filled with irony.

On the day before Preston entered the pulpit, Buckingham suffered a bloody defeat. He had decided to cut his losses and evacuate. First he ordered his army to retreat to an adjoining island separated from the Île de Ré by tidal marshes. Intended to allow his men to board their ships from a sheltered beach, the maneuver was disastrous. To cross the marshes, the army had to file along a narrow, fragile, and defenseless pontoon bridge. The English soldiers fell like late-summer hay before a determined French attack. Fewer than half of Buckingham's men reached England alive, and those who did were wounded, sick, or half-starved.

Preston and his audience knew nothing yet about the calamity, but his sermon probed uncannily close to the truth. Published in 1630, under the title "A Sensible Demonstration of the Deitie," in a collection edited by a man close to John Pocock, it consists of nine thousand words of mesmeric, rhythmical prose. A dense fabric of biblical motifs and metaphors from nature, trade, and science, the sermon seeks to envelop the listener in the all-embracing might of Calvin's God. Nobody has reprinted it since the seventeenth century, but any modern American who read it would find its vocabulary strangely familiar.

Preston hammered out some of the earliest links in a chain of oratory that stretched far into the twentieth century. When the migrating Winthrop gave his own sermon, calling New England "a city upon a Hill," his language strikingly resembled Preston's. Both men drew on a repertoire of imagery that Puritans had developed since the time of Elizabeth. But John Preston gave his diction and his rhetoric new urgency, setting out issues with unprecedented clarity. Preston created a language so definitive that other men had no choice but to employ it as well.

Preston begins ominously. He takes the verses from the sixty-fourth chapter of the Book of Isaiah, words that represent a prayer for help uttered by the stricken people of Israel. Like England, at war with two much larger, richer nations, the Israelites were "oppressed with enemies, more potent and mighty than themselves." They were oppressed, but also sinful, and Preston has no comfort to offer. If the Israelites and England lie beneath the hammer, then they do so because they have departed from the ways of God, a fearful deity of thunder, "a God that doth terrible things that we looke not for."

For Preston, a covenant exists between man and God, the covenant of Abraham and Moses, a covenant that demands faith and obedience. If that covenant is broken, then the "God that doth terrible things" will exact dread retribution. Spanish victories against the Dutch, England's defeat at Cádiz, the French advance on La Rochelle: all these, for Preston, made manifest an awful truth.

"Are not our Allies wasted? Are not many branches of the Church cut off already, and more in hazzard? In a word, have not our enterprises been blasted, and withered under our hands? . . . God is about a great worke, yea, to make a great change in the world," he writes. "While the evill is yet in the clouds, before the storme come, while things are preparing, while the sword is whetting, before the stroake be given, before the decree be come forth, let us search our selves and meet him, to prevent it." England, says Preston, has breached the covenant of the godly, and the only means to repair it is by earnest repentance: "Wisdome stands upon a hill and descryes the danger, and the evills that are a far off, before they approach . . . evill is intended against us and will come upon us, except something be done."[5]

Of course this was deeply offensive to the Crown, and to Buckingham. It implied that they were even more sinful than they were incompetent. Worse was to come. Three days later, news arrived of the retreat from the Île de Ré, at first with little indication of the severity of the English losses. By the end of the week, an unofficial dispatch from the fleet was circulating in London, and it revealed the scale of the defeat. Preston's sermon swiftly acquired notoriety, and so he earned the name of Micaiah. In the words of his biographer, "The totall routing of our army in the Isle of Rhees . . . was such a ratification of his prediction but the Sabbath day before, as made many beleeve he was a Prophet."

Of course, the authorities intervened. Preston apparently invited the overthrow of Buckingham at a time when public hatred of the favorite was exploding into violent demonstrations in the streets. It was widely believed that Buckingham was a secret Spanish agent who had thrown the campaign as a means to deliver England to its enemies. Preston planned to make his sermon the first of two, with the second installment to be delivered at the Chapel Royal the following Sunday. On Friday afternoon, a royal messenger arrived to tell him that he was not required, but the damage had been done. In the words of his biographer, the aborted second sermon was "more talked about . . . than any sermon that he had preached before; for all men enquired what ye sermon was that Dr. Preston was not suffered to preach."[6]

Among them were people who advocated the colonization of New England. For many years Preston had been intimately connected with them, and he had many friends among the preachers of Bread Street. He owed his own evangelical conversion in 1610 to a sermon given by the same John Cotton who later became the pastor of New Boston. John Preston's first wealthy patron was Fulke Greville, the statesman who advocated royal consent for the Pilgrim voyage. Most important of all were his ties to an aristocratic circle that lent early support to the *Mayflower* colonists, and later to John Winthrop. Among Preston's students at Cambridge was the future tax rebel Theophilus Clinton. So close were they that when Preston made his will, he bequeathed to young Theophilus some silver plate, alongside a legacy to Cotton.[7]

When Preston gave his last sermon, he crystallized ideas that pointed directly toward America. *If* a day of decision had dawned—and the military fiascoes of the war with France and Spain suggested as much—*if* the king continued to betray the ideals of the English Reformation, and *if* he sought to rule alone, levying taxes without Parliament and detaining men without trial, then only one path lay open. Old England could no longer claim the fidelity of the godly, but a new Canaan lay before them in New England.

At about the same time, the *Mayflower* investor James Sherley wrote a letter to William Bradford making the same point. "Our estate and condition is much worse than yours," he said. "Wherefore if ye Lord send persecution or trouble heer (which is much to be feared) and so should put into our minds to flye for refuge, I know no place safer than to come to you, for all Europ is at variance, one with another."[8]

This was no exaggeration. With the English beaten, the French forces began the siege of La Rochelle. In the closing days of November 1627, they started to build a fortified wooden barrage to seal the entrance to the port, completing a blockade that would starve the city into surrender. It was this, the long siege of La Rochelle, that led the following year to a decisive renewal of English maritime enterprise in the settlement of North America, led by the western ports of Somerset and Devon.

For the past twenty years, these western havens had made tentative efforts to explore and settle the coast of New England, but as a sideline, not as a preoccupation. Now they suddenly entered the field with determination, in partnership with financiers in London and the *Mayflower* Pilgrims. This occurred as a direct result of the war between Louis XIII and the Huguenots.

Equally important, but less visibly so, was something that occurred on the Lombard plain in Italy in December. The Duke of Mantua died without leaving an undisputed heir, and a succession crisis followed. Because Mantua controlled the valley of the Po, both France and Spain felt obliged to intervene on behalf of rival candidates. The Mantuan succession crisis opened a new phase in European history. Spain and France embarked on destructive conflict first in Italy and then more widely, when France entered the Thirty Years' War in 1635.[9]

War between Spain and France gave England a decade of security, while its former enemies attacked each other elsewhere. Peace released English ships from warfare and privateering to take part in transatlantic trade and to carry emigrants. Like the recoil of a spring, England's merchant navy leaped forward into a postwar boom that brought with it a surge of activity in North America. As we shall see, one of the first and most tangible and direct effects of the boom was the sailing of the Winthrop fleet to Massachusetts Bay.

All this happened at a moment when, for political reasons, the words of John Preston and his friends found an eager audience. Thanks to the catastrophe on the Île de Ré, King Charles in his quest for money had to summon a new Parliament in 1628. The parliamentary session ended the following year with an outcome so frustrating to Puritan opinion that at last exile to America became an inescapable option for settlers in far larger numbers.

Neither Preston nor Buckingham lived to see them go. On August 23, 1628, as he prepared at Portsmouth for another futile attempt at the relief of La Rochelle, the duke fell victim to an assassin's knife. The murderer was an officer wounded during the previous year's defeat, but still unpaid. Buckingham's death fulfilled the prophecy of Micaiah, but Micaiah had also passed away. Four weeks before the death of Buckingham, John Preston succumbed to disease, his lungs choked with thick phlegm. He died "in a cold and clammy sweat" at five in the morning of July 20.[10]

As Buckingham breathed his last, a tiny ship called the *Pleasure* was preparing to leave America for the voyage back to the old country. She carried a cargo of beaver skins from the Pilgrims. From the moment she docked at her home port, on October 17, it was only a matter of time before a second wave of settlers left England to form new Puritan colonies in the west.

Chapter Nineteen

The First Bostonians

I wish I could write . . . good news touching the present state of affairs in this kingdom; but in truth . . . we have more reason to fear an utter downfall, than to hope for a rising.

—the Reverend George Hakewill, rector of Heanton Punchardon, Devon, July 16, 1628[1]

Slung out in the sea like a discus or a jackknife, twelve miles from the coast of North Devon, the island of Lundy guards the approaches to a wide gulf, the great bay of Barnstaple. From the west, the tides fetch in across the full width of the Atlantic. When they reach the granite hulk of Lundy, they split and divide around the shoals that scatter from its corners. Even in sunshine and on a calm day, pale spots of foam mark the location of the rocks, first the Hen and Chickens and then the White Horses, more names awarded by seafarers dead many centuries ago.

To the east, the coast of the mainland sweeps off to form the crescent of the bay. Twenty miles across, it ends at the north in an escarpment of cliffs. The highest in England, they rise to nine hundred feet, divided by plunging chasms, curving and folding away from the eye like the ridge backs of a distant herd of speckled swine. Beneath them, plowed by offshore winds, in the age of sail the waters of the gulf were some of the most hazardous in the British Isles, even more vicious than those off Plymouth Sound, on the opposite side of the same county.

If you stand on the top of Lundy in the winter and look inshore, when the drizzle clears, you will see along the coast a line of surf. For a while, at the innermost middle of the bay, the cliffs dip and vanish, making way for a wide brown expanse of marshes, sand dunes, and mud. In front of them, the line of surf indicates the presence of a bar of silt, with above it shallow water, at the entrance to the estuary of the rivers Torridge and Taw. Crossed at the wrong time, Bideford Bar is fatal, yet another place where wind and tide conspire.

On January 23, 1628, if you had perched like a puffin on Lundy, you would have seen a sailing ship make her way westward from the bar. At two hundred tons, the *White Angel* was a little larger than the *Mayflower,* with a reputation as a craft fit for an attempt to find the Northwest Passage. On this occasion, the *White Angel* was outward bound to the Plymouth Colony, with supplies for the Pilgrims, shipped westward by Isaac Allerton.

Earlier that day, as she dropped down the river with the tide, her crew passed the timbers of a wrecked Dutch ship, the *St. Peter* of Amsterdam. The customs records describe her fate, driven aground that month by a storm, with on board her a cargo of steel, tar, and English woolen cloth. Looking south, the men on board the *White Angel* saw the church at Northam, a fishing village, and in front of the church a plot of high ground called Bone Hill, used as a sandy graveyard for dead sailors. Only twelve months previously, the villagers had buried six fishermen, drowned as they tried to cross the bar in bad weather.[2]

On the low hills above the estuary, a series of church towers offered landmarks to mariners. Signifiers of home and salvation, they guided men back to their wives and safe harbor, at a place where the Taw and the Torridge came together to form a sheltered anchorage. Around it were a series of small townships, not only Northam, but also Appledore, Bideford, Instow, and Heanton Punchardon. They looked for leadership seven miles upstream to Barnstaple, the chief town of the area, the port from which the *White Angel* sailed, and the place that gave its name to the Massachusetts county that now encompasses Cape Cod.

The English Barnstaple stood at the head of the tidal stretch of the Taw, at the place where the first bridge spanned the river. Confident and cosmopolitan, the town was a small Devon replica of La Rochelle. Fiercely independent, this too was a maritime republic, led by an elite of Calvinist merchants. Because of the damage done to trade by the war with France, and because of the new opportunities found by the Pilgrims, in the late 1620s the Barnstaple men in question stepped forward and became the leaders of English commerce in the North Atlantic.

They did so at a moment when at last, like the waters of two estuaries, an array of circumstances converged to permit and to compel a movement out across the ocean much larger than the journey of the Pilgrims in 1620. Suddenly men who had only dabbled or experimented in America found a multitude of new and urgent motives for wanting to make a permanent commitment. Some were shipowners and traders from Barnstaple, or its sister port at Bristol. Some were Puritans from London like John Pocock, and some were Lincolnshire dissidents such as Theophilus Clinton. At the end of 1628 and in early 1629, as it became clear that New England could at last be made to pay its way, thanks to the skin of the beaver, they found a common cause, and the movement began.

At Barnstaple, Isaac Allerton did most of his business with a merchant of fifty-three called William Palmer. In his career, and the town's, we can see how and why events took the course they did.

New Shoes for New England

It seems that William Palmer was sound, because a business partner called him "a just and upright dealer," and he had a loyal following among his fellow citizens. Three times mayor of Barnstaple, Palmer kept the town's archives and its store of gunpowder, and later, during the English Civil War, he led its armed resistance to the Crown. By virtue of his past, and the plight of his town in 1628, he had every reason to offer Allerton the help he needed.[3]

In his late twenties, Palmer lived in the Basque port of San Sebastián in Spain, working as an agent for an older Barnstaple merchant and making regular trips to the French town of Bayonne. Less openly, he spied for the English intelligence service, sending home reports of Spanish shipping movements for the eyes of Sir Robert Cecil. In the Basque Country, Palmer acquired a hatred of Spain that seethes from his letters, but he also found himself among men with the best knowledge available of the North American coast.

For nearly a century the Basque ports had been whaling, fishing, and fur trading as far as Labrador. North American maize grew in the fields around Bayonne, and Native Americans walked the town's streets: a Micmac warrior lodged in the house of Bayonne's mayor, a man Palmer mentioned in his dispatches to Cecil. What's more, William Palmer's employer was a man with American interests by the name of John Delbridge. Another mayor of Barnstaple and several times its member of Parliament, Delbridge dealt in tobacco with Bermuda and with Jamestown. As it happens, Delbridge was a Puritan—an opponent in a lawsuit called him "a man inclyned to Sect and Schisme, and in most things opposite to the government of the Church of England"—and this also had its bearing on the course of events in 1628.[4]

Given his background, in time William Palmer was bound to turn his eyes westward, and so he did. In the early 1620s, when shipowners from Devon began to send fishing expeditions to Maine, Palmer was among the first. As early as 1622, the Council for New England heard complaints of Barnstaple ships fishing without licenses in its territory. The following year, four Barnstaple vessels made the trip on behalf of "Mr. Palmer and others," merchants of the town, fishing and trading for furs, this time with the council's grudging approval. They even applied for their own patent "for the Settling of a Plantacion in New England." No record exists that it was granted, but by 1626 a local man, Abraham Shurt of Bideford, was living at Pemaquid on the coast of Maine. He managed a fishing station, traded, and made sporadic contact with the Pilgrims.[5]

Even so, for the time being these Barnstaple adventures in New England remained modest and marginal. Very few beaver pelts reached the town; they may have come by way of French middlemen, and the ships that went to Maine were small, of eighty tons or less. Until the late 1620s, merchants such as William Palmer had quite enough to keep them occupied much nearer home. During the previous fifty years, they had created a flourishing system of trade across the sea, from Spain to Poland, with Ireland now essential too. As long as it prospered, there was no reason for them to go elsewhere in strength.

Barnstaple had no option but to be pragmatic. To the east lay the barren immensities of Exmoor, which reached the sea to form the cliffs of the bay, while to the south and west the country was too rugged to be worked by the plow for wheat or barley. Tall trees were few and far between. Barnstaple had a population of about three thousand, large enough to make it rank as a populous borough, and so, to feed its people, it had to find grain from elsewhere. To keep its fleet at sea, it needed timber from abroad. In 1615, we find Barnstaple importing rye, flax, iron, and masts for ships on Dutch vessels coming from Norway or the Baltic, while coastal craft ferried in oats, peas, and butter from English regions where the soil was more friendly.

One foreign seaport mattered far more to Barnstaple than any other, and that was La Rochelle. For centuries, ships had left the harbors of North Devon to sail there or to Bordeaux, the wine haven of the old Plantagenet domain of Aquitaine. But by the 1620s, these connections had deepened and intensified, thanks again to the sheep on England's western hills and the weavers who lived in villages inland. Each year, ships leaving Barnstaple made about sixty sea voyages, carrying a new brand of woolen cloth known as "Barnstaple Bayes," to be swapped in foreign ports for wine, salt, iron, figs, prunes, and all the other items the town required. Barnstaple ships sailed also to Cádiz, Lisbon, and the Canaries, but next to La Rochelle they went most often to Ireland. And this, as it turned out, came to be critical too, for the future of New England.[6]

Waterford and County Cork lay only four days' sail away, and behind them were the grasslands of the Irish southeast, the best cattle country in Europe. After about 1610, as English landlords tightened their grip on Ireland, they began to breed livestock. By 1615 shiploads of twenty cows at a time were arriving at Barnstaple from Irish harbors. Soon horses came too, from as far away as Ulster, like the "xvii Yrishe horsses" that arrived from Derry that August.[7]

Thanks to its network of trade, the town of Barnstaple prospered, and its wealth took the tangible form of stone and candles. A preacher called the town "neat Barnstaple," and visitors found the streets lit by lanterns until nine each evening. Travelers remarked on its broad, well-paved streets, its fine houses of stone and brick, and the "sweet and wholesome Air" of this little seaside city-state.[8] When Palmer's business partner died in 1624, he left a rich bequest to found an almshouse for the elderly. The arcaded building still stands, serving the same purpose, just like the Browne almshouses at Stamford.

And then, as a direct consequence of the king's two wars, first with Spain and then with France, the storm clouds began to blow in from Lundy. When Parliament met in 1626, John Delbridge swiftly rose to his feet to list the many grievances afflicting Barnstaple. He spoke out against high taxes on imported wine, and of course he denounced the French for their confiscation of English ships. He raged about the losses suffered at the hands of Turkish pirates and Spanish raiders, and he blamed the Duke of Buckingham. Early the following year, Delbridge delivered the town's petition to the Crown, protesting against the cost of billeted troops. Similar complaints came from many other towns, but most loudly from seaports. For Barnstaple, they reached their worst extent in 1628, after the massacre on the Île de Ré.

In the final weeks of 1627, French engineers at La Rochelle hurried to finish the great barrage that sealed off the port's access to the ocean. The last supplies entered the city in early January, and by the end of that month English agents in France were reporting that the blockade was complete. For the merchants of Barnstaple, the siege removed their most valued trading partner. It dealt the town by far the most serious of the long series of blows it had sustained.[9]

Foreign trade dwindled almost to zero in 1628. That year not a single ship sailed from the Taw estuary to France or Spain, only scraps of woolen cloth left Barnstaple for foreign ports, and until midsummer there were no arrivals from any European port. Two Dutchmen evaded French warships and crept in with salt from Brittany, but the vast bulk of the salt and wine trade from abroad simply vanished. For salt, vital for its fishermen, Barnstaple had to rely on coasters making the long, dangerous voyage from Scotland, under threat from Spanish privateers ranging up and down the North Sea from Dunkirk.[10] The Irish connection remained, but even so the town's seaborne commerce fell to less than half the level seen before the war. "All things are dead with us," said John Delbridge in the Parliament that met in March.[11]

At this very moment, William Palmer found his alternative in the west, in partnership with the Pilgrims. News of the barrage at La Rochelle would have reached North Devon no later than Christmas week. We know from the fate of the *St. Peter* that in Britain's western approaches the weather was bad in January. When it cleared, off from Barnstaple to America went a small fleet of four ships, led by the *White Angel.* She was actually a Bristol ship, but the ports of Barnstaple and Bristol worked in tandem, with small vessels plying back and forth between the two. Both towns sent to sea as many privateers as they could—Palmer and his colleagues had fourteen letters of marque, allowing them to do so—and they used the prize money from taking French and Spanish ships to feed a joint pool of capital. When the time came, it was available to finance the Atlantic trade.[12]

As the Latin of the customs books put it, the *White Angel* was heading "versus Novam Angliam"—toward New England—and she carried a cargo of Irish and Barnstaple-made woolen cloth, haberdashery, and iron. Isaac Allerton was the exporter. The following day a second ship left, the *Eagle,* of fifty tons. For Allerton, she carried two fishing nets and another three hundred pairs of "novorum calceorum," new shoes for the feet of the Pilgrims. Also on board were more haberdashery and groceries, shipped by Palmer.[13]

Two weeks later, on February 7, out sailed the *Content,* a fishing boat of only thirty tons, again bound for New England. Her master was John Witheridge of Instow, aged fifty-five, from a family with long ties to the Palmers. He was perhaps the town's most experienced transatlantic seaman. A Newfoundland veteran, he had fished and traded for fur on the coast of Maine in 1623, where he met Samoset, the Abenaki chieftain who greeted the settlers at New Plymouth.[14]

Last of all, on March 2, the thirty-five-ton *Pleasure* left for America, under the command of a veteran Barnstaple seaman, William Peeters. He took with him a hogshead of brandy, enough for eight thousand shots of liquor. Gunpowder and lead shot made the crossing too, and a mass of tools and trading goods: hatchets, hoes, axes, scythes, scissors, knives, and iron pots. We know this because in his letter book Bradford copied out a set of accounts for the Plymouth Colony drawn up by James Sherley. They match the data from the port of Barnstaple.[15]

Each of the four ships made the journey safely, both ways. When they crossed Bideford Bar on their return, they brought with them a haul of beaver skins of a size hitherto unseen in their home ports. First to reach Devon on July 28 was the *Eagle.* After unloading her supplies for the Pilgrims, she had fished, collected train oil, and then sailed on to Virginia before coming home. She carried no fewer than 274 beaver skins, divided into three consignments for Barnstaple merchants. Of these, 230 went to a consortium led by William Palmer.

Into the Taw on October 2 came the *Content,* and on board John Witheridge brought back another 228 beaver pelts, sixty-five otter skins, and eight tons of wax from Jamestown. All the fur was for Palmer's account. The *Pleasure* was the last to reach harbor, on October 17. Her cargo came directly from the *Mayflower* Pilgrims. Sherley mentioned the *Pleasure,* and Peeters, and two hundred pounds of beaver fur sent back from New Plymouth. Altogether, the *Pleasure* carried four tons of train oil and 726 beaver pelts for five Bristol and Barnstaple merchants. One of them, named John Brand, acted for Sherley. He packed Sherley's pelts off to London to be sold on the colony's behalf.

Nearly thirteen hundred skins from North American beavers arrived in the river Taw that season, more than a third of them imported by Palmer's syndicate. These were remarkable totals. When London ships sailed home from Archangel in the early 1620s, they carried Siberian skins in far greater quantities, but Barnstaple was a small port, with a merchant fleet less than a tenth the size of the capital's, and records list only some of the fur that came home in 1628. The *White Angel* left Lundy on her starboard bow and sailed on to Bristol. The customs books from that town have not survived, but the *White Angel* carried at least three hundred pelts from the Pilgrims alone. She may have picked up still more from other English traders who were making inroads along the coast of Maine. By weight, the skins brought home by the four ships probably amounted to at least three thousand pounds, the pelts of about eighteen hundred of the beavers of Mawooshen.

At this moment, the pattern of events in North America changed fundamentally. For the *Mayflower* Pilgrims, the trading season of 1628 supplied the reward for eight years of effort, often apparently wasted but ultimately worthwhile. That same year, in June, they sent Standish up the coast to eject Thomas Morton by force from his base at Mount Wollaston, on the grounds that he was selling liquor and guns to the Indians: he was packed off to England to be dealt with by the Council for New England, but the affair also stopped Morton competing with the Pilgrims for the Kennebec fur trade.

Meanwhile, back home in London, when the furs were sold, it became clear that the Pilgrims had made their first outright profit, and so they met their first deadline for paying off their debts. At the same time, they found new partners in Bristol and Barnstaple. Another man whose business had suffered because of the French war was a Bristol wine merchant named Giles Elbridge, and now he joined Beauchamp, Pocock, and Sherley in extending additional credit to the Plymouth Colony. Since Elbridge was also a successful privateer, he had the cash to do so, and soon afterward he founded his own colony in Maine. In this way, the momentum created by the Pilgrims began to roll out new settlements all along the New England coast.[16]

Until now, the French had dominated the fur trade of the north, sending back pelts in their thousands from the posts created by Champlain on the St. Lawrence. Suddenly the English stood on the brink of a period in which, for nearly four years, they had the region to themselves. Via their trading post at Cushnoc, and the canoe routes that converged upon it, the Pilgrims had found an avenue that led in and out of the territory, dense with beaver, between the Kennebec, Chaudière, and Penobscot rivers. As we shall see, the English were about to go further, and temporarily elbow the French out of Canada entirely. By doing so, they secured not only the fur supplies of the watershed but also those of the whole St. Lawrence valley. For a while they made the Gulf of Maine an English lake.

All this made possible the Great Migration of Puritans to New Boston. But, before it could occur, a new political crisis had to intervene in England, a crisis that added extra encouragement for those who wavered on the verge of exile. As the Barnstaple ships and their seamen tied up at the quayside in the town in the autumn of 1628, they found the symptoms of the crisis all too visible around them.

Soon after Witheridge dropped anchor in the Taw, a small boat arrived carrying fifteen starving soldiers, English troops who had been trapped in La Rochelle throughout the siege. They were evacuated after the city fell to Louis XIII in October. Similar boatloads of dying men reached many other western ports, and the stories they brought with them intensified a pervasive animosity toward the Crown. On the other side of the county in Plymouth, shipowners, merchants, and mariners began to display open civil disobedience. They refused to commit their men and their hulls to any more futile efforts against the enemy across the channel.

By mishandling the war as they did, the Duke of Buckingham and King Charles laid a trail of gunpowder that led toward New England. All it needed was a lit flame, and the man who struck the match went by the name of Matthew Cradock. Mentioned only briefly by most historians, because he never visited Massachusetts and never saw his land along the Mystic, Cradock founded the new company that settled Massachusetts Bay.

Under his leadership, in the spring and summer of 1629, the company took a series of decisions that led to the voyage of John Winthrop the following year. They were based on the experience of the Plymouth Colony, because Cradock knew the Pilgrims well.

Fur, Politics, and Faith

Up to a point, Matthew Cradock resembled Thomas Weston, but the likeness was very superficial. Like the Westons, the Cradocks came from Staffordshire, where they dealt in wool and woolen cloth, and like Weston the young Matthew Cradock started his career exporting cheap textiles to France. Their names appear beside each other in the customs book for 1617. There the similarity ends, because Cradock rose to become an affluent luminary of the London scene, importing raisins and currants from the Near East. He invested in the East India Company, and he knew the fur trade, since he sat with the beaver king Ralph Freeman on the board of the Muscovy Company. In the spring of 1628, Cradock saw an opportunity to relaunch England's fumbling ventures in America by taking over a failing enterprise that had tried to emulate the *Mayflower* Pilgrims.[17]

The enterprise in question came into existence in 1623. In that year, a group of investors from Dorset, on the south coast of England, decided to found their own Massachusetts fishing colony at Cape Ann. They too were Puritans, haberdashers, and cloth merchants, with a Calvinist preacher called John White at their head. They had a godly aim to bring the Gospel to the people whom they called Indians, but they had a political edge as well. Their number included members of Parliament, patriotic, anti-Catholic, and anti-Spanish, but their business acumen fell far short of their zeal and their national pride.

They sent too few men, in ships that were too small, and only a handful of cattle. They squabbled with the Pilgrims—Miles Standish tried to push them off their jetty in 1624—and in any event they had chosen the wrong place. It was too rocky and too windswept for an enduring post. In 1626, the leader on the spot at Cape Ann, Roger Conant, took them off twenty or thirty strong to a better site at Naumkeag, where Salem stands today. Meanwhile, the investors in England had lost heart, and so John White's project faltered and ground to a halt.[18]

Not for long, however. By the time the Barnstaple men sailed off to New England, in the opening months of 1628, the business community in London had begun to see that the same place might offer solutions for their own dilemmas. They too were losing business, because of the war. So, in March, a group of London merchants including Cradock made what amounted to a takeover bid for White's limping venture. They rebuilt it as the New England Company, with new investors and new capital from the City, and they prepared to send reinforcements to Naumkeag. In June, the *Abigail* left Weymouth in Dorset, a ship of 120 tons, with on board her John Endecott, whose task was to relieve and replace Conant as leader of the colony.

At last, enthusiasm about America north of the Delaware began to take hold in London. In February, even King Charles joined in, with a royal proclamation that called on parish churches to pass round the hat on Sunday to collect donations for a new colony in Casco Bay in Maine, "for the propagacon of the true religion . . . by converting those Ignorant people to Christianity."[19] This was also a matter of military strategy: the king had listened to men who argued that naval bases along the Gulf of Maine were essential, to protect the cod fishing grounds and resources of timber from the French and the Spanish.

Then, during the spring, as Cradock began to revive the White project, some of his near neighbors in London launched the first of two remarkable expeditions to Canada. Like John Pocock, the men concerned came from Bread Street Ward. Their leader, Gervase Kirke, lived in the parish of All Hallows. Another merchant who exported woolens to France, using the same ships as Thomas Weston, Kirke married a Frenchwoman from Dieppe. They had three sons, all of whom trained as navigators in the town. As the war shut down his relationship with France, Kirke became a privateer. In 1628 he saw a superb opportunity to outflank the French, by making a surprise attack on Champlain at Quebec.

Kirke and his partners fitted out three ships, led by his son Captain David Kirke, a young man of only thirty-one. He reached Canada that summer and seized the French trading post at Tadoussac. Then at the mouth of the St. Lawrence he turned to face a French squadron sent out by Richelieu.

Outnumbered by eighteen ships to three, Captain Kirke engaged the enemy closely, sank ten of the French vessels, seized the flagship and captured more than one hundred cannon. In Paris, they burned Captain Kirke in effigy, as a traitor to his mother's homeland. But in London his victory at sea was swiftly recognized for what it was: the most successful English foray to North America since the reign of Queen Elizabeth. The Kirkes swiftly made plans for another, even larger effort the following year, in the spring of 1629.[20]

Meanwhile, as the Barnstaple ships collected their skins from the Pilgrims, and as Cradock sent the *Abigail* to Salem, in June 1628 the political climate became still more unsettled. When Parliament assembled, the House of Commons voted new taxes for the war, but on too small a scale. They would scarcely cover the naval budget if the ships remained in port, let alone pay for a campaign sufficient to relieve La Rochelle. While Buckingham remained at the right hand of the king, the Commons would do no more. The duke became the bottleneck for complaints of all kinds, dating back to the forced loan and before, about imprisonment without trial, about billeting, about the Turkish pirates, about the slump in trade, and about religion.

Members of Parliament began to insist, like John Preston, that if England suffered defeats, it was because the kingdom was ungodly. As the session neared an angry close, a cohort of truculent MPs accused Buckingham of a plot to subvert the Protestant faith and to carry the nation back toward the Church of Rome. The king saw no point in prolonging such nonsense as this. On June 26 he prorogued the session, with the intention of recalling Parliament later that year. To show his critics what was what, he appointed a new bishop of London, William Laud, a latter-day Richard Bancroft. A man close to the duke, Laud was likely to enforce the law strictly against any signs of Puritan dissent. The following month, Buckingham was assassinated. This brought the crisis to a head.

While Buckingham lived, he acted as a lightning conductor for Charles I. His opponents in Parliament could hurl at the duke the blame for every woe from which the kingdom suffered. Among their number were the men most likely to support a new Protestant colony in the west. A list can be made of MPs who called for Buckingham's impeachment in 1626, and on it appear the names of six men who helped finance the early settlement of New England. But with Buckingham dead, they lost their scapegoat, and so if the same woes continued, they would find themselves driven to a much more uncomfortable conclusion: that church and state suffered from a malaise that was chronic, cancerous, and incurable. Worst of all was "the Dilligence of the Papists," as they gnawed away at the base of a Protestant nation.

If, as seemed likely, Laud rose even further, to become archbishop of Canterbury, would he put an end to Calvinism and delete predestination from the doctrine of the Church of England? Would he, like Bancroft, begin a purge of suspect clergymen? Would he punish or dismiss the likes of John Preston, for all their learning and distinction? That too seemed likely. Men such as Pocock would lose the preachers to whom they looked for guidance, the men who maintained godly good order in the parish. Even leaving aside religion—as if anybody could—did England have a future? With its economy in ruins, "impoverished by decay of Trade," how could its people afford Christian charity? In America, they had a charitable mission ready-made, in the duty to bring the Gospel to the Indians, just as Pocock had taken it to Merseyside, by way of Harrison's grammar school.[21]

These were the views of a small Puritan minority, of course. Compared with those who stayed at home, the English who went to America were very few. And, as many historians have argued, as emigration gathered pace in the 1630s, many of those who made the crossing were not really Puritans at all, but entirely economic refugees. But in 1629 that was not the case: again, as with the *Mayflower*, in the beginning numbers mattered less than morale and leadership. In the spring of 1629, the motivation was a compound. Religion stood at the top of the list, but it was inseparable from politics, while business was essential to supply the wherewithal for accomplishing the task.

Parliament met on January 20 and sat for seven weeks. The king wanted money with which to fight the war, while the House of Commons wanted reform. Its members could not quite agree what they meant by the word, but the religious demand was relatively simple: they wanted legislation to defend and to safeguard the Protestant religion as it had been before Laud, Buckingham, and the king's marriage to a French Catholic. The king would not agree, Parliament refused to grant taxes, and so the session ended. Seeing no purpose in further debate, King Charles dissolved Parliament on March 10. In doing so, he gave the last impetus required for Cradock and his colleagues to do the unavoidable and to launch a second, much larger model of the Plymouth Colony. Eleven years passed until Charles ordered a new Parliament to convene.

Six days before the dissolution, the king granted a charter to a new company to found a plantation around Massachusetts Bay. Formed by Matthew Cradock, it absorbed the settlement at Salem, and in March it began to make detailed plans for the future. On the eighteenth of the month, the Massachusetts Bay Company named Cradock as its first governor. With him in the chair, the company took its essential decisions, against a background of rising excitement about the opportunities identified by David Kirke.

On February 4, the Crown issued a patent to the Kirkes that marked another new high point in the scale of British ambition in North America. The king gave them a brief "to displant the French," and if they could do so, then they could keep Canada as a whole. For the Kirkes, possession of the territory offered something of the highest value: "the sole trade of Beaver wools, Beaver skins, Furs, Hides & Skins of wild beasts" from Labrador inland to Lake Ontario and south to Nova Scotia. On August 20, Captain Kirke and his fleet duly captured Quebec, and with it Champlain, his Jesuit companions, his arms and ammunition, and several thousand pelts.

Until the middle of 1632, the English flag flew at Quebec, with the Kirkes standing ready to sink any French ship that approached. Eventually, they had to give back the settlement, under the terms of the treaty that ended the war, but during their period of occupation the English were free to do as they pleased on the far side of the Atlantic. The fur trade of Canada and New England belonged entirely to them. During that space of time the Great Migration began.[22]

Violent though they were, the Kirke expeditions demonstrated that success in North America depended on far bolder ventures than those undertaken hitherto. In reaching the same conclusion, Cradock could also draw upon the lessons taught by the arduous first decade of the Plymouth Colony. Cradock knew and trusted Isaac Allerton, who carried his letters to Endecott at Salem, by way of Barnstaple. He also knew John Pocock. In due course Pocock and three other New Plymouth investors went on to join the board of Cradock's company.[23]

More clearly than anyone else, Cradock recognized that the ships sent to New England needed to be much larger, carrying settlers in parties numbering at least twice as many as the passengers on the *Mayflower.* Cattle had to make the journey too, numbering at least one hundred head. They had to travel with the first colonists, in order to achieve a rapid reproduction of an English diet on the other side of the Atlantic. Speed was essential, and Cradock saw fishing as a distraction: it simply did not make the required financial return.

Rather than wander the coast in search of cod, ships needed to head back to England as swiftly as possible to keep the wage bill to a minimum. On board, they had to carry the items that gave the fastest payback. They should carry fish only if the colonists had it ready and packed on the quayside. "Endevour to gett convenient howsinge, fitt to lodge as manye as you cann," Cradock wrote to Endecott. "And with all what bever, or other comodities, or ffishe, if the meanes to preserve it, can be gotten readie, to returne in the foresaid shippes; and likewise wood . . . there hath not been a better tyme for sale of tymber theise twoe seaven yeres."[24]

During the summer and autumn of 1629, the Massachusetts Bay Company took three essential decisions. First, on July 28, they approved the purchase of a ship called the *Eagle* of nearly four hundred tons, much larger than any used previously by the English in the Gulf of Maine. She was not yet available, because she was privateering in the Mediterranean, looking for Spaniards to sink, but, renamed the *Arbella*, she duly led the Winthrop fleet to America the following year. Still more capacity was needed, but it came within their grasp. With no new taxes from Parliament, Charles had to end the war with France one month later, in April. Soon ships committed to the war effort became free to cross the Atlantic with settlers. Then, as England became a neutral country, seaborne commerce began to thrive, as it carried cargoes for customers from every nation. In the next six years, English shipyards added ten thousand tons of new shipping, and this enabled the Great Migration to accelerate.

The second decision was made on August 29. Cradock and the assistants voted to transfer the company's legal residence and government entirely to America. Why? One motive may have been to lessen the danger of interference by William Laud and the Crown, but another seems equally likely. They simply imitated the Plymouth Colony. It still owed money in London, but in 1626 it shook off the last ties of corporate control from the old country. It entirely ran its own affairs, and since Lyford's departure it had done so with a tranquillity rare among the English overseas. Dual control could never work, causing only friction and disagreement between investors and settlers divided by sea crossings taking many weeks.

Finally, on October 15, they turned their attention to the beaver. Copying the scheme devised by the Pilgrims, they gave the company a monopoly on the fur trade in its territory for seven years, excluding from it the individual settlers. This allowed the company to finance the outlay required for the initial voyages, before the new planters established themselves. In return, the company bore half the cost of fortifications, churches, public buildings, and the salaries of clergymen. From the outset, Cradock and his colleagues understood that only the beaver could pay for the colony that they wanted to establish. Five days later, on October 20, John Winthrop replaced Cradock as governor, because Cradock had so many business interests that tied him to London. Immediately, Winthrop began to organize and to recruit for the fleet expected to sail in the spring of 1630.

Was this enough to create a durable New England? Not quite, but John Witheridge was about to add a last, ambiguous foundation stone. He did so two years later. Again the sequence of events had its origins in Barnstaple. In 1632, Witheridge made the first link between the colonies along the shores of Massachusetts Bay and the slave islands of the Caribbean.

The Voyages of the *Charles*

This phase of the story begins with a minor catastrophe in Boston Harbor. Until World War II, ships heading out from the Charlestown Navy Yard toward the open sea passed a grassy island on their left. Created by glacial debris, and rising to nearly a hundred feet above the water, Governors Island was bulldozed in 1946 to become part of the landfill that now forms Logan Airport. On July 29, 1631, at the time of year when fogs are most frequent, a Bideford fishing ship called the *Friendship* ran aground just here. She beached on the mudflats beyond the island, close to the seaward tip of Logan's longest runway.

She was not a total loss—in 1633, the ship was back home in the Taw, carrying tobacco—but her mishap at Governors Island wrecked an ambitious first attempt to extend the New England trade to the Caribbean. Hired by Allerton and James Sherley, the ship had left Barnstaple the previous winter and spent eleven choppy weeks on the Atlantic before foul weather forced her back to Devon. In May, she set out once more and reached Boston in July. There she landed cattle and sheep. She went aground as she was on her way out again toward the Caribbean island of St. Kitts.[25]

A little cluster of colonies existed in the Lesser Antilles, where sixteen hundred English settlers lived on St. Kitts, using slaves to grow tobacco. The colony had started life in 1624, and the first English slave ship arrived with sixty slaves two years later. Nearby, on the small island of St. Martin, salt ponds supported Dutch pioneers who sold the salt to fishing ships. To the south at Barbados, another new English colony produced tobacco and cotton wool.

If these settlements grew crops to be sold for cash, they would need to import food, and this the Barnstaple men could supply. First they would ship to New England fare-paying emigrants, livestock, and stores, in the form of Barnstaple rugs and woolens. These could be sold for fur. Off the coast, the Barnstaple men would fish for bass and cod. Then they would sail south to the Antilles, sell the fish, and pick up tobacco, salt, and cotton wool. They could head straight back to England, or stop on the way in Ireland or, now that peace had returned, at La Rochelle or in the ports of Spain. The goods could be sold wherever they fetched the best price. The *Friendship* failed in what seems to have been the earliest venture of this kind, but the *Charles* of Barnstaple succeeded.[26]

The master of the *Charles* was the same John Witheridge who sailed for Palmer and the Pilgrims in the tiny *Content* in 1628. His ship this time was a larger vessel, of 150 tons. Preparations apparently began in Barnstaple in September 1631, when Witheridge took delivery of six hundred pounds of peas from Somerset: peas in this sort of quantity were used as cattle feed. On April 10, 1632, the *Charles* duly set off for America, carrying twenty human passengers and some eighty cows and six mares. No comparable cargo of livestock had ever sailed to Massachusetts, and probably none of such a size had ever traveled to Virginia in the twenty-five years since Jamestown began.

To carry animals in these numbers required fine seamanship. When cows and horses traveled from Ireland to Barnstaple, the vessels involved had more than a ton of carrying capacity for each animal, to allow for stall space, fodder, and freshwater. But the two-hundred-mile journey from Cork to Devon took only four days. Even for that short voyage, the number of animals taken on the *Charles* would require 112 tons of shipboard volume, or three-quarters of the space on board. The passage to America was fifteen times longer.

Cattle breeds were scrawny in the seventeenth century, and doubtless the animals were allowed to lose more weight, in the hope of feeding them out in Massachusetts. But even so, and even if Witheridge cut the journey time by loading the cows in Ireland, he would need one thousand bales of hay and forty-five thousand gallons of drinking water to sustain the cattle until they reached New England.* Since the freshwater alone would fill the ship to bursting, the journey could not have been made nonstop. John

---

*Records of three cattle shipments from Barnstaple to America in 1636 show that ships' masters dealt with the problem of transportation by carrying only young livestock, or yearlings. Even so, each animal required 1.3 tons of shipboard capacity, and the largest cargo consisted of no fewer than 115 bullocks.

Witheridge must have sailed by way of the Azores to replenish his stores, and possibly he called at Newfoundland too.

Finding these landfalls was no easy matter. To do so within a tight schedule called for excellence in navigation. Witheridge must have stowed much of his cargo on the open deck, and so he must have loaded his vessel not only with speed but also with great care. This too required skill and experience. And yet John Witheridge took the *Charles* from Barnstaple to Boston in only fifty-six days, ten days faster than the voyage of the *Mayflower.* She arrived on June 5, John Winthrop recorded, with her passengers "all safe and in healthe."

Witheridge showed his caliber again that autumn. The *Charles* lingered off New England until September 22, presumably to fish. Little more than three months later, on December 31, 1632, she reentered the Taw estuary, carrying tobacco from St. Kitts, salt from St. Martin, and wool from Ireland. There are two possibilities. Either Witheridge collected his Caribbean cargo from some middleman in Jamestown or Bermuda, or, and this is more likely, the *Charles* sailed more than five thousand nautical miles in one hundred days, from Boston to the Caribbean and then back across the Atlantic to Devon.*

For the first time, Witheridge completed a vast elliptical circuit of trade between the British Isles, New England, Virginia, and the West Indies: the circuit that eventually came to form the colonial system of the eighteenth century. Other Barnstaple men swiftly followed, while John Pocock helped finance the trade from London. In June 1633, another ship arrived in Barnstaple, aptly named the *Gift.* On board were tens of thousands of pounds of cotton wool from Barbados, and the importers were led by William Palmer. In these voyages, we can see the future in embryo, and more futures than one.[27]

The first Irish immigrants to Boston were skittish cows, oxen, and frightened horses, taken on board at Waterford or Kinsale by ships bound out under masters such as John Witheridge. Between decks crammed with fodder and stinking with filth, they went south to the Azores and then on along the fortieth parallel to the far side of the Atlantic. To understand why the livestock were so essential, and the consequences that they had, we must go back to the Plymouth Colony. We have to return to the colony's soil, and to the special properties of New England's coastal strip, from the Connecticut River to Maine.

---

*The second possibility is more likely because the Barnstaple records specifically name St. Kitts as the point of origin of the tobacco.

Chapter Twenty

The Exploding Colony

We are all free-holders: the rent day doth not trouble us.

—William Hilton, Plymouth colonist, 1621[1]

In the summer of 1633, an epidemic of smallpox struck New England. It lasted until the cold weather returned, and at New Plymouth it killed more than twenty men, women, and children. Among them was Samuel Fuller, their surgeon and physician. He was fifty-three and one of the original settlers from the Leiden community. Like eight other men who died, he left an inventory of his possessions. It shows that by sailing on the *Mayflower,* Samuel Fuller advanced himself in every conceivable way.

He found the religious liberty he needed, he improved his material well-being, and his status was far higher in America. Unusually, and perhaps uniquely, in Fuller's case the evidence exists for an exact comparison between his existence across the sea and his kinfolk's way of life at home.

Samuel Fuller was born in 1580, the third son of a butcher and tenant farmer called Robert Fuller, an unlettered man who signed his name with a mark like an *H.* Being unable to read and write was not yet an infallible symptom of poverty, and the Fuller clan were modestly well-off. They lived in a village in Norfolk called Redenhall. It was located not far from the highway from London to Norwich, and only ten miles from the port of Great Yarmouth, where Separatists were active. As so often, the size of the church is an index of prosperity. Even in a county renowned for great churches, the edifice at Redenhall was special, with a tall flint tower leaping up from the brow of a hill: a little too tall, perhaps, since lightning destroyed the steeple in 1616.

There were two manors at Redenhall, and they belonged to a family called Gawdy. They were successful lawyers, and they lived a mile from the church at Gawdy Hall, later enveloped by a handsome shooting estate of a typically Norfolk kind. If you go in search of the *Mayflower* Fullers today, you must drive carefully, to avoid the plump pheasants that stray out from underneath the hedges. About fifty men rented land from the Gawdys, and they included two Fullers, Robert and John. The latter was either the uncle or the eldest brother of the Pilgrim.

John Fuller ranked near the top of the rent roll, as one of the largest tenants. When he died at the end of 1608, his family made an inventory of his belongings too, listed room by room and marked with Robert's mark. Thanks to this document, and the records left by the Gawdys, we can see precisely how well the Fullers lived at home, and how much better they could do on the other side of the Atlantic.[2]

If Samuel went to prepare the appraisal, first he would pass the stables where John Fuller kept his cart, his plows and harrows, his scythes and mattocks, and the harness for his horses and colts. Four spotted pigs and a sow rooted nearby, while in a barn the Fuller cattle were wintering on hay. Eight lambs sheltered in another barn, while twelve shillings' worth of hens and chickens pecked their way across the yard. Set apart from the house was a dairy, with churns, tubs, and a press for making cheese, and the shed where the Fullers made their beer. It was kitted out with skillets, pots, and "two Brasse thinges." If the family were eating, Samuel Fuller would find them in the hall, the largest room in the house. It served as the kitchen, with an open fire equipped with bellows and iron tongs. They dined around a long table, sitting on benches and four stools.

Six sides of bacon hung from the ceiling, while a musket leaned against the wall. In the corner was a cradle, awaiting an occupant, since John Fuller's widow was three months pregnant when he died. In the parlor, the only room with a carpet, they kept their most valuable item, a four-poster bed, and nine cushions to go with it. Margaret Fuller owned a fine collection of linen, stored in three chests in a separate bedchamber: towels, pillowcases, six tablecloths, four dozen napkins, and thirty-six sheets. Somebody could read, because the inventory listed a desk and five shillings' worth of books.

If he were hardworking, lucky, and an eldest son, this was the way a yeoman farmer might live in old England, but Samuel did far better in the new.

He had two homes—a town house at New Plymouth and a country place by the Smelt River—and he could do far more with his assets. Horses were still in short supply, and so Samuel Fuller rode an ass, but he owned three firearms, a musket for defense and two fowling pieces. It was against the law for his brothers to shoot game birds in Norfolk, thin or fat, but at New Plymouth it was positively encouraged. When the Pilgrims divided up their land in 1628, they made a provision that "ffowling, fishing and hunting be free." To help him hunt and fish, Samuel had a share in a boat.

In 1608, John Fuller had five beds, while in 1633 Samuel possessed only three, and his widow's stock of linen was a little smaller than it might have been in England. Even so, the American Fullers had eight tablecloths, twenty-three napkins, and twelve sheets, and something new, rarely seen in the homes of English farmers: ten yards of calico, cloth sent back from India by traders such as Emmanuel Altham. Both John and Samuel owned much the same by way of tools, pots, pans, brass, and pewter, but in three categories Samuel far outdid his kinsman in England. Each of the three had something in common, because they were goods that conferred status of a special kind on their owner.

Apart from his houses and his livestock, Fuller's most valuable asset was his surgeon's chest. And besides his medical manuals, his inventory listed twenty-six books, including three Bibles and, of course, works by John Robinson and Henry Ainsworth. Finally, while John Fuller's brothers never troubled to itemize his clothes, Samuel's inventory carefully listed his apparel: two cloaks, five suits, a gown, and nine shirts, some of them apparently brand-new and unworn.

His chest, books, and garments showed that Samuel Fuller was an educated, professional man, a distinction denied to him in England. As a Separatist, he had no chance of obtaining a license to practice medicine, since these were granted by the Church of England, and he lacked the money required to become an apprentice barber-surgeon or apothecary. When his father died in 1615, Samuel received only fifteen pounds, since his three sisters needed larger sums if they were to live respectably. Instead, he went to Leiden, where he worked as a weaver. Somehow or other he acquired his medical training, possibly from lectures at the university's medical school, one of the most advanced in Europe. Then he practiced freely in North America.

A learned profession made a man a gentleman, and so Fuller became a gentleman by sailing on the *Mayflower.* He did not use the phrase—none of the nine men who died in 1633 classified themselves by rank, as they would have done in England—but he received the respect a gentleman commanded. Among his bequests were a pair of gloves, which Fuller left to John Winthrop, a member of the English landed gentry, from a background similar to the Gawdy family's. Winthrop and Fuller dealt with each other as equals, something inconceivable on the old side of the Atlantic.

At home, the Fullers were indelibly inferior to the Gawdys, or the Winthrops, because the Fullers belonged to a class of tenants called copyholders. A copyholder occupied his homestead by virtue of a copy of an entry in a document, the court roll of the manor, of the kind that has survived from Jacobean Redenhall. He kept his land for life and handed down his tenancy to his children, but the landlord's demands often increased sharply each time such a transfer occurred. At the tenant's death the landlord could also ask for a due called a heriot, often defined as the tenant's best ox, horse, or ram. Copyholders had rights, litigation was frequent, and it was not one-sided, but this was not the same thing as independence. At New Plymouth, Bradford and his colleagues simply swept copyholding away, along with the rest of the paraphernalia of English manorial law. Men such as Fuller owned land in the colony outright, to buy and sell as they pleased, with no heriots to pay.

By the time of the epidemic, for men like Fuller emigration had accomplished everything they could have wished. Severe though it was, even the rate of mortality from smallpox was less than 10 percent, far lower than in bouts of plague in Leiden or London. In time, it became apparent that life expectancy in New England far outstripped that in the old. And by 1633, beneath the colony lay a bedrock of prosperity, modest but more than adequate. Although Samuel Fuller's inventory was drawn up four months after harvest, it included a hundred bushels of corn, enough to feed nine people for a year, and if grain was plentiful, livestock was ample too.

In 1623, Altham counted only fifty pigs, a few goats, and some hens at New Plymouth. Since poor Altham tended to exaggerate, this must be an upper limit. Although the first cattle arrived the following spring, when Edward Winslow brought them back from England, even in 1628 the cattle still numbered only fourteen. But in the next five years, thanks to voyages like those of the *Charles,* the stock of animals expanded rapidly. Samuel Fuller owned three dairy cows, two calves, eight sheep, and thirty pigs, and he was a long way from being the wealthiest man in the settlement. That distinction belonged to Isaac Allerton, who clearly dealt well for his personal account during his trips to Barnstaple. When the colony levied a tax in 1633, Allerton paid twice as much as Bradford, and four times as much as Fuller.

How had all this been achieved? The beaver played its part, but there was another answer too. To find it, and the implications, we need to interrogate another Pilgrim, the old warrior Miles Standish.

STANDISH THE CATTLEMAN

Perhaps he understood the American landscape best, but if he did so, it was for very English reasons. To Standish, most of all among the Pilgrims, the coastal fringe of land from Cape Cod to Cape Ann promised material opportunities of a kind that the Old World had denied.

Miles Standish was a cattleman, and he lived in a cattleman's homestead. At his death he owned four oxen, five horses, nine cows and heifers, and a calf. In 1863, an early archaeologist unearthed the foundations of his house in Duxbury, Massachusetts, and made a plan of what he discovered. The old soldier had built himself something a modern English hill farmer would recognize: a Devon long house. A long, rectangular structure, it accommodates human beings at one end and animals at the other. Examples, made of stone, still exist on the slopes of Dartmoor today. Since a door between the two segments of the house allowed the stockman to tend his calves without going outdoors, the design was ideal for cold English moorlands and Massachusetts winters too.[3]

Miles Standish fitted perfectly into a New England transformed by cows carried on ships like the *Charles.* They were the last element necessary to allow the Great Migration to prosper in the 1630s, attracting immigrants in thousands, rather than hundreds. Cattle, their manure, and their hauling power for plows allowed the colonies to step away from a lifestyle based on maize, and instead they began to give men and women the quality of life that they aspired to in the old country. Cattle offered independence, status, meat, and a chance to accumulate wealth, and their effects went far beyond those that can be quantified. Cattle farming dispersed the colonists, creating an array of scattered settlements, soon bearing little resemblance to the villages they knew in England. While the physical space in which they lived changed profoundly, their mental landscape underwent a transformation too.[4]

No longer insecure, the Plymouth Colony became an element within a new and dynamic series of townships snaking up the coastline and eventually leading into the interior, unified by buying and selling as much as by shared religion. And while this process alarmed William Bradford, who feared that greed and mobility would subvert the values of the Pilgrim community, the process also contained the seeds of conflict with the native peoples of the region. In 1633, a year after the *Charles* reached

Boston, the demands of the new cattle economy led to the first documented case in New England of the legalized theft of native lands. As we shall see, it occurred with the dispossession of the Pawtucket people. They occupied the best stretch of cow country along the shores of Massachusetts Bay.

Standish and Winslow first entered their territory in 1621, when they went up the Mystic River in pursuit of beaver skins. And because of his background, Standish was ideally qualified to see the possibilities of the coastal strip where the Pawtucket lived. Besides his cattle, his house, and his land in Duxbury, Miles Standish bequeathed to his children another item of property. The old soldier died convinced that he had been cheated of his inheritance in England. In his will, he claimed ownership of estates in six villages in Lancashire. Some unnamed person had swindled his family out of the land, but it was rightfully his, said Standish; and the land in question bore a remarkable resemblance to the place where he settled in America.

Ten miles north of Liverpool, the six villages sat on a wide coastal plain, dotted with moss and peat. In the time of Elizabeth I, two-thirds of the usable land was under grass, for rearing cattle: the sturdy black long-horned beasts for which the county was renowned. Of the six places, the northernmost was Croston, beside an enormous wetland along the estuary of the river Ribble, still today one of the largest salt marshes in the British Isles. Between the spring tides it provided grazing for hundreds more cows. When the waters rose, they could be herded safely to the higher ground where the Standishes had once lived.[5]

So, in England, Standish already knew a kind of terrain that he saw in replica along the shores of Massachusetts Bay. To an English settler, the most striking feature of the new American landscape would have been just this: the long fringes of salt marsh. The grasses cling like a beard to the shore, colored in winter a muddy brown, when the cordgrass has died back, under Boston skies the color of moist mother-of-pearl. Then, in the months of summer sunlight, the whiskers turn a deep amber gold, of a grandeur no Englishman sees at home. Ten degrees of latitude separate his native soil from the wide beaches that reflect the New England sun into a windy blue cloudless sky.

When the *Mayflower* arrived, nearly a quarter of a million acres of salt marsh edged the coast from Rhode Island to Maine. Inside the Provincetown hook, and south toward Wellfleet, along the inner rim of the Cape they found classic locales for creating salt marsh, where the curve of the land depleted the energy of waves rolling in from the Gulf of Maine and allowed sediment to accumulate. It formed habitats ideal for grasses, shellfish, insects, and feeding birds: the environment that Bradford and Winslow described in *Mourt's Relation,* with its salt ponds filled with mud snails and oyster crabs.[6]

A Massachusetts salt marsh in October. This example is at Wellfleet Bay, on Cape Cod, and forms part of the Massachusetts Audubon Society Wildlife Sanctuary. (*Photography: Nick Bunker*)

To begin with, the Pilgrims were more concerned about fish, fur, and corn, but as chance would have it, they blundered into a region where nature created a rich endowment for farming cattle. A North American salt marsh can produce more organic carbon per acre than a tropical rain forest, thanks to the rich blend of nutrients created by the mixing of freshwater from estuaries and salt water from the open sea. Tall cordgrass, which grows in the lowest, wettest part of the marshes, produces more carbohydrate per square yard than wheat or barley.

As it happens, with the exception of Winslow, all the early leaders of the Plymouth Colony came from places close to similar wetlands in the old country. The two Williams, Brewster and Bradford, grew up beside the Humberhead Levels. Allerton apparently came from the coast of Suffolk, where in the years around 1600 landowners and tenants actively reclaimed marshes for grazing land. John Howland's family lived at Fenstanton, north of the city of Cambridge, a mile from the edge of the Great Level. A belt of low-lying bog and swamp twice as large as the salt marshes of Massachusetts, the Level extended all the way to the North Sea, where it joined the fens that reach as far as old Boston in Lincolnshire.

So, when the time and the opportunity were right, the Pilgrims began to farm the marshes along the coast. This process had its origins in 1627, when they divided their livestock. To understand it, we have to step a pace backward, to the land and the fields as they were in the colony's earliest phase.

A Great Deal of Ground

In 1835, a medical doctor called James Thacher published a history of New Plymouth, from the Pilgrims to the age of Andrew Jackson. He gave a candid assessment of the qualities and defects of the place. "The land in this town is hilly, barren and sandy," he wrote. So much so that by the nineteenth century the townspeople preferred not to farm but to ply the sea, make rope, or trade as merchants.

Most of the earth is pretty much the same as it is by Billington Sea, a coarse sand called Carver soil. Very acid, and prone to let water soak straight through, in its natural state it made for meager crops. Even so, a few patches of fertility existed, listed by Thacher with approval. One was called Plain Dealing, the second was Hobbs Hole, and the third was Warren Farm. All possessed excellent earth, said Thacher, and nearby was the beach, with rockweed and kelp as additional manure.[7]

Plot these locations, and what do we find? Plain Dealing is right at the northern limit of modern Plymouth, just inside the town line. Warren Farm lies at the town's very opposite, southern end, four miles from Plain Dealing along the shore. Hobbs Hole sat between Warren Farm and Plymouth Rock, fifteen minutes' walk from Burial Hill. Because of the pattern of the soil, and the need to stay close to water for the sake of natural fertilizer, the town Thacher knew was a strung-out, elongated sort of place. It had been that way for a very long time, since the early days of the colony. That being so, New Plymouth bore very little resemblance to a village of the kind the Pilgrims knew at home.

Bradford made many sensible decisions as governor, and one of his best was to make wills and inventories obligatory, and to insist that title to land be carefully recorded. In 1645, the court made a strict law against forging deeds, altering public records, or bribing officials to do so. Malefactors might be whipped in public and branded on the face with an *F* for "fake" or "forger." Draconian though it was, the system had its merits. In old

England title to land was mostly unregistered, and counterfeit deeds were commonplace.[8] By making the rules he did, Bradford eliminated a source of conflict. He also ensured that later generations could trace exactly who owned what, and how the colony's outline changed. In 1886 another Plymouth historian, William T. Davis, collated the early records and charted the locations against the streets he knew. From his book, and the topography, we can see how the Pilgrims first tried to copy an English village, and then how swiftly they gave up and did something else.[9]

At the very beginning, they had no choice but to cling to the Town Brook and Burial Hill. Too few to cultivate a wide area, they had to use the fields already cleared by Tisquantum's people, and they needed the stream for freshwater and for the fertilizing alewives that swam up it. And since defense remained a paramount concern, men and women working in the open dared not stray over even the lowest ridge, which might conceal them from a sentry on the fort.

Then, in 1623, decisions had to be made. Under the terms of the contract with Thomas Weston, which made the colony a common stock, for the first seven years no individual settler could own a plot of land. To ensure that each farmer received his fair share of good or bad land, the slices were rotated each year, but this was counterproductive. Nobody had any reason to put in extra hours and effort to improve a plot if next season another family received the benefit. So, as Bradford says, they abandoned what he calls the "common course and condition," and began to allocate the soil in lots that, in due course, the owners could keep or sell. This led to a rapid increase in output, and it followed models familiar from their homeland. Side by side with the open field system, fully commercial, individualistic farming had existed in England for at least three centuries. The Pilgrims knew it well.

Also in 1623, the *Anne* arrived with reinforcements, and these new settlers needed land too. So the Pilgrims responded by dividing up a much larger expanse of ground, and in doing so, they copied the layout of an open field village, such as Austerfield. Most of the lots were small, just one or two acres, like the strips laid out within the open fields at home. In Nottinghamshire, each village usually possessed three or four of them, encircling the settlement. At New Plymouth the Pilgrims began by creating something very similar.

About five hundred yards from Burial Hill, on a flat area of ground, watered by two brooks flowing down into the sea, they laid out a North Field. Covered today by a parking lot, where Plymouth keeps its school buses, the field gently slopes down to the water, with one of the brooks still gurgling away beneath it in a sewer. There was also an East Field, between Burial Hill and the sea, and a South Field off in the distance on the good land around Hobbs Hole and a stream called the Wellingsley Brook. The Pilgrims did not use all these field names, but they laid out the lots in these three locations all the same.

It was all very English, but did it make sense? At home, villages like Sturton and Austerfield had evolved over many centuries. They arranged their space as they did because of all sorts of English circumstances, to do with drainage, crop rotation, and the need to stop livestock trampling corn. Landlords set limits to what a tenant might do, and the manor, the parish, and the law knit the villagers together, willingly or not. Since men and women walked to church, the parish could not extend beyond a maximum radius of two miles or so, with a fixed perimeter and fields and houses clustered inside it. Above all, by 1600 in England, a village was a place where there were many people and relatively little land. The puzzle to be solved was how to find an equilibrium between the two.

In America, circumstances differed entirely. At New Plymouth, there were no landlords, and no hedges, and certainly no Anglo-Saxon boundary marks. New England had puzzles of its own, looming conflicts about the earth, but they took an unfamiliar shape. Sooner or later, the Plymouth Colony was bound to veer away from old English models—and all the more rapidly, because they were Separatists. When Brownists made the act of separation, they voted with their feet to abolish the parish system. They did away with the church, its compulsory tithes, and the legal obligation to worship in a single building every Sunday. That being so, how could the Pilgrims insist that men and women remain within a walkable distance of Burial Hill? And if the colony had ample land, and still few people, why should they remain tightly knit, tending fields arranged like satellites around Plymouth Rock, where the soil was scarcely ideal?

In 1627, the Pilgrims began to experience space in a new, un-English manner. They agreed to give each resident twenty acres, each one a perfect rectangle, arrayed in series, with the long side of each one adjoining the water's edge. The colony took on its narrow pencil shape. To the south, a belt of rocky hills fixed a natural boundary, and so the colony marched up the coast to the north, toward the cove at Rocky Nook Point. Up here Fuller owned his second home, and John Howland laid out his farm.

Beyond the river and Rocky Nook lay another waterway, the Jones River. On its far side, Miles Standish discovered what he was looking for: pasture and meadow to replace the birthright he had lost. North of the Jones, a chain of tidal marshes swings off to the right to form a thick margin around the coastline. The belt of marsh extends for eight miles, as far as the town of Marshfield, founded by Winslow in 1632. Even today, when some of it has been reclaimed, Duxbury Marsh encompasses thirteen hundred acres. To its north at Green Harbor the salt marsh is still wider. Standish took the name for his new settlement from Lancashire, where the English Duxbury lies beside the Ribble, near the six townships where he claimed his inheritance.[10]

As cattle started to arrive in quantity in the early 1630s, it began to make even more sense to move northward. "The people of the plantation

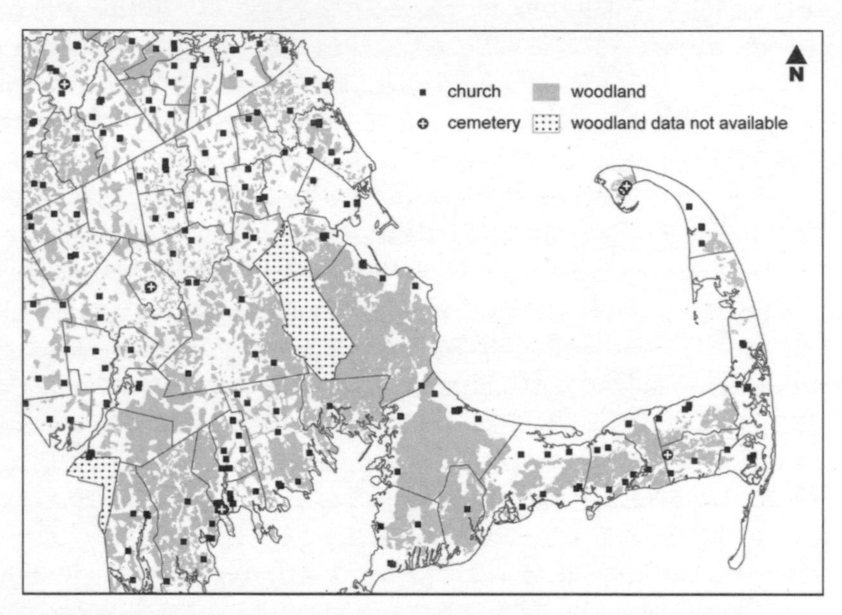

Based on data extracted from maps produced from the Massachusetts state survey of 1830, and then digitized by the Harvard Forest project at Harvard University, this map of Plymouth County in the early nineteeth century shows a very un-English pattern of settlement, following the fringe of salt marsh along the coast.

begane to grow in their outward estats," wrote William Bradford. "No man now thought he could live, except he had catle and a great deale of ground to keepe them." So the migrants laid out their new estates in a long line, from Duxbury to Marshfield. They made not the slightest effort to copy the design of a tightly clustered village in the east of England. As they established their marsh farms, men such as Standish founded a way of life that survived along parts of the New England coast almost unaltered until the 1890s, when men still cut the hay with a scythe. They also deeply worried their governor.

For William Bradford, dispersal was new, and threatening. Many men and women soon lived much too far away to come to the meetinghouse on Sunday. This in itself might undermine the religious mission of the Pilgrims. By 1643, the colony had exploded outward into eight distinct townships, scattered across forty miles, reaching north toward Boston and spilling out eastward toward the elbow of Cape Cod. Although Plymouth remained the largest, with 148 adult males, it accounted for less than a quarter of the total population.

A few years later, as he wrote his history, Bradford made plain his fears that the loss of solidarity endangered the very purpose of New England. His alarm may have been exaggerated: perhaps he had forgotten the quarrelsome nature of the focused villages he knew in the valleys of the Idle and the Trent. By scattering as they did, in all likelihood the colonists eased tensions and made godliness more attainable, rather than less. Even so, Bradford was right to register the fact that disorienting change was under way.[11]

He was far less likely to understand its economic origins on the other side of the Atlantic. Among the Pilgrims, perhaps Robert Cushman saw them most clearly. Born near the most expensive meadow and pasture in the south of England, on the coast of Kent, Cushman possessed the sharpest eye for the material realities of his native land. Transmitted three thousand miles across the ocean, they destroyed the way of life of the Pawtucket along the Mystic River.

George No-Nose and the Marsh

Two marshes bear the name of Romney. One of them forms a green wedge that pokes out into the English Channel, seventy miles from London, with at its farthest extremity the lighthouse at Dungeness. To find the other, simply look down as you drop toward Boston's Logan Airport from the north, at a spot where two blue coils of shining water creep inland amid the brown of the tidal flats. A highway cuts across them in a sweeping arc. The road is the Salem Turnpike, and the water marks the course of two rivers, the Saugus and the Pines. They flow down between the towns of Lynn and Revere, reaching the sea about six miles from downtown Boston. Along the Pines lies the boundary between two counties, Essex and Suffolk, named after coastal shires in England.

Together with Chelsea, the next town to the south, the modern suburbs of Lynn and Revere cover an area that acquired in the 1630s a reputation as the best place to farm in English North America. Winthrop logged the date, 1633, when settlers first reaped a harvest of English wheat. It grew on the American Romney Marsh. The wetland formed the northern extension of a belt of marshes that began on the Mystic at Medford and then curved around the shore to Lynn, encompassing eighteen square miles.

It is hard to imagine what valuable soil this made, now that Greater Boston has swallowed up the region. What remains of the salt marsh lies concealed behind apartment buildings and a state police post, along the boulevard at Revere Beach, where the only vestige of a cow is a stand selling roast beef sandwiches. By far the richest slice of earth was some elevated ground called Oak Island, where many centuries of dying plants and trees created a dark bed of compost. Today it remains the best place to see the dense grass that attracted the early settlers. The island itself has disappeared into suburbia, covered with a grid of streets and houses, but the view of Romney Marsh remains.

Nobody knows who first awarded the name to this corner of Massachusetts, but it must have happened very soon after the earliest settlers arrived. Winthrop used it without any comment, as though it was already familiar. Whoever it was, by doing so he sent a clear message home about the potential of the New World, because the old Romney Marsh was land of the sort that every English farmer wanted most. Nobody understood this better than Robert Cushman.[12]

When he gave his sermon at New Plymouth in 1621, he preached about high rents and greedy landlords, and in his part of Kent the effects of both were very visible. Cushman was born in 1578 at a place called Rolvenden. Under Elizabeth I, this and the nearby village of Cranbrook achieved modest infamy, as a hive of Puritans who clashed with the authorities. But if outsiders had heard of them, the most likely reason lay in their valuable location. Rolvenden stood on a hill above the river that fed Romney Marsh, and the dead center of the marsh lay only ten miles off.

By the early seventeenth century, the reclaimed soil had become a vast ranch, divided into hundreds of smallholdings each of forty acres, with the tenants including Rolvenden men. As many as ninety-five thousand sheep and cattle lived on the rich grassland, in a space less than one-third as large as the salt marshes of Massachusetts. And as the population grew, and the price of grain and cattle feed rose, the cost of land at Romney soared. Rents per acre at Romney were four or five times higher than the English average. They almost doubled in the twenty years before the *Mayflower* sailed.[13]

So, when somebody borrowed the name for the marshes at Revere and Lynn, where nobody need pay rent at all, he issued an invitation that many farmers might find irresistible. Competition for grazing land in England was starting to taper off a little, thanks to the economic slump in Europe and the falling price of wool, but rents dropped only slightly, and the small farmer remained insecure. And for some of them, insecurity was becoming terminal, as more powerful men sealed their dominance of the wetlands that remained.

Since the 1580s, statesmen such as Burghley had worried that so much of England seemed to be infertile wasteland. As far back as 1589, a Dutch engineer proposed a vast plan to drain the fens of eastern England and turn them into cornfields and pasture. When, in the 1590s, disastrous harvests led to appalling hardship, projects such as these came to be seen as urgent necessities.[14]

For the next five decades, schemes to drain English wetlands proceeded in counterpoint with projects for new colonies in North America. Sometimes the same men were involved in both. Most of the fen drainage ventures were failures, for many reasons: costs far exceeded estimates, engineering skills were lacking, and the projects encountered angry opposition. Using a law passed in 1600, the Crown awarded control of immense tracts of wetland to "undertakers," investors from the aristocracy or from the City of London. In return for financing the work, the undertakers received most of the fens they drained: hence their unpopularity among the farmers already occupying the same territory and rearing animals on it.

All of this had a direct bearing on the fate of the Pawtucket. The first colonists arrived on the American Romney Marsh in 1629, in the shape of two men in their twenties, Edmund Ingalls and his younger brother Francis. In England, they came from Skirbeck, by the sea close to the old Boston in Lincolnshire. Skirbeck was a fenland parish, and the two Ingalls boys lived by raising livestock. When their father died in 1617, he left them eight cows, nearly forty sheep, fifteen horses, and a rick full of hay, but prosperity such as this might not last. Here rents were still rising, and the fens around Skirbeck were among those that attracted most attention from outsiders. In 1630, Charles I granted tens of thousands of acres of the Boston fens to a consortium of undertakers, led by a well-connected courtier. Despite angry protests from the residents, the project went ahead amid allegations of corruption among local officials.[15]

The Ingalls brothers left no documentary evidence to say precisely why they left for America, but these were the circumstances from which they came. It seems likely that they were among the farmers displaced by fen drainage. They were also Puritans, with a Puritan vicar. This would have given them a clinching motive for emigration. In Massachusetts, they settled first at Salem and then moved to Lynn. As many as fifty other English families followed in their footsteps in 1630, with "a large stock of cattle, sheep and goats." In doing so, they entered a space far less empty than it must have seemed to them. With its deer, shellfish, herbs, and berries and with ground ideal for maize as well as wheat, Romney Marsh already provided a spacious home to the Pawtucket. They were about to suffer their own catastrophe.

When Standish and Winslow went up the Mystic, they found the grave of Nanepashemet, the sachem of the Pawtucket. When he died, he left not only his widow, the Squa Sachem, but also three sons. They were known to the English as Sagamore John, Sagamore James, and Sagamore George. Of the three, George was by far the youngest, born, it seems, in 1616. The English also called him George No-Nose, though his real name was Wenepoykin. It fell to Wenepoykin to fight to recover Romney Marsh, stolen from his people during the first decade of the new colony beside Massachusetts Bay.

By 1630, because of disease and attacks by the Micmac to the north, the surviving Pawtucket had dwindled to a small but still significant number. Sagamore John led a group of forty warriors based at West Medford. His brother James lived by the Saugus at Lynn, with another forty men, while more made their homes on the marsh between the two. In 1633, the smallpox epidemic devastated those who remained. In the words of Thomas Hutchinson, the New England historian of the 1770s: "John, Sagamore of Winisimet, and James of Lynn, with almost all their people, died of the distemper."

Before the epidemic, tensions had already existed between the Pawtucket and the English, with complaints about cattle trampling fields of maize. What happened afterward is not entirely clear, but as the Ingalls brothers settled down to farm and run a tannery, they attracted envious glances from the south. In 1634, the town of Boston officially annexed Romney Marsh as a whole. Its citizens began to divide up the land, with the lion's share allocated to the wealthiest inhabitants. The Ingalls brothers received 120 acres, but by far the largest tract went to Captain Robert Keayne, commander of the Boston militia. In the end, Keayne owned eight hundred acres—"some of the best land on the New England coast," it was said—including the stretch behind Revere Beach.*

From his brothers, Wenepoykin inherited the title of sachem of

*Keayne was an investor in the Plymouth Colony, and a comrade-in-arms of John Pocock's in the Honourable Artillery Company of London.

Chelsea and Lynn and in due course he began to wage a battle in the law courts at Boston to recover his property. Starting in 1651, the legal proceedings continued fitfully for eighteen years, as Wenepoykin tried to obtain a judgment against the new landowners on Romney Marsh, including Keayne. Although they offered no defense, except right of occupation, Wenepoykin lost his campaign of litigation and took up arms of a different kind. He fought against the English during King Philip's War in 1676. When it ended in defeat for the native people, they shipped him off to Barbados as a convict. Eventually he returned, and died in about 1684. After his death, his family signed away their claim to land at Lynn, in return for silver worth sixteen pounds.[16]

A Western Design

Grievous stories such as that of Romney Marsh have almost too many dimensions. Religion, politics, ecology, and disease, dynastic warfare in Europe, and the ambitions of men and women of many kinds, tanners as well as evangelists, gentlemen landlords as well as fenland farmers: all of them had their roles to play in the making of New England. The foundation of the new colonies resembled a Jacobean drama. It had as many scenes and quite as much ambiguity as a play by Shakespeare, and this book has only covered act 1.

When a story is so complicated, with so much nuance, it serves no purpose to allot praise or blame in simple ways, as though we were slicing up the acres on Romney Marsh. To the south, in the Plymouth Colony, for example, the evidence suggests that Indian rights to land received far more respect. As for the Bostonians, perhaps men like Robert Keayne were acquisitive, or grasping, but if we could place him in the dock, Keayne would have his own case to make. What purpose did it serve, he might say, for a tiny people who lacked livestock to occupy soil that could house so many English families? It was smallpox, not the English farmer, that dispossessed George No-Nose, Keayne might argue, and smallpox killed the European and the native alike. Samuel Fuller died the same death as Sagamore John.[17]

So was the fate of the Pawtucket unavoidable? Did they fall victim not to greedy individuals but to blind and impersonal economic forces? In a sense they did. But this need not have been inevitable. What if cattle had never sailed to Massachusetts? Without them, no evictions would have taken place at Romney Marsh. But livestock could only cross the sea because English mariners had built larger ships and learned to sail them effectively.

That was another story: the evolution of English enterprise by sea. Again, it possessed a logic of its own, but it did not follow anybody's master plan.

Did New England have to happen at all? What if the Duke of Buckingham had brought his men home safely from the Île de Ré? Or what if he and King Charles had never provoked the French cardinal to lay siege to La Rochelle? The war between England and France was not bound to occur. What if it had never broken out, or if Charles I had won some victories? In either case, at home the political temperature would have fallen sharply.

Sea captains from Barnstaple might have proceeded happily on their way, carrying wine and woolens back and forth across the Bay of Biscay. They might never have needed to cross the Atlantic. And would John Winthrop and the Puritans have simply stayed at home? However much they hated Archbishop Laud, it was the crisis in Parliament in 1629 that tipped the balance in favor of departure to America. That crisis would not have occurred without the quarrels about taxation arising from the war.

Of course, this kind of speculation has its limits. Leaving aside the events of the late 1620s, were there deep and chronic flaws in the way England ran its affairs, in matters of religion, politics, and finance? There probably were, and if so, then occasional explosions of discontent were inescapable. Sooner or later men and women would seek an outlet by way of emigration. And the harsh demographics of old England provided another incentive. Even if they did not, there were other strategic reasons to make a push across the ocean.

New England simply offered too many resources—beaver skins, naval stores, and naval bases—for old England to ignore it indefinitely. So perhaps the turning point actually lay in the Canadian expeditions by the Kirkes. Their victories showed that England could challenge France and Spain for control of the North Atlantic. They also made a handsome profit, by way of pelts and captured ships and ordnance.

We could pursue arguments like these indefinitely, but we might end up by explaining nothing at all. The truth is that Calvinist zeal was far more important than any other single factor in bringing about the creation of New England. We cannot simply edit the Puritans out of the picture, however much some historians wish to try. It was the Plymouth Colony that made the essential breakthrough. The Pilgrims invented the model and set the tone for what came later. Investors like Pocock and Cradock would not have persisted with transatlantic projects if they had not seen Bradford and his people show how the job could be done. Even if New England was inevitable, somebody had to be first. And for the task to be accomplished, religion was essential, for two reasons. One had to do with money, while the other concerned morale.

Men such as Cradock and Pocock persevered because they possessed a sort of evangelical superego. It was nurtured in places such as Bread Street Ward, and it goaded them on when others gave up. Many people wished to make money in the City of London, but less hazardous ways existed than the American option, and those who put up the money for Massachusetts were few in number. They were very definitely Puritans, and Puritans of a particular type, the kinds of people who drilled in the Artillery Garden and refused to pay the forced loan demanded by the king.

Morale was necessary too, for leadership and as a means to cope with adversity. Commenced in a dire economic climate, when capital was short and mishaps were many, the *Mayflower* enterprise might have fallen apart at any point in its first seven years if circumstances had been even slightly more adverse. Although they soon learned to feed themselves, the colony could have failed if the Pilgrims ran out of gunpowder, lead, copper, and iron tools, if they provoked Massasoit or lost all their boats, or if a smallpox epidemic as severe as that of 1633 had occurred ten years earlier. Even if complete collapse had not occurred, the Plymouth Colony might have split into fragments, or its demoralized members might have headed south to Virginia. That last option would have been the easiest at any time after 1623. By way of John Pory, they had established good relations with Jamestown, and the start of a boom in the output of tobacco was beginning to make the south seem far more attractive.

Without Separatism, what reason to continue would Bradford, Winslow, and Brewster have possessed? Without an ideology, potent but flexible too, how would they have weathered each of the catastrophes that befell them? That being so, we need to understand exactly what Separatism was, and why it came into being as it did. Sadly, it has become commonplace to skewer the Pilgrims to a blackboard with modern vocabulary such as "fanatic" and "fundamentalist," terms that either did not exist at the time or meant something very different from their modern definitions.

The word "fundamentalist" had no currency before 1910. It came into being in America to refer to evangelical Christians who were defending biblical religion against modern phenomena, such as Darwinism. On the day the *Mayflower* left Plymouth Sound, Darwin remained a very distant prospect far below anybody's horizon. By the standards of our age, everybody was a fundamentalist in the seventeenth century, of some kind or another. When it comes to fanaticism, the Pilgrims could point their finger at many contemporaries far more guilty than they. If we want to find

Preserved at Barnstaple in Devon, this may be the earliest manuscript surviving in England to document the financing of the Massachusetts Bay Colony. It concerns a dispute in 1635 between the London investor John Pocock and the Boston settler John Humfrey, about a cargo shipped on the *Gift* of Barnstaple. (*Barnstaple Town Council and North Devon Record Office, Document B1/4090*) the worst effects of religious hatred in the period, the place to go is central Europe. Over the course of the Thirty Years' War the population of Greater Germany fell by more than seven million.

In any event, Separatism did not originate in religion alone. Its roots lay in the English politics of the early 1580s, when men and women worried about the defense of the realm, about the succession to Queen Elizabeth, and about the best way to run their localities in an age of divisive change. For a William Brewster, Separatism offered a means to respond, in religious language, to a set of situations or a predicament that went far beyond matters of worship. Compounded with ideas about gentility and good government, and seasoned with Greek and Roman ideals of republican virtue, Separatism gave rise to ambitions that had secular consequences. The new colony had to pay its way and govern itself, as well as kneel on the Sabbath.[18]

By any criteria that a Jacobean might recognize, the Plymouth Colony succeeded in all these respects, and remarkably so. Of course, even in 1640 the new English colonies between the Connecticut valley and Maine remained small. There were some twenty thousand settlers at the most, and many of these decided not to stay. Not long ago, a British historian called Susan Hardman Moore published a book correctly showing that a quarter of those who came west across the Atlantic went home again, not least because, in the 1640s, the Puritans seemed to be winning a great victory in the civil war in the old country.* But if we stand the statistic on its head, then 75 percent remained in America. This was quite enough to win a poll in favor of the New World by an overwhelming majority.

Why was this so? In the 1640s, New England suffered its own recession, but it survived, because by then it possessed a flexible, diverse way of life, in a material sense if not in others. Vital in the earliest phase, the trade in beaver fur remained important, but less dominant than it had been. This was because other activities abounded. Men working for Cradock set up the first American shipyard, on the Mystic in 1633. On the Saugus, John Pocock helped finance the first ironworks. Fishing carried on all year round, from places such as Cape Ann, while along the river terraces of the Connecticut valley corn grew in plenty. On the salt marshes of the coast, the herds of cattle multiplied.[19]

New England swiftly became an essential element within the much

---

*Susan Hardman Moore, *Pilgrims: New World Settlers & the Call of Home* (New Haven, CT, and London, 2007).

larger system that evolved from the voyages of the *Charles*. By the 1640s, by far the largest cattleman in New England was another farmer from south Lincolnshire, the freethinking nonconformist William Coddington. Like Pocock, Coddington resisted the forced loan; like the Ingalls brothers, he came to America as a Puritan from old Boston; and in the middle of the 1630s, he migrated to the marshes of Rhode Island. From Narragansett Bay he shipped livestock to the West Indies.[20] Fish and timber made the same journey. English settlers in the Caribbean needed supplies that Massachusetts could provide, and in return they sent sugar and tobacco to New England. There was also the matter of slavery, because slavery was already embedded in the Sugar Islands. That subject lies beyond the limits of this book, but its looming presence must be registered: black slaves came to Boston as well as to Barbados. This was another possibility that John Witheridge created.

All of this happened under the banner of what became the British Empire. It did not yet exist, in a sense that Queen Victoria might recognize, but the flag was rising up the mast and beginning to flap in a strong wind from the west. Sixty years before, when Browne was pondering Separatism, the Spanish had annexed Portugal. By doing so in 1580, Spain apparently gave itself an unshakable grip on the Atlantic trades, because Portugal brought with it Brazil and the Portuguese island territories. When Edward Winslow died, in the 1650s, the place and the circumstances of his death told a very different story.

Miles Standish left his bones at Duxbury, but Winslow's went to the bottom of the Caribbean. They buried him at sea, because the old Pilgrim had made a new career, under Oliver Cromwell, as a diplomat and civil servant in London. Cromwell shipped him out on an English fleet, on its way to seize the Spanish possessions in the West Indies. The expedition carried a grand title: the Western Design.

On May 7, 1655, Winslow died from a fever at sea. His funeral took place the next morning, with a salute of forty cannon. A few days later, the English task force began the invasion of Jamaica. It took time to subdue, but by the end of the century the island of slaves and sugar was by far the most precious British colony of all. Edward Winslow died helping to make Jamaica what it later became. He was a Pilgrim, and an imperialist.

We could never say that about William Bradford. Worrying as he did about spiritual corruption, about greed in the colony, and about the loss of its Christian purpose, Bradford would have had little time for anything as overbearing as Cromwell's imperial agenda. At New Plymouth, Bradford died two years later. They interred his remains on the summit of Burial Hill, in sight of the sand hills of the Cape. What might he have thought, when he heard about his old comrade's death? To find a lesson about the arrogance of empire, William Bradford might open his Bible, turn to the first book of Kings, and ponder what it said about the punishment Jehovah meted out to the proud.

Epilogue

The Last Shaman

The white man will feel it as a duty to his children to seek new lands.

—an Eastern Abenaki prophecy, recorded by Joseph Nicolar in *The Life and Traditions of the Red Man* (1893)[1]

Documents come in many different kinds, and archives take the form of stone as well as paper. The boulder at New Plymouth remains the foremost symbol of the Pilgrims, but there is another significant rock, another slab of memory with its own tale to tell about the same events. A long way from Massachusetts, it rises from the cold middle reaches of the river in Maine where the Pilgrim fur trade had its heart. Forgotten by mapmakers, this second fragment of geology has evaded fame or notoriety, as the finest archives often do. And yet in its own way it serves as a monument every bit as meaningful as Plymouth Rock.

It can be found fifty miles north of Augusta, just inside the boundary of the town of Embden. From the west bank of the Kennebec a ledge of shale pokes forty feet out into rippling blue water. Shaped like a dark gray tooth with a rough blunt tip, the rock makes a natural jetty in a swift, wide, but silent stretch of the river between two bends. On the rock the Eastern Abenaki left an array of carvings, struck into the slanting face of the stone with blows from hammerhead tools.

We cannot read the writing on it as readily as we can decipher the scrawl of a Jacobean manuscript. Even so, the rock at Embden is an archive, just as much as any parchment in a repository in London, York, or Belfast. Mostly submerged, but with its southern face covered with imagery, the legible rock was intended to be seen from a birch-bark canoe coming upstream toward a wild place called Caratunk Falls. And when we examine the art that the Abenaki created on it, we find ourselves gazing at something we did not expect. The rock contains a testament of Native American thinking and belief, made during the earliest days of European entry to the region. It brings to mind new questions about the nature of historical records, and about our winding path toward our knowledge of the past.

For many generations, writers have chronicled the events of the 1620s in New England with the help of a very small range of sources, far too few to make adequate sense of what occurred. For accounts of what transpired, they have chiefly relied on William Bradford, Edward Winslow, Roger Williams, and Captain John Smith, four Englishmen born in the reign of the first Queen Elizabeth.

Each author had talent, sometimes approaching the sublime. They were careful note takers. They did not fabricate their narratives, and they did not make foolish mistakes. Bradford, for instance, carefully transcribed scores of letters, copied verbatim into his history of the Plymouth Colony. His interpretation of events can be challenged, but it is very hard to catch him making a false statement of fact. When new documents come to light, such as the papers describing the Pilgrim flight from Stallingborough, they say much more about what happened, but they also verify the gist of William Bradford's version. The problem lies not with what Bradford and Winslow put in but with what they left out.

Omissions, vacancies, and unexplained allusions abound within the narratives they wrote. Among them, by far the most tantalizing absence relates to the fate of William Bradford's first wife. She died after falling from the *Mayflower* into the wintry sea at Provincetown as the ship lay at anchor, but Bradford passed over the circumstances of her end in complete silence. Why did he exclude a detail so shocking, and so personal?[2]

We might speculate, and many writers have, about the nature of her death and about his motives for leaving it unspoken. If she took her own life, Bradford might well have preferred not to record such a memory, just as modern families at an inquest try to persuade the authorities not to return a verdict of suicide on their loved ones. Perhaps it was an accident: the Pilgrims were not mariners, and a tired, hungry woman with frozen limbs could easily lose her footing. We simply do not know what happened. Bradford might have had any one of many reasons for failing to describe her passing. We have no means of knowing which one was decisive, but the fact of the omission remains significant in itself. It reminds us that we cannot rely on Bradford to tell the whole story.

Does it matter that Winslow and Bradford left so many empty spaces in their chronicles? Does it matter that they tell us so little about the *Mayflower,* about Jones or the ships in Plymouth Sound, about Thomas Weston, about the politics of Leiden, or about their own precise, local reasons for choosing the odd path of Separatism? Do the omissions make a difference, since what they *did* say remains so powerful? The answer to all these questions is yes. Lost in the crevices within their writing lies most of what we need to know if we are to explain how and why the English ended four decades of fitful efforts in North America and made their determined push across the Atlantic.

Maritime economics, advances in navigation, competition for skins, and the reasons why beaver fur became a fetish: essential though these elements were, you will find them neither explored nor explained within the familiar Pilgrim texts. Nor do Bradford and Winslow deal with the motives of King James, or his son, or with those of men and women as essential to the story as John Pocock of Bread Street Ward. Still less do they make clear why Massachusetts became an irresistible compulsion only in 1629, after the blockade of La Rochelle and the political crisis that followed. This was not because Winslow and Bradford thought that these events were insignificant, but because they took their relevance for granted.

To get at these things, we have had to multiply the sources, on both sides of the Atlantic. We have been forced to go backward, sideways, and around and beneath the accepted narratives of migration. We have also been obliged to abandon any yearning for moral fables in the past. It is difficult enough to find out the facts of what happened, and to reproduce them faithfully. Trying to find lessons for the present day is more likely to block the process of understanding than to help it on its way. History is not a stage upon which we are entitled to act out the dramas of our own transitory period.

At this moment we can return to the Embden rock. Among the many gaps in the archives, there is one above all others that anybody who writes about the period must find not merely inconvenient but deeply troubling. No matter how acute Edward Winslow was in his observations of the Native Americans he met, we lack—or rather, we *seem* to lack—a history written by the other side, by the native peoples themselves. In the imagery at Embden, we can find at least some hints about the form that such a narrative might take.

Once upon a time the rock in the Kennebec was longer than it is today. Apparently, in the era when lumbermen drove logs downriver, they found that the rock snagged the timber. They blasted its tip with dynamite. Even so, and even in its wounded form, with a ragged end like a shattered lump of brick, the Embden rock retains a striking, uncanny appearance. This is because of its shape, and because it enters the water at a precise right angle to the bank. Within the angle, on the sheltered downstream side, where the ripples vanish, the water is calm and transparent, but the riverbed is invisible. The rock seems to leap straight out of a void without a bottom. Nothing quite like it exists elsewhere in the central valley of the Kennebec. Because of this, for a very long time indeed the rock has served as a landmark for human beings.

On its southern flank, the rock protects a sheltered little cove. It makes a perfect natural harbor; and nearby, on a flat terrace of pebbles and soil, Native Americans created an encampment, a place to sleep, to wait out bad weather, to repair a canoe, or to skin the pelt from a carcass. Intermittently, they occupied it for more than half a millennium, ending in the seventeenth or eighteenth century. They left behind them at least a hundred implements of stone.

From the cove, the carved mural that gives the Embden rock its significance stands out with sharp clarity. A narrow shelf, no more than a few inches wide, runs along the face of the stone, just above the level of the water. It provides a place to squat. Three feet above it, where the Kennebec in spate has polished the surface of the shale, an image can be seen scored into the rock in a grid pattern of grooves. It unmistakably portrays a square house of the kind built by Europeans, with a front door and a tall pitched roof.

At first, the house seems unique and isolated. But if you splash a little water on the stone, another picture instantly appears. As your eye learns what to look for, images become visible in their dozens. They form a densely populated frieze, placed in such a way that as the level of the river rose and fell with the seasons, the images would seem to vanish into the water or to emerge from its depths. They lead off in a procession outward from the bank: a dog, a serpent, winged figures half-bird and half-human, men with sticklike arms and triangles for bodies, a moose, and a canoe with inside it a crew wielding poles and paddles. Farthest from dry land, we see the running figure of a man with exorbitant genitalia. From his erection he ejaculates four drops of semen, which fall straight into the Kennebec.

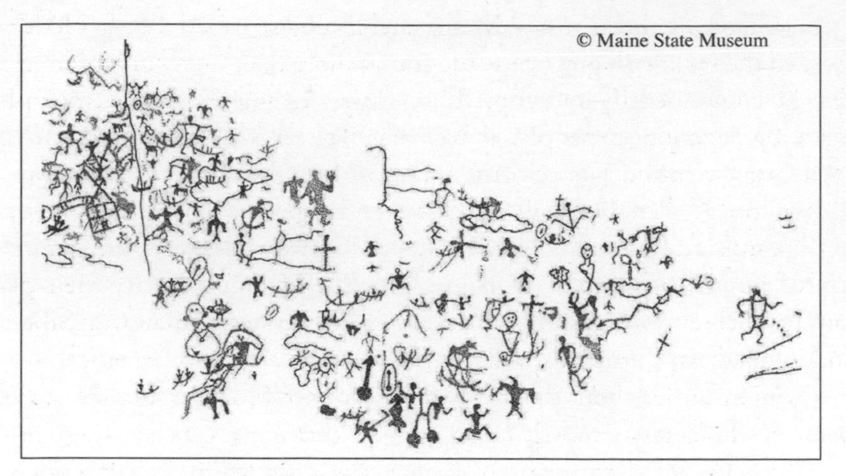

Contrasting examples of Native American and English memorials in stone. Above is the rock at Embden, Maine, covered with Abenaki carvings. Below is the Helwys family monument in the church of St. Martin of Tours, Saundby, Nottinghamshire. The monument was erected in 1599 by Sir Gervase Helwys, cousin of the Separatist Thomas Helwys. (*Photography at Saundby: Nick Bunker*)

Beginning in the 1970s, a Maine archaeologist called Mark Hedden studied the rock with great care. He found more than one hundred images that he could identify and copy. They closely resemble other petroglyphs made by Algonquian people, at Machias Bay on the coast of Maine, in New Brunswick and Nova Scotia, and most lavishly of all at Peterborough in Ontario. At Peterborough, at least nine hundred carvings cover a rock near a canoe trail between the Great Lakes. They contain the same symbolism of bird-men, boats, canoes, and serpents. These icons have their distant parallels elsewhere, similar patterns etched on stone far away in Siberia and in northern Europe, as well as in other parts of North America.

Opinions differ about the meaning of rock art. However, in the last two decades scholars have mostly come to agree that images such as these portray the beliefs of shamanism. A shaman was a seer, a prophet, or a poet, a man or woman who by way of a trance or in a dream could mediate with forces latent in land, river, sky, and ocean. Like the figures in the frieze at Embden, he or she could alter shape, in a chain of metamorphosis, taking the form of a reptile, a beaver, a muskrat, or a bird, and swim underwater or fly through the sky. Shamans could cure sickness, but they could also kill, wounding an enemy by pointing a finger. They foretold the outcome of hunting expeditions. They could conjure fire from water, animals from fire, and corn and tobacco from the soil in winter.[3]

All of this they could do, or so it was said, by way of their access to manitou, the name given in the eastern woodlands of America to the spiritual energy that filled nature like an electric charge. From time to time, manitou flashed visibly, like a spark or a bolt of lightning, when a brilliant creature like a Kennebec eagle displayed its grandeur, or when a comet passed across the sky. More often, manitou made itself present in the landscape, in sites where the elements seemed to promise an epiphany: places, perhaps, like the rock at Embden. By way of its shape, color, oddity, and size, and its location near the foot of the mountains, the rock may have symbolized a point of pregnant intersection. It was a threshold or an orifice. It was a place of passage where a shaman might journey back and forth between the underworld, the heavens, and the earthly home of human beings.

When Winslow made his notes about the native people whom he met in the villages of Massasoit, he found evidence of beliefs of precisely such a kind. Much later, on the Great Plains, researchers in the years around 1900 followed his example and documented the persistence of similar ideas and practices. But among the many records that survive, the rock at Embden has a special quality of relevance and immediacy. This is because we can give at least some of the carvings a date, and because the culture that made them left so much by way of verbal poetry behind.

By its very nature, rock art defies exact chronology. It deposits no organic traces. It might have appeared in any decade within a span of hundreds or even thousands of years. But at Embden, the image of the house tells us that carving must have continued after the first settlers arrived from the other side of the Atlantic. And when archaeologists sifted through the soil, besides stone tools they found European objects: gunflints, clay pipes, trading beads, and a seventeenth-century iron table knife. They also found the remains of fur-bearing mammals. They identified more than forty pieces of bone. All but one came from beaver skeletons.[4]

When beaver pelts traveled to Paris or London, to make costly hats, first they had to come down the Kennebec and past the Embden rock. Perhaps French Jesuits or the English camped at the site, but more likely it was used simply by the Eastern Abenaki who sold skins at Cushnoc or in Quebec. Only twenty miles upstream from the rock, the Kennebec flows past a wide belt of wetlands filled with beavers, around a body of water called Lake Moxie. As late as the 1820s, trappers from the native people on the coast came up to the bogs at Moxie to hunt the animal. They sold its fur to storekeepers at Embden.

So, in the stone, its date, its setting, and its decoration, we find an alternative kind of archive, a window that opens directly into the native world of the 1620s. We also encounter an emblem of mental continuity, between the thinking of the artists who decorated the rock and that of the native people of a much later period.[5] Far into the nineteenth century, the Eastern Abenaki preserved poetic stories that contained motifs identical to those we can see at Embden.

When Henry David Thoreau explored the Maine woods in the 1850s, he met a very unusual old man by the name of John Neptune, the lieutenant governor of the Penobscot tribe. Born as long ago as 1767, Neptune certainly knew the carved rock, because he was one of the men who killed beavers at Moxie. By common consent he was a great shaman, a worker of miracles and dreamer of dreams, perhaps the last among his people. And in his biography, and in the tales told about him, we find another strand of persistence between the seventeenth century and modern times.

Old John Neptune lived in at least two worlds. Recent research has shown that he fought hard by way of politics to defend Penobscot lands from legalized dispossession. But it seems that he owed his fame among his people to the extraordinary legends he inspired. Neptune died in 1865, at the age of ninety-seven, and as late as the 1930s it was still possible to find men and women who remembered him firsthand. At that time, a diligent scholar and gifted writer from Maine called Fannie Hardy Eckstorm collected the Neptune stories. Among them, the strangest of all concerned a serpent of exactly the kind we see carved at Embden.

In the mythology of the Eastern Abenaki, there existed a creature called the *wiwiliamecq,* an underwater monster with horns like a snail. It was said that a shaman from the Micmac, old enemies of the Penobscot, took the form of the monster. To defeat him, John Neptune took the likeness of an eel. Plunging into the water, like the creatures of many kinds at Embden, he entered the pond where the *wiwiliamecq* lived. He killed it after a titanic battle. One of Eckstorm's contacts among the Penobscot even led her to see the pond where the fight took place.

Water serpents often appeared in the stories told by native people in New England. So did the motif of shamans swimming beneath the waves to destroy their enemies. In the 1630s, a shaman in Connecticut threatened to make a submarine attack on an English sailing ship, and the case of John Neptune shows that stories such as these remained as a living tradition hundreds of years after the Pilgrims landed. Nor was it only legends that lived on, but also an independent account of history. It included a narrative of the arrival of the English and the French.

John Neptune had a grandson called Joseph Nicolar, a Penobscot man who served in the state legislature of Maine. In 1893, Nicolar published a remarkable text called *The Life and Traditions of the Red Man.* Very few copies survive, and it was reprinted in the United States only in 2007. Like the icons at Embden, it supplies another alternative archive: a source as worthy of respect as William Bradford or Edward Winslow.

Through his mother's family, Nicolar could trace his genealogy directly from the Kennebec people who lived at Naragooc. His book first appeared at a desperate time in Native American history, soon after the massacre at Wounded Knee. Undaunted and undeterred, Joseph Nicolar composed a strange and wonderful prose epic of his people's past. The Homer of the Abenaki, Nicolar preserved and beautified oral traditions that must date from the earliest contacts between the Eastern Abenaki and the fishermen of England and of France. Like Homer, he may have altered and embellished them, but he did not make up the events he described, any more than Homer invented the city of Troy.

In his Penobscot *Iliad,* Nicolar wrote about blazing stars in the heavens that preceded the arrival of the white newcomers. He described a sailing ship—a "large canoe . . . propelled by a brown colored cloth spread in the wind"—and he chronicled the wars between the native people, between the Abenaki, the Micmac, and the Iroquois. He recorded native memories of kidnapping by the Europeans on the coast. He gave an alternative account of wampum. Nicolar said that it was never intended to be a form of currency, but only to function as a gift, a pledge of goodwill.

Little known and rarely studied, like the rock art at Embden, Nicolar's book records from the native side the beginnings of colonization in New England. Like the rock by the Kennebec, his book reminds us that our knowledge of the past is incomplete, meager, and fragmentary. Both the book and the rock teach us about the extent of what remains to be discovered, about stories and occurrences that seem familiar but that in reality are distant, remote, and strewn with ambiguity.

Far too many sources such as these, Nicolar's book and the rock, lie neglected and ignored, not only by the Kennebec, but also in the record offices of England. In London, the National Archives contains thousands of forgotten papers from the period, documents arising from litigation, from shipping, from taxes, or from diplomacy. Where great matters of politics are concerned, such as the causes of the English Civil War, or where the Crown took a close interest in affairs, as it did with the Virginia plantation, researchers have mined the archives deeply; but the very early settlement of New England was achieved entirely by private enterprise. The traces it left linger in obscure, unfashionable places, in archives relating to trade, lawsuits, and the sea. These are often hardly touched at all.

No single fact, stone, or document will change our picture of the period. History is not a secret code waiting to be cracked with a simple key or a password. We have to examine it from all sides, and find as many sources as we can. Only by doing so can we hope briefly to see things as perhaps they were, for the Eastern Abenaki or for the native people of southern New England, as well as for the Pilgrims. So it is not only in a record office filled with manuscripts but also in the terrain on both sides of the Atlantic.

When we slither down a wooded hillside in Nottinghamshire and come upon a stand of maples or a hedgerow that a Pilgrim might have passed, for an instant the centuries slip away. On a winter afternoon, as darkness falls over an English parish church, we find in a dim corner an alabaster monument, pink and white, made for a family who were allies of William Brewster; so, in that place, a fugitive epiphany occurs. And when we leave a highway in rural Maine and follow a winding trail down through the forest to the stream, suddenly we see beneath the dying autumn leaves the uncanny rock at Embden.

By the water, we have a fleeting intimation of what a shaman meant by manitou. In a small moment of vision of our own, we glimpse the same objects that John Howland might have seen as he came up the Kennebec. We see, as perhaps he first saw them, the foaming river and the white pines, an eagle's nest and the tracks of deer, and, in the distance and the sunset blue slate hills, a glowing palisade against the western sky.

Acknowledgments

The research for this book required three trips to the United States between 2006 and 2008, and my own peaceful expeditions to Holland, La Rochelle, and Ulster. Besides exploring all the locations associated with the Pilgrims on foot or on a bicycle, visiting each one at least twice, I made countless forays to record offices in many different parts of England. In the process I incurred many obligations, to local farmers, churchwardens, bed-and-breakfast landladies, and friendly staff in remote American motels and diners: far too many to list by name.

Principally, I have to express my gratitude to the archive collections referred to in my notes, for access to their material and for the courteous assistance of their staffs. In England, I spent more time at the National Archives at Kew than at any other repository. The speed and efficiency with which it produces documents enabled me to make the most of long and crowded days.

I am particularly grateful to Dr. John Alban, county archivist at Norfolk Record Office, Norwich, and to Dr. Dorothy Johnston, keeper of manuscripts and special collections at the University of Nottingham. Both of them kindly allowed me to use Elizabethan papers that either were too fragile for routine inspection or required conservation work before I could do so.

I would also like to mention help received from Dr. Nicholas Bennett, vice-chancellor and librarian, Lincoln Cathedral; Dr. Glyn Coppack of English Heritage; Robin Harcourt Williams, librarian and archivist to the Marquess of Salisbury, Hatfield House; Steve Hill of Steve Hill Photography, Lincoln; Alice Millea, assistant keeper of the Oxford University

Archives; Helen O'Neill of the London Library; Theresa Thom, librarian, Gray's Inn, London; Katie Vaughan of the Suffolk Record Office, Bury St. Edmunds; Tim Wormleighton, principal archivist, North Devon Record Office, Barnstaple; and Peter Young, archivist to the dean and chapter of York, York Minster.

At Cambridge, I had the benefit of guidance from Dr. Elisabeth Leedham-Green, honorary archivist of Corpus Christi College, and from Malcolm Underwood, her opposite number at St. John's. Also at St. John's, I received invaluable assistance from Jonathan Harrison, the special collections librarian.

My cousin Nigel Bunker, station officer of the Tamar Coastguard Rescue Team, gave me the benefit of his expert knowledge of Plymouth Sound with several days sailing its waters. Captain Paul Jagger, Royal Navy, came with us and explained how it looks to a submariner.

In Dublin, Dr. Raymond Refaussé, librarian and archivist of the Church of Ireland, swiftly identified John Lyford as the prebendary of Loughgall. That led me to Ulster and a little-known eighteenth-century jewel, the Armagh Robinson Public Library, where I received the charming help of Carol Conlin. Dr. Greer Ramsey, acting curator, allowed me to read papers relating to Jacobean Loughgall at the Armagh County Museum.

In the United States, I wish to thank (heading from north to south) Paul du Houx of Polar Bear and Company, Solon, Maine; Bruce Bourque, archaeologist at the Maine State Museum in Augusta; Nick Noyes, head of library services, and his team at the Maine Historical Society in Portland; Professor David Foster, director of the Harvard Forest, Petersham, Massachusetts; Peter Drummey, research librarian, and his colleagues at the Massachusetts Historical Society, especially Tracy Potter; Graham Giese of the Provincetown Center for Coastal Studies, who explained the geology of Cape Cod; and Peggy Baker, director and librarian, Pilgrim Hall, Plymouth, Massachusetts. For expert help with Native American languages, I am very grateful to Dr. Francis J. O'Brien Jr. (Moondancer) of the Aquidneck Indian Council in Rhode Island.

My opening and closing chapters could not have been written without the people who helped me to trace the fur trade on the Kennebec River. Dave Cook, past president of the Maine Archaeological Society, shared his unrivaled knowledge of the canoe trails of his state; Joe Miller of Starks, near Madison, showed me the site of the village at Naragooc; and at Embden, Arthur Arsenault told me where to find the petroglyphs.

For specific permission to cite or to quote from unpublished documents for which they hold the copyright, I am grateful to the Trustees of

Lambeth Palace Library, for the Bacon and Talbot Papers at Lambeth; the Merchant Taylors' Company and the Worshipful Company of Haberdashers, for their records deposited at the Guildhall Library in London; at Cambridge, the masters and fellows of Corpus Christi College, Christ's College, and St. John's College, and the Syndics of the Cambridge University Library; and the Massachusetts Historical Society.

To help in drawing my map of *Mayflower* London, the Historic Towns Trust kindly permitted me to use material from their map of the city in the Tudor period, published in Mary D. Lobel, ed., *The City of London from Prehistoric Times to c. 1520* (Oxford, 1989). I am grateful to the Churches Conservation Trust for permission to reproduce my photograph of the Helwys monument at Saundby.

I am immensely grateful to Professor Patrick Collinson and to Peggy and Jim Baker for reading the typescript, awarding appropriate encouragement and censure, and pointing to errors and omissions. My literary agents, Bill Hamilton of A. M. Heath and Company and George Lucas of InkWell Management, gave enthusiastic support, as did my splendid editors, Carol Janeway of Alfred A. Knopf in New York and Will Sulkin of the Bodley Head in London. Both Will and Carol immediately saw the potential of the book. This would not have happened at all without David Waller, a former colleague of mine at the *Financial Times*, who introduced me to Bill Hamilton. Reginald Piggott drew the maps beautifully, and David Nee and Elizabeth Lee at Knopf and Kay Peddle at the Bodley Head were diligent editorial assistants.

The dedication records an obligation dating back more than twenty-five years. Ms. Mahoney presided over the foundation that awarded me the Harkness Fellowship that allowed me to spend two years in America in the early 1980s. However, my greatest debt of all is to my wife, Sue Temple, who has been a rock of support, love, and friendship since 1985.

Two months before the deadline for submission of the manuscript, my father was suddenly taken ill and died. It is a source of great sadness to my mother and to me that he never saw the book he had waited for.

Notes

Manuscript and Archive Collections: Abbreviations Used in the Notes

BI (York) Borthwick Institute, University of York, UK
BL British Library, London
Bodleian Bodleian Library, Oxford
CKS Centre for Kentish Studies, Maidstone, UK
ECRO Essex County Record Office, Chelmsford, UK
LAO Lincolnshire Archives, Lincoln, UK
LDRO Diocesan Record Office, Lichfield, UK
LPL Lambeth Palace Library, London
LRCRO Leicestershire and Rutland County Record Office, Leicester
NAK National Archives, Kew, UK
NAN Nottinghamshire Archives, Nottingham, UK
NDRO North Devon Record Office, Barnstaple, UK
Norfolk RO Norfolk Record Office, Norwich, UK
Northants RO Northamptonshire Record Office, Northampton, UK
PRONI Public Record Office of Northern Ireland, Belfast
SROB Suffolk Record Office, Bury St. Edmunds, UK
U Nott University of Nottingham, Manuscripts and Special Collections

Other Archive Collections Referred to in the Notes

Archives Départementales de la Charente-Maritime, La Rochelle, France
Armagh County Museum, Armagh, Northern Ireland
Armagh Robinson Public Library, Armagh, Northern Ireland
Cambridge University Archives, University Library, Cambridge, UK
Christ's College, College Archives, Cambridge, UK
Corpus Christi College, Muniment Room, Cambridge, UK
Doncaster Archives, Doncaster, Yorkshire, UK

Guildhall Library, Manuscript Collections, London
Lancashire Record Office, Preston, UK
London Metropolitan Archives
Massachusetts Historical Society, Boston
Massachusetts State Archives, Boston
St. John's College, College Archives, Cambridge, UK
Sheffield Archives, Sheffield, Yorkshire, UK
York Minster Archives, York, UK

Other Abbreviations Used Frequently in the Notes

HMC Historical Manuscripts Commission
NEHGR *New England Historical and Genealogical Register*
ODNB *Oxford Dictionary of National Biography*
PCC Prerogative Court of Canterbury
PMHS *Proceedings of the Massachusetts Historical Society*

Epigraph

1. Robert Ryece to John Winthrop, Aug. 12, 1629, in Massachusetts Historical Society, *Winthrop Papers* (Boston, 1931), vol. 2, p. 130.

Prelude: The Beaver of Mawooshen

1. John Winter to Robert Trelawny, Richmond Island, Me., June 18, 1634, in *Trelawny Papers,* ed. James Phinney Baxter (Portland, ME, 1884), p. 29.
2. Beaver fur prices and ecology: See chapters 12 and 17, below. Land in England: Eric Kerridge, "The Movement of Rent, 1540–1640," *Economic History Review,* n.s., 6, no. 1 (1953), pp. 24–31; and Robert C. Allen, "The Price of Freehold Land and the Interest Rate in the Seventeenth and Eighteenth Centuries," *Economic History Review,* 2nd ser., 41, no. 1 (1988), pp. 33–35.
3. Mark V. Stalmaster, *The Bald Eagle* (New York, 1987), pp. 23–25, 41–42, 56–64, and 113–15.
4. The name Kennebec: Fannie Hardy Eckstorm, *Indian Place Names of the Penobscot Valley and the Maine Coast* (1941; repr., Orono, ME, 1977), pp. 142–43; and Gordon M. Day, "A St. Francis Abenaki Vocabulary," *International Journal of American Linguistics* 30, no. 4 (Oct. 1964), p. 384. Eastern Abenaki: Dean R. Snow, "Eastern Abenaki," in *Handbook of North American Indians,* vol. 15, *Northeast,* ed. Bruce G. Trigger (Washington, DC, 1978), pp. 137–48.
5. "The Description of the Countrey of Mawooshen, c. 1606–7," in *The English New England Voyages, 1602–1608,* ed. David B. Quinn and Alison M. Quinn (London, 1983), pp. 469–76.
6. U.S. Department of Agriculture, *Soil Survey of Somerset County, Maine, Southern Part* (1972), p. 16; digitized soil maps from USDA, Natural Resources Conservation Service, Web Soil Survey; and Howard S. Russell, *A Long, Deep Furrow: Three Centuries of Farming in New England* (Hanover, NH, 1976), pp. 42 and 132–33.
7. For the excavation report, see Ellen R. Cowie, "Continuity and Change at Contact-Period Norridgewock" (Ph.D. diss., University of Pittsburgh, 2002), esp. pp. 15–39 and

336–72. Dr. Cowie led the archaeological investigations carried out in the central Kennebec valley between 1988 and 1995 by the University of Maine at Farmington. Although it has not yet been possible to prove with physical data that maize was cultivated at Naragooc before contact with Europeans, Cowie believes that it probably was, and I have assumed the same. On the important debate about the northern limit of Abenaki maize farming and its earliest date, see Elizabeth S. Chilton, "So Little Maize, So Much Time: Understanding Maize Adoption in New England," *Current Northeast Palaeobotany II*, ed. John P. Hart, *New York State Museum Bulletin* 512 (2008), pp. 53–58.

8. Râle's lexicon: Sebastian Râle, "A Dictionary of the Abnaki Language of North America," ed. John Pickering, *Memoirs of the American Academy of Arts and Sciences*, n.s., 1 (1833); and Day, "St. Francis Abenaki Vocabulary." Taste of beaver: Christopher Levett, *A Voyage into New England* (London, 1628), reprinted in J. P. Baxter, *Christopher Levett of York: The Pioneer Colonist in Casco Bay* (Portland, ME, 1893), p. 110.
9. Canoes: David S. Cook, *Above the Gravel Bar: the Native Canoe Routes of Maine* (Solon, ME, 2007). Birch trees: Charles V. Cogbill et al., "The Forests of Presettlement New England, USA: Spatial and Compositional Patterns," *Journal of Biogeography* 29 (2002), pp. 1279–1304.
10. On English archives relating to Barnstaple, the *White Angel* and the *Pleasure*, and the beaver fur trade in 1628, see chapter 19 below. The English on the coast of Maine: Henry S. Burrage, *The Beginnings of Colonial Maine, 1602–1658* (Portland, ME, 1914), pp. 178–96; and Edwin A. Churchill, "English Beachheads in Seventeenth-Century Maine," in *Maine: The Pine Tree State from Prehistory to the Present*, ed. Richard W. Judd et al. (Orono, ME, 1995), pp. 51–57.
11. Cushnoc excavations, 1985–87: Leon E. Cranmer, *Cushnoc: The History and Archaeology of Plymouth Colony Traders on the Kennebec* (Augusta, ME, 1990), pp. 39–66 and 81–88. Kennebec patent: Samuel Eliot Morison, ed., *Of Plymouth Plantation, 1620–1647, by William Bradford* (New York, 1979), pp. 201–2.
12. Hakluyt (1584), in *The Original Writings and Correspondence of the Two Richard Hakluyts*, ed. E. G. R. Taylor (London, 1935), vol. 2, p. 274.
13. R. G. Thwaites, ed., *Jesuit Relations and Allied Documents*, vol. 36, *Lower Canada, Abenakis, 1650–1651* (Cleveland, 1899), pp. 83–102.
14. Colonial State Papers (American), CO 1/6, fols. 106-10, depositions regarding Edward Ashley, NAK.
15. Fulke Greville, Lord Brooke, *A Dedication to Sir Philip Sidney* (c. 1610), in *The Prose Works of Fulke Greville, Lord Brooke*, ed. J. Gouws, (Oxford, 1986), pp. 69–70.

Chapter One: The Year of the Blazing Star

1. John Bainbridge, *An Astronomicall Description of the Late Comet from the 18 of November 1618 to the 16 of December Following, with Certaine Morall Prognosticks Drawn from the Comets Motion* (London, 1619), pp. 9–10, 19, and 33. Cambridge student: Memoirs of Sir Simonds D'Ewes, Harleian MS 646, fol. 42, BL. French journalist: Estienne Richer, *Le Mercure françois* (Paris, 1620), vol. 5, pp. 290–92.
2. Kepler and the comet: Gary W. Kronk, *Cometography: A Catalog of Comets* (Cambridge, UK, 1999), vol. 1, pp. 338–41. Grassi and Galileo: Stillman Drake and C. D. O'Malley, eds., *The Controversy on the Comets of 1618* (Philadelphia, 1960), pp. 6–7 and 360.

3. A. B. Hinds, ed., *Calendar of State Papers (Venetian)*, vol. 15, 1617–19 (London, 1909), p. 366.
4. Roger Williams, *A Key into the Language of the Indians of New England* (1643), in *Collections of the Massachusetts Historical Society for the Year 1794* (Boston, 1810), vol. 3, pp. 217–18.
5. Kathleen J. Bragdon, *Native People of Southern New England, 1500–1650* (Norman, OK, 1996), pp. 191–93. Ojibwa legends: Thor Conway, "The Conjurer's Lodge: Celestial Narratives from Algonkian Shamans," in *Earth & Sky: Visions of the Cosmos in Native American Folklore,* ed. Ray A. Williamson and Claire R. Farrer (Albuquerque, NM, 1992), pp. 236–37 and 242–44.
6. Edward Johnson, *The Wonder-Working Providence of Sions Saviour: Being a Relation of the First Planting in New England in the Yeare 1628* (New York, 1910), chap. 7.
7. Bainbridge entry in *ODNB.*
8. Bainbridge, *Astronomicall Description,* pp. 31–32.
9. Thomas Birch, *The Court and Times of James I, Illustrated by Authentic and Confidential Letters* (London, 1848), p. 109.
10. Anthony Milton, ed., *The British Delegation and the Synod of Dort* (Woodbridge, UK, 2005), p. 190.
11. Aaron Burckhart, *Cometen Predigt als in diesem 1618 Jahre in Novembr* (Magdeburg, 1618), title page.
12. Conrad Dieterich, *Ulmische Cometen Predigte* (Ulm, 1619), p. 32.
13. Milton, *British Delegation,* p. 191.
14. W. B. Patterson, *King James VI and I and the Reunion of Christendom* (Cambridge, UK, 2000), pp. 191–93 and 268–69.
15. Will of William Staresmore (1636), Archdeaconry of Leicester wills, LRCRO; and baptism of Sabine Staresmore, Aug. 31, 1582, Frolesworth Parish Register, DE 4087/1, LRCRO. Also, William Burton, *The Description of Leicester Shire* (London, 1622), pp. 109–12.
16. Samuel Eliot Morison, ed., *Of Plymouth Plantation, 1620–1647, by William Bradford* (New York, 1979), pp. 353–59.
17. Will of Sir John Wolstenholme (1639), PROB/11/181, PCC Wills, NAK. Also, S. M. Kingsbury, ed., *The Records of the Virginia Company of London* (Washington, DC, 1906–35), vol. 1, pp. 310–11, Feb. 16, 1620. Estimate of twenty pounds as the annual income of a skilled craftsman is based on the sixteen pence paid daily to tapestry weavers by the Crown. Wolstenholme's papers: Notes on the East India trade, CO 77/1 (East Indies), fols. 196–99, and CO 77/2, fols. 68–73, NAK.
18. For the diplomatic correspondence, see Nov. 13 and Dec. 21, 1617, State Papers (France), SP 78/67, fols. 206 and 230, NAK; State Papers (Holland), SP 84/81, fols. 40–43, NAK; and W. N. Sainsbury, ed., *Calendar of State Papers, Colonial Series, East Indies, 1617–1621* (London, 1870), pp. 41, 42, and 69.
19. Petition of Jan. or Feb. 1618, in *The Works of Samuel de Champlain,* ed. H. P. Biggar (Toronto, 1925), vol. 2, pp. 329–45.
20. Pitiscus, *Trigonometry; or, the Doctrine of Triangles,* trans. Rafe Handson (London, 1614), dedication.
21. On Briggs, see typescript notes on fellows of St. John's College, Cambridge, St. John's College Library, and St. John's College Rentals for 1604–5, College Archives; Briggs's will, proved Feb. 11, 1631, PROB/11/159, PCC, NAK; D. M. Hallowes, "Henry Briggs, Mathematician," *Transactions of the Halifax Antiquarian Society* (1962), pp. 87–89.

22. On James and Buckingham, see Jan. 31, 1618, SP 14/95/28, NAK.
23. On the silent revolution, see N. E. McClure, ed., *The Letters of John Chamberlain* (Philadelphia, 1939), vol. 2, pp. 124–26, Jan. 3, 1618; HMC, *Downshire Manuscripts*, vol. 6, *Papers of William Trumbull, 1616–1618* (London, 1995), pp. 342–43 and 357; and John Cramsie, *Kingship and Crown Finance Under James I, 1603–1625* (London, 2002), pp. 142–63.
24. Pirates: State Papers (Spain), SP 94/22, fol. 178, Aug. 22, 1617, and SP 94/22, fol. 236, Dec. 14, 1617, NAK. Spanish rearmament: SP 14/95/22, Jan. 18, 1618, NAK. Navy: N. A. M. Rodger, *The Safeguard of the Sea: A Naval History of Britain, 660–1649* (London, 2004), pp. 368–70.
25. Smith to Francis Bacon, in *The Complete Works of Captain John Smith, 1580–1631*, ed. Philip E. Barbour (Chapel Hill, NC, 1986), vol. 1, p. 378.
26. Edward Winslow, *Hypocrisie Unmasked* (1646), in *Chronicles of the Pilgrim Fathers*, ed. Alexander Young (Boston, 1844; repr. Baltimore, 1974), pp. 382–83.
27. Naunton: Material referred to in note 17, above; and Roy E. Schreiber, *The Political Career of Sir Robert Naunton* (London, 1981), pp. 45–54 and 132. Greville, Coke, and Naunton: HMC, 12th Report, app. pt. 1, *Manuscripts of the Earl Cowper at Melbourne Hall* (London, 1888), vol. 1, p. 110.
28. Thomas Locke to William Trumbull, Aug. 28, 1618, in HMC, *Downshire Manuscripts*, vol. 6, p. 487.
29. Thomas Scott, *Vox Populi; or, News from Spayne* (1620?), pp. 1–3, 1103.c.12, BL.

Chapter Two: Mr. Jones in Plymouth Sound

1. Quoted in Sir John Rennie, *An Historical, Practical, and Theoretical Account of the Breakwater in Plymouth Sound* (London, 1848), p. 13. For the very brief description of the *Mayflower*'s departure given by the Pilgrims, see the opening of their journal, *Mourt's Relation*, either in Dwight B. Heath, ed., *Mourt's Relation: A Journal of the Pilgrims at Plymouth* (Bedford, MA, 1963), p. 15, or in the older, extensively annotated, but sometimes inaccurate edition of Alexander Young, *Chronicles of the Pilgrim Fathers* (Boston, 1844; repr., Baltimore, 1974), pp. 117–18.
2. SP 14/109/78 and SP 14/111/75, NAK.
3. Voyages to America in 1619: The *Bona Nova*, in Exchequer port book (London exports), July 31, 1619, E 190/22/9, NAK; S. M. Kingsbury, ed., *Records of the Virginia Company of London* (Washington, DC, 1906–35), vol. 1, pp. 351–52; and Faith Harrington, " 'Wee Tooke Greate Store of Cod-fish': Fishing Ships and First Settlements on the Coast of New England, 1600–1630," in *American Beginnings: Exploration, Culture, and Cartography in the Land of Norumbega*, ed. Emerson W. Baker et al. (Lincoln, NE, 1994), pp. 203–7. New pattern of trade: Tables in *Merchants and Merchandise in Seventeenth-Century Bristol*, ed. Patrick McGrath (Bristol, UK, 1955), app. D, pp. 279–80.
4. Alicante cargoes: Plymouth port book (new impositions), 1614 and 1616, E 190/1026/15 and E 190/1027/2, NAK. Archaeology: John Allan and James Barber, "A Seventeenth Century Pottery Group from the Kitto Institute, Plymouth," in *Everyday and Exotic Pottery from Europe, c. 650–1900*, ed. David Gaimster and Mark Redknap (Oxford, 1992), pp. 229–35.
5. On Jacobean Plymouth, see Tristram Risdon, *The Chorographical Survey of the County of Devon* (London, 1811), pp. 201–3; and Elisabeth Stuart, *Lost Landscapes of Plymouth: Maps, Charts, and Plans to 1800* (Stroud, UK, 1991).

6. On the ship's design, see Étienne Trocmé and Marcel Delafosse, *Le commerce rochelais de la fin du XVe siècle au debut du XVIIe* (Paris, 1952), pp. 15–21; William A. Baker, *The* Mayflower *and Other Colonial Vessels* (London, 1983), pp. 27–44; and J. R. Hutchinson, "The 'Mayflower,' Her Identity and Tonnage," *NEHGR*, Oct. 1916, pp. 337–42.
7. 1620 port book for Plymouth, Christmas 1619–Christmas 1620, E 190/1029/19, NAK.
8. For Weddell, see W. N. Sainsbury, ed., *Calendar of State Papers, Colonial, East Indies, 1617–1621* (London, 1870), pp. 63, 258, 310, and 332–33; and *ODNB.*
9. Brian Dietz, "The Royal Bounty and English Shipping in the Sixteenth and Seventeenth Centuries," *Mariner's Mirror* 77 (1991), pp. 14–20.
10. Lieutenant-Commander D. W. Waters, *The Art of Navigation in Elizabethan and Stuart England* (Greenwich, UK, 1978), esp. pp. 297–300, 342–44, 425–34, and 478–88.
11. Thomas Dale, *The History and Antiquities of Harwich and Dovercourt in the County of Essex* (London, 1732), p. 250. On Tudor and Stuart Harwich, see H. Hitchman and P. Driver, *Harwich: A Nautical History* (Harwich, UK, 1984), pp. 56–62. Jones's background: Winifred Cooper, *Harwich, the* Mayflower, *and Christopher Jones* (London, 1970), esp. pp. 2–15.
12. Harwich approaches: Cornelis Antoniszoon, *The Safegard of Saylers; or, Great Rutter,* trans. Robert Norman (London, 1612); and Waters, *Art of Navigation,* p. 331. Government of Harwich: Harwich church book, fol. 232, T/P 162/9, ECRO; and Leonard T. Weaver, *The Harwich Story* (Dovercourt, UK, 1975), pp. 18–38. Move to London: B. Carlyon Hughes, *The History of Harwich Harbour* (Harwich, UK, 1939), pp. 152–53. Norway voyage: Hutchinson, " 'Mayflower,' Her Identity and Tonnage," pp. 337–39.
13. Douglas Killock and Frank Meddens et al., "Pottery as Plunder: A 17th-Century Maritime Site in Limehouse, London," *Post-medieval Archaeology* 39, no. 1 (2005), pp. 16–18 and 24–27.
14. On Jones and Wood, see subsidy roll of Brixton Hundred, March 8, 1622, E 179/186/406, NAK; and will of Anthony Wood (1625), PROB/11/148, PCC Wills, NAK.
15. Wine profits: Estimated from details in *Garway et al. v. Rothwell* (1624), E 134/21JasI/HIL25, NAK; and Trocmé and Delafosse, *Le commerce rochelais,* pp. 104–13 and 178–80. Wine trade and Jacobean prosperity: A. M. Millard, "The Import Trade of London, 1600–1640" (Ph.D. diss., London University, 1956), pp. 46–47, and the tables in the app. to vol. 2. Prices: For a mass of useful data regarding Jacobean prices, including those of wine, see John Harland, ed., *The House and Farm Accounts of the Shuttleworths of Gawthorpe Hall, 1582–1621* (Manchester, UK, 1858), esp. pp. 790–92 and 1103–12.
16. For Speight and the *Mayflower,* see London port book (exports), 1617, entries for May 19, 26, and 30, Sackville Papers, U 269/1, OEc 1, CKS; London port book (wine imports), 1620, May 15, E 190/24/3, NAK; Speight's will of 1621, PROB/11/139, NAK; Company of Merchant Taylors, *Memorials of the Guild of Merchant Taylors* (London, 1875), p. 719. The notarial registers at the Archives Départementales de la Charente-Maritime at La Rochelle show that at least ten English merchants were resident there during the reign of James I.
17. On Jennings, see Plymouth port books in note 4 above, and also for 1626 (new impositions), E 190/1031/6, NAK; M. Brayshay, "Royal Post-Horse Routes in South West England in the Reigns of Elizabeth I and James I," *Report of the Transactions of the Devon-*

shire Association 123 (Dec. 1991), pp. 96–97 and 103; Henry S. Burrage, *The Beginnings of Colonial Maine, 1602–1658* (Portland, ME, 1914), pp. 164–66 and 181–82.

18. David B. Quinn and Alison M. Quinn, eds., *The English New England Voyages, 1602–1608* (London, 1983), pp. 340–41.
19. James Phinney Baxter, ed., *Sir Ferdinando Gorges and His Province of Maine* (Boston, 1890), vol. 1, pp. 222–37.
20. Miller Christy, "Attempts Towards Colonization: The Council for New England and the Merchant Venturers of Bristol, 1621–1623," *American Historical Review* 4, no. 4 (July 1899), p. 687.
21. John Pym's notes of speech by Sir Edwin Sandys, Feb. 26, 1621, in *Commons Debates, 1621*, ed. W. Notestein, F. H. Relf, and H. Simpson (New Haven, CT, 1935), vol. 4, pp. 104–6.
22. Barry Supple, *Commercial Crisis and Change in England, 1600–1642* (Cambridge, UK, 1964), pp. 52–64; R. W. K. Hinton, *The Eastland Trade and the Common Weal in the Seventeenth Century* (Cambridge, UK, 1959), pp. 14–32; and Jonathan I. Israel, *The Dutch Republic: Its Rise, Greatness, and Fall, 1477–1806* (Oxford, 1995), pp. 478–82.
23. Edward Misselden, *Free Trade; or, The Means to Make Trade Flourish* (London, 1622), p. 29. Silver shortage: C. E. Challis, ed., *A New History of the Royal Mint* (Cambridge, UK, 1992), pp. 307–17.

Chapter Three: Crossing Sinai

1. John Barlow, *The True Guide to Glory*, funeral sermon for Lady Strode (1618), p. 9, in *An Exposition of the First and Second Chapters* (London, 1632).
2. Details of the night sky over New England on the early morning of November 9, 1620, can be determined using astronomical computer software such as the Alcyone program (www.alcyone.de). The principal source for the landfall itself is (again) the opening of Dwight B. Heath, ed., *Mourt's Relation: A Journal of the Pilgrims at Plymouth* (Bedford, MA, 1963), and Bradford's later account in Samuel Eliot Morison, ed., *Of Plymouth Plantation, 1620–1647, by William Bradford* (New York, 1979), pp. 59–61. November 19 was the date of the landfall using the modern Gregorian calendar. The principal modern American treatment of the voyage and arrival is contained in W. Sears Nickerson, *Land Ho! 1620: A Seaman's Story of the* Mayflower (Boston, 1931).
3. Edward Hayes, *A Treatise Conteining Important Inducements for the Planting in These Parts, and Finding a Passage and Way to the South Sea and China* (London, 1602), p. 16.
4. For conditions on the *Mayflower*, see William A. Baker, *The* Mayflower *and Other Colonial Vessels* (London, 1983), pp. 37–44.
5. M. Oppenheim, ed., *The Naval Tracts of Sir William Monson in Six Books* (London, 1913), vol. 3, p. 434.
6. Morison, *Of Plymouth Plantation*, p. 76; and see chapter 14, note 14, below.
7. "Furthing": K. R. Andrews, "The Elizabethan Seaman," *Mariner's Mirror* 68 (1982), pp. 254–55. Disputes between masters and crew: George F. Steckley, "Litigious Mariners: Wage Cases in the Seventeenth-Century Admiralty Court," *Historical Journal* 42, no. 2 (June 1999), pp. 315–45.
8. Morison, *Of Plymouth Plantation*, p. 78; and G. V. Scammell, "Manning the English Merchant Service in the Sixteenth Century," *Mariner's Mirror* 56 (1970), pp. 149–50.

9. Heath, *Mourt's Relation*, p. 16.
10. Ibid., p. 15.
11. Morison, *Of Plymouth Plantation*, pp. 58–63.
12. New England Society in the City of New York, *Plymouth Church Records, 1620–1859* (New York, 1920–23), vol. 1, pp. 136–37. Ainsworth: *ODNB;* and Michael E. Moody, " 'A Man of a Thousand': The Reputation and Character of Henry Ainsworth," *Huntington Library Quarterly* 45, no. 3 (Summer 1982), pp. 200–214.
13. Hebrew: G. Lloyd-Jones, *The Discovery of Hebrew in Tudor England: A Third Language* (Manchester, UK, 1983), esp. pp. 3–6, 239, and 261. Broughton: *ODNB.*
14. Henry Ainsworth, "Preface Concerning Moses," in *Annotations upon the Five Bookes of Moses, the Booke of the Psalmes, and the Song of Songs or Canticles* (London, 1627). The 1627 edition reprinted the first editions of each work, published in parts in Amsterdam between 1612 and 1619. References to Ainsworth's *Annotations:* The term "exquisite scanning" occurs in the preface, but for other examples see Ainsworth's annotations to Genesis 21:14; Exodus 3:1, 3:18, and 16:1–3; Deuteronomy 8:15; and Numbers 14:29. Midrash: Jacob Neusner and Alan J. Avery-Peck, eds., *Encyclopedia of Midrash* (Leiden, 2005), pp. 400–411 and 520–26.
15. On the prestige of Maimonides, see Jason Rosenblatt, *Renaissance England's Chief Rabbi: John Selden* (Oxford, 2006), p. 79.
16. Ainsworth, "Preface Concerning Moses."
17. Isidore S. Meyer, "The Hebrew Preface to Bradford's History of the Plymouth Plantation," *Journal of the American Jewish Historical Society* (1948–49), pp. 289–301.
18. Barlow, *True Guide*, pp. 16–17.
19. For examples, see John Wood, *The True Honor of Navigation and Navigators; or, Holy Meditations for Sea-Men* (London, 1618), pp. 86–94; Edmund Spenser's account of the voyage to the Bower of Bliss, in bk. 2, canto 12 of the *Faerie Queene* of 1590; and the shipwreck in Sir Philip Sidney's *New Arcadia*, bk. 2, chap. 7. Also see Alain Cabantous, *Le ciel dans la mer: Christianisme et civilisation maritime, XV-XIX siècle* (Paris, 1990), pp. 19–28 and 34–38.
20. W. K. Clay, ed., *Liturgies and Occasional Forms of Prayers Set Forth in the Reign of Queen Elizabeth* (Cambridge, UK, 1847).
21. Ainsworth, *Annotations*, notes on Psalm 107:32. *Birkat ha-gomel:* Ronald L. Eisenberg, *The JPS Guide to Jewish Traditions* (Philadelphia, 2004), pp. 480–81.

Chapter Four: Troublechurch Browne

1. Philip E. Barbour, ed., *The Complete Works of Captain John Smith, 1580–1631* (Chapel Hill, NC, 1986), vol. 3, p. 221.
2. Thomas Twyne, *Discourse on the Earthquake of 1580*, ed. R. E. Ockenden (Oxford, 1936); Edmund Spenser and Gabriel Harvey, *Three Proper and Wittie, Familiar Letters Lately Passed Between Two Universitie Men* (London, 1580), pp. 5–6 and 9–11; R. M. W. Musson, G. Neilson, and P. W. Burton, "The London Earthquake of 1580, April 6," *Engineering Geology* 20 (1984), pp. 113–42.
3. Christopher Haigh, *English Reformations* (Oxford, 1993), pp. 276–77.
4. Edward Arber, *Transcript of the Registers of the Company of Stationers of London, 1554–1640* (London, 1873), vol. 2, pp. 367–73.

5. Robert Lemon, ed., *Calendar of State Papers, Domestic Series* (London, 1856), June 1, 1580, p. 658.
6. Abraham Fleming, *A Bright Burning Beacon, Forewarning All Wise Virgins to Trim Their Lampes Against the Comming of the Bridegroome* (London, 1580), pp. 39–40.
7. Freke to Burghley, April 19, 1581, Lansdowne MS, vol. 33, no. 26, fols. 13–14, BL.
8. Thomas Fuller, *Church History of Britain* (Oxford, 1845), vol. 5, pp. 62–70. Fuller's source for the wife-beating allegation was Robert Baillie, a Scottish Presbyterian of the 1640s hostile to Brownism.
9. Stephen Bredwell, *The Rasing of the Foundations of Brownisme* (London, 1588), "Epistle Dedicatorie" and pp. 134, 138, and 140. Bredwell coined the epithet Troublechurch Browne (p. 112).
10. Property of the Brownes: Postmortem inquisition of Sir Anthony Browne (1591), C 142/229/126, NAK, and his will, PROB/11/76, NAK. Browne and the Pickerings: *Pickering v. Andrewes*, E 133/7/1036 and E 134/35Eliz/East5, NAK. Wealth of the Barrows: Postmortem inquisition of Thomas Barrow (1591), C 142/230/12, NAK. Barrow's income: Gillingham estate accounts, GIL 2/55/1–12, Norfolk RO. Barrow's father, Thomas, as a JP: A. Hassell Smith, *County and Court: Government and Politics in Norfolk, 1558–1603* (Oxford, 1974), pp. 104–5, 203, and 207.
11. Champlin Burrage, *The Early English Dissenters in the Light of Recent Research, 1550–1641* (Cambridge, UK, 1912), vol. 1, pp. 94–117. Also, F. Ives Cater, "Robert Browne's Ancestors and Descendants," *Transactions of the Congregational Historical Society* 2 (1905–6), pp. 151–59; Alan Rogers, ed., *William Browne's Town: The Stamford Hall Book*, vol 1, *1465–1492* (Stamford, UK, 2005), pp. i-x; and S. T. Bindoff, ed., *History of Parliament: The House of Commons, 1509–1558* (London, 1982), vol. 1, pp. 131–32 and 521–22.
12. Beacon: J. Goring and J. Wake, *Northamptonshire Lieutenancy Papers and Other Documents, 1580–1614* (Gateshead, UK, 1975), p. 20. Pickerings: James A. Winn, *John Dryden and His World* (New Haven, CT, 1987), pp. 2–12 and 516–18.
13. H. C. Porter, *Reformation and Reaction in Tudor Cambridge* (Cambridge, UK, 1958), pp. 107–9. Corpus fellows: Lists in Robert Masters and John Lamb, *History of the College of Corpus Christi* (Cambridge, UK, 1831), collated with biographies in J. A. Venn, *Alumni Cantabrigienses.*
14. Porter, *Reformation and Reaction*, chap. 6.
15. John Field and Thomas Wilcox, *The First Admonition: A View of Popish Abuses* (1572), in *Puritan Manifestoes*, ed. W. H. Frere and C. E. Douglas (London, 1907), p. 21.
16. Robert Browne, *A True and Short Declaration* (1583), in *The Writings of Robert Harrison and Robert Browne*, ed. Albert Peel and Leland H. Carlson (London, 1953), p. 397.
17. R. A. Houlbrooke, *The Letter Book of John Parkhurst, Bishop of Norwich* (Norwich, UK, 1975), letter of July 1573, pp. 196–97.
18. Covenant of Asa: George Garnett, ed., *Vindiciae Contra Tyrannos* (Cambridge, UK, 2003), pp. 21–37; Lloyd E. Berry, ed., *John Stubbs's Gaping Gulf* (Charlottesville, VA, 1968), pp. 16–20; Peel and Carlson, *Writings of Harrison and Browne*, pp. 161–62 and 405. Mornay and the *Vindiciae:* Quentin Skinner, *The Foundations of Modern Political Thought* (Cambridge, UK, 1978), vol. 2, pp. 304–6. Bradford on Mornay: William Bradford, *A Dialogue or Third Conference*, ed. Charles Deane (Boston, MA, 1870), pp. 5–6. Brewster's book-

shelves: H. M. Dexter, "Elder William Brewster's Library," *PMHS,* 2nd ser., 5 (1889–90), pp. 37–85.

19. Mornay, Sidney, and Walsingham: *Mémoires de Madame Mornay* (Paris, 1868), pp. 118–19. Mornay and the idea of Protestant colonies: Hugues Daussy, *Les Huguenots et le roi: Le combat politique de Philippe Duplessis-Mornay, 1572–1600* (Geneva, 2002), pp. 87–91 and 282–84.
20. Philippe Duplessis-Mornay, *A Notable Treatise of the Church,* trans. John Field (London, 1579), chap. 10.
21. Jean Morély, *Traicté de la discipline et police chrestienne* (1562; fac. ed., Geneva, 1968), p. 65. Morély as a refugee: Philippe Denis and Jean Rott, *Jean Morély et l'utopie d'une democratie dans l'église* (Geneva, 1993), esp. pp. 73–91.
22. Morély and Ramus: Robert M. Kingdon, *Geneva and the Consolidation of the French Protestant Movement, 1564–1572* (Geneva, 1967), pp. 101–10. Ramus and Sidney: Walter J. Ong, *Ramus, Method, and the Decay of Dialogue: From the Art of Discourse to the Art of Reason* (Cambridge, MA, 1958), p. 302. Browne and Morély: For the closest similarities, see Morély, *Traicté,* pp. 23–27, and compare Peel and Carlson, *Writings of Harrison and Browne,* pp. 161–66.
23. Walsham: K. M. Dodd, ed., *The Field Book of Walsham-le-Willows, 1577* (Ipswich, UK, 1974); D. P. Dymond, "The Parish of Walsham-le-Willows: Two Elizabethan Surveys and Their Medieval Background," *Proceedings of the Suffolk Institute of Archaeology* 33 (1976); Bacon MSS, 4109 and 4121, summaries at SROB; Martineau Papers, D/190 and FL 646/3/18, SROB.
24. John Phillips, *The Wonderfull Worke of God Shewed upon a Chylde, Whose Name Is William Withers* (London, 1581).
25. Robert Harrison, *A Treatise of the Church,* in *Writings of Harrison and Browne,* ed. Peel and Carlson, p. 47.
26. S. H. A. Hervey, *Rushbrooke Parish Registers, 1567–1850* (Woodbridge, UK, 1903), pp. 143–46 and 207–24.
27. C2/1, fol. 6, SROB, Book of Remembrances and Orders for ye Government of Bury.
28. Margaret Statham, ed., *Accounts of the Feoffees of the Town Lands of Bury St. Edmunds, 1569–1622* (Woodbridge, UK, 2003), p. 22.
29. Lansdowne MS 27, no. 70, BL.
30. John Craig, *Reformation Politics and Polemics: The Growth of Protestantism in East Anglian Market Towns, 1500–1610* (Aldershot, UK, 2001), pp. 78–108.
31. Fuller, *Church History of Britain,* vol. 5, p. 64; and Lansdowne MS 33, nos. 67 and 20, BL.
32. Peel and Carlson, *Writings of Harrison and Browne,* p. 424.
33. St. Mary's: Samuel Tymms, *A Historie of the Church of St. Marie, Bury St. Edmunds* (Bury, UK, 1845). Royal arms: H. M. Cautley, *Royal Arms and Commandments in Our Churches* (Ipswich, UK, 1934), pp. 36–39; and Stanley J. Wearing, *Post-Reformation Royal Arms in Norfolk Churches* (Norfolk, UK, 1944), pp. 8–16.
34. Revelation 2:19–20.
35. John Strype, *Annals of the Reformation* (Oxford, 1824), vol. 3, pt. 1, pp. 176–77; Lansdowne MS 36, no. 65, BL; and Albert Peel, ed., *Tracts Ascribed to Richard Bancroft* (Cambridge, UK, 1953), p. xviii.
36. Peel and Carlson, *Writings of Harrison and Browne,* especially pp. 69–74.

37. J. S. Cockburn, *A History of English Assizes, 1558–1714* (Cambridge, UK, 1972), pp. 202–6.
38. On Coppin, see Lansdowne MS 27, no. 28, and MS 38, no. 64, BL.
39. William Bradford, *A Dialogue; or, The Sum of a Conference Between Some Young Men Born in New England and Sundry Ancient Men That Came out of Holland and Old England, 1648,* in Alexander Young, *Chronicles of the Pilgrim Fathers* (Boston, 1844; repr., Baltimore, 1974), pp. 427–28.
40. Rougham parish register: Microfilm, SROB. Will of Sir Robert Jermyn: Hervey, *Rushbrooke Parish Registers,* pp. 143–52; and PROB/11/123, NAK.
41. The Barrows were very close to the events at Walsham le Willows and Bury. Their estates included not only the manor of Westhorpe, a few miles from Walsham, but also a group of manors clustered around the town of Sudbury, within the same archdeaconry.
42. Browne, Barrow, and Separatists in Norfolk and Suffolk: Matthew Reynolds, *Godly Reformers and Their Opponents in Early Modern England: Religion in Norwich, c. 1560–1643* (Woodbridge, UK, 2005), pp. 91–97. For the chain of influence between Browne and Barrow, see Patrick Collinson, "Separation in and out of the Church: The Consistency of Barrow and Greenwood," *Journal of the United Reformed Church History Society* 5, no. 5 (Nov. 1994), pp. 243–46.

Chapter Five: Men and Women of the Clay

1. Dwight B. Heath, ed., *Mourt's Relation: A Journal of the Pilgrims at Plymouth* (Bedford, MA, 1963), p. 30. On the authorship of *Mourt's Relation,* see Heath's introduction, pp. x-xiv.
2. Joseph Hunter, *Collections Concerning the Church or Congregation of Protestant Separatists Formed at Scrooby* (London, 1854), pp. ix-x.
3. Ronald A. Marchant, *The Puritans and the Church Courts in the Diocese of York, 1500–1642* (London, 1960).
4. The population estimate is based on the number of people taking Holy Communion at Easter 1603, from Archdeaconry Records, Presentment Bills, Easter 1603, AN/PB 294/1 224–273, U Nott.
5. Steve Hindle, *The State and Social Change in Early Modern England, 1550–1640* (Basingstoke, UK, 2002), pp. 38–54; Peter Bowden, "Agricultural Prices, Farm Profits, and Rents," in *The Agrarian History of England and Wales,* ed. Joan Thirsk (Cambridge, UK, 1967), vol. 4, pp. 595–99; and Keith Wrightson, *Earthly Necessities: Economic Lives in Early Modern England* (New Haven, CT, 2000), pp. 182–94.
6. E. G. Smith et al., *Geology of the Country Around East Retford, Worksop, and Gainsborough* (London, 1973), esp. pp. 1–4 and 215–32; and Robert Van de Noort and Stephen Ellis, eds., *Wetland Heritage of the Humberhead Levels: An Archaeological Survey* (Kingston upon Hull, UK, 1997), pp. 7–12 and 81–88. Also, D. V. Fowkes, "The Progress of Agrarian Change in Nottinghamshire, c. 1720–1830" (Ph.D. diss., Liverpool University, 1971), pp. 25 and 192–211.
7. David Marcombe, *English Small Town Life: Retford, 1520–1642* (Nottingham, UK, 1993), p. 102.
8. Extract of a subsidy roll for Bassetlaw (1593), Newcastle Papers, Ne S 32, U Nott; and Bassetlaw lay subsidy roll (1600), E 179/160/252, NAK.

9. Meadows: John Norden, *The Surveyor's Dialogue* (London, 1607), bk. 4, pp. 192–95. The Ings: Drainage map of 1769, LA 2 S M.P. 1058, NAN. Rents: Holles estate accounts in miscellany books of Sir John Holles, second Earl of Clare, Portland Papers, PWv4 and PWv5, U Nott.
10. On Gainsborough, see Richard Bernard, *Plaine Evidences* (London, 1610), p. 20; C. W. Foster, ed., *The Parish Registers of Gainsborough* (Horncastle, UK, 1920); Lawrence Stone, *The Family, Sex, and Marriage in England, 1500–1800* (London, 1979), pp. 388–90; and national statistics in E. A. Wrigley and R. S. Schofield, *The Population History of England, 1541–1871: A Reconstruction* (Cambridge, MA, 1981).
11. Proceedings: Lincoln Episcopal visitation journals, Aug. 6, 1607, Vj 19, fol. 52–53, LAO. On illegitimacy: Hindle, *The State and Social Change*, pp. 185–88; and Michael J. Braddick, *State Formation in Early Modern England, c. 1550–1700* (Cambridge, UK, 2000), pp. 143–45.
12. Family trees of the Robinsons and Whites: M. L. Holman, "The Robinson Family," *American Genealogist* 17, no. 4 (April 1941), pp. 207–15; Walter H. Burgess, *John Robinson, Pastor of the Pilgrim Fathers* (London, 1920), pp. 10–26; and Robert S. Wakefield, "The Family of Alexander White of Sturton Le Steeple," *Mayflower Descendant* 43, no. 2 (July 1993), pp. 183–86. Sturton generally: Robert Thoroton, *The Antiquities of Nottinghamshire* (1790–96; fac. ed., Wakefield, UK, 1972), vol. 3, pp. 298–99, and 399–400.
13. J. E. B. Gover, Allen Mawer, and F. W. Stenton, *The Place-Names of Nottinghamshire* (Cambridge, UK, 1940), p. 24.
14. Property of the Whites: Postmortem inquisitions on Alexander White, July 10, 1596, C 142/245/18, NAK; and Charles White, Sept. 3, 1634, C 142/503/25, NAK. Coal mines: Will of Charles White, March 1, 1634, Archdeaconry Wills, East Retford, NAN; and Fillingham of Syerston Papers, DDFM 80/1–13, NAN.
15. Parliamentary survey of Scrooby Manor in 1648: "Assessment of the Manor of Scrooby," Feb. 11, 1648, Ga 11,850, Galway of Serlby Papers, U Nott (quotation from fol. 3). Layout of Scrooby: "A Map of the Parish of Scrooby in the County of Nottingham, 1776," DDRC 14/22, NAN. Will of Richard Torre: Proved May 25, 1602, Archdeaconry Wills, East Retford, NAN.
16. Minutes of the Nottinghamshire Quarter Sessions, East Retford, July 19, 1605, and Jan. 16, 1607, C/QSM/1/66/1–3, NAN.
17. On the Idle valley before the railways, see C. W. Hatfield, *Historical Notices of Doncaster* (Doncaster, UK, 1866), from articles in the *Doncaster Gazette* (1862–65), esp. pp. 18–25 and 92–94. Also, John Raine, *The History and Antiquities of the Parish of Blyth* (Westminster, UK, 1860), pp. 1–2; and John Holland, *The History, Antiquities, and Description of the Town and Parish of Worksop* (Sheffield, UK, 1826), pp. 5–10.
18. T. W. Beastall, *Tickhill: Portrait of an English Country Town* (Doncaster, UK, 1995), pp. 38–39; and Diana Newton, *The Making of the Jacobean Regime* (Woodbridge, UK, 2005).
19. William Bradford's family: W. B. Browne, "Ancestry of the Bradfords of Austerfield," *NEHGR* 83 (1929), pp. 439–64, and 84 (1930), pp. 5–16. Austerfield taxpayers: Subsidy roll, Stratforth and Tickhill Wapentakes (1599), DZ/MZ/85/HP/32/1, Doncaster Archives. Layout of Austerfield: Depositions regarding common lands of Austerfield in 1658, including testimony by William Bradford's stepbrother Robert Briggs, E 134/1658/East34, NAK.
20. Austerfield survey of 1608, LR 2/229, fols. 172–85, NAK.

21. Business relationships: *Noble v. Downes et al.* (1596–98), REQ 2/245/46, NAK. Accounts, with details of crops and cattle: Rent book of Robert Eyre of Blyth and Austerfield, 1593–1602, Clifton Papers, CL A 37, U Nott.
22. Remarkably, the last remaining open-field-farming village in England can still be found about twenty miles from Scrooby, at Laxton in Nottinghamshire. Thanks to this, and the excellent state of the archives relating to the village, we have a very clear picture of open field farming as the Pilgrims would have known it, in two fine books about Laxton: C. S. Orwin and C. S. L. Orwin, *The Open Fields* (Oxford, 1954); and J. V. Beckett, *A History of Laxton* (Oxford, 1989).
23. For the property of the Frobishers, see postmortem inquisition on Francis Frobisher, Sept. 8, 1604, C 142/283/95, NAK. Also, Merchant Taylors' Company, "Register of Apprentice Bindings, 1606–1609," MS 34038/5, p. 112, Guildhall Library.
24. On estate plans, see "G. Stow's Estate at Sturton High Steeple in Nottinghamshire" (1762), Fairbanks Collection, F/STU 1L, 2L, 3L, Sheffield Archives.
25. Sturton fracas of 1594: *Lassells v. Quippe* (1594), STAC 5/L36/16 and 7/25/4, NAK. Lassells family: Surtees Society, *Visitations of Yorkshire and Northumberland in A.D. 1575* (Durham, UK, 1932), pp. 22–24.
26. The manuscript records relating to Sturton are very extensive, with the sad exception of the loss of the parish register. Besides wills, the archives fall into four main categories: Star Chamber litigation, lawsuits in the Courts of Chancery and Exchequer, rolls of taxpayers, and papers from the ecclesiastical courts at York and Retford. The British Library also has a seventeenth-century manuscript history of the Thornhagh family, Add. MS 30997. Containing an especially rich mass of detail, the principal Star Chamber cases at NAK, besides those cited above, are *Lassells v. Lassells* (1594), STAC 5/L33/32; *Thornhagh v. Lassells* (1601?), STAC 5/T36/30; *Thornhagh v. Lassells et al.* (1580), STAC 5/T35/19; *Williamson v. Lassells* (1608), STAC 8/296/17; and *Reyner v. Lassells* (1604), STAC 8/251/30. The principal Exchequer case is *Cherbery et al. v Thornhagh* (1603), E134/1Jas1/Mich14. The Chancery cases are *Lassells v. Thornhagh* (c. 1575?), C3/112/15; and *Thornhagh v. Lassells* (1570s?), C3/181/33. The taxpayer rolls can be found within the E190 series at NAK. Sturton also possesses an excellent village history: John Ford, ed., *The Town on the Street: The Story of the Nottinghamshire Village of Sturton-le-Steeple* (Retford, UK, 1975), based on the work of Samuel Ingham, the village schoolmaster between 1875 and 1920.
27. On Lassells and Biggs, see libel actions (1605) between Biggs, Lassells, and Ostler, *Bigges v. Lascelles* and *Lascelles v. Ostler*, AN/LB 220/6/1, AN/LB 220/6/4 (quotation on fol. 6), and AN/LB 220/6/5, Cause Papers (defamation), Archdeaconry Records, U Nott.
28. *Dickens v. Sturton* (1597–98), HC CP. 1597/II, BI (York).
29. J. Gairdner and R. H. Brodie, *Letters and Papers, Foreign and Domestic, of the Reign of Henry VIII* (London, 1895), vol. 14, pt. 2, p. 359 and vol. 15, pp. 341, 520, and 590–91. Also Holland, *History, Antiquities*, p. 170.
30. *Thornhagh v. Lassells* (1601), CP. H.42 and CP. H.48, BI (York).
31. On Nottinghamshire, see J. E. Neale, *The Elizabethan House of Commons* (Harmondsworth, UK, 1963), pp. 57–63; Alison Wall, "Patterns in English Politics, 1558–1625," *Historical Journal* 38, no. 4 (Dec. 1988), p. 954; and a splendid book about the Talbot/Stanhope feud by two local historians, Beryl Cobbing and Pamela Priestland, *Sir Thomas Stanhope of Shelford: Local Life in Elizabethan Times* (Nottingham, UK, 2003).

Chapter Six: The Making of a Pilgrim

1. Henry David Thoreau, *Cape Cod* (1855; Princeton, NJ, 2004), p. 22.
2. *Brewster v. Ward* (defamation) (1587?), AN/LB 217/2/9/1–2, quotation from fol. 1, Cause Papers, Archdeaconry Records, U Nott.
3. New England Society in the City of New York, *Plymouth Church Records, 1620–1859* (New York, 1920–23), vol. 1, pp. 78–81.
4. Hodgkinson Transcripts, vol. 1, fols.79 and 84, entries for April 29 and May 8, 1592, M461, NAN.
5. C/QSM 1/66/1–5, with the Revell case dated July 17, 1607, NAN.
6. John Smyth, *Paralleles, Censures, Observations* (1609), in *The Works of John Smyth*, ed. W. T. Whitley (Cambridge, UK, 1915), vol. 2, p. 371.
7. Church court cases: Journal of the Archdeaconry of Nottingham, Sept. 1607–Jan. 1608, AN/A 24/11 and AN/A 24/12/2, Archdeaconry Records, U Nott. Retford magistrates, Oct. 9, 1607, and Jan. 15, 1608, C/QSM 1/66/5 and 67/1, NAN. Wise women and mad dogs: Whitley, *Works of Smyth*, vol. 1, pp. 93–96.
8. J. A. Sharpe, *Defamation and Sexual Slander in Early Modern England: The Church Courts at York* (York, UK, 1980), pp. 7–9.
9. James Kelly, *That Damn'd Thing Called Honour: Duelling in Ireland, 1570–1860* (Cork, 1995), pp. 19–24.
10. Charles White in 1614: HMC, *Report on Manuscripts of Lord Middleton* (London, 1911), pp. 178–79. Gentry status: J. P. Cooper, "Ideas of Gentility in Early Modern England," in *Land, Men, and Beliefs: Studies in Early Modern History* (London, 1983); and Felicity Heal and Clive Holmes, *The Gentry in England and Wales, 1500–1700* (Basingstoke, UK, 1994), pp. 7–29.
11. Sir John Ferne, The *Blazon of Gentrie . . . for the Instruction of All Gentlemen Bearers of Armes, Whome and None Other This Work Concerneth* (London, 1586). My quotations are from the dedicatory epistle and from the first part ("The Glory of Generositie"), pp. 3, 7, 13–14, and 89–96.
12. Contested real estate at Doncaster: Brewster's Chancery lawsuit, c. 1580, C2/Eliz/B31/1, NAK. Dispute with the archbishop's widow: *Brewster v. Sandys* (1588/9?), C2/Eliz/B14/11, NAK. Brewster's ancestry: John G. Hunt, "The Mother of Elder William Brewster of the *Mayflower*," *NEHGR*, Oct. 1970, pp. 250–54. John Smythe of Hull: A 1581 lawsuit regarding unpaid customs duties, E134/23Eliz/East4, NAK; and Exchequer port books for Hull, E 190/308/1 (for 1581–82) and E 190/308/4 (for 1583–84), NAK.
13. T. A. Walker, ed., *A Biographical Register of Peterhouse Men, Part II, 1574–1616* (Cambridge, UK, 1930), pp. 71–73.
14. Stefano Guazzo, *The Civile Conversation*, trans. George Pettie and Bartholomew Young (London, 1586), pp. 82, 84, and 91. Bradford on Brewster: See note 3, above.
15. Sturton tax records: "Extract of a Subsidy Roll of Bassetlaw "(1593), NE S 32, Newcastle Papers, U Nott. Quotations: Sir Thomas Smith, *De Republica Anglorum*, ed. Mary Dewar (Cambridge, UK, 1982), p. 72. For an excellent concise account of Elizabethan civic republicanism, including a list of recent scholarly literature, see Michael P. Winship, "Godly Republicanism and the Origins of the Massachusetts Polity," *William and Mary Quarterly*, 3rd ser., 63, no. 3 (July 2006), pp. 427–30.

16. William Nicholson, ed., *The Remains of Edmund Grindal, D.D.* (Cambridge, UK, 1843), pp. 325–26.
17. "Visitation Book of Archdeacon Lowth," 1587, AN/PB 292/1, Archdeaconry Records, U Nott.
18. *Plymouth Church Records,* vol. 1, p. 139.
19. Questionnaires of 1596–98: Steve Hindle, "Dearth, Fasting, and Alms: The Campaign for General Hospitality in Late Elizabethan England," *Past and Present,* no. 172 (Aug. 2001), pp. 44–46, 51–54, and 61–73. Responses by Nottinghamshire churchwardens: Presentment bills (Easter 1598), AN/PB/292/7, fols. 3–72 (Scrooby is fol. 46), Archdeaconry Records, U Nott. Brewster's treatment: Hodgkinson Transcripts, vol. 2, fol. 205, M461, NAN.
20. Lansdowne MS, vol. 27, no. 26, fols. 48–49, BL.
21. Hull: Port books, in note 11, above; E. Gillett and K. A. MacMahon, *A History of Hull* (Oxford, 1980), pp. 116–28, 143–44, and 148–50; and Claire Cross, *Urban Magistrates and Ministers: Religion in Hull and Leeds from the Reformation to the Civil War* (York, UK, 1985), pp. 14–16 and 17–18. Godly republics at Hull and elsewhere: Paul Slack, *From Reformation to Improvement: Public Welfare in Early Modern England* (Oxford, 1999), pp. 30–36.
22. Simon Adams, "A Puritan Crusade? The Composition of the Earl of Leicester's Expedition to the Netherlands, 1585–86," in *Leicester and the Court: Essays on Elizabethan Politics* (Manchester, UK, 2002), pp. 176–95. Adams's 1973 Oxford Ph.D. thesis, "The Protestant Cause" (BLL D0419/74, Bodleian Library), remains an essential source. Except where stated, the following account of events at Flushing is based on the volumes of Sophie Crawford Lomas, ed., *Calendar of State Papers, Foreign Series,* vols. 19 and 20 (London, 1916 and 1921), covering the period 1584–86; Jan Den Tex, *Oldenbarnevelt,* trans. R. B. Powell (London, 1973), vol. 1, pp. 37–73; and Jonathan Israel, *The Dutch Republic: Its Rise, Greatness, and Fall, 1477–1806* (Oxford, 1995), pp. 220–30.
23. Thomas Digges, *A Briefe Report of the Militarie Services Done in the Low Countries by the Erle of Leicester* (London, 1587), p. 6.
24. Harleian MS 285, nos. 99, 102, and 126, BL.
25. Jermyn to Davison, Aug. 25, 1585, Tanner MSS, vol. 78, fol. 73, Bodleian.
26. Briefing paper possibly by Davison: "Reasons to Move Her Majestie to Aid the Lowe Countries" (1585?), Harleian MS 285, no. 48, BL. Sidney's church: HMC, *De L'Isle and Dudley Papers* (London, 1936), vol. 3, pp. 372–74.
27. J. D. Bangs, "The Pilgrims and Other English in Leiden Records: Some New Pilgrim Documents," *NEHGR,* pp. 200–201.
28. Jan van Dorsten et al., *Sir Philip Sidney: 1586 and the Creation of a Legend* (Leiden, 1986), p. 29.
29. Digges, *Briefe Report,* p. 23.
30. Original documents transcribed in Edward Arber, ed., *The Story of the Pilgrim Fathers* (London, 1897), pp. 79–86.

Chapter Seven: The Entrails of the King

1. James VI of Scotland and I of England, *Basilikon Doron* (1603 ed.), in *The Basilicon Doron of King James VI,* ed. James Craigie (Edinburgh, 1944), p. 21.
2. James I's autopsy: Two accounts, in the manuscript memoirs of Sir Simonds D'Ewes

(Harleian MS 646, fol. 77, BL) and in John Nichols, *The Progresses of King James I* (London, 1828), vol. 4, p. 1037. James's health and final illness: Frederick Holmes, *The Sickly Stuarts: The Medical Downfall of a Dynasty* (London, 2005), pp. 49–82. Case notes: Latin text of Mayerne's manuscript notes of 1623, in Norman Moore, *The History of the Study of Medicine in the British Isles* (Oxford, 1908), pp. 162–76.

3. Speech of March 21, 1610, in *King James VI and I: Selected Writings*, ed. Neil Rhodes et al. (Aldershot, UK, 2003), p. 330.
4. James I, *A Meditation Upon the Lord's Prayer* (London, 1619), pp. 14–15; and Craigie, *Basilicon Doron*, pp. 15–17 and 77–82.
5. Speech of May 1607, *Journal of the House of Commons* (1802), pp. 366–68. Jacobean kingship and the language of health and disease: Linda Levy Peck, *Court Patronage and Corruption in Early Stuart England* (London, 1993), pp. 208–15.
6. Richard Bancroft, *Daungerous Positions and Proceedings* (London, 1593), pp. 120–38.
7. Christopher Haigh, "The Taming of Reformation: Preachers, Pastors, and Parishioners in Elizabethan and Early Stuart England," *History* 85, no. 820 (Oct. 2000).
8. Ann Uhry Abrams, *The Pilgrims and Pocahontas: Rival Myths of American Origin* (Boulder, Colo.: Westview Press, 1999), pp. 276–79.
9. William Barlow, *The Summe and Substance of the Conference* (London, 1604), p. 83.
10. Canons of 1604: Archbishop's Commission on Canon Law, *The Canon Law of the Church of England* (London, 1947), pp. 71–78. Text and commentary: Gerald Bray, *The Anglican Canons, 1529–1947* (Woodbridge, UK, 1998), esp. pp. liv-lxi, 276–81, and 408–16 (duties of churchwardens).
11. M. S. Guiseppi, ed., *HMC Salisbury (Cecil) Manuscripts* (London, 1938), vol. 17, pp. 5–6, 39, 46, 66, 73, 83, 92, 104–6.
12. G. W. Marshall, ed., *The Registers of Worksop, Co. Nottingham, 1558–1771* (Guildford, UK, 1894), pp. 109–22.
13. G. P. V. Akrigg, ed., *Letters of King James VI and I* (Berkeley, CA, 1984), p. 3.
14. London College of Physicians, *Pharmacopoia Londinensis* (London, 1618).
15. Joseph Quercetanus (alias Du Chesne), *The Practise of Chymicall, and Hermeticall Physicke, for the Preservation of Health*, trans. Thomas Timme (London, 1605), chiefly pt. 1, chap. 15, from which my quotations come. Chemical medicine: Allen G. Debus, *The English Paracelsians* (London, 1965), pp. 21–39 and 57–89; and Hugh Trevor-Roper, *Europe's Physician: The Various Life of Sir Theodore de Mayerne* (New Haven, CT, 2006).
16. Jacob Soll, "Healing the Body Politic: French Royal Doctors, History, and the Birth of a Nation, 1560–1634," *Renaissance Quarterly* 55, no. 4 (Winter 2000), pp. 1267–81.
17. Robert Burton, *The Anatomy of Melancholy*, 2nd ed. (Oxford, 1624), p. 525.
18. Quoted in Marie Axton, *The Queen's Two Bodies: Drama and the Elizabethan Succession* (London, 1977), p. 144, and chap. 9. Jacobean government: Diana Newton, *The Making of the Jacobean Regime* (Woodbridge, UK, 2005), pp. 98–118.
19. Gypsies: David Masson, ed., The *Register of the Privy Council of Scotland* (Edinburgh, 1877–98), vol. 7, p. 713, and vol. 8, p. 305. The Graemes: C. W. Russell and J. P. Prendergast, *Calendar of State Papers Relating to Ireland, 1608–1610* (London, 1874), pp. xcv–ciii. Exiled ministers: Bannatyne Club, *Original Letters Relating to the Ecclesiastical Affairs of Scotland*, vol. 1, *1603–1614* (Edinburgh, 1851), pp. xxii–xxvi and 28–31; and David Calderwood, *History of the Kirk of Scotland* (Edinburgh, 1842–49), vol. 6, pp. 590–91.

20. Trevor-Roper, *Europe's Physician,* pp. 171–73; and Thomas Russel, *Diacatholicon Aureum* (London, 1602).

Chapter Eight: Disobedience and Contempt

1. The chapel and the mansion at Haughton belonged to the Holles family, whose most famous Jacobean member was Sir John Holles, first Earl of Clare (*ODNB*). His family and the Helwyses: A. C. Wood, ed. *Memorials of the Holles Family* (London, 1937), p. 45; and Elwes of Roxby, in *Burke's Landed Gentry,* 18th ed. Wills: William Elwes (1557) and Edmund Hellwis (1590), York Wills, BI (York); and will of Jeffrey Ellwes (1616), PROB 11/127, NAK. In 1568, Edmund Helwys became the Crown's escheator (or collector of feudal dues owed to the queen) for the counties of Northamptonshire and Rutland: E 112/32/50, NAK. Anti-Catholic tract: Edward Hellwis, *A Marvell Deciphered* (London, 1589). The names Edward and Edmund were sometimes used interchangeably.
2. Quoted in Walter H. Burgess, *John Robinson, Pastor of the Pilgrim Fathers* (London, 1920), p. 82.
3. Brewster at Scrooby: Ronald A. Marchant, *The Puritans and the Church Courts in the Diocese of York, 1500–1642* (London, 1960), pp. 142–46. Thomas Helwys: *Beresford et al. v. Helwys* (1594), C2/Eliz/B16/48, NAK; *Green v. Elwayes* (defamation), n.d, but c. 1590, AN/LB 245/2/23, and presentment bill, Bilborough (1598), AN/PB 292/6/12, Archdeaconry Records, U Nott. Assault: Sessions at Nottingham, Jan. 9 and April 16, 1604, C/QSM 1/66 1–2, NAN.
4. Sir Gervase Helwys: MON 1/15/13, July 13, 1609, LAO; *ODNB; Lists of Sheriffs for England and Wales from the Earliest Times to A.D. 1831* (London, 1898), p. 80, NAK; and the family monument in Saundby Church, Nottinghamshire. Sir Richard Williamson and Nick Fuller: Will of John Williamson (1575), PROB/11/58, NAK; personal communications from Theresa Tom, archivist of Gray's Inn, London, Aug. 2006; and Wilfrid R. Prest, *The Rise of the Barristers: A Social History of the English Bar, 1590–1640* (Oxford, 1986), p. 404. In 1609, Williamson's daughter married one of the Culverwells, the Puritan family in question: Canon A. R. Maddison, ed., *Lincolnshire Pedigrees* (London, 1902), vol. 1, p. 285, and vol. 3, pp. 1085–87.
5. Mark Girouard, *Robert Smythson and the Elizabethan Country House* (London, 1983), pp. 110–15.
6. Wood, *Memorials,* pp. 90–92.
7. Property inventory: Postmortem inquisition of Elizabeth, Countess of Shrewsbury, Dec. 1609, C 142/312, NAK. Talbot at Bawtry: LR 2/229, fols. 172–85, NAK.
8. For the Talbot/Bowes correspondence of Dec. 1603–Jan. 1604, see Talbot Papers, vol. K, fols. 89 and 173, and vol. M, fol. 166, LPL.
9. Normanby: Girouard, *Robert Smythson,* pp. 141–42. Lord Sheffield: Sheffield Papers, esp. B/1, June 16, 1591, LAO; and *ODNB.*
10. M. S. Guiseppi, ed., *HMC Salisbury (Cecil) Manuscripts* (London, 1938), vol. 17, pp. 35, 65, 78–79, and 108–9.
11. J. Raine, ed., *The Correspondence of Dr. Matthew Hutton, Archbishop of York* (London, 1843), pp. 171–75 and 247–48; and Diana Newton, *The Making of the Jacobean Regime* (Woodbridge, UK, 2005), pp. 84–95.

12. Chancery act book, AB 14/1599–1605, fols. 371–78, BI (York); and Marchant, *Puritans and Church Courts,* pp. 296–312.
13. Stephen Wright, *The Early English Baptists, 1603–1649* (Woodbridge, UK, 2006), pp. 13–44.
14. Account books, 1580–1609 and 1585–1604, archives of Christ's College; college register, 1590–1698, and college order book, 1569–1626, Muniment Room of Corpus Christi College.
15. *Dynnys and Gosse v. Hollingworth et al.* (1604), STAC 8/121/12, NAK; City of Lincoln Common Council book, 1599–1638, entries for 1600–1603 and then (Beck's drunkenness) fols. 61–62, Li/1/1/4, LAO; List and Index Society, *Heard Before the King: Registers of Petitions to James I, 1603–1616* (Kew, UK, 2006), p. 19, July 18, 1603.
16. Norwich: Sir John Harington, *A Supplie or Addicion to the Catalogue of Bishops to the Yeare 1608,* ed. R. H. Miller (Potomac, MD, 1979), pp. 127–28. St. Andrew's, Norwich: Thomas Newhouse, *Certaine Sermons* (London, 1614), "Epistle Dedicatory." Newhouse was the parish minister at St. Andrew's from 1602 to 1611, and previously a fellow of Christ's College, Cambridge, next above John Smyth.
17. Registry guard book, UA CUR 4/2, Cambridge University Archives.
18. Ursinus: Zacharias Ursinus, *The Summe of the Christian Religion,* trans. Henry Parry (London, 1595), pp. 265–70 and 765–67. Robinson's essay on faith: John Robinson, *New Essayes or Observations Divine and Morall* (Amsterdam, 1628), pp. 73–83. Robinson's wit: William Hubbard, *A General History of New England from the Discovery to 1680* (Boston, 1848), pp. 42–43. Hubbard began writing it in 1682.
19. John Smyth, *A Patterne of True Prayer* (1605), in *The Works of John Smyth,* ed. W. T. Whitley (Cambridge, UK, 1915), vol. 1, pp. 80–82.
20. Bishop Chaderton's correspondence, B/2/19–20, LAO; and Lincoln Episcopal court book (1605–7), Cj 16, fols. 32 and 97, LAO.
21. Talbot Papers, MS 709, LPL; and Walter Burgess, *John Smyth the Se-Baptist, Thomas Helwys, and the First Baptist Church in England* (London, 1911), pp. 170–71.
22. Incidents in 1607: Retford: Marchant, *Puritans and Church Courts,* p. 157; Gainsborough: Lincoln Episcopal visitation journals, Vj 19, fols. 52–53, Aug. 6, 1607, LAO; Torksey: C. W. Foster, *The State of the Church in the Reigns of Elizabeth and James I* (Lincoln, UK, 1926), vol. 1, pp. lxxvii—lxxviii. The clergyman who gave the "Sodomites" sermon was a protégé of Sir Richard Williamson, who appointed him vicar of Scawby in Lincolnshire. Also, concerning Gainsborough: Jenny Vernon's essay in *Gainsborough Old Hall,* ed. Phillip Lindley (Lincoln, UK, 1991), pp. 27–30.
23. Worksop priory churchwardens' accounts, file PR 22765, NAN.
24. The Drews of Everton: Robert Thoroton, *The Antiquities of Nottinghamshire* (1790–96; fac. ed., Wakefield, UK, 1972), vol. 3, p. 322; presentment bill, Everton (1607), AN/PB/2/227 and AN/PB/294/2/62, archdeaconry records, U Nott; wills of Richard Drew of Harwell Hall (1617) and Robert Drew of Scaftworth (1619), archdeaconry wills, East Retford, NAN; Everton Parish register, microfilm, NAN; and Hodgkinson Transcripts, vol. 2, fol. 306, Oct. 10, 1609, NAN.
25. Many cases relating to Gainsborough survive, but especially relevant are *Hickman v. Williamson, Noble, and Aston et al.* (1610), STAC 8/167/13, and *Williamson v. Hickman* (1610), STAC 8/293/20, NAK.

26. Toby Matthew: Harington, *Supplie or Addicion to the Catalogue of Bishops,* pp. 176–77. Sermons and the archbishop's itinerary: *The Diary and Journal of His Grace Toby Matthew, Lord Archbishop of York,* MS Add. 18, York Minster Archives.
27. For example, High Commission act book, HC AB 15, fols. 42–53, June 2, 1607, BI (York).
28. H. M. Dexter and Morton Dexter, *The England and Holland of the Pilgrims* (Boston, 1906), pp. 53–54 and 85–87.
29. HC AB 15, fols. 116 and 145, BI (York).
30. HC AB 15, fols. 103–4, BI (York).
31. Maddison, *Lincolnshire Pedigrees* (London, 1903), vol. 2, pp. 711–12; K. D. Train, *Lists of the Clergy of North Nottinghamshire* (Nottingham, UK, 1960), pp. 82 and 146; and Marchant, *Puritans and Church Courts,* p. 312.
32. Nicholas Fuller, *The Argument of Nicholas Fuller . . . That the Ecclesiastical Commissioners Have No Power, by Vertue of Their Commission, to Imprison etc.* (Amsterdam?, 1607); Philip Tyler, "The Significance of the Ecclesiastical Commission at York," *Northern History* 2 (1967), pp. 32–34; and *ODNB.*
33. HC AB 15, fol. 117, BI (York).
34. For the fines of twenty pounds on Catholics and on Brewster, see HC AB 15, fol. 60 (June 29, 1607) and fol. 116 (Dec. 1), BI (York).
35. *An Act to Retain the Queen's Subjects in Obedience,* in *Select Statutes and Other Constitutional Documents Illustrative of the Reigns of Elizabeth and James I,* ed G. W. Prothero (Oxford, 1913), pp. 89–92.
36. SPS 460/1/15, LAO. The document was presumably a criminal indictment drawn up for the JPs at Boston, or for the assize judges at Lincoln. It survives as a stray paper among items relating to the Spalding Court of Sewers, which supervised drainage in the Lincolnshire Fens. It appears to be dated November 1609 on the reverse, but it may have been reused, or the paper may be a page torn from a book. By November 1608, Helwys was definitely in Amsterdam. Elizabethan statutes: Note 35 above, and Prothero, *Select Statutes,* pp. 74–76. Will of Leonard Beetson of Boston, signed Dec. 24, 1625, archdeaconry wills, LAO.

Chapter Nine: Stallingborough Flats

1. Humber estuary: University of Hull, Institute of Estuarine and Coastal Studies, *Humber Estuary and Coast* (Hull, UK, Nov. 1994). History of the river and navigation on it: G. de Boer and R. A. Skelton, "The Earliest English Chart with Soundings," *Imago Mundi* 23 (1969), pp. 9–16; and Arthur Storey, *Hull Trinity House History of Pilotage and Navigational Aids of the River Humber (1512–1908)* (Hull, UK, 1971), pp. 2–3 and 25–28. I am also indebted to a lecture about the dynamics of the river given by Jack Hardisty, professor of environmental physics, the University of Hull, on June 17, 2006, at a seminar at Barton-upon-Humber arranged by the Campaign to Protect Rural England (North Lincolnshire).
2. The *Francis:* 1607 Exchequer port book for Grimsby (searcher's book), E 190/312/1, NAK. Coal trade: Simon Pawley, "Lincolnshire Coastal Villages and the Sea, c. 1300–1600: Economy and Society" (Ph.D. diss., thesis, University of Leicester, 1984), pp. 143–44. Cold winter: John Stow and Edmund Howes, *Annales, or a General Chronicle of England* (London, 1631), pp. 891–92.

3. The depositions are on microfilm at NAK, SP 14/32/46 and 47, dated May 13, 1608.
4. Mary Green entry in *ODNB*.
5. A. C. Wood, ed., *Memorials of the Holles Family* (London, 1937), p. 63; and postmortem inquisition of Thomas Hatcliffe, 1610, WARD 7/36/34, NAK.
6. Pawley, "Lincolnshire Coastal Villages," pp. 51–57. Political affairs in the spring of 1608: M. S. Guiseppi and G. D. Owen, eds., *HMC Salisbury (Cecil) Manuscripts* (London, 1968), vol. 20, pp. 112–75.
7. Joan and Thomas Helwys: York High Commission act book, HC AB 15, fols. 144, 167, 177, and 183, Borthwick Institute, York. York assizes: Edmund Hopwood to Thomas Southworth, July 29, 1608, Lancs RO, Kenyon of Peel Papers, DDKE HMC 20. Banishment in 1609: Abstract of the Registers of the Privy Council, 1550–1610, Add. MS 11402, fol. 147r., BL.
8. Hodgkinson Transcripts, vol. 3, fols. 380 and 387, NAN.
9. Journal of Sir Julius Caesar, May 4–July 24, 1608, Lansdowne Papers, MS 168, fols. 297–306, BL. For Cecil's papers, see note 6 above.
10. John McCavitt, *The Flight of the Earls* (Dublin, 2005), pp. 135–53; and O'Doherty's entry in *ODNB*.
11. Add. MS 11402, fols. 140–41, BL.
12. Pauline Croft, "The Religion of Robert Cecil," *Historical Journal* 34, no. 4 (1991), esp. pp. 775–80 and 796.

Chapter Ten: The Tomb of the Apostle

1. Sea approaches to Amsterdam: William Johnson, *The Light of Navigation* (Amsterdam, 1612), bk. 1, p. 12. Eyewitness account: Tadhg Ó Cianáin, *The Flight of the Earls*, ed. Paul Walsh (Maynooth, 1916), pp. 169–87. St. Peter's in 1608: Rudolf Wittkower, *Art and Architecture in Italy, 1600–1750* (New Haven, CT, 1982), pp. 28–29, 111–12, and 190–93. Paul V and Santa Francesca Romana: Ludwig von Pastor, *The History of the Popes from the Close of the Middle Ages* (London, 1891–), vol. 1, pp. 235–37, and vol. 25, pp. 43–49 and 255–58. The date of the canonization was May 19 using the Julian calendar, in force in England in 1608, but May 29 according to the modern Gregorian calendar, which was used in Rome.
2. For Smyth in Amsterdam, see W. T. Whitley, ed., *The Works of John Smyth* (Cambridge, UK, 1915), vol. 1, pp. lxxv–lxxviii.
3. Ó Cianáin, *Flight of the Earls*, pp. 9–11.
4. Micheline Kerney Walsh, *Destruction by Peace: Hugh O'Neill After Kinsale* (Monaghan, 1986), p. 191.
5. J. H. Elliott, *Imperial Spain, 1469–1716* (Harmondsworth, UK, 1970), pp. 305–8.
6. Fernand Braudel, *The Mediterranean and the Mediterranean World in the Age of Philip II* (London, 1973), vol. 1, pp. 334–38 and 415–17.
7. John McCavitt, *The Flight of the Earls* (Dublin, 2005), pp. 200–221.
8. Bancroft to Sir Robert Winwood, Feb. 9, 1606, in *Memorials of Affairs of State in the Reigns of Queen Elizabeth and King James I*, ed. Edward Sawyer (London, 1725), vol. 2, p. 195.

Chapter Eleven: Why the Pilgrims Sailed

1. Philip Yorke, second Earl of Hardwicke, *Letters from and to Sir Dudley Carleton . . . During His Embassy in Holland, from January 1616 to December 1620* (London, 1757), p. 240.

2. For whales and plague, see gazette of 1617, SP 14/95/22, NAK; Yorke, *Letters from and to Carleton,* pp. 89 and 96; HMC, *Downshire Manuscrips,* vol. 6, *Papers of William Trumbull, 1616–1618* (London, 1995), p. 96.
3. S. Groenveld, ed., *De Geschiedenis van een Hollandse Stad* (Leiden, 2003), vol. 2, pp. 44–48.
4. *Says* and Hondschoote: E. Coornaert, *Un centre industriel d'autrefois: La draperie-sayetterie d'Hondschoote* (Paris, 1930), pp. 418–21. Also, Herman Van Der Wee, "The Western European Textile Industries, 1500–1750," in *The Cambridge History of Western Textiles,* ed. David Jenkins (Cambridge, UK, 2003), vol. 1, pp. 433–34 and 452–56. Refugees and textiles: Eric Kerridge, *Textile Manufactures in Early Modern England* (Manchester, UK, 1985), pp. 226–29.
5. N. W. Posthumus, *De Geschiedenis van de Leidsche Lakenindustrie* (The Hague, 1939), vol. 3, pp. 965 and 1175–80.
6. Estienne Richer, *Le Mercure françois* (Paris, 1617–18), vol. 4, pp. 415–18; Jonathan I. Israel, *The Dutch Republic: Its Rise, Greatness, and Fall, 1477–1806* (Oxford, 1995), pp. 436–38; and Jonathan I. Israel, *The Dutch Republic and the Hispanic World, 1606–1661* (Oxford, 1982), pp. 57–60.
7. Jeremy Dupertuis Bangs, "Pilgrim Homes in Leiden," *NEHGR* 154 (Oct. 2000), pp. 412–23.
8. Kees van der Wiel, *Leidse Wevershuisjes: Het Wisselende lot van zeventiende-eeuwse Leidse arbeiderswoningen* (Leiden, 2001), pp. 35–38, 124–26, and 144–45; and Groenveld, *De Geschiedenis,* vol. 2, pp. 21–22 and 31–32.
9. Richer, *Le Mercure françois,* vol. 5, pp. 25–26; Yorke, *Letters to and from Carleton,* p. 184; P. J. Blok, *Geschiedenis eener Hollandsche Stad: Die Republiek* (The Hague, 1916), pp. 106–8; an annotated print, *d'Arminianze Schans tot Leyden* (1618), in the British Museum; and Joke Kardux and Eduard van de Bilt, *Newcomers in an Old City: The American Pilgrims in Leiden, 1609–1620,* 3rd ed. (Leiden, 2007), pp. 37–40.
10. Yorke, *Letters to and from Carleton,* p. 163. Oldenbarnevelt, Prince Maurice, and the crisis of 1617–18: Jan Den Tex, *Oldenbarnevelt,* trans. R. B. Powell (London, 1973), vol. 2, pp. 423–66 and 566–73; and Israel, *Dutch Republic: Its Rise, Greatness, and Fall,* pp. 433–59 and 461–62.
11. Yorke, *Letters to and from Carleton,* p. 435.
12. Ibid., p. 307.
13. Peter Lake, *Moderate Puritans and the Elizabethan Church* (Cambridge, UK, 1982), pp. 68–75.
14. HMC, *Downshire Manuscripts* (1940), vol. 4, p. 454.
15. HMC, *Downshire Manuscripts* (1988), p. 353; and *Isaaci Casauboni Corona Regia* (London, 1615), pp. 113–14.
16. *ODNB;* and Alan R. Macdonald, "James VI and I, the Church of Scotland, and British Ecclesiastical Convergence," *Historical Journal* 48 (2005), pp. 893–99.
17. Yorke, *Letters to and from Carleton,* pp. 345, 346–53, 379–80, 385–99, 405–10, 423, and 437. Also: Anthony Milton, ed., *The British Delegation and the Synod of Dort* (Woodbridge, UK, 2005), pp. 211–12.
18. Samuel Eliot Morison, ed., *Of Plymouth Plantation, 1620–1647, by William Bradford* (New York, 1979), pp. 23–27.
19. Entries in London port books for 1617, E 190/21/2, NAK; and U 269/1 Oec 1, CKS.
20. Simon Hart, *The Prehistory of the New Netherland Company: Amsterdam Notarial Records of the First Dutch Voyages to the Hudson* (Amsterdam, 1959), pp. 17–38.

21. J. R. Brodhead and E. B. O'Callaghan, eds., *Documents Relative to the Colonial History of the State of New York* (Albany, NY, 1856), vol. 1, pp. 21–24.

Chapter Twelve: The Beaver, the Cossack, and Prince Charles

1. Pierre de La Primaudaye, *The French Academie* (London, 1618), p. 836.
2. J. C. Jefferson, ed., *Middlesex County Records, 1549–1688* (London, 1886–92), vol. 1, p. 191, and vol. 2, pp. xvii–xxii; and Digby entry in *ODNB.*
3. Philip Stubbes, *The Anatomie of Abuses,* 3rd ed. (London, 1585; repr., 1836), pp. 50–51.
4. Bernard Bailyn, *The New England Merchants in the Seventeenth Century* (Cambridge, MA, 1979), pp. 23–26; Bernard Allaire, *Pelleteries, manchons et chapeaux de castor: Les fourrures nord-américaines à Paris, 1500–1632* (Paris, 1999), esp. pp. 67–83 and 157–74.
5. Bacon Papers, MS 650, fols. 222 and 286; MS 651, fols. 76, 147, 184, 235, and 281; MS 657, fols. 103 and 188; MS 658, fol. 172; MS 659, fol. 79; MS 661, fol. 236, LPL. Also, regarding beaver hat alterations: May 16, 1622, Lancs RO, Kenyon of Peel Papers, DDKE HMC 51. Anthony Bacon: Daphne du Maurier, *Golden Lads: A Study of Anthony Bacon, Francis, and Their Friends* (London, 2007), esp. pp. 144–48.
6. Arnolds: Wills of Samuel Arnold, Aug. 20, 1618, PROB 11/132, PCC, NAK, and Richard Arnold, May 24, 1621, PROB 11/138, PCC, NAK; Minutes of the Court of Assistants of the Haberdashers' Company, MS 15842, vol. 1, fols. 208 and 214, Guildhall Library; and R. G. Lang, ed., *Two Tudor Subsidy Assessment Rolls for the City of London: 1541 and 1582* (London, 1993), pp. 114 and 236. Haberdashers and Puritans: Ian Archer, *The History of the Haberdashers' Company* (Chichester, UK, 1991), pp. 74–80, with references to Richard Arnold on p. 237.
7. Berthold Laufer, "The Early History of Felt," *American Anthropologist,* n.s., 32, no. 1 (1930), pp. 1–18.
8. On the natural history and anatomy of the beaver, see Lewis H. Morgan, *The American Beaver and His Works* (Philadelphia, 1868), pp. 17–29 and 46–51; and Dietland Müller-Schwarze and Lixing Sun, *The Beaver: Natural History of a Wetland Engineer* (Ithaca, NY, 2003), esp. pp. 10–21.
9. Ben Jonson, *A Celebration of Charis in Ten Lyric Pieces: Her Triumph,* in *Ben Jonson: The Complete Poems,* ed. George Parfitt (Harmondsworth, UK, 1975), p. 129.
10. J. F. Crean, "Hats and the Fur Trade," *Canadian Journal of Economics and Political Science* 28, no. 3 (Aug. 1962), pp. 379–82.
11. "Chapeau," in Denis Diderot, *Encyclopédie; ou, Dictionnaire raisonné des sciences, des arts et des métiers* (Paris, 1751–65); Thierry Lefrançois, "L'art du chapelier," in *La Traite de la fourrure: Les Français et la découverte de l'Amérique du Nord* (La Rochelle, France, 1992); Allaire, *Pelleteries,* pp. 125–31 and 188–92; and Michael Sonenscher, *The Hatters of Eighteenth-Century France* (Berkeley, CA, 1987), pp. 20–25.
12. Thomas Mun, *England's Treasure by Forraign Trade* (first printed in 1664, but probably written in 1626 or 1627), in *Early English Tracts on Commerce,* ed. J. R. McCulloch (Cambridge, UK, 1954), p. 132. Luxury trades: Chapter 1 of an excellent recent book by Linda Levy Peck, *Consuming Splendor: Society and Culture in Seventeenth-Century England* (Cambridge, UK, 2005).
13. Wardrobe accounts of Prince Charles: E 101/434/9 (1617–18); E 101/434/14 (1618–19);

E 101/436/1 (1622–23); E 101/436/9 (1623–24); and E 101/435/20 (extraordinary expenses for the journey to Spain, 1623), NAK.

14. On fur from Russia, see London Port Book (imports) for 1621, entries for Oct. 20–Nov. 17, esp. the entry for the *Encrease* on Oct. 31, E 190/24/4, NAK.
15. Will of Ralph Freeman (1634), PROB/11/165, NAK.
16. Paul Bushkovitch, *The Merchants of Moscow, 1582–1701* (Cambridge, UK, 1980), pp. 44–45.
17. Tar, ropes, and cordage and their cost and sources of supply (1610–18) in the papers of Sir John Coke, Add. MSS 69895, fols. 109–10, 146–49, 152, and 168–69, BL.
18. Siberian fur: Raymond H. Fisher, *The Russian Fur Trade, 1550–1700* (Berkeley, CA, 1943), esp. pp. 4–29, 49–78, 113, and 153–55. Political background: George Vernadsky, *The Tsardom of Moscow, 1547–1682* (New Haven, CT, 1969), pt. 1, pp. 276–91.
19. London port book (exports) for 1617, Sackville Papers, U 269/1 OEC1, CKS. Bullion shipments are listed in a special section at the back of the port book.
20. Collapse of the Muscovy Company: The events are chronicled in the *Calendar of Colonial State Papers, East Indies, China, and Japan, 1617–1621*, ed. W. N. Sainsbury (London, 1870), esp. pp. 350 and 453–54. Freeman in the 1620s: Samuel Purchas, *Hakluytus Posthumus; or, Purchas His Pilgrimes* (Glasgow, 1906), vol. 13, pp. 24–26; and J. Kotilaine and M. Poe, eds., *Modernizing Muscovy: Reform and Social Change in Seventeenth-Century Russia* (New York, 2004), pp. 191–92.
21. S. M. Kingsbury, ed., *Records of the Virginia Company of London* (London, 1906–35), vol. 3, p. 308.

Chapter Thirteen: In the Artillery Garden

1. Philip E. Barbour, ed., *The Complete Works of Captain John Smith, 1580–1631* (Chapel Hill, NC, 1986), vol. 1, p. 429.
2. Bill of complaint of Edward Pickering, 1622, E 112/104/1502, NAK.
3. Peter Wilson Coldham, "Thomas Weston: Ironmonger of London and America, 1609–1647" *National Genealogical Society Quarterly* 62, no. 3 (Sept. 1974), pp. 163–72. Coldham made errors in dating the documents, and he overlooked the Sackville Papers, and hence his account of events is imperfect. Even so, his article shines a brilliant light on the unsentimental realities of Jacobean London.
4. Weston and Welsh cottons: *Rowland & Rudge v. Vaughan et al.* (1622), E 134/20JasI/Mich30, deposition of Andrew Weston, NAK; and lists of Shrewsbury drapers' apprentices in *Transactions of the Shropshire Archaeological Society* 50 (1939–40), p. 26. On the Welsh cotton trade: T. C. Mendenhall, *The Shrewsbury Drapers and the Welsh Wool Trade in the XVIth and XVIIth Centuries* (Oxford, 1953), esp. pp. 13–17, 34–48, and 56–68.
5. Donald F. Harris, "The More Children of the *Mayflower*: Their Shropshire Origins and the Reasons Why They Were Sent Away," *Mayflower Descendant* 43, no. 2 (July 1993), pp. 123–32, and 44, no. 1 (Jan. 1994), pp. 11–19, and no. 2 (July 1994), pp. 109–18.
6. See note 4 to chapter 15, below.
7. L. M. Midgley, ed., *A History of the County of Stafford* (London, 1959), vol. 5, pp. 155–57 and 160–61.
8. Staffordshire Parish Registers Society, *Rugeley Parish Register, Part 1* (Stafford, UK, 1928);

1616 Metropolitical Visitation: Excommunication book B/V/2/8, LDRO; and W. N. Landor, "Staffordshire Incumbents and Parochial Records (1530–1680)," in *Collections for a History of Staffordshire, 1915* (London, 1916), pp. 381 and 392.

9. Statistics: Richard Grassby, *The Business Community of Seventeenth-Century England* (Cambridge, UK, 1995), pp. 76–81. Will of Ralph Weston: Aug. 12, 1605, LDRO.
10. Grassby, *Business Community*, pp. 82–91.
11. For discussion of credit and bills of exchange, see P. McGrath, ed., *The Merchants Avizo* (Cambridge, MA, 1957), pp. 48–51; and Robert Ashton, *The Crown and the Money Market, 1603–1640* (Oxford, 1960), pp. 1–4.
12. London port book (exports), eleven entries, Sackville Papers, U269/1/Oec 1, CKS.
13. Astrid Friis, *Alderman Cockayne's Project and the Cloth Trade* (Copenhagen, 1927), esp. pp. 306–26; also, Cokayne entry in *ODNB*.
14. Interlopers: Friis, *Alderman Cockayne's Project*, pp. 108–12. Marshalsea: Chamberlain to Carleton, in *The Letters of John Chamberlain*, ed. N. E. McClure (Philadelphia, 1939), vol. 2, p. 131. Will of Edward Pickering (1623): PROB 11/142, NAK.
15. In the 1950s, the American scholar Ruth A. McIntyre conducted some excellent research into the business affairs of the Plymouth Colony, examining the background of many of the investors. Her book *Debts Hopeful and Desperate: Financing the Plymouth Colony* (Plymouth, MA, 1963) remains a fine source, but much more can now be said.
16. Will of Thomas Beacham (1614), PROB/11/123, NAK; will of Christopher Beachom (1623), archdeaconry of Northampton wills, 2nd ser., M247, Northants RO; Northants Record Society, *A Copy of Papers Relating to Musters, Beacons, Subsidies, etc., in the County of Northampton, A.D. 1586–1623* (Kettering, UK, 1926), pp. 44, 60, 92, 117, 130, 177, and 178; J. J. Howard, ed., *Visitation of London, 1633–4* (London, 1880), vol. 1, p. 59; will of John Beauchamp (the Plymouth Colony investor) (1655), PROB/11/245, NAK.
17. For the business dealings of Beauchamp and Sherley, see London Port Book (exports) for 1617, numerous entries, Sackville Papers, U269/1/Oec 1; London Port Book (imports) for 1621, E 190/24/4, NAK; and London Port Book for 1626, E 190/31/3, NAK.
18. W. F. Craven, *The Dissolution of the Virginia Company* (Oxford, 1932), pp. 222–30.
19. Artillery company: G. A. Raikes, *The Ancient Vellum Book of the Honourable Artillery Company* (London, 1890); G. Goold-Walker, *The Honourable Artillery Company, 1537–1987* (London, 1986), pp. 25–39; Thomas Adams, *The Souldiers Honour* (London, 1617), "Epistle Dedicatorie." Bingham and the Dutch connection: Jean Tsushima, "Members of the Stationers' Company Who Served in the Artillery Company Before the Civil War: Ralph Mabbe and His Network," in *The Stationers' Company and the Book Trade, 1550–1990*, ed. R. Myers and M. Harris (Winchester, UK, 1997), pp. 69–74.
20. Kenneth Rogers, "Bread Street, Its Ancient Signs and Houses," *London Topographical Record* 16 (1932), pp. 52–76.
21. Merchant Taylors' Company, "Register of Apprentice Bindings, 1606–1609," MS 34038/5, p. 101, May 18, 1607, Guildhall Library; wills of John Harrison, Ralph Longworth, Nathaniel Wade, and Edward Pocock, PROB 11/133, 11/135, 11/136, and 11/164, NAK; postmortem inquisition of John Pocock Sr., July 24, 1627, C142/436/34, NAK; *Longworth v. Pocock* (1629–30), DL4/79/57, NAK; and *Memorials of the Guild of Merchant Taylors* (London, 1875), pp. 714–21.

22. Stock: *ODNB;* Tom Webster, *Godly Clergy in Early Stuart England: The Caroline Puritan Movement, c. 1620–1643* (Cambridge, UK, 1997), pp. 80–83; and Stock's will (proved 1626), PROB/11/149, NAK.
23. Christopher Hill, "Puritans and 'the Dark Corners of the Land,' " *Transactions of the Royal Historical Society,* 5th ser., 19 (1963), pp. 91–97.
24. James I to Sir Walter Aston, Jan. 5, 1620, SP 94/23, fols. 279–90, NAK.
25. Charles P. Kindleberger, "The Economic Crisis of 1619–1623," *Journal of Economic History* 51, no. 1 (March 1991), pp. 149–75.
26. Mendenhall, *Shrewsbury Drapers,* pp. 190–96; and also Barry Supple, *Commercial Crisis and Change in England, 1600–1642* (Cambridge, UK, 1964), pp. 54–58; Joan Thirsk and J. P. Cooper, eds. *Seventeenth-Century Economic Documents* (Oxford, 1972), pp. 1–4; and tables of data on wages, rents, and prices in the appendices to Joan Thirsk, ed., *The Agrarian History of England and Wales* (Cambridge, UK, 1967), vol. 4.
27. Archbishop Abbot's account book: Midsummer 1620, MS 1730, fol. 114, LPL.

Chapter Fourteen: Comfort and Refreshing

1. Samuel Eliot Morison, ed., *Of Plymouth Plantation, 1620–1647, by William Bradford* (New York, 1979), p. 72. For this chapter, the principal narrative sources are Bradford's history and Dwight B. Heath, ed., *Mourt's Relation: A Journal of the Pilgrims at Plymouth* (Bedford, MA, 1963).
2. Benjamin Bangs, diary, Oct. 28, 1747, typewritten transcript, Massachusetts Historical Society; Simeon Deyo, ed., *History of Barnstable County, Massachusetts* (New York, 1890), p. 791; and Theresa M. Barbo, *Cape Cod Bay: A History of Salt and Sea* (Charleston, SC, 2008), pp. 90–92.
3. Thomas Prince, *A Chronological History of New England* (Boston, 1852), p. 165.
4. U.S. Bureau of the Census, *A Century of Population Growth: From the First Census of the United States to the Twelfth* (Washington, DC, 1909), p. 191.
5. Wendell S. Hadlock, "Three Contact Burials from Eastern Massachusetts," *Bulletin of the Massachusetts Archaeological Society* 10, no. 3 (April 1949), pp. 63–66.
6. N. J. G. Pounds, *A History of the English Parish* (Cambridge, UK, 2000), pp. 417–29; and Nigel Llewellyn, *Funeral Monuments in Post-Reformation England* (Cambridge, UK, 2000), pp. 6–14 and 146–63.
7. Heath, *Mourt's Relation,* p. 17.
8. SP 14/130/106, NAK.
9. *Theological Miscellanies of David Pareus,* trans. A.R. (London, 1645), p. 735.
10. S. M. Kingsbury, ed., *Records of the Virginia Company of London* (Washington, DC, 1906–35), vol. 3, pp. 130–35 and 623.
11. Town book of Blyth, 1560–94, Clifton Papers, CL M 62, U Nott.
12. Sir Thomas Smith, *De Republica Anglorum,* ed. Mary Dewar (Cambridge, UK, 1982), p. 57.
13. William Hubbard, *A General History of New England from the Discovery to 1680* (Boston, 1848), p. 67.
14. Levett (1628), in J. Phinney Baxter, *Christopher Levett of York* (Portland, ME, 1893), pp. 102 and 119.
15. Thomas Hunt: His will of 1619, PROB/11/134, NAK. His voyage to Russia: Sackville

Papers, U269/1 Oec1, April 23, 1617, CKS; and Philip E. Barbour, ed., *The Complete Works of Captain John Smith, 1580–1631* (Chapel Hill, NC, 1986), vol. 2, p. 401. The Thomas Hunt who left the will and sailed to Archangel must have been the same as the Hunt who kidnapped Tisquantum, because only one ship's master of that name appears in the port books of the period.

Chapter Fifteen: The Mystic and the Thames

1. N. E. McClure, ed., *The Letters of John Chamberlain* (Philadelphia, 1939), vol. 2, p. 405.
2. Samuel Eliot Morison, ed., *Of Plymouth Plantation, 1620–1647, by William Bradford* (New York, 1979), p. 66; and draft warrant for Weston's arrest, 1622, Sackville Papers, U269/1 OE 1247, CKS.
3. R. B. Turton, *The Alum Farm* (Whitby, UK, 1938), pp. 88–91.
4. The legal documents relating to Thomas Weston fall into four categories. First, the official records concerning Guest and Weston's alum smuggling are among Lord Cranfield's papers at CKS Sackville Papers, files U269/1 OEc180, and OE 682, 779, 1135, and 1247. Second, details of Weston's business activities can be found in the files relating to the Exchequer lawsuit *Rowland and Rudge v. Vaughn et al.* (1622), E 112/103/1414 and E 134/20JasI/Mich30, NAK. His legal quarrel with the Separatist haberdasher Edward Pickering gave rise to the third set of documents, in the case of *Pickering et al. v. Weston et al.* (1622–25). These files can be found at NAK, E 112/104/1502 and 1569; E 124/32/254; E 124/33/74; E 124/34/22–23; E 124/35/268; E 134/22Jas1/Hil8; E 134/22JasI/Mich22 and Mich59; and E 178/5451. Finally, Privy Council orders relating to Weston are in *Acts of the Privy Council of England, 1621–1623* (London, 1932), pp. 136–37, and *Acts of the Privy Council of England Colonial Series, Vol. I, 1613–1680* (London, 1908), pp. 50–51.
5. Slany and the Merchant Taylors: Court Minutes of the Merchant Taylors' Company, 1611–20, MS 34010/5, Guildhall Library; and List of Freemen, MS 34037, Guildhall Library. Humphrey Slany and the *Mayflower*: J. R. Hutchinson, "The 'Mayflower,' Her Identity and Tonnage," *NEHGR*, Oct. 1916, p. 341.
6. Fynes Moryson, "Of the Turkes, French, English, Scottish, and Irish Apparrell," in *An Itinerary . . . Containing His Ten Yeeres Travell* (London, 1617), pt. 3, bk. 4, chap. 2.
7. Samuel Hartlib, *Samuel Hartlib His Legacie* (London, 1651), pp. 46, 79, and 88–90.
8. Caleb H. Johnson, *The* Mayflower *and Her Passengers* (Philadelphia, 2006), p. 73.
9. Charles Brooks, "Indian Necropolis in West Medford, Mass.," *PMHS*, 1st ser., 6 (1862–63), pp. 362–64; and Carl Seaburg and Alan Seaburg, *Medford on the Mystic* (Medford, MA, 1980), pp. 3–4 and 93–95.
10. Alonzo Lewis and James R. Newhall, *History of Lynn, Essex County, Massachusetts* (Boston, 1865), pp. 32–42; and Richard S. Dunn, James Savage, and Laetitia Yeandle, eds., *The Journal of John Winthrop, 1630–1649* (Cambridge, MA, 1996), pp. 47–49 and 105.
11. Dexter, in the notes to his edition of *Mourt's Relation*, published in Boston in 1865.
12. Morison, *Of Plymouth Plantation*, p. 65.
13. W. N. Sainsbury, *Calendar of Colonial State Papers, American, 1574–1660* (London, 1860), p. 124; and Alan James, *The Navy and Government in Early Modern France, 1572–1661* (Woodbridge, UK, 2004), pp. 25–28.
14. J. Gardner Bartlett, "John Peirce of London and the Merchant Adventurers," *NEHGR* 67 (1913), pp. 147–53.

15. "Records of the Council for New England," *Proceedings of the American Antiquarian Society* (1867), pp. 91–93, entry for March 25, 1623.
16. Beale's output: Edward Arber, *A Transcript of the Registers of the Company of Stationers of London, 1554–1640* (London, 1875–94), vol. 3, entries under Beale's name. Background: Carolyn Nelson and Matthew Seccombe, "The Creation of the Periodical Press, 1620–1695," in *The Cambridge History of the Book in Britain,* ed. J. Barnard and D. F. McKenzie (Cambridge, UK, 2002), vol. 4, pp. 533–37.
17. On Butter, Bourne, and Bellamy, see Leona Rostenberg, *Literary, Political, Scientific, Religious, and Legal Publishing, Printing, and Bookselling in England, 1551–1700: Twelve Studies* (New York, 1965), pp. 75–91 and 97–129; *ODNB* entries for Butter and Bourne; and Bellamy's entry in Henry R. Plomer, *A Dictionary of the Booksellers . . . from 1641 to 1667* (London, 1968).

Chapter Sixteen: Diabolical Affection

1. Alexander Young, *Chronicles of the Pilgrim Fathers* (Boston, 1844; repr., Baltimore, 1974), pp. 272–73.
2. Arrival of Massasoit: Letter of Emmanuel Altham, Sept. 1623, in *Three Visitors to Early Plymouth: Letters About the Pilgrim Settlement in New England During the First Seven Years,* ed. Sydney V. James Jr. (Plymouth, MA, 1963), pp. 29–32. Map of Plymouth, 1830: The Bourne map, Massachusetts State Archives, vol. 68, no. 2161, p. 7.
3. *Sherley and Andrewes v. Weston et al.* (1623), E 112/104/1569, NAK.
4. C. M. Andrews, *The Colonial Period in American History,* vol. 1, *The Settlements* (New Haven, CT, 1934), pp. 332–34; and the comprehensive account in William Heath, "Thomas Morton: From Merry Old England to New England," *Journal of American Studies* 41, no. 1 (2007), esp. pp. 143–47.
5. Personal communication, April 2008, from Francis J. O'Brien Jr. (Moondancer) of the Aquidneck Indian Council.
6. Roger Williams, *A Key into the Language of America* (1643), in *Collections of the Massachusetts Historical Society for the Year 1794* (Boston, 1810), vol. 3, p. 228.
7. London Port Book (exports) for 1619, entry for July 31, 1619, E 190/22/9, NAK.
8. Kathleen L. Ehrhardt, *European Metals in Native Hands: Rethinking the Dynamics of Technological Change, 1640–1683* (Tuscaloosa, AL, 2005), pp. 57–59 and 76–81; Laurier Turgeon, "The Tale of the Kettle: Odyssey of an Intercultural Object," in *Ethnohistory* 44, no. 1 (winter 1997), pp. 1–21.
9. The various accounts of Wessagussett are Bradford's, in *Of Plymouth Plantation, 1620–1647, by William Bradford,* ed. Samuel Eliot Morison (New York, 1979), pp. 113–19; Winslow's, in Young, *Chronicles of the Pilgrim Fathers,* pp. 296–311 and 327–41; the narrative of Phineas Pratt, in *Collections of the Massachusetts Historical Society,* 4th ser., 4 (1858), pp. 476–79; and Thomas Morton's, in *New English Canaan* (Amsterdam, 1637). Morton's text is now easily available as an e-book, via Google Books and other portals, in an edition first published in 2000 by Jack Dempsey.
10. CLIMOD statistics for Plymouth-Kingston (1893–2007) from Northeast Regional Climate Center, Cornell University, Ithaca, NY.
11. Appraisal of the *Little James*'s armament, anchors, rigging, and so forth (1624?), HCA 24/81/120, NAK.

12. All quotations from Altham's letters are from James, *Three Visitors to Early Plymouth*, pp. 21–59.
13. Wills of Edward Altham (1605) and Elizabeth Altham (1623), PROB 11/106 and PROB/11/139, NAK. On the Althams: Harleian Society, *Visitations of Essex Part II* (London, 1879), pp. 538–39; and transcripts of the Altham family papers, T/A 531/1, ECRO. The Altham family had strong kinship ties to the leading Puritan families of eastern England: the most important was the marriage of Emmanuel's eldest brother, Sir James Altham, to Elizabeth Barrington. The Barringtons were active Puritan politicians in successive Parliaments and closely related by marriage to Oliver Cromwell and John Hampden.
14. Records of the lawsuit *Stephens and Fell v. the ship* Little James *et al.* (1624), HCA 24/81/40, 41, and 158, NAK.
15. Letters of John Bridges and Emmanuel Altham, 1623–24, *PMHS* 44 (1910–11), pp. 178–89.
16. Will of Emmanuel Altham (1638): PROB/11/178, NAK. Altham at Armagon: W. Foster, ed., *The English Factories in India, 1630–1633* (Oxford, 1910), pp. 183–84, and *The English Factories in India, 1634–1636* (Oxford, 1911), pp. 47–48, 296, and 327; and E. B. Sainsbury, ed., *A Calendar of the Court Minutes of the East India Company, 1635–1639* (Oxford, 1907), p. 318.
17. Pelts imported into Plymouth, Devon, in 1622: See the Plymouth Port Book (new impositions), Easter 1622–Michaelmas 1622, E 190/1030/10, NAK. For 1624: E 190/1030/19, NAK. The first record of substantial imports of beaver skins into Plymouth comes in July 1626, when Abraham Jennings shipped home more than one thousand pelts on the *Consent*: E 190/1031/6, NAK.
18. Bradford's narrative of the Lyford affair, from which all my quotations come unless otherwise indicated, is in Morison, *Of Plymouth Plantation*, pp. 146–70.
19. "Malignant" entry in *The Oxford English Dictionary.*
20. Winthrop: Francis J. Bremer, *John Winthrop: America's Founding Father* (New York, 2003), pp. 72–73 and 98–99. Winslow: Jeremy Dupertuis Bangs, *Edward Winslow: New England's First International Diplomat* (Boston, 2004), pp. 1–2. Slany: Court Minutes of the Merchant Taylors' Company, 1611–20, MS 34010/5, pp. 77, 108, 150–51, and 173–75, Guildhall Library.
21. W. H. Rylands, ed., *The Four Visitations of Berkshire* (London, 1907), vol. 1, p. 244, and vol. 2, pp. 172–73; William Page and P. H. Ditchfield, eds., *The Victoria County History of Berkshire* (London, 1924), vol. 4, pp. 81–84 and 110–14; and J. Foster, ed., *Alumni Oxonienses, 1500–1714* (Oxford, 1891–92), vol. 3.
22. Puritan clergy in Ireland: Alan Ford, "The Church of Ireland, 1558–1634: A Puritan Church," in *As by Law Established: The Church of Ireland Since the Reformation*, ed. Alan Ford, J. I. McGuire, and Kenneth Milne (Dublin, 1995), pp. 56–67. Armagh cathedral prebendaries: J. B. Leslie, *Armagh Clergy and Parishes* (Dundalk, Ireland, 1911), pp. 59–73. On the Ulster Plantation generally: S. J. Connolly, *Contested Island: Ireland, 1460–1630* (Oxford, 2007), pp. 290–302.
23. For Lyford at Loughgall, see Diocese of Armagh, "Visitation Royal 1622," fols. 54r–55, showing appointment of Lyford as prebendary on Oct. 21, 1613, Armagh Robinson Public Library; List of the Temporalities of 1622, file DIO/4/4/2, fol. 40, entry regarding Levalleglish, PRONI; and Leslie, *Armagh Clergy*, p. 351.

24. The O'Neills and the confiscation of Loughgall: John McCavitt, "Rebels, Planters, and Conspirators: Armagh, 1594–1640," in *Armagh: History and Society,* ed. A. J. Hughes and William Nolan (Dublin, 2001), pp. 253–58; and R. J. Hunter, "County Armagh: A Map of Plantation, c. 1610," in the same volume, pp. 268–73. Copes at Loughgall: "A Book of the Plantation of Ulster" (1619), in *Calendar of the Carew Manuscripts, 1603–1624,* ed. J. S. Brewer and William Bullen (London, 1873), pp. 415–16; *ODNB;* and will of Anthony Cope (1633), Cope Papers (28–1975), Armagh County Museum.
25. Lyford and Church land: Entry regarding John Lyford in Robert C. Anderson, *The Pilgrim Migration: Immigrants to Plymouth Colony, 1620–1633* (Boston, MA, 2004), p. 313; map of Loughgall in 1834, OS/6/2/8/1, PRONI; and James Morrin, ed., *Calendar of the Patent and Close Rolls of Chancery in Ireland in the Reign of Charles I* (Dublin, 1863), p. 322. Hampton and long leases: Sir James Stuart, *Historical Memoirs of the City of Armagh* (Newry, UK, 1819), pp. 308–10; and "Orders Concerning the Church of Ireland 1623," inside the manuscript "Visitation Royal 1622," Armagh Robinson Public Library.
26. Pory's letters: James, *Three Visitors to Early Plymouth.* Bradford on Pory: Morison, *Of Plymouth Plantation,* pp. 112–13.

Chapter Seventeen: If Rochelle Be Lost

1. Massachusetts Historical Society, *Winthrop Papers,* vol. 2, *1623–1630* (Boston, 1931), pp. 58–59.
2. State Papers (France), SP 78/80, fol. 83 (Oct. 12, 1626); fol. 97 (Oct. 13); fols. 114–16 (Nov. 6); fol. 163 (Nov. 30); and SP 78/81, fol. 187 (1627), NAK. Also, Francisque Michel, *Histoire de commerce et de la navigation à Bordeaux* (Bordeaux, 1870), vol. 2, pp. 52–54 and 61–62; and Thomas R. Cogswell, "Prelude to Ré: The Anglo-French Struggle over La Rochelle, 1624–1627," *History* 71 (1986), pp. 13–14.
3. SP 78/80, fol. 116, NAK; and Charles de la Roncière, *Histoire de la marine française* (Paris, 1923), vol. 4, pp. 558–628.
4. François de Vaux de Foletier, whose book first appeared in 1931.
5. MP: Sir Benjamin Rudyerd, April 1, 1628, in *Commons Debates, 1628,* ed. R. C. Johnson and M. J. Cole (New Haven, CT, 1977), vol. 2, p. 228. French commerce in French hulls: See, for example, "Declaration du roy," in Etienne Cleirac, *Les us et coutumes de la mer* (Rouen, 1671), pp. 2–3. La Rochelle, its defenses, and the preliminaries of the siege: François de Vaux de Foletier, *Le siège de La Rochelle* (La Rochelle, France, 1978), pp. 16–18, 81–94; and Cogswell, "Prelude to Ré."
6. Barnstaple: SP 16/51/25–26, Jan. 26, 1627, NAK. Sailors: J. F. Larkin, *Stuart Royal Proclamations,* vol. 2, *1625–1646* (Oxford, 1983), pp. 127–128.
7. Samuel Eliot Morison, ed., *Of Plymouth Plantation, 1620–1647, by William Bradford* (New York, 1979), p. 34; and S. M. Kingsbury, ed., *The Records of the Virginia Company of London* (Washington, DC, 1906–35), vol. 1, pp. 221 and 228.
8. Clinton's pamphlet, SP 16/54/82.i, Jan. 24, 1627, NAK; and Richard Cust, *The Forced Loan and English Politics, 1626–1628* (Oxford, 1987), esp. pp. 32–39, 102–3, 170–76, and 298–99.
9. Wincob, Coddington, and Lincolnshire loan refusers: SP 16/56/39, March 8, 1627, NAK; and the 1625 certificate of residence of "*John Wincope . . . gent,*" E 115/46/56,

NAK. Dudley and the loan: SP 16/72/36, July 28, 1627, NAK. Identification of John Wincob: Records relating to taxpayers in Lincolnshire have survived in large numbers and in very good condition. They list only one gentleman with a name like John Wincob or Weyncopp. He was registered as a taxpayer in the parish of Kirkby Underwood. The village is eight miles from Sempringham, where the Clintons owned a manor house, and three miles from Folkingham, where they owned land and which they later chose as their principal residence.

10. Bread Street Ward forced loan refusers: SP 16/71/15, July 16, 1627, NAK. Other City wards: SP 16/72/60, 61, 62, 64, and 65, NAK. Pocock's arrest warrant, July 19, 1627: *Acts of the Privy Council of England (January–August 1627)* (London, 1938), p. 424.
11. Deposition against Archbishop Laud, SP 16/500/4, NAK.
12. The *Marmaduke*: London port book (exports) for 1627, E 190/31/1, fol. 113, NAK. John Gibbs and the Plymouth Colony: Morison, *Of Plymouth Plantation*, p. 197.
13. Lynn Ceci, "Native Wampum as a Peripheral Resource in the Seventeenth-Century World-System," in *The Pequots in Southern New England: The Fall and Rise of an American Indian Nation*, ed. Laurence M. Hauptman and James D. Wherry (Norman, OK, 1990), pp. 48–63.
14. For example, see household accounts of Lord Bayning, Jan. 30 and Oct. 17, 1634, SP 46/77, NAK.
15. Robert Le Blant, "Le commerce compliqué des fourrures canadiennes au début du XVII siècle," *Revue Historique de l'Amérique Française* 26, no. 1 (June 1972). I have converted the French prices in silver into English shillings of the period, using data from the history of the Royal Mint in London and in Natalis de Wailly, *Mémoire sur la variation de la livre tournois* (Paris, 1857). The price of twenty shillings in the late 1620s matches details given by Bradford.
16. William Hubbard, *A General History of New England from the Discovery to 1680* (Boston, 1848), p. 68.
17. On the restructuring of the Plymouth Colony's finances, see Morison, *Of Plymouth Plantation*, pp. 184–86 and 194–96.
18. "Plymouth Company Accounts," *Collections of the Massachusetts Historical Society*, 3rd ser., 1 (1907), pp. 200–201.

Chapter Eighteen: The Prophecy of Micaiah

1. John Preston, "A Sensible Demonstration of the Deitie," in *Sermons Preached Before His Maiestie* (London, 1631), p. 56.
2. E. W. Harcourt, ed., *The Life of the Renowned Doctor Preston, Writ by His Pupil, Master Thomas Ball . . . in the Year 1628* (Oxford, 1885). Also Irvonwy Morgan, *Prince Charles's Puritan Chaplain* (Oxford, 1957), esp. pp. 111 and 126.
3. The probate inventory of Miles Standish is available on the Web site of Pilgrim Hall, Plymouth, MA: www.pilgrimhall.org.
4. H. M. Colvin, ed., *The History of the King's Works, Vol. 4, 1485–1660*, Part 2 (London, 1982), pp. 304–41; and Peter E. McCullough, *Sermons at Court: Politics and Religion in Elizabethan and Jacobean Preaching* (Cambridge, UK, 1998), pp. 31–42.
5. Preston, *Sermons Preached Before His Maiestie*, pp. 47 and 52–61.

6. Harcourt, *Renowned Doctor Preston,* pp. 158–62.
7. Will of John Preston, signed 1618, proved 1628, PROB/11/154, NAK. When Preston's sermon appeared in print in 1631, the volume was edited by the Puritan minister John Davenport, a London friend of John Pocock's brother Edward. Davenport had close ties to the leading investors in the Massachusetts Bay Company.
8. Samuel Eliot Morison, ed., *Of Plymouth Plantation, 1620–1647, by William Bradford* (New York, 1979), p. 382.
9. N. M. Sutherland, "The Origins of the Thirty Years' War and the Structure of European Politics," *English Historical Review* 107 (July 1992), esp. pp. 590–91 and 618–22; and David Parrott, "The Mantuan Succession, 1627–1631: A Sovereignty Dispute in Early Modern Europe," *English Historical Review* 112 (Feb. 1997), pp. 20–25, 48–50, and 64–65.
10. Harcourt, *Renowned Doctor Preston,* p. 174.

Chapter Nineteen: The First Bostonians

1. Hakewill to Archbishop Ussher of Armagh, in *The Whole Works of the Most Rev. James Ussher, D.D.,* ed. C. R. Elrington (Dublin, 1847–64), vol. 15, p. 418. Hakewill, a fellow of Exeter College, Oxford, preached often at Barnstaple, where he married the daughter of the merchant and mayor, John Delbridge.
2. Regarding the *St. Peter* and the *White Angel:* Barnstaple port book (overseas) for 1628, entries for Jan. 7 and Jan. 23, E 190/947/5, NAK; and Patrick McGrath, ed., *Records Relating to the Society of Merchant Venturers in the City of Bristol in the Seventeenth Century* (Bristol, UK, 1952), p. 203. Drowned fishermen: Todd Gray, ed., *Early-Stuart Mariners and Shipping: The Maritime Surveys of Devon and Cornwall, 1619–35* (Exeter, UK, 1990), p. xvi.
3. Will of John Penrose, former mayor of Barnstaple (1624), PROB/11/145, NAK.
4. Letters to Cecil, 1603–4: HMC, *Salisbury,* vol. 15 (London, 1930), pp. 337–38, and vol. 16 (London, 1933), pp. 6, 116, 127, 136, and 345. Delbridge and Palmer: Will of Anthonie Palmer (1596), PROB/11/87, PCC Wills, NAK. Micmac chieftain at Bayonne: This was a man called Messamouet; see Bruce J. Bourque and Ruth R. Whitehead, "Trade and Alliances in the Contact Period," in *American Beginnings: Exploration, Culture, and Cartography in the Land of Norumbega,* ed. Emerson W. Baker et al. (Lincoln, NE, 1994), pp. 136–39. Delbridge and religion: *Eastman v. Delbridge,* STAC 8/134/5 (1616), NAK.
5. For Barnstaple's activities in New England in 1622–23, see *Records of the Council for New England* (Cambridge, MA, 1867), pp. 71, 83–84, and 96. Evidence of only very modest imports of beaver fur before 1628 comes from the Barnstaple port books recording payment of the customs duties on cargoes subject to the so-called new impositions, which included beaver skins. These are: Barnstaple Port Book (new impositions), Easter 1624–Michaelmas 1624, E 190/946/3, NAK; Barnstaple Port Book (new impositions), Michaelmas 1625–Easter? 1626, E 190/946/8, NAK; and Barnstaple Port Book (new impositions), Michaelmas 1626–Easter 1627, E 190/946/10, NAK. Three port books recording new impositions collected at Barnstaple survive from the years 1614–16 and show no beaver fur imports. On Barnstaple generally, see J. R. Chanter and Thomas Wainwright, *Reprint of the Barnstaple Records* (Barnstaple, UK, 1900); Lois Lamplugh, *Barnstaple: Town on the Taw* (South Molton, UK, 2002); and Todd Gray, ed., *The Lost Chronicle of Barnstaple, 1586–1611* (Devonshire Association, 1998).

6. Barnstaple's trade by sea is clearly displayed in the town's overseas port book for 1615, E 190/942/13, NAK. Also see contributions by Alison Grant and Todd Gray to *The New Maritime History of Devon,* ed. Michael Duffy et al. (London, 1992), vol. 1.
7. Barnstaple port book (overseas) for 1620, entry for Aug. 30, E 190/944/8; and entries for Aug. 28 and Sept. 11, 1615, E 190/942/13, NAK. Irish livestock: Donald Woodward, "The Anglo-Irish Livestock Trade of the Seventeenth Century," *Irish Historical Studies* 18 (1972–73), pp. 489–91.
8. Richard W. Cotton, *Barnstaple and the Northern Part of Devonshire During the Great Civil War, 1642–1646* (London, 1889), pp. 5–6 and 41.
9. SP (France), 78/83, Jan.–Dec. 1628, NAK.
10. E 190/947/5, NAK, shows only 37 outward voyages from Barnstaple to overseas ports in 1628, compared with about 60 in other years for which the port books survive. Of the 37, some 25 went to Ireland. Inward voyages from abroad numbered 67, compared with the usual total of about 160. Taking these figures together, we see the number of voyages falling from about 220 in a normal year to 104 in 1628.
11. R. C. Johnson and M. J. Cole, eds., *Commons Debates, 1628* (New Haven, CT, 1977), vol. 2, p. 304.
12. Bristol-Barnstaple connection: Barnstaple Port Book (coastal) for 1615. The *White Angel* as privateer: John Bruce, ed., *Calendar of State Papers, Domestic Series, 1628–1629* (London, 1859), pp. 439–42, letters of marque issued Nov. 4, 1628.
13. All of these details come from E 190/947/5, NAK.
14. On Witheridge in Maine, and his contacts with Samoset, see James Phinney Baxter, *Christopher Levett of York: The Pioneer Colonist in Casco Bay* (Portland, ME, 1893), pp. 101–3.
15. For Sherley's accounts, see Chapter Seventeen, note 18, above.
16. Elbridge: Henry S. Burrage, *The Beginnings of Colonial Maine, 1602–1658* (Portland, ME, 1914), pp. 180–82 and 217–20; and also David Harris Sacks, *The Widening Gate: Bristol and the Atlantic Economy, 1450–1700* (Berkeley, CA, 1992), chap. 7. Regarding the trading season of 1628: Sherley to Bradford, Nov. 17, 1628, in Samuel Eliot Morison, ed., *Of Plymouth Plantation, 1620–1647, by William Bradford* (New York, 1979), pp. 197–98. Morton in 1628: Morison, *Of Plymouth Plantation,* pp. 204–10; and the sources referred to in Chapter Sixteen above, note 9.
17. Cradock: *Collections for a History of Staffordshire* (London, 1920 and 1922), vol. 2, pp. 22–23; and Sackville Papers, U 269/1, OEc 1, CKS. Cradock, Russia, and fur: Minutes of the Muscovia Company (1630), State Papers (Russia), SP 91/2, fols. 182–84, NAK, where Cradock's name appears alongside that of Ralph Freeman among the company's directors.
18. Frances Rose-Troup, *John White: Founder of Massachusetts* (London, 1930), pp. 64–99. Rose-Troup made occasional errors, and so caution is required in matters of detail.
19. Baxter, *Christopher Levett of York,* pp. 68–70.
20. Will of Gervase Kirke (1631), PROB/11/159, NAK; London port book (exports), 1617, as in note 17; and Henry Kirke, *The First English Conquest of Canada* (London, 1908), esp. pp. 70–97.
21. Massachusetts Historical Society, *Winthrop Papers* (Boston, 1931), vol. 2, pp. 145–49.
22. Bannatyne Club, *Royal Letters, Charters, and Tracts Relating to the Colonization of New Scotland* (Edinburgh, 1867), p. 47.

23. In addition to Pocock, the investors were Christopher Coulson, Thomas Goffe, and John Revell.
24. Cradock to Endecott, quoted in Sidney Perley, *The History of Salem, Massachusetts* (Salem, MA, 1924), pp. 102–4.
25. The *Friendship* of Bideford: Barnstaple port book (overseas) for 1630–31, Dec. 29, 1630, E 190/947/8, NAK; Barnstaple port book (overseas) for 1633, March? 1633, E 190/948/10, NAK; Richard S. Dunn, James Savage, and Laetitia Yeandle, eds., *The Journal of John Winthrop, 1630–1649* (Cambridge, MA, 1996), pp. 53–55. Governors Island: Pre-1945 editions of the *United States Coast Pilot;* and Nancy S. Seasholes, *Gaining Ground: A History of Landmaking in Boston* (Cambridge, MA, 2003), pp. 375–79.
26. St. Kitts and the early English Caribbean colonies: Sir Alan Burns, *History of the British West Indies* (New York, 1973), pp. 187–[illegible]. Slaves at St. Kitts in 1626: V. T. Harlow, ed., *Colonising Expeditions to the West Indies and Guiana, 1623–1667* (London, 1925), p. 26.
27. Voyages of the *Charles* and the *Gift*: SP 16/203/48, NAK; Dunn, Savage, and Yeandle, *Journal*, pp. 69–70 and 81; Barnstaple Port Books (overseas) for 1632–33, E 190/948/10 and E 190/948/11, NAK. Pocock, Barnstaple, and Massachusetts: Bill of exchange of 1635, B1/4090, NDRO.

Chapter Twenty: The Exploding Colony

1. Quoted in Alexander Young, *Chronicles of the Pilgrim Fathers* (Boston, 1844; repr., Baltimore, 1974), pp. 250–51.
2. The Redenhall archives are held at Norfolk RO. Probate inventory of John Fuller (1608): Microfilm, DN/INV 22/102. Manorial records: Court book of Redenhall Manor, 1615–25, file MC 584/7; and court book of Coldham Hall in Redenhall, 1564–1649, file MC 584/2. Redenhall church records: List of churchwardens, 1573–1852, continued to 1893, file PD 295/158. Also, for Fuller entries in the parish register: Francis H. Fuller, "Fullers of Redenhall, England," *NEHGR*, Oct. 1901, pp. 401–6. Genealogy of the Fullers: Robert C. Anderson, *The Pilgrim Migration: Immigrants to Plymouth Colony, 1620–1633* (Boston, MA, 2004), pp. 212–21.
3. James Deetz and Patricia Scott Deetz, *The Times of Their Lives: Life, Love, and Death in the Plymouth Colony* (New York, 2000), pp. 230–35.
4. Virginia DeJohn Anderson, *Creatures of Empire: How Domestic Animals Transformed Early America* (New York, 2004), esp. chaps. 3 and 5.
5. F. Walker, *Historical Geography of Southwest Lancashire Before the Industrial Revolution* (Manchester, UK, 1939), pp. 11–12; and Charles Foster, "Farmers and the Economy in Cheshire and Lancashire," *Transactions of the Lancashire and Cheshire Antiquarian Society* 101 (2005), pp. 25–31.
6. Keryn D. Bromberg and Mark D. Bertness, "Reconstructing New England Salt Marsh Losses Using Historical Maps," *Estuaries* 28, no. 6 (Dec. 2005), pp. 823–32.
7. James Thacher, *History of the Town of Plymouth* (1835; fac. repr., Yarmouth Port, MA, 1972), pp. 312–14; also, William S. Russell, *Pilgrim Memorials and Guide to Plymouth* (Boston, 1860), p. 158.
8. Benjamin Shurtleff and David Pulsifer, eds., *Records of the Colony of New Plymouth in New England*, vol. 11, *Laws, 1623–1682* (Boston, 1855–61), pp. 15 and 48.

9. William T. Davis, *Ancient Landmarks of Plymouth: Part 1, Historical Sketch* (Boston, 1883), pp. 49–54.
10. Cynthia Hagar Krusell, *Marshfield: A Town of Villages* (Marshfield, MA, 1990), esp. pp. 5–9.
11. Dispersal of the Plymouth Colony: Darrell B. Rutman, *Husbandmen of Plymouth: Towns and Villages in the Old Colony, 1620–1692* (Boston, 1967), p. 23. Abandonment of English manorial law: S. C. Powell, *Puritan Village: The Formation of a New England Town* (Middletown, CT, 1963), pp. 142–44.
12. For early comments about the Romney Marsh of Massachusetts, see Howard S. Russell, *A Long, Deep Furrow: Three Centuries of Farming in New England* (Hanover, NH, 1976), p. 41.
13. Puritans in Cranbrook and Rolvenden: Patrick Collinson, "Cranbrook and the Fletchers: Popular and Unpopular Religion in the Kentish Weald," in *Godly People: Essays on English Protestantism and Puritanism* (London, 1983), pp. 399–428. Romney Marsh and English wetlands: Stephen Hipkin, "Tenant Farming and Short-Term Leasing on Romney Marsh, 1587–1705," *Economic History Review*, n.s., 5, no. 4 (Nov. 2000), pp. 666–72; and Oliver Rackham, *The History of the Countryside* (London, 1986), pp. 374–94.
14. Sir William Dugdale, *The History of Imbanking and Drayning of Divers Fens and Marshes* (London, 1662), pp. 374–416; and H. C. Darby, *The Draining of the Fens* (Cambridge, UK, 1956), pp. 22–32 and 263–69.
15. Will of Robert Ingols (1618), Consistory Court Wills, 1618, vol. 2, 317, LAO; probate inventory of Robert Ingols, INV 121/118, LAO; Dugdale, *History of Imbanking*, pp. 422–23; and Clive Holmes, *Seventeenth-Century Lincolnshire* (Lincoln, UK, 1980), pp. 25–27 and 121–30.
16. On Romney Marsh and the Pawtucket: Mellen Chamberlain, *A Documentary History of Chelsea, 1624–1824* (Boston, 1908), pp. 60–76, 86–109, and 635; Alonzo Lewis and James R. Newhall, *History of Lynn, Essex County, Massachusetts* (Boston, 1865), pp. 32–42, 51–58, and 76–78; Benjamin Shurtleff, *The History of the Town of Revere* (Boston, 1937), pp. 11–13.
17. Jeremy D. Bangs, *Indian Deeds: Land Transactions in Plymouth Colony, 1620–1691* (Boston, 2002), introduction.
18. For a similar argument, see Keith Wrightson and David Levine, *Poverty and Piety in an English Village: Terling, 1525–1700*, 2nd ed. (Oxford, 1995), pp. 204–11.
19. New England in the 1640s: Stephen Innes, *Creating the Commonwealth: The Economic Culture of Puritan New England* (New York, 1995), chap. 7. Population: Carla Gardina Pestana, *The English Atlantic in the Age of Revolution, 1640–1661* (Cambridge, MA, 2004), pp. 229–34.
20. Carl Bridenbaugh, *Fat Mutton and Liberty of Conscience: Society in Rhode Island, 1636–1690* (Providence, 1974), pp. 19–31.

Epilogue: The Last Shaman

1. Joseph Nicolar, *The Life and Traditions of the Red Man* (Bangor, ME, 1893; repr., Durham, NC, 2007, ed. by Annette Kolodny), p. 115.
2. Cotton Mather mentioned Dorothy Bradford's death in his *Magnalia Christi Americana* of 1702, but even he makes only the briefest reference to it.
3. Shamanism and rock art in North America: James L. Pearson, *Shamanism and the Ancient Mind: A Cognitive Approach to Archaeology* (Walnut Creek, CA, 2002), pp. 53–64. Petro-

glyphs at Embden and elsewhere: Dean R. Snow, "The Solon Petroglyphs and Eastern Abenaki Shamanism," in *Papers of the Seventh Algonquian Conference,* ed. William Cowan (Ottawa, 1975); Edward Lenik, *Picture Rocks: American Indian Rock Art in the Northeast Woodlands* (Hanover, NH, 2002), pp. 51–57; and Joan Vastokas and Romas Vastokas, *Sacred Art of the Algonkians: A Study of the Peterborough Petroglyphs* (Peterborough, ON, 1976), pp. 121–29. Shamanism in New England: Kathleen J. Bragdon, *Native People of Southern New England, 1500–1650* (Norman, OK, 1996), pp. 200–216; and Frank Speck, "Penobscot Shamanism," *Memoirs of the American Anthropological Association* 6 (1919), pp. 239–88.

4. Eric Lahti et al., "Test Excavations at the Hodgdon Site," *Man in the Northeast* 21 (1981), pp. 19–36.
5. F. H. Eckstorm, *Old John Neptune and Other Maine Indian Shamans* (Portland, ME, 1945), esp. pp. 33–39; and two articles about Eckstorm and Neptune by Jacques Ferland and Pauleena MacDougall in *Reconstructing Maine's Wabanaki History,* a special issue of *Maine History* 43, no. 2 (Aug. 2007).

Further Reading

For reasons of space, the notes to this book chiefly comprise references to primary sources, most of them unpublished. Because so many may be unfamiliar even to experts in the field, I have given full details of all of them. I have mentioned secondary works by modern scholars only when it seemed entirely necessary.

Nevertheless, I wish to record my debt to some excellent books that have provided indispensable assistance. Within their pages readers will find more information, and alternative views, about the very early history of New England and the origins of the Pilgrims. Each book contains a bibliography and notes that will take the reader in most of the directions he or she might wish to travel.

With regard to Puritanism, and the wider religious history of England in the sixteenth and early seventeenth centuries, the most comprehensive recent survey is Felicity Heal's *Reformation in Britain and Ireland* (Oxford, 2003). It should be used in conjunction with the opening chapters of Michael Braddick, *God's Fury, England's Fire: A New History of the English Civil Wars* (London, 2008). An equally important book is Alexandra Walsham's *Providence in Early Modern England* (Oxford, 1999), especially chapter 3. A brilliant analysis of the way in which people interpreted their experience in religious language, it supplements the description of the origins of Separatism contained in *Making Haste from Babylon.*

Sooner or later, every student of the period must turn to Professor Patrick Collinson. First published in 1967, his book *The Elizabethan Puritan Movement* remains a classic of English historiography. His concise treatment of Elizabeth I in the *Oxford Dictionary of National Biography* is essential too: by far the best account of that overexposed celebrity. For those seeking to understand two complicated subjects—Calvinism and Separatist attitudes to the Church of England—Collinson supplies an eloquent shortcut, in chapters 2, 3, 6, and 7 of his collection of essays *From Cranmer to Sancroft* (London, 2006). They supersede most earlier work on these vexed issues.

There are so many penetrating books about the politics of the period between 1580 and 1630 that a full list would require a volume of its own. John Guy's *My Heart Is My Own: The Life of Mary, Queen of Scots* (London, 2004) covers far more than its title suggests. However, if readers want to know more about the 1580s, they might try Blair Worden's controversial but fascinating book about Sir Philip Sidney, *The Sound of Virtue: Philip Sidney's Arcadia and Elizabethan Politics* (New Haven, CT, 1996).

For later decades, Ronald Hutton supplies a road map through the jungle in his *Debates in Stuart History* (Basingstoke, UK, 2004). I also recommend Conrad Russell's *Parliaments and English Politics, 1621–1629* (Oxford, 1979), another modern classic, and Kevin Sharpe's *Personal Rule of Charles I* (New Haven, CT, 1992). I do not agree with everything Sharpe says, but his account of the crisis of 1628 and 1629 is essential. So are Richard Cust's excellent biography, *Charles I: A Political Life* (Harlow, UK, 2005), and Roger Lockyer's *Buckingham: The Life and Political Career of George Villiers, First Duke of Buckingham, 1592–1628* (London, 1981).

American historians have produced an immense body of work dealing with the first Puritan settlements. To my mind, the finest literary account of early New England is still Charles Francis Adams Jr.'s *Three Episodes of Massachusetts History*, published as long ago as 1892. A man who fought at Antietam and Gettysburg before coming home to regulate railroads in his state, Adams had some excellent credentials to write the book in question. For those who prefer something more recent, free from Adams's errors, Francis J. Bremer gives us a splendid start in his *John Winthrop: America's Forgotten Founding Father* (Oxford, 2003). So does David Hackett Fischer in *Champlain's Dream* (New York, 2008), another book that does much more than it says on the label.

With more direct relevance to the Pilgrims, by far the most reliable narrative can still be found in the first volume of C. M. Andrews's *Colonial Period of American History* (New Haven, CT, 1934). It should be read alongside the elegant book by Bernard Bailyn, *The New England Merchants in the Seventeenth Century* (Cambridge, MA, 1955). They provide a solid introduction before one opens William Bradford's history of the Plymouth Colony.

The best edition of that is contained in the annotated volumes published by the Massachusetts Historical Society: William Bradford, *History of Plymouth Plantation, 1620–1647* (Boston, 1912). However, because the society's edition is hard to find except in university libraries, in my notes I have preferred to cite Samuel Eliot Morison's 1979 edition. Morison made small mistakes in his own annotations, but none of them were fatal.

Besides Andrews and Bailyn, and other books mentioned in my notes, the American works to which I have turned most often have been Virginia DeJohn Anderson, *New England's Generation: The Great Migration and the Formation of Society and Culture in the Seventeenth Century* (Cambridge, UK, 1991); Karen Ordahl Kupperman, *The Jamestown Project* (Cambridge, MA, 2007); Mark A. Noll, *America's God: From Jonathan Edwards to Abraham Lincoln* (New York, 2002); Daniel K. Richter, *The Ordeal of the Longhouse: The Peoples of the Iroquois League in the Era of European Colonization* (Chapel Hill, NC, 1992); Neal Salisbury, *Manitou and Providence: Indians, Europeans, and the Making of New England, 1500–1643* (New York, 1982); and David A. Weir, *Early New England: A Covenanted Society* (Grand Rapids, 2005).

However, to my mind some of the most relevant American scholarship in recent years has come from archaeologists and scientists. I am referring especially to Professor David R. Foster and his team at Harvard University's Harvard Forest project. Their research can be found in David R. Foster and John D. Aber, eds., *Forests in Time: The Environmental Consequences of 1,000 Years of Change in New England* (New Haven, CT, 2004). An excellent account of New England salt marshes can be found in the essential textbook by Professor Mark Bertness of Brown University, *Atlantic Shorelines: Natural History and Ecology* (Princeton, NJ, 2007). I also recommend two recent publications that deal with the interaction between ecology, geography, Native American culture, and the arrival of European colonists. The first is by Lisa Tanya Brooks, *The Common Pot: The Recovery of Native Space in the Northeast*

(Minneapolis, 2008). The second is an article by W. Jeffrey Bolster, "Putting the Ocean in Atlantic History: Maritime Communities and Marine Ecology in the Northwest Atlantic, 1500–1800," *American Historical Review* (Feb. 2008).

I cannot count the number of times that I have delved into the Web site of the New England Historic Genealogical Society, www.newengland ancestors.org. For biographical facts about the *Mayflower* Pilgrims, another excellent source is the Web site maintained by Caleb Johnson, at www.mayflowerhistory.com. Johnson sets high standards of accuracy, both on his Web site and in his privately printed book, *The* Mayflower *and Her Passengers* (2006).

I have a last intellectual debt to repay. For many years, much of the best work in the field of North Atlantic history has come from French scholars, whether in metropolitan France or in French Canada. My text and notes refer to Bernard Allaire, Laurier Turgeon, and three La Rochelle historians of a much earlier generation: Marcel Delafosse, Étienne Trocmé, and François de Vaux de Foletier. Behind them lie the great masters of modern historical writing: Lucien Febvre, Marc Bloch, and Fernand Braudel. My account of the voyage of the *Mayflower* owes much to another French historian, Alain Cabantous. I adapted the title of his book *Le ciel dans la mer: Christianisme et civilisation maritime (XVIe–XIXe siècle)* (Paris, 1990) for the title of the first part of my own.

Since the 1970s, Jeremy Dupertuis Bangs has plowed a deep but perhaps a lonely furrow, as a historian committed to using careful archival research to enhance our understanding of the Pilgrims and the Plymouth Colony. His wide learning in art history and theology have assisted him greatly in the task. In September 2009, when *Making Haste from Babylon* was entering its final stages of preparation, Dr. Bangs published his important book *Strangers and Pilgrims, Travellers and Sojourners: Leiden and the Foundations of Plymouth Plantation* (General Society of Mayflower Descendants, Plymouth, Massachusetts, 2009). Although it appeared too late for me to use it as a source, *Strangers and Pilgrims* provides additional perspectives of the highest value.

Index